CENTRAL STATISTICAL OFFICE

SOCIAL TRENDS

No. 7   1976

Edited by ERIC J. THOMPSON

Associate Editor: CHRIS LEWIS

A publication of the Government Statistical Service

LONDON : Her Majesty's Stationery Office

ISBN 0 11 630156 2*

Contents

		Page
Editorial		6
Social commentary: social change in Britain: 1970-1975 Central Statistical Office		8
Crime in England and Wales Dr Charles Glennie, Home Office		32
Crime in Scotland Dr David Bruce, Scottish Home and Health Department		43
Subjective measures of quality of life in Britain: 1971 to 1975 John Hall, Survey Unit, Social Science Research Council		47

Tables and charts
* New in this issue of *Social Trends*

Population

Table 1.1	Sex and age structure of the population	62
Chart 1.2	Population structure: by age, sex, and marital status, 1974	63
Table 1.3	Population changes and projections	63
Chart 1.4	Population changes and projections	64
*Table 1.5	Variant population projections, 1974-based	64
*Chart 1.6	1974-based variant population projections, 1961–2011	65
Table 1.7	Birth rates	65
*Table 1.8	Standardised death rates	66
Chart 1.9	Net migrants beyond the British Isles	66
Table 1.10	Net migrants beyond the British Isles	67
Table 1.11	Marriage	67
Table 1.12	Divorce	68
*Table 1.13	Marital status of household population over 15	68
Table 1.14	Families by size and by age of head, 1971	69
Table 1.15	Average family size at specified durations of marriage	69
*Table 1.16	Family size distributions after 10 years of marriage	69
Chart 1.17	Women childless by duration of marriage	70
*Table 1.18	Legitimate live births to women married once only: by number of previous liveborn children	70
*Chart 1.19	Abortions: by age group and marital status of woman	71
*Table 1.20	Mid-year estimates of the population of New Commonwealth and Pakistani ethnic origin, 1966–1975	71
Table 1.21	Live births: by country of birth of mother, 1970 to 1974	72
Table 1.22	Populations of new standard regions	72

Households

Table 2.1	Households, 1951–1971	73
Table 2.2	Institutional population and non-family households, 1961 and 1971	74

		Page
*Table 2.3	Household projections	74
*Table 2.4	People by household size	75
*Table 2.5	Age of head of household	75
*Table 2.6	Family type: families with dependent children	75
*Table 2.7	Type of household	76
*Table 2.8	Socio-economic group of head of household	76

Children

Table 2.9	Children: by age group	77
*Chart 2.10	Children: projections, 1974–2011	77
*Table 2.11	Children: population projections	78
*Table 2.12	Women with own children in households	78
*Table 2.13	Children: by household accommodation, 1973	78
Table 2.14	Children's services	79
Table 2.15	Children received into care of local authorities: circumstances of admission	79
Table 2.16	Children in care of local authorities: type of accommodation and age groups	80
Chart 2.17	Children in care of local authorities	80

Elderly

*Table 2.18	Elderly people: population projections	81
Chart 2.19	Persons supported by the local authorities in residential accommodation	81
Table 2.20	Residential and other services mainly for the elderly and handicapped	82
Chart 2.21	Household expenditure, 1974	82
Table 2.22	Income of persons over retirement age, 1974	83
Chart 2.23	Source of household income, 1974	83
Table 2.24	Household expenditure: average weekly expenditure on goods and services: by household composition, 1975	84

Coloured population

*Table 2.25	Age and colour of household population, 1975	84
*Table 2.26	Age and colour of head of household	85
*Table 2.27	Size of household: by colour, 1974 and 1975	85
Table 2.28	Households with chief economic supporter born outside the United Kingdom, 1971	85

Education

Table 3.1	Education for the under-fives	87
*Chart 3.2	Children under school age by socio-economic grouping of head of household, 1973	87
Chart 3.3	Pupils under 5 as a percentage of age group population, all schools	87
Table 3.4	School pupils: summary	88
Table 3.5	Pupils: projections and age distribution	88
*Table 3.6	Secondary education: England and Wales	89

1

		Page
Table 3.7	Secondary education: Scotland and Northern Ireland	89
*Table 3.8	Courses taken in secondary schools	89
Chart 3.9	School leavers: by type of school and examination achievement, 1973/74	90
Table 3.10	Destination of school leavers: by type of school, 1973/74	90
*Table 3.11	Intentions of 16 year old school children, 1975	91
Chart 3.12	Advanced level passes	91
Table 3.13	Further education	92
Table 3.14	Higher education: number and age of students	92
*Table 3.15	Destination of UK graduates at GB universities	93
Table 3.16	Selected statistics of manpower employed in education	93
Table 3.17	Public expenditure on education	94
*Table 3.18	Satisfaction with education: by qualification	94

Employment

		Page
*Table 4.1	New entrants to employment	95
*Table 4.2	Young people under 18 on day release from work, at November	95
Table 4.3	Economic activity: summary, 1961 to 1971	96
*Chart 4.4	Distribution of people at work	96
Chart 4.5	Population aged 15 and over: economic activity	97
*Table 4.6	Economic activity rates by age and sex	97
*Table 4.7	Employment by sector	98
*Chart 4.8	Public sector: total employees in employment	98
*Chart 4.9	First permanent employment of all UK university degree holders	98
*Table 4.10	Qualified population: by age, 1971	99
*Table 4.11	Qualified population: by subject group, 1971	99
Table 4.12	Highest qualification level of those not in full-time education	100
Table 4.13	Income by selected highest qualification levels: males in full-time employment	100
*Table 4.14	Occupational change, 1970 to 1971	101
Table 4.15	Job mobility in the last twelve months	101
Chart 4.16	Unemployed	102
Table 4.17	Unemployment	102
Chart 4.18	Training under government schemes	103
*Table 4.19	Open University students: by occupation	103
Table 4.20	Total weekly hours, April 1975	104
Chart 4.21	Total weekly hours, April 1975	104
Table 4.22	Job satisfaction: by sex and age group	105
*Table 4.23	Immigrants' contribution to labour supply, 1971	105
*Table 4.24	Geographical distribution of economically active immigrants, 1971	106
*Table 4.25	Shiftwork by country of origin: males, 1974	106

Personal income and wealth

		Page
*Table 5.1	Income and expenditure account of the personal sector, excluding private non-profit-making bodies	107
Chart 5.2	Annual changes in real personal disposable income per head	108
Chart 5.3	Distribution of personal incomes before and after tax, 1973–74	108

		Page
Table 5.4	Distribution of personal incomes before and after tax, 1973–74	109
Table 5.5	Sources of total income	109
*Chart 5.6	Distribution of personal incomes, quantile shares, 1961 to 1973–74	110
Table 5.7	Household income by main household type, 1975	110
*Chart 5.8	Distribution of household incomes: active and non-active households, 1974	111
*Chart 5.9	Distribution of household incomes: active households with and without children, 1974	111
Table 5.10	Household income: average weekly income by source, 1975	112
Table 5.11	Redistribution of income through taxes and benefits, 1974, all households	113
*Chart 5.12	Average taxes paid and benefits received by retired and non-retired households in different income ranges, 1974	114
Chart 5.13	Original income and income after all taxes and benefits, 1961 to 1974	115
*Chart 5.14	Average taxes paid and benefits received, 1961 to 1974	115
Table 5.15	Gross weekly earnings of full-time workers	116
*Chart 5.16	Relative changes in median gross weekly earnings of full-time workers	116
Table 5.17	Cumulative distribution of gross weekly earnings of full-time workers, April 1975	117
Table 5.18	Gross weekly earnings of full-time workers: by age, April 1975	117
Chart 5.19	Distribution of gross weekly earnings, April 1975	118
Table 5.20	Percentage increases in average gross weekly earnings of full-time workers, April 1974 to April 1975	118
*Table 5.21	Proportion of income taken in tax in the case of a married couple with two children under 11, with no income except the husband's earnings from employment and family allowances	118
Table 5.22	Persons receiving national insurance benefits and extent supplemented	120
Table 5.23	Persons receiving supplementary benefit	120
Chart 5.24	Persons receiving supplementary benefit	121
Chart 5.25	Persons receiving retirement pensions	121
Table 5.26	Family income supplement: families receiving: by size and weekly rate, 30 December 1975	121
Chart 5.27	Total income support: marginal net benefit	122
Table 5.28	Estimated number of families theoretically liable to receive various levels of net benefit from an additional £1 of earnings, December 1974	123
*Table 5.29	Trends in the numbers of families and persons normally with low net resources	123
Table 5.30	Families and family allowances	123
Table 5.31	Families and persons normally with low net resources, December 1974	124
Table 5.32	Retirement pensions (and supplementary benefits) related to average net earnings, 1960 to 1975	124

Table 5.33	Percentage of net income represented by social security payments to unemployed or sick men	125
Table 5.34	Public expenditure on social security benefits	125
Table 5.35	Distribution of wealth among identified wealth owners	126
Table 5.36	Distribution of wealth among adult population	127
*Table 5.37	Composition of personal wealth by asset value, 1960 to 1974	127
Table 5.38	Selected regional characteristics	128

Personal expenditure

Chart 6.1	General index of retail prices	129
*Table 6.2	Index of retail prices	130
Table 6.3	Internal purchasing power of the pound	130
Chart 6.4	Expenditure patterns: by type of household	131
Table 6.5	Household expenditure: average weekly expenditure on goods and services	132
Table 6.6	Consumers' expenditure: indices at constant prices	132
Chart 6.7	Availability of durable goods, 1974	133
*Table 6.8	Possession of, and attitudes towards, consumer durables, 1973 and 1975	133
*Chart 6.9	Consumption of alcohol	133
Chart 6.10	Changes in household food consumption, 1965–1975 and 1973–1975	134
Table 6.11	Household food consumption	134

Health

*Table 7.1	Summary of mortality statistics, 1951–1974	135
Chart 7.2	Infant and maternal mortality	135
Table 7.3	Deaths by selected causes: standardised mortality ratios	136
Chart 7.4	Deaths by selected causes	136
Table 7.5	Death at various ages: death rates for selected causes: by sex	137
*Chart 7.6	Morbidity: reported sickness, 1973	138
Table 7.7	Morbidity: chronic sickness: by marital status, 1973	138
Table 7.8	Morbidity: acute sickness: by marital status, 1973	138
Table 7.9	Hospital summary: all specialties	139
Table 7.10	Selected types of illness: non-psychiatric hospitals	139
Chart 7.11	Hospital summary: by specialty, 1974	140
*Table 7.12	Resident patients in mental illness hospitals and units: by age and duration of stay at 31 December 1974	140
Chart 7.13	Private medical insurance	141
Chart 7.14	Number of health centres	141
*Chart 7.15	Family practitioner services: shares in total cost	141
Table 7.16	Persons consulting general practitioners (NHS): by marital status, 1973	142
Table 7.17	Selected regional health statistics	142
Table 7.18	Maternity services	143
*Table 7.19	Family planning services	143
Table 7.20	Abortions	144
Table 7.21	Venereal diseases: new patients seen at hospital clinics	144
Chart 7.22	Smoking habits, 1973	145
Chart 7.23	Alcoholism: admissions to mental illness hospitals and units	145

Table 7.24	Dangerous drugs: registered addicts	145
*Table 7.25	Health visitor, home nursing, and chiropody services	146
*Table 7.26	Services provided for the disabled	146
*Chart 7.27	Cervical cytology: examinations and positive cases detected	147
Table 7.28	Preventive medicine: vaccination	147
Table 7.29	Manpower in the health and local authority social services	148
Table 7.30	Public expenditure on the health and personal social services	149

Housing

Chart 8.1	Stock of dwellings: by tenure	150
*Chart 8.2	Slum clearance	150
Table 8.3	Stock of dwellings: by region, December 1975	151
Table 8.4	Stock of dwellings: change and tenure	151
Chart 8.5	Stock of dwellings and housing completions: by region, 1975	152
*Table 8.6	Housing conditions: availability of amenities	152
*Table 8.7	Housing amenities: by colour of head of household	152
*Chart 8.8	Households: tenure by type of accommodation	153
*Table 8.9	Households: tenure profile of heads, 1974	153
*Chart 8.10	Households: colour of head: by tenure and bedroom standard, 1971–1973	154
Chart 8.11	Distribution of households: by income and tenure, 1974	154
*Table 8.12	Length of residence of head of household: by tenure, 1974	155
Chart 8.13	Households: actual and potential movers	155
Table 8.14	Households: number of moves made by the head of household in the last five years: by current tenure	156
Table 8.15	General improvement areas declared	156
Table 8.16	House renovation grants	156
Table 8.17	House prices: by region	157
Chart 8.18	Rent and mortgage payments: by region, 1973	157
Table 8.19	Public expenditure on housing	158
Table 8.20	Housing subsidies and tax relief on mortgages	158
*Table 8.21	Homeless households: applications, acceptances, and action taken	159
*Table 8.22	Homeless households: applicants housed: by type of permanent accommodation	159
*Table 8.23	Homeless households: by type of last accommodation and by reason for loss of accommodation	160
*Table 8.24	Homeless households: applications for accommodation accepted; January–June 1975	160

Environment

*Chart 9.1	General values of sunshine	161
*Chart 9.2	Rainfall	161
Chart 9.3	Cleaner air	162
Table 9.4	Air pollution	162
*Map	Winter mean concentrations of sulphur dioxide (opposite page 162)	
Table 9.5	Air pollution: by region	164
Table 9.6	Estimates of pollutants from road vehicles	164
Table 9.7	Radioactivity in milk	164

Table 9.8 River pollution 165
Chart 9.9 River pollution 165
*Table 9.10 Population in conurbations 1951–1974 166
*Table 9.11 Population in the London Metropolitan Region, 1901–1971 167
*Table 9.12 Resident labour force in conurbations, 1951–1971 167
Table 9.13 Population density 168
Table 9.14 Agricultural land in use 168
*Map Conservation of the countryside (opposite page 168)
*Chart 9.15 Agricultural land: changes 170
*Table 9.16 Gipsy site provision: by region, at 31 December 1975 170
*Table 9.17 Accessibility of facilities, 1972 170
Chart 9.18 Passenger transport: use and prices 171
Table 9.19 Passenger transport: use, resources, and prices 171
Table 9.20 Recycling: quantities of selected materials recovered as a proportion of consumption, 1973 172
Table 9.21 Public expenditure on environmental services 172
*Table 9.22 Satisfaction with district, by length of residence 172

Leisure
Chart 10.1 Weekly hours of work 173
Chart 10.2 Annual paid holiday 173
Table 10.3 Weekly hours of work and paid holidays: manual workers 174
Table 10.4 Accessibility: journeys to work: time taken, 1966 and 1973 174
*Chart 10.5 Journeys to work: means of travel, 1966 and 1971 175

Tourism
Chart 10.6 Holidays: numbers taken each year by adults resident in Great Britain 175
Table 10.7 Holidays 176
Chart 10.8 Profile of holidays abroad taken by adults resident in Great Britain 176
Chart 10.9 Holidays taken by adults resident in Great Britain: accommodation used 176
Table 10.10 Overseas visitors 177

Membership of organisations
Table 10.11 Outdoor activities: membership of organisations 177
Table 10.12 Organisations for young persons 178
Table 10.13 Church membership and attendance 178

Leisure activities
Table 10.14 Books: number of titles issued 180
Table 10.15 Attendances at art galleries, museums, and theatres 180
Table 10.16 Circulation of newspapers 181
*Table 10.17 Selected leisure activities: by age and sex, 1973 181
*Table 10.18 Leisure activities: by socio-economic group, 1973 182
*Table 10.19 Gambling 182
Table 10.20 Television viewing 183
Table 10.21 Public expenditure on libraries, museums, and the arts 183
*Table 10.22 Ownership of pets 183

Public safety
Table 11.1 Crime: offences, persons proceeded against, and persons found guilty 184

Table 11.2 Persons found guilty of indictable offences or crimes per 100,000 of the population: by age and sex 185
Table 11.3 Persons found guilty of indictable offences: by age, sex, and type of offence, 1975 185
Table 11.4 Receptions into prison establishments and population in custody 186
Chart 11.5 Adult male sentenced prison population, June 1975 186
Table 11.6 Public expenditure on justice and law 187
Table 11.7 Strength of police forces 187
Table 11.8 Road accident casualties 188
Chart 11.9 Serious road casualties: traffic index 189
*Chart 11.10 Road accident casualties: averages by hour of the day, 1973–1975 189
Chart 11.11 Serious road casualties: class and age of user 190
Table 11.12 Railway accidents: casualties 190
Table 11.13 Industrial accidents 191
Table 11.14 Deaths from accidents occurring in the home and residential accommodation 191
*Table 11.15 Search and rescue operations at home 192
Table 11.16 Fatal fire casualties: by age and sex 192
Chart 11.17 Casualties from fireworks 193
Table 11.18 Northern Ireland: deaths and injuries connected with the civil disturbances, 1969–1976 193

Social participation
Table 12.1 Parliamentary elections, 1964 to 1974 195
*Table 12.2 Parliamentary by-elections 195
Chart 12.3 General elections results 196
*Table 12.4 Local elections, 1973 and 1976 196
*Table 12.5 Public Bills considered in Parliament: by session 197
*Chart 12.6 Education of Conservative and Labour MPs 197
*Table 12.7 Activities of charities and other organisations 197
*Chart 12.8 Trade unions: membership 198
*Table 12.9 Membership of trade unions 198
Table 12.10 Citizens' Advice Bureaux 198
Table 12.11 Civil justice: summary 199
Table 12.12 Civil justice: County Courts 199
Chart 12.13 Civil justice: County Courts 200
Table 12.14 Civil justice: Sheriff Courts 200
Chart 12.15 Civil justice: Sheriff Courts 201
Chart 12.16 Crown Court: persons tried by type of plea 201
Table 12.17 Complaints to Parliamentary Commissioner for Administration 202
Table 12.18 Administrative tribunals 202
Table 12.19 Crime: legal aid applications 203
Table 12.20 Civil justice: legal aid 203
*Table 12.21 Immigration Act 1971: appeals disposed of, 1973 to 1975 204
*Chart 12.22 Marriages: manner of solemnisation 204

Resources
Chart 13.1 Pattern and source of public expenditure, 1974 205
Table 13.2 Public expenditure summary: analysis by economic category 206
Table 13.3 Public expenditure summary: analysis by function 206
Table 13.4 Local authority income: by source 206
Table 13.5 Local authority expenditure summary: analysis by function 207

		Page
Chart 13.6	Local authority income and expenditure	207
*Table 13.7	Public spending: annual average rates of increase	207

International

Table 14.1	Population and population density: 1950–1975	209
Chart 14.2	Population changes, 1950–1974	210
Chart 14.3	Birth rates	210
Chart 14.4	Infant mortality	211
Table 14.5	Life expectation	211
*Chart 14.6	*Per capita* domestic product	212
Table 14.7	Consumer spending at current prices, 1973	212
Chart 14.8	Consumer spending, 1963–1973	213
Table 14.9	Consumer price index numbers	213
*Chart 14.10	Cars, freezers, and dishwashers, May 1975	214
Table 14.11	Average formal educational experience of population	214
Table 14.12	Economically active population	215
Table 14.13	Unemployment	215
Chart 14.14	Industrial disputes	216

		Page
Calendar of events		217
Appendix A	Statistical notes	230
Appendix B	Definitions and terms	234
Appendix C	Sources and further references	254
Alphabetical Index		263
Articles published in previous issues		inside of back cover

Symbols and conventions used

Rounding of figures. In tables where figures have been rounded to the nearest final digit, there may be an apparent discrepancy between the sum of the constituent items and the total as shown.

Symbols. The following symbols have been used throughout *Social Trends*.

   .. = not available

   – = nil or negligible (less than half the final digit shown)

n.e.i. = not elsewhere included

Editorial

Introduction

Since *Social Trends* was first published in 1970, social reports have been produced in many other countries. These include France, Germany, Italy, the Netherlands, Norway, Spain, and Sweden in Europe; and Canada, Japan, Malaysia, the Philippines, and the United States of America elsewhere. Reading other social reports, and talking about them with some of their editors,[1] it becomes clear that they can fulfil more than one function. *Social Trends* differs from some of the other social reports – such as, for example, that produced in the Social and Cultural Planning Office in the Netherlands – in that it does not try to specify which are the most important problems facing our society, let alone try to recommend policies to solve them. Its main purpose is to provide essential background data needed by those concerned with policy formulation and monitoring. It aims to show where society has got to, and how it is changing: and it tries wherever possible to highlight interactions and changes in relationships.

Social Trends is thus designed to present a wide range of information which all sides in the political arena can accept as setting the factual context within which divergent political forces and pressure groups can argue about policy.

However, when topics are omitted from *Social Trends* this does not necessarily mean that they are not thought important. Space limits the coverage; lack of data is perhaps even more important; but in some cases, of course, lack of imagination may be the trouble. The need to keep the publication down to a manageable size means that tables have often to be dropped to make way for new data. Issues of *Social Trends* are designed to be used as a series; and, although there are data on most major subject areas each year, important items are sometimes left out of one issue because they have been covered relatively extensively in a previous year or because no new data are available. For example, the present issue contains little on social class differences simply because they were covered in some detail in *Social Trends No. 6* last year.

We are always being asked for more of something. Data on regional differences are a favourite request, but to cover them adequately in *Social Trends* would mean increasing its length – and

price – considerably; and there is already another CSO annual, *Regional Statistics*. Another publication which readers will find useful for further information is *Population Trends*. It is produced quarterly by the Office of Population Censuses and Surveys, and includes articles on population subjects as well as the latest data. Sources of other information can be traced through the references given in Appendix C to *Social Trends* (starting on page 254 this year) or through the CSO's new *Guide to Statistical Sources*, first published in November 1976.

This year's articles

This year *Social Trends* includes the fifth Social Commentary. This looks back over the period since 1970 and tries to identify some social developments characterising that period. Before looking separately at some of the main areas of social change – population; education; employment; income, wealth, and expenditure; health; personal social services; housing; public safety; civil administration and justice; and political change – an introductory section presents a more individual overview, including aspects of the period which are not easily summarised in statistical form. It is perhaps only fair to say that not all members of the *Social Trends* Editorial Board would accept the emphasis and choice of topics, but the Board felt that it would be valuable if a rather more personal viewpoint were to be developed in the Social Commentaries. Another change – this time resulting from a self-denying ordinance – is that the Commentary, though illustrated with graphs, has no tables. It is hoped that these changes have produced a more generally interesting article, and readers' views will be welcomed on this and any other aspects of *Social Trends*.

The Social Commentary does not cover the field of crime, as it is followed by two articles on aspects of that subject: Dr Glennie of the Home Office deals with problems of measurement and gives examples of some of them for England and Wales, while Dr Bruce of the Scottish Home and Health Department describes the Scottish situation. Because of the different legal systems of Scotland and of England and Wales, crime is one of the areas where it is particularly difficult to present a coherent picture for the United Kingdom as a whole; but producing national totals is becoming an increasing problem in other areas too.

The article by John Hall, formerly of the Social Science Research Council's (SSRC) Survey Unit,

---

[1] See the August 1976 issue, No 34, of *Statistical News* for an account of a seminar on 'Social Reports: their Contribution to Integrated Development Planning' held in April 1976 under the auspices of the Division of Social Affairs of the United Nations Office at Geneva.

looks at subjective social indicators of individual well-being resulting from the three *Quality of Life Surveys* – in *1971, 1973*, and *1975* – mentioned briefly in Mark Abrams's note in last year's *Social Trends*. Some of the indicators (eg on housing) seem to have been stable; others (eg those relating to freedom) seem to have been volatile. John Hall also discusses the way in which subjective reactions can be related to 'objective' measures apparently covering similar areas. This is an important area for research; but the article is designed not just to show how research is developing, but also to provide a background to tables derived from the SSRC surveys which have been included in some of the later sections of *Social Trends*.

Tables and charts

This issue contains about 220 tables and 110 charts. Around 30 per cent of each are new. It is not always possible to bring data up to date – particularly when they come from the Census of Population – but, where it is possible, updated versions of tables included in previous issues but omitted this time can normally be supplied on request by the CSO Social Monitoring Branch. Similarly, where data presented in chart form are not also given in tables, the figures will be made available if required.

This year's *Social Trends* includes a number of time series derived from the annual General Household Survey conducted since 1971 by the Social Survey Division of the Office of Population Censuses and Surveys. No dramatic trends can be expected in social data over such a short period (generally 1971–74, though preliminary 1975 data have been included in a few cases), and some apparent changes may result from sampling variations. Nevertheless, the inclusion of more than 30 tables or charts showing trends based on data from the GHS is a reflection of its increasing value as results accumulate over time.

In extending the coverage of *Social Trends* a special effort has been made this year to include data relevant to the problems of ethnic minorities in those sections – Population, Employment, Leisure, Households, Housing, and Social participation – where such data were available. On the other hand, the International section has been shortened, largely because so many qualifications are needed when attempting international comparisons. Consideration will, however, be given to producing a separate publication should readers' reactions show that that would be a useful step for the CSO to take.

The period covered by the Social Commentary is also covered by the Calendar of Events which follows the International section. The Calendar's layout has been changed, by separating out references to legislation; and some of the major events mentioned in the Calendar have now been included in the Index.

Acknowledgements

A formal list of acknowledgements for a publication such as this would be almost never ending; but the *Social Trends* team in the CSO Social Monitoring Branch would like to place on record again their thanks to statistical departments throughout UK central government for their continuing support, help, and advice.

Thanks are also due to other organisations (including the SSRC, the National Readership Survey, and numerous charities, pressure groups, and trade unions) for making their data available.

Within the CSO, a special word of thanks is due to the draughtsmen who have co-operated as splendidly as ever in producing the diagrams, and who this year have provided some extra illustrations too. The Social Commentary draws, as always, particularly widely for contributions from social statistics departments; but the work of bringing it together has been undertaken by John Evans in the CSO, to whom the editor is particularly grateful.

ERIC J. THOMPSON

Central Statistical Office
Great George Street
London SW1P 3AQ

Social change in Britain: 1970–1975[1]

Central Statistical Office

Introduction

It is now six years since *Social Trends* first appeared, and this year's Social Commentary looks back at some of the changes in British society during that period. It is too soon for an historical perspective, but the first half of the seventies exhibited a number of changes which at least seemed significant at the time of writing, however they may eventually be assessed. Most of this Commentary looks separately at the various subject areas into which *Social Trends* is divided. To start with, though, it seems worthwhile gathering together some rather more subjective impressions, including comments on some items which do not fit into the statistical framework used in the rest of *Social Trends*. Many of the changes discussed had started before 1970, but when taken together they nevertheless appear to characterise the first half of the 1970s.

Looking back from mid-1976, the last few years seem to have been overshadowed by two economic factors: inflation and unemployment. All the main economic indicators – including the rate of change of price levels and money earnings, unemployment, the balance of payments, the external value of the pound sterling, stock market prices, and money supply – had exceptionally large fluctuations. Most of these reached record post-war levels, some all-time record levels; and, for the first time for decades, the United Kingdom experienced falls in gross domestic product and in average real income levels. Most of these changes seem to have had large cyclical components – the most violent since the 1939–45 war. External factors had major impacts, most prominent, perhaps, the oil crisis which began in 1973. (However, by the end of the period oil was being produced from the UK Continental Shelf.) The oil crisis coincided with an increasing appreciation of the finite nature of natural resources at both individual and international levels.

In the United Kingdom there seemed to be a marked change in the attitudes of some people to what can reasonably be expected from society, and what local and central government is able to do. This was associated with a wider questioning of the extension of state intervention, which may or may not be due to the fact that more and more people found themselves paying increasing amounts of direct taxes. These taxes were required to help finance the increasing proportion of the Gross Domestic Product represented by public expenditure – an increase partly accounted for by the increase in transfer payments. Generally speaking the early 1970s seem to have been a period of increasing state intervention in many social and economic areas, including government sponsored policies for incomes.

These incomes policies took several different forms. Some were statutory and some were maintained only by voluntary agreement. One feature of some of the incomes policies was that they involved payments of increases up to a maximum allowable amount consisting of a cash element with or without a percentage increase. This tended, at least temporarily, to make the overall distribution of earnings more equal in percentage though not in absolute terms. Indeed, during the period there was evidence of a significant alteration in the distribution of earnings, a development discussed in more detail in the Income sub-section.

The development of national incomes policies was largely a response to rapid inflation. The first area of rapid price increases was housing, and in 1971–73 the practice of 'gazumping' appeared to become temporarily widespread in England and Wales. The rise in commodity prices led to steep increases in the cost of items such as sugar, which almost disappeared from shops for a short time in 1973–74. We were perhaps used to paying higher prices by 1975 – and the introduction of decimal currency in February 1971 was sometimes blamed for making it harder for some people to retain standards of comparison –, but the rapid increase

---

[1] Figures in bold refer to tables or charts on pages 61 to 216. Definitions of terms used in this Commentary are given in Appendix B.

in the cost of vegetables, especially potatoes, caused concern again in early 1976.

In the social field some people seem to have felt that what they thought to be trends towards a 'permissive society' had gone far enough. Certainly, there were few changes in the early 1970s which could correspond to those of the late 1960s, which saw, for example, the abolition of the death penalty for murder; changes in the abortion, divorce, and homosexuality laws; reform of theatre censorship; new gaming laws; and the voting age together with the right to marry without seeking parental consent in England and Wales lowered to age 18. The Sunday Theatres Act of 1972 was almost the only legislation of this type in the 1970s, together, perhaps, with the introduction of non-custodial sentences in the Criminal Justice Act of the same year. (Looking at areas of the 'permissive society' which aroused vocal comment, the social statistician observes that the percentage of births conceived outside marriage declined a little – and that actual numbers of such births fell considerably –, that the number of induced abortions under the 1967 Act to residents of this country, after increasing for some years, began to decline slightly by the mid-1970s, and that the increasing number of new patients seen at hospital clinics dealing with venereal diseases will have reflected increasing willingness to consult doctors as well as the spread of these diseases.)

There were, however, a large number of legal changes in the early 1970s. Many of these seemed to be in the direction of increased government intervention. This was so both in the economic area – ranging from extensions to the rent acts to equal pay legislation and incomes policies – and in the social area. The growing consumer movement led to both social and economic changes. The Trades Descriptions Act of 1968 was followed by the Fire Precaution Act 1971 and the Unsolicited Goods and Services Act of 1971; another Trades Descriptions Act in 1972; the Fair Trading Act of 1973; and the Town and Country Amenities and Control of Pollution Acts of 1974. Important legislation in the field of education supported the raising of the school leaving age from 15 to 16, and the final commitment of the Government to comprehensive education. Measures concerned with protecting people included the Tattooing of Minors Act of 1969; and a higher age for riding motor cycles in 1971, followed by the compulsory wearing of crash helmets in 1973. At the time of writing a further measure to make wearing seat belts generally compulsory in cars was before Parliament. The Health and Safety at Work, etc, Act, 1974, was designed to produce a comprehensive and integrated system of law to deal with the health and safety of virtually all people at work, and the protection of the public where they might be affected by the activities of people at work.

Many minority groups became more vocal than before, and the role of pressure groups for minorities was increasingly accepted by both public and government. They included campaigns for rights of the poor, the old, and the disabled, as well as for immigrants, gipsies, and homosexuals (for whom the word 'gay' acquired more general use especially after a fortnightly newspaper called *Gay News* started publication in 1972). The issue of the number of families in poverty became much more prominent, partly as a result of the actions of the Child Poverty Action Group. The plight of those families in the so-called 'poverty trap' (where, owing to the interaction of means-tested benefits and direct taxes, the net effect of a small rise in wages was zero or even negative) was also brought to the public's attention (**5.27**). The campaign for rights for women was reflected in the Equal Pay Act of 1970 which broadly aimed to achieve equal pay for equal work by the end of 1975. Some women began to use the abbreviation 'Ms'. Measures designed to increase equality for women included the Sex Discrimination Act 1975, and the setting up of the Equal Opportunities Commission in 1976. Immigration remained in or near the centre of political controversy during the period. The Immigration Act of 1971 introduced the concept of patriality, and the expulsion of Asians from Uganda in 1972 led to the need to absorb 26 thousand immigrants in a few months. In 1976 a Bill to strengthen the law against racial discrimination was introduced into Parliament.

A further significant feature of the early 1970s was the implementation of the central recommendations of the Seebohm Report by means of the Local Authority Social Services Act 1970. This required local authorities (through amalgamation of the old Children's and Welfare Departments into new Social Services Departments) to provide integrated personal social services, ideally community based, instead of dealing with the problems of individuals and families on a client group basis.

New legislation, particularly the Chronically Sick and Disabled Persons Act 1970 and the Children and Young Persons Act 1969, together with growing public concern over social problems and the desire to apply preventive and community based measures, all contributed to the growth of social services and especially in the manpower needed to provide these services. Subsequent reorganisation of both local government and the National Health Service (which generally resulted in coterminous boundaries) also increased the scope for improved collaboration between these services and between statutory and voluntary organisations.

Expanded social service provision was in part a reflection of the fact that social service commitments grew, as did the publicity given to social problems such as homelessness, teenagers coming alone to London, one-parent families (particularly following the Finer Report), and battered wives. Inflation had important effects in this area, too, as local authorities found it difficult to fund their activities without increasing both the rates and their borrowing requirement.

Protests grew against lack of public participation in some decision making. This exhibited itself at various levels; ranging from squatting, local planning inquiries into such problems as motorway routes, through regionalism to nationalism in Scotland and in Wales. Although nationalism's increased impact on the larger UK political parties was associated with the first post-war minority government in 1974, the practical implementation of devolution within Great Britain was still at the planning stage in mid-1976. The United Kingdom joined the European Economic Community (EEC) at the start of 1973 and this was endorsed in the United Kingdom's first national referendum in 1975.

One part of the United Kingdom – Northern Ireland – had had its own devolved assembly for decades, but increasing unrest there led to its prorogation in March 1972 and again in May 1974. Disorder, which had started with civil rights demonstrations, developed into severe rioting; and in 1971 the Irish Republican Army began a widespread campaign of terrorism, using guns and explosives against the security forces and civilian targets. With retaliatory action from paramilitary organisations on the 'loyalist' side, violence became a major feature of life in Northern Ireland in the 1970s. Terrorism occurred in Great Britain too, though on a much smaller scale. In 1970 and 1971 there were outbreaks of bombings for which the so-called 'Angry Brigade' claimed responsibility. In 1974 there was a much more serious and widespread outbreak caused by the spread of Northern Ireland terrorist activity to Great Britain. As a result bomb scares and explosions entered the experience of many ordinary people on this island for the first time for three decades.

Violence was by no means as dominant a social theme in Great Britain as in Northern Ireland, however. In many ways one of the most surprising features of the mid-1970s was the lack of violent protests about record post-war levels of unemployment. This may have been influenced by the higher levels of benefit available to unemployed people. Industrial unrest, however, there certainly was; and industrial action by the miners in 1972 and 1973–74 and by workers in Northern Ireland in 1974 had major effects on politics during the period. One result seems to have been an even greater governmental acceptance of the important role of trade unions in formulating national economic policy, and this was given institutional recognition when, in the April 1976 budget, proposed tax changes were made explicitly dependent on the acceptance of further wage restraint by the Trades Union Congress (TUC).

There was also an increasing tendency to use strikes, sit-ins, etc. for openly political ends; for example, in 1971 there was a one-day protest strike against the Industrial Relations Bill, and later there was further protest after the Bill became law as the National Industrial Relations Act, 1971. Again, in 1975 some health service employees refused to serve private patients in National Health Service (NHS) hospitals. Unrest among student teachers at the likelihood of a significant proportion of them not being able to find a job in teaching led to protests and sit-ins in the middle of 1976. Such militancy was not confined to students and manual workers, and the increase in white-collar unionism and industrial action by such groups as hospital doctors or civil servants was another feature of the first half of the seventies.

The physical environment was the subject of increasing public and governmental awareness. This was reflected in the introduction of several important and comprehensive items of legislation, such as the Water Act of 1973 and the Control of Pollution Act of 1974, and also in the early work of the standing Royal Commission on Environmental Pollution. The levels of some pollutants were reduced in both air and fresh water and new controls on the disposal of waste were implemented. Nevertheless, although there was no major nationwide environmental disaster during the period, there was concern that, amongst the many chemical substances being released into the environment, there would inevitably be some which would cause significant environmental problems. Certainly, some forms of pollution increased over the period in environmental sectors in which there was a more concentrated use of resources or facilities.

The amount of leisure time potentially available to people continued to increase as paid holidays per year increased. Data showing trends in leisure activities are rather scarce, but those that are available point to an increase in active leisure participation. Membership of most organisations for leisure activities increased over the period, particularly those for young people and those concerned with outdoor activities such as camping walking, water sports, and so on (**10.11**). However, television-watching remained by far the most popular leisure pastime, with the number of viewing hours continuing to increase steadily (**10.20**). The demand for continuing educational and recreational classes was met by the growth of attendances at evening classes and by the highly successful innovation of the Open University. Both 1975 and 1976 had particularly hot summers, 1976 in particular breaking many records. The early and mid-1970s were also a period of low average rainfall, and water rationing became necessary in some areas in the second half of 1976. Concern was expressed about possible long-term climatic changes – though the fears of different groups were often inconsistent.

In the light of all these developments it would perhaps be rash to attempt to single out one as having the greatest potential long-term significance. A strong candidate for that title must, however, be the continued fall in the birth rate. The associated changes in family structure and the consequences in all social areas of a static or slowly declining population were beginning to be seen to have potentially very far-reaching effects indeed.

While declining population numbers were a new feature at the national level, many localities had had much longer experience of this: some of the major cities, for instance, had been experiencing a loss of resident population for a decade or more, an important factor in this case being the spreading out of population to suburbs or adjacent smaller towns or rural areas.

Population

Changes in overall numbers
Between mid-1970 and mid-1976 the total population of the United Kingdom grew by a little over half a million. However, as shown in Figure I, almost all of this growth took place before 1974; and there has been virtually no change in the total numbers since then. The population stopped growing because of the fall in the number of births. The trend in the numbers of births is shown in

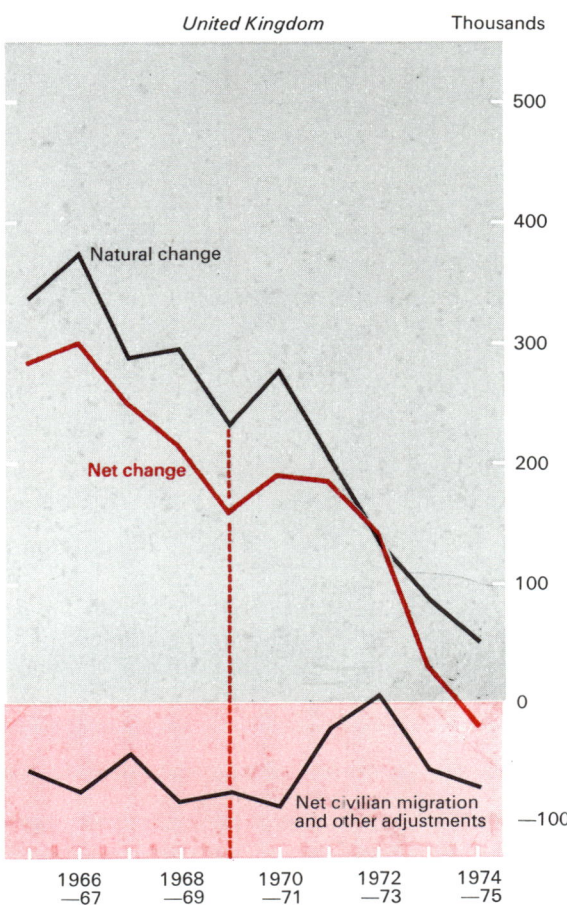

Figure I   *Population changes: mid-year to mid-year*

United Kingdom   Thousands

Natural change

Net change

Net civilian migration and other adjustments

1966 —67   1968 —69   1970 —71   1972 —73   1974 —75

Source: Population Trends No. 3, Office of Population Censuses and Surveys

Figure II. Although the number of births per thousand total population was unprecedentedly low in 1975, lower even than the levels of the 1930s, the fertility rate (births per thousand women aged 15–44 years) was still above that of the 1930s (**1.3** and **1.7**).

The other two factors affecting changes in overall population size are changes in the numbers of deaths and in migration into and out of the country. During the period the number of deaths remained broadly constant and so had no significant effect on the movements in population size. (Deaths are discussed further in the Health subsection.) Net outward migration continued, although for the year ending in mid-1973 migration was nearly balanced owing to the exceptional inflow of Ugandan Asians (**1.10**). Nevertheless, the effect of variations from year to year in migra-

Figure II   Total live births

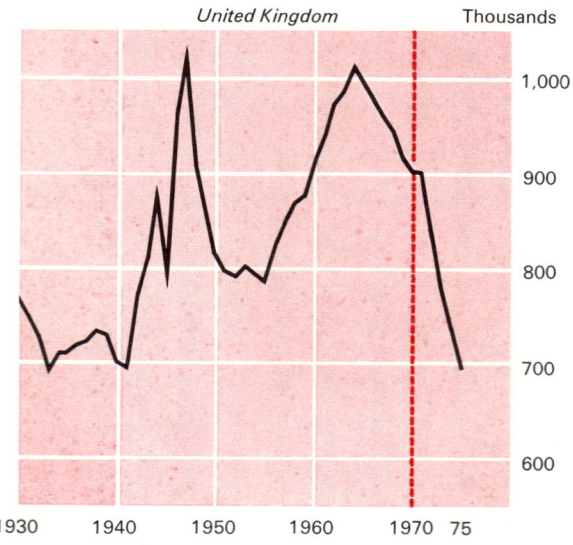

United Kingdom   Thousands

Source: Office of Population Censuses and Surveys

tion at the national level was far smaller than that of changes in the number of births (though the reverse is often true at the sub-national level).

During the early part of the period considerable public attention had been focused upon the issue of population growth. The Government set up the Population Panel in 1971 to examine the implications of continued population growth and its report was published in 1973. One of its conclusions was that in the long-term Britain would do better with a stationary rather than an increasing population. By the mid-1970s, when population growth had, at least temporarily, stopped, there was little public debate about the implications of a static or declining population. Nevertheless, many public policies, involving both long- and short-term plans, were already being re-examined. Provision of school teachers is one such policy; plans for new towns is another. At a personal level, attitudes towards the ideal number of children in a family seem to have changed, though presumably as a cause rather than an effect of changes in national population growth (**1.5**).

Changes in population structure

Changes in overall population size brought with them changes in the structure of the population, changes which may of course continue whether the population size remains static or falls. These showed themselves in various forms of population distribution – by region, by age group, and by ethnic group, for example.

The regional distribution of the population in the first half of the 1970s changed largely as a result of migration between different parts of the country. Figure III shows the percentage changes in population for the standard regions. The metropolitan counties generally showed substantial falls in population, as shown in Figure IV. In particular, the population of Greater London fell by over half a million between mid-1970 and mid-1975.

At the national level, there was not only a reduction in the number of children because of the falling birth rate since 1964, but also an increased number of elderly people, the latter reflecting birth patterns in the early years of this century and in the final decades of the last century. Between mid-1970 and mid-1975 the number of people in the United Kingdom aged over the National Insurance retirement ages (65 for men and 60 for women) rose by 9 per cent, from 8,912 thousand to 9,518 thousand. Proportionally, there was a particularly large increase in the number of people in the age group 85 and over: 17 per cent, from 439 thousand to 515 thousand, over the same period. These are people who are generally especially in need of medical care (**1.1**).

Figure III   Home population: estimated percentage changes mid-1970 to mid-1975: standard regions

Source: Office of Population Censuses and Surveys

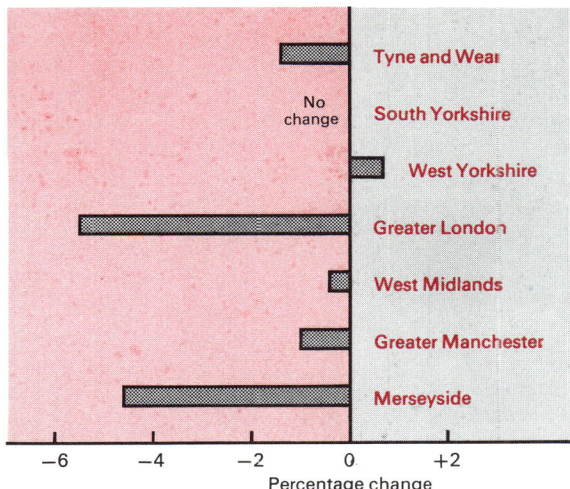

*Figure IV   Home population:
estimated percentage changes
mid-1970 to mid-1975:
metropolitan counties*

Tyne and Wear
South Yorkshire
West Yorkshire
Greater London
West Midlands
Greater Manchester
Merseyside

No change

−6   −4   −2   0   +2

Percentage change

Source: Office of Population Censuses and Surveys

People of New Commonwealth and Pakistani ethnic origin formed a higher proportion of our population in mid-1975 than they had in mid-1970; their numbers rose from 2·6 to 3·3 per cent of the population of Great Britain between these dates. Migration accounted for almost half of this increase, and natural increase for the remainder. The population of New Commonwealth and Pakistani ethnic origin has a higher proportion of young people than the rest of the population, and, as a result, has had a smaller proportion of deaths and a higher proportion of births than the population as a whole. The proportion of births which were of New Commonwealth or Pakistani ethnic origin rose from 5·9 per cent in 1970–71 to 6·4 per cent in 1974–75. The numbers of these births thus fell, but not as quickly as those of the Great Britain population as a whole. This difference may be accounted for at least in part by the comparatively young age structure of the population of New Commonwealth and Pakistani ethnic origin (**1.20**).

Marriage and divorce

The trend to younger first marriage, which had been noticeable throughout the 1960s, was boosted in 1970 when the Family Law Reform Act lowered to 18 the age at which people could marry without having to obtain parental permission (for England and Wales). As a result of this there was a sharp rise in the number of people marrying at ages under 20, in particular at 18, and

this contributed to an increase in marriages between teenagers. In 1970 the average ages at marriage for bachelors and spinsters in England and Wales were lower than at any time since the beginning of civil registration, 140 years ago. Subsequently there was a slight rise; and in 1975 the average ages at marriage were 25·0 and 22·8 for bachelors and spinsters respectively, the same as the mid-1960s. After 1972 a fall in the proportion of the unmarried population marrying was seen in every age group. The biggest fall was in the 20–24 year age group.

The fairly steady growth (averaging 9 per cent annually) in the number of divorces in the 1960s accelerated in the early 1970s following the 1971 Divorce Law Reform Act. (This applied only to England and Wales.) In 1972 the number of divorces in England and Wales was double that of 1970. The number fell back in 1973 but rose by about 7 per cent in each of the two succeeding years. It reached 120 thousand in 1975, slightly more than in 1972. This rapid increase led to a sharp rise in the number of divorced persons in the population and the number of young divorcees increased especially quickly. Most of them remarried quite quickly, however, particularly the younger ones, so the rise in the number of divorces was followed by an increase in remarriages in the United Kingdom. The number of these marriages, where one or both of the partners had previously been married, rose by nearly a half (from 82 thousand in 1970 to 125 thousand in 1975). In contrast the number of first marriages (of both partners) fell steadily from 389 thousand in 1970 to 306 thousand in 1975, a figure close to the lowest annual total of the post-war period. The result was that after 1970 the total number of marriages rose to a peak in 1972 but then fell; while the proportion of marriages which were remarriages rose sharply from 17 per cent in 1970 to 29 per cent in 1975 (**1.11**, **1.12**).

Births

The decline in the number of births during the period occurred alongside many other social developments which may have had a bearing on it. Examples of these are the developments in family planning services and in contraceptives, and the increase in the number of abortions up to 1972 (when the numbers began to level off). There were also changes in attitudes towards the ideal number of children to have, as discussed below. It is difficult to estimate the impact of these factors, since they tend to interact. The increasing use of more efficient contraceptives should have made it easier for families to achieve the number and spacing of births that they wanted, and this in turn

13

may have been a factor behind the changes in attitudes towards the ideal family size, as well as the changes in practice. There were two changes in child-bearing patterns within families which had major effects on the numbers of births. These were: first the trend towards delaying the birth of the first child until later in marriage, and second the trend towards the decrease in the number of births which were the families third or fourth child. The first trend resulted in an increase in the proportion of women childless two and three years after marriage, and the second resulted in a fall in the proportion of families with three or more children (**1.15** to **1.17**).

Apart from changes in actual child-bearing patterns, there were also changes in the number of children expected by married couples, and in the number of children they considered to be the ideal number to have. There is evidence that the proportion of parents wanting three or more children was very much lower in 1973 than in 1968[2], and, further, that the proportion of women, married between 1960 and 1967, considering three or more children an ideal number for couples similar to themselves and their husbands, halved between 1967 and 1973[3]. Results from the General Household Survey are in line with this.

The continued decline in family size, which reduced the length of time spent in building families and in bringing up small children, and the tendency for births to be delayed until later in marriage, are linked with the increased employment of married women, which is discussed in the Employment sub-section.

The number of illegitimate births declined sharply in absolute terms, though rising from 8·2 per cent of all live births in Great Britain in 1970 to 9·1 per cent in 1975. Premarital conceptions fell both absolutely and also as a proportion of all live births, representing 9·0 per cent of live births in 1970 and 6·9 per cent in 1975. In 1975, 14 per cent of recently married women had a premaritally conceived birth, as opposed to 20 per cent in 1970. The 1975 figure was the lowest since 1955. (These figures apply to first marriages only.) (**1.7**)

Households

The private household population in Great Britain increased by 1·1 per cent between mid-1970 and mid-1975, while the number of private households (based on Census definitions) increased by 4·7 per cent. This difference is linked with the

continuing rise in the proportion of smaller households, containing one or two people, and the decline in the number of larger households. The increase in the number of smaller households was partly due to the trend in the formation of single person households among the younger age groups, partly to the increased number of elderly people, many of whom live just with their spouses or on their own, and partly to the increased number of divorced individuals (**2.4**, **2.7**).

Education

Generally speaking, the period was one of expansion in education, though the pace of expansion was slower than in the 1960s. A 10-year programme of expansion announced by the Government in December 1972 was reduced in 1975 owing to the economic situation, revised estimates of the school population, and the tendency for participation in higher education to increase less rapidly than had been expected. One major event during the period was the raising of the school leaving age from 15 to 16 in the academic year 1972/73. There were also changes in the educational institutions; for example in 1974 the Government announced its commitment to a fully comprehensive system of education in schools in England and Wales and declared its intention to eliminate the grant paid to the direct grant and assisted schools giving them the choice to become fully state-maintained schools or to become independent schools. (In Scotland, where the educational system differs in many respects, virtually all public sector schools were comprehensive by 1974.) Some teacher training colleges were integrated with other higher education institutions and a few were closed.

There was considerable debate over the type of education given in educational institutions, and one focus of this debate was the discussion over the effect which changes in teaching methods and changes in the types of schools used have had on the standards of education in schools. Particular developments were the Bullock Committee's inquiry into the teaching of reading and the other uses of English in schools, the report of which was published in 1975, and the formation of the Assessment of Performance Unit by the Department of Education and Science (DES) to improve the methods available for assessing educational achievement. Concern over the difficulties of the educationally disadvantaged was reflected in the launching of the Adult Literacy Programme, designed to combat adult illiteracy, and in the establishment of the Educational Disadvantage Unit to act as the central reference point in the DES for all matters concerned with the educationally disadvantaged and the education of immigrants.

---

[2] *How Many Children?* Ann Cartwright. Institute for Social Studies in Medical Care.
[3] *Families Five Years On.* Myra Woolf and Sue Pegden. HMSO.

What follows in this sub-section has to be concerned with the educational system of the country since this is the source of almost all our statistics. The numbers in the educational system, at its various levels, are determined not only by government policy but also by the numbers in the population at the relevant age levels and, particularly at the higher ages, by personal choice. Figure V shows the proportion of the population in full-time education at several different age levels. (The jump in some of the series is due to the raising of the school leaving age.) The flattening off of the trends towards increased participation at the higher age levels in recent years is noticeable.

Figure V   *Percentage of population in full-time education[1]: by age*

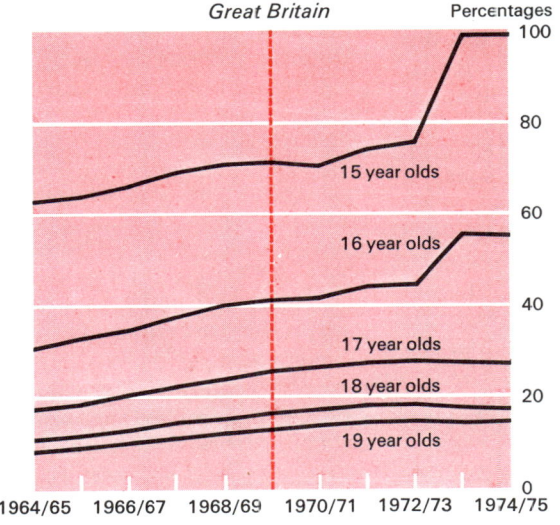

Great Britain   Percentages

15 year olds
16 year olds
17 year olds
18 year olds
19 year olds

1964/65   1966/67   1968/69   1970/71   1972/73   1974/75

[1] As at 1 January each year.

Source: Department of Education and Science

In order to study the main trends more closely it is best to look at the different institutions in turn.

Schools

During the period state provision for nursery education increased substantially, despite the fall in the numbers in the under-five population caused by the decline in births after 1964. The number of places in United Kingdom public sector nursery schools rose from 34 thousand in 1970 to 45 thousand in 1975 (**3.4**). Including nursery and other classes in primary schools and in the independent sector, the proportion of the 2–4 age group attending school in 1975 rose from 12·4 per cent in 1970 to 20·8 per cent in 1975 (**3.1**).

Between the ages of five and the minimum school leaving age education is compulsory, and so the number of pupils aged five and over in primary schools is almost totally determined by the numbers of births in earlier years. Owing to the pattern of these births, the numbers of primary school pupils aged five and over reached a peak in 1974 in England and Wales (1973 in Scotland) and the decline after 1974 will be continued for some years to come (**3.4**).

The pattern of births in still earlier years – the late 1950s and 1960s – caused the numbers of pupils in secondary schools to rise during the period at each age level below the minimum school leaving age. The total was further increased by the raising of the school leaving age from 15 to 16 in the academic year 1972/73 (**3.4**).

Above the school leaving age, the numbers in school depend not only on the numbers in the population in that age group, but also on the proportion of children staying on at school. An indication of the proportion of children wishing to stay on at school after the school leaving age is given by the proportion of 17-year olds at school. This fell between January 1973 and January 1974 and had fallen again by January 1975 (**3.5**). At the same time there was an increase in the numbers of young people taking 'A' levels at colleges of further education rather than in school (**3.12**). The longer-term effect on the raising of the school leaving age on voluntary staying-on rates is not yet clear.

Despite the increase in the numbers of pupils, the average pupil/teacher ratios in public sector schools in Great Britain continued to fall. In primary schools the figure fell from 27·7 in 1970 to 24·9 in 1974, and in secondary schools from 17·7 in 1970 to 17·3 in 1974.

The number of children leaving school without having passed any public examination fell during the period. In 1974 four out of five children leaving school in England and Wales had some such qualification compared with three out of five only two years before. The rise was mainly accounted for by the numbers with no GCE passes but with CSE pases of grade five or better, and this itself was probably due to the raised school leaving age, altered in 1972/73. There was little change in the proportion of leavers with 5 or more 'O' levels (including CSE grade 1) or in the proportion with 1 or more 'A' level passes. In Scotland, where there is no system of examinations parallel to the CSE examinations, the extra year at school resulted in a significant increase in the number of 'O' grade examination entries; the proportion of leavers with 5 or more 'O' grades and the proportion with one or more 'H' grades, both showed increases up to 1974. The overall output of pupils and students passing one or more 'A' levels while at school or further education establishments in England and Wales was 132 thousand (26 thousand from the latter) in 1973/74, 500 more than in 1972/73 and 6,200 more than in 1970/71. The proportion of school leavers passing two or more 'A' levels in a combination of arts and science subjects continued to increase, reaching nearly one in five in 1973/74.

The proportion of school leavers continuing directly to full-time higher and further education remained at approximately 20 per cent during the period.

Higher and further education

The proportion of young home students entering higher education courses after rising sharply during the 1960s, remained at about 13·4 per cent of the 18 year old population after 1969. Because of this, the number of full-time students in higher education in Great Britain grew much more slowly during the period than it had in the previous five years, although the slackening in demand for places from home students was partly off-set by a rapid increase in the number of overseas students. The number of young men entering higher education courses remained constant, but the number of young women entrants rose steadily after 1970, by about 2 per cent a year (**3.14**).

Within the higher education sector the pattern of courses began to alter considerably. The number of students admitted to courses of initial training at teacher training colleges fell from the peak reached in 1972 in England and Wales, and 1971 in Scotland, as a result of the government policy to reduce the numbers of teachers in training substantially. This followed the decline in the numbers of births, which, as mentioned above, led to a fall in the numbers of pupils in primary schools after 1974 and will have an increasing effect on the overall numbers in the school population for some years to come. Although some colleges were closed, and some amalgamated with polytechnics and to a lesser extent universities, others introduced courses leading to a non-teaching qualification, and new courses, such as a two year diploma of Higher Education, were being developed.

The number of students at universities continued to grow, though not as quickly as in the 1960s. The proportion of overseas students at universities in Great Britain increased considerably, rising from 3·8 per cent of undergraduates and 25·6 per cent of postgraduates in 1970/71 to 6·5 per cent and 33·4 per cent, respectively, in 1975/76. Science subjects continued to attract a higher proportion of overseas students than the average for all subjects. However, in general, science subjects lost ground to the social sciences. Women increased their share of university places from 28 per cent to 33 per cent.

There was a steady growth in the number of full-time and sandwich students at polytechnics in England and Wales (apart from their departments of education). The total numbers of such students rose from 61 thousand in 1970 to 77 thousand in 1974. There was a particularly marked rise in the numbers on Council for National Academic Awards (CNAA) degree courses, and graduates with CNAA degrees accounted for 14 per cent of all new first degree graduates in 1975. This rise (together with the rapid expansion of the Open University, which had some 50 thousand students following courses in 1975) led to a fall in the proportion of graduates with traditional university degrees.

In further education, at lower levels, there were considerably more students on full-time non-advanced courses in 1974 than there had been in 1970 (**3.13**). As most of these students were in the 16–19 age group this growth was no doubt partly because further education courses were increasingly seen as an alternative to staying on at school. In times of recession, and particularly in Autumn 1975, the numbers entering further education may well have been further increased because of the difficulties that many school leavers would have had in finding employment. The numbers of workers attending day release and block release courses decreased by just over 20 per cent between 1970 and 1975, reflecting a similar fall in the proportion of young people in employment.

Employment

As mentioned in the introduction, the generally high level of unemployment, which reached levels not previously seen since the war, seems to have been one of the dominating features of the mid-1970s. The level of unemployment generated much discussion, both about the reasons for the rise and measures required to bring the level down, and also about the composition of the population of registered unemployed. For example, there was a debate about the proportion of the total who were moving between jobs and about the number not actively seeking work. Efforts were made to preserve jobs in the labour market by government intervention, sometimes against short-term commercial considerations. Apart from unemployment, there were significant changes in the working population during the period, particularly noteworthy being the rise in the number of wives working in paid employment.

In some years there was considerable industrial unrest. Following industrial action by the coalminers, industry was required to work a three-day week for a short period in 1974. Measures introduced by one government to regulate the affairs of the trades unions were repealed by another, and governments increasingly accepted that the consent of the trades unions was essential to an effective industrial relations policy. Within the trade union movement itself, one significant change was the growth of the 'white-collar' unions.

The working population

Over the period 1970 to 1975 the working population of Great Britain increased slightly from 24·7 million to 25·2 million: the fall in the number of men in employment was less than the increase in the number of women. The distribution of the civilian labour force continued to change between industries. Between 1970 and 1975 the number of employees in manufacturing fell from 8·16 million to 7·33 million, or from 37·1 per cent to 33·0 per cent of all employees in civilian employment. Both the level of employment in manufacturing and its share of all employees in employment fell during the 1971–72 recession: neither the level nor the share had recovered by mid-1976. While the number of people in employment declined between 1970 and 1975, output (as measured by the change in the index of production over the whole period) did not; and the rise in output per head in the production industries was over 9 per cent.

The structure of the labour force was principally affected by three factors: changes in the flow from full-time education to employment, the increased proportion of wives in paid employment, and the rise in the numbers of part-time employees. These are discussed below.

The most significant change in the output of the educational system was caused by the raising of the school leaving age from 15 to 16 in the academic year 1972/73, resulting in the loss of 15-year olds to the labour market from September 1972 onwards. The proportion of school leavers going on to formal full-time post-school education or training increased: even though the proportion going on to higher education showed little change

the proportion (generally of the younger leavers) entering further education courses rose. As a consequence of these changes there was a steady fall in the proportion of people in the age ranges 16 to 18 in, or looking for, jobs, an increase in the average age of first entry to employment, and an increase in the proportion of new entrants to employment with formal educational qualifications.

The increase in the proportion of married women in paid employment was associated with long run changes in women's employment patterns and in their roles within the family. A high proportion of women continued to work after marriage until the arrival of their first child; and so the trend to postponement of the start of child-bearing tended to increase the proportion of younger married women in paid employment. A proportion of women have always worked more or less continuously throughout their child-bearing period (this proportion was higher in 1971 than a decade earlier, though it was still fairly low in absolute terms). The greatest change was in the proportion of women returning to work after a spell at home looking after their children while their children were still very young. At the same time, smaller family sizes, and shorter periods of child-bearing, meant fewer years during which very young children were in the family. The number of women prepared to return to employment once their children were old enough to attend school apparently increased, while a higher proportion of children under five attended nursery schools or day nurseries.

However, these increased tendencies for married women to undertake paid employment were undoubtedly a reflection of other factors as well. During the period attitudes towards the employment of women changed, and many women felt it more appropriate for them to go out to work than they had done in the past. Career opportunities for women improved, partly as a result of the increased scope for employment in the service industries. Indeed, the demographic changes mentioned above may have been due to some extent to deliberate choice by women to free themselves for employment.

Many married women who had paid jobs, particularly those with children, engaged in part-time employment only. The number of part-time workers in the labour force increased considerably between 1971 and 1975, and their share of employment rose from 14 per cent to 17 per cent. The greater part of this increase was due to the increase in the number of female part-time workers (particularly in the service industries), from 2·76 million in 1971 in Great Britain to 3·55 million in

1975; but the number of male part-time workers also increased, from 0·58 million to 0·70 million, over the same period.

Unemployment

Unemployment was significantly higher than earlier in the post-war period, though not unusually high by contemporaneous international standards in the Western World. In March 1972 the unemployment rates in Great Britain (seasonally adjusted and excluding school leavers and students) reached 3·9 per cent, and the level in the 1975 recession was even higher. At the beginning of 1976 the numbers of unemployed stood at 1·16 million, 5·1 per cent of employees. The lowest level of unemployment recorded between 1970 and 1976 was not far below half a million people, at a level representing about 2·1 per cent of employees. As is usual, the average duration of unemployment increased during the periods of recession and increased more markedly during the more severe recession of 1975 than in the recession of 1971–72 (Figure VI) (**4.17**).

Unemployment levels and rates must, of course, be interpreted carefully. It seems likely that at the end of the period the figures above were affected by a greater propensity for women to register as unemployed in circumstances where in earlier years they would not have done so, while figures for school leavers were affected by a propensity for school leavers unable to find work to register more quickly than before. Nevertheless, it does seem clear that the peaks of unemployment affected younger workers disproportionately, particularly

during 1975, and that the 1975 recession also saw a disproportionate increase in unemployment among women, this latter being partly associated with the large proportion of younger workers in the female workforce. Very large numbers of school leavers registered as unemployed in

Figure VI   Unemployed[1]

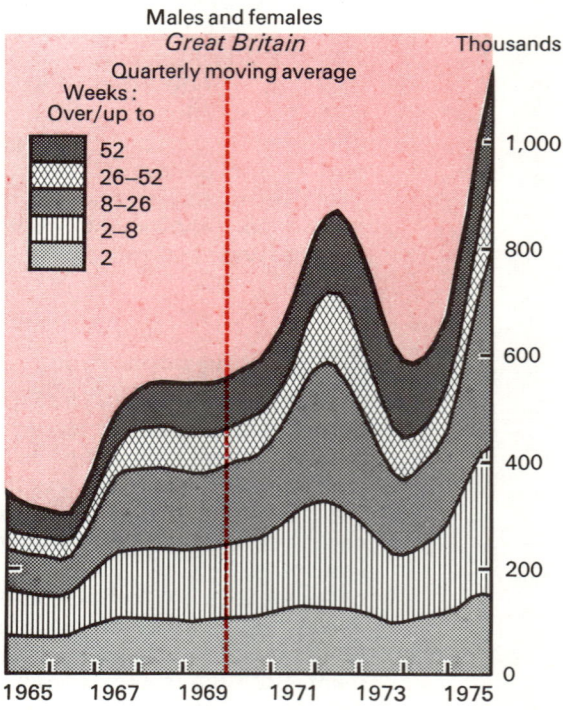

By duration of unemployment

[1] Casuals were excluded prior to April 1972. Adult students registered for vacation employment were excluded from October 1975 onwards.

Source: Department of Employment

Figure VII   Number of school leavers unemployed in July, August, September and October 1970–1975

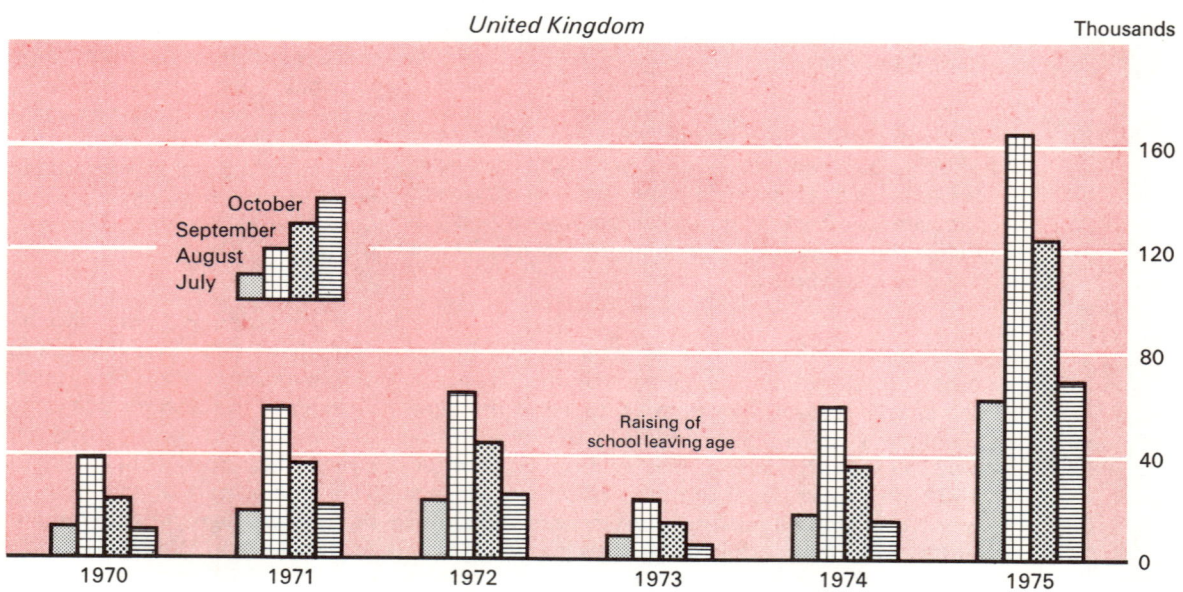

Source: Department of Employment Gazette, Department of Employment

1971–72 and what was then a record number in 1975, as shown in Figure VII. (The figures for 1975 will have been affected by the tendency, already noted, for school leavers to register as unemployed earlier than in previous years.) The 1975 record was broken in 1976.

Regional disparities in unemployment were considerable, with Northern Ireland having the highest rates relative to the national average in the period 1970–75. Since Northern Ireland, and other regions with unemployment rates in excess of the national average, tended to move towards the national average, regional disparities in unemployment rates were reduced between 1970 and 1975. However, this may be at least partly accounted for by the tendency, seen in previous economic cycles, for regional disparities in unemployment to widen in times of boom and contract in times of recession.

In order to alleviate unemployment and to provide short-term jobs to bridge the period until demand for labour increased, the Government initiated a programme of temporary employment measures in 1975.

Hours of work and holidays

The number of normal basic hours of work for men in manual jobs remained steady at about 40 hours a week during the period 1970–75. Average weekly hours actually worked by men fell with the onset of the 1971–72 recession, when they averaged about 45, increased by 1973 with the upturn from the recession, but later fell back again. (**10.1 and 10.3**).

There was a marked increase in the period 1970–75 in the number of manual workers having an entitlement to receive more than three weeks paid holiday in a year. At end-1970 only 3 per cent had a holiday entitlement of more than three weeks, but by end-1975 this had increased to about 80 per cent[4]. Two-thirds of non-manual workers were already entitled to this length of holiday by 1970; by April 1974, the latest date for which figures are available, the proportion had risen to three-quarters[4]. There were also changes in the pattern of holidays taken during the period. The number of people taking holidays away from home, either in Great Britain or abroad, continued to increase, from $40\frac{1}{4}$ millions in 1970 to $48\frac{3}{4}$ millions in 1973, falling slightly in 1974 due to the rise in travel costs after the oil price rises. The fall, which is accounted for by the fall in holidays taken

---

[4] The figures for manual workers relate to basic holiday entitlements as laid down in national collective agreements and wages board and council orders, and understate actual holiday entitlements. The figures for non-manual workers relate to actual entitlements and to men only.

abroad, coincided with a change in the way people travelled, with a drop in the proportion going on package tours (**10.6 to 10.9**).

Industrial training

The majority of Government sponsored industrial training is effected through the various Industry Training Boards which were set up before 1970 and which are funded through levies on employers. It is estimated that in 1974 roughly 2 million people were receiving industrial training, mostly under the aegis of these Boards. There is also, however, a separate system of industrial training, mainly on retraining programmes, to meet the excess demand for certain skills. In the late 1960s approximately 10 thousand people each year were trained under such schemes. In 1975 the system was reorganised as the Training Opportunities Scheme (TOPS) under the auspices of the new Training Services Agency and the numbers trained increased sevenfold – to roughly 68 thousand in 1975. This was coupled with an overhaul of the Government's employment services which began in 1972. The two developments were linked in concept: one provided an improved information service about skills in demand and on offer, and the other an improved system of teaching the skills to meet demand (**4.18**).

Industrial disputes

There was some change in the pattern, and a marked change in the incidence, of working days

Figure VIII   Working days lost due to industrial disputes

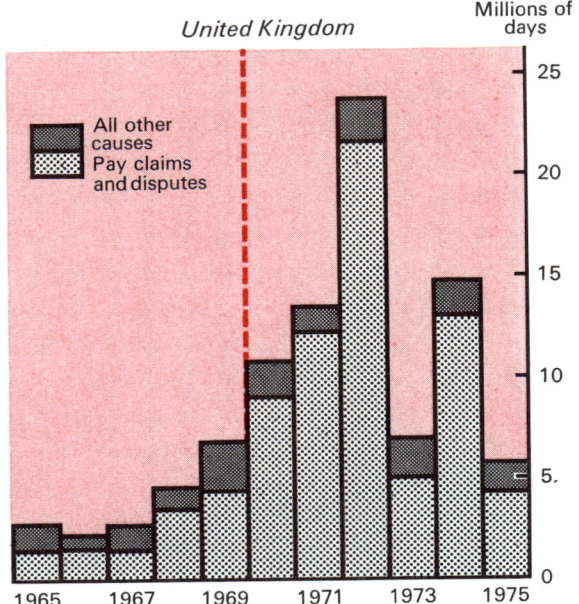

Source: Department of Employment

lost in industrial disputes in the period 1971 to 1975 relative to the period 1966 to 1970 (Figure VIII). In the earlier period disputes over pay were responsible for nearly 75 per cent of days lost, against nearly 90 per cent in the period 1971 to 1975. Even if the effect of the miners' strikes in 1972 and 1974 are removed there were almost twice the number of days lost through industrial disputes over the period 1971 to 1975 than in the period 1966 to 1970. However in 1975 the number of working days lost was the lowest since 1968 and this improved trend, which was also reflected in the number of stoppages and workers involved, continued into 1976.

Income and Wealth

During this period, for the first time in many years, there was a significant alteration in the distribution of earnings, with the differentials between those with the highest and the lowest earnings being gradually eroded. There were also significant changes in relative price levels. These trends tend to be obscured by the very high rate of inflation during the period. The general rate of inflation, as measured by the rate of increase of the General Index of Retail Prices, rose to unprecedented levels in 1975, before slackening off rela-

tively in the first half of 1976. Figure IX shows this very rapid increase in both retail prices and gross earnings. The period can be divided roughly into two parts, with the second being distinguished by the very much higher rate of inflation. Figure IX indicates that average gross earnings increased faster than average prices until the end of 1974 (except during the first quarter of 1974, when many people were working a three-day week).

Other effects of inflation were the erosion of almost all forms of savings and investments in real terms and the worsening of the financial situation of people dependent on fixed incomes for support. During the period attention was often focused upon the problems of people in poverty, usually defined as people in families with incomes below, or just above, Supplementary Benefits level (**5.29**). One problem, for a relatively small number of families on low incomes was the so-called 'poverty trap', illustrated in Chart **5.27** and its accompanying text. The proportion of average earnings taken in tax increased; but, on average, gross earnings rose fast enough for take-home pay to have been higher in 1975 than in 1970 even after taking inflation into account.

Figure IX   Indices of average earnings and retail prices

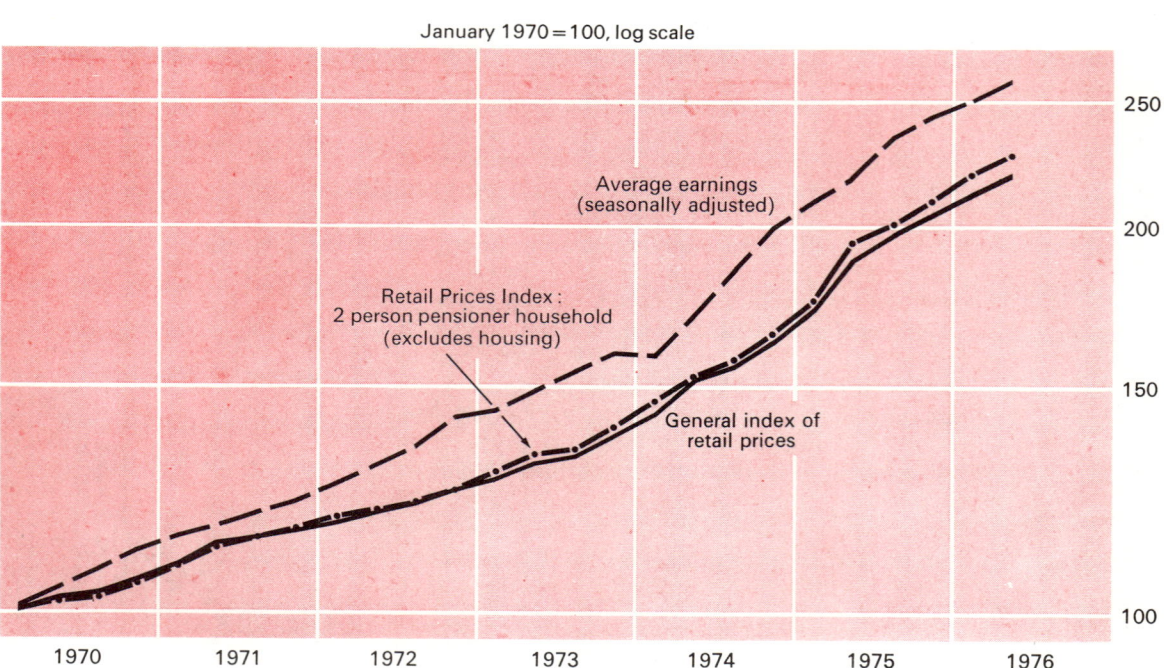

January 1970 = 100, log scale

Average earnings (seasonally adjusted)

Retail Prices Index: 2 person pensioner household (excludes housing)

General index of retail prices

Source: Department of Employment

Aggregate personal income

Real personal disposable income (the total income of the personal sector after deduction of tax contributions and calculated at the prices of 1970) rose by 18 per cent between 1970 and 1974. The main source of total personal income continued to be employment, though its share, like that of the category 'rents, dividends and net interest, etc.', fell, while the share of income from categories 'self-employment' and 'national insurance benefits and other current grants' rose.

The statistics available for earnings from employment, which represents a substantial part of total personal income, allow comparatively recent trends to be analysed. Average gross earnings from employment rose rapidly between April 1970 and April 1975, as shown in Figure IX; but the rise was not the same for all categories of earners. Between April 1970 and April 1975 median earnings of manual workers increased faster than the (higher) median earnings of non-manual workers, women's median earnings increased faster than men's – to some extent in anticipation of the implementation of the Equal Pay Act by the end of 1975 –, and median earnings of young workers increased faster than median earnings of older workers. The increases are compared in Figure X, which indicates that the median earnings of the five groups tended to converge in proportionate terms, since the large percentage increases were generally obtained by groups with the lower median wage levels.

This movement towards greater equality of earnings can be seen within groups as well. In the case of both manual and non-manual workers the differentials between the highest and lowest paid decreased during the period. (More precisely, expressed as a proportion of median earnings, the top earnings deciles tended to decline, while the bottom ones increased.) This closing of the differentials is particularly striking for male non-manual workers.

The effect of taxation on gross earnings varies according to individual circumstances, but it may be illustrated by taking a hypothetical case. Taking, for example, the case of a family consisting of a married couple with two children under 11 years of age, whose income comes only from the husband's manual occupation and family allowances, it is possible to calculate the net earnings that would be obtained from different levels of gross earnings after deducting direct taxes and national insurance contributions. The change in net earnings over the period, resulting from a given series of gross earnings, can then be divided by the corresponding change in the Retail Price Index to give the change in *real disposable earnings*. Figure XI shows the changes in *real disposable earnings* since 1970 for families with 5 different levels of gross earnings, and shows clearly the greater increases in the case of those families with lower gross earnings. The proportion of gross income which would have gone in *direct* taxes for a household, of the type described above, whose gross earnings were equal to the median gross earnings of manual workers, rose during the period, from 18·7 per cent in 1970 to 23·3 per cent in 1975.

Household income

The hypothetical household discussed above is of course by no means typical of all households. Data from the Family Expenditure Survey may be used to study trends in the income of actual households, taking into account a far wider range of household income than earnings and family allowances alone. Analyses of this kind carried out in the Central Statistical Office show the average income and taxes paid for several different household types. The income definitions used in this work are *original income* (which is the total combined income of the members of the household from employment, self-employment, and investment – including occupational pensions) and *disposable income* (which is original income plus direct cash benefits less both direct taxes and employees' own national insurance contributions). Original income plus cash benefits may be thought of as the *gross income* of the household.

Figure X   *Percentage increase in median gross weekly earnings of full-time employees[1]: April 1970 to April 1975*

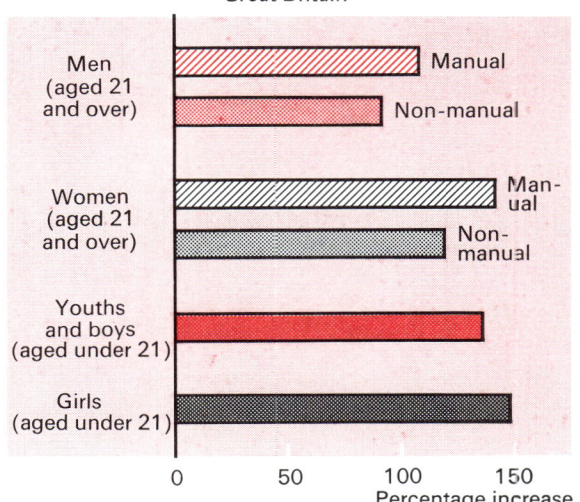

Great Britain

Men (aged 21 and over) — Manual / Non-manual
Women (aged 21 and over) — Manual / Non-manual
Youths and boys (aged under 21)
Girls (aged under 21)

0   50   100   150
Percentage increase

[1] Excluding those whose pay was affected by absence.

Source: New Earnings Survey, Department of Employment

Figure XI   Indices of 'real disposable earnings' at 1970 prices: at certain levels of the earnings distribution

Married couple with two children aged under 11[1]

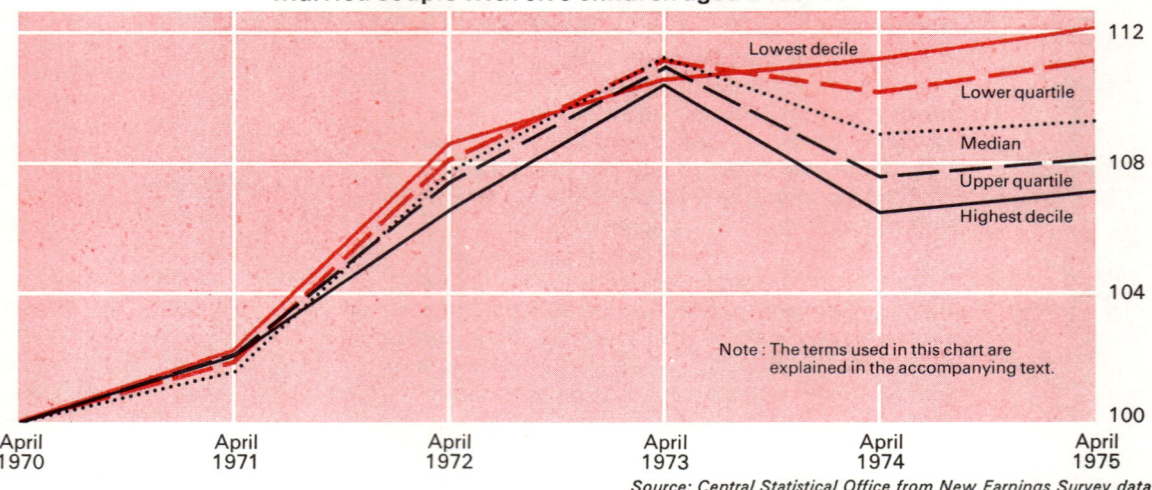

Source: Central Statistical Office from New Earnings Survey data

The average levels of original income and disposable income are markedly different for different types of households; and the relationship between income, taxation, and benefits is also different. In particular, for the hypothetical case used above disposable income is less than original income; but the reverse might be true if the household were unemployed. Disposable income is again, on average, more than original income for single retired person households (**5.11 to 5.14**).

During the period 1970–1975 the disposable income of all households taken together rose by 97 per cent, which compares with an increase of 84 per cent in the General Index of Retail Prices over the same period. The average change for households containing two adults and two children was 99 per cent, and for single retired person households, 117 per cent. Direct taxes (income tax plus employees' national insurance contributions) accounted for 20 per cent of gross household incomes (more precisely original incomes plus cash benefits) in 1975, compared with 16 per cent in 1970 and only 15 per cent in 1972. Total taxes (both direct and indirect) accounted for 36 per cent of gross household incomes in 1975, the same as in 1970, after a fall to 32 per cent in 1973. There was thus a change in the relative magnitudes of direct and indirect taxation, which respectively accounted for 16 per cent and 20 per cent of gross household incomes in 1970, but 20 per cent and 16 per cent in 1975.

Taking all households together, there was a rise in the proportion of disposable income represented by cash benefits. Movements in the levels of cash benefits and in the numbers receiving them are discussed below.

Social security and income support

The early 1970s saw some selectivity in the improvement of social security benefits, favouring the elderly, the chronically sick, and the disabled. Many of the trends in the numbers receiving the various benefits were closely connected to the changes discussed in the Population sub-section and elsewhere in this Commentary. For example, the rise in the number of elderly was reflected in a steady rise in the number of retirement pensions in the United Kingdom between 1970 and 1975, by about half a million in all, to 8·3 million (**5.22**).

The number of recipients of unemployment benefit was higher at the end of 1975 than 1970, by 223 thousand, but in this case there were considerable fluctuations rather than a steady rise. This reflects the movements in the total numbers registered as unemployed, shown in Figure VI.

There was an increase of 200 thousand, to over 4·4 million, in the number of families receiving family allowances. The total number of children attracting allowances, however, scarcely changed (**5.30**). This implies a drop in the average size of the families who received the allowances, another facet of the trends in family size discussed in the Population sub-section.

In August 1971, Family Income Supplement (FIS), a new benefit aimed specifically at families with children, came into being. It was designed to supplement the income of a family whose head is in full-time employment and earns below the prescribed amount, which has been uprated roughly in line with prices. In December 1975 the

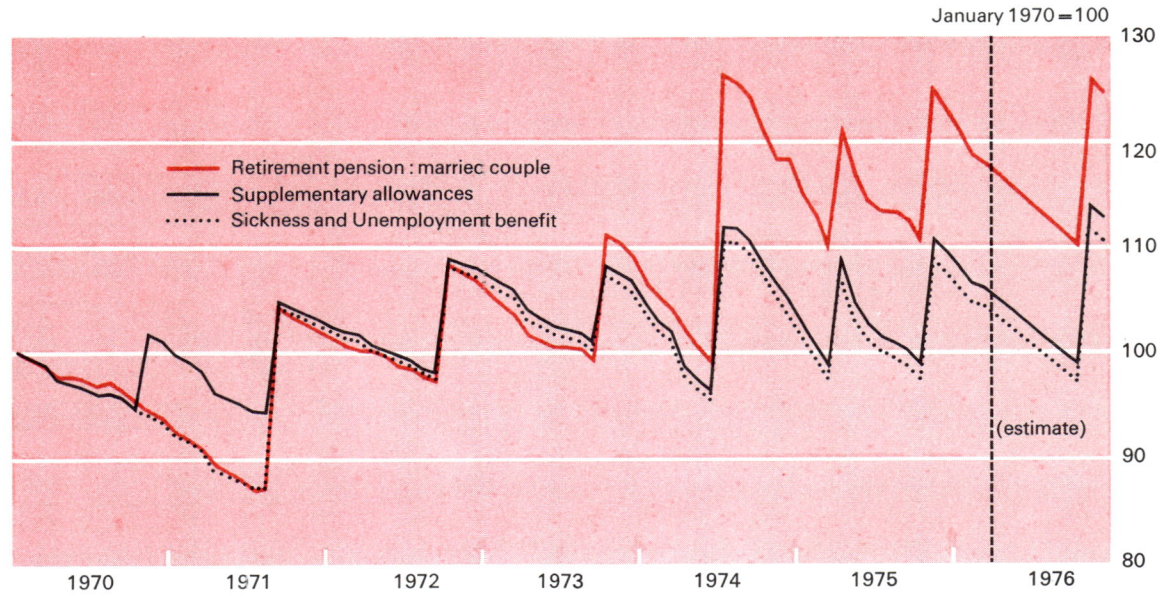

Figure XII   Real value[1] of pensions and benefits

January 1970 = 100

Retirement pension : married couple
Supplementary allowances
Sickness and Unemployment benefit

(estimate)

1970   1971   1972   1973   1974   1975   1976

[1] Deflated by General Index of Retail Prices.

Source: Central Statistical Office

number of families in the United Kingdom receiving FIS was 68 thousand, considerably lower than the levels of over 100 thousand which were reached in 1972 and 1973. The reason for this fall appears to have been a decline in the number of families eligible for FIS – caused in turn by an improvement in the pay of many low wage earners relative to prices. Take-up rates for FIS are estimated to have risen from roughly 50 per cent in 1972 to 75 per cent in 1974. Over half the families receiving FIS in 1975 had only one parent (**5.26**).

Among new benefits introduced for the chronically sick and disabled was attendance allowance, a benefit payable to severely disabled people requiring frequent attention or continual supervision, which came in by stages between 1971 and 1973. In December 1975 this was being paid in respect of 220 thousand disabled persons who had certain specified attendance requirements.

The number of people receiving supplementary benefit at the end of 1975 was, at 2·8 million, much the same as at the end of 1970, although the number of their dependants was 200 thousand more at 1·6 million. Within the roughly unchanged total of recipients, the number of retirement pensioners receiving a supplement to their retirement pensions declined. This was in spite of the rise in the number of retirement pensioners, since many of them elected to receive other benefits instead of supplementary benefits. The number of sick

and disabled under retirement age also fell. However the number of unemployed and of single parent families being helped by supplementary allowances were higher at the end of 1975 than of 1970. Taken together these changes in the composition of those receiving supplementary benefits explain the rise in the number of their dependants (**5.23**).

Figure XII shows changes in the 'real value' of retirement pensions, the flat-rate of unemployment and sickness benefit, and the ordinary scale rate of supplementary allowance. The 'real value' of a benefit as calculated for Figure XII shows how much its value has increased (or decreased) compared with average prices: if the amount of benefit paid rose or fell each month exactly in line with prices, the real value would always be the same; if the amount paid remained the same while prices rose, the real value would fall. Changes in the average value of prices were derived from the General Index of Retail Prices. During the period the levels of benefits were reviewed periodically. The inevitable consequence of accelerating inflation was an increasingly rapid rate of fall in the real value of benefits between successive upratings, but these were more frequent in the second half of the period. There was a particularly large increase in the value of retirement pensions and other long-term benefits in July 1974. (The relationship between retirement pensions, supplementary benefit, and average earnings is shown in Table **5.32**.)

Wealth

Many different definitions of wealth are possible and the statistics available are much less detailed than those about incomes. Official estimates of the distribution of wealth are derived from Inland Revenue estate duty statistics. These are based on a survey of the estimated values of estates left at death. The method is explained in the Personal Income and Wealth section and Appendix B. These estimates do not cover non-marketable wealth, for example the entitlement to a state pension, which, it can be argued, should be included in a comprehensive definition of wealth. Furthermore the estimates do not cover the whole adult population. Nevertheless the trends in the estimates are thought to give a reliable guide to trends in the shape of the distribution of wealth (as defined for the purposes of calculating estate duty). On this basis, the figures available indicate a continuing slow trend towards greater equality in the distribution of personal wealth during the period (**5.35, 5.36**).

Prices and expenditure

As well as increases in the average level of prices, there were significant changes in the relative prices of different commodities during the period. Figure XIII shows the price increases for each of the main groups of expenditure covered by the *Family Expenditure Survey*. The largest increases were for the 'Food' group and for the group 'Meals bought and consumed outside the home'. The next largest were for the 'Fuel and light' and 'Transport and vehicles' groups, both of which were influenced by the rise in oil prices which followed the oil crisis of 1973–74. The smallest increases were in the 'Alcoholic drink' and 'Tobacco' groups. These were just over half the increase for the 'Food' group (**6.2**).

Owing to the rises in prices, the amount of expenditure rose for all the groups. However, the proportions of total household expenditure going on each of the groups changed far less than the changes in relative prices. It is also possible to look at the changes in expenditure 'at constant prices', that is, expenditure revalued in the prices of a standard base year, at present 1970. Changes in expenditure at constant prices reflect changes in the volume of consumption of the various groups. Figures, derived from the National Accounts, showing the changes in expenditure at constant prices for broad categories of consumers expenditure (that is, the expenditure of the personal sector, the major part of which is expenditure by households) are shown in Table **6.6**. They show rises in all the major categories of

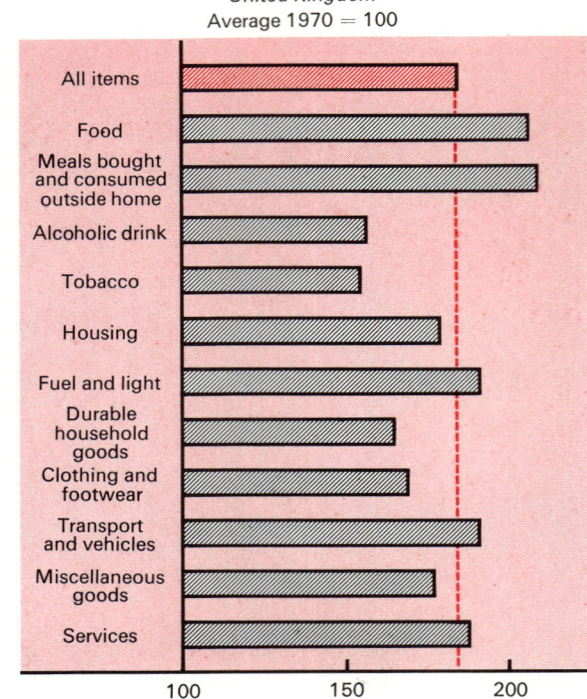

*Figure XIII   Retail price index:
main groups, averages 1975*

United Kingdom
Average 1970 = 100

Source: Department of Employment

consumers expenditure between 1970 and 1975. Measured at constant prices, expenditure on food rose only slightly, by one per cent, while expenditure on alcohol rose by 34 per cent (**6.9**). Expenditure on durable goods (comprising motor vehicles, furniture, floor coverings, and radio and electrical goods) also rose substantially, by 22 per cent. Despite a relatively low rise in average prices of tobacco goods, expenditure at constant prices on tobacco rose by only two per cent.

Health

Mortality

In spite of their obvious limitations, death rates still provide the most useful indicators of the health of a country. In 1970–74 the general level of mortality in Great Britain continued to decline at much the same slow rate as in the previous 20 years. As the age structure of the population changed during the period, in order to study changes in mortality it is best to look at the changes in Standardised Mortality Ratios (SMRs). All SMRs in this section are based on 1968 =100 and, unless otherwise stated, are for males and females combined. They thus relate the situation in the year in question to that of 1968. They are calculated according to the formula shown in Appendix B, page 234. The SMR for all causes stood at 95 for both men and women in 1974. There was consequently only a slight increase in the expectation of life; for males at birth this was still short of the biblical threescore years and ten, at 69·3 years in 1974, although for females the expected span was some six years longer at 75·5 years (**7.1**).

Three-quarters of all deaths are of men and women aged 65 and over, and it was the steady decrease of mortality at these ages that was the main contribution to the general decline referred to above. Below the age of 65 there was no consistent picture; and in the middle age range, 45 to 54 years, the rates levelled out, or even increased marginally. Infant mortality continued to decrease (although not so fast as in some other developed countries), and the rate for Great Britain fell by about 10 per cent between 1970 and 1974. Childhood mortality (ages 1 to 14) declined slightly less (**7.5**).

Though great changes in the pattern of mortality attributable to different diseases are not to be expected in so short a period as 5 years, some noteworthy developments did occur. Among diseases which had been increasing over the past decades, interest centred around lung cancer and coronaries (ischaemic heart disease) which together accounted for almost one in every three deaths. Although the general level of lung cancer mortality continued to be much lower in women than in men, the female rate increased more rapidly; and in 1974 the SMR for women was 130 as opposed to 105 for men. However it is a hopeful sign that in men younger than 65 and in women younger than 45 the rates began to decrease. Trends in coronaries are more difficult to detect and interpret owing to problems of diagnosis and classification. However it seems that between 1972 and 1975, rates for both men and women continued to rise. Rates for men were higher than the rates for women, and in the middle age range, 45 to 54 years, rates for men rose faster than rates for women (**7.3**).

Mortality due to respiratory disease in any one year depends heavily on whether there was an epidemic of influenza in that year (the epidemic of 1969–70 was the worst for more than 10 years). Apart from deaths attributed to influenza there was an increase in mortality attributed to pneumonia, the SMR in 1974 being 105 for men and 106 for women. However this was more than counterbalanced by fewer bronchitis deaths for which the 1974 SMRs were 76 for males and 75 for females. Among other important diseases with declining

mortality were strokes (cerebrovascular disease) and high blood pressure (hypertensive disease) with SMRs in 1974 of 89 (males) and 91 (females), and 73 (males) and 68 (females), respectively (**7.3**).

Morbidity

Unlike deaths – which are required to be registered and to be assigned a cause and date – non-fatal illnesses are not clearly definable, instantaneous events, and they are therefore much more difficult to monitor than deaths. Furthermore, most of the available information stems from records of health care, and so trends in the pattern of illness are confounded with changes in the provision of services and in the threshold of demand. Studies of morbidity statistics from general practice suggest some lowering of this threshold over the past 15 years. As with mortality, major changes in the pattern of morbidity are unlikely to have occurred within as short a period as five years, except among the infectious diseases as a result of epidemics or successful control measures. For example a reduction in the frequency of occurrence of measles followed the introduction of measles vaccination in the late 1960s. An epidemic of meningitis (meningococcal), which started in the late 1960s and reached its peak in 1974, was noted in several other European countries and elsewhere. The rapid decline in the frequency of tuberculosis since 1950 slowed down in the last few years. In some areas the majority of new cases in recent years were found among certain immigrant groups. Immigration and foreign travel also contributed to the sharp increase in the frequency of malaria.

Hospital statistics show an increase in the frequency of in-patient spells due to the effects of poisons and other chemical substances. The increased admissions of children may be the result of an increasingly cautious admission policy; the increase in adult admissions is almost entirely due to self-administered overdoses of sleeping pills, tranquillisers, and other psychotropic medicines. Fewer children were admitted for removal of tonsils and adenoids, though this reflected a change in doctors' views on the need for this operation rather than a change in morbidity.

The number of new patients with sexually transmitted diseases who were seen at hospital clinics increased substantially between 1970 and 1975. This was mainly due to the large increase in the numbers of patients attending clinics with symptoms not attributable (at least until recently) to specific diseases, and also to increased willingness to consult doctors about sexually transmitted diseases (**7.21**).

After a fall in the late sixties the number of registered drug addicts in the United Kingdom rose in the 1970s by 37 per cent, from 1,426 in 1970 to 1,954 in 1975. The increase was largely accounted for by the 25–30 age group, and the under 20 age group showed a decline of 73 per cent (**7.24**). This may, in part at least, reflect a particular group of addicts getting older and passing through the age group statistics.

The numbers of people admitted to mental illness hospitals and units in England and Wales for treatment for alcoholism or alcoholic psychosis rose at an increased rate in the period and in 1974 stood at 12,495, an increase of 54 per cent since 1970 (**7.23**).

The National Health Service

The period 1970–75 was an unsettled one for the National Health Service. In August 1972 a White Paper, *National Health Reorganisation; England*, set out the Government's proposals for an integrated health service to facilitate the plannng and operation of the service. The administrative changes were incorporated in the National Health Reorganisation Act 1973 which came into force on 1 April 1974. This brought together in a single structure the hospital services, the local authority health services including the school health and ambulance services, and the family practitioner services. Fourteen Regional Health Authorities were established in England with 90 Area Health Authorities with boundaries coterminous with those of the new local authorities. A further 8 Area Health Authorities were set up in Wales. Where necessary Areas were subdivided into two or more districts each with a District Management Team responsible to the Area Health Authority. The creation of new authorities and the transfer of (mainly administrative) staff from the former authorities to the new authorities raised a number of staffing and accommodation problems at the end of the period.

Reorganisation took a somewhat different form in Scotland and Northern Ireland. For example, in Scotland a Common Services Agency was established to carry out a variety of tasks (including research, statistics, and computer development) on behalf of the Scottish Home and Health Department and the health boards.

During the period there was the first widespread industrial action in the National Health Service, taken by ancillary staff early in 1973. Following this there were a number of cases of industrial unrest in various staff groups for a complex of reasons, including action by junior hospital doctors in support of their claim for new contracts defining precisely their working hours, and, in some places, by consultants over the Government's decision to reduce and eventually eliminate the number of pay beds in NHS hospitals.

The trend for general practitioners to work as members of co-ordinated primary health care teams continued, and more doctors worked in group practices. In 1970 56 per cent of doctors were in group practices, while in 1974 the figure was 65 per cent. By 1975 there were places for 17 per cent of doctors to practise in Health Centres built and maintained by health authorities, and the number of Health Centres rose sharply during the period (**7.14**).

Within the hospital service, the decline in the number of beds available continued. In 1974 there were 483 thousand in Great Britain; 30 thousand fewer than in 1970. This resulted mainly from a reduction in the number of beds in mental illness hospitals in line with the Government policy of caring for the mentally ill, wherever possible, in psychiatric units of general hospitals, day units, out-patient departments, and community homes and hostels, rather than in the traditionally large long-stay institutions. Despite the overall fall in the number of beds, certain hospital departments expanded and the number of beds available for some specialities (eg traumatic and orthopaedic surgery) increased. Within acute hospitals the pattern of activity continued to change. Average duration of stay continued to fall for all specialities and major disease categories, and as a result discharge rates rose slightly. This was in spite of the fall in available beds and industrial action by health service staff towards the end of the period.

The number of new out-patients increased slightly from 1970 to 1973, but fell back to below the 1970 level in 1974 although total attendances continued to rise. New accident and emergency cases also continued to rise throughout the beginning of the period, but there was a slight drop in 1974.

Family planning

There was a rise of 57 per cent between 1971 and 1974 in the number of patients at Family Planning Association clinics. From April 1974 a free family planning service was available to all, irrespective of age, sex, or marital status, through National Health Service family planning clinics. A similar service was available through hospital and family doctors from July 1975, when the terms under which this service would be provided were settled.

Personal social services

The personal social services are the responsibility of local authority social services departments. They are directed towards many different groups of people in need. Three of the most important groups are children, the handicapped, and the elderly, and services provided for them are discussed below.

Children

Sessional and full-day care for children under 5, provided either in nurseries and play groups or by registered child minders, expanded considerably in the early 1970s. The maximum number of children provided for rose from some 300 thousand in England and Wales at the end of 1969 to some 490 thousand in March 1975. There were signs that this rapid growth was flattening out, since the number of children in the care of registered child minders remained stable at about 90 thousand after 1972 and the number of children permitted to be cared for in registered premises increased by only 8 thousand (2 per cent) between March 1974 and March 1975 (**2.14**).

Trends in the numbers of children recorded as being in the care of local authorities in England and Wales were affected by the introduction of the provisions of the Children and Young Persons Act 1969, which made the figures for the year ending 31 March 1971 not strictly comparable with earlier years. (A similar situation obtained in Scotland, where Part III of the Social Work (Scotland) Act, 1968, setting up the children's hearings system, also came into force in 1971.)

After 1971 the total number of children in care in England and Wales rose by some 3 thousand each year, the greater part of the overall increase being due to children brought into care under the provision of the 1969 Act. The number of children in care accommodated with parents, guardians, relatives, or friends in England and Wales trebled between 1970 and 1975, rising from 6 thousand to 18 thousand (**2.16**).

The handicapped

Partly as a result of the Chronically Sick and Disabled Persons Act 1970, the number of persons in England and Wales who were registered as disabled under the National Assistance Act 1948 doubled in the first five years of the 1970s. There were 406 thousand at 31 December 1969 and 811 thousand at 31 March 1975. Information about the assistance given to handicapped persons is still incomplete, but has recently been extended. The figures show that the number of households receiving assistance from Social Services Departments by means of communication equipment, television or radio, personal aids, or adaptations to buildings rose from approximately 150 thousand in the year ended March 1973 to 247 thousand in the year ended March 1975. In addition, handicapped persons were helped by local authority Social Services Departments through the provision of home help and meals services, holidays, and the assistance of social workers. Help was also provided by other local and central government services (**2.20**).

The elderly

The considerable increase in the number of elderly in the population, and especially in the number of those aged 85 and over, placed higher demands on the social services. Generally speaking, personal social services delivered to the homes of the elderly by local authorities more than kept pace with this growth in population, but residential care in homes for the elderly tended to lag. The number of meals served to the elderly in England and Wales increased by more than 60 per cent between 1970 and 1975, measured in terms of the rate per 1,000 population aged 65 and over. This expansion was primarily directed towards giving meals to more people, and the proportion of people provided with meals at home rose by over a half (while the number of meals per person increased by about 10 per cent). There was also a marked increase in the proportion of the elderly receiving the aid of home helps. This proportion rose by a third in England and Wales during the period and in 1975 more than 8 per cent of the population aged 65 and over received this benefit. In Scotland the number of households receiving home help provided for people aged 65 and over increased by nearly 15 per cent per year between 1970 and 1974.

In contrast, the rate of provision of residential accommodation for the elderly, measured in terms of residents per 1,000 population aged 65 and over, was much the same in 1975 as it was in 1970. Indeed, if the age and sex structure of the population is taken into account, the rate in 1975 was marginally less. There was, however, on average a reduction in the size of the homes. In 1975 only 7 per cent of the residents were living in homes with 70 places or more compared with 12 per cent in 1970 (**2.20**).

Housing

During the period there was considerable concern about the cost of housing to the public. This was reflected in the short-term aid given by the central government in 1974 to the building societies to forestall an imminent rise in interest rates and as a first step towards arrangements which were developed for mortgage stabilisation. Action was also taken that year, first to freeze, and later to moderate, increases in both council and private rents. The public expenditure provision for subsidies to local authorities rose sharply throughout the period as did the total sum of tax relief on mortgage interest payments by owner occupiers. Mandatory schemes for rent allowances and rent rebates were introduced, and the Rent Act 1974 extended the protection afforded to "unfurnished" tenants under previous legislation to "furnished" tenants of absentee landlords. Conflicting opinions were expressed about the long-term effects of this on the supply of private rented accommodation.

Demand for housing

In certain areas the stock of housing still fell short of requirements, even though the period witnessed the end of the absolute national housing shortage. The continuing deficiencies of housing tend to be concentrated in particular conurbations and in specialised types of dwellings such as housing designed specifically for young people or the disabled.

Changes in stock of dwellings

The total net gain in housing stock between end-1970 and end 1975 in the United Kingdom was 1,132 thousand. The main gains were due to new construction. The public sector contributed 714 thousand dwellings, and the private sector 885 thousand dwellings. However, the level of both public and private house-building was lower than had been achieved in the late 1960s. Losses from the housing stock totalled 506 thousand, mainly as a result of slum clearance even though the rate of slum clearance was lower after 1973 (**8.4**).

Housing conditions

During the first part of the period the number of improvement grants to local authorities and private owners for improvement and conversion of property increased very rapidly from 126 thousand approvals in 1969 to 456 thousand in 1973 in the United Kingdom. This was partly as a result of the higher grants available for such work in development and intermediate areas from late-1971 until mid-1974. Approvals fell to 303 thousand in 1974 and 161 thousand in 1975, but since then there

has been a general switch of emphasis from major redevelopment schemes to rehabilitation of existing properties. Building of 'high rise' flats by public authorities continued to decline (**8.15** and **8.16**).

Reflecting this improvement activity and the continued clearance of unfit properties, the proportion of households living in accommodation lacking basic amenities continued to decline. Nevertheless, in 1973, there were still 12 per cent of households which did not have an internal WC solely for their own use (**8.7**).

Tenure

The proportions of owner-occupied and local authority housing in the United Kingdom has increased for many years, and the proportion of the stock which is privately rented has correspondingly decreased. It is not yet possible to assess the effects which the 1974 Rent Act may have had on the proportion of privately rented stock. The proportion of houses which were owner-occupied – almost half of which were owned outright – rose from 49 per cent at the end of 1970 to 53 per cent five years later. Although owning only a small part of the stock, housing associations began to play a larger part in the provision of both new and improved housing. The 1974 Housing Act increased the provisions for financing housing associations' activities, and in 1975 they accounted for 6 per cent of new dwellings and 4 per cent of renovation grant approvals.

Prices and rents

In 1972 and 1973 house prices rose very rapidly, much faster than the general rate of inflation, though they levelled off after the second half of 1973. Substantial regional differences continued, although the spread between the highest average regional price (Greater London) and the lowest (Yorkshire and Humberside), which widened in 1971 and 1972, was narrower in 1975 than in 1970. As a result of this rise in prices and the general rise in interest rates, the average value of mortgage interest payments, net of tax relief, rose faster than the General Index of Retail Prices until mid-1974. In 'real' terms (that is, after dividing by the increase in the General Index of Retail Prices) the average level of net mortgage interest payments fell between 1974 and 1975; but the level in 1975 was still 20 per cent higher than in 1970. In contrast the average 'real' value of local authority rents net of rebate, after rising between 1970 and 1973, fell between 1973 and 1975 to a level 10 per cent below that in 1970. These changes are shown in Figure XIV. (**8.17**)

Figure XIV *Indices of average mortgage interest payments and local authority rebated rents deflated by the General Index of Retail Prices*

United Kingdom
1970 = 100

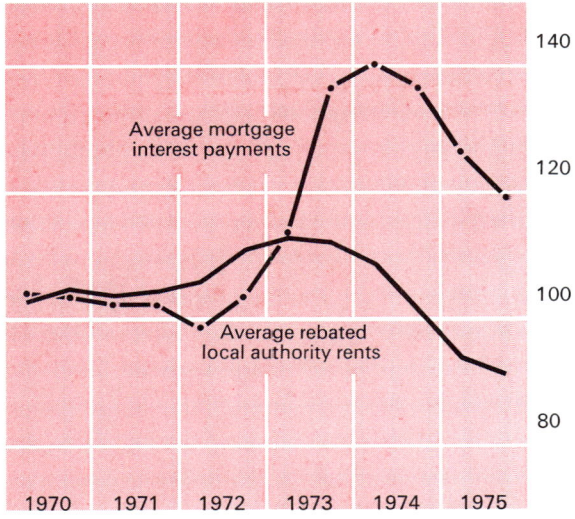

Average mortgage interest payments

Average rebated local authority rents

Sources: Mortgages index from the Department of the Environment. local authority rents index from the Department of Employment

Public safety

The incidence of crime would need to be given prominence in any comprehensive study of public safety. The subject is very complex, and requires a very careful analysis; and, as it is treated in two articles elsewhere in this issue of *Social Trends,* crime is not covered in this Commentary. There remain a number of topics relevant to public safety, including the incidence of road casualties, fire casualties, and accidents at work and in the home. There are also the Northern Ireland troubles, which have a bearing not only on public safety in Northern Ireland, but also on the spread of terrorist activities to the rest of the United Kingdom.

Road casualties

The incidence of road casualties was lower between 1970 and 1975 than in the previous six years. The total number of casualties from road accidents fell during the period, while deaths, which numbered 6·4 thousand in 1975, had also declined. The movements of the numbers of casualties and deaths, which were not identical, are shown in Table **11.8**. There were restrictions on speed limits after the oil crisis of 1973, and some of these were still in operation in 1976. The oil price rise of 1973–74 resulted in a fall in private passenger car mileage. Another consequence may have been the increased usage of 2-wheeled motor vehicles. The number of killed or seriously injured motor cyclists rose by approximately 15 per cent between 1973 and 1975 after showing a steady decline since 1964; but in terms of numbers killed or seriously injured per hundred million vehicle kilometres the decline continued (**11.8, 11.9**).

Accidents at work and at home

The rate of severe accidents at work per 100,000 employees in manufacturing industries declined steadily from 670 to 550 between 1970 and 1974 (**11.13**) and the numbers of deaths fell from 278 to 254. The numbers of deaths from accidents in the home and in residential accommodation in England and Wales also declined, from 6·5 thousand in 1970 to 5·7 thousand in 1974. Most of these deaths were due to falls (**11.14**).

Fire

From 1972 onwards the annual numbers of casualties, both fatal and non-fatal, resulting from fires in buildings were approximately 25 per cent greater than during the immediately preceding years. Fatal casualties rose from 714 in 1970 to 926 in 1974, while non-fatal casualties rose from 4,472 to 5,458 in the same period. The increase in casualties was due to an increase in the numbers of fires in buildings (particularly in dwellings) rather than in the severity of fires. The increases in fatal casualties caused by burns, inhalation of gas and smoke, and physical injuries were roughly similar to one another. However, in non-fatal casualties, there was a greater increase in the number of people overcome by gas and smoke than in the number who suffered other types of injury (**11.16**).

Northern Ireland

The number of deaths in Northern Ireland from causes connected with the civil disturbances there reached a peak yearly figure during the period of 468 in 1972, but fell to 247 in 1975. The majority of these deaths were civilian deaths, but there were 103 army deaths in 1972. The number of persons injured in connection with the disturbances fell from 4,876 in 1972 to 2,474 in 1975 (**11.18**).

Civil administration and justice

Court proceedings – civil

The number of proceedings commenced in Courts of First Instance and Courts of Appeal in Great Britain, excluding petitions or actions initiated for divorce, increased by some 4 per cent between 1970 and 1975. Divorce petitions or actions initiated for divorce increased by 92 per cent during the same period. In England and Wales, only 9 per cent of monetary claims in County Courts in 1970 were for amounts of more than £100. By 1975 this proportion had increased to 27 per cent. From October 1973 it became possible to deal with small claims by means of a less formal, arbitration process within the County Court system. The growth in this method of dealing with disputes is indicated by the 60 per cent increase in the number of cases disposed of by this procedure between 1974 and 1975. There was a rise in the number of legal aid certificates issued in respect of civil actions in Courts of First Instance. In Great Britain the number rose from 154 thousand in the financial year 1969–70 to 212 thousand in 1974–75 (**12.11 to 12.14, 12.20**).

Court proceedings – criminals

For criminal offences, most detected offenders are proceeded against in court, but some are given oral cautions. The use of cautioning increased over the period 1970–1975, particularly for young offenders and for female offenders. The number of persons cautioned, as a proportion of all persons found guilty or cautioned for offences other than motoring offences, rose from 11 per cent in 1970 to 14 per cent in 1975. In England and Wales the number of offenders found guilty by the courts increased by 19 per cent over the period 1970–1975. There was an increase in the proportion of persons found guilty of indictable offences who were fined and a decrease in the proportion dealt with by probation, supervision, or immediate imprisonment. Throughout the period some 90 per cent of those found guilty of non-indictable offences were fined. Certain new measures were introduced for dealing with some types of offenders. Most of the provisions of the Children and Young Persons Act 1969 came into force on 1 January 1971. Under this Act supervision orders were substituted for probation orders for young people, and care orders for approved school and fit person orders. In Scotland the Social Work (Scotland) Act 1968 provided new procedures, available from 15 April 1971, whereby the majority of child offenders were to be dealt with by non-court procedures. The Criminal Justice Act 1972, which came into force on 1 January 1973, gave the Courts the power, *inter alia*, to make community service orders, to require offenders to attend day training centres, and to defer passing sentence for up to 6 months. In 1975, 336 thousand applications for legal aid in criminal court proceedings were granted in England and Wales. This was approximately double the corresponding number for 1970

Custody

In Great Britain the proportion of convicted persons given prison sentences fell between 1970 and 1975 for all the main categories of offence. In spite of this, the numbers of receptions into custody of people under sentence, after declining from 1970 to 1973, rose in 1975 to the highest figure recorded since 1918. The average daily population in custody (including Borstal trainees and those in detention centres) fell during 1972 and 1973, but it rose in 1975 to almost 45 thousand, much the same level as 1970 and 1971 (**11.4**).

Political structure and elections

The first half of the 1970s saw far-reaching changes in the political organisation of the United Kingdom. At the international level there was the United Kingdom's entry into the European Economic Community on 1 January 1973. This was endorsed by the results of the referendum held in June 1975. The referendum was the first of its kind to be held in the United Kingdom. Within the United Kingdom itself there was considerable debate over the devolution of power to Scotland and Wales. The Government set out their proposals in a White Paper of November 1975 (*Cmnd 6348*, supplemented by *Cmnd 6585* in August 1976) and intended to introduce a Bill into Parliament early in the 1976/77 session. At the local level, the structure of local authorities in England and Wales was changed by the Local Government Act, 1972, which came into effect on 1 April 1974. Local Government in Scotland was changed in 1975. The reorganisation, which resulted in different structures in England and Wales and Scotland, was not as extensive as hoped for in some quarters, but there were some major changes, and, in particular, some counties disappeared off the political map. Following the changes there was concern about the staffing levels of the new authorities. The first elections for the new authorities took place in 1973 (England and Wales) and 1974 (Scotland) (**12.4**).

Parliamentary elections

There were three parliamentary elections during the period, in June 1970, and in February and October 1974. The percentage of the vote gained by the two major parties was significantly lower in the 1974 elections than in 1970. It is usual to include the Ulster Unionist vote with the Conservative vote in the case of the elections before and during 1970, but to exclude it in the case of the 1974 elections. On this basis the Conservative and Labour parties obtained between them 89 per cent of the votes cast in 1970 (very close to the corresponding figure for the two elections of the 1960s) but only 75 per cent in the elections of 1974. The share of the vote accounted for by parties other than Labour and Conservative thus rose. Taking the three elections of 1970 and 1974 in turn, the Liberals' share of the votes went from $7\frac{1}{2}$ per cent to $19\frac{1}{2}$ per cent and then to 18 per cent, and the Scottish and Welsh Nationalist shares, taken together, rose from $1\frac{3}{4}$ per cent to $2\frac{1}{2}$ per cent and then to $3\frac{1}{2}$ per cent. As a result of the elections there was a minority Labour Government in February 1974 (in spite of the fact that the Conservatives obtained 1 per cent more of the total votes cast than Labour) and, because of the greater geographical concentration of their votes, the Scottish and Welsh Nationalists won 14 seats in October 1974 compared with the 13 won by the Liberals, though nationally the Nationalist vote was only 19 per cent of that for the Liberals in October 1974. Within Scotland and Wales, however, the Scottish Nationalist Party and Plaid Cymru obtained, respectively, 30 per cent and 11 per cent of the votes cast in October 1974. The percentages of votes gained by the Nationalist and Liberal parties are compared in Figure XV (**12.1, 12.2**).

Figure XV   Shares of votes cast for minor parties: 1970 and 1974

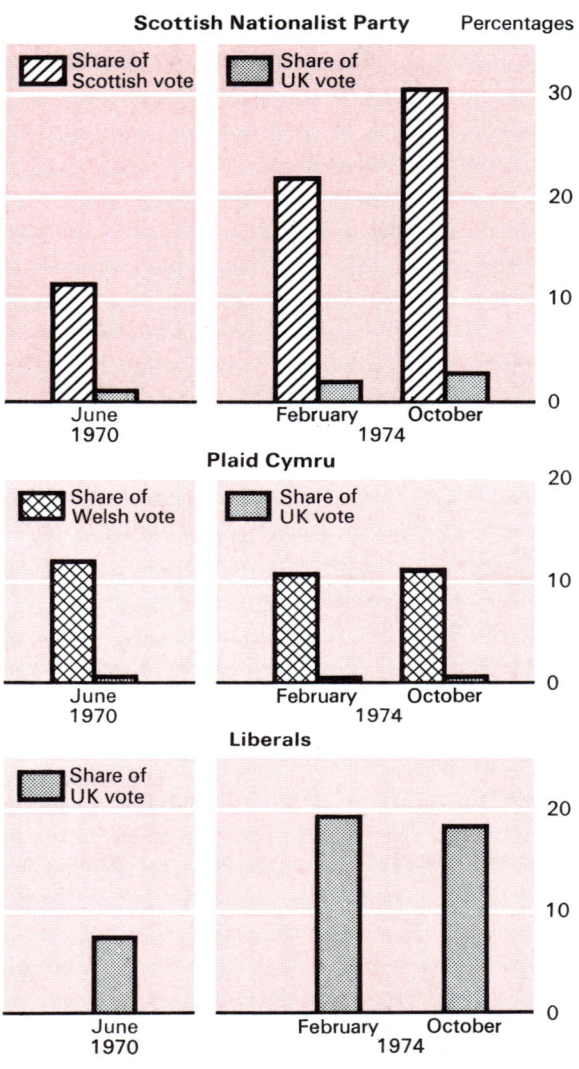

Source: Home Office

Crime in England and Wales

Dr Charles M Glennie
Home Office

Editorial Note

This article, and the article on Crime in Scotland on page 43, approach the problem of measuring crime in different ways. It is convenient to have two articles because the legal system in Scotland is substantially different from that in England and Wales; indeed, many of the problems which arise when attempting to compare crime statistics between two countries such as France and Germany can be seen in comparing Scotland with the rest of Great Britain.

Dr Glennie's article deals with the problems of how to define and how to measure crime, going on to discuss how many offenders there are, and what happens to them. Although the tables which illustrate his discussion are drawn from England and Wales, much of the discussion of the problem of measurement is appropriate to Scotland, and to many other countries.

Dr Bruce's approach is to describe the main characteristics of crime in Scotland; the upsurge since the mid-1950s; characteristics of offenders; sentences; and growth in prison population. These points are covered in Dr Glennie's tables in this article, or in the case of prisons can be found in Table 11.4 of the Public Safety section.

What is crime?

It is often said that 'There should be a law against it'. And so there very often is. But just what 'it' is remains very often in the mind of the speaker vague and unclear. One task, which courts throughout the land spend a lot of time discharging, is that of clarifying the law; indeed, through case law, the courts themselves create a great deal of the law. It is, generally speaking, a criminal offence for a person to take an action of which society disapproves if society has expressed its disapproval by passing a law against such action. It is unrealistic to suppose that one can, *a priori*, define clearly what a criminal offence is simply in terms of the action taken by the apparent offender. Examples can be given to show what type of action would normally be a criminal offence. But

for the action actually to constitute a criminal offence it is, in general, necessary that the circumstance of the offence and the intention of the person taking action should satisfy certain criteria.

For many criminal offences it is necessary that *mens rea* should be present. That is, the offender must have a 'guilty mind'; he must have a certain intention to carry out the action. Other offences are offences of strict liability: in such offences, it is not necessary for *mens rea* to be present. Examples of the offences for which *mens rea* is necessary include murder, burglary, theft, and assault; there are many more. Two examples of offences of strict liability are failing to display a road fund licence disc on a car windscreen and causing poisonous, noxious, or polluting matter to enter a stream.

The majority of the offences with which we are familiar are offences created by statute law, ie created under Act of Parliament. Let us consider some possible examples of such criminal offences. Under Section 1 of the Theft Act 1968 a person is guilty of theft if he dishonestly appropriates property belonging to another with the intention of permanently depriving the other of it. Under Section 9 of the same Act a person is guilty of burglary if, (a) he enters any building or part of a building as a trespasser and with intent to commit any such offence as is mentioned in another part of the same Act; or, (b) having entered any building or part of a building as a trespasser he steals or attempts to steal anything in the building or that part of it or inflicts or attempts to inflict on any person therein any grievous bodily harm. Under Section 1 of the Criminal Damage Act 1971 a person who without lawful excuse destroys or damages any property belonging to another, intending to destroy or damage any such property, or being reckless as to whether any such property would be destroyed or damaged shall be guilty of an offence. Under the Offences Against the Person Act 1861, Section 20, whosoever shall unlawfully and maliciously wound or inflict any grievous bodily harm on any other person, either with or without any weapons or instrument, is guilty of an offence. And so we could go on. Generally, the law seeks to protect an individual or a group of individuals within society from the actions of others or seeks to control the actions of individuals or groups for what is perceived to be 'the good of society'.

Offences somewhat different in character from those mentioned in the previous paragraph are those dealing with, for example, such matters as failing to take out a television licence, not having the proper certificate for a firearm, committing an offence under an Act for the Protection of Wild Birds, or possessing cannabis.

In talking about criminal offences we are talking about behaviour of individuals when attempts are made by society as a whole to control or influence that behaviour. In the last analysis, an action taken by an individual amounts to a criminal offence only if it is decided by a properly constituted court of law that that action has, under the law prevailing at the time, amounted to an offence. It will be readily appreciated that, in order to establish that an action has amounted to a criminal offence, it is necessary to establish not only the facts as to what took place and the intention of the person taking the action but also the law as it stood at the time.

The law of the land is not immutable. New Acts of Parliament are passed, old Acts of Parliament are repealed, and the courts are continually refining the interpretation of the law. For example, the Theft Act 1968 substantially altered the law relating to theft and related offences; this caused major difficulties of comparability in the statistics, as did also the Criminal Damage Act 1971. These were, perhaps, the most spectacular changes in the law in recent years so far as the statistics are concerned, but there is a steady stream of legislation affecting the criminal law. It is against this background that measures have to be devised for use in trying to assess the extent of criminal behaviour within the country at any one time. It is a truism that an apparent change in the amount of measured crime may be due to any one, or more, of a number of factors such as: (a) an actual increase in criminal activities; (b) a change in the extent to which the criminal activity is perceived or recorded, and (c) a change in the definition of what is criminal.

How can crime be measured?

There are, essentially, two main units in which crime can be counted. These are offences and offenders. For each of these there are two basic questions which should be answered before any system of collecting statistical information is instituted. These questions are: (a) who will be in a position to know about the numbers of offences and offenders? (b) what information is it relevant to collect about the offences and the offenders?

For the collection of information about offences there is in this country a well established system by which the police submit monthly returns to central government of the numbers of certain offences which have come to their notice. Clearly, the police cannot report those offences which do not come to their notice: the amount of crime which remains undiscovered is often referred to as 'the dark figure'. There are, of course, various reasons why certain crimes remain undiscovered.

In the first place, the fact that a crime has been committed may not be appreciated by the person committing the offence or by his victim – if any. In the second place, the victim, assuming there is one and that he knows he is a victim, may not wish to bring to the attention of the police the fact that he has been involved, even innocently, in criminal activity. An obvious example would be the case of a victim of blackmail where the victim is frightened of his blackmailer; another example would be the victim of an assault who knows his assailant and does not wish the assailant to be charged by the police. Thirdly, it is, of course, perfectly possible for the police to be deceived into believing that facts reported to them do not have the necessary ingredients to constitute a criminal offence when, in fact, they do. But this possibility is less likely than the converse, since the police, partly by training, partly from experience, are inclined to view with suspicion events which might disclose a criminal offence. Their usual practice would be to record the event as a criminal offence in the first instance and only to downgrade it later to 'no crime' if satisfied that no crime had been committed.

In any case where an action, or evidence that there has been an action (or, conversely, failure to take a required action), comes to the notice of the relevant authorities the judgement to be made is whether that action would, if tested in a court of law with full knowledge of the facts, amount to a criminal offence. Thus, for example, if a person is found by the roadside badly injured, there are two clear possibilities: either that person has been the victim of a deliberate attack, which would in all probability amount to a criminal offence, or that person has been the victim of a genuine accident. Even if it were established that the injuries were the result of an accident it could be that a criminal offence was associated with the accident without being the direct cause of the injuries. For example, the victim might have been struck by a car which had defective brakes without the fact that the brakes were defective contributing to the accident.

Some crime comes to police attention because the police have gone looking for it; inspection of unoccupied premises could reveal evidence of a burglary. In a not dissimilar spirit of enquiry some criminological research workers have attempted to establish some value for 'the dark figure' by conducting self-report studies, in which those being examined are, in essence, invited to identify themselves as having committed offences, or by conducting victim studies in which the attempt is to identify people who have been victims of crime. Some such studies have suggested that the crime coming to the notice of the police forms only a small proportion of that actually committed: by their very nature, however, it is difficult to assess the accuracy of such studies.

Turning now to the question of what information should be collected about offences which do come to the notice of the police, the first point to make is that, having established that an offence has apparently been committed and, by that very establishment having made a decision, possibly implicit but more likely explicit, as to what criminal offence has been committed, the main interest of the police is to collect such information as will enable them to clear up the offence, that is, attribute the offence to an offender. It is an arguable proposition that only such information as will enable the police to achieve that end should be collected by them; it is equally arguable that other ends, such as crime prevention or the furtherance of criminological research, can be served by the

collection of further relevant information at this stage.

As regards information about offenders, the situation is similar in one respect to that of collecting information about offences but different in another. It is similar in that the question of what information to collect is difficult to answer; it is dissimilar in that there is not a need to collect information to 'solve' a crime. The two main options open to the police in dealing with an offender, or alleged offender, are (a) to caution him and (b) to bring him to court. A formal caution is used as an alternative to court proceedings in certain cases where the offender admits his guilt and, in the view of the police, the interests of justice are best served by a caution rather than by taking the offender to court. Where an offender is taken to court there are two main stages. The first stage is for the prosecution to establish, if it can, to the satisfaction of the court, the guilt of the offender. For this purpose the prosecution requires information about the circumstances of the offence and the intentions of the offender. The second stage is the sentencing stage which is reached only if the defendant is found guilty. At this stage information, which may be collected by the police or the probation service, or be given in court by witnesses, is required by the court about the character, background, and previous criminal history of the offender in order to determine the sentence which appears to the court to be the most appropriate.

Having discussed the various stages at which information is collected about offences and offenders we turn now to look at the central question: how is crime to be measured? By counting the number of offences? By counting the number of offenders? If the former, is more weight to be given to some offences than to others? If the latter, is the number of offences committed by each offender to be taken into account? The published *Criminal Statistics* gives the number of indictable offences recorded as known to the police, in various categories, but with little attempt to weight the offences by any scale of seriousness. There is, at present, no way commanding widespread support of assigning a measure of seriousness to offences. Various attempts have been made to draw up such scales: clearly, this is a very difficult problem as the extent of seriousness of an offence is a matter of subjective judgment. What is perhaps not generally recognized is that the question of what should constitute a criminal offence is also a matter of subjective judgment. The crucial distinction between the two judgments is that society has evolved, over the centuries, a sophisticated system (Parliament) for deciding what actions should be criminal offences and a sophisticated system (the courts) for testing an individual action to see whether it amounts to an offence, but has to date evolved only a rudimentary system (the setting of maximum penalties) for deciding collectively how serious an offence is. There is, for example, a single offence of theft, with a statutory maximum penalty of 10 years imprisonment; the majority of people would, however, probably agree with the simple statement that some thefts are more serious than others.

How much crime is there?

Granted that we are prepared to settle for a simple system of measuring crime – no weighting for seriousness, no attempt to find out about the dark figure, just a simple counting of offences known to the police – we still face a number of difficulties. The most fundamental difficulty is simply that of deciding what constitutes a single criminal offence. If two injured people are found, should that event be counted, assuming that it is thought to be the result of criminal activity, as one criminal offence or as two? And if, subsequently, it is established that more than one offender was responsible does that increase the number of offences? If one person steals within a space of twenty minutes from a number of cars owned by different people but parked in the same car park should that constitute one criminal offence or a number of different criminal offences? Over the years a number of conventions have been developed to cope with these difficulties, but the figure of offences known to the police is still subject to quite a bit of interpretation. The general practice in England and Wales in recent years has been to collect the number of indictable offences known to the police. The indictable offences are, in essence, those that can (or must) be tried at the Crown Court, though

many can be dealt with at a magistrates' court if the accused consents to this. Table I shows the number of such offences recorded in selected recent years.

In the classification system used in Table I, no distinction is, in general, made between, on the one hand, a conspiracy, threat, or attempt to commit an offence and, on the other hand, the completed substantive offence. The groupings employed help to show (with, of course, the exception of the 'Other indictable offences' group) that, in at least one sense, there are very few essentially different actions which constitute criminal offences. There are attacks upon another person (which need not involve an unwilling victim), there are thefts or takings, there are offences of damage to property, and there are offences of dishonesty such as fraud. There are, of course, such other offences as riot and offences against public order, but these are small in number in comparison with the big groups, namely burglary and theft. Amongst the non-indictable offences – those not included in the figures regularly published as 'known to the police' – there is a greater variety since these include, for instance, such offences as failure to take out the correct dog licence, TV licence, or motor vehicle licence; offences related to drunkenness, to prostitution, to betting and gaming, to vagrancy, and to motoring, to name but a few.

Of the offences recorded as known to the police some are said to be 'cleared up', that is, attributed *by the police* to an offender. Table II shows, for the same years as Table I, offences cleared up expressed as percentages of the numbers of offences recorded as known to the police in the same groups.

Table I   Indictable offences recorded as known to the police

				England and Wales							Thousands
	1955	1960	1965	1970		1972		1974			
Offence group:											
Violence against the person	8	16	26	41		52		64			
Sexual offences	17	20	20	24		24		25			
Burglary				431		439		484			
Robbery	427[1]	751[1]	1,179[1]	6	1,480	9	1,565	9	1,800		
Theft and handling stolen goods				953		1,009		1,190			
Fraud and forgery				89		108		117			
Criminal damage	2	5	9	18		42		67			
Other indictable offences	6	6	2	5		7		8			
Total	460[1]	797[1]	1,235[1]	1,568		1,690		1,963			

[1] The Theft Act 1968 redefined many offences of dishonest appropriation of property; and certain previously non-indictable offences of stealing were made indictable. It is not possible to provide the full breakdown for the relevant groups for the years before 1969 but adjusted totals are shown for comparison.   *Source: Home Office*

Table II Offences cleared up, expressed as a percentage of offences recorded as known to the police

England and Wales   Percentages

	1955	1960	1965	1970		1972		1974	
Offence group:									
Violence against the person	89·5	88·0	85·0	82·2		80·8		80·2	
Sexual offences	83·0	80·7	76·1	76·2		77·4		77·8	
Burglary	44·9[1]	41·0[1]	36·2[1]	36·1	43·3	36·6	44·2	34·0	42·5
Robbery				42·0		42·7		42·1	
Theft and handling stolen goods				42·9		43·4		42·1	
Fraud and forgery				82·5		82·6		82·4	
Criminal damage	63·5	63·5	44·2	38·9		37·2		37·9	
Other indictable offences	97·7	97·5	85·1	93·5		93·6		91·1	
All indictable offences	47·9[1]	43·5[1]	38·0[1]	44·9		45·8		44·2	

[1] See footnote [1] to Table I.

Source: Home Office

To say that an offence is cleared up does not necessarily mean that an offender has been convicted for that offence: the reasons for this are, *inter alia*, that the police may have decided not to take action against the offender, they may have cautioned him, or the offence may have been taken into consideration when sentence was passed for other offences. Except in the case of murder, the statistics of offences recorded as known to the police or recorded as 'cleared up' are not altered in the light of subsequent court decisions. Thus, even if the alleged offender is acquitted by a court the offence remains in the statistics both as 'known' and as 'cleared up'.

How many offenders?
Before discussing how many offenders there are in any given year we must first consider just what we mean by an offender. It is convenient to distinguish six different classes:
  a. those people who commit offences which do not come to the notice of the police,
  b. those people who commit offences which do come to the notice of the police but of which the police are not able to discover the perpetrator,
  c. those people who are believed by the police to have committed offences but against whom the police take no action (eg because the person concerned has left the country and it is not thought worthwhile bringing him back, or because he is already detained in a mental hospital under a long restriction order),
  d. those people who admit that they have committed offences and are cautioned by the police,
  e. those people who are prosecuted and acquitted although in fact guilty, and
  f. those people who are prosecuted and plead guilty to the charge or charges, or are found guilty by the court.

It is, of course, quite possible that amongst those people classified as offenders under *c* or *f* there are some who are not offenders at all. It is virtually impossible to estimate what proportions of groups *c* and *f* such people would form, though there is no reason to suppose they are other than small.

The offences committed by offenders in the first category in the preceding paragraph are not, by definition, included amongst those recorded as known to the police, while those committed by offenders in the second category are precisely those which are recorded as known to the police but not cleared up. Offences committed by offenders in the remaining four categories are all recorded as known and cleared up; so also are 'offences' alleged to have been committed by people who are correctly acquitted by the court (apart from murder).

It is an extremely difficult task to measure, or even to estimate, the number of people in classes *a* and *b*. Various attempts have been made to do this, principally, as mentioned earlier, by means of self-report studies in which those participating are asked to say how many criminal offences they themselves have committed; or by means of victim studies, that is, finding out how many offences there are of which the respondents to the study have been victims. For the latter technique the number of offences has to be converted to numbers of offenders and this in itself requires assumptions about the similarity between the offender/offence ratio for those offences which do come to the notice of the police and are solved by them, and those which do not.

It will be readily appreciated that in the absence of data about the offenders whose offences do not come to police notice or about the offenders who remain uncaught it is not possible to make statements about the proportions of crime *committed* by people of different ages or having different social characteristics. The best that can be done is to examine the age structure of the population of known offenders. There is no upper limit beyond which a person is deemed legally incapable of committing a criminal offence but there is a lower

Table III *Persons cautioned for or found guilty of indictable offences per 100,000 of population, 1971–1974: by sex and age*

England and Wales

Rates per 100,000

	Persons cautioned				Persons found guilty			
	1971	1972	1973	1974	1971	1972	1973	1974
Males								
Under 14	1,962	2,105	2,156	2,408	1,248	1,229	1,246	1,406
14–16	2,060	2,198	2,341	2,773	4,432	4,597	4,738	5,418
17–20	283	273	284	256	5,558	5,775	5,522	5,952
21–29	65	67	65	60	2,472	2,427	2,349	2,509
30 and over	23	25	25	26	570	567	543	587
Total	303	333	347	396	1,485	1,484	1,464	1,603
Females								
Under 14	479	603	646	771	121	124	129	152
14–16	586	679	704	863	521	490	505	626
17–20	41	46	45	49	628	639	639	745
21–29	22	23	24	22	354	368	356	400
30 and over	20	23	21	23	133	137	126	151
Total	80	97	100	119	214	219	210	247

Source: Home Office

limit, the so-called 'age of criminal responsibility'. This is now 10, having been raised from 8 in 1964. Acts committed by children under 10 may well appear to be criminal offences (damage to property and theft are obvious examples) and may indeed be recorded by the police as such; the police may, or may not, later ascertain the ages of the alleged offenders. The numbers of offenders found guilty of, or cautioned for, indictable offences per head of population in different age groups is one measure of the criminality of different age groups. Table III gives figures for the years 1971–1974, for males and females separately.

The three main features of the table are:
  a. that the peak of the distribution occurs amongst teenagers,
  b. that there is a very marked fall-off with age (either there is a tendency to become more law abiding with advancing years or the probability of getting caught diminishes), and

c. there are many fewer known female than male offenders per 100,000 of population at all ages.

For most age groups there has been a strong upward trend in these rates in recent years. Changing patterns over the years of dealing with the youngest age groups have almost certainly rendered figures for these groups incomparable. The fact that the majority of known offenders (for indictable offences, which cover those offences commonly regarded as 'crime', such as burglary, theft, damage, and serious assaults) are males aged between mid-teens and late twenties is an important point to be borne in mind when comparing crime rates in different areas.

Table IV shows the numbers of indictable offences which have come to the notice of the police in certain years in the period 1965 to 1974, the proportions of those offences which were cleared up, and the numbers of offenders who were either cautioned or prosecuted for those cleared up

Table IV *Indictable offences known to the police, offences cleared up, and persons prosecuted or cautioned*

England and Wales

Thousands and percentages

	1955	1960	1965	1970	1972	1974
Offences known to the police (thousands)	438	744	1,134	1,556	1,690	1,963
Percentage cleared up	48	44	39	45	46	44
Persons prosecuted or cautioned:						
Percentage prosecuted	90	88	89	86	81	79
Percentage cautioned	10	12	11	14	19	21
Total number prosecuted or cautioned (=100%) (thousands)	128	199	263	406	460	511

Source: Home Office

37

offences. From Table III it will be seen that two changes which have occurred are:

    a. an increase in the number of offences known to the police coupled with an increase in the number of offenders, and

    b. a marked change in the proportions dealt with by caution and by prosecution.

It is interesting to note the relative constancy of the ratio of cleared up offences to offenders (1·7) over this period.

Table V shows, for those offenders who were prosecuted for indictable offences, the proportions who were committed for trial at the Crown Court, who were acquitted or whose cases were dismissed at the magistrates' court, and the proportion found guilty at the latter court. It further shows the proportion found guilty at the Crown Court of those tried there and gives an estimate for the proportion of the total number of offenders prosecuted who were found guilty at one or other court. It is interesting to note that this has fallen only slightly and that the proportion of those prosecuted who were committed for trial has risen.

Table VI shows, for offenders cautioned or prosecuted for non-indictable offences, other than motoring offences, that there has not been a switch from prosecution to cautioning for this group in the way that there has been for the group of offenders dealt with for indictable offences. The total proportion found guilty in this group has, however, remained remarkably constant.

Table V   Persons prosecuted for indictable offences

England and Wales					Thousands and percentages
	1955	1960	1965	1970	1972	1974
Persons prosecuted at magistrates' courts:						
Percentage acquitted or whose case was dismissed	5·8	5·1	6·2	6·4	7·4	6·2
Percentage found guilty at magistrates' courts	79·2	77·7	83·4	81·4	79·5	80·8
Percentage committed for trial at the Crown Court	15·0	17·2	10·4	12·2	13·1	13·0
Total (=100%) (thousands)	115	175	235	351	373	406
Persons found guilty at magistrates' courts:						
Percentage sentenced by magistrates' courts	97·6	97·7	96·3	95·1	95·7	96·4
Percentage committed to the Crown Court for sentence	2·4	2·3	3·7	4·9	4·3	3·6
Total (=100%) (thousands)	91	136	196	285	297	328
Percentage of persons found guilty at the Crown Court after trial there	89·8	91·0	83·2	85·0	83·1	83·0
Percentage[1] of all persons prosecuted who were convicted at magistrates' courts or Crown Court	93·3	93·6	92·9	91·8	90·4	91·7

[1] Because of the counting rules used (see discussion of Table VII) this figure is an estimate.   *Source: Home Office*

Table VI   Persons prosecuted or cautioned for non-indictable non-motoring offences

England and Wales					Thousands and percentages
	1955	1960	1965	1970	1972	1974
Persons prosecuted at magistrates' courts:						
Percentage acquitted or whose case was dismissed	7·3	7·3	7·8	8·2	7·9	6·3
Percentage found guilty at magistrates' courts	92·6	92·5	91·8	90·7	90·9	92·2
Percentage committed for trial at the Crown Court	0·1	0·2	0·4	1·1	1·2	1·6
Number prosecuted (=100%) (thousands)	353	313	314	420	437	418
Persons found guilty at magistrates' courts:						
Percentage sentenced at magistrates' courts	..	..	99·97	99·7	99·8	99·5
Percentage committed to the Crown Court for sentence	..	..	0·02	0·3	0·2	0·5
Number found guilty (=100%) (thousands)	327	290	288	381	397	386
Number of persons cautioned by the police (thousands)	55	47	32	30	34	31
Percentage of those found guilty or cautioned who were cautioned	14·5	14·2	10·0	7·3	7·9	7·4

Source: Home Office

Table VII   *Persons prosecuted for non-indictable motoring offences*

	England and Wales				Thousands and percentages	
	1955	1960	1965	1970	1972	1974
Persons prosecuted at magistrates' courts:						
Percentage acquitted or whose case was dismissed	3·2	2·3	2·3	3·3	3·4	4·0
Percentage found guilty at magistrates' courts	96·6	97·5	97·4	96·4	96·2	95·6
Percentage committed for trial at the Crown Court	0·2	0·2	0·3	0·3	0·4	0·4
Number of persons prosecuted (=100%) (thousands)	307	585	862	1,006	1,131	1,227
Persons found guilty at magistrates' courts:						
Percentage sentenced at magistrates' courts	..	..	99·98	99·78	99·81	99·83
Percentage committed to the Crown Court for sentence	..	..	0·02	0·22	0·19	0·17
Number of persons found guilty (=100%) (thousands)	296	570	839	971	1,089	1,173

Source: Home Office

Table VII deals only with those prosecuted for non-indictable motoring offences. The vast majority of offenders dealt with by the criminal courts come within this category. Figures for numbers cautioned, comparable to those given in earlier tables, are not available for this group. The overall proportion found guilty is once again fairly constant but is at a noticeably higher level for this group than for the two previously discussed.

Table VIII brings together from Tables V, VI and VII the number committed for trial at the Crown Court. The numbers recorded as having appeared for trial at the Crown Court are consistently lower than the totals of the numbers committed for trial from the magistrates' court. This is in part due to cases being dropped between the one stage and the next and in part to defendants dying or disappearing, but it is mainly due to the counting methods adopted within the *Criminal Statistics*. These counting methods are:

a. at the magistrates' court a person committed for trial for an indictable offence and for a non-indictable offence is counted once in each group, whereas at the Crown Court he is counted once only; this results from a decision to treat indictable and non-indictable offences at magistrates' courts separately for statistical purposes as it was felt important at the time that there should be full counts both of persons found guilty of indictable offences and persons found guilty of non-indictable offences,

b. a person may be committed for trial to a single sitting of the Crown Court from several different magistrates' courts or from a single magistrates' court sitting on several occasions: in either of these cases he will be counted several times at the magistrates' court stage but only once at the Crown Court stage, and

c. at a time when the number of persons prosecuted is increasing each year the time lag between committal for trial and reception at the Crown Court for trial causes an apparent shrinkage.

Table VIII   *Persons for trial at the Crown Court*

	England and Wales				Thousands and percentages	
	1955	1960	1965	1970	1972	1974
Persons committed for trial by magistrates courts (thousands):						
Indictable offences	17·2	30·5	26·8	42·9	48·9	53·0
Non-indictable non-motoring offences	0·2	0·4	1·3	4·7	5·4	6·6
Non-indictable motoring offences	0·7	1·7	3·7	2·9	4·2	5·1
Total committed for trial	18·3	32·8	31·9	50·4	58·6	64·8
Persons received for trial at the Crown Court:						
Persons received for trial (thousands)	18·0	30·5	26·8	44·1	51·9	56·4
Persons received as a percentage of persons committed	98·6	93·3	84·2	87·6	88·6	87·0
of which:						
persons found guilty (percentages)	*89·8*	*91·0*	*83·2*	*85·0*	*83·1*	*83·0*
persons acquitted (percentages)	*10·2*	*9·0*	*16·8*	*15·0*	*16·9*	*17·0*

Source: Home Office

What happens to the offenders?

When a person commits a criminal offence any one (or more) of a number of possibilities may result. In the first place, the fact that a criminal offence has been committed may remain unknown even to the offender. In the second place, even if the fact that a criminal offence appears to have been committed does come to the notice of other people no official action may result. This could be, for example, because the offence has not been brought to the notice of the authorities whose job it is to investigate and deal with crime. It often happens that a victim, on discovering that a theft has taken place, does not trouble to report the matter to the police, possibly in the belief that the police would be powerless to do anything about the theft and that by reporting it no useful purpose would be served. If the offence does come to the notice of the police, either because it has been reported to them or because they have themselves witnessed or discovered it, it is always possible that the offender will remain undiscovered. For over half of the offences recorded by the police as known to them in the last few years no offender has been traced. But we are concerned here with those people who are thought to have committed offences and with what subsequently happens to them.

The two main ways in which the police deal formally with offenders are by cautioning them or by prosecuting them. The decision whether to caution or to prosecute is, generally speaking, one for the police (advised, where necessary, by the Director of Public Prosecutions). In making this decision, they will have in mind a number of considerations such as the age of the offender, the apparent seriousness of the offence, the mental state of the offender, the past record of the offender, and, by no means least in order of importance, whether or not the offender admits the offence.

Table IX   Persons for trial at the Crown Court, numbers pleading not guilty to principal offence, and numbers acquitted

England and Wales		Thousands and percentages	
	1972	1973	1974
Persons for trial (thousands):			
Pleading not guilty to principal offence	17	18	18
Acquitted	8·5	9·3	9·0
Total for trial	52	54	56
Of those pleading not guilty, persons acquitted (percentages)	51	51	51

Source: Home Office

A high proportion of the offenders who are taken to court either plead guilty to, or are found guilty by the courts of, one or more of the offences for which they are prosecuted. This proportion has not dropped below 90 per cent in the last few years. Recent public discussion of acquittal rates has tended to concentrate on acquittal rates at the Crown Court, with jury trials, for those persons who plead not guilty; for such people the proportion acquitted of all offences is of the order of 50 per cent. Table IX gives some relevant figures.

The range of sentences and orders available to the criminal courts for dealing with offenders found guilty is much wider at the present time than in the past. Subject to statutory limitations, which in general relate to the offence and the offender's age and/or previous history, the powers of criminal courts for dealing with offenders range from an absolute discharge to life imprisonment. The main types of sentence or order are:

a. monetary penalties such as fines and compensation orders,

b. orders such as probation orders, care orders, supervision orders, and certain types of hospital order,

c. conditional or suspended sentences such as conditional discharges and suspended sentences of imprisonment, in which the court takes no further action provided that the offender does not commit a further offence within a specified period,

d. custodial or restrictive sentences such as imprisonment, borstal, or detention centre training and certain types of hospital order, and

e. community service orders under which the offender is required to perform unpaid work.

Probation orders may or may not have requirements attached to them such as a requirement that the offender should undergo treatment for a mental condition or that he should attend at a day training centre.

Typical of the factors taken into account by a court when passing sentence are the following:

a. the range of sentences available under the law,

b. the nature and gravity of the particular offence of which the offender has been found guilty,

c. the character and past record of the offender,

d. the present circumstances of the offender, including, for example, whether or not he is employed and what his home circumstances are,

e. the prevalence of such offences as those of which the offender has been convicted,

f. the range of penalties which it is usual to impose on offenders for similar offences, and

g. the recommendations of probation officers.

Fuller information about sentencing is contained in the handbook prepared by the Home Office and published by HMSO entitled *The Sentence of the Court*.

In 1973 some 300,000 people were found guilty at magistrates' courts of indictable offences. For both the males and the females, the most frequently used sentence was the fine; rather more than half of the offenders of each sex being fined. The second most popular sentence was the conditional discharge which was given to some 12 per cent of the males and 20 per cent of the females. Imprisonment, either immediate or suspended, was awarded to some 8 per cent of the males and 3·5 per cent of the females. For the non-indictable offences the fine was used even more frequently. Amongst offenders convicted of motoring offences (and there were over a million of them in 1973) all but 2 per cent were fined. For those found guilty of non-indictable offences other than motoring offences the proportion fined was also high, just over 90 per cent. At the Crown Court which deals, roughly speaking, with persons accused of the most serious 2 or 3 per cent of offenders, the pattern of disposals is, as one might expect, quite different from that of the magistrates' court. Custodial sentences figure much more prominently: in 1973, some two-thirds of the males of all ages sentenced by the Crown Court (some after committal from the magistrates' court for sentence) were given custodial sentences, albeit that rather over a fifth of these custodial sentences were suspended. The proportion of females given custodial sentences, at approximately 39 per cent, with about 45 per cent of these sentences suspended, was much lower than the corresponding proportion for males.

A great deal of attention has been given in recent months to the problems of overcrowding in prisons. In 1973 nearly 25,000 men aged 21 and over were sentenced to imprisonment (either immediate or suspended) at magistrates' courts, and some 19,000 after trial at the Crown Court. Magistrates' courts are only able to give sentences of imprisonment of up to six months, while the Crown Court may give any sentence up to the maximum permissible in law. Table X shows for the years 1970 and 1974 the proportion of men aged 21 and over found guilty at the Crown Court who were given prison sentences either suspended or immediate. It also shows the proportion of the total found guilty formed by those found guilty in each offence group. The offence groups are those used in *Criminal Statistics* with one exception: the offences of causing death by dangerous driving, reckless or dangerous driving, driving while unfit through drink or drugs, and other motoring offences have been removed from the groups in which they normally appear and have been placed in a single group in the table. It will be seen that the proportion of men imprisoned for motoring offences by the Crown Court is very much lower than the proportion imprisoned in any other offence group. Caution should be exercised in drawing conclusions from this difference, particularly in view of the number of different factors which are normally taken into account by courts when sentencing and which are spelt out above.

Table X   Men aged 21 and over receiving prison sentences[1], expressed as a percentage of those found guilty, by court and offence type

	England and Wales			Numbers and percentages
	After trial and sentence at magistrates' courts		After trial at the Crown Court	
	1970	1974	1970	1974
Percentage in each offence type:				
Violence against the person	20	12	73	69
Sexual offences	17	9	65	69
Burglary	41	31	81	82
Robbery	0[2]	0[2]	92	95
Theft and handling stolen goods	20	13	74	59
Fraud and forgery	29	22	77	77
Criminal damage	29	8	60	51
Motoring offences	25	20	38	31
Other indictable offences	15	9	64	65
All indictable offences	23	15	72	66
Numbers sentenced to imprisonment[1]	28,048	18,810	18,165	20,173

[1] Either immediate or suspended sentences of imprisonment.

[2] Robbery cannot be tried at magistrates' courts – hence no men aged 21 and over were found guilty there.

Source: Home Office

Reconvictions

There are those who, having committed a crime and having been dealt with for it by the police or the courts, do not commit further criminal offences. There are also those, of course, who do in fact commit criminal offences and who may, or may not, be subjected once again to the process of being cautioned by the police or dealt with in the courts. Table XI, which is based on a sample of adult prisoners discharged in 1971, shows that the proportion of such prisoners reconvicted within two years of discharge decreased as the length of sentence from which they were discharged increased. It might be tempting to think that this shows that in certain respects longer sentences were more successful at preventing reconvictions than shorter sentences. But this temptation should be strongly resisted. There are many factors which affect the likelihood of reconviction; not least is the age of the offender. If we assume a simple model in which frequency of offending diminishes with age, and length of sentence awarded increases with the number of previous convictions (both of which assumptions have evidence to support them), then we would expect a higher incidence of reconviction amongst those released from the shorter sentences simply because, in general, they would have been awarded to the younger and hence more criminally active offenders.

There are two further aspects to studies of reconviction rates which deserve consideration. The first is that, as we have seen above, the commission of a criminal offence is by no means the same as a conviction for that criminal offence. Thus the fact that a person who has been through the criminal justice system once as an offender is or is not reconvicted may have as much as or more to do with the criminal justice system than with the actual commission of crime by that person. The more criminally sophisticated the person becomes the less, on the one hand, may be his chances of getting caught and the more, on the other hand, may be his chances of being known to the police. The second factor is that, even allowing for the difference between the commission of an offence and conviction for that offence, it may be imprudent to suppose that the 'success' or 'failure' of a particular sentence is correctly measured by the commission or non-commission of further criminal offences. Certainly these are important elements, but it has to be borne in mind that we are dealing with human behaviour in human situations and that the commission of criminal offences reflects the behaviour of the individual, the pressures of the environment, and the attitude of society to that behaviour as expressed in the criminal law. There may be many factors which it would be proper to take into account, following a person's conviction, as measures of the 'success' or 'failure' of the sentence awarded to that person. Such factors in addition to reconviction could include, for example, the extent to which the ex-offender was dependent on social security, the stability of the ex-offender's personal relationships and, in general, the extent to which the ex-offender could be seen as being a person making a contribution to society and the extent to which he was in need of support from society. There are real problems of measurement involved in a number of these concepts.

Table XI   *Men aged 21 and over discharged from prison in 1971; reconviction within 2 years of discharge, results of a sample study*

England and Wales		Numbers and percentages
	Total sample size	Percentage reconvicted
Length of sentence from which discharged:		
Up to and including 3 months	534	60
Over 3 months, up to and including 6 months	554	53
Over 6 months, but less than 18 months	575	47
18 months	505	45
Over 18 months, up to and including 4 years	555	45
Over 4 years, up to and including 10 years	373	39
Over 10 years and life imprisonment	69	19

Source: Home Office

Crime in Scotland

Dr David Bruce

Scottish Home and Health Department

The increase in crime

As in most western European countries there has been an upsurge of crime in Scotland since the mid-1950s. The official statistics do not provide accurate information on the amount of crime occurring in the country since not all breaches of the law are brought to the attention of the police. The official statistics are of more value for the study of trends but even in that context their use is restricted by a number of factors: for example, the public's readiness to report incidents, the general level of tolerance to certain forms of anti-social behaviour, the amount of police resources allotted to different aspects of their work, may all vary over time. Whilst any conclusion based solely on trends in the recorded statistics must therefore be treated with considerable caution, all the evidence points to there having been a substantial increase in the level of crime in Scotland since the mid-1950s. At present there is about one crime or offence[1] per annum per 10 persons in Scotland, which is nearly 3 times the number recorded twenty years ago.

Of all crimes and offences recorded in Scotland well over half are road traffic offences, theft, or housebreaking. Table I which lists the different crimes and offences as percentages of the total, shows that the most common types of crime or offence have changed little in their proportional contribution to the total. The proportionate increase in certain types of incidents which currently attract public attention, vandalism, drunk driving, and unlawful removal of motor vehicles, has however been substantial.

Accepting the limitations of the criminal statistics as an index of trends in crime (and even more so as an index of trends in particular forms of crime) the statistics in Table II serve to indicate the considerable changes that have taken place in the

Table I   Crimes and offences as a percentage of total number recorded

Scotland	Percentages and thousands	
	1959	1974
Crime or offence (percentages):		
Road traffic offences	27·8	28·1
Theft (excluding motor theft)	15·5	14·4
Housebreaking	16·8	13·9
Breaches of Order (Breaches of the peace and byelaws, drunk and disorderly)	19·7	19·5
Vandalism	2·6	5·7
Drunk driving	1·2	2·6
Revenue and Excise Law contraventions	1·2	2·2
Theft of a motor vehicle and taking and driving away a motor vehicle	0·3	4·4
Crimes against the person with violence	0·5	0·7
Crimes against the person without violence	0·9	0·8
Non-payment of TV licences	0·8	0·7
Other crimes	3·0	3·3
Miscellaneous offences	9·7	3·8
Total crimes and offences (=100%) (thousands)	256·8	538·8

Source: Scottish Home and Health Department

incidence of both crimes and offences over the past twenty years. There has been a fairly sustained growth in all the main groups of crimes and offences over the period.

It is not possible in this article to provide information on the trends over the years for every type of crime and offence; however the annual volumes of the *Scottish Criminal Statistics* do give details. Crimes of violence are the subject of public concern and the following reviews the trends. The information on the main categories making up crimes of violence against the person is shown in Table III.

The data in Tables II and III show that whilst, in comparison with other crimes and offences and in particular with crimes of dishonesty, the incidence of crimes of violence remains small, between 1955 and 1967 the number quadrupled; between 1967 and 1974 however the total number

---

[1] For statistical purposes contravention of the law in Scotland is divided into Crimes: roughly the more serious contraventions, and Offences: the less serious or technical contraventions.

Table II   Crimes and offences made known to the police

	Scotland					Thousands
	1955	1960	1965	1970	1972	1974
Crimes	74·8	102·6	140·1	167·2	178·4	192·2
of which						
Crimes of violence	*0·9*	*1·5*	*2·6*	*3·2*	*3·7*	*3·8*
Offences	121·0	180·0	224·3	263·8	302·8	346·6
of which						
Breach of the peace	*21·1*	*27·2*	*36·6*	*46·4*	*56·7*	*70·1*
Against intoxicating liquor laws	*13·3*	*14·8*	*15·6*	*15·5*	*17·3*	*22·2*
Motor vehicle	*49·9*	*84·3*	*105·3*	*129·9*	*145·4*	*165·6*
Total crimes and offences known	195·8	282·7	364·4	431·0	481·2	538·8

Source: Scottish Home and Health Department

Table III   Violence against the person

	Scotland						Numbers
	1955	1960	1965	1967	1970	1972	1974
Crimes of violence	862	1,528	2,623	3,535	3,204	3,724	3,765
of which							
Murder	*11*	*16*	*32*	*41*	*29*	*47*	*38*
Culpable homicide	*24*	*19*	*31*	*29*	*54*	*38*	*40*
Attempts to murder, etc.	*7*	*10*	*37*	*49*	*93*	*90*	*121*
Serious assaults	*497*	*966*	*1,763*	*2,440*	*2,108*	*2,593*	*2,442*

Source: Scottish Home and Health Department

has remained relatively static. The interpretation of the figures for the less frequent but more serious crimes of violence must be general because of the variability exhibited by the smaller numbers; it must be seen against the background of the partial and complete abolition of the death penalty in 1959 and 1965 respectively. Murders and culpable homicides are now running at higher levels than in 1955 to 1960 but the period of rapid growth to 1967 has passed. It is clear however that the proportionate increase in murder and culpable homicide taken together over the whole period has been less than for other crimes of violence though not dissimilar from that for crime overall. There is reason to believe that the steep rise in attempts to murder is largely due to changes in charging practice as a result of an important High Court decision; if this had not occurred many of these attempts to murder would have been classified as serious assaults.

The offenders

As already mentioned, the statistics of crimes and offences made known to the police are an incomplete record of the actual crimes and offences which actually occur. Of those which are known to the police however, offenders are identified for only about 40 per cent of crimes and 90 per cent of miscellaneous offences. The group of people who are identified as being responsible is biased towards the less expert offender. Thus official statistics of persons dealt with for crime relate only to a select subset of all offenders.

Since 1971 procedures not involving prosecution in Court have been available for dealing with children. Prior to that time most children who were officially dealt with for crime were proceeded against in Court. These new procedures were designed to encourage the public to present for treatment those children responsible for crime. Thus comparison over the whole age range of persons dealt with for crime is somewhat complicated. It is perhaps sufficient here to record that in 1974 the number of children aged under 16 years dealt with for crime was 24,074 while the number of persons over 16 against whom a criminal charge was proved was 31,155. Crimes (largely housebreaking and theft) are in general those events which require police investigation, and from this about 40 per cent of persons apprehended by the police for crime are below the age of 16. However, when miscellaneous offences (largely motor vehicle offences) are included the proportion falls to about 15 per cent. The number of children of each age group dealt with increases with age up to the age of 15.

The nearest equivalent in Scotland to the practice in England and Wales of cautioning is that of official oral and written warnings by the police or the Procurator Fiscal (Public Prosecutor). In Scotland, official warnings by the police can only be administered on the instructions of the Procurator Fiscal, who has sole responsibility for instituting prosecutions, unlike the position in England and Wales where the police have this responsibility and complete discretion to issue a caution. The actual number of adults dealt with by official warnings in Scotland is about 2 per cent of the number prosecuted and does not vary greatly with offence type.

Thus in Scotland 98 per cent of adult offenders dealt with are proceeded against in Court, and of these 94 per cent have a charge proved against them. Table IV shows the distribution between the sexes of persons against whom charges are proved expressed as rates per thousand of the population above the age of criminal responsibility (8 years). While the proportion of persons in violent crimes (including housebreaking) who are female is under 5 per cent, the proportion dealt with in theft and similar crimes rises to over 20 per cent.

As a measure of male criminality of each age group over the last twenty years the number of males with crimes proved against them each year has been related to the number of males in the (home) population at mid-year. This is shown as a rate per thousand of the population in Figure 1. The highest probability of having a crime proved is at age 16, after which the probability decreases fairly continuously. Over the period there has been a fairly continuous increase in all age groups of population though the rate of increase has been greater for younger ages.

Table IV Sex of persons against whom charges proved expressed as a rate per thousand of the population, 1974

Scotland	Rate per thousand	
	Male	Female
Crimes against the person (mainly violence and sex)	1·4	0·1
Crimes against property with violence (mainly housebreaking)	3·3	0·1
Crimes against property without violence (mainly theft)	6·9	1·7
Other crimes	1·2	0·1
Miscellaneous offences	80·8	7·2
All crimes and offences	93·5	9·1

Source: Scottish Home and Health Department

Figure I Males per 1,000 of the population of each age group with crimes proved against them each year

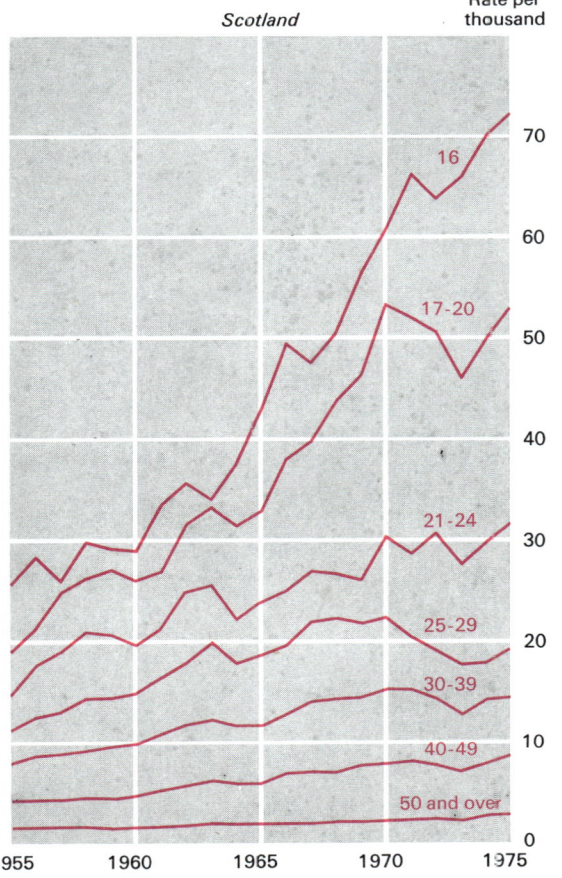

Source: Scottish Home and Health Department

The sentences imposed on those dealt with in Court

The use made by the Scottish Courts of the main penalties available to them in the sentencing of persons aged 17 or over against whom a charge has been proved is shown in Table V in percentages.

Table V Sentencing of persons, aged 17 and over, against whom charge proved

	Scotland					Percentages
	1955	1960	1965	1970	1972	1974
Custodial sentences	5·0	4·9	4·3	6·7	6·0	4·9
Fines	84·8	86·7	85·6	84·1	83·6	84·6
Probation	1·0	1·2	1·3	1·3	1·3	1·0
Other	9·2	7·3	8·9	7·9	9·2	9·4

Source: Scottish Home and Health Department

The proportionate use of the different sentences by Scottish Courts has not changed decisively over the last twenty years; there was however a peak in the use of custody around 1970. The fine remains by far the most frequently used Court sentence; around 85 per cent of persons are dealt with by this sentence.

In 1955 the total number of persons fined was 89,974 and the average fine imposed £2.40 (almost identical to that for 1931 when the change in the value of money over the period is taken into account). By 1974 the number fined had risen to 187,230 and the average fine imposed was £16, which in constant money values was just over double the 1955 figure. Thus both the number of

Table VI   Custodial sentence: by default and direct

						Scotland	Numbers
	1955	1960	1965	1970	1972	1974
Persons imprisoned for non-payment of fine	3,099	4,409	4,720	7,850	8,662	8,632
Persons receiving direct sentence of imprisonment	5,634	6,571	7,328	10,654	10,343	9,426

Source: Scottish Home and Health Department

persons fined and the level of fine in constant money values has increased by a factor of more than 2 in the last twenty years. Not all those who are fined pay their fine and some serve a prison sentence in default of payment. The number of fine defaulters sent to prison and the number of persons receiving direct prison sentences have for many years been of comparable size, as can be seen from Table VI.

In 1955, 3·4 per cent of those persons fined went to prison in default, in 1965, 3·3 per cent went to prison, and in 1974, 4·6 per cent.

The average length of sentences of those received into Scottish prison institutions (excluding borstal and detention centres) has increased from about 100 days in 1955 to about 110 days in 1974.

Prison population

Prison population in Scotland has risen from an average daily population of 2,176 persons in 1955 to 4,689 in 1974 (with a peak of 5,338 in 1971). This could be seen as one effect of the combination of:—

(a) the increased incidence of crime,
(b) the increased number of persons convicted,
(c) the maintained proportion of custodial sentences used by the Courts, and
(d) the slightly increased length of sentences.

Subjective measures of quality of life in Britain: 1971 to 1975 Some developments and trends

John Hall[1,2]
Polytechnic of North London, formerly of the Survey Unit, Social Science Research Council

During its short, but fruitful, life, the Social Science Research Council (SSRC) Survey Unit conducted one small pilot survey and three reasonably large surveys of the adult general population as part of its research programme to develop subjective indicators of quality of life. The pilot was conducted with a national quota sample (N=213) in March 1971 and the first of the major studies with a quota sample (N=593) in seven major conurbations during October and November 1971. Two further national surveys using probability samples drawn from the electoral register were conducted in urban areas of Great Britain in October–December 1973 (N=966) and March–May 1975 (N=932). A fifth survey, intended to re-interview in 1976 a sample of respondents from the 1973 and 1975 surveys, was cancelled, partly as a result of the decision by SSRC to close the Survey Unit, and partly because of cut-backs in expenditure. The 1973 survey was replicated simultaneously in Stoke-on-Trent (N=753) and Sunderland (N=770). Preliminary findings have already been published in earlier issues of *Social Trends* and accounts of other work or justification for research using subjective indicators have been published by the SSRC Survey Unit (Abrams, 1973 and 1976; Hall, 1973 and 1976; Hall and Perry, 1974; Hall and Ring, 1974).

An extremely important application for subjective indicators is that of measuring changes in attitudes over time. One of the major justifications cited by Campbell for this kind of work was to measure the 'psychological correlates of social change'. Since some of the measures were used in more than one survey, it is now possible to compare two, and in some cases three or even four, points in time.

In considering changes in indicators over time, it should be remembered that change may take place only slowly, if at all, in some areas; whilst in others it may take place rapidly, either in one direction or in many. Thus subjective measures in some domains might be expected to be stable across time, in others less so. The data from our surveys would appear to support such a view. This means that satisfaction with domains such as health, housing, and education may remain relatively unchanged within specific categories of healthiness, tenure, or educational experience; whereas in domains such as finance or politics we might expect changes in income or government to be reflected in changes of satisfaction, and such indeed appears to be the case. Of course, even the most reliable and valid indicators of satisfaction would have to take into account changes in expectations or in values as possible sources of variation.

It is relatively easy to demonstrate a stable relationship between a subjective measure and a related objective condition for certain domains such as housing, environment, and health. To some extent, the same kinds of relationships can be demonstrated in domains where objective indicators are more difficult to define and measure (eg education, leisure, and work). The really difficult task is to determine such relationships when the relevant domain is intangible. We have no difficulty in obtaining satisfaction ratings with the 'level of freedom and democracy' in a country, but we face practically insuperable problems, either of measurement when there is consensus of definition, or of definition when there is not, of what constitutes equity, or tolerance, or acceptable censorship. Again, we may have no difficulty

[1] The author would like to express thanks to Dr Mark Abrams, with whom he was co-director of the Quality of Life Survey in the SSRC Survey Unit from 1970 to 1976; and to James Ring, David Lord, and Dr Graham Dann for their invaluable assistance in data storage, retrieval, and analysis. The data for all the surveys have now been deposited in the SSRC Survey Archive at Essex University and are available for teaching and, on certain conditions, for research. A full set of user manuals has been published by the SSRC Survey Unit (Hall *et al.*, 1976). The concepts and methods used in the surveys carried out by the SSRC Survey Unit were described in a full-length

article in *Social Trends No 4, 1973*. The results quoted in this article and in the sections of *Social Trends* come from two further national quality of life surveys carried out in October–December 1973 and March–May 1975. Both surveys were conducted in the same primary sampling units, but with a different sample of individuals. Some questions were replicated in both surveys.

[2] The author is Principal Lecturer in Sociology in the Department of Applied Social Studies, Polytechnic of North London and an Alderman of the London Borough of Haringey.

obtaining *satisfaction with* equality or tolerance, but how does one measure the *amount of* justice or tolerance in a society, or the equity of pay differentials? If there are measurable objective changes in a country's social or economic conditions, how does one determine whether changes in subjective measures are related to these changed conditions? And if a relationship can be demonstrated, can a directional causality be determined? It is not proposed to answer such questions in this article but results from our surveys begin to throw some light on the problems involved.

The subjective measures used in the surveys are broadly:

    direct measures of satisfaction using single items (the majority);

    indirect measures in that they involve some measure of discrepancy between a perceived and a desired state of affairs;

    some measures including an element of perceived time (in that respondents were asked to give ratings for past, present, and future situations);

    and another type of measure represented by various global indices of psychological well-being.

Examples of the behaviour of the various subjective measures over time to be described in this article will focus on areas of life for which there already exist highly developed and much used objective indicators (material standard of living, health, and housing), on areas for which perceptual measures cannot at present be avoided (the British polity and the equity of differential material rewards), and on general measures of well-being. Any programme of research in this area should test new measures or set new baselines, and consequently some measures are reported which have only one time point in the hope that they will be replicated later. As well as the tables in this article, various sections of *Social Trends* include satisfaction indicators by objective conditions drawn from our surveys.

What is 'Quality of Life'?
The late Tom Harrisson, founder of Mass Observation, once wrote 'You cannot, yet, take a census of love in Liverpool, or random sample the effect that fear of the future has on the total pattern of contemporary life in Leeds'. For several years now a number of researchers on both sides of the Atlantic have been trying to do just that. Bradburn in Chicago; Campbell, Converse, and Rodgers and Andrews and Withey in Michigan; Allardt in Helsinki; Abrams and Hall in London: all have severally and jointly been working towards the definition and measurement of 'quality of life' as experienced by individual human beings rather

than as indexed by some cash value such as GNP or by official statistics derived from censuses. The work abroad has had a distinctly psychological flavour, often venturing into such realms as music, love, fresh air and sunshine, and being with or near nature. The SSRC work has tended more towards social policy areas, since, although we are aware that the non-policy areas may be better determinants of a sense of well-being, it is the policy areas which allow of intervention to correct inequalities and injustices.

In the 1975 survey we asked a fully-probed open-ended question to elicit respondents' own definitions of 'quality of life'. (*There's a lot of talk these days about the 'Quality of Life' in Britain and in other countries. Of course, 'Quality of Life' means different things to different people. What does it mean to you? – What sort of things do you think of now when you hear the words 'Quality of Life'?*)

Definitions of 'Quality of Life' ranged from single-word answers to philosophical treatises, and seem to vindicate the life-domains approach adopted in the earlier surveys. The largest single category of references was to family, home-life, marriage, etc. (23 per cent). A large number of respondents (19 per cent) were unable to be specific and referred to simply being contented, happy, or 'being satisfied inside yourself'. Money and prices were specifically mentioned (18 per cent) as also was standard of living or decent conditions of life (17 per cent). Of these last, a strikingly large number of answers specifically *excluded* luxuries. Social values, social *mores*, and decent standards of behaviour (16 per cent) comprised the only other areas referred to by more than 15 per cent of respondents. At the other end of the scale the fewest references were to social equality and social justice (2 per cent), altruism (2 per cent), complaints and negative statements about others (2 per cent), and worries, cares, or mental health (2 per cent) (Table I).

Men and women tended to give similar replies, but there were some notable differences. Women were more likely to mention home-life and health, and to give the generalised non-specific answer. Men were more likely to mention living standards, work, and freedom. Younger people were more likely to mention money, living standards, and work; whilst older people referred more to values and to the past. Middle class people tended to think of social relationships, living standards, environment, freedom, and leisure, and to give a greater number of answers than did working class people, who were more likely to refer to money, or to give 'don't know' replies.

Table I Definition of 'Quality of Life', 1975

Great Britain — Percentages

Reference to:	All	Men	Women	18–29	30–44	45–59	60+	AB	C1	C2	D	E
Family and home life	23	18	26	22	24	26	21	26	20	25	22	20
General contentment	19	17	21	26	15	18	18	16	18	22	20	18
Money and prices	18	18	18	28	21	13	12	15	18	20	21	12
Living standards	17	23	13	20	23	19	8	22	19	16	17	13
Social values and standards	16	14	17	7	11	22	21	16	20	14	17	12
Personal beliefs, religion	11	10	12	9	11	12	11	12	10	10	13	10
Social relationships	10	9	11	10	8	10	12	18	12	7	8	7
Housing	10	9	10	12	11	10	8	13	10	9	12	7
Health	10	8	11	8	12	12	7	10	9	10	14	3
Work	9	12	6	14	12	8	2	10	8	12	8	1
Freedom of all kinds	7	9	5	7	9	5	6	12	7	7	2	5
Leisure, holidays, travel	6	8	5	6	12	5	3	9	7	7	5	3
Environment, nature	4	4	4	5	4	4	3	11	4	3	2	1
Education and culture	4	2	4	4	5	2	4	7	5	4	1	0
Comparison with past and other countries	4	4	4	2	1	3	7	5	4	3	3	4
Consumer goods, luxuries	3	4	3	6	2	5	1	5	3	4	2	2
Pressures of life	3	3	3	4	3	3	2	3	4	4	2	1
Worries, cares, mental health	2	2	3	2	2	2	2	0	4	2	4	2
Negative statements	2	2	3	2	2	2	4	2	2	2	2	4
Altruistic statements	2	2	2	1	1	2	3	3	3	1	0	3
Equality and justice	2	2	2	2	2	1	2	1	2	1	2	4
Other	3	4	3	5	1	3	3	3	7	2	2	3
Don't know	10	8	11	11	8	8	11	3	5	10	13	18

Column group headers: Sex (Men, Women); Age groups (18–29, 30–44, 45–59, 60+); Social class of head of household (AB, C1, C2, D, E).

Quality of life in Britain and other countries

Because of the referendum campaign and the cross-national nature of the research, a new section was included on perceived quality of life in Britain and in other countries. This was also designed to provide a baseline for time trends, and perhaps to encourage other countries to produce similar data. Thus, after defining their own meanings for 'Quality of Life', our respondents were asked to rate the quality of life in different countries using an eleven-point scale on which 0 represented the 'lowest possible' and 10 represented the 'highest possible'.

After careful consideration nine countries were selected. These represented the third world (India), the EEC (France, Germany, Holland), a European social democracy with a high standard of living (Sweden), Eastern Europe (Russia), North America (USA), and the Old Commonwealth (Australia), plus, of course, Britain. Australia was ranked the highest (7·7) and India the lowest (2·5). After Australia came Sweden (7·5), Germany and Holland (7·4), with Britain (7·2) following. Second and third lowest were Russia (4·9) and France (6·4). The USA was rated 7·1.

Perceived trends in Quality of Life

As well as rating the 'Quality of Life' in Britain now, respondents also gave ratings for 'Quality of Life' 5 years ago, 'Quality of Life' in 5 years time, and what people thought they deserved. The general picture is of a country sliding rapidly down from 8·0 5 years ago, through 7·2 now, to 6·0 in 5 years time. This contrasts with individual respondents' estimations of their personal standard of living (which seem to be maintained at about the same level of 6·6 over the reference period) and of life-satisfaction (perceived to be on the increase, from 7·3 through 7·8 to 8·1) (Table II).

When asked what was the *one* thing they would most like to change to improve the quality of life in Britain today, respondents made most references to prices and inflation (11 per cent) closely followed by government and politics (10 per cent). Trade unions could claim third place since 6 per cent thought there were too many strikes and 3 per cent thought the unions had too much power. Seven per cent thought people should be made to work and 6 per cent that people were too greedy or selfish. A further 6 per cent wished to reduce levels of crime and violence. Whatever the others thought, 6 per cent wanted to change nothing: for them Britain was definitely best.

Table II Perceived trends of 'Quality of Life': 1975

Great Britain   Various units

	Mean[1] rating	Grouped scale ratings Percentages					Total sample (=100%)
		(0–4)	(5–7)	(8–9)	(10)	DK	
(a) Level of 'Quality of Life' in Britain							
5 years ago	8·0	3	29	49	17	2	932
Now (1975)	7·2	7	43	38	11	2	932
5 years time	6·0	25	39	22	9	5	932
Entitled	8·9	1	9	40	47	3	932
(b) Level of 'your own standard of living'							
5 years ago	6·5	12	54	26	6	2	932
Now (1975)	6·6	8	60	28	3	1	932
5 years time	6·7	12	42	34	7	5	932
Deserved	8·0	–	28	52	17	2	932
(c) Satisfaction with 'your life as a whole'							
5 years ago	7·3	7	40	36	16	1	932
Now (1975)	7·8	3	29	48	20	1	932
5 years time	8·1	3	22	46	25	4	932
Entitled	8·8	–	10	50	38	2	932

[1] 0–10, 0=lowest possible, 10=highest possible.

Self-reported satisfaction

The list of domains for which global satisfaction ratings were obtained between 1971 and 1975 is shown with the mean satisfactions and other measures in Table III. Not all domains were used in each survey, and the October 1971 survey ratings have been recalculated to 0–10 from the 1–7 scale actually used for comparability with a sister study in the USA (Campbell, Converse, and Rodgers, 1976). This makes it difficult to compare ratings from 1971 with those for 1973 and 1975, especially since both the 1971 samples were of the quota-type, and neither was designed to represent urban Great Britain. With these reservations it seems reasonable to claim that the rank order of mean satisfaction ratings has remained fairly stable; that satisfaction with family life, leisure, health, and job has remained steady; and

that satisfaction with standard of living, general financial situation, and the level of freedom and democracy in this country has improved. There would also appear to be a modest improvement in satisfaction with education received. If genuine, some of these improvements may be due simply to the passage of time (eg later samples will include people with longer education in better facilities); others may well be due to changes in personal or national circumstances, such as increases in real income and changes in the composition and policies of central and local government. In 1975 lowest satisfaction was with 'The Quality of Life in Britain today'. In view of the economic crisis, cut-backs, and unemployment rates experienced in Britain during 1976 the absence of data from the planned follow-up survey seems unfortunate.

Table III Satisfaction with major life domains and with life as a whole (1971–1975)

Great Britain   Various units

	Mean satisfaction rating			Proportion dissatisfied			Proportion completely satisfied			Correlation with overall life satisfaction		
	1971	1973	1975	(1–3) 1971	(0–4) 1973	(0–4) 1975	(7) 1971	(10) 1973	(10) 1975	1971	1973	1975
Marriage	9·2	..	..	3	..	..	68	..	..	0·23	..	..
Family life	8·5	..	8·8	5	..	4	52	..	55	0·39	..	0·37
Job[1]	8·3	8·3	8·0	5	2	2	41	32	29	0·34	0·46	0·42
Town	..	7·8	8·1	..	8	6	..	32	36	..	0·31	0·25
Health	7·9	7·7	7·8	10	10	8	41	31	27	0·25	0·35	0·38
District	7·9	7·5	7·9	6	11	9	29	28	33	0·23	0·27	0·28
Being a housewife[2]	7·9	..	8·1	11	..	7	42	..	38	0·34	..	0·54
Leisure	7·6	7·5	7·7	11	7	6	34	22	27	0·41	0·41	0·52
House	7·4	7·8	7·8	8	7	8	26	28	28	0·18	0·35	0·37
Standard of living	6·9	7·4	7·7	13	7	5	19	19	23	0·37	0·56	0·53
Education	6·5	6·7	6·9	17	13	13	20	14	18	0·27	0·34	0·23
Democracy	6·1	6·7	7·3	18	9	6	12	9	13	0·26	0·22	0·23
Financial situation	5·5	6·6	7·3	30	15	10	10	12	19	..	0·51	0·52
Life in Britain	..	..	6·5	..	..	15	..	..	10	..	..	0·32
Life as a whole	7·8	7·6	7·8	4	4	3	26	19	20	–	–	–

[1] All working including part-time.   [2] All full-time housewives.

50

Relationship between objective and subjective measures

Some idea of the relationship of subjective satisfaction measures to actual or reported differences in objective circumstances can be obtained from the data on housing and health shown below. Any strong and systematic linear relationships should be revealed by differences in mean scores in that we would expect higher scores for 'better', advantageous, or desirable circumstances and lower scores for the less advantageous or desirable. The inclusion of objective and subjective measures in linear models to predict variation in satisfaction with housing, local district, or life as a whole is reported elsewhere (Hall and Ring, 1974; Hall, 1975).

At sub-domain levels there is a high degree of sensitivity of reported satisfaction with a specific aspect of a domain to measurable differences in that aspect. At the global level of domain satisfaction these differences remain, but tend to be smaller; and at the level of satisfaction with life as a whole they may disappear altogether. A question for researchers would be to ask whether there exists a set of objective circumstances which will give the enormous differences in reported satisfaction with life as a whole as, for instance, not having a bath in the house makes to reported satisfaction with facilities for baths. Whilst we ourselves have not yet mounted a search for such objective measures, we doubt that we shall find them in our data.

What do make for big differences in life satisfaction are large differences in subjective measures. It may well be that subjective measures are as objective as 'objective' measures and can be used in the same way by policy makers and policy-evaluators. But if not, at least subjective indicators may be used to weight objective indicators when decisions need to be made in a *ceteris paribus* situation. A crude example would be that, subjectively, it is much worse not to have a bath at all than to have to share one, but sharing a kitchen is just as bad, subjectively, as not having a kitchen at all. A more complex example might indicate that expensive improvements to immediate environment will make no difference to community satisfaction if every other house in the neighbourhood has 3 children under 5 years old living in it. Whilst it may be difficult to attach a money cost to these situations, it seems plausible to attach a satisfaction or distress cost.

Housing

In addition to the global measures of satisfaction with 'your house or flat' and 'local district', satisfaction ratings were obtained in 1973 and 1975 for a number of aspects of each, some specific, some more generalised. The aspects

chosen for study were mostly derived from the more frequent responses to open-ended questions in the 1971 studies, but items were also deliberately constructed to represent the various need-levels outlined by Maslow (1954) even if these may not have been present in earlier responses. Respondents were thus encouraged to think of their housing and their immediate local environment in wider terms than might otherwise have been the case. The 1975 survey was deliberately used to collect substantial and detailed information on housing and health with the specific intention of investigating the relationship of objective and subjective measures.

The items eventually used in the list for housing satisfaction and the results obtained are shown in Table IV.

Table IV   Satisfaction with house or flat, 1973–1975

Great Britain

	Mean satisfaction rating with specified aspect		Zero-order correlation with overall housing satisfaction	
	1973	1975	1973	1975
Number of rooms	8·3	8·2	0·41	0·50
Baths or showers	8·1	8·4	0·47	0·52
Keeping it clean and tidy	8·1	8·2	0·42	0·46
Privacy from neighbours	7·9	8·3	0·41	0·41
Damp and condensation	7·3	7·6	0·49	0·51
Warmth in winter	7·1	7·0	0·46	0·52
Noise	7·0	8·1	0·38	0·35
View from windows	6·7	7·2	0·46	0·42
Kitchen	6·7	6·7	0·47	0·49
Cost	6·6	6·5	0·34	0·23
Size and shape of rooms	..	7·9	..	0·57
Internal repair and decoration	..	7·7	..	0·58
External appearance	..	7·4	..	0·58

In both 1973 and 1975 the average house-satisfaction rating for the whole sample was 7·8, with 28 per cent indicating complete satisfaction. In addition to the subjective satisfaction ratings for the various aspects of housing, we have hard data relating to the dwelling itself. These data together with multivariate analysis offer some validation of the subjective measures and the final global rating as an overall measure of housing satisfaction. The hard measures show expected association with both the overall satisfaction with dwelling and, where obtained, satisfaction with the relevant aspect. Owner-occupiers are more satisfied than council tenants who in turn are more satisfied than private-unfurnished tenants (Table V).

As would be expected, those who do not have, or have to share, a bath, a toilet, or kitchen are much less satisfied with their dwelling than those who

Table V   Housing tenure and housing satisfaction, 1971–1975

Great Britain				Means and numbers
	1971a	1971b	1973	1975
Mean satisfaction with house or flat				
Owners	} 8·2	7·6	{ 8·7	8·6
Mortgagees			8·2	8·2
Council rented	6·9	7·2	7·2	7·4
Rented unfurnished	7·5	6·9	6·8	6·9
Number in sample	213	593	966	932

have exclusive use. Sharing a toilet or kitchen, or not having a separate kitchen, is associated with particularly low levels of dwelling satisfaction. Those who have a garden, garage, or central heating are, naturally, more satisfied than those who have not.

Occupants of detached houses score higher than those in semi-detached, who in turn score higher than those in terraced houses, and these latter are more satisfied than people who live in flats or maisonettes.

More internal evidence of validity is given by the enormous differences in satisfaction with particular aspects of their housing of those for whom the relevant objective condition differs. In houses with no fixed bath or shower, satisfaction with facilities for baths or showers was 1·5 in 1973 and 2·2 in 1975 as against 8·6 and 8·7 in houses with exclusive use of fixed baths. In houses without inside flush WCs the figures were 3·3 and 4·5 as against 8·6 and 8·7. In 1975 those who had piped hot water for their baths scored 8·8 but those who had to heat water in a kettle or pan scored only 3·9 (Table VI).

The detailed data on other housing circumstances for 1975 show a similar pattern to those for standard amenities; but the relationships between satisfaction ratings and related conditions, whilst consistent, are not in all cases so strongly marked. Thus respondents living in houses built before 1945 are generally, but only slightly, less satisfied with 'the general state of repair and decoration inside' than are those living in more modern houses. Those who live in detached houses are more satisfied with 'its appearance from the outside' than are those who live in other types of housing. The greater the cost of rent or mortgage payments plus annual repairs and maintenance costs, the less satisfied people are with housing costs. Central heating is associated with higher satisfaction for 'keeping it warm in winter' than other types of heating (in the main living room). Those whose houses front open country or residential areas with gardens and trees are more satisfied with 'the view from your windows' than those who look out into treeless or gardenless housing, factories, or shops and offices.

Table VI   Mean satisfaction ratings for specified housing conditions, 1975[1]

Great Britain			Means
	Mean overall satisfaction with house	Mean satisfaction with specific aspect	Satisfaction item
Building type			
Detached	(8·7) 8·6	8·4	'Its appearance
Semi-detached	(8·1) 8·1	7·9	from the
Terrace	(7·4) 7·4	6·9	outside'
Flat or maisonette	(7·3) 7·3	6·6	. .
Fixed bath or shower			
None	(5·8) 5·5	(1·5) 2·2	'Facilities for
Shared	(7·3) 7·3	(7·1) 6·9	baths or
Exclusive	(8·0) 8·0	(8·6) 8·7	showers'
Inside flush toilet			
None	(6·4) 6·5	(3·3) 4·5	''
Shared	(7·2) 6·9	(6·9) 6·7	
Exclusive	(7·9) 8·0	(8·6) 8·7	
Hot water for bath or shower			
Piped	8·1	8·8	
Geyser	7·5	8·2	
Kettle	6·0	3·9	
Method of heating living-room in winter			
Central heating	8·3	8·4	'Keeping it
Electric storage	8·9	8·1	warm in
Solid fuel	7·9	6·8	winter'
Gas fire	7·6	6·5	
Electric fire	7·1	5·4	
Other	6·4	4·5	
Cost of rent, rates, etc.			
Under £5 p.w.	7·7	7·2	'The cost of
£5 under £10	7·6	6·4	(rent/mort-
£10 under £15	7·7	5·9	gage) rates,
£15 under £25	7·8	6·0	repairs, etc.'
£25 under £35	8·0	4·9	
£35 or more	8·1	5·3	
Date of construction			
1899 or earlier	7·5	7·2	'The general
1900–1918	7·7	7·9	state of repair
1919–1944	7·8	7·6	and decoration
1945–1964	8·1	8·3	inside'
1965 or later	8·2	8·0	
View from front			
Open country, trees	7·8	8·4	'The view
Gardens, trees	8·1	7·6	from your
No gardens or trees	7·4	6·4	windows'
Industrial	7·2	5·4	
Commercial, shops	7·4	5·4	
Other	7·7	3·9	

[1] 1973 figures in brackets.

One promising type of subjective indicator tried out in 1975 seems to be strongly related to satisfaction ratings and may well be more acceptable to sceptics, while retaining the essentially *experiential* component. Respondents were asked to indicate the extent to which, during the past few weeks, they had been bothered by ten types of nuisance, five of which related to noise and five to other sources of nuisance. Those who claimed to have been bothered 'a lot' or 'a great deal' by noise from neighbours or industry were least satisfied (5·6) with their housing. Noise from children or traffic and trains was associated with slightly less dissatisfaction (6·5, 6·7), but noise from aircraft does not appear to be associated with anything like the same degree of dissatisfaction (7·3). Satisfaction with 'noise' in the neighbourhood drops significantly for those claiming to be bothered by noise, and again noise from industry seems to generate greatest dissatisfaction (3·0) and noise from aircraft the least (5·9) (Table VII).

Housing satisfaction ratings associated with high levels of other nuisances were 5·4 for damp, 5·6 for 'rats or mice', 6·3 for 'insects getting in the house' and 'smoke, soot, fumes, smells, dirt or dust in the air outside', and 6·6 for 'condensation or ventilation problems'. A *Housing Nuisance Index* was derived from these items which has a striking association with levels of housing satisfaction. Respondents not bothered at all by any kind of nuisance scored 8·5 whereas those reporting four or more sources scored 2.8. (Noise items were collapsed to a single measure for this purpose.)

Table VII   Housing nuisance index, 1975

	Great Britain	Means and percentages
	Percentage bothered 'a lot' or 'a great deal'	Mean satisfaction with house
Component items:		
Noise from:		
Traffic or trains	13	6·7
Children	11	6·5
Neighbours	5	5·6
Aircraft	4	7·3
Industry	2	5·6
Other:		
Condensation	20	6·6
Air pollution	12	6·3
Damp	11	5·4
Insects	3	6·3
Vermin	2	5·6
	Percentage in category	Mean satisfaction with house
No. of sources of nuisance:		
(Noise once only)		
None	57	8·5
One	25	7·6
Two	11	6·7
Three	4	6·1
Four or more	3	2·8
Total	100	7·8

Health
The second area in which we examined the relationship between subjective and objective indicators was health. Most people would agree that good health is a prerequisite in any index of individual or national well-being. All our surveys included the question *Do you yourself have any long-standing physical disability or health trouble?* (IF YES) *Does it keep you from doing things you might like to do?* This yields three categories of self-reported disability: first, those reporting no long-term disability; second, those reporting such disability but who do not feel limited by it; third, those who claim to be limited

in their normal activities by some long-standing disability or health problem. In all three surveys satisfaction with health is highest for the first group and lowest for the third.

Table VIII   Health condition and health satisfaction

	Great Britain		Means and percentages		
	Percentage in category			Mean satisfaction with health	
	1971	1973	1975	1971	1973	1975
No chronic problem	72	68	74	8·7	8·6	8·6
Problem, not limiting	12	7	8	6·9	7·5	7·3
Limiting problem	16	25	19	4·9	5·4	5·2

Partly on the grounds of providing more 'objective' measures of health, and partly as a means of measuring stress, the 1975 survey included the battery of health symptoms used by Bradburn (1969) with three extra items added. From these it is possible to construct general indices of poor physical health and of anxiety. Since a great deal of work in the mental health field purports to show high diagnostic value of scores on such scales for identifying persons possibly in need of psychiatric help, such a scale, if it were robust, valid, and reliable, should provide a major 'objective' tool for the measurement of quality of life.

At least half the sample were free of each symptom, except for 'aches and pains' (44 per cent), and more than three-quarters were free of some of the more severe symptoms. Seventeen per cent were bothered 'a lot' or 'a great deal' by 'aches and pains' and 'getting to sleep', 14 per cent by 'nervousness', and 13 per cent by 'headaches', 'cold or flu', or 'feeling run down'. Of the more severe symptoms, only 3 per cent had been bothered by skin rashes, 4 per cent by rapid heart-beat, and 5 per cent by sweating hands. The highest correlations with health satisfaction were for 'feeling run down' (0·55) and 'nervousness' and 'aches and pains' (0·49); the lowest were for 'cold or flu' (0·15) and 'skin rashes' (0·17) (Table IX).

An index of poor physical health was calculated as the sum of endorsements of the five items 'Dizziness', 'General aches and pains', 'Hands sweating and feeling damp and clammy', 'Headaches', and 'Rapid heart-beat'. An index of anxiety was calculated in the same way from the three items 'Nervousness or tenseness', 'Trouble getting to sleep at night', and 'Not having enough energy to do all the things you would like to do'.

As in the case of housing, the single item measuring satisfaction with health is highly sensitive to differences in the number of symptoms admitted and on indices derived from the symptoms.

Table IX   Health symptoms, 1975
'To what extent, if any, were you bothered by . . . . . during the past few weeks?'

Great Britain   Various units

	'Not at all'	'A little'	'Quite a lot' and 'A great deal'	Total in sample (=100%)	Zero-order corr. with overall sat. with health
Percentage bothered by:					
Aches and pains	44	38	17	924	0·49
Headaches	53	34	13	930	0·30
Feeling run down	55	33	13	930	0·55
Cold or flu	56	31	13	922	0·15
Nervousness	56	30	14	930	0·49
Trouble getting to sleep	65	18	17	931	0·42
Upset stomach	71	22	7	930	0·34
Trouble staying asleep	75	13	12	930	0·37
Shortness of breath	77	15	7	930	0·43
Dizziness	82	12	6	929	0·34
Twitching or trembling	82	12	7	929	0·34
Rapid heart-beat	85	11	4	928	0·35
Sweating hands	86	9	5	928	0·25
Skin rashes	89	8	3	928	0·17

Differences in health indices are also associated, but less strongly, with differences in self-reported life-satisfaction. Respondents with high levels of symptom admission are more likely to have consulted their doctors within the last four weeks and to have taken medication prescribed by a doctor (Table X).

Table X   Health indices, 1975

Great Britain   Various units

		Mean satisfaction with health	Percentage taking prescribed medicine	Total in sample
Number of the five symptoms[1] indicating poor health exhibited	None	9·1	13	237
	One	8·2	32	280
	Two	7·5	43	231
	Three	6·9	51	113
	Four	5·6	68	47
	Five	4·8	88	24
Number of the three symptoms[1] indicating anxiety exhibited	None	9·1	15	320
	One	8·3	34	287
	Two	6·8	48	203
	Three	5·1	73	122
Index of limitation by recent illness or chronic disability	None	8·8	18	562
	No limitation	7·6	48	92
	Some limitation	6·0	68	275
Most recent consultation with doctor: within last 7 days		7·1	67	111
,, ,, 4 weeks		7·0	69	214
,, ,, 3 months		7·7	39	173
,, , 12 months		8·1	14	220
a year or more ago		8·9	5	205

[1] As defined in paragraph above.

Satisfaction with health fell steeply, from 9·1 for those with none of the symptoms in either index, to 4·8 for those with all five symptoms of poor health and 5·1 for those with all three symptoms of anxiety. Similarly, the proportion of respondents taking medication prescribed by a doctor climbed steeply, from 15 per cent and 13 per cent to 88 per cent and 73 per cent respectively. Those who had experienced no recent illness or chronic disability scored 8·8 for satisfaction with health, and 18 per cent of them had taken prescribed medication; but those whose activities were limited by recent or chronic ill-health scored only 6·0, and 68 per cent of them were on prescribed medication. The longer the interval since the last visit to a doctor the higher the satisfaction with health and the lower the proportion taking prescribed medication. As with housing, it would seem that the health symptom index might substitute for satisfaction ratings and overcome the scepticism of some policy-makers.

Perceived equity in standard of living

Instead of attempting to measure evaluations directly, it is sometimes useful to measure indirectly by obtaining some measure of distance from a desired or ideal condition. Using a scale in which the top represented 'highest possible' and the bottom 'lowest possible' we asked respondents in both 1973 and 1975 to estimate the present standard of living[3] of fourteen broadly defined occupational groups and one ethnic group. This measure gave both a comparative ranking of public perception of each group's present standard of living and a ranking of its perceived comparative deprivation. The scale was also used to obtain ratings of the respondents' perceptions of their own standard of living, not only present and deserved, but also past and anticipated. From these data all manner of relative deprivations and advantages can be calculated, and changes in rank over time can be measured. Since we also asked respondents which of the groups they themselves came in, or were closest to, we can obtain a measure of how closely they

[3] *Standard of living* had been defined thus: 'The things that people can buy and do – their housing, furniture, food, cars, recreation, and travel – make up their standard of living'.

identified themselves with the fortunes of the group they said they were in.

In terms of present standard of living the groups emerge clearly ranked, with professional and executive groups at the top and welfare recipients and pensioners at the bottom. The top five ranks and the bottom three were the same in both 1973 and 1975. In our respondents' ideal society the rank orders would remain largely the same, but with some exceptions. Investors and shareholders would be demoted from second place to seventh or eighth, and pensioners would be promoted from fourteenth to ninth. Uniformed public service workers improved their rank from eighth to sixth in present standard of living and from fourth to equal second in entitlement. Skilled workers ranked fifth for present and second for deserved standard of living in both surveys. Thus, even though changes in absolute levels appeared desirable, these only marginally affect the relative placings of the groups. Coloured people living in Britain were perceived as having a low place both in present and deserved standards of living (Table IX).

In 1975 most groups were perceived to be closer to their entitlement than in 1973, usually because of a perceived increase in present ratings. However, the shortfall between present and entitlement was seen to have widened for two groups. In the case of shopkeepers and small proprietors this was due to a drop in present ratings, and in the case of professional people such as doctors and lawyers to an increase in entitlement. It should be remembered that, during the 1975 fieldwork, the hospital consultants were working to rule. Three groups apparently closer to their entitlement had achieved this by a reduction in perceived entitlement in the eyes of the public: these were students, welfare recipients, and coloured people.

Examination of the perceptions each group had of the standard of living of the other groups reveals one potentially alarming trend. In 1973 only two groups were thought to be getting more than they deserved, not only by the whole sample but also by each of the other groups; these were 'investors and shareholders' and 'company directors and business executives'. In 1975, as things began to get tight in Britain, negative shortfalls began to appear elsewhere, and this may be evidence of scape-goat seeking and incipient polarisation. Civil servants were thought to be overprivileged by labourers, company executives, professional people, policemen, and welfare recipients; labourers and unskilled workers were thought to be so by company executives. Welfare recipients enjoyed too high a standard of living for company executives, civil servants, small proprietors, and policemen; and coloured people's

standard of living was too high for policemen and labourers. In view of the recent electoral advances of ultra-right candidates and increased community tensions, such as seen during the Notting Hill Carnival, 1976, it seems unfortunate that no replication of the survey was available for mid-1976.

Perceptions of trends in personal standard of living have changed so that people, instead of expecting a steady and significant improvement as in 1973, had switched to a steady but maintained level in 1975. Had data been available for 1976 it is possible that these would have shown a steady, but significant, decline.

Table XI   Comparison of perceived levels of living in 1973 and 1975

	Great Britain				Means	
	Now		Deserved		Shortfall	
	1973	1975	1973	1975	1973	1975
(a) – Mean ratings of standard of living ascribed to various groups by whole sample:						
Directors and executives	9·1	9·0	8·4	8·5	−0·7	−0·5
Doctors and lawyers	8·9	8·5	9·2	9·4	0·3	0·9
Investors and shareholders	8·7	8·4	7·6	7·7	−1·1	−0·7
Civil servants	7·4	7·6	7·8	7·7	0·4	0·1
Skilled workers	7·2	7·4	8·4	8·5	1·2	1·1
Teachers	6·9	6·7	8·1	8·0	1·2	1·3
Small businessmen	6·9	6·6	8·0	8·1	1·1	1·5
Uniformed public service	6·4	6·7	8·3	8·5	1·9	1·8
Clerks	6·2	6·3	7·4	7·4	1·2	1·1
Personal service	5·4	5·5	7·3	7·3	1·9	1·8
Labourers	5·2	5·6	7·0	6·9	1·8	1·3
Students	5·0	5·3	6·3	6·1	1·3	0·8
Welfare recipients	4·6	5·0	5·6	5·4	1·0	0·4
Pensioners	3·8	4·5	7·4	7·4	3·6	2·9
Coloured people	5·3	5·7	6·5	6·2	1·2	0·5
Yourself	6·4	6·6	8·0	8·0	1·6	1·4

(b) – Perceived trends in personal standard of living:		
	1973	1975
5 years ago	6·0	6·5
Now	6·4	6·6
5 years time	7·0	6·7
Entitled	8·0	8·0

Perceived political equity

It is a central tenet of a social democracy that a just society is necessary for human fulfilment. A number of items were included from 1971 onwards intended to measure perceptions of various aspects of the British political system. In 1971 a numbered scale, ranging from 'None or not at all' to 'A very great deal', was used to ask people how much they thought there was in Britain of certain elements assumed to be desirable. In 1973 and 1975 the number of elements was increased and the metric extended to ask not only how much people thought there was at the present time, but also how much they thought there *ought* to be.

Table XII   Comparison of perceived levels of freedom and democracy in Britain

Great Britain   Means and proportions

| | Mean rating[1] | | | | | | | Proportion stating | | | |
| | Now | | | Ought to be | | Shortfall | | Should be at least one point less | | Should be at least two points more | |
	1971	1973	1975	1973	1975	1973	1975	1973	1975	1973	1975
Freedom of speech	7·8	7·5	8·3	8·9	9·1	1·4	0·8	6	8	28	13
Democracy	6·1	6·9	7·3	.9	8·9	1·9	1·6	3	5	35	26
Pride in being British	..	..	6·9	..	9·4	..	2·5	..	1	..	44
Equality for women	..	..	6·9	..	8·6	..	1·7	..	7	..	32
Government information	..	..	6·4	..	5·2	..	−1·2	..	47	..	9
Tolerance	5·9	5·7	6·4	8·3	8·4	2·6	2·0	6	9	50	38
Social equality	..	5·5	6·0	8·6	8·4	3·3	2·4	2	3	58	45
Censorship	..	..	5·3	..	6·2	..	0·9	..	22	..	30
Easy to understand politics	5·1	5·3	5·2	8·9	8·9	3·6	3·7	−	1	64	63
Influence of voters	3·6	4·8	5·3	8·8	8·7	4·0	3·4		1	67	58
Respect for law and order	..	..	4·8	..	9·4	..	4·6	..	−	..	78

[1] On 0–10 scale.

The two measures can then be compared and a discrepancy measure generated for each element.

From 1971 to 1975 there were improvements in perceived levels of freedom of speech, tolerance, democracy, and influence of voters. However, ease of understanding politics and government remained depressingly low throughout. There was a small increase in perceived social equality between 1973 and 1975. All improvements were due to perceived increases of the present levels, since the desired levels remained steady. It is the shortfalls between present and desired levels which are important, since a low value for a particular element may be highly desirable to some people or even to many. Thus, voter influence and understanding of politics were still a long way short of ideal; and there was a fair way to go for social equality, tolerance, and democracy in spite of improvements between 1973 and 1975. To judge by the items asked only in 1975, there was nowhere near enough respect for law and order, nor was there sufficient pride in being British. Women's equality had a little way to go, censorship was about right, and the government should have collected and kept less information on individual citizens (Table XII).

Any set of political values is bound to have dissidents as well as adherents. Thus, even in 1975 there were those who thought there should be less tolerance (9 per cent), less freedom of speech (8 per cent), and less equality for women (7 per cent), that Britain should be less democratic (5 per cent), and that the government should collect and keep more information on individuals (9 per cent). Censorship is the most contentious issue since, although its shortfall of 0·9 is the second smallest, the 22 per cent who thought there should be less were outnumbered by the 30 per cent who thought there should be a lot more.

Small area data

In recent years there has been a great deal of interest in small area indicators (Holtermann, 1975) and some of the standard census indicators have been subjected to great scrutiny in order to identify areas of privilege and deprivation. An advantage of the subjective approach is that it becomes possible to measure people's feelings about the areas they live in and to relate these to census indicators. Subjective indicators may then be used to modify the interpretation of objective measures and perhaps suggest priorities for intervention or new types of objective indicators.

Hall and Ring (1974) appealed for survey interviews to be coded by geographical location so that sociological and psychological measures could be mapped in space and related to other variables. Whilst they did not expect the 1-metre National Grid references already used by some local authorities, they did suggest a practicable goal of always coding the wards of local authorities in which the interviews were conducted.

An advantage of this is that in those areas where government and local authorities collect and publish statistics at ward level, every survey is immediately open to enrichment by the addition of known data about the locality in which it took place. Moreover, it also enriches the stock of data on wards themselves which can then become units of analysis. Localised social indicators are already submitted to regression analysis to determine the needs element of the Rate Support Grant and subjective indicators have been used to inform and evaluate social policy in Cleveland, Newcastle-upon-Tyne, Strathclyde, and Thamesdown.

Table XIII *Relationship of satisfaction with local district to variations in level of census indicators*

Sunderland, Nov. 1973–Feb. 1974   Various units

Census indicator (percentages unless shown)	Level of indicator	Mean satisfaction with district (of respondents living in wards with specified level of indicator)
Population		
Aged 0–4	Less than 8%	8·5
	8% or more	7·0
Children aged 0–4 per 1,000 women aged 15–44	Less than 420	8·3
	420 or more	7·0
Aged 0-14	Less than 25%	8·1
	25% or more	7·3
Aged 60 or over	Less than 19%	7·2
	19% or more	8·2
Single person households	Less than 17%	7·6
	17% or more	7·9
Households with 6 or more persons	Less than 7%	8·1
	7% or more	7·3
Households at more than 1½ persons per room	Less than 3%	8·1
	3% or more	7·1
Other		
Households in owner-occupation	Less than 26%	7·3
	26% or more	8·0
Households renting from local council	Less than 30%	8·1
	30% to 59%	7·8
	60% to 79%	7·8
	80% or more	6·8
Households with exclusive use of basic amenities	Less than 76%	7·4
	76%–90%	8·3
	91% or more	7·5
Households with access to car	0%–30%	7·1
	31%–40%	8·1
	41% or more	8·5
In Social Class I or II	Less than 5%	6·7
	5%–9%	7·6
	10%–19%	7·9
	20% or more	9·3
In Social Class IV or V	Less than 20%	9·3
	20%–29%	7·7
	30%-34%	7·3
	35% or more	7·2

The 1973–74 Sunderland Quality of Life survey[4] was enriched in this way by the addition of census and planning data available at ward level. Whilst there is a problem that wards tend to be quite large in area and that we have no smaller sub-divisions for which data are available, it is encouraging that, even at this crude level of precision, the relationships which emerge between hard measures and subjective survey responses, though unsurprising, are quite striking.

[4] The SSRC Survey Unit was contracted by the Department of the Environment to replicate the Quality of Life survey in Stoke-on-Trent and Sunderland simultaneously with the national urban survey in 1973 (Contract No. DGR/B/44). The report to the DOE on the leisure aspects has been published separately (Hall & Perry, 1974).

Sunderland is a much surveyed town, and the Birmingham University study of perception of local areas in 1973 outlines the problems of measuring associated with words such as 'area' and 'district' (Donnelly, Goodey, and Menzies, 1973). Whilst we are aware that ward boundaries in no case ever coincide with the boundaries of 'this local district', and that indeed most people will not know where ward boundaries are, the overall satisfaction rating for district appears to be sensitive to differences in the characteristics of wards as measured by census indicators. Differences in satisfaction with specific aspects of local district are also consistently and systematically related to ward census indicators, especially those related to class or wealth, or to the indicators used as measures of social malaise.

Thus, higher satisfaction with local district is expressed by those living in wards with low proportions of young children, higher proportions of older people, lower proportions of large households, and lower levels of overcrowding. Those living in wards with high levels of home and car ownership, with high proportions of professional and managerial workers and corresponding lower proportions of semi-skilled and unskilled workers, are more satisfied than their less well endowed counterparts. However, the proportion of single person households and level of household amenities does not seem to be associated with satisfaction in the same way. A selection of indicators and associated satisfaction levels is given in Table XIII. It remains to be seen whether a similar pattern emerges for the national survey or for the parallel survey of Stoke-on-Trent.

Global measures of well-being

Of course, 'satisfaction' is only one dimension of the many needed to give a full account of human fulfilment and happiness, and satisfaction can change its meaning depending on its context. McKennell (1973) has already isolated cognitive and affective (roughly intellectual and emotional) components in data from Britain and the USA. Awareness of this led us to include other measures designed to tap a general sense of well-being, such as the extent to which people feel they wish to change their present lives, or have choice and control over the way life has turned out for them. They have also been asked how much they worried 'these days', how well they felt they were doing in achieving life's goals, and also how happy they felt. Other more complex measures were used in 1975 to measure personal efficacy, disposition to trust other people, and the balance of positive over negative mood states during the recent past. These latter were the ten item 'Affect Balance Scale' described by Bradburn (1969), and a three item 'Trust in Others' scale together with a four

Table XIV Measures of affect and syndromes, 1975

Great Britain   Various units

a. Endorsement of items composing scales (percentages)

Positive affect		Negative affect	
Excited	40	Restless	24
Proud	43	Lonely	18
Pleased	60	Bored	28
On top of the world	41	Depressed	24
Things going your way	60	Upset	14

b. Scores on subscales

	0	1	2	3	4	5	Sample total (=100%)	Mean
	(percentages)							
Positive affect	15	16	20	20	17	12	932	2·5
Negative affect	45	25	14	10	5	1	932	1·1

c. Affect balance (positive affect minus negative affect)

−5	−4	−3	−2	−1	0	+1	+2	+3	+4	+5	Sample total (=100%)	Mean
					(percentages)							
0	1	3	6	7	14	18	19	16	12	4	932	1·4

d. Personal competence (4 equals high)

0	1	2	3	4	Sample total (=100%)	Mean
		(percentages)				
13	25	29	24	9	932	1·9

e. Trust in others (3 equals high)

0	1	2	3	Sample total (=100%)	Mean
	(percentages)				
18	19	28	35	932	1·8

item 'Personal Competence' scale used by the University of Michigan in 1971 (Campbell, Converse, and Rodgers, 1976).

The Affect Balance Scale consists of five positively-worded and five negatively-worded items, the endorsements to which are summed to yield two measures, 'positive affect' and 'negative affect'. Affect Balance is calculated as the extent to which positive affect is greater or less than negative affect. Scores on the two components have been found to be completely uncorrelated in the USA, and this finding is replicated in the British data (Pearson product moment coefficient = 0·002). The distribution of scores for positive affect was very flat, but that for negative affect closely resembled a Poisson distribution. The distribution of affect balance appeared to be approximately normal, with a slight skew towards a positive score, and a long tail for high negative scores.

Personal competence levels were evenly spread in the centre of the range, with only 13 per cent scoring zero and only 9 per cent the maximum score of five. Trust in others tended to be high, with 35 per cent obtaining the maximum score, but nonetheless 18 per cent remaining very untrusting. Whilst affect balance scores varied markedly according to age, sex, or class, there

was no such variation for competence or trust. All three types of measure were strongly and systematically related to other subjective measures. Detailed analysis of these measures is reported elsewhere (Hall, 1976). The Affect Balance Scale was particularly sensitive to differences in personal circumstances and may well be preferable to other measures as a dependent variable. Only further fieldwork will test its robustness and reliability (Table XIV).

A word of caution

In pursuing the development and application of sophisticated and complex indicators, or the use of advanced scaling techniques, it is important not to overlook the simple indicators which can be of equal if not greater relevance to the quality of life as experienced by individual Britons. Loneliness can often be relieved by the reassuring presence of a pet, and holidays are well known for their tonic value.[5] Large numbers of our citizens still live in bad housing conditions, have dirty or dangerous jobs, suffer from poor health or other disabilities, and face a daily struggle to survive in spite of the availability of state benefits. Of those whose weekly household incomes were less than £15 in 1975, only half had had a holiday in the previous twelve months and 15 per cent had not had one

[5] For objective data see the Leisure section, pages 173 to 183.

for ten years or more. In contrast, four fifths of those with household incomes of £80 a week or more had had a holiday in the last year and only 2 per cent not for ten years. Of those whose heads of households were in the higher social grades, 26 per cent had had a holiday abroad in the last twelve months, 3 per cent no holiday for ten years, and there was not a single case of anyone in that category who had never had a holiday: the corresponding figures for those dependent on welfare benefits and state pensions were 4 per cent, 14 per cent, and 10 per cent. These and other indicators show clearly how it is better to be middle-class or highly paid in Britain today (Table XV).

Table XV   Holidays, class, and income, 1975

Great Britain   Percentages and numbers

	Year of most recent holiday			Never had a holiday	Sample size (=100%)
	1974/75		1965 or earlier		
	Abroad	Britain			
Social class of head of household: (percentages)					
AB	26	54	3	–	152
C1	12	55	3	1	187
C2	10	49	3	5	295
D	10	44	8	6	173
E	4	42	14	10	125
Gross household income: (percentages)					
Under £15	4	46	15	7	68
£15 but under £25	1	47	9	8	106
£25 „ „ £35	9	38	8	6	88
£35 „ „ £45	8	45	4	4	104
£45 „ „ £60	14	56	3	3	148
£60 „ „ £80	15	57	3	2	112
£80 or more	30	49	2	3	113

Conclusions and proposals for future

If one were to think in terms of a 'best buy' in the subjective indicators field from among those reported here, it would seem to be valuable to emphasise the Housing Nuisance Index and the Health Symptom Index as potentially useful policy tools. For the political scientists the concept of equity shortfalls in democracy and material rewards for occupational groups seems to offer rich pickings, and the measures described appear to be sensitive to changes in national mood. For the psychometricians the Affect Balance Scale and the syndrome measures afford many analytical possibilities, together with various semantic differential techniques tried out between 1971 and 1975. The 'satisfied–dissatisfied' metric appears to be reasonably efficient, but the length of the scale needs to be investigated, as does the semantic content of each pole. Responses on 1–7 scales tend to bunch at the upper end, and those on 0–10 scales are unevenly distributed in peaks and

troughs. The Ornauer and Galtung 1–9 scale[6] appears to avoid bunching and also to yield distributions approaching a normal curve. Unfortunately Cantril omitted Britain from his large cross-national study and so it is still necessary to ask the British what, for them, constitute the best possible and the worst possible futures (Kilpatrick and Cantril, 1960).

The range of life-domains needs expanding to include role-performance, self-fulfilment, personal relationships, culture, and other areas not yet investigated in Britain. We have consciously avoided any attempt at measurement of intelligence or sexual behaviour and satisfaction, or at psychiatric diagnosis, believing these to be properly the sphere of other professional competences than our own. However, joint investigations relating such areas to our own indicators would be more than welcome.

The programme of research followed by the SSRC Survey Unit on a limited budget and with limited resources has demonstrated both the feasibility of subjective indicators and their legitimacy, not only as an area of academic social research, but also as an integral part of policy formulation and evaluation. It is important to have a degree of flexibility to be able to react to external events. The social researcher, unlike the laboratory scientist, is unable to manipulate the context in which he carries out his research. Sometimes an event occurs which materially affects his results, and if he is able to monitor the situation before and after such an event this is a useful bonus: for example, Bradburn was conducting a survey in 1963 when President Kennedy was assassinated, and was able to measure attitudes before and after that event.

While the 1973 survey was in the field, Mr Heath decided to go to the country in the General Election of February 1974. If fieldwork could have been extended through the hustings it would have been possible to have obtained an additional 1,000 interviews for around £7,000. However, the money was not available. In early and mid-1976 Britain faced its toughest economic crisis since the 1930s, unprecedented publicity was given to falling standards of living, there were campaigns to 'Save it', and coloured immigration flared up as an ugly issue in by-elections and in the shape of race-killings. A further £9,000 would have given readings on subjective indicators for 1976 from 1,000 of our 1973 and 1975 respondents, and incidentally have transformed our respondents into a panel to yield genuine time measures. In this case also the money was not available

[6] As used in a survey 'Images of the World in the year 2000', 1967, by H Ornauer and T Galtung. Data deposited at SSRC Survey Archive, University of Essex.

because of the very economic crisis which would have made the survey valuable to academics and policy makers alike.

What is needed now is guaranteed funding[7] for a programme of data collection over a period of at least ten years with large samples, preferably a

panel, together with sufficient staff to work full time on development, analysis, and reporting. Such a programme would be likely to cost upwards of £250,000; but it would provide not only a rich source of data for years to come to enhance our understanding of society but also assist in the development of a scientific approach to formulation and evaluation of social policy, something we badly need at the present time.

[7] The 1971 British pilot surveys cost £460 and £1,600 respectively; in contrast the American pilot survey was funded to the tune of $250,000 and a Canadian study has just been awarded almost $1,000,000.

References and further reading

M A Abrams	'Subjective social indicators', *Social Trends No. 4*, ed. M Nissel. HMSO, 1973.
	'Subjective measures of equity'. Paper given in Cambridge in June 1974 (OECD Seminar on 'Social inequality').
	'Changing political values', *Encounter*, Oct. 1974.
	'The development and background of subjective social indicators' and 'A comparison of some findings from social indicators research in Britain and the Netherlands', Chaps. 2 and 4 in *Measures of Welfare*, Netherlands Institute of Statistics. The Hague, Nov. 1974.
	'A review of work on Subjective Social Indicators 1971–1975', *Occasional Papers in Survey Research, No. 8, SSRC Survey Unit*, 1976.
M A Abrams and J Hall	'The condition of the British people—A report on a pilot survey using self-rating scales'. Paper given at Ditchley in May 1971 at a joint conference on Social Indicators, organised by the SSRCs of the UK and USA.
	'Life satisfaction of the British people'. Paper given at OECD, Paris, in May 1972.
E Allardt	'About Dimensions of Welfare'. Research Report No. 1. Research Group for Comparative Sociology, University of Helsinki, 1973.
F M Andrews and S B Withey	'Developing measures of perceived life quality': Results from several national surveys. *Social Indicators Research 1*, 1–26 1974. Elsevier, Amsterdam.
N Bradburn	*The Structure of Psychological Well-Being*. Aldine, 1969.
A Campbell and P Converse	'Monitoring the Quality of American Life' – Research Proposal to Russell Sage Foundation, 1970.
	(Eds) *The Human Meaning of Social Change*. Russell Sage, 1972.
A Campbell, P Converse and W Rodgers	*The Quality of American Life*. Russell Sage, 1976.
D Donnelly, B Goodey, and M Menzies	'Perception Related Survey for Local Authorities: a Pilot Study in Sunderland', *Research Memorandum 20*, Centre for Urban and Regional Studies, University of Birmingham, 1973.
J Hall	'Measuring the quality of life using sample surveys', in *Technology Assessment and Quality of Life*, ed. G Stöber and D Schumacher. Elsevier, 1973.
	'The relationship between subjective and objective indicators of individual well-being – a linear modelling approach'. Paper to joint seminar 'Subjective Measures of Quality of Life' sponsored by SSRCs of UK and USA – Fitzwilliam College, Cambridge, England, September, 1975.
	'The Quality of Life in urban Britain, 1971 to 1975: an analysis of the relationship between subjective and objective indicators'. *Occasional Papers in Survey Research No. 9*, SSRC Survey Unit, 1976.
J Hall and J Ring	'Indicators of environmental quality and life satisfaction: a subjective approach'. Paper given at Toronto, August 1974 at the Eighth World Congress of Sociology, ISA.
J Hall and N Perry	'Aspects of leisure in two industrial cities'. *Occasional Papers in Survey Research No. 5*, SSRC Survey Unit, 1974.
J Hall *et al.*	Users Manuals for Quality of Life Surveys, SSRC Survey Unit, 1976.
S Holtermann	'Areas of urban deprivation in Great Britain: an analysis of 1971 Census data', *Social Trends No. 6*, ed. E J Thompson, HMSO, 1975.
F Kilpatrick and H Cantril	'Self Anchoring Scaling: A Measure of Individuals' Unique Reality Worlds', *Journal of Individual Psychology*, Vol. 16, No. 8, 1960.
A Marsh	'The Silent Revolution: Value Priorities and the Quality of Life in Britain', *American Political Science Review*, Vol. LXIX, No. 1, March 1975.
A Maslow	*Motivation and Personality*. Harper & Row, 1954.
A McKennell	'Monitoring the Quality of American Life – Commentary'. Paper prepared for SSRC Survey Unit in 1971 and published in Strumpel B (1974).
	'Cognition and Affect in Judgements of Subjective Well-being'. ISR, University of Michigan, 1973.
I Miles	'Survey Research, Psychological Variables and Social Forecasting'. Science Policy Research Unit, University of Sussex, 1974.
C O'Muircheartaigh and B Whelan	'Statistical Aspects of Subjective Measures of Life-Satisfaction: some results from analysis of a pilot survey'. *Occasional Papers in Survey Research, No. 4*, SSRC Survey Unit, 1976.
J Robinson	Chapter on measures of happiness and well-being in Robinson J & Shaver P. *Measures of Social Psychological Attitudes*. ISR, University of Michigan, 1970.
B Strumpel (Ed)	*Subjective Elements of Well-being*. OECD, Paris, 1974.

TABLES AND CHARTS

Population

Since an understanding of the changing size and structure of the population is an essential part of any study of economic or social well-being of the country as a whole, this section sets the scene for the whole of *Social Trends*. Up-to-date demographic information is of great importance for the efficient deployment of resources and for the satisfaction of the varying needs of different parts of the community. Knowledge of the direction in which changes are taking place is important for future planning. For example, changes in the birth rate occurring now have important implications for the planning of the number of school teachers.

The assessment of future longer-term trends in the population, while very difficult, will be essential for long-range planning. Accordingly, this section contains basic information about the structure of the population and the changes which are taking place. Apart from information on the three factors which directly influence the size of the whole population – births, deaths, and migration – there are tables and charts on marriage and divorce, the present and projected regional distribution, migrant flows, and some on the characteristics of the population born overseas. There is also a series of tables on family size.

The figures in this section are derived from several sources. First there are the full population censuses which have occurred every 10 years since 1801 up to 1971, except for 1941. Although these were all complete enumerations, some questions in 1961 and 1971 were tabulated for only 10 per cent

of households. In addition, in 1966 a sample census on 10 per cent of the population was taken. A second source of data is the registration of births, marriages, and deaths. These provide data on trends in nuptiality, fertility, and mortality; and they are used to arrive at estimates of the population in the intercensal years. Details of migrants are obtained from the *International Passenger Survey*, and a great deal of household information is collected in the *General Household Survey*.

There are fewer tables and charts than in previous editions because of the introduction, since the last *Social Trends* was compiled, of the Office of Population Censuses and Survey's *Population Trends*. The reader is referred to *Population Trends*, a quarterly journal, for more detailed tables, charts, and articles on population topics.

Each series of tables and charts in this section is preceded by a short note listing any relevant points about sources, breaks in the series, assumptions made, etc. For general comments on recent demographic trends, the reader is referred to the Population section of the Social Commentary, pages 8 to 31, which describes changes in the period 1970–1976. More technical points on the statistics, and definitions are found in Appendix B, and a list of sources and further reading in Appendix C.

Sex and age structure: population changes: variant projections

Table 1.1 and Chart 1.2 show the trend and the 1975 situation regarding the sex and age structure of the population. The projections in Table 1.1 are mid-1975 based but the variant projections in Table 1.5 but in Chart 1.6 are mid-1974 based. Technical points on these projections will be found in Appendix B. Population projections begin from an estimate of the population at a particular time-point. To derive figures for a future period it is then necessary to make assumptions about the future movements of fertility, mortality, and migration. Of these, fertility is most likely to vary, and Table 1.5 and Chart 1.6 show the effects of four different fertility assumptions on the 1974-based projections. Details of these can be found in *Variant Population Projections 1974–2011*. Table 1.3 and Chart 1.4 show population changes; of particular interest is the grey area of Chart 1.4 showing the variation in natural increase this century.

Table 1.1 Sex and age structure of the population

United Kingdom   Various units

	Census enumerated				Mid-year estimates					Projections[4,5]			
	1901	1911	1921	1931	1941	1951	1961	1971	1975[6]	1981	1991	2001	2011
Total population[1] (millions)													
All persons	38·2	42·1	44·0	46·0	48·2	50·6	53·0	55·7	56·0	55·9	57·3	58·3	59·0
By sex and age group													
Males:													
Under 15	6·2	6·5	6·2	5·6	5·1	5·8	6·3	6·9	6·7	5·9	6·1	6·5	6·0
15–29	5·2	5·4	5·3	5·8	5·8	5·3	5·3	6·0	6·2	6·6	6·6	5·7	6·6
30–44	3·6	4·3	4·3	4·5	5·5	5·5	5·3	4·9	5·0	5·5	6·1	6·6	5·7
45–64[2]	2·7	3·2	4·1	4·6	5·0	5·6	6·4	6·5	6·3	6·1	6·1	6·7	7·7
65–74	0·6	0·7	0·9	1·1	1·4	1·6	1·6	2·0	2·2	2·2	2·2	2·0	2·2
75 and over	0·2	0·2	0·3	0·3	0·5	0·7	0·7	0·8	0·9	1·0	1·1	1·2	1·1
All ages	18·5	20·4	21·0	22·1	23·3	24·4	25·7	27·1	27·3	27·3	28·1	28·8	29·2
Females:													
Under 15	6·2	6·5	6·1	5·5	5·0	5·6	6·0	6·5	6·4	5·6	5·8	6·1	5·6
15–29	5·6	5·8	5·9	6·0	5·8	5·2	5·1	5·8	6·0	6·3	6·3	5·4	6·2
30–44	3·9	4·6	5·0	5·2	5·8	5·7	5·3	4·8	4·9	5·4	5·9	6·4	5·4
45–59[2]	2·4	2·9	3·6	4·2	4·6	5·1	5·5	5·2	5·0	4·8	4·7	5·4	5·8
60–74	1·3	1·5	1·9	2·4	3·0	3·5	3·9	4·5	4·6	4·5	4·2	3·9	4·4
75 and over	0·3	0·4	0·5	0·5	0·8	1·1	1·5	1·8	1·9	2·1	2·4	2·4	2·3
All ages	19·7	21·7	23·0	24·0	24·9	26·1	27·3	28·6	28·7	28·6	29·2	29·6	29·8
Sex ratio (males per 1,000 females):													
All ages	937	937	915	920	933	934	941	947	950	953	963	972	978
Under 45 years	955	957	928	949	990	1,008	1,027	1,038	1,043	1,045	1,046	1,049	1,050
45 years and over	866	869	877	852	819	808	811	810	812	815	830	854	878
Age distribution: range of middle 50 per cent[3] **of population:**													
Upper quartile	40·1	41·9	45·2	48·1	50·3	51·8	53·7	55·0	55·0	*55·8*	*54·7*	*54·4*	*55·6*
Median	23·4	25·6	27·8	30·0	33·0	34·8	35·4	34·0	33·9	*34·5*	*34·7*	*36·2*	*37·8*
Lower quartile	11·3	12·0	13·5	15·5	17·6	16·9	16·1	15·6	16·1	*17·6*	*18·5*	*17·3*	*18·7*

Note: See also Table 14.1 (International).
[1] Figures relate to the *home* population until 1931, thereafter they relate to the *total* population. [2] Retirement ages 65 and over for men, 60 and over for women. [3] Figures up to 1941 relate to Great Britain only. [4] Figures in italics are based partly on the assumptions made about future fertility rates. [5] 1975-based. [6] Provisional.

Sources: *Census of Population Reports; Population Projections, 1975–2015, Office of Population Censuses and Surveys*

**Chart 1.2
Population
structure: by age,
sex, and marital
status, 1974**

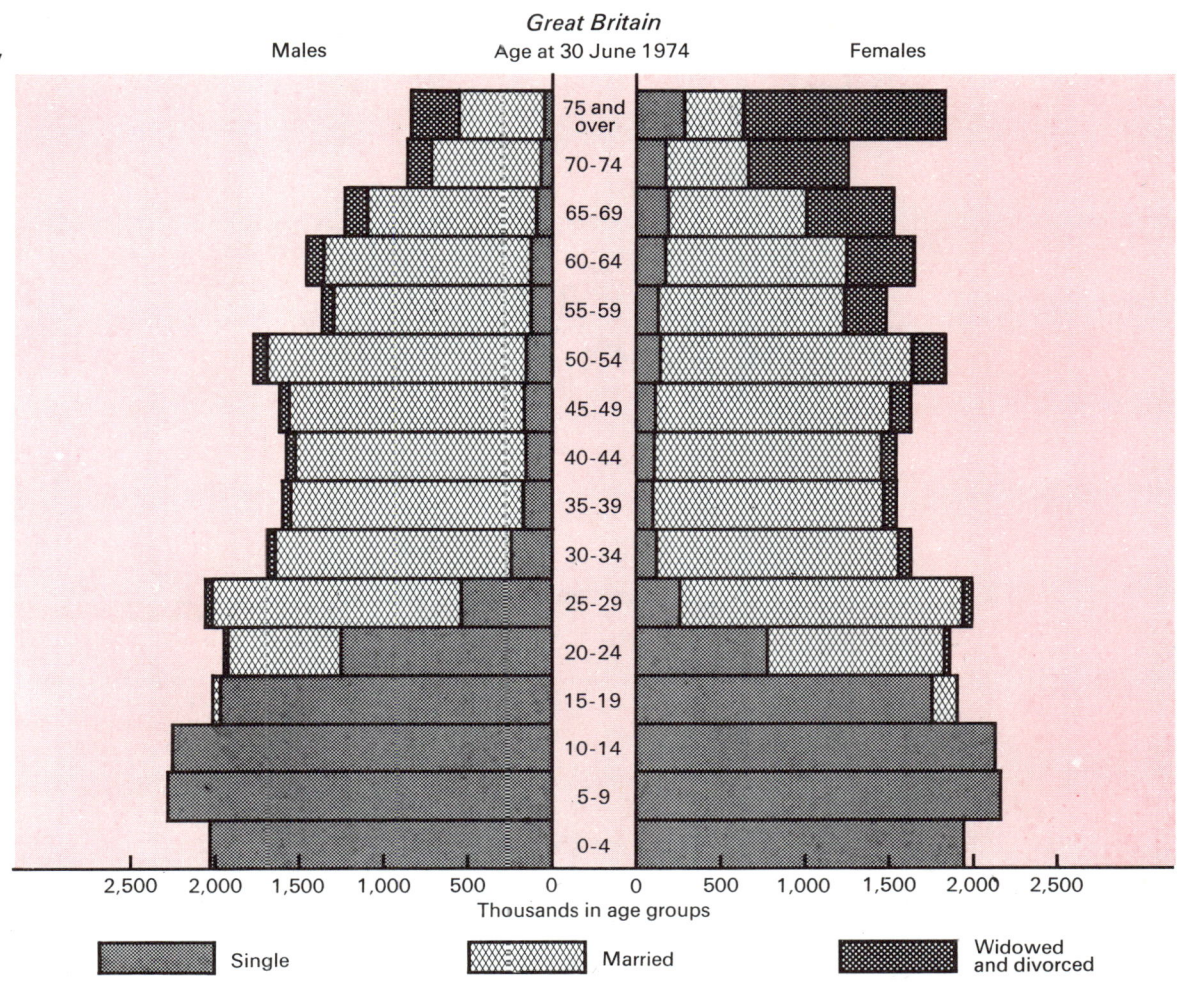

Great Britain
Age at 30 June 1974

Males · Females

Source: Office of Population Censuses and Surveys

Table 1.3 Population changes and projections

United Kingdom

	Census enumerated			Mid-year estimates							Projections[1]			
	1901 –11	1911 –31	1931 –51	1951 –61	1961 –71	1971 –72	1972 –73	1973 –74	1974 –75	1975 –76[2]	1975 –81	1981 –91	1991 –2001	2001 –11
Home population at start of period (millions)	38·2	42·1	46·0	50·3	52·8	55·6	55·8	55·9	56·0	**55·9**	56·0	55·9	57·3	58·3
Average annual change (thousands):														
Live births	1,091	899	785	839	962	862	808	752	721	**688**	694	882	847	793
Deaths	624	622[3]	598[3]	593	638	661	672	664	671	**681**	689	712	709	693
Net natural change	467	277	188	246	324	202	136	88	50	**7**	5	170	138	100
Net civilian migration	} −82	−79	+22 {	−7	−32	−44	−5	−77	−72	..	} −26	−32	−32	−32
Other net changes				+13	−12[4]	+26	+9	+20	−	..				
Overall annual change	385	198	213	252	280	184	140	31	−22	..	−22	138	106	68

Projections based on the mid-1975 estimate of *total* population.   [2] Figures in bold, are provisional.   [3] Including deaths of non-civilians and merchant seamen who died outside the country.   [4] The England and Wales component includes changes in armed forces, in visitor balance and balancing adjustments to reconcile population increase between 1961 and 1971 Censuses with estimates of natural increase and net civilian migration.

Sources: Census of Population Reports: Population Projections 1975–2015, Office of Population Censuses and Surveys

**Chart 1.4
Population
changes
and projections**

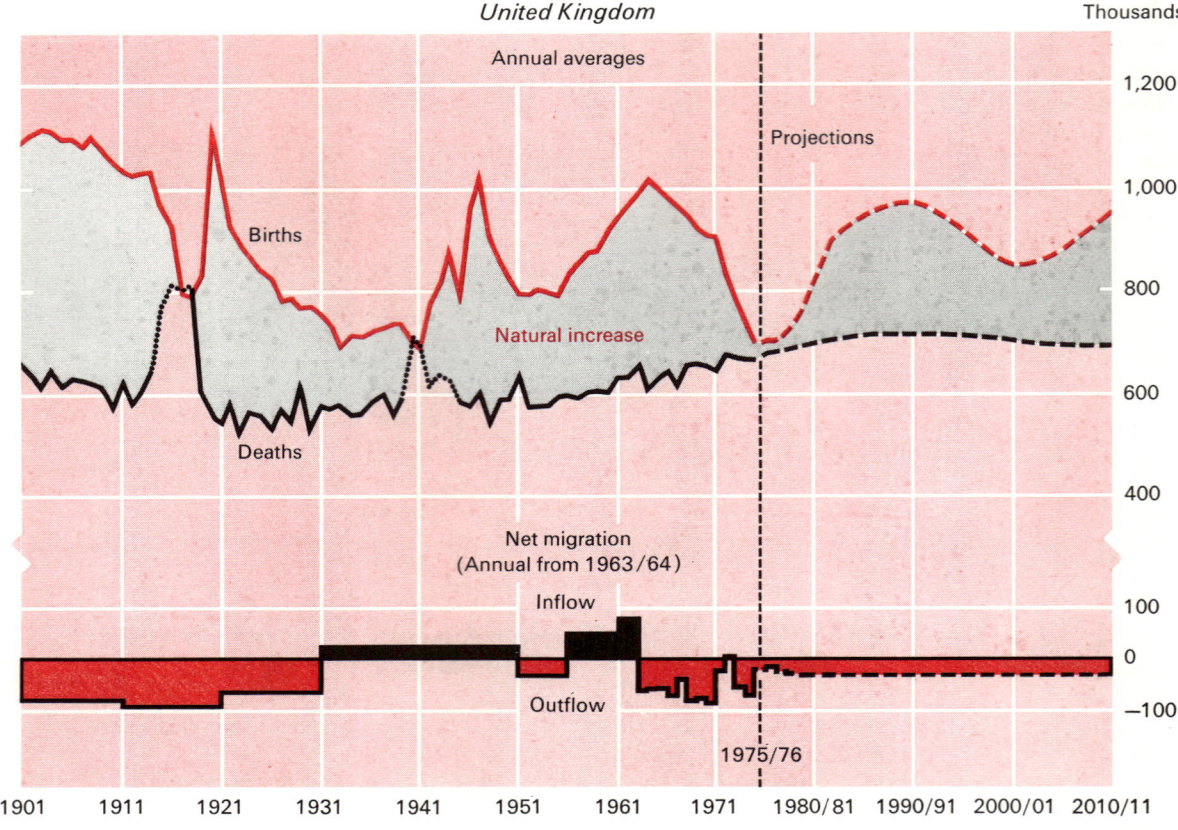

United Kingdom

Annual averages

Projections

Births

Natural increase

Deaths

Net migration
(Annual from 1963/64)

Inflow

Outflow

1975/76

Thousands

1,200

1,000

800

600

400

100

0

−100

| 1901 | 1911 | 1921 | 1931 | 1941 | 1951 | 1961 | 1971 | 1980/81 | 1990/91 | 2000/01 | 2010/11 |

Source: Office of Population Censuses and Surveys

Table 1.5   Variant population projections, 1974 based

	Great Britain					Thousands
	1974 (base)	1976	1981	1991	2001	2011
High variant						
Persons aged:						
0–14	12,800	12,500	12,074	13,305	13,736	13,721
15–64/59[1]	32,522	32,745	33,694	34,633	36,713	38,725
65/60 and over[2]	9,200	9,360	9,588	9,680	9,275	9,804
All ages	54,522	54,605	55,356	57,618	59,724	62,250
Central variant						
Persons aged:						
0–14	12,800	12,438	11,419	12,319	12,995	12,400
15–64/59[1]	32,522	32,745	33,694	34,573	35,859	37,481
65/60 and over[2]	9,200	9,360	9,588	9,680	9,275	9,804
All ages	54,522	54,542	54,700	56,572	58,129	59,685
Low variant						
Persons aged:						
0–14	12,800	12,408	10,981	11,428	12,229	11,181
15–64/59[1]	32,522	32,744	33,694	34,543	35,167	36,339
65/60 and over[2]	9,200	9,360	9,588	9,680	9,275	9,804
All ages	54,522	54,512	54,263	55,652	56,671	57,324
Continuing low variant						
Persons aged:						
0–14	12,800	12,408	10,970	10,275	10,453	9,143
15–64/59[1]	32,522	32,744	33,694	34,542	34,634	34,591
65/60 and over[2]	9,200	9,360	9,588	9,680	9,275	9,804
All ages	54,522	54,512	54,251	54,497	54,362	53,538

[1] 15–64 for males; 15–59 for females.   [2] 65 and over for males; 60 and over for females.

Source: Variant Population Projections, Office of Population Censuses and Surveys

**Chart 1.6
1974-based variant
population
projections,
1961-2011**

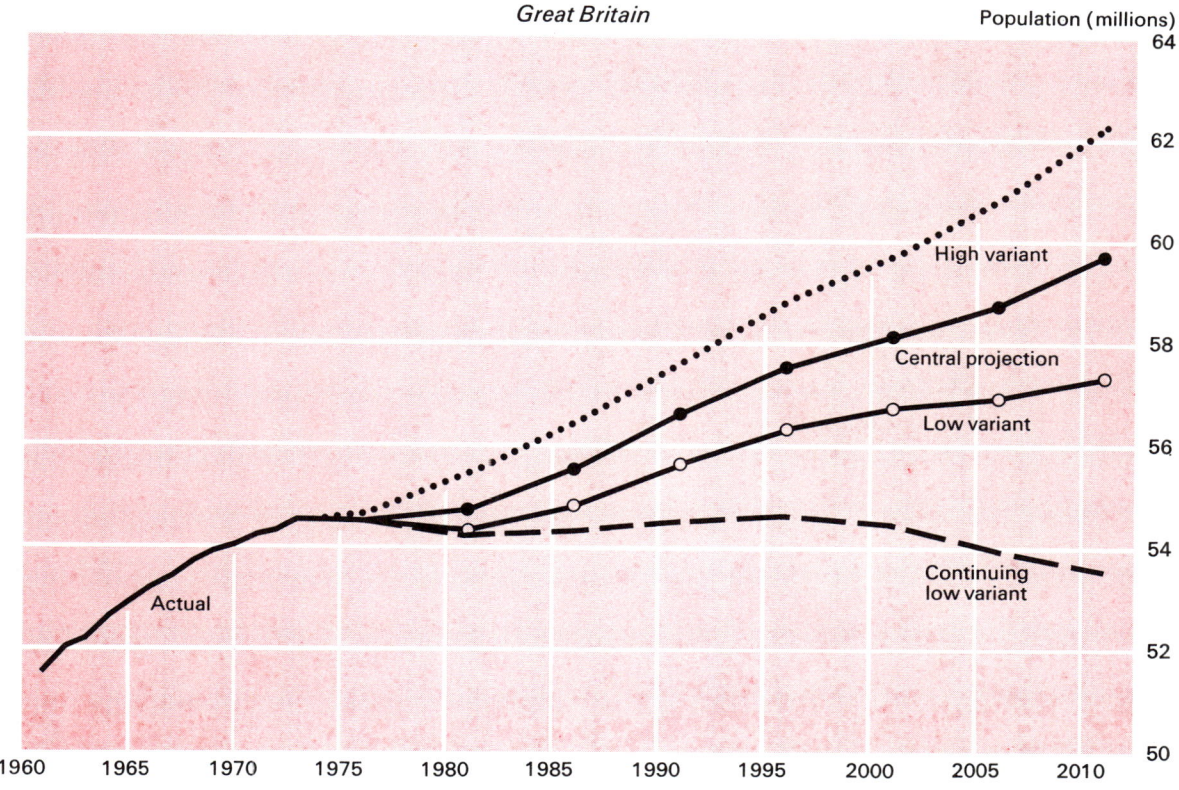

Great Britain

Source: Variant Population Projections, 1974–2011

Components of population change

The next four tables and charts summarise the three components of population change: births, deaths, and migration. Table 1.7 shows birth rates, Table 1.8 death rates, and there are a table and a chart on net migrant flows.

Table 1.7   Birth rates

United Kingdom   Rates and percentages

	1951	1961	1966	1971	1972	1973	1974	1975[4]
Birth rates								
Live births per 1,000:								
Crude birth rates (persons all ages)	15·8	17·9	18·0	16·2	14·9	13·9	13·2	12·4
Fertility rates[1]								
Women aged 15–19	21	37	48	51	48	44	41	37
20–24	126	173	177	155	142	132	124	115
25–29	135	178	175	155	143	136	130	124
30–34	91	104	98	78	70	64	60	58
35–39	47	49	46	33	29	25	22	20
40–44	14	14	12	8	7	6	5	5
All ages (15–44)	72·5	90·0	91·1	84·2	77·5	71·8	67·6	63·5
Live births								
Illegitimate as percentage of all live births	4·8	5·7	7·6	8·2	8·4	8·4	8·7	9·0
Percentage of legitimate live births to women married once only occurring within eight months of marriage[2]:								
Mother aged under 20	55·0[3]	56·5	54·9	56·9	56·0	54·5	53·2	51·2
20–24	12·2[3]	10·5	10·7	10·4	9·9	9·2	8·6	8·2

[1] The quinary rates relate to Great Britain only. Births to mothers under 15 or 45 and over have been included in the All ages (15–44). Births to mothers aged under 15 have been included in the 15–19 age-group.   [2] Relates to Great Britain only.   [3] England and Wales maternities only.   [4] Provisional.

Source: Office of Population Censuses and Surveys

Table 1.8   Standardised death rates[1]

	Great Britain								Rate per 1,000 population
	1930–32	1950–52	1960–62	1966	1968	1970	1972	1973	1974
Males in age group:									
Under 1	79·5	34·5	26·0	22·4	21·8	21·4	19·1	18·9	18·8
1–14	3·7	0·9	0·6	0·6	0·6	0·5	0·5	0·5	0·5
15–44	4·0	1·9	1·5	1·5	1·4	1·4	1·4	1·4	1·4
45–64	17·4	15·8	14·7	14·4	14·1	14·1	13·9	13·7	13·5
65 and over	88·3	83·9	80·2	79·6	79·9	77·6	78·7	76·9	76·1
All ages	17·2	14·1	13·1	12·9	12·8	12·5	12·6	12·3	12·2
Females in age group:									
Under 1	59·7	26·5	19·9	17·1	16·2	16·3	14·9	14·5	14·2
1–14	3·3	0·7	0·5	0·4	0·4	0·4	0·4	0·4	0·4
15–44	3·4	1·5	1·0	0·9	0·9	0·9	0·9	0·8	0·8
45–64	13·0	9·1	7·8	7·5	7·5	7·5	7·6	7·4	7·5
65 and over	82·3	71·3	62·9	59·4	59·4	56·9	56·5	56·1	55·2
All ages	19·1	14·6	12·6	11·9	11·9	11·5	11·4	11·3	11·2

[1] Standardised on 1971 Census age-distribution.

Source: Office of Population Censuses and Surveys

**Chart 1.9
Net migrants
beyond the
British Isles**

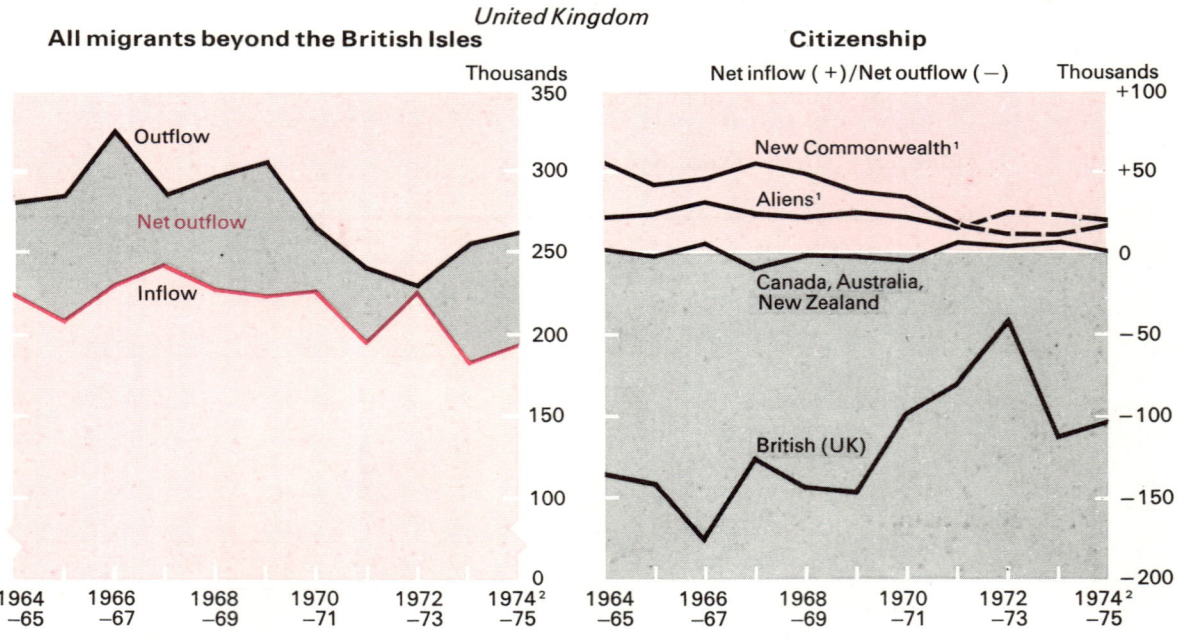

United Kingdom

All migrants beyond the British Isles

Thousands

Citizenship

Net inflow (+)/Net outflow (−)   Thousands

Note: See notes to Table 1.10 from which these figures are taken.
[1] Pakistani citizens are included in 'New Commonwealth' up to and including 1971–72, but in 'Aliens' in 1972–73 and thereafter.
[2] Provisional. These figures include 3,000 people from Cyprus; 2,400 are in 'British (UK)' and 600 in 'New Commonwealth'.

Source: Office of Population Censuses and Surveys

Table 1.10 Net migrants beyond the British Isles[1]

United Kingdom   Thousands

	1964 –65	1966 –67	1968 –69	1970 –71	1972 –73	1973 –74	1974[5] –75
Citizenship[2]							
Aliens	+22	+30	+21	+21	+24	+23	+20
Old Commonwealth	+ ·	+ 5	− 2	− 5	+ 3	+ 6	0
New Commonwealth[3]	+55	+45	+48	+33	+11	+11	+17[6]
United Kingdom citizens	−136	−175	−136	−88	−42	−112	−104[6]
of which							
UK passport holders from East Africa[3]	−	−	+ 8	+ 9	+34	+10	+13
All migrants beyond the British Isles[4]	−58	−95	−68	−39	−5	−72	−67
of which: inflow	223	231	228	227	225	183	194
outflow	28·	326	296	266	230	255	261

[1] See note in Appendix A.   [2] Pakistani citizens are included in 'New Commonwealth' up to and including 1971–72, but in 'Aliens' in 1972–73 and thereafter.   [3] These figures were, in previous *Social Trends*, included in 'New Commonwealth'.   [4] Excluding net immigration due to direct traffic with the Irish Republic which may have averaged some 10,000 persons per annum during the 1961–1971 intercensal period.   [5] Provisional.   [6] Includes 3,000 people from Cyprus; 600 are in the 'New Commonwealth' stream and 2,400 in the 'UK citizens'.

Source: Office of Population Censuses and Surveys

Marriage, divorce, and family size

Tables 1.11 to 1.19 detail trends affecting marriage patterns and family sizes. Tables 1.11 and 1.12 show trends in marriages and divorces, while Table 1.13, from the *General Household Survey*, shows changes in marital status during recent years. Table 1.14 is the latest full count of families, by size, from the *1971 Census*, while Table 1.15 relates size of family to length of marriage, for a run of years. Table 1.16 shows the distribution of size of family after 10 years of marriage, where the decline in proportions of such families with 3 or more children is noticeable: this point is brought out again in Table 1.18, a table which shows the decline in the annual number of first and second order births. It is likely that the current decline in births partly reflects a change in the timing of family formation.

Table 1.11 Marriage

Great Britain   Various units

	1901	1911	1931	1951	1961	1971	1972	1973	1974
Marriages									
Total (thousands)	291	307	344	402	387	447	468	442	426
of which:									
First marriage for both parties	253	272	307	329	331	357	349	323	305
First marriage for one party only	28	25	28	51	36	54	70	68	69
Second (or later) marriage for both parties	10	9	10	22	21	36	50	51	52
Remarriage[1] as a percentage of all marriages	13·1	11·4	11·0	18·1	14·6	20·2	25·5	27·1	28·3
First marriages									
Average age of marrying (years)									
Bachelors	27·2	27·3	27·4	26·8	25·6	24·6	24·8	24·8	24·8
Spinsters	25·6	25·6	25·5	24·6	23·3	22·6	22·8	22·7	22·7
Remarriages									
Average age of remarrying (years)									
Men	45·5	46·2	49·2	46·5	49·1	45·5	45·2	43·9	43·2
Women	40·6	41·5	44·3	40·9	42·9	41·1	40·7	39·9	39·3
Estimated number of married persons (thousands)									
Males	6,289	7,240	9,364	12,110	13,001	13,739	13,780	13,817	13,821
Females	6,408	7,393	9,492	12,230	13,070	13,748	13,783	13,816	13,795
All persons	12,697	14,633	18,857	24,340	26,070	27,486	27,563	27,633	27,616

[1] Remarriage for one or both parties.   *Source: Office of Population Censuses and Surveys*

POPULATION

Table 1.12   Divorce[1]

Various units

	1951	1961	1970	1971	1972	1973	1974
England and Wales							
Petitions filed (thousands)	38·4	31·9	71·7	110·9	110·7	115·5	131·7
Decrees nisi granted (thousands)	30·5	26·9	62·0	89·3	110·7	107·3	118·2
Decrees absolute granted:							
Thousands	28·8	25·4	58·2	74·4	119·0	106·0	113·5
Rate per thousand married population	2·6	2·1	4·7	6·0	9·5	8·4	9·0
Scotland							
Divorces granted (thousands)	2·0	1·8	4·6	4·8	5·5	7·1	7·2
Great Britain[2,5]							
Percentages of all divorces by duration of marriage (in years):							
Up to 4	10·3	11·3	14·5	13·4	13·1	15·5	16·5
5 to 9	31·5	30·6	33·1	30·5	28·4	29·4	29·8
10 to 14	24·4	22·9	20·9	19·4	18·4	18·9	18·6
15 to 19	14·1	13·9	12·9	12·6	12·9	13·1	13·0
20 and over	19·7	21·2	18·6	24·2	27·2	23·0	22·1
Divorce rate per thousand married women aged, at divorce:							
16 to 24	2·9	2·4	6·7	7·8	11·5	11·8	11·6
25 to 29	5·3	4·3	10·9	12·6	18·1	17·1	18·2
30 to 34	4·8	3·6	8·6	10·2	15·0	14·1	15·3
35 to 39	3·6	2·9	6·2	7·4	11·6	11·0	12·0
40 to 44	2·8	2·3	4·4	5·6	9·0	8·0	9·0
All ages	2·6	2·1	4·6	5·8	9·0	8·2	8·7
Dissolved marriages where there were children[3] as percentage of all divorces	65·6	68·3	73·9	72·5	74·1	75·2	74·6
Average number of children per couple divorcing[3]	1·23	1·37	1·61	1·57	1·64	1·70	1·68
Estimated numbers of divorced persons[4] (thousands)							
Males	79·5	101·0	201·4	199·7	236·7	282·1	318·2
Females	130·1	183·9	314·1	317·0	363·7	418·0	461·0
All persons	209·6	284·9	515·5	516·7	600·4	700·1	779·2

[1,2] See notes in Appendix A.   [3] England and Wales only. See note in Appendix A.   [4] Divorced persons who have not remarried.
[5] Data for 1951 are for England and Wales only.

Source: Office of Population Censuses and Surveys

Table 1.13   Marital status of household population over 15[1]

Great Britain   Percentages and numbers

	1971	1972	1973	1974	1975[2]
Marital status:					
Males					
Married	71·8	72·6	72·3	72·6	73·4
Single	22·6	21·3	21·2	21·1	20·6
Widowed	4·0	4·4	4·5	4·4	3·9
Divorced/separated	1·5	1·7	2·0	1·8	2·0
Females					
Married	65·3	65·5	66·1	65·0	65·8
Single	17·8	17·0	15·8	16·6	15·8
Widowed	14·0	14·3	14·8	15·0	14·8
Divorced/separated	2·9	3·2	3·3	3·3	3·7
Total					
Married	68·4	68·9	69·0	68·6	69·4
Single	20·1	19·0	18·4	18·7	18·1
Widowed	9·3	9·6	9·9	10·0	9·6
Divorced/separated	2·2	2·5	2·7	2·6	2·9
Total sample size, people (=100%) (numbers)	25,761	24,553	24,209	22,591	24,673

[1] Over 14 in 1971 and 1972.   [2] Unedited data.

Source: General Household Survey

68

Table 1.14   Families by size and by age of head, 1971

Great Britain   Thousands and means

	Under 30	30–44	45–64	65 and over	All families	Total dependent children
Married couples with dependent children:						
None	741	546	3,543	1,868	6,697	—
1	622	820	968	32	2,443	2,443
2	468	1,439	485	6	2,399	4,798
3	127	725	176	2	1,030	3,090
4	30	282	64	1	377	1,508
5 or more	9	151	37	—	196	1,083
Total married couples	1,997	3,964	5,273	1,909	13,142	12,922
Mean number of dependent children	*1·1*	*2·0*	*0·6*	—	*1·0*	
Total dependent children	2,105	7,839	2,925	54	12,922	
Lone parents[1] with dependent children:						
Total lone parents	153	305	423	494	1,375	1,110
of whom: male lone parents	12	57	107	77	253	196
female lone parents	140	249	316	417	1,123	914
Mean number of dependent children	*1·6*	*1·9*	*0·6*	—	*0·8*	
Total dependent children	252	576	258	24	1,110	
All families	2,149	4,269	5,696	2,403	14,518	14,032

[1] For female lone parents age 60 has been used and not 65.

Source: Census of Population, 1971, 10% sample, Office of Population Censuses and Surveys

Table 1.15   Average family size at specified durations of marriage

Great Britain   Averages

	1935 –39	1940 –44	1945 –49	1950 –54	1955 –59	1960 –64	1965 –69	1971	1972
Average number of live births[1] at marriage duration:									
2 years	0·55	0·50	0·65	0·60	0·63	0·69	0·64	0·52	0·48
5 years	1·05	1·10	1·26	1·24	1·37	1·48	1·37		
10 years	1·67	1·73	1·83	1·92	2·07	2·10			
15 years	1·96	1·98	2·11	2·20	2·30				
Completed family size	2·07	2·09	2·22	2·30	2·38[2]				

[1] To women married once only before the age of 45.
[2] Estimate.

Source: Office of Population Censuses and Surveys

Table 1.16   Family size distributions after 10 years of marriage[1]

England and Wales   Percentages

	1951	1956	1961	1963	1964	1965[2]
Number of liveborn children:						
0	14	11	8	9	9	10
1	27	22	18	17	17	18
2	35	38	44	46	48	49
3	16	19	22	21	19	18
4 or more	8	11	9	8	6	5
Total	100	100	100	100	100	100

[1] For women married at ages 20–24 and married once only.   [2] Provisional.

Source: Office of Population Censuses and Surveys

**Chart 1.17
Women childless
by duration of
marriage**

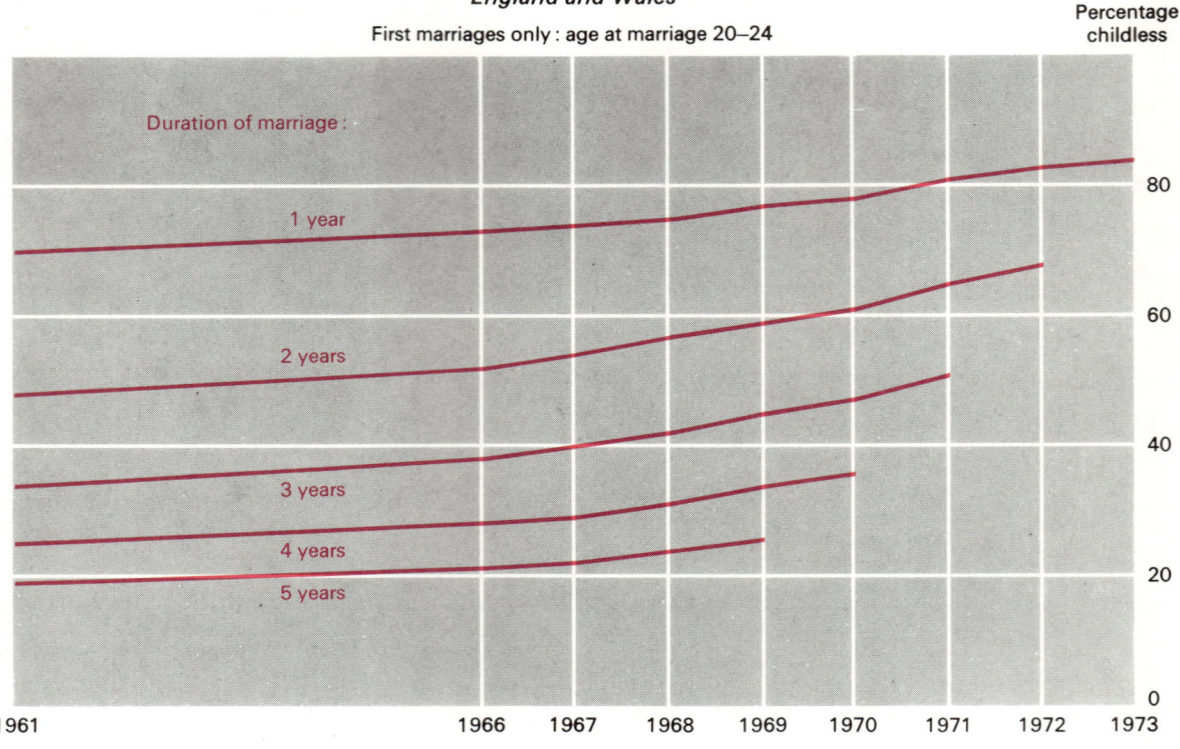

England and Wales

First marriages only : age at marriage 20–24

Percentage
childless

Duration of marriage :

1 year

2 years

3 years

4 years

5 years

80

60

40

20

0

1961   1966   1967   1968   1969   1970   1971   1972   1973

Source: Office of Population Censuses and Surveys

Table 1.18   Legitimate live births to women married once only: by number of previous liveborn children

	England and Wales		Percentage change from preceding year	
	1972	1973	1974	1975[1]
Number of previous liveborn children:				
0	− 6·5	− 4·9	− 4·7	− 6·9
1	− 4·8	− 3·6	− 3·5	− 4·8
2	−12·4	−14·0	−10·8	− 6·7
3	−15·3	−18·8	−16·3	−10·8
4	−18·6	−22·9	−17·8	−14·2
5 and over	−21·1	−22·8	−19·7	−14·5
Total	− 8·0	− 7·3	− 6·1	− 6·5

[1] Based on provisional figures for 1975.

Source: Office of Population Censuses and Surveys

**Chart 1.19
Abortions¹ : by
age group and
marital status of
woman**

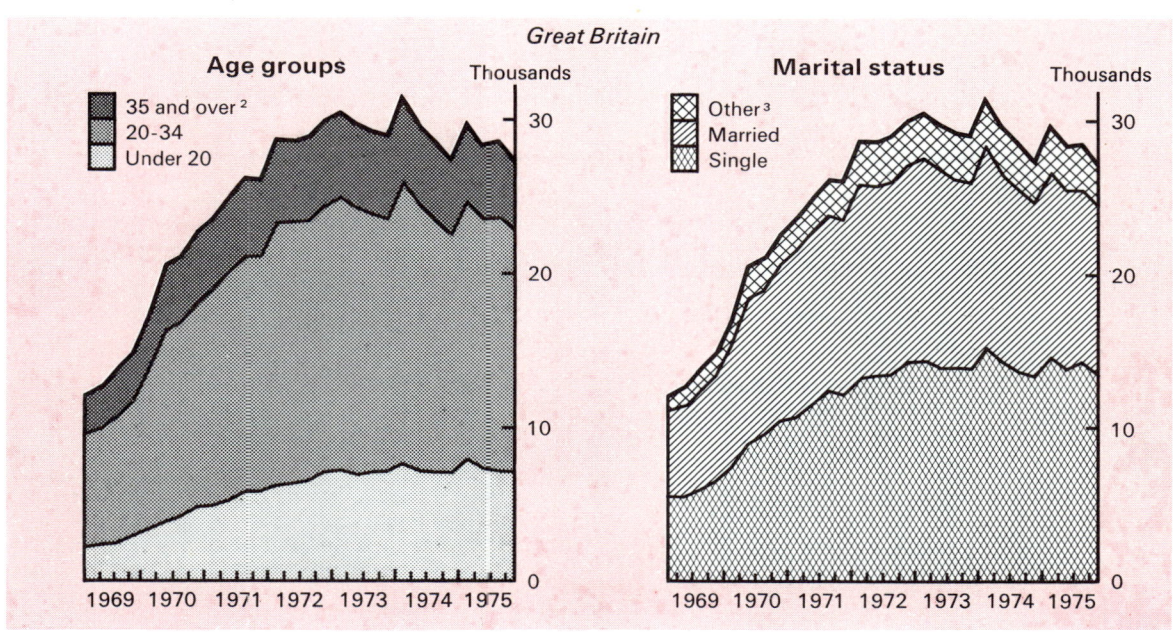

¹ Abortions carried out within Great Britain on women resident within the United Kingdom: data for England and Wales relate to occurrences from 1969 to 1973 and to notifications for 1974 and 1975; for Scotland they relate to notifications throughout. ² Includes those whose age was not stated. ³ Includes those widowed, divorced, separated, and those whose marital status was not stated.
Sources: Office of Population Censuses and Surveys; Scottish Health Service; Common Services Agency

Country of birth

Tables 1.20 and 1.21 show the population of New Commonwealth and Pakistani ethnic origin 1966–75, and live births by country of birth of mother.

The methodology on which the estimates in Table 1.20 are based is complex and details can be found on pages 2–8 of *Population Trends 2, 1975.*

Table 1.20   Mid-year estimates of the population of New Commonwealth and Pakistani ethnic origin, 1966-1975

	Great Britain								Thousands and percentages
	Mid-year to mid-year								
	1966–67	1967–68	1968–69	1969–70	1970–71	1971–72	1972–73	1973–74	1974–75
Population at beginning of period	1,016	1,103	1,217	1,320	1,411	1,501	1,576	1,665	1,729
Births	+45	+47	+50	+52	+52	+49	+47	+45	+44
Deaths¹	−3	−3	−4	−4	−4	−4	−5	−5	−5
Natural increase	+42	+44	+46	+48	+48	+45	+42	+40	+39
Migration	+45	+70	+57	+43	+42	+30	+47	+24	+32²
Change in year	+87	+114	+103	+91	+90	+75	+89	+64	+71
Population at end of period	1,103	1,217	1,320	1,411	1,501	1,576	1,665	1,729	1,800
Per cent of home population at end of period	2·1	2·3	2·5	2·6	2·8	2·9	3·1	3·2	3·3

¹ Including deaths of children of New Commonwealth ethnic origin born in the United Kingdom.   ² Provisional.
Source: Office of Population Censuses and Surveys

Table 1.21   Live births: by country of birth of mother, 1970 to 1974

England and Wales   Thousands and percentages

	Number (thousands)					Percentage of all live births				
	1970	1971	1972	1973	1974	1970	1971	1972	1973	1974
Country of birth of mother:										
Irish Republic[1]	23·5	21·6	18·9	16·4	14·6	3·0	2·8	2·6	2·4	2·3
Australia, Canada, New Zealand	2·3	2·4	2·4	2·4	2·3	0·3	0·3	0·3	0·4	0·4
New Commonwealth[2]	46·0	45·2	43·0 ▎34·1		33·1	5·9	5·8	5·9 ▎5·1		5·2
of which										
India, Pakistan[2], Bangladesh	*21·3*	*21·6*	*21·2 ▎13·6*		*13·2*	*2·7*	*2·8*	*2·9 ▎2·0*		*2·1*
West Indies[3]	*14·1*	*12·5*	*10·8*	*9·1*	*8·1*	*1·8*	*1·6*	*1·5*	*1·3*	*1·3*
Pakistan				6·8	6·8				1·0	1·1
Other foreign	19·7	19·6	18·6	17·7	17·6	2·5	2·5	2·6	2·6	2·7
Total with mother born outside UK	91·5	88·8	83·0	77·5	74·5	11·7	11·3	11·4	11·5	11·6
United Kingdom	684·5	689·7	640·0	596·9	564·2	87·3	88·1	88·2	88·3	88·2
Not stated	8·5	4·6	2·5	1·6	1·2	1·1	0·6	0·3	0·2	0·2
Total births	784·5	783·2	725·4	676·0	639·9	100·0	100·0	100·0	100·0	100·0

[1] Including Ireland, part not stated.   [2] From 1973 data for Pakistan are not included in those of the New Commonwealth.   [3] Including Guyana and Belize (formerly British Honduras).

Source: Office of Population Censuses and Surveys

Table 1.22   Populations of new[1] standard regions

United Kingdom   Millions

	Mid-year estimates[2]						Projections[2] (1974-based)			
	1961	1971	1972	1973	1974	1975[3]	1976	1981	1986	1991
North	3·1	3·1	3·1	3·1	3·1	3·1	3·1	3·1	3·1	3·1
Yorkshire and Humberside	4·7	4·9	4·9	4·9	4·9	4·9	4·9	4·8	4·9	4·9
East Midlands	3·3	3·6	3·7	3·7	3·7	3·7	3·8	3·9	4·0	4·1
East Anglia	1·5	1·7	1·7	1·7	1·8	1·8	1·8	1·9	2·1	2·2
South East	16·1	17·0	17·0	17·0	17·0	16·9	16·9	16·8	17·0	17·1
Greater London Council	*8·0*	*7·4*	*7·3*	*7·3*	*7·2*	*7·1*	*7·0*	*6·5*	*6·1*	*5·7*
Outer South East	*3·7*	*4·4*	*4·4*	*4·5*	*4·5*	*4·5*	*4·6*	*4·9*	*5·1*	*5·4*
Outer Metropolitan Area	*4·4*	*5·2*	*5·2*	*5·3*	*5·3*	*5·3*	*5·3*	*5·5*	*5·7*	*6·0*
South West	3·7	4·1	4·1	4·2	4·2	4·2	4·2	4·4	4·5	4·7
West Midlands	4·8	5·1	5·2	5·2	5·2	5·2	5·2	5·2	5·3	5·3
North West	6·4	6·6	6·6	6·6	6·6	6·6	6·6	6·4	6·4	6·5
Wales	2·6	2·7	2·7	2·7	2·8	2·8	2·8	2·8	2·9	2·9
England and Wales	46·2	48·9	49·0	49·2	49·2	49·2	49·3	49·4	50·1	50·9
Scotland	5·2	5·2	5·2	5·2	5·2	5·2	5·3	5·3	5·5	5·6
Great Britain	51·4	54·1	54·2	54·4	54·4	54·4	54·5	54·7	55·5	56·6
Northern Ireland	1·4	1·5	1·5	1·5	1·5	1·5	1·5	1·6	1·6	1·6
United Kingdom	52·8	55·6	55·8	55·9	56·0	56·0	56·1	56·3	57·1	58·2

[1] As at 1 April 1974 (England and Wales), and 31 May 1975 (Scotland).   [2] Mid-year estimates and projections of the home population.   [3] Provisional.

Source: Office of Population Censuses and Surveys

Households

This section includes information, drawn mainly from the *Census* and from the *General Household Survey* (*GHS*), on households, and in particular on the characteristics of children, elderly people, and the coloured population. This type of analysis is a move away from the 'subject by social group' approach of much of the rest of *Social Trends*, where topics are arranged under 'subjects' such as Education, Health, Environment, etc. The section is interdepartmental in the sense that there is no Ministry for Households or for Children or for the Elderly. It is hoped that this fresh approach will be of value to both the statistician and administrator.

Much of this section is new: in particular there are several trend tables from the *GHS* on basic characteristics of households. Although a great deal of data has already been published from the *GHS* (*General Household Survey Reports* for 1971, 1972, and 1973), most of this is on an annual basis, and the *GHS* tables in this section cover the years 1971–75. It is the intention to update these trend tables as soon as the later *GHS* data tapes have been analysed.

Some of the basic full counts of households from the *1971 Census* have been reproduced here. Although estimates of total numbers of various types of household are made for each year, as in Table 2.3, full counts by size will not be available again until the results of the *1981 Census*.

Information on size of families can be found in the Population section as this can be best looked at in the context of the study of fertility.

The first two tables concentrate on information collected from the *Censuses of Population* held in 1951, 1961, 1966, and 1971. Table 2.1 gives information on the different types of household and household size. Table 2.2 shows the institutional population by type of institution and the non-family household population, both expressed as percentages of the total population. As well as being analyses of households these tables can be regarded as analyses of the population by the type of household in which they lived.

Table 2.3 shows projections of total numbers of households of various types from 1976 to 2001 based on 1973 assumptions. The increases shown here are mainly due to the growing proportion of one person potential households, both under and over pension age. Similar trends are shown in the first of the *GHS* tables, Table 2.4, where the proportion of individuals living alone has risen from 6 per cent in 1971 to 8 per cent in 1974. Tables 2.5 to 2.8 are all trend tables from the *GHS* for 1971 to 1975 showing age of head of household, only families with dependent children, type of household, and socio-economic group of head of household. Care must be taken in interpreting trends in these tables; for one thing, four years is too short a time, some movements may be in the same direction simply due to chance alone: there is also a small error attached to each figure, because the figures are estimated from a sample survey. Details of these errors are given in the Introductory Section to the *GHS*, *1973*. Thus, although, in Table 2.8, it looks as if the proportion of households with professional worker heads has increased, taking into account the short number of years, and the error associated with the sample survey, there is not yet enough evidence to be sure that this has actually happened.

Table 2.1   Households, 1951–1971

Great Britain   Percentages and thousands

	Percentage of all households				Thousands of households			
	1951	1961	1966	1971	1951	1961	1966	1971
Households:								
No family households	..	16·8	19·4	22·2	..	2,724	3,287	4,068
One family households	..	80·5	78·7	76·4	..	13,026	13,334	13,986
of which								
Married couple, no children	..	*25·6*	*25·8*	*26·7*	..	*4,147*	*4,377*	*4,890*
Married couple with children[1]	..	*43·1*	*46·1*	*43·0*	..	*7,790*	*7,801*	*7,869*
Lone parent with children[1]	..	*6·7*	*6·8*	*6·7*	..	*1,089*	*1,156*	*1,227*
Two or more family households	..	2·7	1·9	1·4	..	439	317	263
Total households	..	100·0	100·0	100·0	14,554	16,189	16,937	18,317
Households – by size:								
1 person	10·7	11·9	15·2	18·1	1,563	1,919	2,572	3,320
2 persons	27·3	29·8	30·4	31·5	3,974	4,820	5,158	5,771
3 ,,	25·1	23·3	21·2	18·9	3,653	3,780	3,592	3,458
4 ,,	19·0	19·1	18·0	17·2	2,763	3,100	3,042	3,148
5 ,,	9·7	9·2	8·7	8·3	1,414	1,489	1,480	1,515
6 or more persons	8·2	6·7	6·5	6·0	1,187	1,079	1,093	1,106
Total households	100·0	100·0	100·0	100·0	14,554	16,189	16,937	18,317

[1] Never-married children of any age.   *Source: Censuses of Population, 1951–1971, Office of Population Censuses and Surveys*

Table 2.2 Institutional population[1] and non-family households, 1961 and 1971

Great Britain   Numbers and percentages

	1961	1971
Institutional population[1] enumerated in (numbers):		
Hotels	397,664	304,070
of which		
Resident guests	*136,607*	*58,680*
Visitor guests	*118,352*	*134,695*
Hospitals	621,530	555,820
Homes for the old and disabled	121,726	177,790
Children's homes	50,669	47,385
Educational establishments	130,149[2]	240,620
Places of detention	45,295	55,515
Defence establishments	168,722	101,420
Others	182,494	135,530
Total institutional population	1,718,249	1,618,155
as a percentage of total population	3·35	3·00
Non-family households		
(Number of persons in household):		
1	1,919,480	3,319,620
2	647,530	622,750
3	118,080	91,040
4	27,080	23,580
5 or more	11,430	11,160
Total number of persons in non-family households	3,740,110	4,995,380
as a percentage of total population	7·48	9·45

[1] Population enumerated in institutions on Census night. [2] The 1961 Census was held during the Easter holiday, therefore on Census night a considerable number of pupils were at home.

Source: Censuses of Population, 1961, 1971 Office of Population Censuses and Surveys

Table 2.3 Household projections

England and Wales   Thousands

	Mid-year estimates						
	1973	1976	1981	1986	1991	1996	2001
Potential households:							
Married couple families	11,720	11,875	12,109	12,431	12,720	12,895	13,012
Lone parent households	1,127	1,125	1,130	1,136	1,144	1,173	1,190
One-person potential households	3,222	3,577	4,127	4,602	4,986	4,936	4,906
Other households	876	833	785	754	732	722	716
Total	16,946	17,410	18,151	18,923	19,582	19,726	19,825
Private household population	47,733	47,861	48,061	48,742	49,589	50,349	50,878
Average potential household size (numbers)	2·82	2·75	2·65	2·58	2·53	2·55	2·57
Census-type households:							
Married couple households	11,457	11,613	11,841	12,151	12,427	12,599	12,718
Lone parent households	1,127	1,125	1,130	1,136	1,144	1,173	1,190
One-person households	3,521	3,844	4,344	4,773	5,118	5,067	5,036
Other households	876	833	785	754	732	722	716
Total	16,981	17,415	18,099	18,814	19,421	19,561	19,661

[1] Using 1973-based population projections. For definitions see Appendix B page 237.

Source: Department of the Environment

Table 2.4   People by household size

	Great Britain				Percentages and numbers
	1971	1972	1973	1974	1975[1]
Number of persons in household (all ages):					
1	6	7	7	8	7
2	22	22	23	23	23
3	20	19	19	18	19
4	25	25	25	25	25
5	}28	14	14	13	14
6 or more		13	13	13	11
Total sample size, people (=100%) (numbers)	34,849	33,322	33,033	30,892	33,504

[1] Unedited data.   Source: General Household Survey

Table 2.5   Age of head of household

	Great Britain				Percentages and numbers
	1971	1972	1973	1974	1975[1]
Age group:					
Under 25	4·2	4·5	4·1	4·2	4·3
25–29	7·2	8·8	8·3	7·9	8·7
30–44	26·2	24·7	24·5	24·3	25·3
45–59	29·2	27·4	28·0	26·7	26·3
60–64	10·0	9·7	9·8	10·2	9·7
65–69	8·4	8·9	9·4	9·5	8·9
70–79	11·2	12·1	11·7	13·1	12·8
80 and over	3·6	3·9	4·2	4·1	4·0
Total sample size, households (=100%) (numbers)	11,949	11,649	11,638	11,058	12,067

[1] Unedited data.   Source: General Household Survey

Table 2.6   Family type: families with dependent children

	Great Britain			Percentages and numbers
	1971	1972	1973	1974
Type of parent (percentages):				
Married couple[1]	91	91	90	90
Lone mother[2]	8	8	8	9
Lone father	1	1	1	1
Number of dependent children in families (percentages):				
1	37	37	37	37
2	37	38	38	38
3	17	16	16	16
4 or more	9	9	8	9
Total sample of families (=100%) (numbers)	4,855	4,673	4,567	4,309

[1] Includes cohabitees.   [2] About 5 per cent of lone mothers are married, and only temporarily separated from their husband, usually because of the husband's work.   Source: General Household Survey

Table 2.7   Type of household

	Great Britain				Percentages and numbers
	1971	1972	1973	1974	1975[1]
Households:					
One person households					
Aged 16–59	5·1	5·3	5·5	5·6	5·6
Aged 60 or over	11·9	13·4	13·5	15·4	14.7
Two person households					
Both aged 16–59	14·0	13·7	14·1	13·0	14·0
Both aged 16 or over, one or both aged 60 or over	16·6	17·0	17·3	17·7	16·6
Three or more person households					
Youngest aged 0–4	18·1	18·5	} 37·8	37·2	{ 15·6
Youngest aged 5–15	21·1	20·3			22·3
Three or more aged 16 or over	13·3	11·9	11·8	11·1	11·2
Total sample size, households (=100%) (numbers)	11,934	11,647	11,642	11,060	12,064

[1] Unedited data.   *Source: General Household Survey*

HOUSEHOLDS AND FAMILIES   2.H.4

Table 2.8   Socio-economic group of head of household

	Great Britain			Percentages and numbers
	1971	1972	1973	1974
Socio-economic group of head of household (percentages):				
Professional	3·9	4·1	4·2	4·3
Employers and managers	14·6	13·5	13·2	15·0
Intermediate and junior non-manual	19·8	21·4	19·9	20·0
Skilled manual (incl. foremen and supervisors) and own-account non-professional	33·3	33·3	33·9	31·9
Semi-skilled manual and personal service	19·5	18·2	19·4	19·8
Unskilled manual	6·6	6·8	6·5	6·4
Never worked	1·9	2·2	2·3	2·0
Full-time students	0·4	0·5	0·6	0·5
Total sample size, households (=100%) (numbers)	11,591	11,319	11,349	10,852

Source: General Household Survey

Children

Tables 2.9 to 2.17 give details of children in various categories. The first three tables and chart show population by sex and age group from 1951 to 2011. The projections used in the tables are the central variant of the 1975 estimates. The data for Chart 2.10 are drawn from the 1974 projections. The red lines on the chart have been drawn to give an indication of the uncertainty of the projections. Information to the right of the lines is based entirely or in part on projections of births.

Tables 2.12 and 2.13 are again drawn from the *GHS*. Table 2.12 shows the trend in proportions of households with mothers and children, and

Table 2.13 shows, for 1973, the type of accommodation in which children live, ie 80 per cent of children under the age of 2 live in houses, and 20 per cent in flats, whereas 89 per cent of children aged 10–14 lived in houses and only 11 per cent in flats.

The sub-section ends with three tables containing statistics from several sources including the Department of Health and Social Security. Table 2.14 displays data on services devoted to children and Tables 2.15 to 2.17 give information about the care of children by local authorities.

Table 2.9   Children: by age group

Great Britain   Thousands

	Census enumerated		Mid-year estimates				
	1951	1961	1961	1966	1971	1974	1975[1]
Boys							
0–4	2,145	2,086	2,118	2,369	2,231	2,044	1,962
5–9	1,819	1,886	1,888	2,108	2,318	2,274	2,230
10–14	1,624	2,137	2,116	1,890	2,100	2,250	2,293
15–16	633	757	771	768	768	833	845
17–18	608	733	739	836	764	784	808
Total under 19	6,829	7,599	7,632	7,971	8,181	8,185	8,138
Girls							
0–4	2,044	1,980	2,008	2,262	2,117	1,933	1,852
5–9	1,741	1,797	1,798	1,990	2,202	2,162	2,115
10–14	1,574	2,037	2,018	1,787	1,987	2,134	2,177
15–16	617	725	739	740	724	792	801
17–18	616	718	724	813	730	752	777
Total under 19	6,592	7,257	7,286	7,591	7,759	7,773	7,722

[1] Provisional.   Source: Census of Population Reports, Office of Population Censuses and Surveys

Chart 2.10 Children: projections, 1974-2011

Great Britain

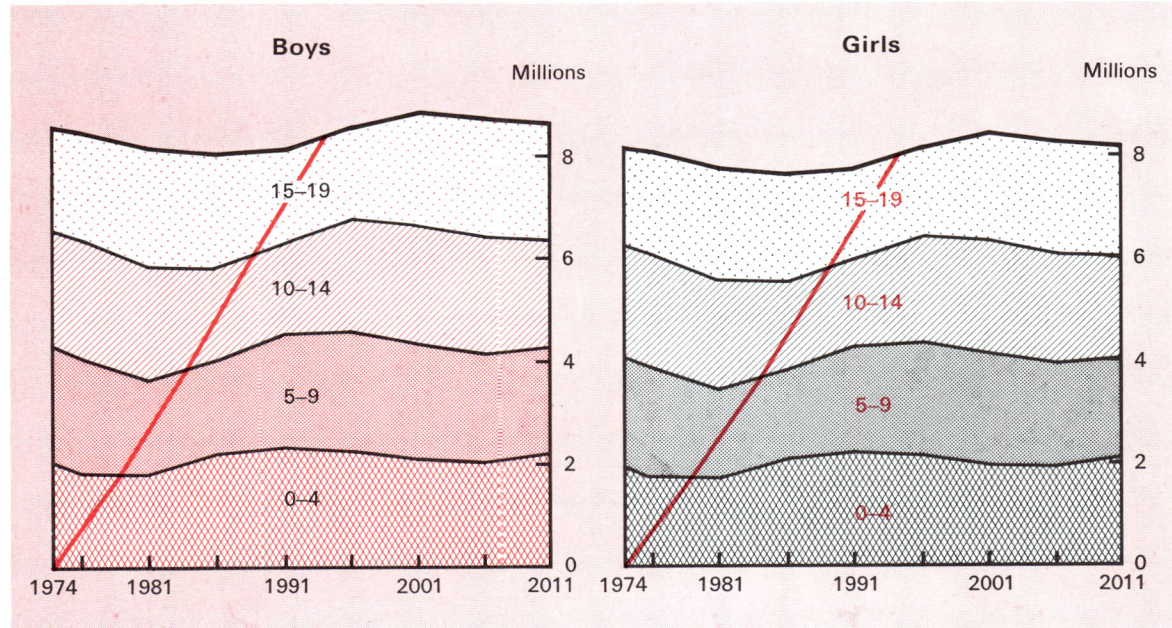

Source: Variant Population Projections, 1974–2011, Office of Population Censuses and Surveys

HOUSEHOLDS

Table 2.11 Children: population projections[1,2]

United Kingdom Thousands

	1975 (base)	1976[1]	1981[1]	1986[1]	1991[1]
Boys					
0– 4	2,035	1,925	1,743	2,137	2,293
5– 9	2,309	2,282	1,900	1,718	2,111
10–14	2,373	2,390	2,271	1,889	1,707
15–19	2,128	2,183	2,402	2,282	1,901
Total under age 20	8,845	8,780	8,316	8,026	8,012
Girls					
0– 4	1,919	1,812	1,648	2,021	2,169
5– 9	2,189	2,165	1,789	1,623	1,996
10–14	2,252	2,269	2,155	1,778	1,613
15–19	2,017	2,070	2,281	2,166	1,789
Total under age 20	8,377	8,316	7,873	7,588	7,567

[1] 1975-based projection.   [2] See note in Appendix B, page 235.

Source: Population Projections, 1975–2015, Office of Population Censuses and Surveys

Table 2.12 Women with own children in households

Great Britain Percentages and numbers

	1971	1972	1973
Women with own children in household:			
Number of children aged 0–15[1]:			
1	12	13	13
2	13	13	13
3	5	5	5
4 or more	3	3	3
All non-married children aged 16 or over[2]	13	12	11
Total sample size, all women[3] (=100%) (numbers)	13,587	12,953	12,473

[1] Children aged 0–14 in 1971 and 1972.   [2] Children aged 15 or over in 1971 and 1972.   [3] Includes women who had no children, or had children all of whom lived outside the household, or had children who had themselves been married or had children.

Source: General Household Survey, 1971–1973

Table 2.13 Children: by household accommodation, 1973

Great Britain Percentages and numbers

	Flats[1] by floor level					Houses	Total sample size (=100%) (numbers)
	(Semi-) Basement	Ground floor	1st floor	2nd floor or higher	All floors		
Age of children (percentages):							
Under 2 years	–	7	7	5	20	80	985
2–4 years	–	6	5	4	15	85	1,639
5–9 years	–	5	5	2	12	88	2,849
10–14 years	–	4	4	2	11	89	2,787

[1] Excluding (semi-) detached and terraced houses, but including purpose-built and converted flats, caravans, and farms with attached outbuildings.

Source: General Household Survey, 1973

Table 2.14 Children's services

United Kingdom Thousands

	England and Wales					Scotland	Northern Ireland
	1961	1972	1973	1974	1975	1974	1975
Child health centres (total children attending)	1,619	1,783	1,735	1,773	. .	120	. .
Maintained day nurseries[1]—places (end-year)	22	23	24	25	26	4[7]	–[8]
Registered nurseries[2]—places (end-year)	18	296	335	362	370	1[7]	–[8]
Registered child-minders[2,3]—places (end-year)	14	90	92	87	87	. .	5[8]
Nursery education[4,5] (January)—full-time	226	296	325	334	338	11	21
—part-time	. .	86	101	122	141	17	
Special schools[6] (excl. hospital schools) (January)	62	114	118	121	122	13	2
of which: educationally sub-normal children	*34*	*78*	*80*	*80*	*73*	*10*	*1*

[1–8] See notes in Appendix A. Sources: Various, see Appendix C, page 256

Table 2.15 Children received into care of local authorities[1,2]: circumstances of admission

United Kingdom Thousands

	England and Wales				Scotland	Northern Ireland
	1961	1973	1974	1975	1974	1974[5]
Admissions to care of local authorities[1]						
Abandoned or lost	0·3	1·0	1·0	1·2	0·5	0·04
Death of, or deserted by, mother	4·2	5·4	5·2	4·3	0·1	0·15
Incapacity of parent or guardian	27·4	20·3	17·6	15·8	1·6	0·29
Child illegitimate—mother unable to provide	1·7	2·0	1·9	1·8	. .	0·21
Parent or guardian in prison or remanded in custody	0·7	1·0	0·9	0·8	. .	0·01
Family homeless—through eviction	2·0	0·9	0·8	0·4	0·2	–
—through cause other than eviction	1·1	1·9	1·6	1·2	0·4	0·03
Unsatisfactory home conditions	1·0	4·4	4·7	4·9	. .	0·05
Fit person orders—offenders[3]	1·1				. .	0·01
—non-offenders[3]	3·0					0·09
Care orders		9·3	10·0	11·3		–
Interim care orders or remand to care[4]		9·9	10·1	10·7	. .	–
Other reasons	2·6	7·4	9·0	9·8	2·3	0·10
Total admissions to care	45·2	63·5	62·8	62·3	12·1[5]	0·99

[1–5] See notes in Appendix A. Sources: Various, see Appendix C, page 256

Table 2.16   Children in care of local authorities: type of accommodation and age groups[1]

United Kingdom   Thousands

	England and Wales				Scotland	Northern Ireland
	1972	1973	1974	1975	1974[3]	1974
Total of all children in care	90·6	93·2	95·9	99·1	20·6	1·74
Manner of accommodation						
Boarded out	29·9	29·8	30·7	31·9	5·6	0·75
In lodgings or residential employment	2·3	2·5	2·3	2·0	0·2	0·01
In community homes provided, controlled, or assisted by local authorities[2]:						0·32[6]
with observation and assessment facilities	4·2	4·8	4·8	5·3		..
with education on the premises	6·7	7·0	6·7	6·2		..
residential nurseries providing accommodation for children under seven	2·3	2·2	2·1	2·0	2·5	..
other homes	16·6	17·1	19·4	21·0		..
Voluntary homes	5·7	5·6	5·2	4·3	2·2	0·45
Accommodation for handicapped children	2·3	2·5	2·7	2·7	..	0·02
Hostels	1·6	1·5	1·2	0·7	..	0·06
Under charge of parent, guardian, relative, or friend	15·2	16·1	16·6	18·0	8·3	0·13
Other accommodation	3·8	4·1	4·2	4·9	1·9	..
By age groups						
Under 2 years	3·8	4·0	3·9	4·0	2·3	0·19
Two years but not of compulsory school age	8·3	8·6	7·9	8·3		0·18
Compulsory school age	51·9	59·3	63·6	66·9	6·0[4]	1·16
Over compulsory school age	26·6	21·3	20·5	19·9	12·2[5]	0·20

[1]–[6] See notes in Appendix A.   Sources: Various, see Appendix C, page 256

Chart 2.17   Children in the care of local authorities

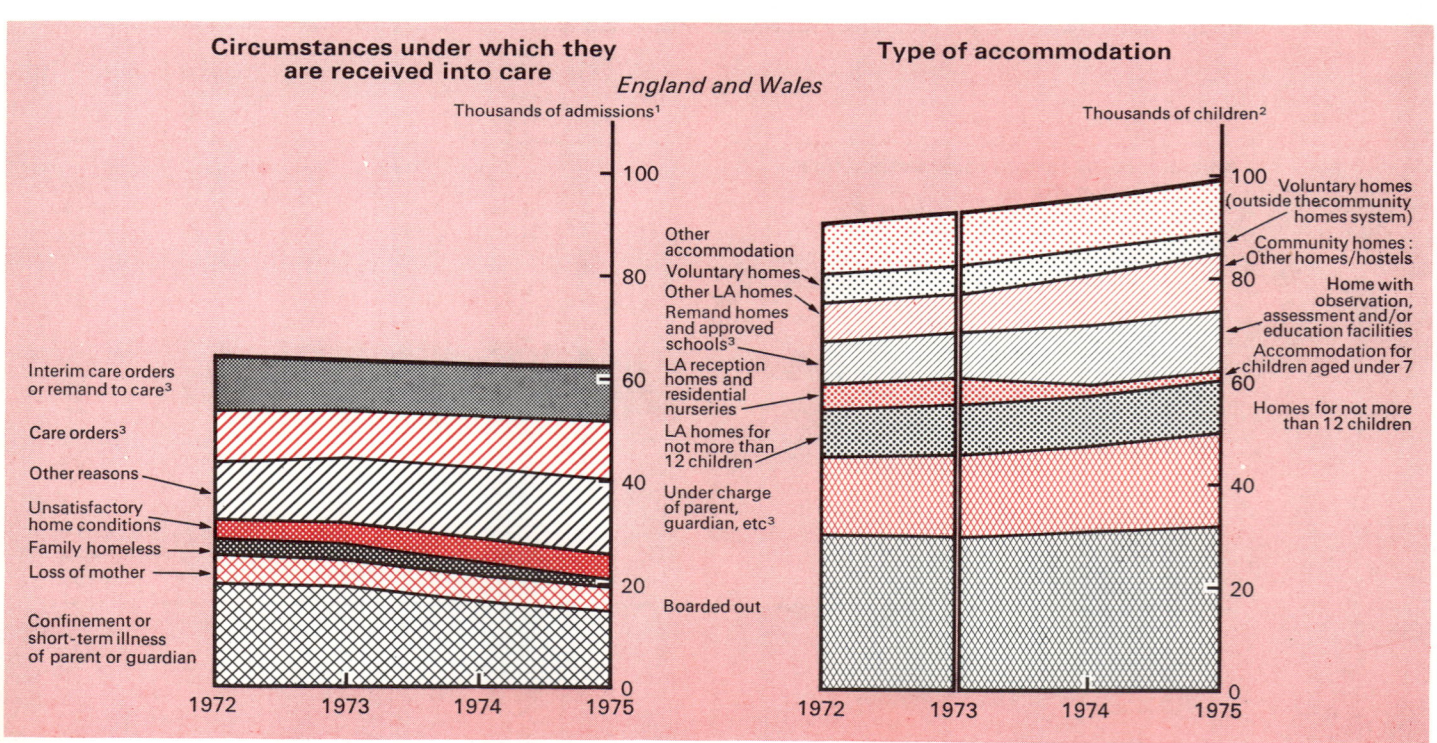

[1] During years ending 31 March.   [2] At 31 March.   [3] See note in Appendix B regarding the provisions of the
Children and Young Persons Act 1969.   Sources: Department of Health and Social Security; Welsh Office

The elderly

This subsection (Tables 2.18–2.24) contains a brief selection of tables and charts on the elderly (aged over 65 for men and over 60 for women). Basic demographic data are shown in Table 2.18, detailing the growth in numbers over retirement age, recently and in the future. Information on services for the elderly, where the growth in services reflects the growth in numbers, is shown in Chart 2.19 and Table 2.20. There are also 2 tables and 2 charts showing how the pattern of elderly household finance differs from that of the rest of the population. Table 2.22 on income of retired persons has been estimated from Family Expenditure data, and the 100 per cent totals are estimates with considerable standard errors attached.

Table 2.18   Elderly people: population projections[1]

United Kingdom   Thousands

	1975 (base)	1976[1]	1981[1]	1986[1]	1991[1]
Males					
60–64	1,488	1,458	1,375	1,453	1,358
65–69	1,262	1,265	1,233	1,172	1,240
70–74	899	916	966	946	910
75–79	496	518	607	644	633
80–84	248	247	279	328	349
85 and over	127	129	130	144	167
Total aged 60 and over	4,520	4,533	4,590	4,687	4,657
Females					
60–64	1,690	1,653	1,556	1,604	1,480
65–69	1,569	1,574	1,526	1,443	1,489
70–74	1,313	1,324	1,379	1,342	1,278
75–79	950	975	1,057	1,108	1,085
80–84	574	583	657	718	759
85 and over	387	393	420	471	521
Total aged 60 and over	6,483	6,502	6,595	6,686	6,612

[1] 1975-based projection. See note in Appendix B, p. 235.   *Source: Population Projections, 1975–2015, Office of Population Censuses and Surveys*

Chart 2.19 Persons supported by the local authorities in residential accommodation

England and Wales

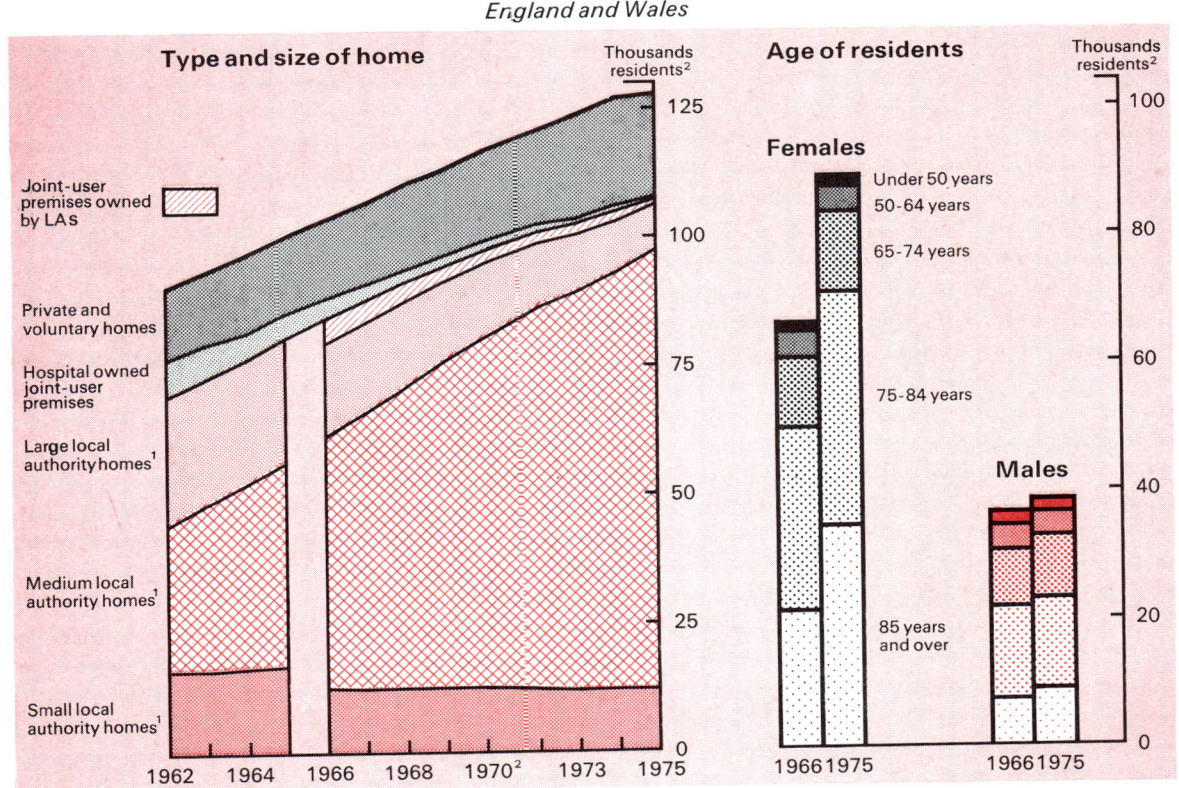

[1] There is a discontinuity between 1965 and 1966. See note in Appendix A. relate to 31 March.

[2] Up to 1970, data relate to 31 December; from 1972 they *Sources: Department of Health and Social Security; Welsh Office*

Table 2.20 Residential and other services mainly for the elderly and handicapped

Thousands

	All persons						Persons aged 65 and over					
	England and Wales[1]				*Scotland*[7]	*N. Ireland*	*England and Wales*[1]				*Scotland*[7]	*N. Ireland*
	1961	1973	1974	1975	1974	1974	1961	1973	1974	1975	1974	1974
Residents (on 31 December) in accommodation of:												
Local authorities, etc.[2]	74	103	105	108	9	2	66	97	98	102	8	2
Voluntary organisations[3]	13	20	21	20	6	1	10	15	15	16	5	1
Home nursing—cases attended	882	2,208[4]	..	..	192	..	431	942[4]	..	..	81	..
Home helps—cases attended	328	555	596	648	56	13	249	476	513	562	47	9
Meals on wheels—persons served during one week[5]	..	172	181	185	16	3	..	168	177	180	..	3
Chiropody—persons treated	..	1,110	..	..	190	..	..	1,066	..	..	188	..
Overall population (millions)	*46·2*	*49·2*	*49·2*	*49·2*	*5·2*	*1·5*	*5·5*	*6·8*	*6·9*	*7·0*	*0·7*	*0·2*
Total persons registered as[6]:												
Blind	96·7	104·8	105·6	106·7	..	..	65·1	75·5	76·6	77·9	..	..
Deaf	23·8	27·2	27·1	26·9	..	0·9	3·7	5·8	6·1	6·3	..	..
Other handicap	151·1	482·1	588·7	677·1	..	10·1	53·2	274·4	348·9	411·2	..	..

[1]–[7] See notes in Appendix A.

Sources: Various, see Appendix C, page 256

**Chart 2.21
Household
expenditure, 1974**

United Kingdom

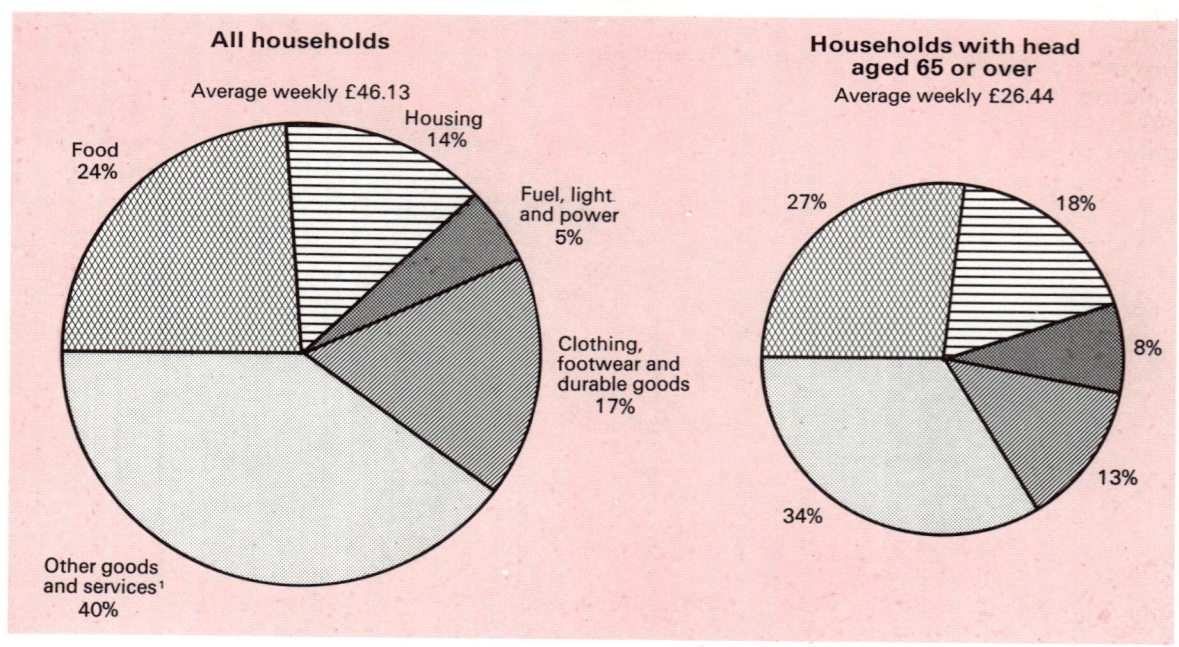

All households

Average weekly £46.13

Food
24%

Housing
14%

Fuel, light
and power
5%

Clothing,
footwear and
durable goods
17%

Other goods
and services[1]
40%

**Households with head
aged 65 or over**

Average weekly £26.44

27%

18%

8%

13%

34%

[1] Includes alcohol and tobacco.

Source: Family Expenditure Survey, Department of Employment

Table 2.22   Income of persons over retirement age[1], 1974

Great Britain   Various units

		Gross weekly income[2]			Weekly income from occupational pensions		
		Married couples	Single[3] males	Single[3] females	Married couples	Single[3] males	Single[3] females
Less than £5	(Percentages)				45	52	53
£5 and under £7					12	15	14
£7 „ „ £8		–	1	3	4	4	5
£8 „ „ £9					4	6	3
£9 „ „ £10					4	2	2
£10 „ „ £12		–	22	27			
£12 „ „ £14		–	18	23			
£14 „ „ £16		–	15	20	17	13	15
£16 „ „ £18		8	11	8			
£18 „ „ £20		11	7	4			
£20 „ „ £25		23	9	6	8	4	6
£25 „ „ £30		15	6	2			
£30 „ „ £35		9	2	3	3	4	2
£35 „ „ £40		6	2	1			
£40 and over		18	7	4	4	1	1
Total (=100%) (thousands)		2,090	720	3,350	1,080	280	660
Median (£)[4]		24·6	15·2	13·8	5·8	4·8	4·7

[1] Excludes people in institutions.   [2] Includes income from occupational pensions as at date of interview. All other income adjusted to 31 December 1974.   [3] Includes all single, widowed, and divorced persons.   [4] Calculated from banded data.

Source: Department of Health and Social Security, Family Expenditure Survey data

Chart 2.23 Source of household income, 1974

United Kingdom

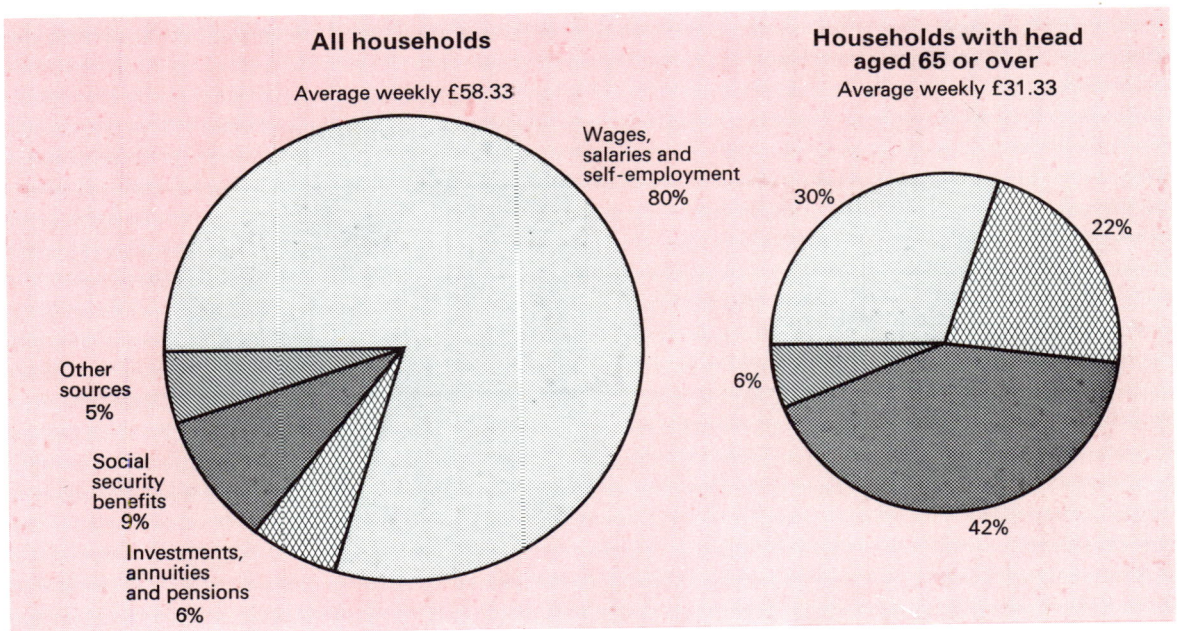

All households
Average weekly £58.33
Wages, salaries and self-employment 80%
Other sources 5%
Social security benefits 9%
Investments, annuities and pensions 6%

Households with head aged 65 or over
Average weekly £31.33
30%
22%
6%
42%

Source: Family Expenditure Survey, Department of Employment

Table 2.24   Household expenditure: average weekly expenditure on goods and services: by household composition, 1975

United Kingdom   Percentages

| | Total expenditure on goods and services (=100%) | Percentages of all goods and services | | | | | | | | | Percentage of all households |
		Housing	Fuel, light and power	Food	Alcohol and tobacco	Clothing and footwear	Durable house-hold goods	Other goods	Transport and vehicles	Services and mis-cellaneous	
Household composition, 1975											
One man:											
aged under 65	39·40	15·6	4·7	17·9	11·9	5·4	4·4	6·2	17·3	16·6	3·2
aged 65 and over	20·56	20·7	9·9	26·3	11·3	3·3	2·2	6·2	8·2	11·9	2·5
One woman:											
aged under 60	32·78	21·9	5·3	18·7	4·9	9·2	8·0	7·8	12·4	11·8	3·3
aged 60 and over	19·97	23·7	10·2	26·4	2·5	7·0	6·0	7·5	5·2	11·5	11·0
Man and woman:											
Head aged under 65	57·26	13·7	4·9	22·1	8·8	7·6	8·5	7·6	15·7	11·1	18·0
Head aged 65 and over	34·80	16·8	8·3	27·7	7·9	6·8	4·9	6·8	9·7	11·1	9·9
Man, woman, one child	59·71	12·5	5·3	24·3	9·0	8·7	8·8	8·0	14·2	9·2	9·5
Man, woman, two children	63·83	13·0	5·5	25·8	7·6	8·5	7·8	7·6	14·9	9·3	14·4
Man, woman, three children	68·97	11·3	5·0	27·9	7·5	9·0	7·7	7·7	13·3	10·6	5·3
Two adults, four or more children	70·65	10·2	5·3	30·8	8·5	10·1	6·9	6·7	12·1	9·4	2·9

Source: Family Expenditure Survey, Department of Employment

Coloured population

In the *GHS* the interviewer makes his own assessment of the colour of his respondent. Tables 2.25 to 2.27 are drawn from the 1971 to 1975 results of the *GHS* and show how the coloured household population (as assessed by the interviewer) differs from the rest of the household population. The two characteristics that stand out here are the younger overall age of the coloured population, and the greater tendency for coloured people to live in larger households. This latter characteristic is confirmed by Table 2.28 which is a census count of households by country of birth of chief economic supporter, showing 5·9 per cent of New Commonwealth households in 1971 had 2 or more families living in them.

Table 2.25   Age and colour of household population, 1975[1]

Great Britain   Percentages and numbers

| | Age | | | | | Total sample size (people) (=100%) numbers |
	0–15	16–19	20–44	45–64	65 or over	
Interviewer's assessment of colour (percentages):						
White	23	5	31	24	14	30,474
Coloured	38	8	39	14	2	896

[1] Unedited data.

Source: General Household Survey

Table 2.26   Age and colour of head of household

Great Britain   Percentages and numbers

	Age					Total sample size (households) (=100%) numbers
	Under 25	25–29	30–44	45–64	65 or over	
Interviewer's assessment of colour (percentages):						
1971-73						
White	4	8	24	38	25	33,090
Coloured	5	13	51	25	6	662
1974-75[1]						
White	4	8	24	37	27	21,684
Coloured	8	11	49	27	4	467

[1] Unedited data.   *Source: General Household Survey*

Table 2.27   Size of household: by colour[1], 1974 and 1975

Great Britain   Percentages and numbers

	Number of household members (all ages)						Total sample size (households) (=100%) numbers
	1	2	3	4	5	6 or more	
Interviewer's assessment of colour of head of household (percentages):							
White	21	32	17	17	8	5	21,699
Coloured	16	18	14	16	12	24	472

[1] Unedited data.   *Source: General Household Survey*

Table 2.28   Households with chief economic supporter born outside the United Kingdom, 1971

Great Britain   Percentages and numbers

	Type of household				All types (=100%) (numbers)
	No family	1 family	2 families	3 or more families	
Country of birth of the chief economic supporter:					
Irish Republic	22·6	76·1	1·2	–	309,700
Old Commonwealth	29·9	68·7	1·4	–	48,490
New Commonwealth	19·7	74·4	5·3	0·6	367,610
Europe (excluding USSR)	25·2	72·9	1·8	0·1	234,780
Rest of the world	29·6	69·4	1·0	–	132,640
All countries (outside UK)	23·4	73·7	2·7	0·2	1,093,220
All households	22·2	76·4	1·4	–	18,317,160

Source: Census of Population, 1971, 10% sample tables, Office of Population Censuses and Surveys

Education

In previous years the sections on Education and Employment have been separated from each other and have mainly reflected the way in which government has administered the departments dealing with these two subjects. This is to some extent inevitable, as statistics from which we draw our data are mainly collected by the Departments of Education and Science and of Employment (or equivalent departments in Scotland). However, this year we have attempted to integrate the two sections so that they follow a natural progression, starting with the learning of basic skills at school, following on to further education, or to learning skills through an apprenticeship or day-release. Most people then enter employment and continue for forty years or more in a job. However, as the chart below shows, many groups of people are likely to drop out of employment for a shorter or longer period; married women will stop to have a family; some people become unemployed; others will move from employment into retraining as the skills which they possess become redundant due to declining industry or changes in technology. There are also many people who, rather than remaining in one trade or skill their whole working life, change spontaneously from one job to another.

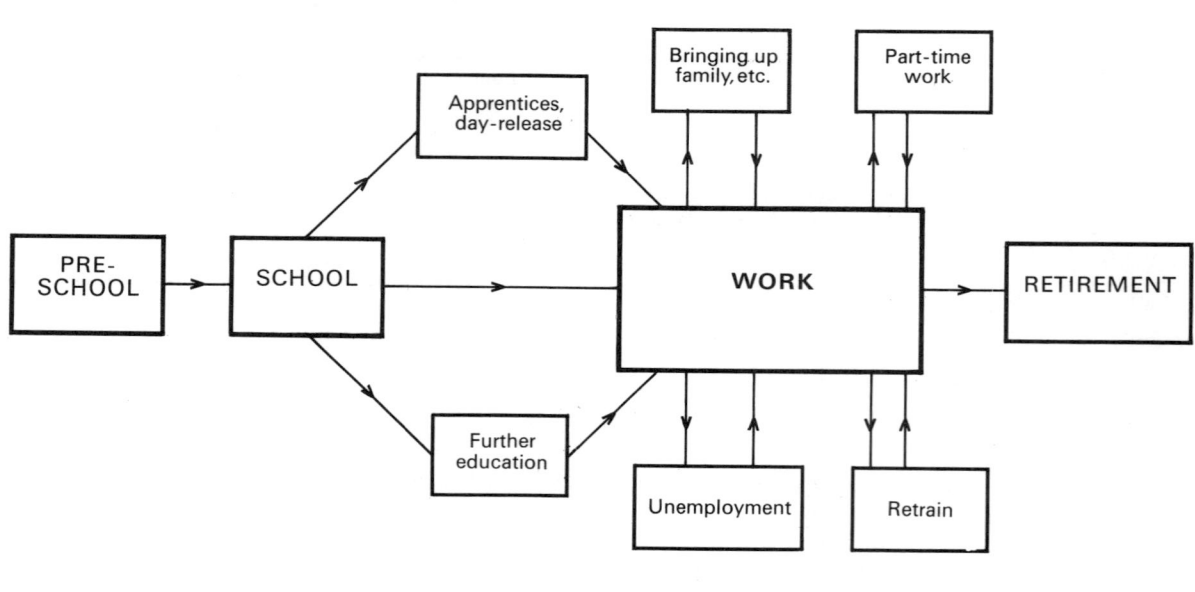

Ideally we should like to be able to show the stock of people, by age, sex, socio-economic group, etc. in each box, and the flows between them (there are, of course, many other subsidiary boxes and flows not listed here), but the statistics are not available in such a systematic way. They exist for some stocks and flows, but not for others, and in differing degrees of detail where they do exist. One particular problem on the education side is that there are differences in the structure and administration of the educational system in each of the four constituent countries of the United Kingdom. This makes impossible a unified statistical treatment. For anyone requiring a more detailed analysis the publications in Appendix C, together with the sources and definitions in Appendix B, should be read.

Although education is not compulsory until a child is 5, a growing number of children are attending some form of educational activity before then. (Other children under 5 attend play-groups or nurseries outside the educational system. In the years from 1961 to 1975 the number of places in registered nurseries in England and Wales rose from 18 to 370 thousand.) Table 3.1 and Chart 3.3 show how the proportion of children aged 2, 3, and 4 in school has risen in the same period. Chart 3.2 shows that, in 1973, children of professional class parents were more likely to be attending a nursery school or play-group.

Table 3.1 Education for the under-fives[1]

	United Kingdom					Percentages and thousands
	1967	1969	1971	1973	1975[2]	Thousands of children 1975
Full-time and part-time pupils in all schools as a percentage of all children:						
Aged 2	0·4	0·4	0·4	0·6	0·5	4·0
Aged 3	4·0	4·4	5·7	8·2	10·7	90·6
Aged 4	26·6	29·2	34·1	43·5	49·5	437·0
Total aged 2–4	10·1	11·5	13·6	17·6	20·7	531.6
Total (thousands)	296·1	336·9	383·8	474·1	531·6	

[1] As at January each year; part-time pupils counted as 1.
[2] Figures for Scotland are taken from the count held in September 1974.

Sources: Department of Education and Science; Scottish Education Department; Department of Education, Northern Ireland

Chart 3.2
Children under school age by socio-economic grouping of head of household[1], 1973

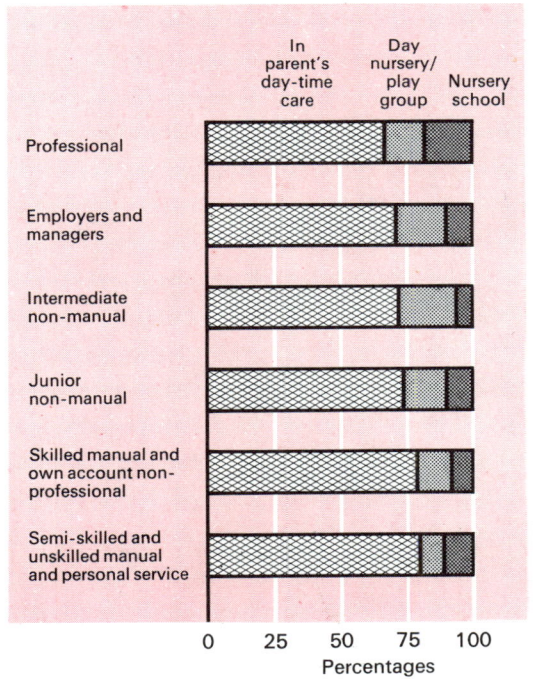

England and Wales

[1] Normally the father, but the socio-economic grouping of the head of household has been used where the father was not a member of the household.
Source: General Household Survey, 1973

Chart 3.3
Pupils under 5[1] as a percentage of age group population, all schools

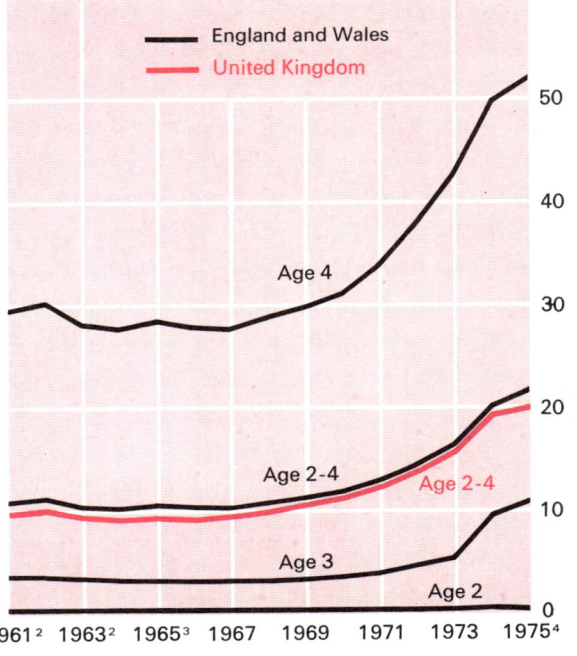

For footnotes see Appendix A.

Source: Department of Education and Science

EDUCATION

Education is compulsory from the age of 5 until 16, and Tables 3.4 and 3.5 show the numbers of children at school by type of school and age of child. Projections of school population are given which show the decline in numbers of school children which began for the 5–10 year old age group in 1974 and is expected to continue so that by 1985 the total number of school children of these ages will be 25 per cent less than in 1975.

Table 3.4 School pupils[1] : summary

United Kingdom — Thousands

	Actual							Projections		
	1961	1966	1971	1972	1973	1974	1975	1976	1980	1985
Nursery schools										
Public sector	29	31	35	38	40	43	45	56	68	87
Assisted and independent	8	7	5	5	5	5	2	2	2	2
Total	37	38	40	43	45	48	47	58	70	88
Primary schools										
Public sector	4,903	5,151	5,883	5,989	6,032	6,046	5,986	5,954	5,391	4,748
Assisted and independent	295	272	260	259	260	264	264	245	242	240
Total	5,198	5,423	6,143	6,248	6,292	6,310	6,250	6,199	5,633	4,988
Secondary schools										
Public sector	3,165	3,165	3,555	3,675	3,801	4,205	4,333	4,408	4,585	4,172
Assisted and independent	371	362	349	350	354	361	366	388	405	415
Total	3,536	3,527	3,904	4,025	4,155	4,566	4,699	4,796	4,990	4,587
Special schools[2]	78	88	103	137	143	146	147	150	155	152
All schools – total pupils	8,848	9,076	10,190	10,453	10,635	11,070	11,143	11,203	10,848	9,815

[1] Part-time pupils counted as 0·5.
[2] Including, from 1972, establishments transferred from the health service on 1 April 1971.

Source: Education Statistics for the United Kingdom, Department of Education and Science

Table 3.5 Pupils[1] : projections and age distribution

United Kingdom — Thousands and percentages

	Actual							Projections		
	1961	1966	1971	1972	1973	1974	1975	1976	1980	1985
All schools										
Thousands of boys and girls in January each year aged:										
2–4	244	263	344	379	417	448	452	491	536	645
5–10	4,550	4,891	5,544	5,623	5,639	5,614	5,549	5,448	4,875	4,205
11–14[2,3]	3,484	3,044	3,286	3,386	3,470	4,391	4,493	4,604	4,662	4,163
15	282	475	534	567	599					
16	172	226	272	282	292	400	429	433	499	498
17	87	128	157	161	163	163	167	171	205	222
18 and over	29	49	53	56	55	54	53	56	71	84
All ages	8,848	9,076	10,190	10,453	10,635	11,070	11,143	11,203	10,848	9,815
As percentage of age group:										
Boys										
16	22·6	28·7	36·3	36·5	36·7	48·4	50·4	50·5	52·7	55·4
17	13·1	16·2	21·3	21·3	21·5	20·6	20·5	20·5	22·3	24·5
18 and over[4]	5·4	6·4	8·3	8·2	8·0	7·8	7·5	7·6	8·6	9·8
Girls										
16	20·4	26·7	35·0	35·6	36·5	48·7	51·1	50·7	53·3	56·0
17	10·3	13·2	19·3	20·2	20·5	20·0	20·0	20·0	21·9	24·2
18 and over[4]	2·7	3·7	5·6	5·8	5·9	6·0	5·8	6·0	7·0	8·1
Boys and girls										
2–4[5]	9·9	9·3	12·3	13·9	15·7	17·0	17·7	20·2	26·1	26·0
16	21·5	27·7	35·6	35·9	36·6	48·5	50·8	50·6	53·0	55·7
17	11·7	14·8	20·3	20·7	21·0	20·3	20·2	20·2	22·1	24·3
18 and over[4]	4·1	5·1	7·0	7·2	7·1	6·9	6·7	6·8	7·8	9·0

[1] Part-time pupils counted as 0·5. [2] In Scotland 11 year olds are customarily in primary schools. The numbers of Scottish 11 year olds included above were 93,285 in 1975 and are expected to decrease to 71,000 in 1985. [3] The statutory leaving age was raised by one year to 16 in the educational year 1972/73. January 1974 (January 1973 for Scotland) figures are the first to reflect this change and hence age group 11–15 is taken from 1974 onwards. [4] As a percentage of the 18 years age group. [5] As a percentage of the 2–4 age group although there are very few pupils aged 2 (see table 3.1).

Source: Education Statistics for the United Kingdom, Department of Education and Science

Recent trends in the types of school attended are shown in Tables 3.6 and 3.7 for England and Wales, Scotland, and Northern Ireland separately. In 1975 nearly two-thirds of pupils in England and Wales were in comprehensive schools, compared with almost 100 per cent in Scotland. The courses taken at school are shown in Table 3.8. During the last 10 years, there has been a substantial increase in social science and vocational subjects.

Table 3.6 Secondary education: England and Wales

Percentages and numbers

	1970	1971	1972	1973	1974	1975
Public sector secondary schools (percentages):						
Middle deemed secondary	1·2	1·8	2·3	3·7	4·6	5·4
Modern	40·3	37·0	33·4	28·7	23·0	18·2
Grammar	19·9	18·2	16·6	14·8	11·0	9·0
Technical	1·4	1·2	1·0	0·8	0·6	0·5
Comprehensive	30·8	35·9	41·1	47·0	57·4	64·3
Others	6·5	5·9	5·5	5·1	3·3	2·6
Total – thousands of pupils (=100%)	3,046·0	3,143·9	3,251·4	3,362·6	3,723·7	3,826·6
Average number of pupils per qualified teacher[1]	*17·8*	*17·9*	*17·6*	*17·1*	*17·5*	*17·2*

[1] Including full-time equivalent of part-time and visiting teachers.

Source: Statistics of Education, Volume I, Schools, Department of Education and Science

Table 3.7 Secondary education: Scotland and Northern Ireland

Percentages and numbers

	1970	1971	1972	1973	1974	1975
Scotland						
Public sector secondary schools						
3–4 year selective	19·3	14·3	8·2	3·5	1·6	1·1
6 year selective	17·2	14·0	10·1	6·0	0·4	0·3
Comprehensive	51·9	58·7	68·8	77·9	84·7	86·7
Part comprehensive/part selective	11·5	13·0	12·9	12·5	13·3	11·9
Total – thousands of pupils (=100%)	304·0	314·4	324·4	338·1	370·9	393·0
Average number of pupils per qualified teacher[1]	*16·4*	*16·1*	*15·6*	*15·1*	*15·5*	*15·7*
Northern Ireland						
Public and assisted sector secondary schools						
Secondary intermediate	63·7	64·6	65·3	65·7	67·7	67·5
Grammar	35·6	35·0	34·6	34·3	32·3	32·5
Technical intermediate	0·7	0·4	0·1	–	–	–
Total – thousands of pupils (=100%)	126·9	130·9	133·8	135·8	146·4	148·8
Average number of pupils per qualified teacher[1,2]	*18·6*	*18·2*	*17·9*	*17·4*	*17·3*	*17·2*

[1] Including full-time equivalent of part-time and visiting teachers. [2] Excluding technical intermediate schools.

Sources: Scottish Education Statistics, Scottish Education Department; Northern Ireland Education Statistics, Department of Education, Northern Ireland

Table 3.8 Courses taken in secondary schools

	England and Wales						Thousands
	1963	1966	1969	1971	1972	1973	1974
Numbers of school children sitting summer 'O' level examinations in the following subjects:							
Arts	1,158·8	1,103·4	1,114·6	1,087·0	1,116·5	1,144·0	1,206·1
of which Modern languages	*218·3*	*211·6*	*207·0*	*202·3*	*206·7*	*207·5*	*214·8*
Science and technical	729·0	700·7	734·3	758·7	789·2	802·3	845·1
of which Mathematics	*271·3*	*257·2*	*266·1*	*273·1*	*280·5*	*281·4*	*293·8*
Social science	191·5	196·3	234·4	246·0	262·2	268·9	287·0
Vocational	106·0	119·4	127·9	132·2	137·0	136·8	139·1
Total all subjects	2,185·3	2,119·8	2,211·3	2,223·8	2,304·9	2,352·0	2,477·3

Source: Statistics of Education, Volume 2, School Leavers, CSE and GCE, Department of Education and Science

School leavers

Children can leave school at the age of 16, although many stay on to complete examination courses. A table and a chart, 3.9 and 3.10, show examination success by type of school, and destination of school leavers. A new table, 3.11, from the school intentions survey shows the attitudes of school children at the age of 16. The results are summarised as:

a. Sixty per cent of the children of fathers in non-manual occupations are likely to continue in full-time education beyond 16 years of age compared with only 32 per cent of children of manual workers.

b. Thirty-four per cent of the children of fathers in non-manual occupations have 5 or more 'O' level certificates (or its equivalent) by 16 years of age compared with only 11 per cent for children of manual workers.

c. At all levels of attainment children of non-manual workers are more likely to continue in full-time education than are children of manual workers.

d. The daughters of manual workers are more likely than sons to continue in full-time education.

**Chart 3.9
School leavers:
by type of school
and examination
achievement,
1973/74**

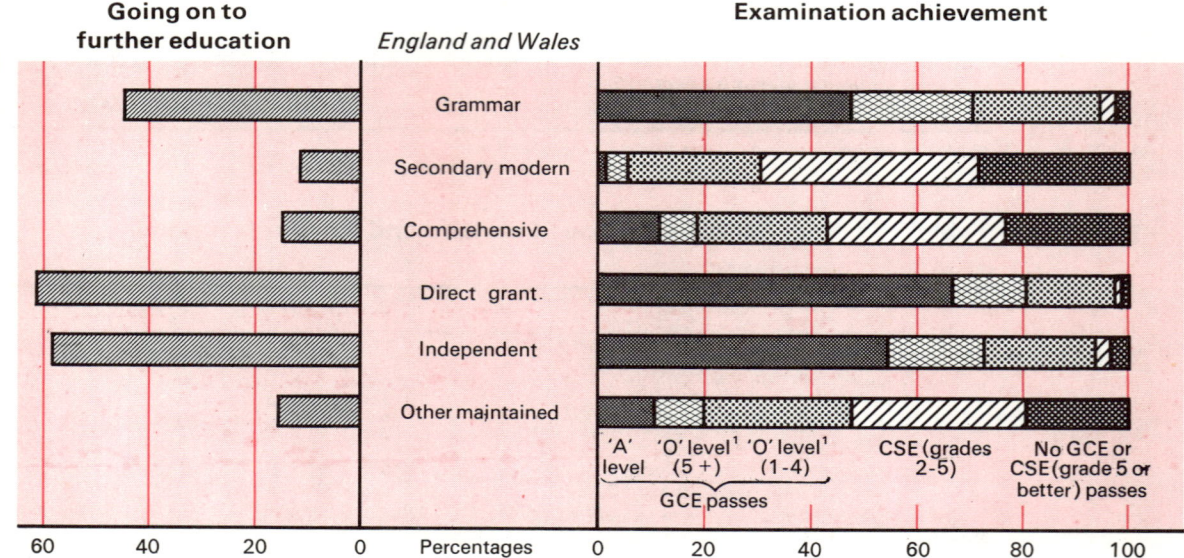

¹ Including Grade 1 results in the CSE examination and 'A' level passes on 'A' level papers.

Source: Statistics of Education, Volume 2, School Leavers, CSE and GCE, Department of Education and Science

Table 3.10   Destination of school leavers: by type of school, 1973/74

England and Wales   Percentages and numbers

	Universities	Colleges of Education	Polytechnics	Other full-time further education	Employment¹	Total (=100%) (numbers)
Boys (percentages):						
Grammar	21·3	2·5	7·1	8·8	60·3	34,370
Comprehensive	4·3	0·8	1·8	5·2	87·9	195,630
Modern	0·3	0·1	0·2	7·5	91·9	82,530
Other secondary	3·2	1·0	2·3	7·3	86·2	14,130
Direct grant	38·4	2·4	9·9	10·1	39·2	8,070
Independent	31·6	0·7	6·1	17·5	44·1	14,910
Girls (percentages):						
Grammar	14·0	11·6	4·1	20·0	50·3	36,150
Comprehensive	2·6	3·4	1·0	10·6	82·4	184,520
Modern	0·1	0·6	0·3	13·7	85·3	77,870
Other secondary	1·6	3·3	0·6	11·9	82·6	13,300
Direct grant	26·0	12·6	5·2	18·6	37·6	7,970
Independent	14·8	5·5	3·8	36·9	39·0	11,990

¹ Includes those entering temporary employment, pending entry into full-time further education not later than September–October 1975, and those who left for other reasons and whose destinations were not known.

Source: Statistics of Education, Volume 2, School Leavers, CSE and GCE, Department of Education and Science

Table 3.11   Intentions of 16-year-old school children, 1975

England and Wales   Percentages and numbers

	Father's occupation Non-manual			Father's occupation Manual			Total		
	Boys	Girls	Total	Boys	Girls	Total	Boys	Girls	Total
Percentage of students who wish to stay on in full-time education									
High attainment[1]	..	..	88	..	..	75	..	..	83
Medium attainment[2]	..	..	59	..	..	45	..	..	50
Low attainment[3]	..	..	30	..	..	17	..	..	20
All students	62	58	60	26	39	32	38	45	41
Percentage of students who have certain levels of attainment									
High[1]	35	33	34	10	12	11	18	19	18
Medium[2]	32	37	34	30	33	32	31	35	33
Low[3]	33	30	32	60	55	57	51	46	49
Total sample size (=100%) (numbers)	144	121	265	288	253	541	432	374	806

[1] 5 or more GCE 'O' level or CSE Grade 1 passes.   [2] 1–4 GCE 'O' level or CSE Grade 1 passes.   [3] No GCE or CSE Grade 1 passes.

Source: School Intentions Survey, Department of Education and Science

Further education

Tables 3.12 to 3.14 show various aspects of education for the 16 to 21 year old population after leaving school. The increase in 'A' levels taken at college rather than at school is shown in Chart 3.12, the growth in further (non-university) education in Table 3.13, and the general levelling out in the number of students at universities and on advanced courses is shown in Table 3.14.

**Chart 3.12
Advanced level
passes**

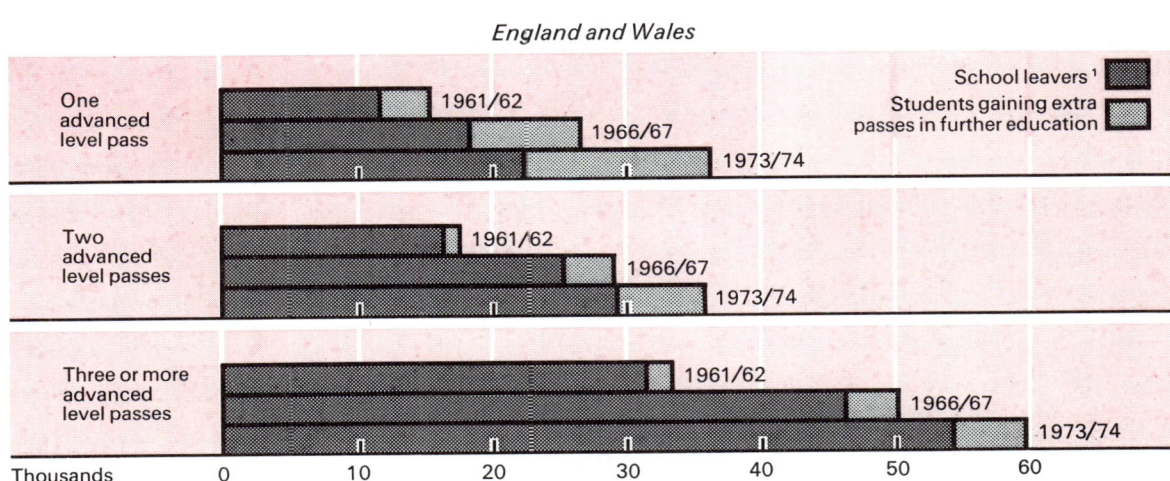

England and Wales

[1] Including estimated numbers leaving from independent schools not recognised as efficient.

Source: Department of Education and Science

Table 3.13   Further education

United Kingdom   Thousands

	United Kingdom				*England and Wales* 1974	*Scotland* 1974	*Northern Ireland* 1974
	1969	1971	1973	1974			
Students in public sector and assisted establishments[1]							
Major establishments:							
Full-time	260	282	295	328	292	25	11
Sandwich	35	43	45	48	43	4	1
Day release	727	661	613	625	553	60	12
Other part-time day	117	138	174	188	174	13	1
Evening only	765	792	829	828	785	31	12
Total	1,904	1,915	1,957	2,017	1,847	133	37
of which—men	*1,198*	*1,144*	*1,099*	*1,104*	*994*	*88*	*22*
—women	*706*	*771*	*857*	*914*	*853*	*46*	*15*
of which aged—15 to 17	*536*	*498*	*450*	*467*	*406*	*46*	*15*
—18 to 20	*493*	*476*	*470*	*473*	*420*	*43*	*10*
—21 and over	*875*	*941*	*1,036*	*1,077*	*1,021*	*44*	*12*
Evening institutes[2]							
Total	1,402	1,561	1,744	1,854[3]	1,841	13	..
Total students in major establishments and evening institutes	3,306	3,476	3,700	3,871	3,688	146	37
of which:							
on courses leading to recognised qualifications:							
advanced	*219*	*222*	*233*	*249*	*222*	*23*	*4*
non-advanced	*1,129*	*1,078*	*1,032*	*1,048*	*912*	*107*	*29*
on other courses	*1,958*	*2,176*	*2,436*	*2,574*	*2,554*	*16*	*4*
Students taking courses of adult education provided by Responsible Bodies[4,5]	247	255	267	269	269	..	..

[1] See note in Appendix A defining these establishments.   [2] Excluding students on non-vocational courses in Scotland.   [3] Great Britain only.   [4] Universities, Workers' Educational Association and the Welsh National Council of YMCA.   [5] England and Wales only.
[6] Includes the following students: Under 15 – 100,123; 15 – 67,079; and 16–17 – 118,146.

Sources: Department of Education and Science; Scottish Education Department; Department of Education, Northern Ireland

Table 3.14   Higher education: number and age of students

United Kingdom   Thousands

	Men					Women				
	1965/66	1971/72	1972/73	1973/74	1974/75	1965/66	1971/72	1972/73	1973/74	1974/75
Full-time students:										
Universities[1]	128·1	170·2	170·5	170·8	172·4	46·1	72·3	76·3	80·4	85·3
Colleges of education[1,2]	24·2	35·9	37·5	38·8	32·5	61·0	90·3	89·7	91·5	85·0
Further education advanced courses[2]	39·1	77·4	78·1	80·6	84·1	11·8	27·3	29·9	33·4	37·4
Total full-time students	191·4	283·5	286·1	290·2	289·0	118·9	189·9	195·9	205·3	207·7
of which:										
18 and under	..	30·3	30·2	29·9	30·1	..	32·3	32·5	32·1	32·2
19–20	..	101·5	101·8	102·7	101·6	..	85·4	87·8	89·4	89·7
21–24	..	106·9	105·0	106·7	104·6	..	46·5	48·8	54·8	55·4
25 and over	..	44·9	49·1	51·0	52·5	..	25·8	26·8	28·9	30·4
Part-time students:										
Universities	14·6	18·4	18·2	18·5	19·0	3·0	5·1	5·3	5·9	6·4
Further education: advanced courses										
Part-time day courses	56·9	69·4	68·5	69·7	76·5	3·1	7·6	8·7	10·6	12·9
Evening only courses	47·9	37·0	34·5	33·4	33·7	2·3	4·7	4·9	5·1	5·4
Total part-time students	119·4	124·8	121·2	121·6	129·2	8·4	17·4	18·9	21·6	24·7

[1] Students in university departments of education are included under universities.   [2] Students in art teacher training centres in further education establishments and departments of education in polytechnics are included under further education.

Source: Statistics of Education, Volume 3, Further Education, and Volume 6, Universities, Department of Education and Science

Table 3.15 shows the first destinations of UK graduates. About a quarter of men and a third of women continue some further study. A significant feature of this table is the growth in public sector employment as the first job for graduates; 15 per cent of men and 21 per cent of women go into the public sector or education now compared with 10 per cent and 16 per cent 5 years ago. To these must be added the percentage who will go into the public sector or education when they complete their higher degree or teacher training. Numbers employed in education are shown in Table 3.16. It is important to consider this increase in numbers employed in education when looking at the large increase in public expenditure on education in Table 3.17.

Table 3.15   Destination of UK graduates at GB universities

Percentages and numbers

	Men				Women			
	1968/69	1971/72	1972/73	1973/74	1968/69	1971/72	1972/73	1973/74
Teacher training	8·1	9·4	8·4	6·9	25·8	26·4	24·1	21·3
Other further education or training[1]	25·0	20·3	18·9	17·5	22·3	19·1	18·3	16·6
Already in employment	5·6	5·4	6·3	6·1	1·6	2·0	2·2	2·3
Gained UK employment:								
Public service	5·1	11·3	10·0	11·5	8·0	13·9	14·2	16·3
Education	5·1	5·0	4·9	4·3	7·7	5·2	5·1	5·4
Other UK employment[2]	33·2	30·0	33·1	33·9	14·8	14·5	17·4	18·2
Employment overseas	4·5	3·0	3·0	3·3	4·3	3·3	3·5	3·3
Other destinations[3]	13·4	15·7	15·3	16·5	15·5	15·5	15·2	16·6
Total (=100%) (numbers)	36,259	42,480	42,468	43,559	13,890	16,967	18,230	19,325

[1-3] See Appendix A.   *Source: 'First Destination of University Graduates', University Grants Committee*

Table 3.16   Selected statistics of manpower employed in education

England and Wales   Thousands

	1960	1970	1971	1972	1973	1974
Full-time teachers[1] in grant-aided schools and establishments, men and women						
Maintained primary and secondary schools:						
Primary and nursery[2]	144	163	173	181	189	194
Secondary[3]	123	162	171	181	194	207
Others[4]	1	3	3	3	3	3
Total	268	328	347	365	386	404
Direct grant grammar schools	6	7	7	7	7	7
Special schools	5	9	9	11	12	13
Further education establishments	20	50	52	56	59	61
Colleges of education	3	11	11	11	11	11
Others	1	2	3	3	3	4
Total	302	407	428	452	478	500
Academic staff in universities[5]	11	23	24	24	25	26

[1] At 31 March.   [2] Including middle schools deemed primary.   [3] Including middle schools deemed secondary.   [4] Including teachers whose full-time service was divided between primary and secondary schools.   [5] These figures are for academic years. 1960 refers to the academic year 1959–60, etc.

Source: Statistics of Education England and Wales, Department of Education and Science

93

EDUCATION

Table 3.17   Public expenditure on education [1]

United Kingdom   £ million and percentages

	£ million						Percentages	
	1961 –62	1971 –72	1972 –73	1973 –74	1974 –75	1975 –76	1961 –62	1975 –76
Current expenditure								
Schools maintained by education authorities:	531	1,401	1,666	1,914	2,799	3,725	*50·1*	*53·2*
of which:								
Nursery	*2*	*8*	*10*	*13*	*18*	..	*0·1*	*–*
Primary	*246*	*639*	*748*	*843*	*1,234*	..	*23·2*	*–*
Secondary	*269*	*699*	*838*	*975*	*1,434*	..	*25·4*	*–*
Special	*14*	*55*	*70*	*83*	*113*	..	*1·3*	*–*
School health [2]	15	37	44	48	..	..	*1·4*	*–*
Transport of pupils	14	43	48	55	80	103	*1·4*	*1·5*
Fees and grants to direct grant and independent schools	21	48	50	59	75	90	*2·0*	*1·3*
Further and adult education	87	351	416	466	604	769	*8·2*	*11·0*
Teacher training	25	129	146	162	185	224	*2·4*	*3·2*
Universities (including CATs):								
Grants to universities	60	259	325	315	417	548	*5·7*	*7·8*
Grants and allowances to students	27	77	77	84	111	146	*2·5*	*2·1*
Youth service and physical training	10	27	34	41	57	81	*0·9*	*1·2*
Other current expenditure [3]	87	289	327	418	481	581	*8·2*	*8·3*
Total current expenditure	877	2,661	3,133	3,562	4,809	6,267	*82·7*	*89·5*
Capital expenditure								
Schools:								
Expenditure by education authorities	105	299	377	453	348	439	*9·9*	*6·3*
Grants and loans by central government	9	28	32	37	54	65	*0·8*	*0·9*
Further and adult education	31	64	65	69	65	75	*2·9*	*1·1*
Teacher training	12	12	11	12	18	25	*1·1*	*0·4*
Grants to universities	26	81	87	70	83	98	*2·5*	*1·4*
Other capital expenditure	–	9	12	25	26	33	*–*	*0·5*
Total capital expenditure	183	493	584	666	594	735	*17·3*	*10·5*
Total public expenditure on education	1,060	3,154	3,717	4,228	5,403	7,002	*100·0*	*100·0*

[1] Excluding current expenditure on school meals and milk.   [2] From 1 April 1974, included in the National Health Service.   [3] Includes administration, selective employment tax, value added tax paid by local authorities, and imputed rents for the use of buildings of schools and colleges maintained by education authorities.

Sources: National Income and Expenditure, Central Statistical Office; Department of Education and Science

Table 3.18 shows that people with higher qualifications tend to be more satisfied with their education than people with no qualifications. However, there is very little variation compared with results of satisfaction with other areas of life; eg see the article by John Hall on Subjective Indicators.

Table 3.18   Satisfaction with education: by qualification [2]

England and Wales   Numbers

	1973			1975		
	Mean [1] score	Standard [1,2] deviation	Number in sample	Mean [1] score	Standard [1,2] deviation	Number in sample
Satisfaction by qualification [2]:						
Higher	7·60	1·64	65	7·68	2·21	60
Further	6·94	2·14	31	7·66	1·77	56
Basic only	7·04	1·75	53	7·83	2·38	81
Other	6·45	2·35	168	6·85	2·32	114
No qualifications	6·62	2·39	629	6·67	2·44	605
All people	6·69	2·31	946	6·92	2·36	916

[1] On a 0–10 scale, 0 = completely dissatisfied, 10 = completely satisfied.   [2] See note in Appendix B, page 235.   *Source: SSRC Survey Unit*

Employment

This section continues directly from the last section with tables showing people's activities in the employment field after they have left full-time education. Table 4.1 shows the new entrants to employment and numbers apprenticed, since 1961. Apart from 1973, when the school leaving age was raised and fewer people entered employment, the percentage apprenticed has remained fairly constant, about 40 per cent of boys, and 7 per cent of girls. Other forms of training are given in day-release to attend college, and numbers and percentages in this area are in Table 4.2.

Table 4.1 New entrants to employment

	Great Britain				Thousands and percentages	
	1961	1966	1971	1972	1973[1]	1974
Boys aged under 18 (thousands):						
Boys entering apprenticeship to skilled craft	114·7	114·4	95·6	100·2	66·0	118·2
Total boy entrants	302·5	270·2	242·1	258·9	140·5	274·8
Percentage apprenticed	37·9	42·4	39·5	38·7	47·0	43·0
Girls aged under 18 (thousands):						
Girls entering apprenticeship to skilled craft	20·5	16·7	16·7	18·0	5·0	15·5
Total girl entrants	284·9	251·7	220·4	228·2	107·0	237·8
Percentage apprenticed	7·2	6·7	7·6	7·9	4·7	6·5

[1] School leaving age raised to 16 years in September 1972 affecting the number of new entrants in 1973.

Source: Department of Employment Gazette

Table 4.2 Young people under 18 on day release from work, at November

	England and Wales						Numbers and percentages			
	Men					Women				
Industry:	1971[1] as % of no. insured	1971	1972	1973	1974	1971[1] as % of no. insured	1971	1972	1973	1974
Agriculture, forestry, and fishing	39	6,017	6,474	5,281	5,482	9	311	343	298	364
Mining and quarrying	53	5,249	3,867	2,992	3,587	24	124	116	105	131
Manufacturing industries	42	82,136	69,916	63,427	69,572	7	12,153	9,957	9,215	10,302
Construction	48	22,874	27,810	31,180	27,149	8	424	449	404	397
Gas, electricity, and water	96	5,178	4,606	3,750	3,862	35	932	796	773	983
Transport and communication	46	8,650	7,704	6,630	7,065	18	1,840	1,846	1,328	1,592
Distributive trades	6	5,414	5,446	4,425	4,373	2	3,387	3,398	2,527	2,570
Insurance, banking and finance, and business services	9	754	693	970	1,319	2	692	619	727	1,220
Professional and scientific services	37	4,270	4,411	4,638	4,330	26	7,990	7,407	6,662	6,366
Miscellaneous services	36	20,191	21,129	19,626	17,275	24	12,646	13,785	10,586	10,073
Public administration and defence	107	10,289	10,778	10,030	10,418	74	7,511	7,258	6,108	7,781
Total	36	171,022	162,834	152,949	154,432	10	48,010	45,974	38,733	41,779

[1] Numbers on day release at November 1971 as a percentage of those insured at June 1971. No equivalent figures available for later years.

Source: Statistics of Education, Volume 3, Department of Education and Science

Table 4.3   Economic activity: summary, 1961 to 1971

Great Britain   Thousands and percentages

	Total			Males			Females		
	1961	1966	1971[2]	1961	1966	1971[2]	1961	1966	1971[2]
Population aged 15 and over[1]	39,569	40,041	40,935	18,811	19,030	19,496	20,758	21,011	21,439
Economically active									
In employment[3]:									
Self-employed and employers	1,717	1,586	1,843	1,385	1,231	1,472	331	355	371
Employees	21,622	22,583	21,890	14,363	14,344	13,560	7,257	8,239	8,330
Part-time workers (incl. above)[4]	2,066	3,121	3,724	174	373	572	1,892	2,748	3,152
Out of employment[3]:									
Sick	297	216	291	216	133	190	81	82	101
Other	378	472	997	268	287	662	110	186	335
Total	24,014	24,857	25,021	16,232	15,994	15,884	7,782	8,863	9,137
Economically inactive									
Students	994	1,265	1,745	540	675	933	454	591	812
Retired	2,448	2,411	5,346[5]	1,808	1,911	2,304	639	500	3,043[5]
Housewives and other persons	12,113	11,508	8,822[5]	230	450	376	11,883	11,058	8,446[5]
Total	15,555	15,184	15,914	2,578	3,036	3,613	12,976	12,148	12,301
As percentage of population aged 15 and over.									
Economically active	*60·7*	*62·1*	*61·1*	*86·3*	*84·0*	*81·5*	*37·5*	*42·2*	*42·6*
Students	*2·5*	*3·2*	*4·3*	*2·9*	*3·5*	*4·8*	*2·2*	*2·8*	*3·8*
Retired	*6·2*	*6·0*	*13·1[5]*	*9·6*	*10·0*	*11·8*	*3·1*	*2·4*	*14·2[5]*
Housewives and other persons	*30·6*	*28·7*	*21·6[5]*	*1·2*	*2·4*	*1·9*	*57·2*	*52·6*	*39·4[5]*

[1]–[5] See notes in Appendix A.

Source: Census of Population Reports, Office of Population Censuses and Surveys

General economic activity

The series of charts and tables 4.4 to 4.9 show various aspects of economic activity. The increase in public sector employment shown in Table 4.7 must be noted, although there have been some changes in definition. These are partly noted in Appendix B, but the reader is also referred to an article in *Economic Trends* for February 1976.

Chart 4.4
Distribution of people at work

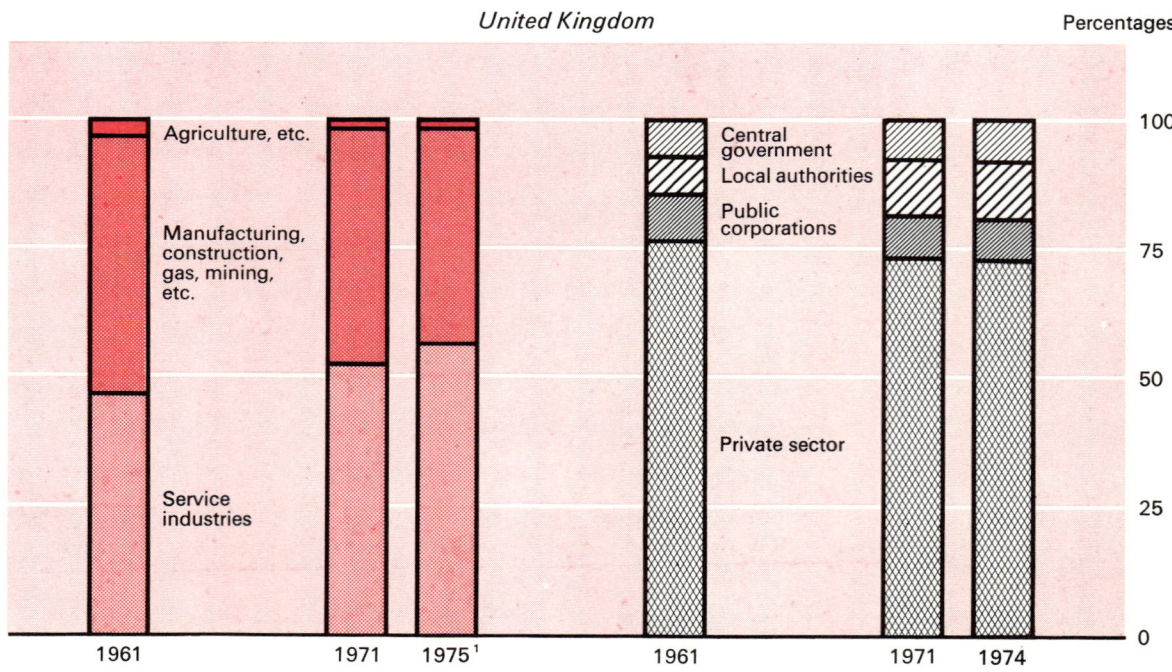

Distribution of total employees in employment

Distribution of total employed labour force

United Kingdom

Percentages

Agriculture, etc.

Manufacturing, construction, gas, mining, etc.

Service industries

Central government

Local authorities

Public corporations

Private sector

1961   1971   1975[1]   1961   1971   1974

[1] Provisional.

Source: Census of Employment, Department of Employment

Source: Economic Trends, February 1976, Central Statistical Office

Chart 4.5
Population aged
15 and over:
economic activity

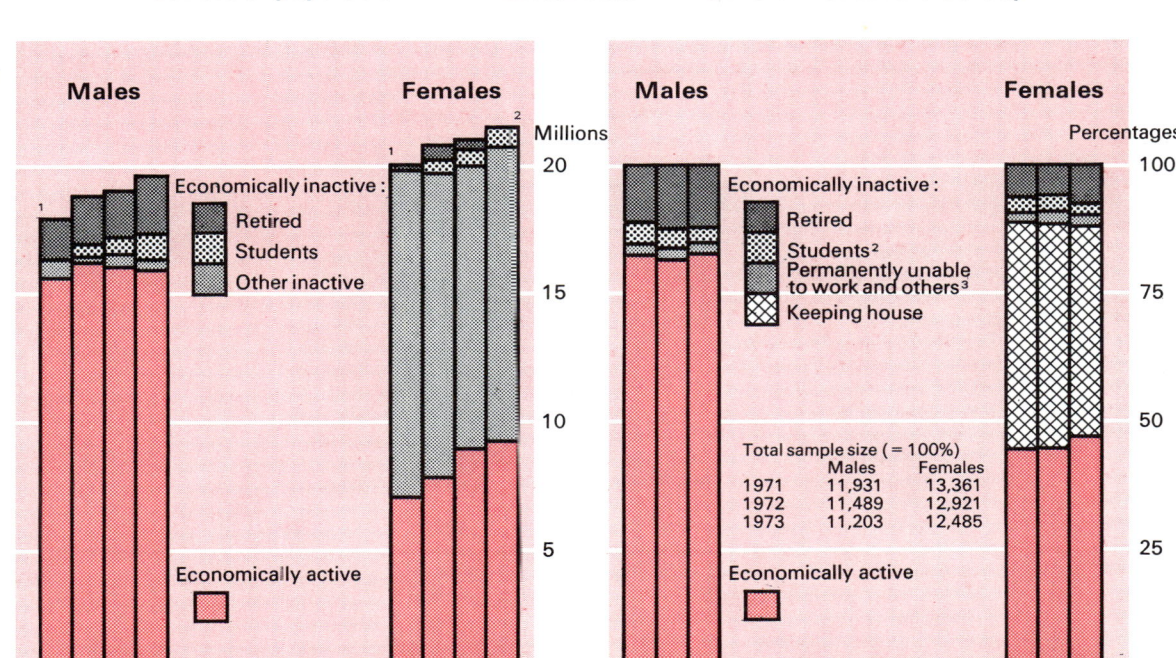

Census of population   *Great Britain*   General Household Survey

¹ Students included with other inactive.
² Retired included with other inactive.

Source: Census of Population Report, Office of Population Censuses and Surveys

¹ Aged 16 and over in 1973.   ² Excludes part-time students who were working in the reference week.   ³ Includes 0·3, 0·2, and 0·1 per cent, respectively, for 1971, 1972, and 1973, males who were keeping house.

Source: General Household Survey, 1973

Table 4.6   Economic activity rates by age and sex¹

Great Britain   Percentages and numbers

	1971	1972	1973	1974[5]	Total sample size (=100%) (numbers) 1974[5]
Percentage economically active:					
Males					
15–17[2]	48·2	52·0	62·7	55·6	408
18–24	91·0	91·7	90·6	89·7	1,247
25–44	98·9	98·5	98·2	97·9	3,622
45–64	94·6	92·9	94·0	92·8	3,313
65 or over	16·8	16·2	19·2	18·4	1,640
Total	82·3	81·1	82·3	80·8	10,230
Married females					
15–17[2,3]	. .	. .	. .	. .	. .
18–24	45·7	45·7	49·7	49·2	652
25–44	48·6	49·0	53·9	56·7	3,219
45–59	54·2	56·7	58·7	60·3	2,165
60 or over	13·8	14·1	15·0	16·2	1,492
Total	44·0	44·4	47·8	49·0	7,539
Unmarried females[4]					
15–17[2,3]	48·8	48·8	57·0	51·8	407
18–24	85·6	84·0	83·5	78·3	600
25–44	79·3	76·2	79·2	76·5	486
45–59	73·9	74·2	72·0	72·9	561
60 or over	11·3	11·9	11·2	12·2	1,954
Total	45·3	44·4	44·9	42·4	4,008

1–4 See Appendix A.   ⁵ Unedited data.   *Source: General Household Survey*

Table 4.7 Employment by sector

	Total employment (thousands)				Total employment (percentages)			
United Kingdom							Thousands and percentages	
	1961[1]	1971	1974	1975	1961[1]	1971	1974	1975
Total public sector	5,843	6,566	6,861	7,278	23·9	26·9	27·4	29·1
Central Government	1,773	1,929	2,087	2,246	7·3	7·9	8·3	9·0
of which								
HM Forces and Women's Services	*474*	*368*	*345*	*336*	*1·9*	*1·5*	*1·4*	*1·3*
Civilian	*1,299*	*1,561*	*1,742*	*1,910*	*5·3*	*6·4*	*7·0*	*7·6*
Local authorities	1,870	2,651	2,844	3,024	7·6	10·9	11·3	12·1
Public corporations	2,200	1,986	1,930	2,008	9·0	8·1	7·7	8·0
Total private sector	18,610	17,833	18,199	17,690	76·1	73·1	72·6	70·9
of which								
Employees	*16,859*	*15,924*	*16,274*	*15,765*	*68·9*	*65·3*	*64·9*	*63·1*
Employers and self-employed	*1,751*	*1,909*	*1,925*	*1,925*	*7·2*	*7·8*	*7·7*	*7·7*
Total employed labour force	24,453	24,399	25,060	24,968	100·0	100·0	100·0	100·0

[1] Data for 1961 have been revised since last published in *Economic Trends No. 268, February 1976.*   *Source: Central Statistical Office*

Chart 4.8
Public sector: total employees in employment

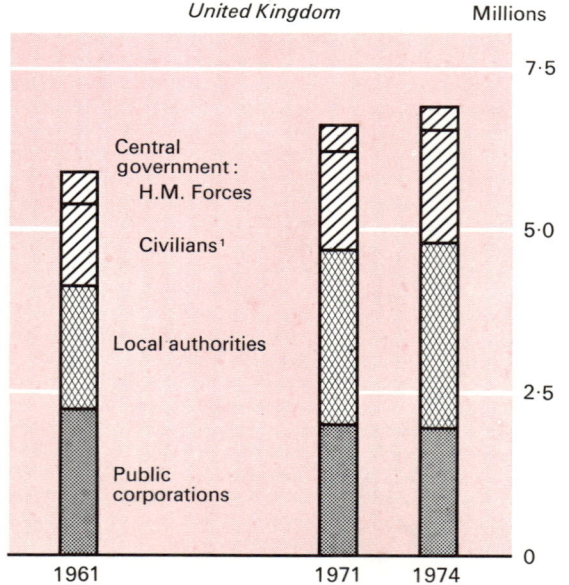

Includes civil servants.

Source: Economic Trends, February 1976

Chart 4.9
First permanent employment of all UK university degree holders

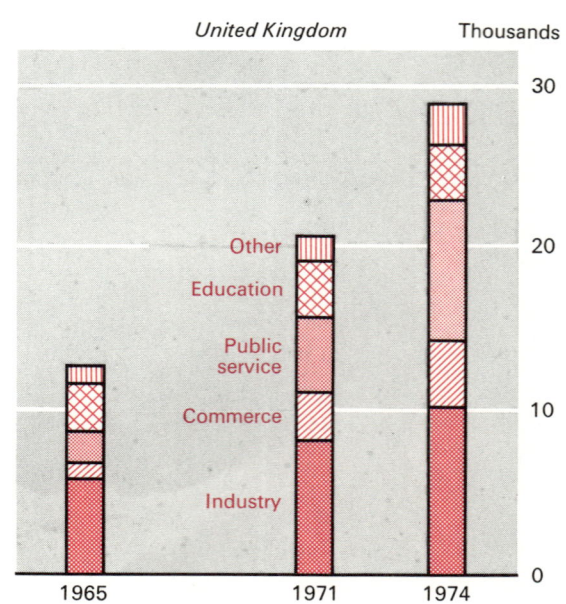

Source: Institute of Manpower Studies

Qualified population

Tables 4.10 to 4.13 show qualifications of both the whole population, by age, sex, subject group, and income. Tables 4.10 and 4.11 are from the *1971 Census*, and 4.12 and 4.13 show more recent data from the *GHS*. Special care needs to be taken in interpreting the *GHS* tables, particularly 4.13. Table 4.11 shows the general increase in percentages of people who have qualifications; these people are generally the younger age group, entering the labour force, although more and more older people (see Table 4.19 below) are taking

Open University and other courses later in life. Young people also tend to earn less than older people; this, together with the problem of inflation, makes the trends in 4.13 difficult to interpret. However, there is no doubt that those with higher qualifications, on average, earn more than people with no qualifications, although there is a large overlap in the distribution so that, in 1973, 20 per cent of people with at least a degree earned less than 25 per cent of people with no qualifications.

Table 4.10 Qualified population: by age, 1971

Great Britain   Percentages

	Males		Females		Total	
	Qualified	Highly qualified	Qualified	Highly qualified	Qualified	Highly qualified
Percentage of the population who are qualified[1] or highly qualified[2], by age:						
18–19	0·1	0·0	0·2	0·0	0·1	0·0
20–24	8·0	4·5	8·2	2·3	8·1	3·4
25–29	13·7	8·1	10·3	2·8	12·1	5·5
30–34	12·6	7·5	9·4	2·1	11·0	4·8
35–39	11·5	6·7	8·5	1·8	10·0	4·2
40–44	10·4	6·3	7·1	1·7	8·8	4·0
45–49	8·5	5·0	5·6	1·1	7·0	3·0
50–54	7·3	4·1	5·1	1·0	6·1	2·5
55–59	6·9	4·0	4·9	1·0	5·8	2·5
60–64	6·0	3·6	4·4	1·0	5·2	2·2
65–69	5·0	3·1	4·0	1·0	4·4	1·9
All ages (18–69)	8·7	5·1	6·5	1·5	7·6	3·3

[1] All qualifications obtained after age 18.   [2] First degree or higher.

Source: Census Volume of Qualified Manpower Tables, Office of Population Censuses and Surveys

Table 4.11 Qualified population: by subject group, 1971

Great Britain   Thousands and percentages

	Higher degree or equivalent	First degree or equivalent	of which[1] percentage male	Other qualifications obtained after age 18	Total	of which percentage male
Qualified manpower aged 18–69 by subject:						
Education	3·7	24·6	57	492·9	521·1	27
Health	8·6	118·2	75	508·4	635·2	24
Technology	13·7	242·6	99	205·5	461·7	99
Agriculture	1·8	13·7	84	11·7	27·2	81
Science	36·0	148·8	76	23·5	208·3	76
Social studies	13·2	231·8	83	153·1	398·2	86
Vocational studies	1·3	43·5	69	56·0	100·7	72
Language studies	9·3	112·1	45	3·3	124·7	45
Arts	6·7	52·5	64	4·6	63·8	65
Music and visual arts	1·5	46·8	38	22·6	70·9	41
Total	95·8	1,034·7	76	1,481·6	2,612·1	56

[1] i.e. first or higher degree or equivalent.
Source: Census Volume of Qualified Manpower Tables, Office of Population Censuses and Surveys
Note: Data relate to whole population over 18.

Table 4.12   Highest qualification level of those not in full-time education

	Great Britain				Percentages and numbers	
	1972			1973		
	Persons aged			Persons aged		
	30–39	40–49	50–59	30–39	40–49	50–59
Males						
Higher qualification[1]	14	7	9	13	12	9
Other qualification[2]	34	31	25	35	29	26
No qualification	52	61	66	52	59	65
Total sample size (=100%)	1,802	1,764	1,689	1,720	1,813	1,741
Females						
Higher qualification[1]	10	6	5	10	8	6
Other qualification[2]	25	20	14	27	19	16
No qualification	65	74	82	63	73	78
Total sample size (= 100%)	1,854	1,962	1,929	1,818	1,932	1,905

[1] Qualification levels 1–5 as shown in Appendix B; generally HNC and above; corresponds to census a, b, c levels.   [2] All other qualification levels 6–14 in Appendix B, page 239.   Source: General Household Survey

Table 4.13   Income by selected highest qualification levels: males[1] in full-time employment[2]

	Great Britain						Percentages and numbers		
	Degree or equivalent[3]			GCE 'O' level/ CSE Grade 1			No qualifications		
	1971	1972	1973	1971	1972	1973	1971	1972	1973
Gross annual earnings (percentages):									
Less than £500	1	1	2	8	5	5	5	5	3
£500, less than £1,000	3	4	2	19	12	12	24	15	10
£1,000 „ „ £1,500	6	7	4	28	24	18	42	38	32
£1,500, „ „ £2,000	11	10	12	24	25	23	20	27	30
£2,000, „ „ £2,500	16	13	10	11	17	20	6	10	15
£2,500, „ „ £3,000	18	18	16	4	9	11	2	3	5
£3,000 and over	44	46	54	6	9	11	2	2	5
Total sample size (=100%) (numbers)	357	364	440	1,070	745	958	4,650	4,103	4,021

[1] Aged 15 and over in 1971 and 1972; aged 16–64 in 1973.   [2] Working 31 hours or more per week (26 hours or more for teachers and lecturers).   [3] Includes professional qualifications.   Source: General Household Survey, 1971–1973

Change in jobs

Tables 4.14 and 4.15 both show changes in job or occupation during the previous 12 months. Table 4.14 is from the *1971 Census*, showing for all males, and all occupation groups, the percentage who were in the same occupation, 12 months before. Table 4.15, from the *GHS* shows that 15 per cent of all workers had changed job (but not necessarily occupation) in 1974. Other results from the *GHS*, although not included here as a table, show that people find their employment more often through informal means rather than by going through an employment agency. In 1974 56 per cent of people heard of their new job through friends or by direct approach to an employer.

Table 4.14 Occupational change, 1970 to 1971

Great Britain   Percentages and numbers

		Position in 1970				
		In same occupation	Different occupation	No occupation	Occupation not stated	Total (=100%) (thousands)
Males in employment 1971:						
I	Farmers, foresters, fishermen	91·6	3·7	3·0	1·7	623
II	Miners and quarrymen	92·3	4·0	2·1	1·6	233
III	Gas, coke, and chemical makers	90·5	6·6	1·5	1·4	122
IV	Glass and ceramic makers	88·2	6·8	2·7	2·3	60
V	Furnace, forge, foundry, rolling mill workers	90·8	5·4	1·9	1·9	151
VI	Electrical and electronic workers	91·0	4·2	3·6	1·2	514
VII	Engineering and allied trade workers nec	89·1	5·7	3·4	1·8	2,404
VIII	Woodworkers	91·0	3·9	3·2	1·9	397
IX	Leatherworkers	89·8	4·6	3·7	1·9	55
X	Textile workers	86·4	7·6	3·1	2·9	135
XI	Clothing workers	89·0	4·7	4·3	2·0	75
XII	Food, drink, and tobacco workers	88·1	5·7	4·1	2·1	250
XIII	Paper and printing workers	91·7	4·2	2·8	1·3	213
XIV	Makers of other products	84·0	8·5	4·8	2·7	198
XV	Construction workers	90·6	4·9	2·3	2·2	517
XVI	Painters and decorators	91·4	3·9	2·8	1·9	259
XVII	Drivers of stationary engines, cranes, etc.	90·2	6·4	1·6	1·8	291
XVIII	Labourers nec	80·0	9·3	6·1	4·6	964
XIX	Transport and communications workers	87·7	7·9	2·2	2·2	1,209
XX	Warehousemen, storekeepers, packers, bottlers	84·0	9·2	4·3	2·5	478
XXI	Clerical workers	86·4	7·5	5·0	1·1	1,042
XXII	Sales workers	86·3	9·1	3·1	1·5	1,146
XXIII	Service, sport, and recreation workers	84·9	8·5	4·3	2·3	864
XXIV	Administrators and managers	89·8	8·4	1·2	0·6	829
XXV	Professional, technical workers, artists	88·4	6·4	4·5	0·7	1,651
XXVI	Armed Forces (British and Foreign)	–	–	–	100·0	239
XXVII	Inadequately described occupations	44·4	3·9	4·5	47·2	99
Total		86·1	6·7	3·5	3·7	15,031

Source: Census of Population Report 1971, Office of Population Censuses and Surveys

Table 4.15 Job mobility in the last twelve months

Great Britain   Various units

	Changed jobs[1] (percentages)		Number of job changes (averages)		Total sample size (=100%) (numbers)	
	1972	1974	1972	1974	1972	1974
Age group:						
16–17	24	31	0·38	0·45	766	541
18–24	25	31	0·37	0·46	2,087	1,871
25–34	16	20	0·22	0·29	3,033	2,837
35–44	11	12	0·15	0·15	2,850	2,744
45–54	6	8	0·08	0·10	3,121	2,972
55–64	4	5	0·05	0·07	2,160	2,016
65 and over	6	6	0·08	0·06	447	464
Total	13	15	0·18	0·21	14,464	13,445
Marital status:						
Not married[2]	18	20	0·26	0·30	4,078	3,703
Married	11	13	0·15	0·17	10,386	9,751

[1] A job change means a change of employer.   [2] The 'not married' are people who are single, widowed, divorced or separated.

Source: General Household Survey, 1972 and 1974

Unemployment and retraining

The next four tables and charts are drawn from administrative data, and show trends in unemployment and retraining. Table 4.19, showing Open University students and graduates can be regarded as a type of retraining, although it is not yet clear how many students are intent on studying to obtain a new job and how many are studying for its own sake.

Chart 4.16
Unemployed [1]

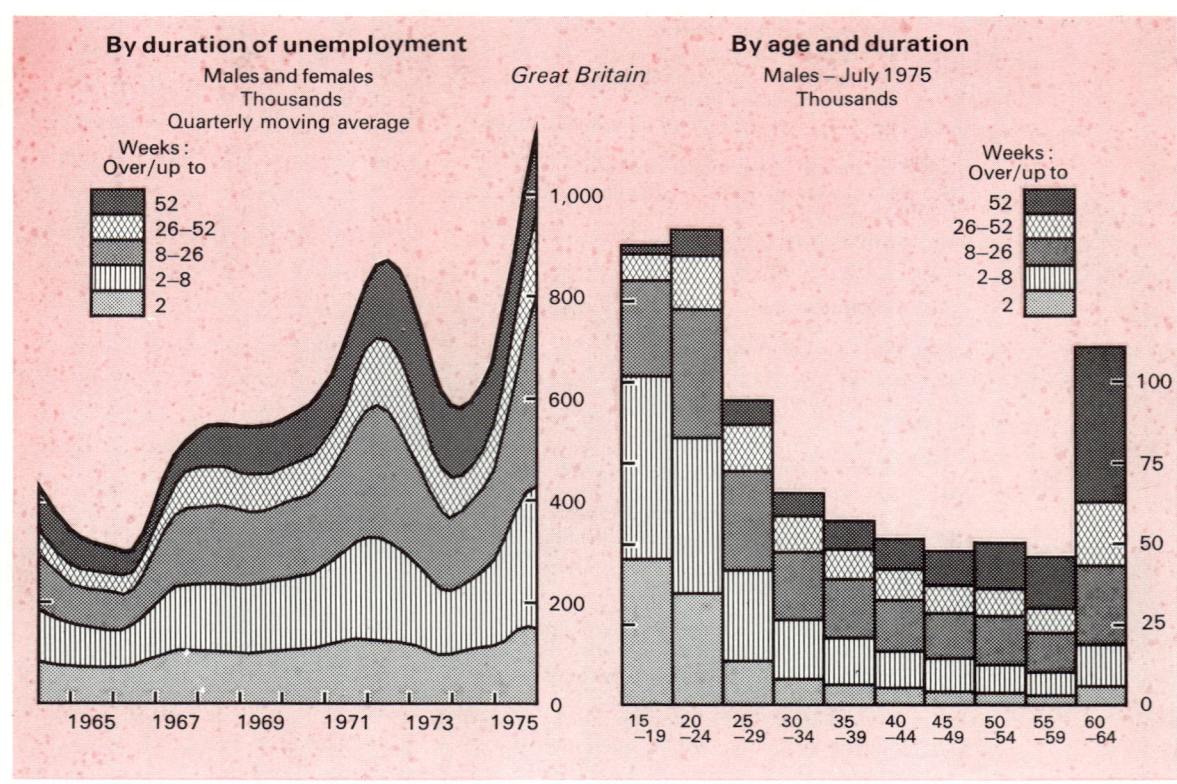

[1] Casuals were excluded prior to April 1972.

Source: Department of Employment

Table 4.17   Unemployment

	United Kingdom						Thousands and rates	
	Monthly averages						1976	
	1971	1972	1973	1974	1975		January	July
Total unemployed[1]	792·1	875·7	618·8	614·9	977·6		1,303·1	1,463·5
Percentage rate[2]	*3·5*	*3·8*	*2·7*	*2·6*	*4·2*		*5·6*	*6·3*
Total unemployed excluding school leavers— seasonally adjusted[1]	775·9	854·9	611·0	599·4	929·3		1,262·6	1,255·0
Percentage rate – seasonally adjusted[2]	*3·4*	*3·7*	*2·6*	*2·6*	*4·0*		*5·2*	*5·4*
Unemployed school leavers	16·3	20·7	7·7	15·1	48·6		40·7	208·5
Adult students registered for vacation employment	7·0	9·8	11·5	16·0	36·1		127·1	108·8

[1] Excludes adult students registered for vacation employment.   [2] As percentages of numbers of employed/unemployed employees at appropriate mid-year. The figures for 1974 include an average of 11 months for the data for Great Britain.

Sources: Department of Employment; Department of Manpower Services (Northern Ireland)

**Chart 4.18
Training under
government
schemes**

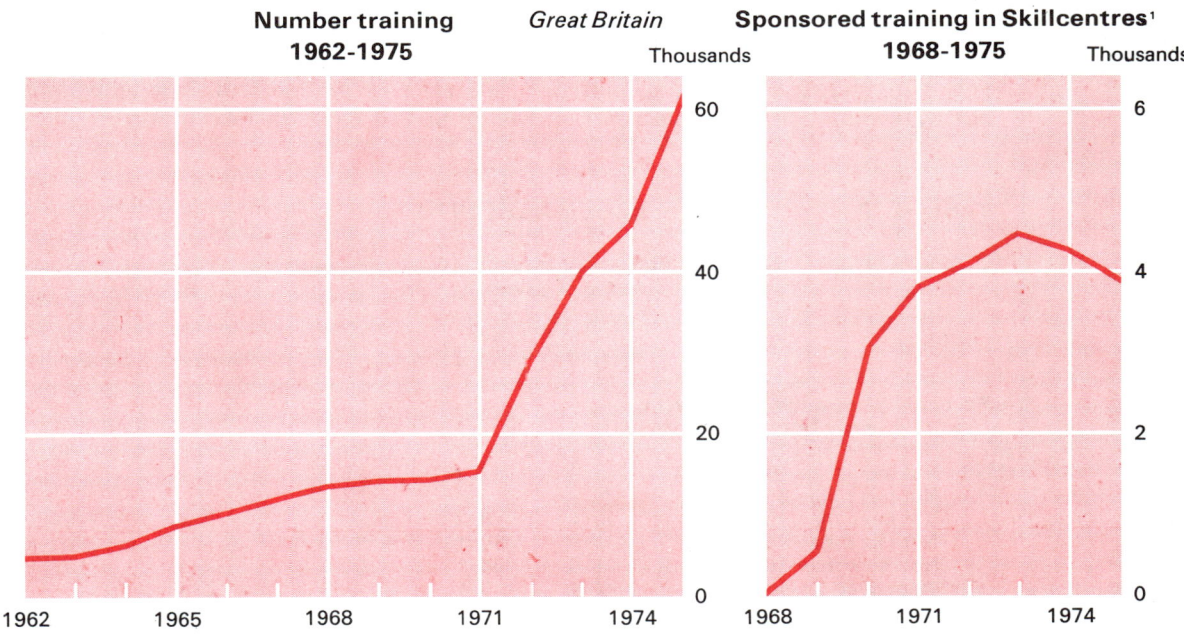

Number training *Great Britain* **Sponsored training in Skillcentres**[1]
1962-1975 **1968-1975**
Thousands Thousands

[1] Apart from trainees under the Training Opportunities Scheme (TOPS), Skillcentres also offer opportunities to employers to nominate members of their staffs for upgrading training in the construction, engineering, and certain other trades. The right-hand chart shows the numbers trained under this sponsorship scheme since its introduction in 1968.

Source: Training Services Agency

Table 4.19 Open University students: by occupation

United Kingdom Percentages and numbers

	Finally registered new students[1]				Registered continuing students[1]		
	1971	1972	1973	1974	1972	1973	1974
Housewives	10·1	13·2	13·6	14·1	10·4	12·2	13·3
Armed forces	1·7	1·9	2·7	3·1	1·7	1·8	2·0
Administrative and managerial	5·0	4·8	4·1	3·9	4·8	4·6	4·5
Teachers and lecturers	40·1	33·2	34·7	33·6	42·3	40·4	38·4
Scientific and professional	14·9	16·0	14·2	14·2	14·8	14·9	14·8
Industrial, farming, and transport	15 5	17·5	17·7	16·9	14·8	14·9	15·6
Clerical and office staff	6 4	7·8	7·6	8·3	6·2	6·6	6·8
Sales and services staff, recreation workers	2·9	3·4	3·4	3·0	2·7	2·8	2·9
Retired, independent means, students	1·5	1·8	1·5	2·2	1·4	1·4	1·4
In institutions (eg prisons, chronic sick, etc.)	0·3	0·3	0·4	0·5	0·4	0·1	0·2
No information	1·6	0·1	0·1	0·2	0·5	0·3	0·2
Total (=100%) (numbers)	19,5&1	15,716	12,680	11,336	16,186	25,744	31,300
Registered continuing students	—	16,186	25,744	31,300			
Total students	19,581	31,902	38,424	42,636			
Total graduating					903	3,630	5,026

[1] For explanation of these terms see Appendix B, page 239.

Source: Open University

Working conditions

Statistics on working conditions are difficult to obtain, as there are no easy indicators of 'bad' or 'good' conditions. We should like to measure numbers of people working underground, in wet, hot, or unpleasant conditions, but such data are not available. The indicators used in this group of tables and charts are total weekly hours (4.20 and 4.21), job satisfaction from the GHS (4.22), and industrial disputes, often a measure, albeit an inadequate one, of working conditions. A measure of amounts of shift-working is shown in Table 4.25 in the next group.

Table 4.20 Total weekly hours, April 1975[1]

	Great Britain					Percentages and averages	
	Full-time men[2]		Part-time men[2]	Full-time women[3]		Part-time women[3]	
	Manual	Non-manual		Manual	Non-manual	Manual	Non-manual
Percentage of each group with total weekly hours (percentages):							
Not more than 8	–	–	12·2	–	–	3·8	3·6
Not more than 16	–	–	35·9	–	–	20·0	17·0
Not more than 24	–	–	82·8	–	–	66·0	68·5
Not more than 32	0·1	5·2	98·6	2·7	9·6	98·7	99·0
Not more than 40	39·8	80·1	99·8	84·4	93·8	99·8	99·9
Not more than 48	72·6	94·5	100·0	97·2	99·3	100·0	100·0
48 or over	27·4	5·5	–	2·8	0·7	–	–
Average total weekly hours	*45·5*	*38·7*	*18·2*	*39·4*	*36·6*	*21·4*	*21·4*
Quantiles of total hours							
Lowest decile	*39·1*	*34·3*	*7·3*	*34·2*	*32·2*	*12·7*	*13·8*
Median	*43·0*	*37·4*	*19·6*	*39·4*	*36·7*	*20·8*	*20·6*
Highest decile	*55·5*	*44·5*	*27·2*	*42·6*	*39·8*	*29·6*	*29·6*

[1] Total weekly hours means the number of basic hours which the employee was expected to work in a normal week (normal basic hours) plus the number of hours (per week in the pay-period) for which the employee received overtime pay. People whose pay for the reference period was affected by absence are excluded.
[2] Aged 21 and over.   [3] Aged 18 and over.   Source: New Earnings Survey, 1975, Department of Employment

**Chart 4.21
Total weekly
hours, April 1975**

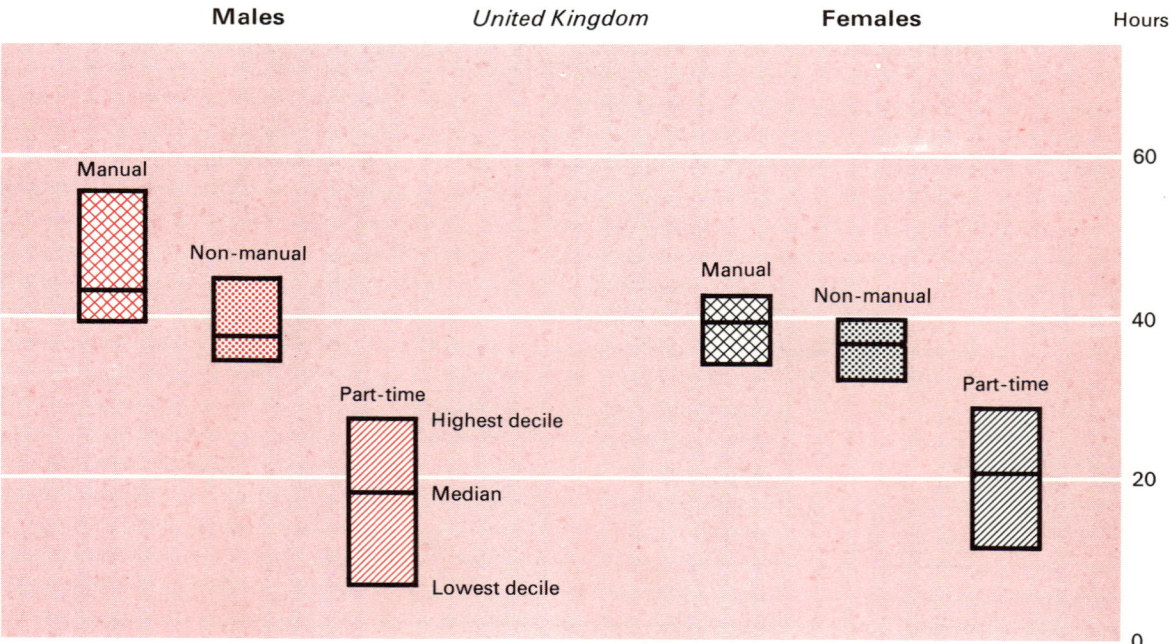

Source: New Earnings Survey, 1975, Department of Employment

Table 4.22 Job satisfaction: by sex and age group

Great Britain — Percentages and numbers

	1971 Satisfied	1971 Not satisfied[1]	1972 Satisfied	1972 Not satisfied[1]	1974 Satisfied	1974 Not satisfied[1]	Total sample size (=100%) (numbers)
By sex (percentages):							
Males	87·0	13·0	84·4	15·6	84·8	15·2	7,619
Females	91·8	8·2	88·8	11·2	89·4	10·6	4,614
By age group (percentages):							
16–17[2]	90·6	9·3	82·4	17·7	88·0	12·0	434
18–24	84·6	15·4	81·7	18·4	80·3	19·7	1,735
25–34	88·2	11·7	84·9	15·1	84·2	15·8	2,605
35–44	89·5	10·5	87·6	12·3	88·2	11·8	2,497
45–54	89·4	10·7	87·7	12·4	88·3	11·7	2,759
55–64	90·1	9·8	87·5	12·4	89·1	10·9	1,854
65 and over	95·8	4·2	93·6	6·5	95·0	5·0	340
In full-time work (percentages):	87·8	12·3	85·3	14·7	85·8	14·2	10,064
In part-time work[3] (percentages):	93·3	6·7	89·2	10·8	89·9	10·1	2,169

[1] Including those 'neither satisfied nor dissatisfied'.
[2] Prior to 1973, 15 year olds were included; the minimum school leaving age was raised to 16 from 1 September 1972.
[3] Part-time is defined here as those working 30 hours or less per week.

Source: General Household Survey

Immigrant labour force

Tables 4.23 to 4.25 show the contribution of immigrants to the labour force, as measured by the *1971 Census* and by a more recent PEP Survey: *The Facts of Racial Disadvantage, a National Survey*, D. Smith. About 6 per cent of the labour force in 1971 were immigrants, 2·2 per cent from the New Commonwealth, 1·7 per cent from Ireland, and 1·3 per cent from the rest of Europe. Table 4.24 showed how this varied from 1·3 per cent in the North of England to over 15 per cent in Greater London. Table 4.25 shows the greater tendency for immigrants to work shifts.

Table 4.23 Immigrants' contribution to labour supply[1], 1971

Great Britain — Numbers and percentages

	Males Number	Males As a percentage of all economically active males	Females Number	Females As a percentage of all economically active females	Total Number	Total As a percentage of all economically active persons
Country of birth						
New Commonwealth	384,930	2·4	170,590	1·9	555,520	2·2
of which:						
West Indies	*112,080*	*0·7*	*81,260*	*0·9*	*193,340*	*0·8*
India	*110,920*	*0·7*	*37,180*	*0·4*	*148,100*	*0·6*
Pakistan	*72,300*	*0·5*	*4,240*	*0·0*	*76,540*	*0·3*
East Africa	*17,190*	*0·1*	*9,410*	*0·1*	*26,600*	*0·1*
Rest of Africa	*21,340*	*0·1*	*13,240*	*0·1*	*34,580*	*0·1*
Other	*51,100*	*0·3*	*25,260*	*0·3*	*76,360*	*0·3*
Old Commonwealth	16,020	0·1	14,690	0·2	30,710	0·1
Irish Republic	259,990	1·6	161,140	1·8	421,130	1·7
Other EEC Countries	76,010	0·5	77,150	0·8	153,160	0·6
Other European Countries	119,630	0·8	65,710	0·7	185,340	0·7
Elsewhere	90,520	0·6	32,210	0·4	122,730	0·5
Total	947,100	6·0	521,490	5·7	1,468,590	5·9

[1] Economically active persons born outside the United Kingdom and with both parents born outside the United Kingdom.
Source: 1971 Census of Population, Office of Population Censuses and Surveys

EMPLOYMENT

Table 4.24   Geographical distribution of economically active immigrants, 1971

Great Britain   Numbers and percentages

Region/Conurbation	Economically active persons born outside the UK and with both parents born outside the UK (numbers) (a)	Total economically active population (numbers) (b)	(a) as a percentage of (b)
North	18,690	1,471,995	1·3
Tyneside Conurbation	*5,250*	*368,115*	*1·4*
Yorkshire and Humberside	90,540	2,199,595	4·1
West Yorkshire Conurbation	*60,090*	*817,685*	*7·3*
North West	130,830	3,144,630	4·2
Merseyside Conurbation	*16,970*	*579,670*	*2·9*
South East Lancashire Conurbation	*73,900*	*1,150,890*	*6·4*
East Midlands	76,640	1,593,115	4·8
West Midlands	176,530	2,464,215	7·2
West Midlands Conurbation	*119,650*	*1,171,950*	*10·2*
East Anglia	32,520	753,060	4·3
South East	828,940	8,302,075	10·0
Greater London	*602,450*	*3,845,135*	*15·7*
South West	47,780	1,654,215	2·9
Wales	24,240	1,170,680	2·1
Scotland	41,880	2,349,330	1·8
Central Clydeside Conurbation	*17,460*	*783,505*	*2·2*
Great Britain	1,468,590	25,102,915	5·9

Source: 1971 Census of Population, Office of Population Censuses and Surveys

Table 4.25   Shiftwork by country of origin: males, 1974

England and Wales   Percentages and numbers

	Whites	Ethnic minorities				
		West Indian	Pakistani/ Bangladeshi	Indian	African, Asian	Total
Type of shift worked (percentages):						
Permanent nights	1	1	8	4	3	3
Alternate two-shift system (day and night)	3	7	8	5	4	6
Alternate three-shift system	5	10	10	9	5	9
Total night shifts	9	19	27	18	12	19
Double day	3	6	9	7	7	7
Others	2	3	2	2	–	2
Type not stated	–	3	–	3	1	2
Total day shifts or type not stated	5	13	11	12	9	12
Total working shifts	15	31	38	30	20	31
Total sample size[1] (= 100%) (numbers)	1,553	2,835	1,347	1,833	1,019	7,033

[1] See note in Appendix B, page 240.   *Source: 'The Facts of Racial Disadvantage: a National Survey', Political and Economic Planning, 1976*

Personal income and wealth

This section considers statistics on income and wealth. The tables on income statistics are grouped into six sub-sections, which broadly correspond to the sources of the statistics they contain. There are several reasons for this sub-division. In the first place no single definition of income could be satisfactory for all purposes. For example, the definition of income required for an analysis of immediate command over resources would be narrower than that required for a discussion of economic welfare in a more general sense. Again the choice of income unit used, whether the individual, the family, tax unit, or household, must depend on the purpose for which the statistics are required. Although there is a wide range of income statistics available, the information does not allow a complete treatment of all sources of incomes – for example there is little on fringe benefits. Furthermore the fall in the value of money makes it difficult to analyse trends in the distribution of incomes. Statistics of wealth holdings are much less complete than those for incomes.

The recent reports of the Royal Commission on the Distribution of Income and Wealth discuss the subject in more detail and present a wider selection of statistics, on both income and wealth, than given here.

National income

The information in these two tables and charts is taken from National Accounts data published in the annual *National Income and Expenditure* Blue Book. These data are the source of estimates of the total income of the personal sector and of the economy as a whole. Table 5.1 shows the income and expenditure account of the personal sector of the economy, excluding private non-profit making bodies, and so relating to households. Chart 5.2 shows annual changes in real personal disposable income per head (see definition in Appendix B, page 240).

Table 5.1 Income and expenditure account of the personal sector, excluding private non-profit-making bodies

United Kingdom   Percentages and £ million

	1966	1968	1970	1972	1974	1975
Income						
Income from employment	71·6	70·5	71·1	70·2	70·1	72·1
Income from self-employment[1]	8·4	8·6	8·8	10·1	10·5	9·2
Rent, dividends, and net interest	11·3	11·0	10·3	9·2	9·4	8·4
Current grants from public authorities	8·2	9·5	9·4	10·1	9·7	10·0
Current transfers from non-profit-making institutions	0·5	0·4	0·4	0·4	0·3	0·3
Total personal income (=100%) (£ million)	31,845	36,052	42,815	53,576	74,940	94,554
Expenditure						
Expenditure on consumption	74·0	73·6	71·7	71·9	67·1	65·1
Current transfers to non-profit-making institutions	1·3	1·4	1·3	1·3	1·1	1·0
National Insurance and other contributions	5·7	6·0	6·2	6·2	6·7	7·2
UK taxes on income and additions to reserves	11·7	12·9	13·8	13·0	14·8	16·5
Net transfers and taxes paid abroad	0·1	0·2	0·1	0·1	0·1	0·1
Balance: saving before providing for depreciation and stock appreciation but after providing for additions to tax reserves	7·2	5·9	6·9	7·5	10·2	10·1
Total personal expenditure (=100%) (£ million)	31,845	36,052	42,815	53,576	74,940	94,554

[1] Before providing for depreciation and stock appreciation.

Source: National Income and Expenditure, Central Statistical Office

**Chart 5.2
Annual changes[1]
in real personal
disposable income
per head**

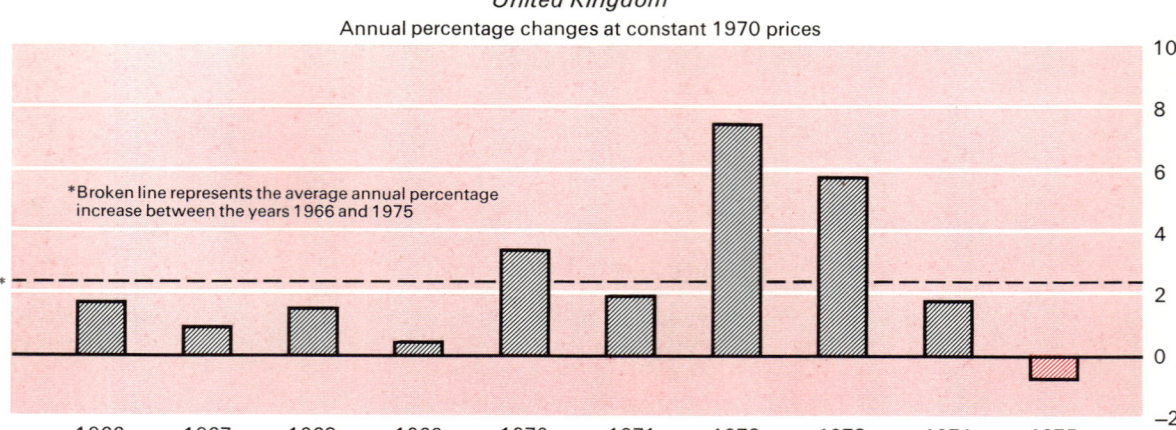

United Kingdom
Annual percentage changes at constant 1970 prices

*Broken line represents the average annual percentage increase between the years 1966 and 1975

[1] The changes shown in this chart are based on figures which have been revised in *National Income and Expenditure, 1965–1975.*

Source: National Income and Expenditure, Central Statistical Office

Personal incomes

The first three tables and charts in this section are derived from the distribution of income statistics compiled by the Central Statistical Office (CSO) and published, like the previous figures in this section, in the *National Income and Expenditure* Blue Book. The CSO distribution is the most comprehensive available, and is the only set of official statistics compiled solely for the purpose of presenting information about the distribution of personal income. The method used is described in detail in articles in *Economic Trends* in August 1975 and June 1976.

The CSO estimates are based on a number of sources, but mainly on the Survey of Personal Incomes (SPI), carried out by Inland Revenue, and the Family Expenditure Survey (FES). The SPI is a survey of administrative tax records and the FES is a personal interview survey. The reason for producing the composite, CSO, estimates is to produce a more comprehensive distribution than that provided by existing single data sources. For example the SPI, although giving comparatively good coverage of the upper tail of the income distribution, has the disadvantage that many incomes below the effective tax exemption limit

(the level at which a single person's income is subject to tax) are omitted, as are certain categories of income not liable to tax, for example supplementary benefits. Trends derived from the SPI data are affected by changes in tax provisions. Again, the FES, from which information may be derived about income below the tax threshold, national insurance benefits, and some income in kind, has a comparatively very poor coverage of high incomes, and has too low a sample size to give reliable estimates of the distribution of income. The two sources are thus deficient by themselves but together they are complementary. In addition to these sources, National Accounts data was used, providing control totals. The CSO distribution, like the SPI, is based on tax units. (Tax units are mainly individuals paying tax, but where a husband and wife's incomes are assessed together for tax purposes they are treated as one tax unit.) There is a break in the CSO data between 1967 and 1972–73, and the most recent data available are for 1973–74. No disaggregation of the CSO data has yet been carried out, and so in order to show trends in the composition of income from the various sources, and in particular the increasing importance of wives' earnings, Table 5.5 uses data from the SPI.

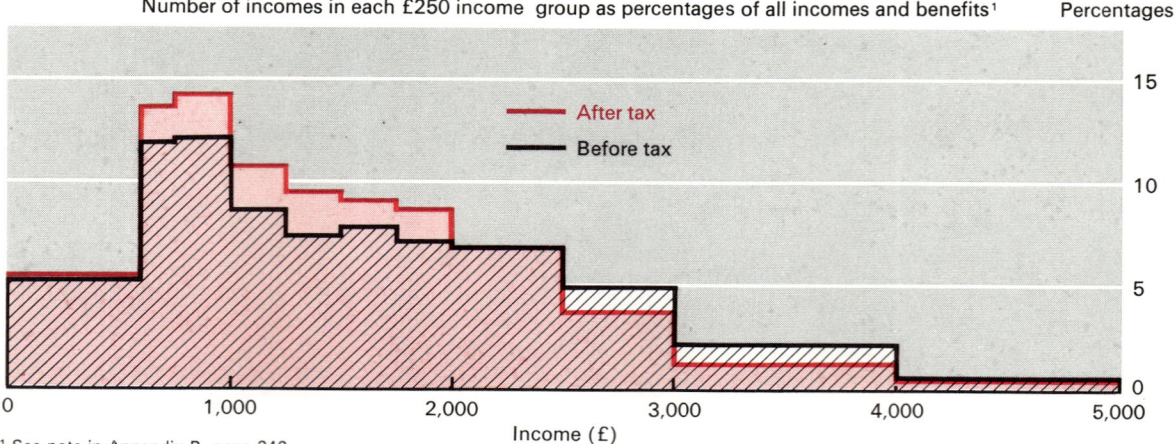

Number of incomes in each £250 income group as percentages of all incomes and benefits[1]   Percentages

After tax
Before tax

Income (£)

[1] See note in Appendix B, page 242.

Source: Central Statistical Office

Table 5.4 Distribution of personal incomes before and after tax, 1973–74

United Kingdom   Various units

	Pre-tax income by pre-tax range		Post-tax income by post-tax range	
	Numbers (thousand tax-units)	Amounts (£million)	Numbers (thousand tax-units)	Amounts (£million)
Income ranges				
Lower limit of range (£)				
Under 595	3,579	1,800	3,589	1,803
595	2,091	1,486	2,364	1,674
750	3,408	3,027	3,964	3,499
1,000	2,420	2,723	2,981	3,351
1,250	2,068	2,838	2,657	3,642
1,500	2,184	3,546	2,524	4,101
1,750	2,036	3,814	2,417	4,524
2,000	3,800	8,509	3,755	8,370
2,500	2,764	7,534	2,035	5,539
3,000	2,415	8,209	1,229	4,181
4,000	699	3,102	288	1,280
5,000	234	1,279	133	726
6,000	204	1,409	125	858
8,000	85	760	41	365
10,000	49	530	13	137
12,000	38	505	5	72
15,000	27	456	2	32
20,000 and over	22	692	1	18
All ranges	28,123	52,219	28,123	44,172

	Pre-tax income	Post-tax income
	(Percentages)	(Percentages)
Quantile shares		
Top 1%	6·5	4·5
2– 5%	10·6	9·8
6–10%	9·7	9·3
Top 10%	26·8	23·6
11–20%	15·6	15·5
21–30%	13·0	13·2
31–40%	11·2	11·2
41–50%	9·3	9·5
51–60%	7·5	7·8
61–70%	5·8	6·4
71–80%	4·7	5·4
81–90%	3·5	4·1
91–100%	2·6	3·2
Median (£)	*1,550*	*1,348*

Source: Central Statistical Office

Table 5.5 Sources of total income[1]

United Kingdom   Percentages

	1959–60	1964–65	1969–70	1970–71	1971–72	1972–73	1973–74
Profits and professional earnings	7·9	7·2	7·6	7·6	7·7	7·6	8·0
Employment income excluding wives'	72·6	73·3	72·1	71·9	70·6	71·6	70·6
Wives' employment income	6·8	7·3	8·0	8·6	9·9	9·7	9·9
Pensions	3·2	3·9	4·6	4·4	4·9	4·8	4·8
Family allowances	0·8	0·7	1·0	0·9	0·8	0·7	0·6
Investment income[2]	8·7[3]	7·6	6·7	6·6	6·1	5·6	6·1

[1] Above the deduction card limit.   [2] Includes the tax charged at the composite rate on interest paid by building societies from 1969–70 onwards.   [3] Includes the imputed income from owner-occupied houses.

Source: Survey of Personal Incomes, Board of Inland Revenue

**Chart 5.6
Distribution of
personal income,
quantile shares,
1961 to 1973-74**

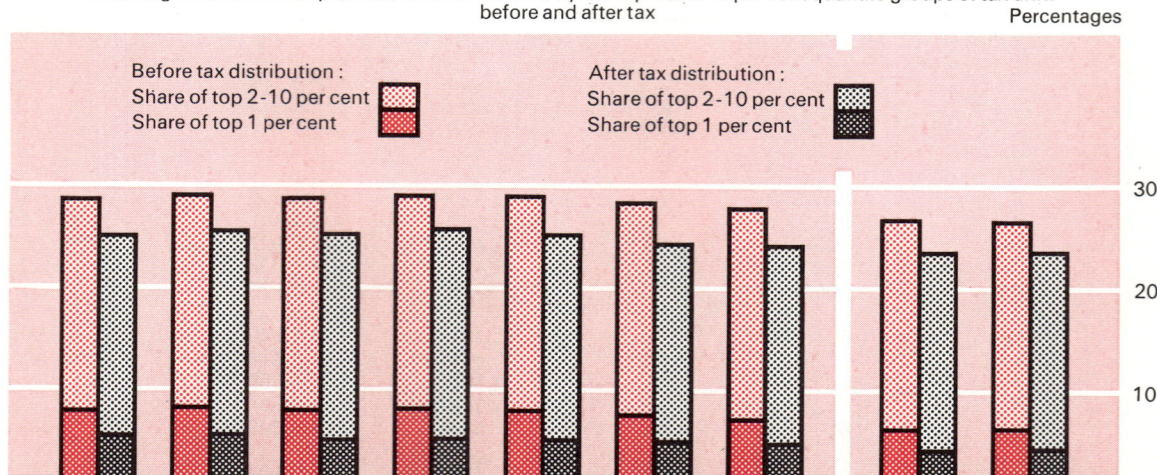

United Kingdom
Percentage shares of total personal income received by the top 1 and 10 per cent quantile groups of tax units
before and after tax
Percentages

Before tax distribution :
Share of top 2-10 per cent
Share of top 1 per cent

After tax distribution :
Share of top 2-10 per cent
Share of top 1 per cent

1961 1962 1963 1964 1965 1966 1967 1972-73 1973-74

Source: Central Statistical Office

Household income

The previous set of tables and charts was based on tax units. However for many purposes the most practical unit to take, when considering resources available to people, is the household. The main source of data on household incomes is the Family Expenditure Survey (FES). This is a continuous, personal interview survey which covers all types of private households in the United Kingdom. Its primary purpose is the analysis of expenditure patterns for use in the construction of the Retail Price Index, but the range of questions in the survey also includes questions on income. The FES covers a wide range of household income, including incomes below the effective tax limit and some forms of income not liable to tax.

Imputed rent based on rateable values is added to the income of owner-occupied households. Like any other voluntary sample survey, the FES suffers from the problems of non-response and sampling error.

Table 5.7 shows the distribution of household income for each of the main household types. Chart 5.8 shows the distribution of income for active and non-active households separately and Chart 5.9 shows the distribution of income for active households with and without children. The contributions of each of the main sources of household incomes are illustrated in Table 5.10.

Table 5.7 Household income by main household type, 1975

United Kingdom   Percentages and numbers

Type of household	Under 20	20 –30	30 –40	40 –50	50 –60	60 –80	80 –100	100 –120	over 120	Total in sample (=100%) (numbers)
One adult aged 65 or over	67	18	7	3	2	1	1	–	1	811
One adult aged under 65	24	14	14	13	12	13	5	3	2	630
One man, one woman, head aged 65 or over	3	42	23	10	7	7	4	1	3	714
One man, one woman, head aged under 65	2	3	5	8	11	24	20	13	14	1,297
One man, one woman, one child	–	3	4	8	13	33	19	10	10	684
One man, one woman, two children	–	2	4	7	11	29	25	11	11	1,034
One man, one woman, three children	–	1	1	6	11	29	23	13	16	380
Two adults, four or more children	–	2	6	9	12	27	23	10	11	211

Source: Family Expenditure Survey, Department of Employment

hart 5.8
istribution of house-
old incomes: active
nd non-active house-
olds, 1974

United Kingdom

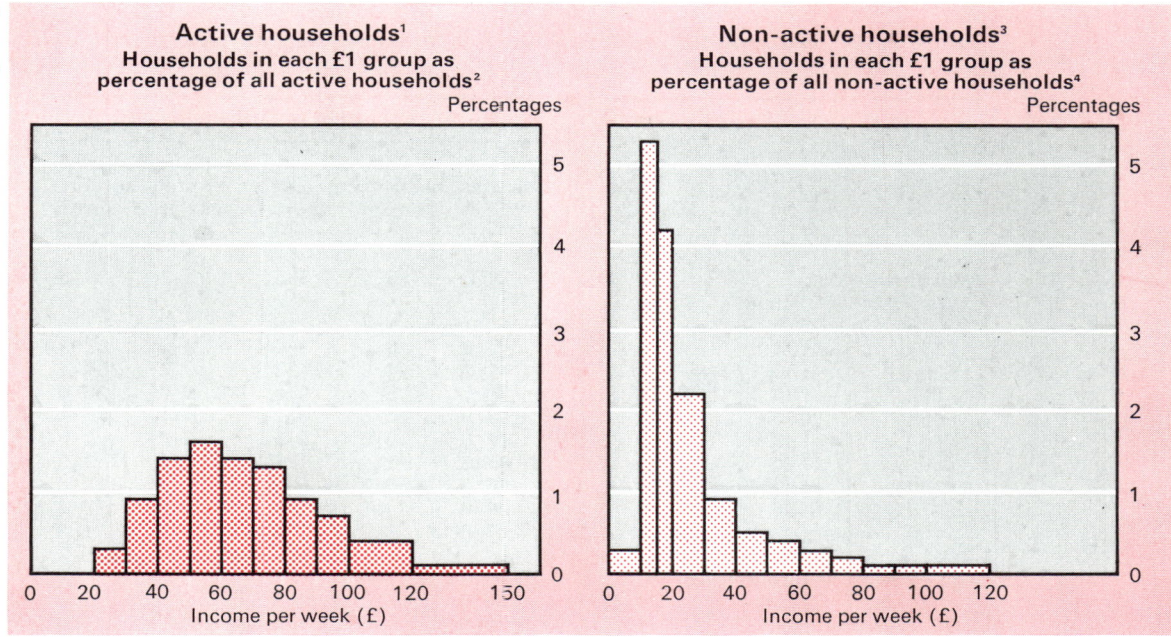

Active households[1]
Households in each £1 group as
percentage of all active households[2]
Percentages

Non-active households[3]
Households in each £1 group as
percentage of all non-active households[4]
Percentages

Income per week (£)

Income per week (£)

[1] Active households are defined here to be households where the head is in full-time employment. with incomes over £150 per week are not shown. [3] Non-active households are defined here to be households where the head is over the national insurance pension age, is retired, and unoccupied. [4] The 0·5 per cent of non-active households with incomes over £150 per week are not shown.

[2] The 3 per cent of active households

Source: Family Expenditure Survey, Department of Employment

hart 5.9
istribution of house-
old incomes: active
ouseholds[1] with and
ithout children, 1974

United Kingdom

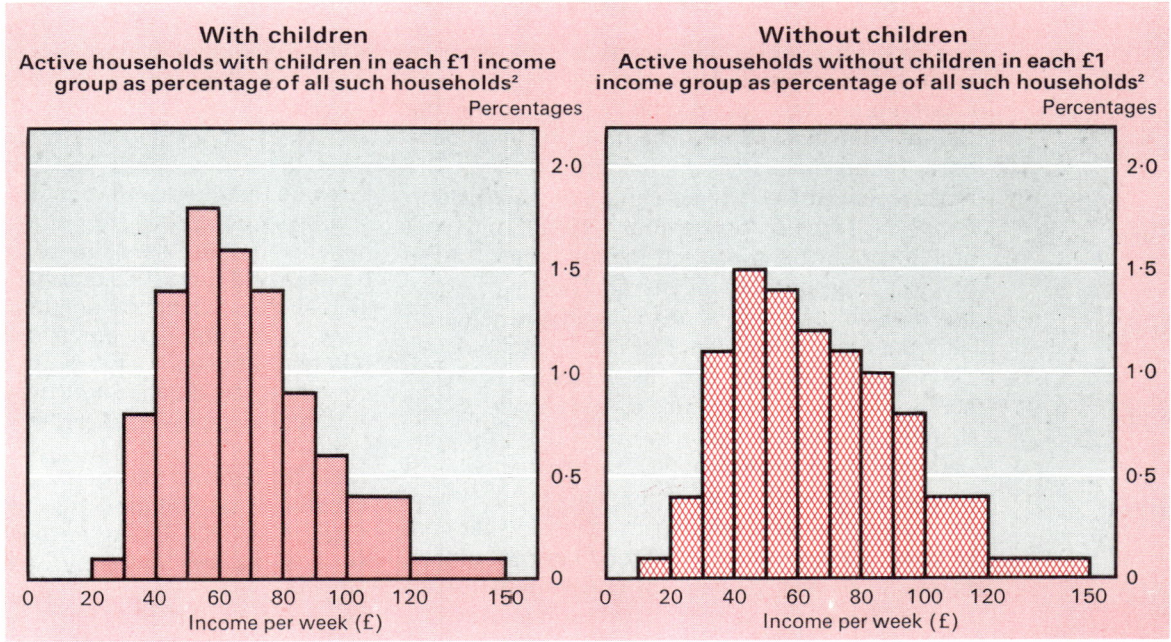

With children
Active households with children in each £1 income
group as percentage of all such households[2]
Percentages

Without children
Active households without children in each £1
income group as percentage of all such households[2]
Percentages

Income per week (£)

Income per week (£)

[1] Active households are defined here to be households where the head is in full-time employment. incomes over £150 per week are not shown. [2] The 3 per cent of households with

Source: Family Expenditure Survey, Department of Employment

Table 5.10 Household income: average weekly income by source, 1975

United Kingdom   £s and percentages

	Average total weekly income (=100%)	Percentages of total weekly income						Percentage of all households
		Wages and salaries	Self-employ-ment	Invest-ments	Annuities and pensions	Social security benefits	Other sources	
	£							
All households:	72·87	74·8	5·5	3·5	2·3	9·6	4·3	100·0
Weekly income range:								
Under £15	12·79	1·1	1·7	2·9	1·8	85·3	7·2	3·7
£15 but under £20	17·46	2·8	0·6	3·0	3·0	83·3	7·3	7·0
£20 „ „ £30	24·83	11·1	4·0	4·3	6·3	67·1	7·2	9·7
£30 „ „ £40	34·96	35·5	5·2	6·1	9·0	36·6	7·6	7·4
£40 „ „ £60	50·73	66·5	7·0	3·7	4·2	13·1	5·5	16·1
£60 „ „ £80	69·83	79·9	5·5	2·2	2·4	5·8	4·2	18·8
£80 „ „ £100	89·41	85·3	4·0	1·9	1·6	3·3	3·9	14·5
£100„ „ £120	108·93	86·3	3·8	2·3	1·3	3·0	3·3	9·6
£120„ „ £150	133·15	85·0	4·8	3·0	1·2	2·4	3·6	7·0
£150 or more	195·87	77·0	9·3	7·4	1·2	1·8	3·3	6·2
Age of head of household:								
Under 30	73·88	86·6	5·7	0·8	–	2·4	4·5	14·6
30 and under 50	91·58	83·6	6·8	1·5	0·2	3·6	4·3	34·3
50 and under 65	80·63	78·0	5·1	4·4	2·4	6·7	3·4	26·5
65 and over	37·86	24·3	2·1	11·4	12·0	44·7	5·5	24·6

Source: Family Expenditure Survey, Department of Employment

Redistribution of income

The following tables and charts are drawn from extended analyses of household income and expenditure data performed annually by the Central Statistical Office. The basic information is drawn from the Family Expenditure Survey. The most recent analysis is contained in an article in *Economic Trends* of February 1976, and that article should be consulted for full details of the analysis. The purpose of the analysis is to show the redistributive effect of taxes and benefits on different types of households. The households are divided up according to a classification which in some respects approximates to a life-cycle classification. It is not possible to find a basis for allocating all taxes or all benefits to particular types of households and, indeed, in the most recent estimates available, relating to 1974, 37 per cent of total public expenditure and 52 per cent of total taxation were allocated to households. These figures have no special significance but one consequence of them is that, on average, house-

holds are shown in the tables as paying more in taxes than they receive in benefits.

The taxes concerned are of three types: direct, indirect on final goods and services, and indirect taxes on intermediate products. Corporation taxes and taxes on capital are not included. Half of the benefits are in the form of cash benefits and housing and food subsidies. Others are benefits in kind such as education and health services. Many benefits in kind are not allocated between the different household types: the main categories concerned are defence and environment spending, and capital expenditure on the social services.

Table 5.11 shows the combined effect of taxes and benefits at several different income levels. These data are also illustrated in Chart 5.14 which gives an analysis by household type as well as by income range. Charts 5.12 and 5.13 illustrate trends in the pattern of taxes and benefits and in their effects on original income.

Table 5.11 Redistribution of income through taxes and benefits, 1974, all households[1,2]

United Kingdom
Numbers and £ per year

	Under 381	381–	557–	816·	1,194–	1,749–	2,561–	3,750–	5,490 and above	Average over all income ranges
					Range of original income					
Average in each range of original income (£ per year):										
Original income[3]	104	462	678	1,011	1,488	2,175	3,120	4,466	7,639	2,719
Direct benefits in cash: (+)										
Family allowance	6	5	7	9	20	23	28	26	25	20
Pensions[4]	551	649	510	445	216	115	75	45	70	209
Unemployment benefit	5	4	15	20	19	9	8	5	4	8
Sickness and industrial injury benefit	4	10	8	20	30	21	17	13	9	15
Family income supplement	–	–	–	2	4	1	–	–	–	1
Supplementary benefit	157	42	67	34	38	14	10	11	2	40
Other cash benefits[5]	5	1	8	5	6	6	4	2	1	3
Original income and cash benefits	833	1,172	1,292	1,546	1,820	2,364	3,263	4,570	7,752	3,017
Direct taxes: (−)										
National insurance, employees' contributions	1	4	7	26	60	100	138	181	223	105
Income tax and surtax	3	18	54	90	143	260	421	693	1,458	402
Disposable income	828	1,151	1,233	1,432	1,617	2,004	2,704	3,696	6,071	2,509
Indirect benefits (housing and food subsidies) (+)	95	61	68	71	90	71	67	63	50	72
Indirect taxes (−)	173	238	263	317	371	452	578	726	1,019	507
Income after all taxes and transfers	750	973	1,037	1,185	1,336	1,623	2,193	3,033	5,101	2,074
Direct benefits in kind: (+)										
Education	82	60	97	131	176	207	258	269	346	208
National health service	143	166	144	145	153	162	158	156	168	156
Welfare foods	6	5	8	6	9	11	13	11	12	10
Income after all taxes and benefits	981	1,203	1,285	1,468	1,675	2,003	2,623	3,470	5,627	2,448
By type of household										
Average net benefits received (+) less average taxes paid (−):[6]										
1 adult – retired	+ 656	+450	+345	+129	+ 93	–203				+555
2 adults – retired	+1,016	+848	+675	+541	+363	+ 79	365			+750
1 adult – non-retired	+ 814	+427	+251	+ 13	– 315	–716	–1,016	–1,668	–3,021	–365
2 adults – non-retired	+ 796	+881	+673	+477	– 32	–459	–892	–1,450	–2,592	–836
2 adults, 1 child				+668	+ 70	–323	–676	–1,162	–3,008	–642
2 adults, 2 children	+1,890				+331	–116	–430	–823	–1,757	–435
2 adults, 3 children					+736	+237	– 58	–397	–1,646	– 89
2 adults, 4 children					+1,140	+796	+344	– 93	–1,240	+424
All households	+ 877	+740	+607	+457	+187	–172	–496	–996	–2,012	–271
Number in sample	1,116	177	213	262	502	1,112	1,580	1,178	555	6,695

[1] These estimates are based on the Family Expenditure Survey. See definition in Appendix B, page 241.
[2] Includes some types of household covered by the Survey but not here specified in detail.
[3] See definition in Appendix B, page 241.
[4] National insurance, retirement and widows' pensions, including supplementary allowances where these are not separately distinguished, war and disability pensions, and invalidity pensions and allowances.
[5] Including maternity benefit, death grant, redundancy payments, and supplementary allowances where separately distinguished.
[6] Blank spaces indicate sample size too small for estimate to be made.

Source: Central Statistical Office

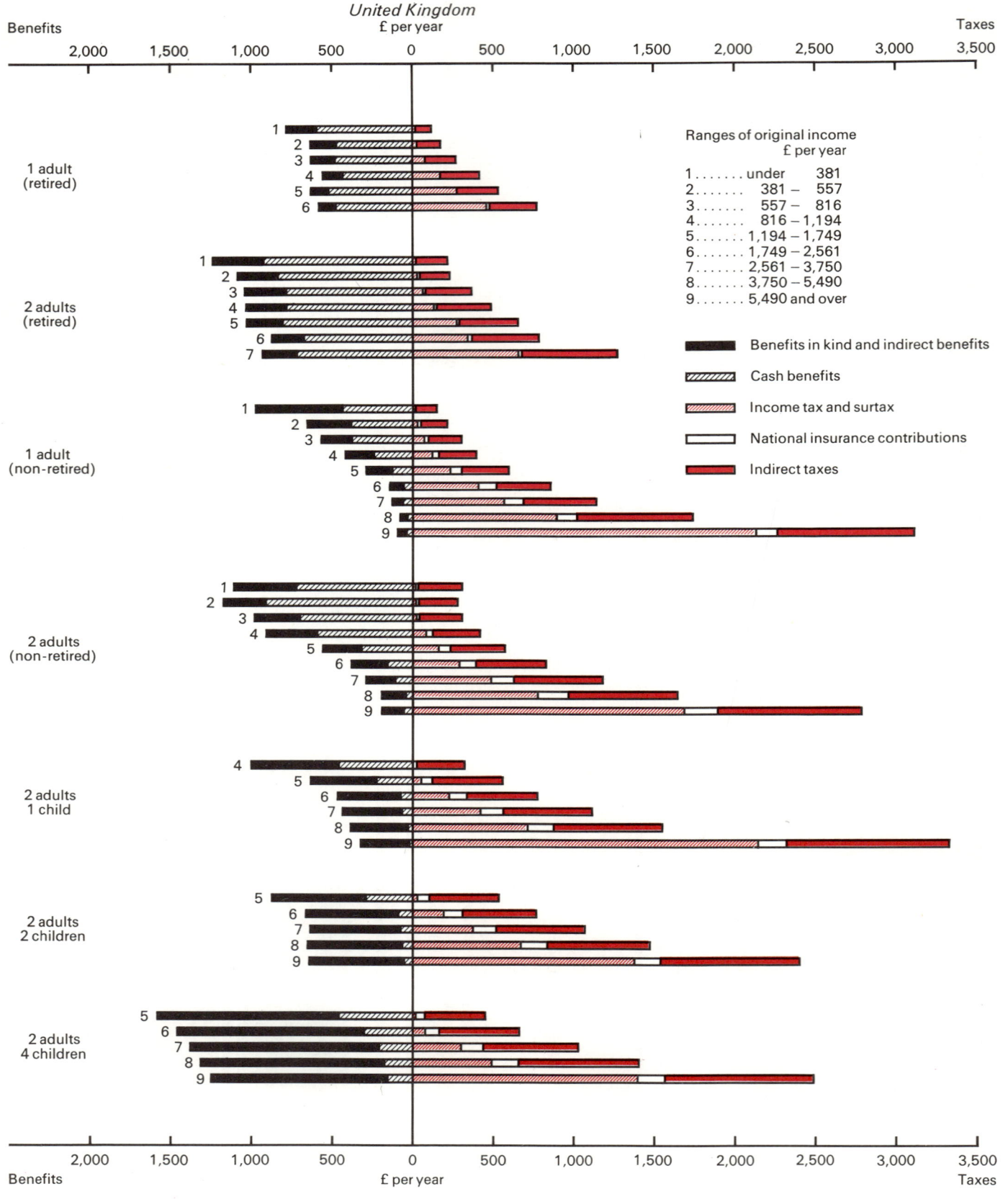

Chart 5.12   Average taxes paid and benefits received by retired and non-retired households in different income ranges, 1974

United Kingdom
£ per year

Benefits — Taxes

Ranges of original income
£ per year

1 . . . . under   381
2 . . . . . .   381 —   557
3 . . . . . .   557 —   816
4 . . . . . .   816 — 1,194
5 . . . . . . 1,194 — 1,749
6 . . . . . . 1,749 — 2,561
7 . . . . . . 2,561 — 3,750
8 . . . . . . 3,750 — 5,490
9 . . . . . . 5,490 and over

Benefits in kind and indirect benefits

Cash benefits

Income tax and surtax

National insurance contributions

Indirect taxes

1 adult
(retired)

2 adults
(retired)

1 adult
(non-retired)

2 adults
(non-retired)

2 adults
1 child

2 adults
2 children

2 adults
4 children

Source: Central Statistical Office

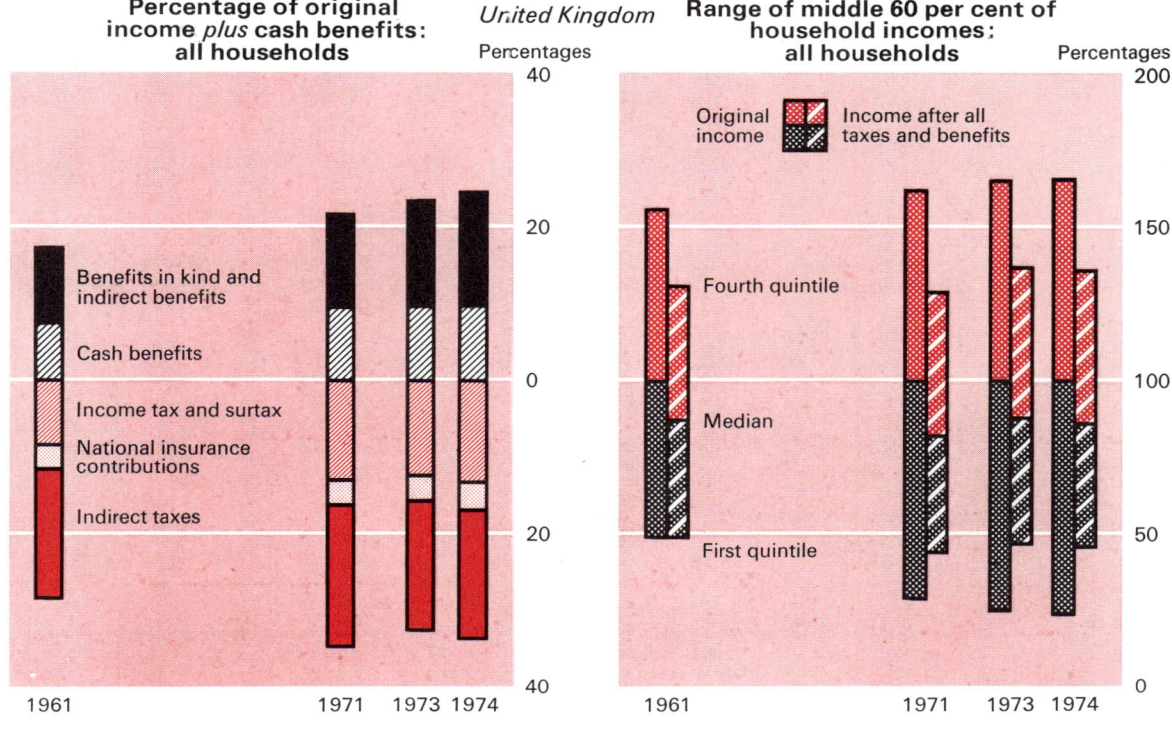

Chart 5.13
Original income and income after all taxes and benefits, 1961 to 1974

Percentage of original income *plus* cash benefits: all households

United Kingdom
Percentages

- Benefits in kind and indirect benefits
- Cash benefits
- Income tax and surtax
- National insurance contributions
- Indirect taxes

1961   1971 1973 1974

Source: Central Statistical Office

Chart 5.14
Average taxes paid and benefits received 1961 to 1974

Range of middle 60 per cent of household incomes: all households

Percentages[1]

Original income / Income after all taxes and benefits

Fourth quintile

Median

First quintile

1961   1971 1973 1974

[1] Figures are expressed as percentages of median of the original income for each year.

Source: Central Statistical Office

Earnings

As shown in Table 5.1, about 70 per cent of total personal income (excluding private non-profit-making bodies) comes from the category 'Employment'. Statistics on earnings thus cover a considerable part of total personal income, and the New Earnings Survey (NES) carried out by the Department of Employment allows the distribution of earnings to be analysed in some detail, in particular into distributions for manual and non-manual workers separately. The first six tables and charts are taken directly from the NES, and all relate to the gross weekly earnings of full-time workers. Table 5.15 shows the changes in the dispersion of gross weekly earnings in the most recent years and Chart 5.16 shows the relative changes in median gross earnings for some major groups of workers. Table 5.20, showing the percentage increases in median gross earnings, is drawn from the matched sample of the NES. The rises in gross earnings may be compared with the rises in the General Index of Retail Prices shown in the Expenditure section, and trends in the two series for the last five years are also shown in the Social Commentary (Figure IX).

The effect of taxation on gross earnings varies according to individual circumstances. Trends in net earnings for a hypothetical case are shown in the Social Commentary (Figure XI). Table 5.21 shows trends in the proportion of income taken in direct taxation for the same hypothetical household at various levels of income. This household consists of a married couple, with two children under 11 years of age, whose income comes only from the husband's occupation and family allowances. For any given level of the husband's earnings it is then possible to calculate the proportion of income taken by direct taxation. This proportion is shown in Table 5.21 for several different years and for four different income levels, which are related to the average gross weekly earnings of manual workers, as derived from the Department of Employment's October earnings enquiry. (Figures from the October earnings enquiry are available for a long run of years, while the NES began only in 1970.)

Table 5.15 Gross weekly earnings of full-time workers[1]

Great Britain   £ and percentages

	Men aged 21 and over					Women aged 18 and over				
	1968	1970	1972	1974[2]	1975	1968	1970	1972	1974[2]	1975
Manual workers										
£										
Highest decile	33·1	37·7	45·9	60·3	76·9	16·0	18·5	23·9	32·5	43·8
Upper quartile	27·4	31·3	38·3	50·6	64·5	13·1	15·4	19·9	27·2	37·1
Median	22·4	25·6	31·3	41·8	53·2	10·8	12·8	16·4	22·7	31·0
Lower quartile	18·2	20·8	25·5	34·4	44·1	9·0	10·6	13·5	18·8	25·8
Lowest decile	15·1	17·2	21·2	28·7	36·8	7·7	8·8	11·3	15·7	21·2
As percentage of median										
Highest decile	*147·8*	*147·2*	*146·6*	*144·1*	*144·4*	*148·3*	*144·8*	*145·9*	*143·4*	*141·4*
Upper quartile	*122·3*	*122·3*	*122·3*	*121·0*	*121·3*	*121·1*	*120·1*	*121·6*	*119·8*	*119·6*
Lower quartile	*81·0*	*81·1*	*81·3*	*82·2*	*82·8*	*83·4*	*83·0*	*82·5*	*83·0*	*83·3*
Lowest decile	*67·3*	*67·3*	*67·6*	*68·6*	*69·2*	*71·1*	*69·0*	*68·9*	*69·1*	*68·4*
Non-manual workers										
£										
Highest decile	49·6	55·0	66·8	83·1	103·1	24·8	27·6	34·4	42·3	61·6
Upper quartile	36·5	41·1	50·5	63·1	80·2	18·3	20·6	26·0	33·4	45·7
Median	27·8	31·4	38·5	48·5	61·8	14·1	15·9	20·1	26·1	35·9
Lower quartile	21·1	24·2	29·6	37·6	47·9	11·1	12·4	15·8	20·7	28·8
Lowest decile	17·0	19·4	23·7	30·5	38·7	9·3	10·2	12·9	17·4	23·9
As percentage of median										
Highest decile	*178·5*	*175·1*	*173·7*	*171·6*	*166·7*	*175·5*	*173·7*	*170·9*	*162·0*	*171·5*
Upper quartile	*131·1*	*130·8*	*131·3*	*130·2*	*129·6*	*129·3*	*129·4*	*129·1*	*127·9*	*127·2*
Lower quartile	*75·9*	*77·1*	*76·8*	*77·6*	*77·5*	*78·8*	*78·3*	*78·2*	*79·4*	*80·3*
Lowest decile	*61·2*	*61·8*	*61·7*	*62·9*	*62·6*	*65·4*	*64·2*	*64·0*	*66·5*	*66·5*

[1] These figures relate to men aged 21 and over and women aged 18 and over whose pay for the survey period was not affected by absence. The survey period was in September in 1968, and in April in 1970 and subsequent years.   [2] Estimates for 1974 were affected by under-representation of local authority and National Health Service employees in the New Earnings Survey sample.

Source: New Earnings Survey, 1975, Department of Employment

Chart 5.16
Relative changes in median gross weekly earnings of full-time workers

Great Britain

Ratios of median gross weekly earnings[1,2]

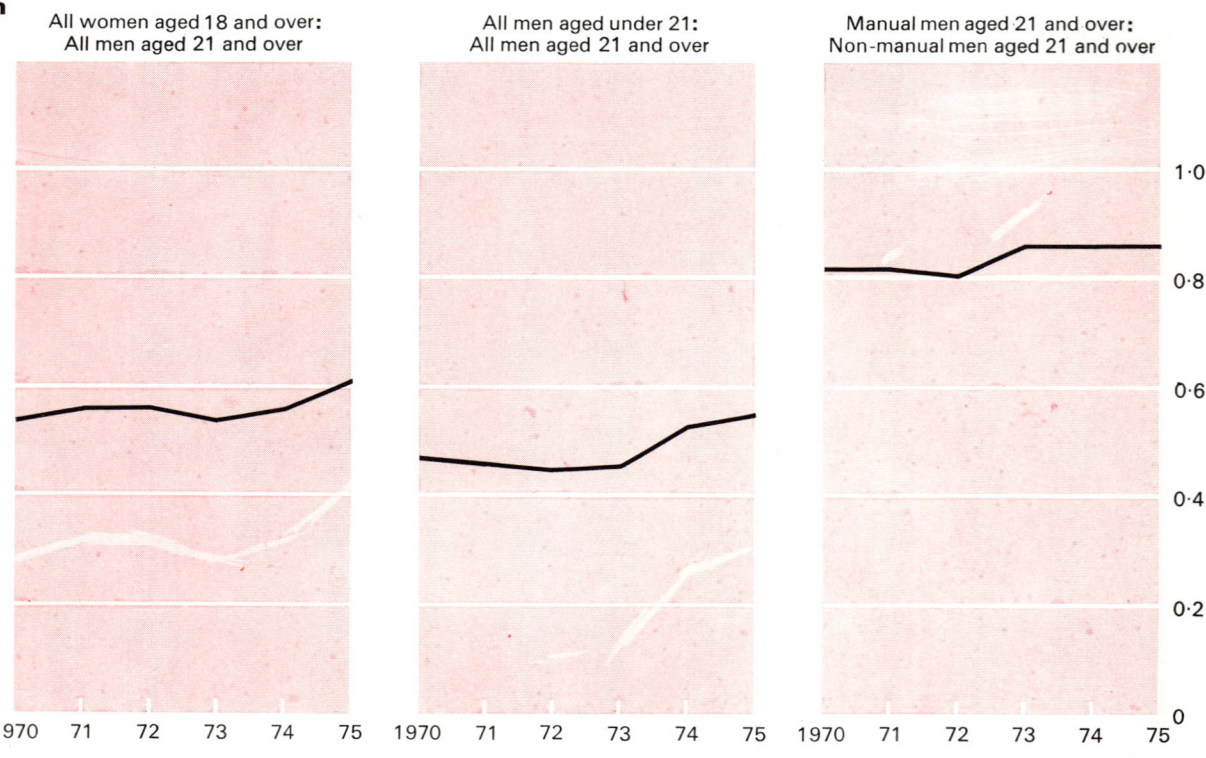

All women aged 18 and over:
All men aged 21 and over

All men aged under 21:
All men aged 21 and over

Manual men aged 21 and over:
Non-manual men aged 21 and over

[1] Full-time workers whose pay during the survey period was not affected by absence.   [2] The figures relate to April each year.

Source: New Earnings Survey, 1975, Department of Employment

Table 5.17 Cumulative distribution of gross weekly earnings of full-time workers, April 1975

Great Britain — Millions

	Men (21 and over)			Women (18 and over)		
	Manual	Non-manual	Total	Manual	Non-manual	Total
Total employees in employment	7·2	4·3	11·5	1·7	3·5	5·2
Employees in employment excluding those whose pay for the survey reference period was affected by absence						
—total	6·2	4·1	10·3	1·3	3·3	4·7
—with gross weekly earnings[1] less than: £						
20	—	—	—	0·1	0·1	0·2
25	—	—	0·1	0·3	0·4	0·7
30	0·1	0·1	0·2	0·6	1·0	1·6
35	0·4	0·2	0·7	0·9	1·6	2·5
40	1·0	0·5	1·5	1·1	2·1	3·2
45	1·7	0·8	2·5	1·2	2·5	3·7
50	2·5	1·2	3·7	1·3	2·7	4·0
55	3·4	1·6	5·0	1·3	2·9	4·2
60	4·1	1·9	6·0	1·3	3·0	4·3
70	5·1	2·6	7·7	1·3	3·1	4·5
80	5·7	3·1	8·8	1·3	3·2	4·6
100	6·1	3·7	9·8	1·3	3·3	4·6
200	6·2	4·1	10·3	1·3	3·3	4·7

[1] Earnings include overtime pay and other additions relating to the survey reference period. They exclude earnings from subsidiary employment, income in kind, and tips.
Source: New Earnings Survey, 1975, Department of Employment

Table 5.18 Gross weekly earnings of full-time workers[1]: by age, April 1975

Great Britain — £

	Manual workers			Non-manual workers		
	Lower quartile	Median	Upper quartile	Lower quartile	Median	Upper quartile
Males						
Under 18	19·4	23·4	28·9	18·6	22·2	26·2
18 and under 21	30·6	38·0	47·3	25·9	31·0	38·1
21 „ „ 25	40·9	49·2	59·3	37·3	44·5	53·1
25 „ „ 30	44·3	53·8	64·9	47·5	57·0	68·6
30 „ „ 40	46·9	56·2	67·9	54·5	67·5	83·9
40 „ „ 50	45·7	55·1	66·8	54·6	70·6	90·7
50 „ „ 60	43·2	52·4	63·4	49·0	64·6	85·9
60 „ „ 65	39·9	48·4	58·4	41·7	54·8	73·7
65 and over	33·4	42·3	51·6	36·2	47·1	64·3
All ages	41·3	51·7	63·4	45·8	60·1	78·6
Females						
Under 18	19·1	23·0	28·2	18·3	20·8	24·5
18 and under 21	23·0	28·1	33·5	23·8	27·8	32·4
21 „ „ 25	26·4	31·7	37·4	29·9	35·1	41·5
25 „ „ 30	26·3	32·2	38·6	32·3	39·6	49·6
30 „ „ 40	25·8	31·7	38·4	31·1	38·8	52·1
40 „ „ 50	26·3	31·6	37·6	30·1	37·9	50·8
50 „ „ 60	26·4	31·0	36·8	30·3	38·1	48·9
60 „ „ 65	25·3	30·7	36·8	27·5	37·7	48·7
65 and over	21·2	26·3	31·0	24·5	31·4	40·7
All ages	25·3	30·7	36·8	27·7	34·9	44·7

[1] Whose earnings in the reference period were not affected by absence.
Source: New Earnings Survey, 1975, Department of Employment

**Chart 5.19
Distribution of
gross weekly
earnings,
April 1975[1]**

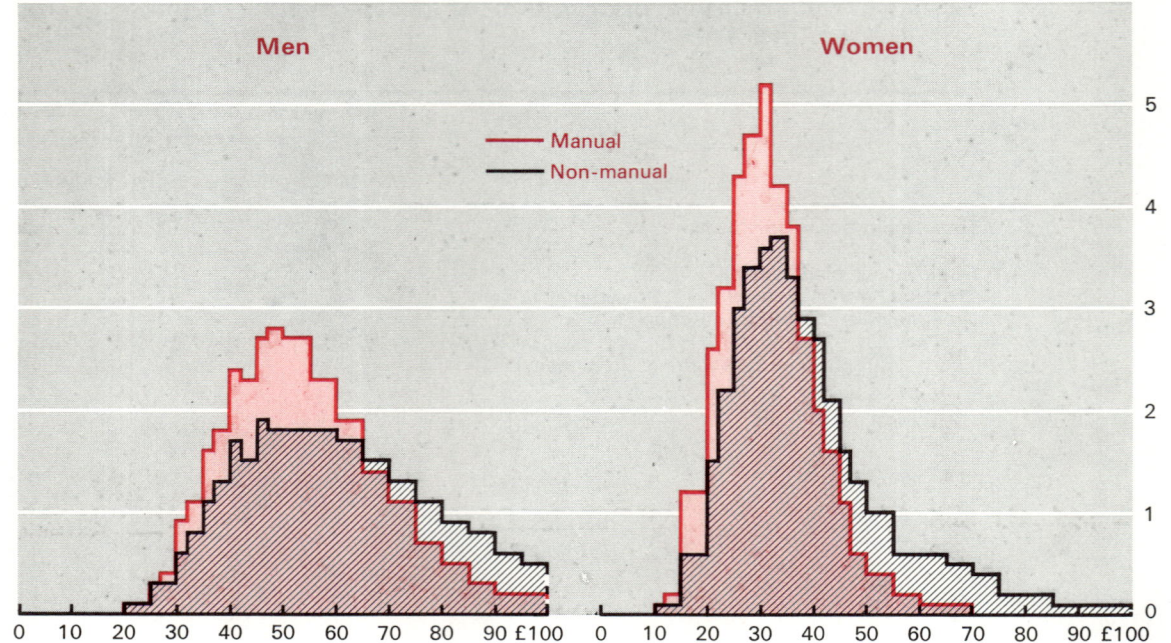

Great Britain

Earners in each £1 earnings group as percentage of all full-time workers

Percentages

Men

Women

— Manual
— Non-manual

[1] These figures relate only to men aged 21 and over and women aged 18 and over whose pay for the survey reference period was not affected by absence.

Source: New Earnings Survey, 1975, Department of Employment

Table 5.20   Percentage increases in average gross weekly earnings of full-time workers[1], April 1974 to April 1975

Great Britain   Percentages

	All industries and services		All manufacturing industries	
	Men (21 and over)	Women (18 and over)	Men (21 and over)	Women (18 and over)
Percentage increase including overtime pay				
Manual workers	29·2	35·6	25·7	33·7
Non-manual workers	27·5	38·8	26·5	38·2
All workers	28·4	38·0	26·0	35·6

[1] Of those whose pay for either survey period was not affected by absence. These figures are based upon the matched sample of the New Earnings Survey. See note in Appendix B, page 241.

Source: New Earnings Survey, 1974 and 1975, Department of Employment

Table 5.21   Proportion of income taken in tax in the case of a married couple with two children under 11, with no income except the husband's earnings from employment and family allowances[1]

Great Britain   Percentages

	1966 –67	1967 –68	1968 –69	1969 –70	1970 –71	1971 –72	1972 –73	1973 –74	1974 –75	1975 –76
Earnings level:										
Multiples of median earnings of full-time male manual workers aged 21 and over[2]										
2/3	–	0·6	3·2	4·8	5·7	4·8	4·2	7·2	8·4	12·5
1	6·6	7·5	10·9	12·6	14·2	13·0	12·6	14·7	16·5	19·8
3/2	14·8	15·6	17·8	18·9	20·1	18·6	18·4	19·7	21·9	24·8
2	19·0	19·7	21·3	22·2	23·0	21·5	21·3	22·2	24·7	27·6
Income tax threshold[3] as a percentage of median earnings[2]	69·2	65·8	57·1	55·9	57·4	58·5	59·6	52·3	51·0	44·5
Median earnings[2] (£)	1,059	1,115	1,203	1,295	1,463	1,613	1,873	2,134	2,536	3,107

[1] The tax deduction includes family allowance 'clawback'.   [2] The earnings figures are derived from the Department of Employment October earnings enquiries, converted to an annual rate. They relate to all industries covered by the survey.   [3] Taking account of the effects of earned income relief where appropriate.

Source: Board of Inland Revenue from Department of Employment data

Social security and income support

This group of tables and charts comes mainly from national insurance and supplementary benefit sources. However, these administrative statistics have been supplemented by three tables using data from the Family Expenditure Survey (FES).

The first group of tables and charts, 5.22 to 5.26 and 5.30, illustrate statistics about main types of benefits. Weekly rates of the main national insurance benefits, family allowances, and supplementary benefits are shown in Appendix B.

Some families receiving means-tested benefits may find that an increase in earnings is wholly or substantially offset by reductions in these means-tested benefits, together with increases in income tax and national insurance contributions. This situation has become known as the 'Poverty trap': its potential importance is illustrated in Chart 5.27 and Table 5.28. The reductions in means-tested benefits would occur if claims for these benefits were renewed at the same time or soon after receiving an increase in earnings. The cumulative effects of taxes and benefits are illustrated in the charts for a hypothetical family of a married couple with two children aged 4 and 6 living in typical (not GLC) local authority accommocation. The first half of Chart 5.27 shows the total net effect of benefits, taxes, and earnings at different levels of earnings, and the second, the potential marginal effect of a £1 pay rise.

In practice a family's benefits will not always change immediately after a pay rise. For example, Family Income Supplement is awarded for a 12-month period and it is thus unlikely that a family will have to renew their claim immediately following a pay rise. For illustration we have shown what could happen after a few months (the medium term) if either all benefits and taxes were reassessed or all those with the exception of Family Income Supplement were reassessed. The medium term (taking account of administrative practices) is assumed to be at least 2 months, and at most (as long as there is no Budget or change in the needs levels of benefits) 11 months, after any change in gross earnings. This graph also assumes a certain level of rent and rates for the family (£4.72 per week rent and £1.90 per week rates) for which the cut-off points for rebates are about £56[1] of earnings per week. The shape of the graph would alter if rent and rates were higher since rebates are a function of both amount of income and housing costs. For example, if a family had rent of £8 per week and rates of £2.50 per week the head of the family could have earnings of up to about £69[2] per week before losing housing rebates entirely. Another assumption is that the gross income of the family is earned solely by the husband. If the wife were earning, part of her income would be disregarded for some of the means-tested benefits and this would also affect the shape of the chart. Again other types of family would produce different results.

Table 5.28 gives estimates of the numbers of families potentially affected by the 'Poverty trap', assuming an immediate recalculation of benefits following a £1 pay rise. These figures overestimate the numbers affected, since in practice adjustments to net income due to changes in tax, national insurance, and benefits may not take place in the short-term (ie within 2 months following a pay rise). In the long term (ie more than 11 months) adjustments for inflation in the Budget and in the needs levels of benefits would shift the chart to the right. It is very unlikely that a family getting an average percentage pay rise would, in the long-term, have lost most of this increase through the effects of tax and loss of benefits; but in the medium-term some families might temporarily have done so. Budget tax changes and upratings of social security benefits normally ensure that families whose gross incomes rise roughly in line with average earnings will eventually get larger increases in their total income support than the charts and table imply.

Table 5.31 shows the numbers of families, of various types, with low resources. These families have disposable incomes (net incomes less net housing costs) either below supplementary benefit level or just above. By using the supplementary benefit level as a basis for need, it is possible to adjust income to take account of family composition. It should be noted that these figures do not attempt to assess whether families are entitled to supplementary benefit or not. Details are given in Appendix A.

Table 5.29 shows the variations in the numbers of poor families and persons over the four years 1972–1975.

Trends in the values of some of the principal benefits as compared with the changes in the Retail Price Index are shown in Figure XII of the Social Commentary on page 23. Tables 5.32 and 5.33, included in this section, relate the values of benefits to earnings; Table 5.32 showing the ratios of retirement pensions and supplementary benefit to average earnings and Table 5.33 the percentage of net income that social security payments provide for unemployed or sick men.

Finally, Table 5.34 shows trends in public expenditure on social security benefits.

---

[1] Since Chart 5.27 was drawn, new housing needs alowances have been introduced. From November 1976 the corresponding cut-off point will be about £60 earnings per week.

[2] Using the new housing needs allowances introduced in November 1976.

Table 5.22   Persons receiving national insurance benefits and extent supplemented

United Kingdom   31 December   Thousands and percentages

	1951	1961	1971	1972	1973	1974	1975
National insurance beneficiaries (thousands)							
Unemployment benefit[1]	207[6]	227	485	371	211	294	525
Sickness benefit[2]	941	964	578	598	605	597	552
Invalidity benefit[3]			421	442	458	467	441
Retirement pensions and contributory old age pensions *plus*							
widows aged 60–64 receiving widows' benefit	4,224	5,941	7,982	8,123	8,253	8,383	8,356
—*of which: males*	*1,465*	*1,930*	*2,672*	*2,732*	*2,799*	*2,848*	*2,866*
females	*2,759*	*4,011*	*5,310*	*5,392*	*5,454*	*5,535*	*5,490*
Widows' benefit (excluding widows aged 60–64)[4]	467	460	460	456	419	413	395
Guardians' allowances, orphans' pensions and individual							
children's allowances	26	6	5	5	5	5	5
Maternity allowance	49	72	84	85	78	75	75
Injury benefit[2]	59	62	57	55	59	60	45
Industrial disablement benefit	81	183	209	208	207	207	199
Industrial death benefit	6	21	30	31	31	32	30
NI beneficiaries also receiving national							
assistance/supplementary benefit (percentages):							
Unemployment beneficiaries	16	14	23	24	21	27	23
Sickness/invalidity beneficiaries	13	13	13	11	9	8	6
Retirement pensioners *plus* widow beneficiaries aged 60–64	22	22	28	28	26	25	22
Widow beneficiaries (excluding widows aged 60–64)[4]	23	14	15	14	13	10	7
Earnings-related supplement[5] **(males only)** (percentages):							
Unemployment beneficiaries				39	37	41	39	46[6]
Sickness/invalidity beneficiaries				27	26	28	27	25
Injury beneficiaries				56	58	59	61	57

[1] As at the first Monday in November.
[2] Average of monthly figures.   [3] Invalidity benefit commenced 23 September 1971.   [4] Includes widow basic pensioners.
[5] Earnings-related supplement was not payable until 1966. At June of each year for sickness and injury benefit and at November for unemployment benefit. Of those not receiving earnings-related supplement some will not yet be entitled because the twelve absolute waiting days have not been served, others will have exhausted their entitlement having received it for 6 months while others are outside the age and earnings limits set.
[6] GB only.   *Source: Social Security Statistics, Department of Health and Social Security*

Table 5.23   Persons receiving supplementary benefit[1]

United Kingdom   Thousands

	National assistance			Supplementary benefits				
	1951[2]	1961	1965	1966	1972	1973	1974	1975
Retirement pensioners and national insurance widows								
60 years and over	767	1,089	1,258	1,668	1,857	1,796	1,761	1,635
Others over pension age	202	234	212[3]	203	112	107	106	104
Unemployed with national insurance benefit	33	48	35	79	91	50	76	138
Unemployed without national insurance benefit	33	94	85	111	320	212	240	418
Sick and disabled with national insurance benefit	121	138	153	161	142	122	98	80
Sick and disabled without national insurance benefit	98	142	147	151	171	173	175	175
Women under 60 with dependent children	41	78	110	128	232	233	250	281[7]
National insurance widows under 60	86[4]	60	58	62	65	56	44	32
Others	81[5]	18	17	17	24	24	27	27
Total persons receiving supplementary benefit	1,462	1,902	2,075	2,580	3,014	2,772	2,778	2,891
of whom wage stopped[6] (unemployed)	..	15	19	25	27	12	10	

[1] The figures in the table relate to times close to the ends of the years shown.   [2] Great Britain only.   [3] Includes 18,000 unsupplemented non-contributory old-age pensioners.   [4] Includes some widows aged 60 years and over.   [5,6] See notes in Appendix A.
[7] Now defined as one-parent families (includes families headed by a man under pension age).
Source: Social Security Statistics, Department of Health and Social Security

Chart 5.24
Persons receiving supplementary benefit

Chart 5.25
Persons receiving retirement pension

Great Britain

¹ National assistance. ² Provisional.

Source: Social Security Statistics, Department of Health and Social Security

Table 5.26 Family income supplement: families receiving: by size[1] and weekly rate, 30 December 1975

United Kingdom Thousands

	Weekly rate in range (£)										All families	Average weekly rate (£)
	0·20 to 0·90	1·00 to 1·90	2·00 to 2·90	3·00 to 3·90	4·00 to 4·90	5·00 to 5·90	6·00 to 6·90	7·00 to 7·90	8·00 to 8·90	Over 9·00		
Two-parent families												
1 child	0·8	1·0	0·7	1·0	0·8	0·9	0·4	1·0	–	–	6·6	3·81
2 children	1·0	1·6	1·0	0·8	1·3	0·6	0·5	1·3	–	–	8·2	3·68
3 children	0·9	1·2	1·1	0·8	0·9	0·7	0·5	0·4	0·8	–	7·4	3·89
4 or more children	1·2	1·6	1·4	1·7	1·7	1·1	0·9	0·8	1·4	1·3	13·1	4·71
All two-parent families	4·0	5·3	4·2	4·4	4·6	3·4	2·2	3·5	2·2	1·3	35·2	4·13
One-parent families												
1 child	1·2	2·4	2·3	2·9	3·0	2·6	1·7	2·8	–	–	19·0	4·15
2 children	0·7	1·1	1·0	1·3	1·2	1·1	0·9	1·2	–	–	8·5	4·14
3 or more children	0·3	0·6	0·6	0·5	0·7	0·7	0·5	0·3	0·5	0·1	4·9	4·55
All one-parent families	2·2	4·1	4·0	4·7	4·9	4·4	3·1	4·4	0·5	0·1	32·3	4·21

[1] Number of children in two-parent families is 110,800 and in one-parent families is 53,000.

Source: Social Security Statistics, Department of Health and Social Security

**Chart 5.27
Total income
support: marginal
net benefit**

**The relationship between total income support[1] and gross earnings of the husband
as at July 1976 for a married couple with 2 children aged 4 and 6**

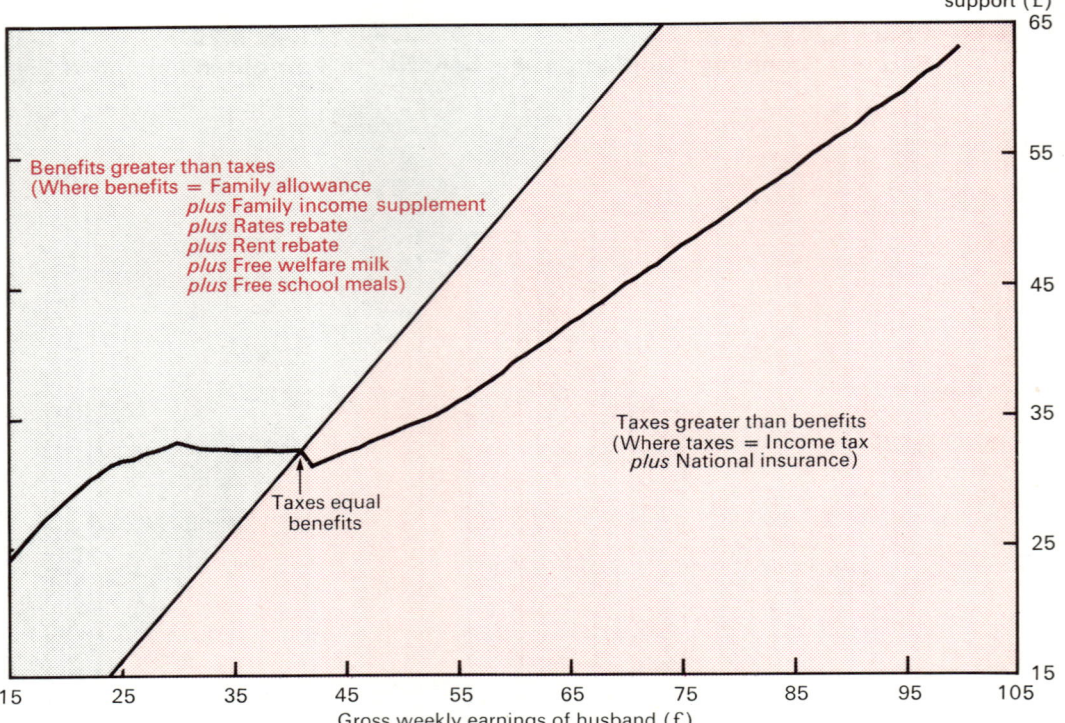

Total income
support (£)

Benefits greater than taxes
(Where benefits = Family allowance
plus Family income supplement
plus Rates rebate
plus Rent rebate
plus Free welfare milk
plus Free school meals)

Taxes greater than benefits
(Where taxes = Income tax
plus National insurance)

Taxes equal
benefits

Gross weekly earnings of husband (£)

**Marginal net benefit from £1 increase in gross earnings, as at July 1976
Medium term effect on a married couple with 2 children aged 4 and 6**

Marginal net
benefit (£)

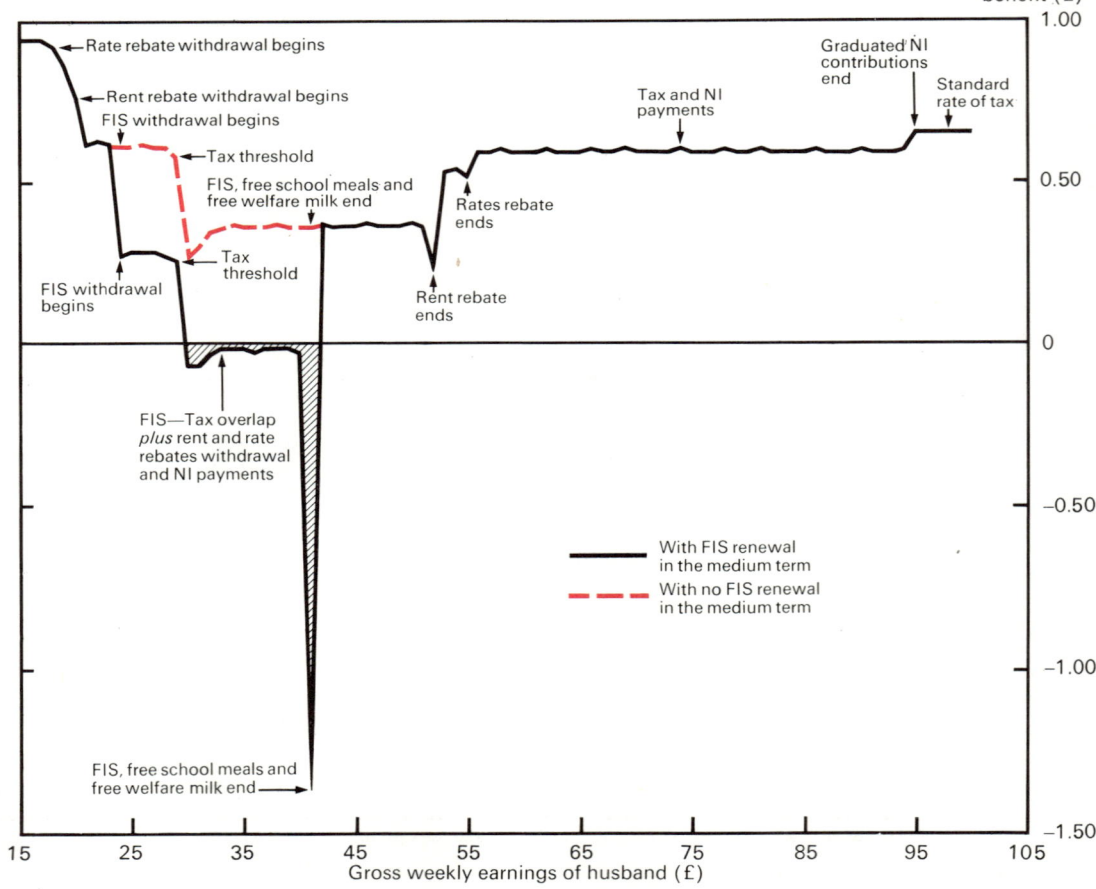

Rate rebate withdrawal begins

Rent rebate withdrawal begins
FIS withdrawal begins

Tax threshold

FIS, free school meals and
free welfare milk end

Tax
threshold

FIS withdrawal
begins

Rates rebate
ends

Rent rebate
ends

Graduated NI
contributions
end

Tax and NI
payments

Standard
rate of tax

FIS—Tax overlap
plus rent and rate
rebates withdrawal
and NI payments

With FIS renewal
in the medium term
With no FIS renewal
in the medium term

FIS, free school meals and
free welfare milk end

Gross weekly earnings of husband (£)

[1] For definition of total income support see note to Table 5.31 in Appendix A.

Source: Department of Health and Social Security

Table 5.28   Estimated number of families[1] theoretically liable to receive various levels of net benefit[2] from an additional £1 of earnings[3], December 1974

Great Britain   Thousands

	Marginal net benefit from £1 increase in earnings			
	Negative	Up to 24p. increase	25–49p. increase	All families
Families with children – head in full-time employment	[20][4]	[30][4]	250	6,560
Families without children – head in full-time employment	–	[10][4]	120	10,230

[1] For the definition of the term family as used here see Appendix B, page 243.
[2] No account has been taken of higher tax rates for those with high incomes. See notes on page 119.
[3] Similar estimates published in *Social Trends No. 6* are now thought to have overestimated these numbers.
[4] Figures in square brackets are subject to considerable sampling error.

Source: Department of Health and Social Security, from Family Expenditure Survey data

Table 5.29   Trends in the numbers of families[1] and persons normally with low net resources[2]

Great Britain   December   Thousands[3]

	1972	1973	1974[4]	1975[4]
Families	5,210	4,980	4,740	5,250
Persons	8,350	7,890	7,300	8,880

[1] Including families in receipt of supplementary benefit as estimated from the Annual Statistical Enquiry of supplementary benefit recipients. For definition of 'family' as used here see Appendix B, page 243.   [2] Families are included in this table if the head is either normally receiving supplementary benefit or if the family's net income less housing costs less work expenses is less than 120% of their supplementary benefit scale rate.
[3] Rounded to the nearest 10,000.   [4] In 1974 the self-employed were included in the analysis for the first time. The effect of this was to give figures higher by 100,000 for families and 300,000 for persons than would otherwise have been the case. This method of analysis was continued in 1975.   *Source: Department of Health and Social Security analysis of the Family Expenditure Survey*

Table 5.30   Families and family allowances

United Kingdom   At 31 December   Thousands

	1951	1961	1971	1972	1973	1974
Families receiving allowances						
All families	3,219	3,743	4,463	4,502	4,595	4,606
Families with:						
2 children	2,051	2,269	2,649	2,705	2,785	2,844
3 children	757	910	1,147	1,152	1,165	1,153
4 children	256	337	433	426	427	414
5 or more children	156	225	234	220	218	195
Total number of children (including first child) in						
families receiving allowances	8,273	9,906	11,775	11,772	11,979	11,873
Families with one child (estimated)	3,024	3,004	3,075	3,075	3,075	2,785

Source: Social Security Statistics, Department of Health and Social Security

Table 5.31 Families[1] and persons normally with low net resources, December 1974[2]

Great Britain   Thousands and percentages

	Family resources					
	Below supplementary benefit level and normally not receiving supplementary benefit		Normally on supplementary benefit[3]		Above supplementary benefit level but within 20% of it	
	Families	Persons	Families	Persons	Families	Persons
						Thousands[4]
Families under pension age						
Married couples with children	90	390	80	390	120	580
Single persons with children	20[5]	70[5]	260	760	20[5]	60[5]
Married couples no children	30	70	80	150	30	70
Single persons no children	330	330	300	300	100	100
Families over pension age						
Married couples	90	200	320	650	330	660
Single persons	350	350	1,480	1,480	700	700
All families	920	1,410	2,530	3,730	1,300	2,160
					Percentage of all families of each type	
Families under pension age						
Married couples with children	1	2	1	2	2	2
Single persons with children	4[5]	4[5]	41	44	3[5]	3[5]
Married couples no children	1	1	2	2	1	1
Single persons no children	5	5	4	4	1	1
Families over pension age						
Married couples	5	5	15	15	16	16
Single persons	9	9	36	36	17	17
All families	4	3	10	7	5	4

[1] For the definition of the term family as used here see Appendix B on page 243.
[2] Families are included in this table if the head is either normally receiving supplementary benefit or if the family's net income less net housing costs less work expenses is less than 120% of their supplementary benefit scale rate. For definition of net income see Appendix A.
[3] This analysis of the FES treats respondents according to their normal income and employment situation within the three months preceding the interview; these figures exclude persons who have received supplementary benefit for less than three months in order that the information should be consistent with that obtained from the FES. See also notes to Table 3.1 in Appendix A.   [4] Rounded to the nearest 10,000.
[5] Subject to considerable sampling error.   *Source: Analysis of the Family Expenditure Survey, Department of Health and Social Security*

Table 5.32 Retirement pensions (and supplementary benefits) related to average net earnings, 1960 to 1975

United Kingdom   £

	Standard rate of retirement pension for a married couple (A)	Supplementary benefit basic scale rate for a married couple (B)	Average net earnings after deducting tax and NI contrib. for a married couple (C)	(A)/(C) (%)	(B)/(C) (%)
As at October					
1960	4·00	4·25	12·55	32	34
1962	4·63	4·77½	13·29	35	36
1964	5·45	5·22½	14·92	37	35
1966	6·50	6·27½[1]	16·21	40	39[1]
1968	7·30	7·45	17·88	41	42
1969	7·30[2]	7·45[3]	19·10	38[2]	39[3]
1970	8·10	7·85[4]	21·09	38	37[4]
1971	9·70	9·45	23·22	42	41
1972	10·90	10·65	27·36	40	39
1973	12·50	11·65	30·71	41	38
1974	16·00	13·65	35·15	46	39
1975	18·50[5]	15·65[6]	41·86	44[5]	37[6]

[1] Increased to £6.65 on 28 November 1966 – percentage becomes 41.   [2] Increased to £8.10 on 3 November 1969 – percentage becomes 42.
[3] Increased to £7.85 on 3 November 1969 – percentage becomes 41.   [4] Increased to £8.50 on 2 November 1970 – percentage becomes 40.
[5] Increased to £21.20 on 17 November 1975 – percentage becomes 51.   [6] Increased to £17.75 on 17 November 1975 – percentage becomes 42.
Source: Department of Health and Social Security

Table 5.33 **Percentage of net income[1] represented by social security payments to unemployed or sick men[2]**

Great Britain   £s and percentages

	Single men	Married men[3]				
		No children	1 child	2 children	3 children	4 children
Nov. 1975: Men with average earnings						
Net income when working[5] (£)	40·58	42·46	44·08	46·32	48·56	51·04
Percentage of net incomes:						
provided by sickness/unemployment benefit[4]:						
—without ERS[7]	27	42	49	54	59	63
—with ERS[7]	48	63	68	72	76	79
provided by supplementary benefit level[6]	39	56	61	66	73	82
Nov. 1975: Men with half average earnings						
Net income when working[5] (£)	22·57	24·46	26·07	28·31	30·55	33·03
Percentage of net incomes:						
provided by sickness/unemployment benefit[4]:						
—without ERS[7]	49	74	82	88	93	97
—with ERS[7]	66	74	82	88	93	97
provided by supplementary benefit level[6]	69	97	103	108	115	127

[1] Net incomes comprise gross earnings *plus* family allowances where appropriate *less* income tax and NI contributions.   [2] 1975 weekly rates of national insurance and supplementary benefits are given in Appendix B, page 243.   [3] Children's ages have been assumed to be respectively 4 years; 4 and 8 years; 4, 8, and 11 years; and 4, 8, 11, and 16 years.   [4] Includes family allowance where appropriate. [5] Includes family income supplement where appropriate.   [6] The national assistance and supplementary benefit level of requirements, ie scale rates according to family composition plus the following average rent additions: April 1961: £1.12 single men; £1.35 married men; £1.40 married men plus children. Nov. 1975: £4.78 single men; £5.92 married men; £6.02 married men plus children.   [7] Earnings related supplement.   *Source: Department of Health and Social Security*

Table 5.34 **Public expenditure on social security benefits**

United Kingdom   Various units

	£ million					Percentages		
	1951 –52	1961 –62	1971 –72	1974 –75	1975 –76	1961 –62	1974 –75	1975 –76
Current expenditure by central government								
National insurance:								
Retirement pensions	281	800	2,091	3,661		47·8	51·1	
Widows' benefits and guardians' allowances	25	83	203	324		5·0	4·5	
Sickness benefits	66	161	434	711	6,323	9·6	9·9	64·8
Maternity benefits	9	25	44	48		1·5	0·7	
Death grants	3	6	14	14		0·4	0·2	
Unemployment benefits	16	41	250	227	479	2·4	3·2	4·9
Industrial injuries benefits	16	60	117	170	248	3·6	2·4	2·2
War pensions	77	103	136	206	260	6·1	2·9	2·7
Non-contributory old-age pensions[1]	25	10	–	–	–	0·6	–	–
Supplementary benefits[1]:								
Old persons	34	89	286	326	420	5·3	4·5	4·3
Unemployed persons	6	22	155	200	344	1·3	2·8	3·5
Sick persons	18	32	84	118	136	1·9	1·6	1·4
Other persons in need	16	25	140	232	345	1·5	3·2	3·5
Old persons' pensions	..	..	24	32	36	..	0·4	0·4
Family income supplement	..	..	5	14	14	..	0·2	0·2
Attendance allowance	..	..	6	66	100	..	0·9	1·0
Lump sums to pensioners	..	..	..	93	–	..	1·3	–
Family allowances	66	140	359	360	547	8·4	5·0	5·6
Administration	45	78	230	369	533	4·6	5·2	5·5
Total public expenditure on social security benefits	703	1,675	4,578	7,171	9,755	100·0	100·0	100·0

[1] Non-contributory old age pensions and national assistance ceased after 26 November 1966, when they were replaced by supplementary benefits The analysis of supplementary benefits grants is not exact; the estimates are derived from average numbers in receipt of benefits and average amount of grants paid.   *Sources: National Income and Expenditure, Central Statistical Office; Department of Health and Social Security*

Personal wealth

The distribution of wealth in Great Britain has been the subject of considerable interest in recent years. A good deal of discussion about the concept of wealth itself, and about the small range of statistics available, is to be found in the first report of the Royal Commission on the Distribution of Income and Wealth (Cmnd 6171). The concept of wealth used is crucial to the estimates of the distribution of wealth. This is shown very clearly in Figure 14 of Report No 1, mentioned above. The Royal Commission show that, by including the entitlement to State and occupational pensions in the definition of wealth, the resulting distribution is, as might be expected, much more equal than the distribution obtained from the definition of wealth used for estate duty purposes, which, apart from the treatment of life insurance policies, corresponds broadly to marketable wealth.

The only official statistics available for the distribution of wealth are the Inland Revenue estimates based on estate duty statistics, and these are used for Tables 5.35, 5.36, and 5.37. The figures are subject to fairly wide margins of error, as explained in Appendix B, which also gives more details of the definition of wealth used. When interpreting trends in the figures relating to wealth ranges, the effects of inflation should be borne in mind, since the figures are in current terms.

The reason why there are two tables showing the distribution of wealth stems from the fact that estate duty statistics cover only the estates which are probated. Since the method used (which is explained further in Appendix B) involves the assumption that the estates of people dying in a given period are a representative sample of the estates of the living in that period, it follows that the estimates of the distribution of wealth derived solely from estate duty statistics refer to only a part of the whole population, viz., those for whom probate would be obtained on death. The Inland Revenue refer to this group of people as 'identified wealth owners'. Table 5.35 shows the trends in the distribution of wealth among them. The proportion of the adult population identified as wealth owners has varied from year to year but, as the figures at the bottom of Table 5.35 show, it has consistently been less than half the population aged 15 and over in recent years. It was reduced, for several years after 1965, as a result of the Administration of Estates (Small Payments) Act, 1965, and this makes the interpretation of trends in the tables more difficult. Table 5.36 shows the

Table 5.35   Distribution of wealth among identified wealth owners[1]

Great Britain   Percentages

	1962	1965	1966	1973	1974	1974 Males[2]	1974 Females[2]
Distribution of wealth among wealth owners							
Percentage of wealth owned by:							
Most wealthy 1 per cent of owners	27·2	24·4	23·6	21·8	18·4	17·5	19·6
„ „ 2 „ „ „ „	35·6	32·7	31·0	27·7	24·9	24·0	26·3
„ „ 5 „ „ „ „	48·8	46·4	43·7	38·8	36·7	35·7	38·1
„ „ 10 „ „ „ „	60·7	58·6	56·0	50·9	49·0	47·4	51·6
„ „ 25 „ „ „ „	78·5	77·7	75·1	72·6	71·0	69·0	73·9
„ „ 50 „ „ „ „	92·2	92·5	90·9	91·4	90·5	89·2	91·9
Total wealth (£ thousand million)	*58·3*	*74·3*	*76·8*	*163·7*	*157·1*	*98·2*	*58·9*
Distribution of owners by individual net wealth							
Percentage of owners with assets covered by estate duty statistics valued:							
Over — Not over (£)							
— 1,000	48·3	41·1	35·3	18·8	18·1	15·0	22·6
1,000 — 3,000	29·5	28·4	31·2	25·1	25·3	23·6	27·9
3,000 — 5,000	10·9	14·0	15·3	11·9	11·8	12·9	10·3
5,000 — 10,000	6·2	9·7	10·9	21·3	21·9	23·9	19·2
10,000 — 25,000	3·4	4·7	5·2	17·9	17·7	19·6	15·0
25,000 — 100,000	1·5	1·9	1·8	4·4	4·6	4·7	4·6
100,000 —	0·2	0·2	0·2	0·6	0·5	0·5	0·5
Total owners of wealth – thousands	18,448	18,560	17,921	19,140	18,837	11,072	7,765
as percentage of home population aged 15 and over	*46·1*	*45·6*	*43·9*	*46·2*	*45·3*	*55·7*	*35·7*

[1] See introductory notes above and notes in Appendix B, page 243.

[2] In interpreting the greater inequality of distribution of wealth for females than for males it should be remembered that the distributions are affected by the fact that for married couples a large proportion of the property is owned by the husband although it may be used by both partners.

Source: Inland Revenue Statistics

distribution of wealth in the whole adult population which would be obtained from the previous information under the extreme assumption that the part of the adult population not identified as wealth owners have no wealth at all. Since the 'wealth owners' form less than half the adult population the figures in the two tables differ considerably; but, subject to the reservations mentioned in Appendix B, the figures in Table 5.36 provide an upper limit to the actual degree of inequality in the ownership of wealth as defined for the purposes of calculating estate duty.

Appendix B also contains two series of Gini coefficients, which are measures of concentration of wealth, derived from the two distributions shown in the tables. These figures, together with the tables they are derived from, indicate that there has been a long-term trend towards greater

equality in the distribution of personal wealth, but that, on this definition, personal wealth is very much less evenly distributed than personal income.

The third table in this sub-section shows trends in the composition of estates. These figures are based on the relative values of the different assets, rather than on their volumes, and so the rise in the proportion of the values of total estates accounted for by dwellings reflects not only the rise in home ownership but also the rapid rise in house prices in the last few years. The distributions of the different assets among the population, although not shown here, vary considerably; the distribu- of wealth in the form of land is very markedly concentrated amongst the wealthiest in the population, but no comprehensive data on this are available.

Table 5.36 Distribution of wealth among adult population[1,2]

Great Britain   Percentages

	1962	1965	1966	1973	1974	1974 Males[3]	1974 Females[3]
Distribution of wealth among adult population[1]							
Percentage of wealth owned by:							
Most wealthy 1 per cent of adult population[1]	36·7	33·9	32·2	28·6	26·0	22·9	30·2
" " 2 " " " " "	46·6	44·2	42·2	36·9	34·9	31·0	40·1
" " 5 " " " " "	62·2	60·3	58·5	52·5	51·1	45·4	59·0
" " 10 " " " " "	75·4	74·7	73·1	68·6	67·5	60·1	77·0
" " 25 " " " " "	93·7	94·0	93·2	93·1	92·8	86·1	97·0
" " 50 " " " " "	100·0	100·0	100·0	100·0	100·0	99·6	100·0

[1] Defined as the home population aged 15 and over.   [2] On the assumption that the added population has no wealth (see notes introducing these tables).   [3] See footnote 2 to Table 5.35 above.   Source: Inland Revenue Statistics

Table 5.37 Composition of personal wealth by asset value, 1960 to 1974[1]

Great Britain   Percentages

Asset/liability	Proportion of estimated total wealth[2]								
	1960	1962	1964	1966	1968	1970	1972	1973	1974
Physical assets									
Dwellings	20·7	18·7	24·2	26·3	26·7	30·3	35·2	38·2	42·7
Land	2·1	2·5	2·7	2·7	3·3	2·9	3·8	4·3	4·5
Other physical assets	7·7	8·6	7·7	7·2	7·0	7·6	6·5	6·2	6·8
All physical assets	30·5	29·8	34·6	36·2	37·0	40·8	45·5	48·7	54·0
Financial assets									
Listed ordinary shares	15·2	15·0	16·3	13·8	15·0	13·0	13·8	11·0	6·3
Other company securities	7·8	6·8	7·1	6·5	6·4	5·7	5·4	5·0	4·0
Life policies	11·9	12·7	13·9	14·8	14·8	16·5	14·8	14·3	14·9
Building society deposits	5·4	5·2	4·9	6·5	7·4	7·4	6·9	7·2	7·5
Other financial assets	37·6	38·4	34·1	33·2	29·4	28·3	23·3	23·1	23·4
All financial assets	77·9	78·1	76·3	74·8	73·0	70·9	64·2	60·6	56·1
Liabilities	−8·4	−7·9	−10·9	−11·0	−10·0	−11·8	−9·7	−9·3	−10·1
Total	100·0	100·0	100·0	100·0	100·0	100·0	100·0	100·0	100·0

[1] See introductory notes above and notes in Appendix B, page 243.   [2] The figures are affected by the fact that, unlike other assets, estate duty on real property (land and buildings) does not have to be paid until a year after death. Thus, at a time of rising real property values, the proportion of real property tends to be understated, and vice versa.   Source: Inland Revenue Statistics

Table 5.38 Selected regional characteristics

	North	Yorkshire and Humberside	East Midlands	East Anglia	South East		South West	West Midlands	North West	Wales	Scotland	Northern Ireland	United Kingdom
					Greater London	Other S East							
Median earnings (£ per week) April 1975:													
Full-time men aged 21 and over	56·6	54·4	53·9	51·4	63·1	55·8	51·9	55·5	54·6	55·4	56·2	49·9	55·8
Full-time women aged 18 and over	32·8	32·4	32·4	31·8	41·3	33·9	32·6	32·3	32·9	32·8	32·7	31·9	34·1
Average weekly household income (£) 1974 and 1975[1]	60·8	59·5	64·0	63·3	72·2	75·9	63·4	66·7	61·6	60·3	63·6	53·4	65·9
Source of household income (percentages) 1974 and 1975[1]													
Wages and salaries	75·7	77·0	72·2	70·1	75·2	72·5	68·1	78·2	73·0	71·5	76·0	67·0	73·8
Self-employment	5·6	4·3	7·4	8·5	6·1	7·1	9·2	5·3	5·7	6·5	5·0	9·0	6·4
Investments	2·3	2·6	4·6	3·8	3·1	4·4	5·4	2·1	2·8	3·1	3·8	1·6	3·5
Annuities and pensions (other than social security)	2·2	1·8	2·1	2·5	2·4	3·0	2·9	1·5	2·3	3·0	2·3	2·7	2·4
Social security benefits	10·5	10·5	9·3	9·7	7·8	7·5	9·7	8·6	11·5	12·1	10·5	16·4	9·5
Sub-letting and imputed income from owner/rent-free occupancy	2·7	3·0	3·7	4·0	4·1	4·4	4·1	3·8	3·7	2·9	1·5	2·1	3·5
Other sources	1·0	0·8	0·7	1·4	1·3	1·1	0·6	0·5	1·0	0·9	0·9	1·2	0·9
Distribution of weekly household income (percentages) 1974 and 1975[1]													
Under £15	8·7	7·7	5·5	6·7	4·8	4·0	4·7	5·8	6·6	9·4	5·5	14·1	6·1
£15 and under £20	7·1	7·7	7·3	7·3	6·7	5·6	5·1	7·4	8·2	6·5	6·7	6·9	6·8
£20 and under £30	9·4	10·8	9·8	10·2	10·1	8·2	11·0	7·6	11·5	10·2	10·0	9·6	9·8
£30 and under £40	6·5	7·7	9·4	7·5	7·5	8·9	10·4	8·9	9·1	8·2	11·2	11·0	8·8
£40 and under £50	11·3	11·1	10·7	11·8	8·2	7·7	12·0	7·4	8·8	11·3	8·6	11·3	9·4
£50 and under £60	12·4	10·6	11·1	10·0	10·1	10·1	10·2	10·3	10·0	9·2	9·5	6·9	10·2
£60 and under £70	10·6	10·9	9·4	11·0	9·2	8·9	10·7	10·7	8·9	10·9	11·1	12·0	10·0
£70 and under £80	8·8	8·9	9·8	8·1	8·0	8·5	9·2	9·8	9·6	9·1	8·6	8·6	8·9
£80 and under £90	5·6	7·7	6·1	6·7	6·9	7·9	8·2	8·8	7·8	5·8	6·8	6·2	7·3
£90 and under £100	5·6	4·7	5·6	5·9	5·7	6·7	4·4	6·3	4·5	4·8	6·3	3·1	5·6
£100 and under £120	6·1	6·1	7·6	6·3	8·8	9·2	6·7	7·6	7·4	7·7	7·6	6·2	7·6
£120 or more	7·9	6·1	7·7	8·5	14·0	14·3	7·4	9·4	7·6	6·9	8·1	4·1	9·5
Principal social security benefits 1973–74 as percentage of total expenditure (Great Britain = 100%)													£ million[2]
Retirement pensions	5·8	8·9	6·0	3·4	32·6		8·2	8·2	12·4	5·3	9·1		2,749
Sickness and invalidity benefit	8·6	11·3	6·2	1·8	20·8		6·4	9·1	15·9	9·1	10·8		548
Widow's benefit	6·1	9·0	6·1	3·3	32·2		7·3	9·0	12·7	5·3	9·0		243
Unemployment benefit	10·9	9·7	5·1	2·3	20·0		6·3	8·6	17·1	6·9	13·1		174
Maternity benefit	4·9	9·8	7·3	2·4	31·7		7·3	9·8	12·2	4·9	9·8		42
Disablement benefit	11·5	10·6	5·8	1·9	18·3		3·8	9·6	14·4	10·6	13·5		105
Injury benefit	11·8	14·7	8·8	2·9	14·7		5·9	8·8	11·8	8·8	11·8		34
Supplementary benefit	7·6	9·2	5·3	2·2	27·7		6·0	8·8	15·5	5·8	12·0		686
Family allowances	6·1	9·0	6·4	3·2	30·4		7·0	9·9	12·8	4·6	10·7		344
War pensions	7·3	7·9	6·0	2·6	31·1		8·6	7·3	13·9	5·3	9·9		151
Total	6·8	9·3	5·9	2·9	29·6		7·4	8·6	13·5	5·9	10·0		5,076
Home resident population: Percentage of Great Britain at mid-1975[3]	5·7	9·0	6·8	3·3	31·1		7·8	9·5	12·1	5·1	9·6		

[1] Figures relate to the two calendar years 1974 and 1975 taken together.
[2] Figures are of Great Britain total expenditure and exclude payments to beneficiaries resident outside Great Britain.
[3] Provisional.

Sources: Various, see Appendix C

Personal expenditure

This section complements the previous one on Personal income and wealth. Four areas are covered: rising prices; expenditure patterns; possession of durables; and household food consumption.

As is discussed in the Social Commentary on page 8, the effects of inflation have been of extreme significance during the most recent few years. Chart 6.1, and Tables 6.2 and 6.3 show recent changes in retail prices, brought as up to date as possible, with Table 6.3 showing the fall in the internal purchasing power of the pound.

Chart 6.4 and Table 6.5 show household expenditure patterns for the last few years, using data from the *Family Expenditure Survey*. For more detailed information on both income and expenditure patterns, the reader is referred to the annual reports of the *Family Expenditure Survey*. As well

as looking at the spending patterns of a sample of households it is also possible to look at total consumer spending, and Table 6.6 shows changes in constant prices since 1961. Both Table 6.4 and 6.6 show the greater proportions of expenditure being spent on housing, transport, and services, and the smaller proportions being spent on food.

Chart 6.7 on the possession of durables is again taken from the *Family Expenditure Survey*. A new source of data is used for Table 6.8, the results of Social Science Research Council Survey Unit *Quality of Life Surveys 1973 and 1975*. This table shows not only possession of durables, but also attitudes to them, whether one expects to have a colour television in the future, etc.

This section concludes with a table and a chart on household food consumption, taken from the *National Food Survey*.

**Chart 6.1
General index
of retail prices**

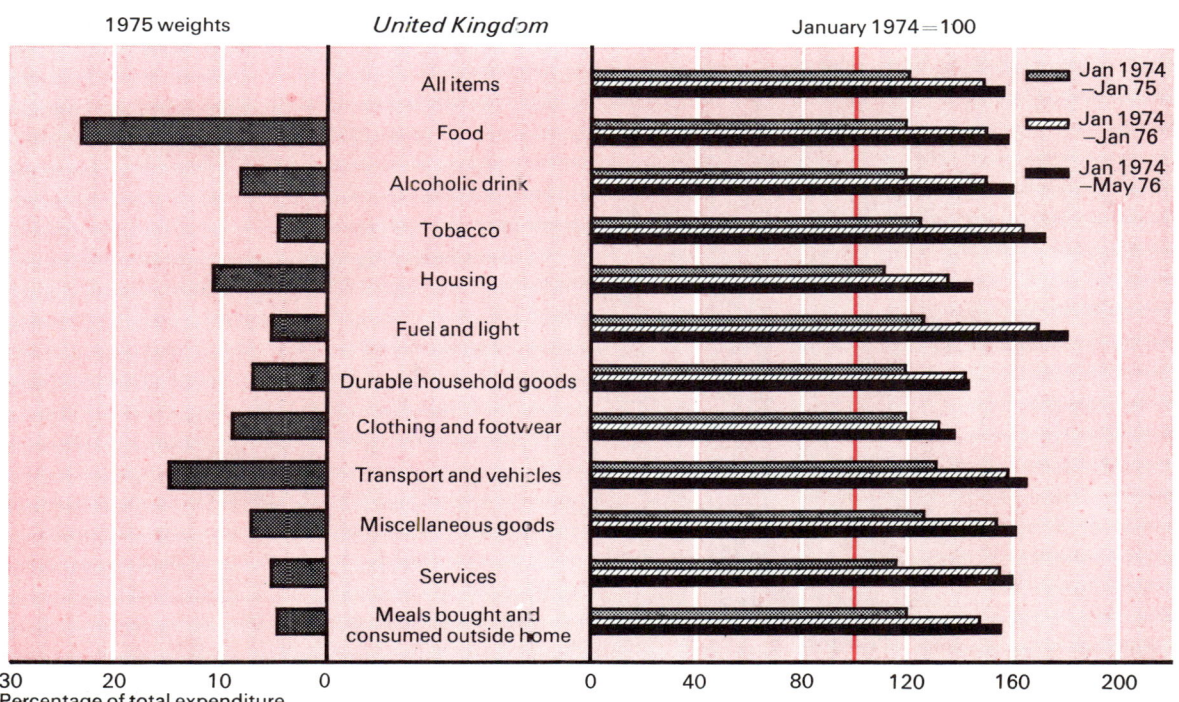

Source: Department of Employment

Table 6.2 Index of retail prices

United Kingdom   Index numbers and weights

	January 1974 = 100							
	12-month averages				January 1976	March 1976	July 1976	Weights 1976
	1966[5]	1970[5]	1974	1975				
General								
All items	60·7	73·1	108·5	134·8	147·9	150·6	156·3	1,000
Food	53·3	64·7	106·1	133·3	148·3	153·8	153·4	228
Alcoholic drink	73·3	86·7	109·7	135·2	149·0	151·9	162·4	81
Tobacco	85·0	95·9	115·9	147·7	162·6	162·8	175·3	46
Housing	57·1	70·2	105·8	125·5	134·8	136·3	143·8	112
Fuel and light	64·1	77·3	110·7	147·4	168·7	169·7	185·6	56
Durable household goods	67·7	79·6	107·9	131·2	140·8	141·9	142·7	75
Clothing and footwear	66·0	74·3	109·4	125·7	131·5	135·9	138·3	84
Transport and vehicles	62·8	75·5	111·0	143·9	157·0	157·4	166·9	140
Miscellaneous goods	61·7	78·4	111·2	138·6	152·3	154·7	162·0	74
Services	56·6	72·3	106·8	135·5	154·0	155·7	160·1	57
Meals bought and consumed outside home[1]		63·4	108·2	132·4	146·2	149·5	158·0	47
Pensioner households								
All items excluding housing[2]								
One-person households	59·0	71·1	107·3	135·0	152·3[3]	158·3[4]	..	
Two-person households	59·0	71·1	107·4	134·6	151·5[3]	157·3[4]	..	

[1] Not separately identified until 1968.   [2] No account is taken of housing costs in constructing these indices for pensioner households
[3] Relates to the first quarter, 1976.   [4] Relates to the second quarter, 1976.   [5] Converted to January 1974 = 100 by Central Statistical Office.
Source: Department of Employment Gazette

Table 6.3 Internal purchasing power of the pound[1]

United Kingdom   £.p

	1965	1967	1969	1970	1971	1972	1973	1974	1975
1965	1.00	1.06½	1.17½	1.25	1.37	1.46½	1.60	1.86	2.31
1967	0.94	1.00	1.10½	1.17½	1.28½	1.37½	1.50½	1.74	2.16½
1969	0.85	0.90½	1.00	1.06½	1.16½	1.24½	1.36	1.58	1.96
1970	0.80	0.85	0.94	1.00	1.09½	1.17	1.28	1.48½	1.84½
1971	0.73	0.78	0.86	0.91½	1.00	1.07	1.17	1.35½	1.68½
1972	0.68	0.72½	0.80	0.85½	0.93½	1.00	1.09	1.26½	1.57½
1973	0.62½	0.66½	0.73½	0.78	0.85½	0.91½	1.00	1.16	1.44
1974	0.54	0.57½	0.63½	0.67½	0.73½	0.79	0.86	1.00	1.24
1975	0.43½	0.46	0.51	0.54	0.59	0.63½	0.69½	0.80½	1.00

[1] This table is based upon the retail price index shown in Table 6.2. The estimated purchasing power of the pound has been calculated for each of the years 1965 to 1975, taking the value as £1.00 in each year in turn. The figures given in the rows of the table can be used to express the changes in a slightly different way. For example, using the 1969 row a pound in 1969 could purchase what it required only 85p to purchase in 1965, or, using the 1965 row, it required £1.17½ in 1969 to purchase what a pound could purchase in 1965. This table applies to purchases in the UK only.
Source: Central Statistical Office

**Chart 6.4
Expenditure
patterns: by
type of
household**

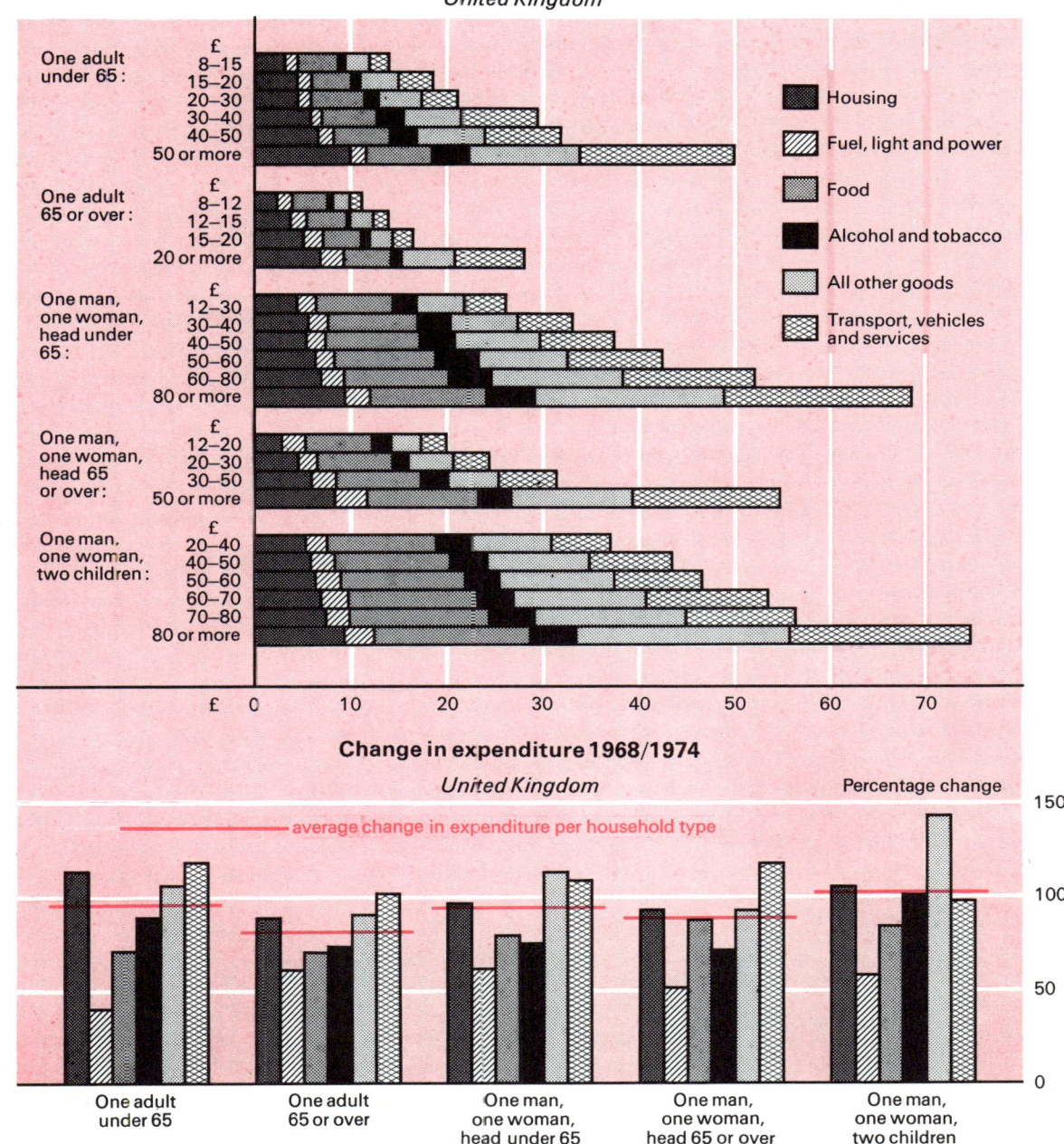

Average weekly expenditure (£), 1974
United Kingdom

One adult
under 65:
£
8–15
15–20
20–30
30–40
40–50
50 or more

One adult
65 or over:
£
8–12
12–15
15–20
20 or more

One man,
one woman,
head under
65:
£
12–30
30–40
40–50
50–60
60–80
80 or more

One man,
one woman,
head 65
or over:
£
12–20
20–30
30–50
50 or more

One man,
one woman,
two children:
£
20–40
40–50
50–60
60–70
70–80
80 or more

Legend:
- Housing
- Fuel, light and power
- Food
- Alcohol and tobacco
- All other goods
- Transport, vehicles and services

£ 0   10   20   30   40   50   60   70

Change in expenditure 1968/1974
United Kingdom

Percentage change

— average change in expenditure per household type

150

100

50

0

One adult
under 65

One adult
65 or over

One man,
one woman,
head under 65

One man,
one woman,
head 65 or over

One man,
one woman,
two children

Source: Family Expenditure Survey, Department of Employment

131

Table 6.5   Household expenditure: average weekly expenditure on goods and services

United Kingdom   £ and percentages

	Total expenditure on goods and services (=100%)	Percentages of all goods and services								
		Housing	Fuel, light and power	Food	Alcohol and tobacco	Clothing and footwear	Durable household goods	Other goods	Transport and vehicles	Services and mis-cellaneous
All households:	£									
Three-year periods										
1965–1967	22·29	11·5	6·3	27·8	9·7	9·2	6·4	7·1	12·2	9·8
1966–1968	23·51	11·9	6·2	27·3	9·6	9·0	6·5	7·2	12·5	9·8
1967–1969	24·88	12·2	6·4	26·6	9·4	8·9	6·5	7·2	13·2	9·6
1968–1970	26·55	12·5	6·4	26·1	9·3	9·0	6·5	7·3	13·6	9·3
1969–1971	28·67	12·6	6·3	25·9	9·2	9·0	6·4	7·4	13·8	9·4
1970–1972	31·62	12·7	6·0	25·5	8·9	9·1	6·8	7·4	13·9	9·7
1971–1973	35·14	13·0	5·8	25·0	8·7	8·9	7·3	7·3	13·8	10·2
1972–1974	40·11	13·4	5·5	24·6	8·4	8·9	7·7	7·4	13·7	10·4
1973–1975	46·75	13·4	5·4	24·6	8·5	8·9	7·7	7·5	13·6	10·4

Source: Family Expenditure Survey, Department of Employment

Table 6.6   Consumers' expenditure: indices at constant prices

United Kingdom   Index numbers and £m

	At constant prices[1] 1961 = 100						At current prices 1975 £ million
	1961	1966	1971	1973	1974	1975	
Food (household expenditure)	100	105	109	109	110	109	12,092
Bread and cereals	100	100	95	93	93	92	1,512
Meat and bacon	100	105	110	102	105	107	3,379
Fish	100	116	107	102	94	99	433
Oils and fat	100	105	105	102	104	103	475
Sugar, preserves, and confectionery	100	100	98	107	103	93	1,224
Dairy products	100	106	115	118	120	121	1,598
Fruit	100	111	115	111	107	105	690
Potatoes and vegetables	100	111	118	126	124	124	1,529
Beverages	100	108	119	127	140	148	830
Other manufactured food	100	105	110	126	124	123	422
Alcoholic drink	100	115	147	179	185	185	4,902
Tobacco	100	98	93	104	103	98	2,741
Housing	100	115	133	140	142	142	9,201
Fuel and light	100	119	127	135	138	137	2,927
Clothing and footwear	100	112	130	145	144	146	5,320
Motor vehicles—purchase	100	162	258	299	216	214	1,932
—running costs	100	175	231	267	267	264	3,940
Furniture and floor coverings	100	113	122	136	119	121	1,387
Radio, electrical, and other durables	100	117	166	248	242	226	1,539
Other household goods	100	114	127	141	139	134	1,795
Books, magazines, and newspapers	100	100	93	99	96	91	973
Chemists' goods	100	119	139	180	190	186	1,048
Communications: postal, telephone, and telegraph	100	122	156	201	217	241	976
Travel	100	103	107	121	116	114	1,989
Entertainment and recreational goods and services	100	122	139	169	180	184	2,710
Consumers' expenditure abroad	100	125	121	130	113	123	1,089
Other expenditure[2]	100	113	111	118	119	115	6,812
Total consumers' expenditure	100	114	126	140	138	138	63,373

[1] Using 1970 weights (ie derived from a series of expenditures at 1970 prices).
[2] Net of all expenditure by foreign tourists in the United Kingdom. Includes catering (meals and accommodation).

Source: National Income and Expenditure, Central Statistical Office

**Chart 6.7
Availability of
durable goods,
1974**

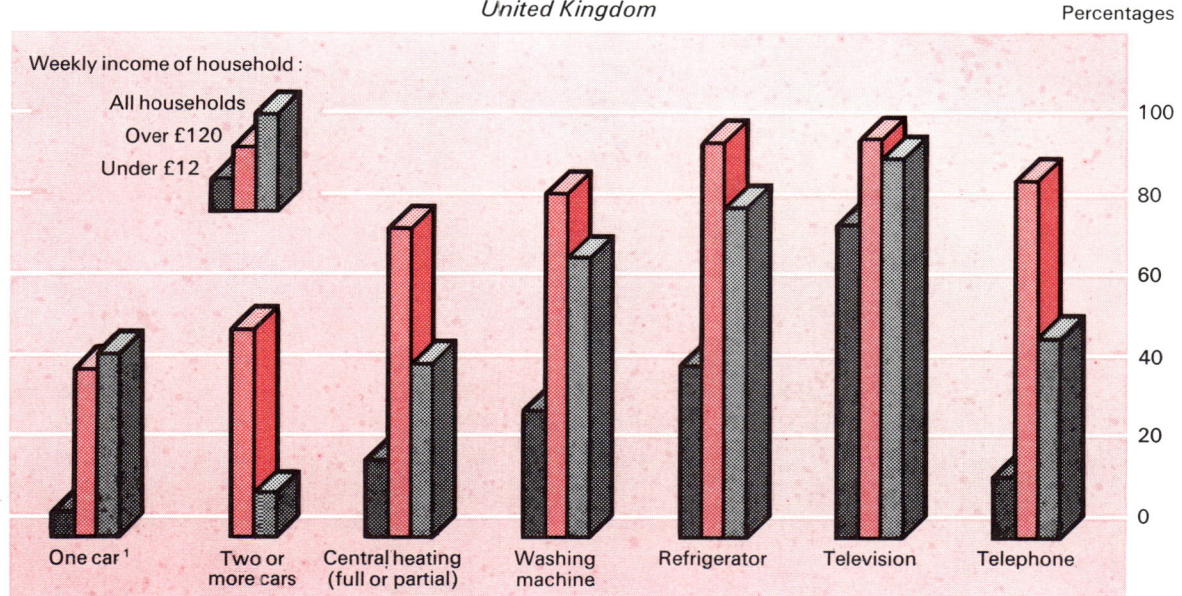

United Kingdom   Percentages

Weekly income of household:

All households
Over £120
Under £12

One car [1]   Two or more cars   Central heating (full or partial)   Washing machine   Refrigerator   Television   Telephone

[1] This means only one car.

Source: Family Expenditure Survey, Department of Employment

Table 6.8 Possession of, and attitudes toward, consumer durables, 1973 and 1975

Great Britain   Percentage of all households

	Possesses durable	Does not possess durable		
		And does not want	Would like to possess and expects to soon	Would like to possess but does not expect to soon
1975[1] (1973 data[1] in brackets)				
Washing machine	75 (74)	16 (16)	4 (4)	4 (5)
Central heating	42 (41)	29 (28)	6 (8)	19 (20)
Car	56 (56)	30 (27)	3 (5)	9 (10)
Refrigerator	86 (82)	7 (7)	3 (5)	3 (4)
Colour TV	42 (30)	31 (32)	7 (15)	15 (19)
Own telephone	54 (49)	24 (25)	3 (6)	15 (17)
Second home	4 (5)	58 (52)	2 (3)	32 (36)

[1] Figures do not add to 100 due to 'don't know' replies.

Source: Social Science Research Council Survey Unit, Quality of Life Surveys

**Chart 6.9
Consumption
of alcohol**

Consumption of alcohol per head of adult population

Beer   *United Kingdom*   Wines and spirits

Year

1911-1912
1931-1932
1961-1962
1971-1972
1974-1975

British wine
Imported wine
Spirits

40   30   20   10   0   0   0·5   1·0   1·5   2·0

Gallons   Wines: gallons; spirits: proof gallons

Source: HM Customs and Excise

**Chart 6.10
Changes in
household food
consumption,
1965-1975 and
1973-1975**

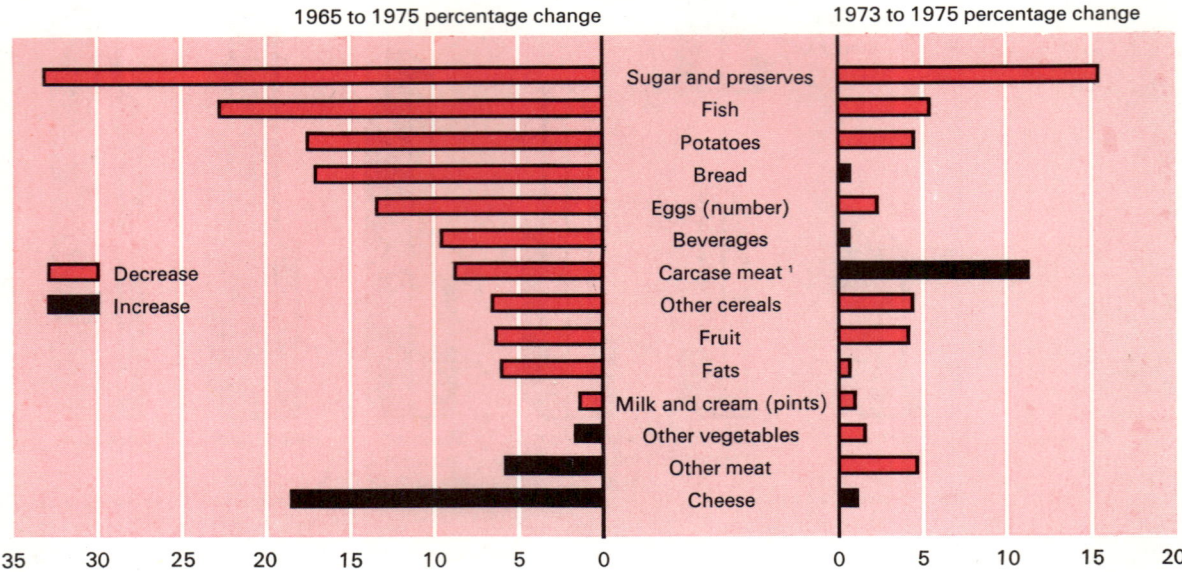

Change in average quantity by weight per head for all households
Great Britain

1965 to 1975 percentage change   1973 to 1975 percentage change

■ Decrease
■ Increase

Sugar and preserves
Fish
Potatoes
Bread
Eggs (number)
Beverages
Carcase meat [1]
Other cereals
Fruit
Fats
Milk and cream (pints)
Other vegetables
Other meat
Cheese

35 30 25 20 15 10 5 0   0 5 10 15 20

[1] In 1973 carcase meat was in short supply in an abnormal market situation. The average consumption figures per head (per week) were 1965: 16·78 ozs; 1973: 13·75 ozs; 1975: 15·30 ozs.   *Source: National Food Survey, Ministry of Agriculture, Fisheries and Food*

Table 6.11   Household food consumption

Great Britain   Index by weight: all households 1975=100

	Milk and cream (pints)	Cheese	Eggs (number)	Carcase meat	All other meat	Fish	Fruit	Bread	Potatoes	Beverages
All households:										
1955	99	75	101	119	72	133	92	164	136	114
1965	101	84	115	110	94	130	107	121	121	111
1974	100	99	99	96	97	97	99	99	104	104
1975	100	100	100	100	100	100	100	100	100	100
Gross weekly income of head of household, 1975:										
Pensioner households[1]	109	104	116	116	93	119	110	101	90	156
Under £28										
—with earners	98	90	100	122	105	103	79	108	112	111
—without earners	107	94	107	107	96	112	120	100	93	148
£28 and over without earners	102	134	120	103	102	125	167	96	91	128
£28 and under £49, with earners	98	94	99	94	103	95	83	107	109	96
£49 „ „ £82, „ „	99	100	96	98	100	98	99	99	99	93
£82 „ „ £110, „ „	101	110	99	107	95	100	128	83	93	83
£110 and over, „ „	103	118	101	99	90	101	146	78	72	77
Composition of household (consumption per head):										
1 adult	120	140	133	110	109	126	148	106	90	175
1 adult, 1 or more children	102	81	91	67	96	78	89	109	109	96
2 adults	103	126	115	136	119	132	129	105	97	137
2 adults, 1 child	106	98	97	91	106	98	102	97	97	89
2 adults, 2 children	101	85	88	83	86	79	84	88	89	73
2 adults, 3 children	94	72	83	91	80	73	78	94	101	68
2 adults, 4 or more children	91	69	84	61	79	64	63	103	114	66

[1] Households solely or mainly dependent on state retirement pensions (contributory) or non-contributory old age pensions.
        Source: National Food Survey, Ministry of Agriculture, Fisheries and Food

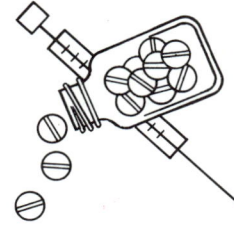

Health

This section presents statistics on some aspects of the state of health of the population of the United Kingdom; and it demonstrates services available to those who are sick or socially disadvantaged in some way. It also includes information on some aspects of preventive medicine.

The section has been organised in four main areas – mortality, morbidity, the provision and use of health services, and preventive medicine. There are four main sources of statistics. First, the records of the Registrars General give standard mortality information. Secondly, the records of

the health services give the use made of such services and, in particular, the *Hospital In-patient Enquiry* and its Scottish equivalent give a sample survey of in-patients which is used for several tables in this section. Thirdly, the national insurance records provide information on absence from work for those who are entitled to sickness benefit (though these statistics are not very representative for women). Finally, the *General Household Survey* (*GHS*), a sample survey of interviews with the public, provides information both on morbidity and on the use of services.

Table 7.1 Summary of mortality statistics, 1951-1974

		1951	1961	1966	1970	1971	1972	1973	1974
		Great Britain							*Various units*
SMRs[1] (all ages: 1968 = 100)	Males	114	103	101	98	95	98	97	95
	Females	128	106	100	97	94	97	96	95
Expectation of life[2]:									
At birth	Males	66·2	67·9	68·5	68·6	68·7	68·8	69·1	69·3[6]
	Females	71·2	73·3	74·7	74·9	74·9	75·1	75·4	75·5[6]
At age 30	Males	40·2	40·9	41·2	41·2	41·3	41·4	41·5	41·7[6]
	Females	44·5	46·1	46·7	46·8	46·9	47·0	47·2	47·2[6]
At age 60	Males	14·7	15·0	15·2	15·1	15·2	15·3	15·4	15·2[6]
	Females	18·0	19·0	19·7	19·7	19·8	19·9	20·1	20·1[6]
Infant mortality per 1,000 live births									
Neonatal[3]		19·3	15·6	13·1	12·4	11·8	11·6	11·3	11·2
Post-neonatal[3]		11·5	6·3	6·3	6·0	5·9	5·8	5·8	5·4
Maternal mortality[4] per 1,000 births									
Deaths due to abortion		0·16	0·06	0·06	0·04	0·03	0·04	0·02	0·02
Other maternal deaths[5]		0·63	0·27	0·20	0·15	0·13	0·12	0·12	0·12

[1] Standardised mortality ratios.   [2] These figures have been obtained by weighting the separate expectations for England and Wales and for Scotland in proportion to the respective home populations for the relevant year. They make no allowance for any future improvement in mortality thereafter.   [3] Neonatal relates to the deaths occurring under the age of 4 weeks and post-neonatal to those of 4 weeks and under 1 year.
[4] See notes in Appendix B, page 245.   [5] Excludes associated maternal deaths.   [6] Provisional figures only.
Sources: Office of Population Censuses and Surveys; Government Actuary's Department

Chart 7.2 Infant and maternal mortality

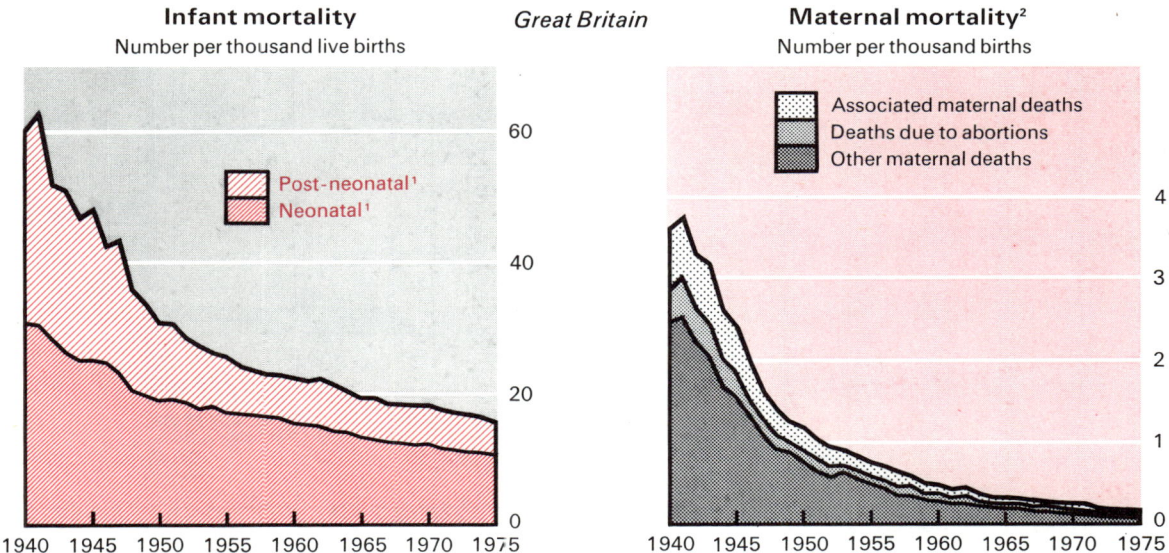

Infant mortality
Number per thousand live births

Great Britain

Maternal mortality[2]
Number per thousand births

[1] Neonatal relates to the deaths occurring under the age of 4 weeks and post-neonatal to those of 4 weeks and under 1 year.
[2] See notes in Appendix B, page 245.   *Source: Office of Population Censuses and Surveys*

Table 7.3   Deaths by selected causes: standardised mortality ratios[1]

Great Britain   SMRs base year 1968 = 100

	Males				Females				All persons: percentage of total deaths 1974
	SMRs			Number of deaths in 1974	SMRs			Number of deaths in 1974	
	1961	1966	1974		1961	1966	1974		
Tuberculosis, all forms	174	115	57	1,000	162	116	63	450	0·22
Meningococcal infections	115	99	209	147	169	106	231	102	0·04
Cancer:									
Digestive system	102	100	98	22,326	105	100	95	21,565	6·75
Lung, bronchus, trachea	88	97	105	29,379	72	90	130	7,418	5·66
Breast	105	121	104	90	97	98	107	12,332	1·91
Cervix uteri					105	102	83	2,278	0·35
Prostate	101	103	101	4,733					0·73
Leukaemia	93	96	95	1,795	91	95	95	1,584	0·52
Diabetes	82	91	106	2,219	98	100	98	3,556	0·89
Chronic rheumatic heart disease	139	109	81	2,429	134	105	81	4,149	1·01
Hypertensive disease	156	108	73	4,098	170	112	68	5,187	1·43
Ischaemic heart disease	90	97	104	98,472	97	97	102	73,806	26·50
Other forms of heart disease	..	..	80	11,624	..	..	77	18,366	4·61
Cerebrovascular disease	105	103	89	34,230	105	100	91	54,800	13·70
Influenza	190	95	27	588	141	79	24	792	0·21
Pneumonia	84	91	105	21,513	76	88	106	28,264	7·66
Bronchitis, emphysema, and asthma	101	104	76	21,337	108	105	75	7,791	4·48
Peptic ulcer	118	98	87	2,803	106	98	106	1,947	0·73
Congenital anomalies	123	103	92	2,388	128	103	97	2,205	0·71
Motor vehicle accidents	114	120	98	4,964	99	107	97	2,255	1·11
All other accidents	126	123	92	5,209	115	110	89	5,907	1·71
Suicide	117	106	85	2,540	115	113	86	1,796	0·67
All causes	103	101	95	328,037	106	100	95	321,995	100·00

Note: See also Table 11.8 (road casualties).
[1] See notes in Appendices A and B.

Sources: General Register Office for Scotland; Office of Population Censuses and Surveys

Chart 7.4 Deaths by selected causes[1]

Great Britain

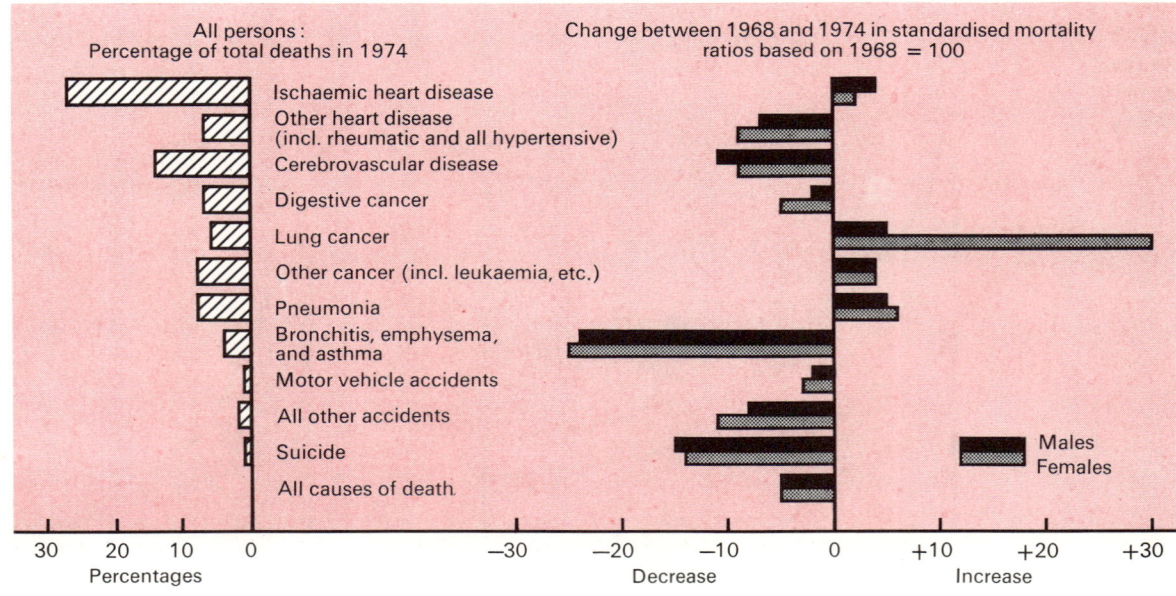

[1] See notes in Appendix A.

Source: Office of Population Censuses and Surveys

Table 7.5 Death at various ages: death rates for selected causes: by sex

Great Britain   Rate per 100,000 population in each age group

	Males				Females			
	1950–53 average	1961	1973[1]	1974[1]	1950–53 average	1961	1973[1]	1974[1]
Ages under 1 year								
Infective, etc., diseases	249	75	78	67	199	71	57	51
Pneumonia	527	320	160	149	416	254	113	108
Congenital anomalies	460	460	380	403	430	455	381	401
All non-motor vehicle accidents[2]	122	73	62	56	95	53	38	40
All other causes	1,936	1,522	1,209	1,208	1,415	1,087	859	819
All causes	3,293	2,450	1,889	1,884	2,554	1,920	1,448	1,419
Ages 1–14 years								
Infective, etc., diseases	15	4	3	3	14	3	2	2
Cancer, including leukaemia	8	8	7	6	7	7	5	5
Pneumonia	7	6	3	3	7	5	3	3
Motor vehicle accidents	11	9	9	7	5	5	5	5
All other accidents[2]	13	12	9	8	7	5	4	4
All other causes	30	24	19	18	27	20	15	15
All causes	85	62	49	45	67	44	34	34
Ages 15–34 years								
Infective, etc., diseases	26	3	1	1	33	3	1	1
Cancer, including leukaemia	15	15	13	13	13	12	12	11
Motor vehicle accidents	19	31	30	28	3	6	8	7
All other accidents[2]	21	16	17	15	3	3	4	4
Suicide	6	8	8	8	3	4	4	4
All other causes	49	36	30	30	51	31	22	21
All causes	136	108	99	96	105	59	50	47
Ages 35–44 years								
Infective, etc., diseases	42	9	3	3	27	6	2	3
Cancer, including leukaemia	58	53	48	46	71	68	66	64
Heart diseases[3]	54	68	78	78	34	27	20	21
Motor vehicle accidents	11	15	15	13	2	4	5	4
All other accidents[2]	21	20	18	18	4	4	7	8
Suicide	12	15	13	12	7	9	8	7
All other causes	93	69	57	58	83	62	51	51
All causes	288	248	231	227	228	180	159	158
Ages 45–64 years								
Infective, etc., diseases	89	27	10	10	26	10	5	5
Cancer, including leukaemia	350	384	382	380	266	271	297	300
Heart diseases[3]	417	484	567	563	196	179	180	181
Cerebrovascular diseases	115	109	95	91	121	96	74	75
Bronchitis	114	113	70	63	26	21	20	20
Suicide	25	24	15	16	13	17	11	11
All other causes	329	270	224	220	198	165	150	150
All causes	1,439	1,412	1,365	1,343	848	759	737	742
Ages 65–74 years								
Infective, etc., diseases	126	71	25	23	34	18	9	11
Cancer, including leukaemia	1,053	1,186	1,357	1,348	655	620	652	658
Heart diseases[3]	1,924	1,912	1,938	1,945	1,204	1,072	928	909
Cerebrovascular diseases	725	678	568	551	653	579	439	428
Pneumonia	184	236	265	256	108	136	160	154
Bronchitis	461	549	408	389	158	117	72	69
All accidents, poisonings and violence[2]	115	113	80	84	64	79	63	63
All other causes	899	784	574	593	584	523	397	393
All causes	5,487	5,530	5,214	5,190	3,462	3,145	2,719	2,685

[1] Figures for 1973 and 1974 are based on the eighth revision of the International Classification of Diseases, while those for earlier years are based on the seventh revision categories most similar to them. Comparability between the two periods may therefore be approximate in some cases.
[2] Includes injury undetermined whether accidentally or purposely inflicted.
[3] Includes all terms of hypertension for 1973 and 1974, but not for earlier years.

Source: Office of Population Censuses and Surveys; General Register Office of Scotland

**Chart 7.6
Morbidity:
reported
sickness, 1973**

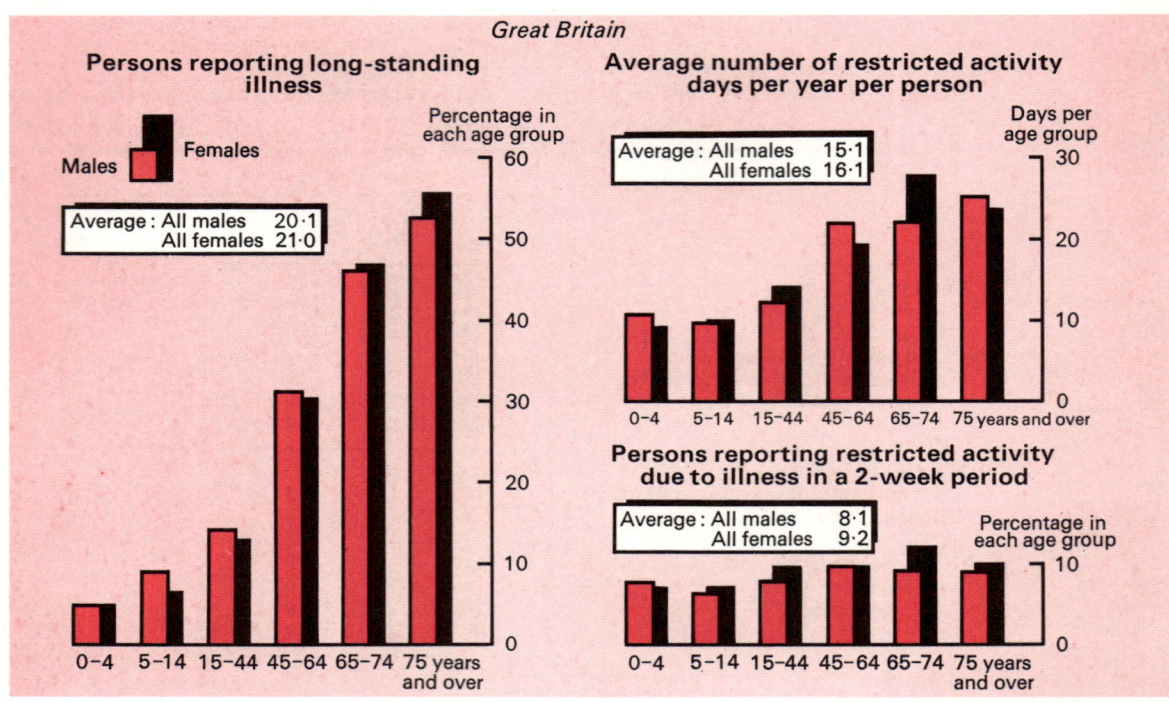

Source: General Household Survey, 1973

Table 7.7 Morbidity: chronic sickness[1]: by marital status, 1973

Great Britain   Percentages in each sub-group

	Males aged			Male observed rates as a percentage of expected rates[2]	Females aged			Female observed rates as a percentage of expected rates[2]
	15–44	45–64	65 and over		15–44	45–64	65 and over	
Persons reporting long-standing illness: by marital status:								
Single	12·9	31·3	39·0	92	12·4	34·7	48·8	101
Married	14·9	30·5	48·8	101	12·6	27·9	46·0	95
Other	14·4	40·3	47·1	104	18·2	38·6	52·9	111
All persons	14·2	31·0	47·8	100	12·7	30·2	50·0	100
Persons reporting limiting long-standing illness: by marital status:								
Single	5·5	21·0	32·0	96	5·1	23·3	35·3	102
Married	6·3	18·3	35·2	100	5·8	15·5	32·9	93
Other	4·8[3]	26·7	33·6	105	11·9	25·6	36·0	112
All persons	6·0	18·9	34·6	100	5·9	17·7	34·8	100

[1]–[3] See notes in Appendix A.   *Source: General Household Survey, 1973*

Table 7.8 Morbidity: acute sickness[1]: by marital status, 1973

Great Britain   Percentages in each sub-group

	Males aged			Male observed rates as a percentage of expected rates[2]	Females aged			Female observed rates as a percentage of expected rates[2]
	15–44	45–64	65 and over		15–44	45–64	65 and over	
Persons reporting acute sickness: by marital status:								
Single	7·5	8·0	6·0[3]	93	10·5	14·0	8·3	109
Married	8·1	9·5	9·7	101	8·9	9·0	11·3	94
Other	7·2[3]	16·0	8·0	111	14·6	10·5	11·8	113
All persons	7·8	9·7	9·1	100	9·5	9·6	11·2	100

[1]–[3] See notes in Appendix A.   *Source: General Household Survey, 1973*

Table 7.9 Hospital summary: all specialties

United Kingdom

	Units	1961	1966	1971	1973	1974	1975
In-patients							
Discharges and deaths	Thousands	5,007	5,736	6,437	6,385	6,447	6,214
of which private in-patients[1]		84	102	115	116	114	98
Average number of beds occupied daily	Thousands	472	461	436	414	407	396
of which private in-patients[1]		3	3	3	2	2	2
Average length of stay							
—all patients	Days	34·5	29·4	24·7	23·7	23·0	23·3
—excluding psychiatric, geriatric, and chronic sick patients	Days	14·5	12·4	10·4	10·0	9·9	9·9
Waiting lists	Thousands	..	604	596	624	629	704
of which surgical patients		..	557	554	587	593	657
Out-patients[2] (excl. accident and emergency)							
New patients	Thousands	..	8,935	9,572	9,608	9,509	9,714
Average attendances per new patient	Number	..	4·1	4·2	4·2	4·2	4·2
Accident and emergency patients[2]							
New patients	Thousands	..	7,909	9,358	10,018	9,870	9,989
Average attendances per new patient	Number	..	1·9	1·6	1·6	1·6	1·5
Rates per 1,000 population							
In-patients							
Discharges and deaths	Number per 1,000 population	94·6	104·7	115·8	114·0	115·1	111·0
Waiting lists		..	11·1	10·7	11·2	11·2	12·6
Out-patients[2] (excl. accident and emergency) New patients		163	164	172	172	170	173
Accident and emergency patients[2] New patients		105	144	168	179	176	179

[1] Figures relate to England and Wales only. [2] Figures for out-patients in Scotland include ancillary departments.

Sources: Scottish Home and Health Department; Welsh Office; Department of Health and Social Services (Northern Ireland); Department of Health and Social Security

Table 7.10 Selected types of illness: non-psychiatric hospitals

Great Britain — Discharges per 10,000 population

Diagnostic group	Mean duration of stay (days) 1973	Mean waiting time[1] (weeks) 1973	1968 Males	1968 Females	1973 Males	1973 Females
Infective and parasitic diseases	18·0	6·4	26·4	21·0	22·7	18·6
All malignant neoplasms	18·3	4·5	50·7	46·9	58·4	54·5
Benign neoplasms and neoplasms of unspecified rature	7·5	11·2	15·7	40·4	11·5	34·3
Endocrine, nutritional, and metabolic diseases	20·7	8·8	12·8	21·4	14·6	22·3
Diseases of nervous system	45·6	8·3	17·0	16·5	17·6	17·5
Diseases of eye	8·7	16·2	20·6	22·6	20·3	22·9
Rheumatic fever, hypertensive disease, and heart disease	24·0	6·3	56·6	41·2	65·6	45·3
Diseases of peripheral circulatory system	43·3	16·4	44·6	47·7	47·5	49·1
Diseases of respiratory system	12·2	22·1	117·5	86·3	102·4	74·3
Diseases of digestive system	9·8	13·0	121·3	88·0	114·9	88·8
Male genital disorders	8·8	14·6	32·8	–	33·6	–
Diseases of breast and female genital system	6·0	12·1	0·5	104·7	0·7	104·4
Conditions of pregnancy, childbirth, and puerperium	6·5[2]	1·5[2]	–	964·9[3]	–	962·2[3]
Diseases of skin and subcutaneous tissue	12·4	12·3	17·4	15·1	17·9	15·4
Congenital anomalies	12·1	19·0	18·2	11·8	20·7	13·4
Symptoms and ill-defined conditions	11·6	10·8	64·3	63·2	80·0	78·1
Fractures, dislocations, and sprains	21·9	11·1	43·1	29·8	41·2	33·2
Other injuries and reactions	5·4	11·1	74·8	46·9	80·2	58·0
All causes	14·1[2]	13·7[2]	822·9	1,160·8	859·2	1,208·1

[1] Mean waiting time of those patients admitted from the waiting list. [2] Excludes ante-natal care in Scotland.
[3] Rate based on female population 15–44.

Sources: Scottish Hospital In-patient Statistics, Scottish Health Service; Hospital In-patient Enquiry, Department of Health and Social Security

**Chart 7.11
Hospital
summary: by
specialty, 1974**

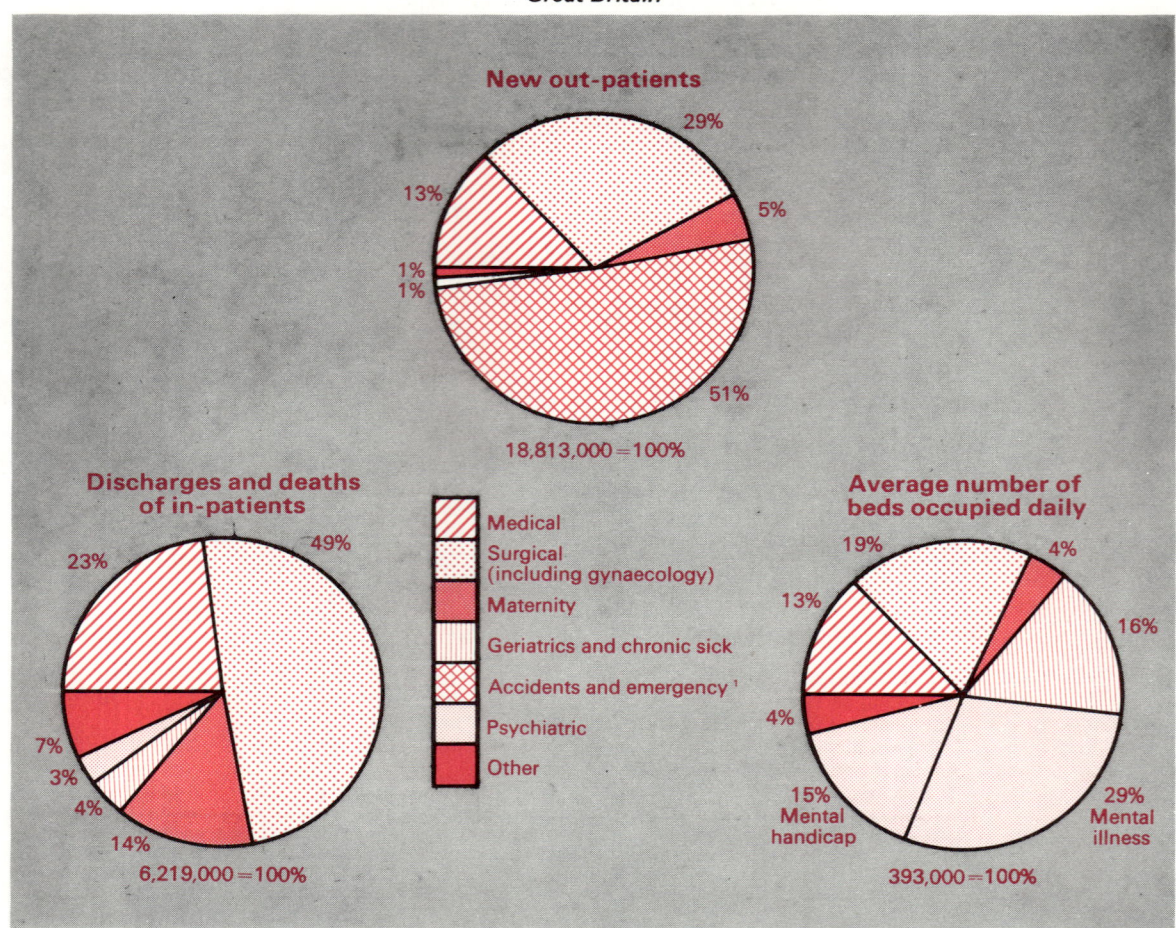

Great Britain

New out-patients

29%

13%

5%

1%
1%

51%

18,813,000 = 100%

**Discharges and deaths
of in-patients**

49%

23%

7%

3%

4%

14%

6,219,000 = 100%

Medical

Surgical
(including gynaecology)

Maternity

Geriatrics and chronic sick

Accidents and emergency [1]

Psychiatric

Other

**Average number of
beds occupied daily**

19%

4%

13%

16%

4%

15%
Mental
handicap

29%
Mental
illness

393,000 = 100%

[1] The specialty 'Accidents and emergency' applies to out-patients only. On admission, these cases are allocated to their respective in-hospital specialty.

Sources: Various, see Appendix C

**Table 7.12   Resident patients in mental illness hospitals and units: by age and duration
of stay at 31 December 1974**

England and Wales   Rates and thousands

	Duration of stay						Total resident patients (thousands)
	Under 1 year	1 year	2 years	3 years	5 years	All durations	
Age group (rates per 100,000 population):							
Under 20	10	2	1	–	–	13	2·0
20–34	56	8	4	5	10	83	8·4
35–44	61	10	7	8	50	136	7·7
45–54	67	15	11	16	131	240	14·9
55–64	70	19	14	18	215	335	18·1
65–74	110	39	25	33	291	497	22·0
75 and over	223	101	66	95	439	925	22·5
All ages	58	16	10	14	96	194	95·6
Total resident patients (thousands)	28·8	7·8	5·1	6·7	47·2	95·6	

Sources: Department of Health and Social Security; Welsh Office

Chart 7.13
Private medical insurance

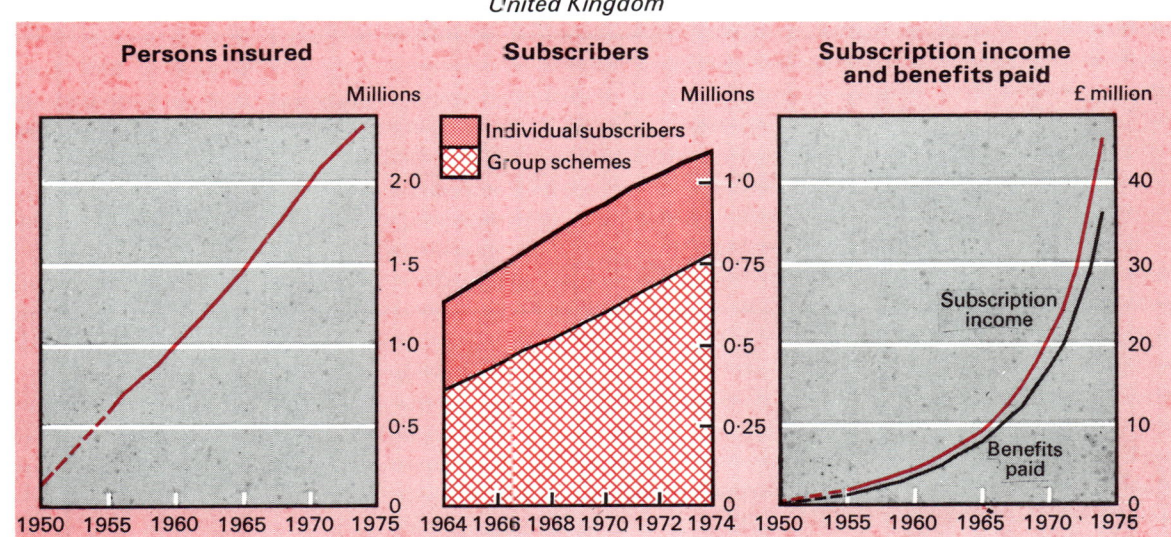

United Kingdom

Persons insured — Millions

Subscribers — Millions
- Individual subscribers
- Group schemes

Subscription income and benefits paid — £ million
Subscription income
Benefits paid

Source: UK Private Medical Care, Provident Schemes Statistics, 1974, Department of Health and Social Security

Chart 7.14
Number of health centres[1]

Chart 7.15
Family practitioner services: shares in total cost[1]

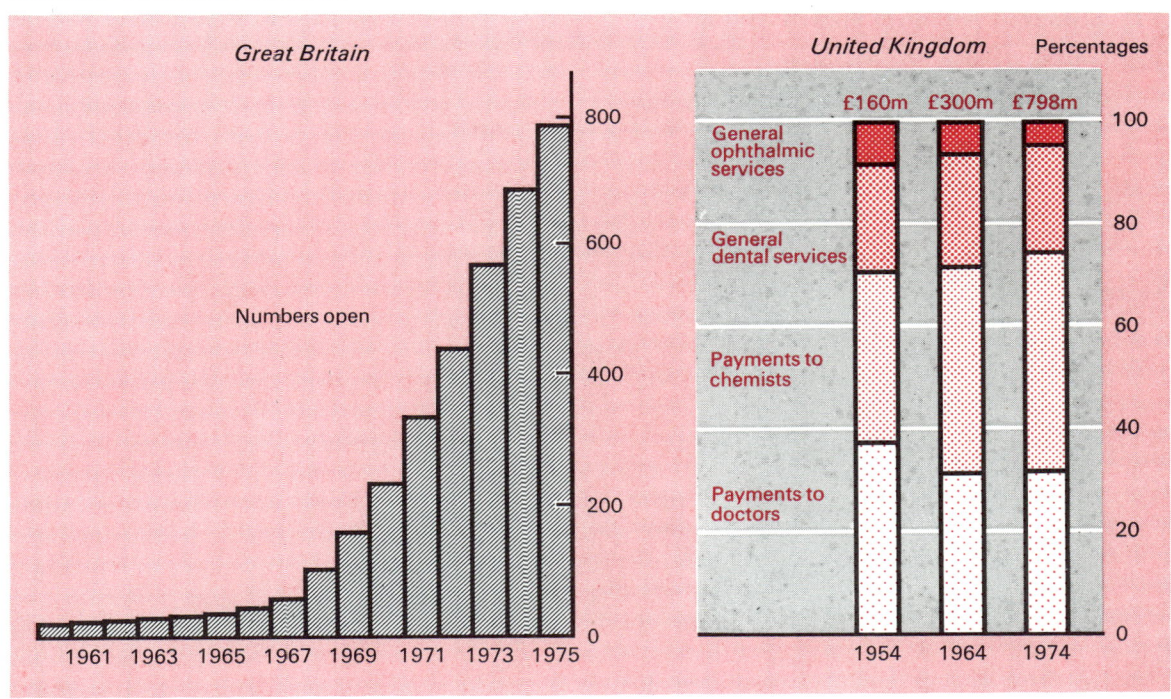

Great Britain

Numbers open

United Kingdom — Percentages

£160m   £300m   £798m

- General ophthalmic services
- General dental services
- Payments to chemists
- Payments to doctors

1954   1964   1974

[1] Number of health centres open at the end of each year.
Sources: Department of Health and Social Security;
Welsh Office; Scottish Health Service, Common Services Agency

[1] Excludes administrative costs and includes patients' charges.
Source: Annual Abstract of Statistics, 1975,
Central Statistical Office

Table 7.16   Persons consulting general practitioners (NHS)[1] : by marital status, 1973

Great Britain   Percentages in each sub-group

	Males aged			Male observed rates as a percentage of expected rates[2]	Females aged			Female observed rates as a percentage of expected rates[2]
	15–44	45–64	65 and over		15–44	45–64	65 and over	
Marital status								
Single	6·6	6·9	12·0	82	11·4	17·7	14·2	92
Married	8·4	11·5	15·0	105	14·5	10·7	14·8	101
Other	6·4[3]	14·6	13·5	99	15·4	12·8	15·5	105
All persons	7·7	11·3	14·5	100	13·7	11·6	15·1	100

[1]–[3] See notes in Appendix A.   *Source: General Household Survey, 1973*

Regional variations

Table 7.17 shows that there are regional variations in both health services, and in morbidity and mortality. Although the mortality figures have been presented as a rate per 1000 men aged 45–64, the data in this table are not adjusted for any differences in age/sex structure of the population. Even if they were, regional variations would still exist for many other economic, industrial, and sociological reasons: for example, morbidity in Wales is high whatever measure is taken.

Table 7.17   Selected regional health statistics

	Morbidity			Services		Mortality				
	Persons reporting acute sickness per thousand population[1] 1973	Persons reporting long-standing illness, per thousand population[1] 1973	Certified sickness: males – days of incapacity per person at risk[2] 1972/73	General medical practitioners Average list size[3] 1975	General dental service Persons per dentist[4] 1975	Deaths per thousand males aged 45–64 1975[7]				Infant mortality 1975[7]
						Lung cancer	Other cancers	Heart disease	Bron-chitis[5]	
Standard regions:										
North	91	224	25·3	2,434	5,650	2·0	2·3	6·2	0·8	15·0
Yorkshire and Humberside	77	217	21·5	2,450	5,078	1·7	2·0	6·1	0·7	17·3
East Midlands	86	225	15·9	2,495	5,662	1·5	1·9	5·2	0·6	15·1
East Anglia	83	202	12·9	2,302	4,941	1·4	1·8	4·4	0·4	14·6
South East										
Greater London	98	208 ⎫	10·5	2,309	3,234	1·7	2·0	5·2	0·6	16·0
Other South East	88	190 ⎭				1·3	1·9	4·7	0·4	14·3
South West	77	191	16·0	2,188	3,617	1·4	2·0	5·0	0·5	14·4
West Midlands	88	198	14·8	2,424	5,216	1·8	2·0	5·4	0·7	16·8
North West	86	219	21·0	2,454	4,947	2·0	2·3	6·4	0·8	17·2
Wales	106	259	32·2	2,208	5,194	1·6	2·1	6·6	0·8	14·5
England and Wales	88	210	16·4	2,373	4,248	1·6	2·0	5·5	0·6	15·7
Scotland	79	177	20·0	1,939	4,611	1·9	2·2	6·5	0·6	17·2
Great Britain	87	205	16·7	2,329	4,263	1·7	2·0	5·6	0·6	15·8
Northern Ireland	..	..	27·1[6]	2,105	4,880	1·2	2·1	7·0	0·9	20·4

[1] See notes on the General Household Survey in Appendix B.   [2] Figures are for 7 June 1972 to 3 June 1973.   [3] As at 1 October.   [4] As at 30 September.
[5] Figures for bronchitis relate to ICD Nos. 490–492 (Bronchitis and Emphysema), a different classification from that used in Tables 7.3 and 7.5.
[6] From 1 June 1972 to 31 May 1973.   [7] Provisional.   *Sources: Various, see Appendix C*

Maternity services

These are related to the number of births, and thus there has been a general downward trend as the birth-rate has fallen. Very few mothers now have their babies at home, although as recently as 1961, one-third did so. The average length of stay in hospital has fallen from over 9 to under 7 days in the same period.

Table 7.18   Maternity services

Great Britain   Various units

	Unit	1961	1966	1971	1972	1973	1974	1975
Births								
Total births	Thousands	930	961	881	814	759	718	678
of which:								
Percentage at home	Per cent	33	24	10	8	6	4	..
NHS hospitals in-patient maternity service								
Average daily number of beds occupied	Thousands	18	20	19	18	17	17	16
Average length of stay	Days	9·3	8·1	7·0	7·0	6·8	6·9	6·8
Other maternity services								
Women receiving ante- or post-natal care:								
NHS hospitals	Thousands	806	936	973	936	896	857	825
Community health clinics		423	324	285	279	226	..	..
Ante-natal mothercraft and relaxation classes		..	145	150	147	136	131	128
Domiciliary midwives — early discharge cases		..	308	476	509	533	504	526

Sources: Department of Health and Social Security; Common Services Agency of the Scottish Health Service ; Welsh Office

Family planning

The new table below replaces previous versions based on information from family planning agencies. Area Health Authorities are scheduled to complete the takeover of the former agency arrangements with the Family Planning Association by 1 October 1976; the table is now based on AHA returns. By no means all family planning advice comes from the NHS, however. Statistics for all non-NHS clinics are not available, but, for example, in 1975 the Brook Advisory Centres gave advice to 44,218 clients who made 123,014 visits to their clinics. Such visits were mainly in London (37,155) and Birmingham (42,365).

Table 7.19   Family planning services

Great Britain   Thousands

	1971	1972	1973[1]	1974[2]	1975
Clinic services (community and hospital)					
New patients[3]	329·8	384·9	456·0	1,142·3	1,617·9
Attendances	2,146·1	2,463·8	2,912·7	2,743·9	4,116·0
Domiciliary services					
New patients[3]	..	..	..	14·1	21·0
Visits by family planning staff	..	..	..	54·3	77·4

[1] 1973 figures for Scotland are estimates based on the first quarter of the year only.   [2] 1974 figures are for period 1 April to 31 December 1974.
[3] 1971–1973, each patient counted in the year of attendance if no visits during previous three years. 1974, new patients counted at first visit during the period 1 April to 31 December 1974.   *Source: Health and Personal Social Services, Department of Health and Social Security*

Table 7.20 Abortions[1]

	Great Britain					Thousands
	Women residents of the United Kingdom					
	1970	1971	1972	1973	1974	1975[3]
Total number of abortions	81·7	102·1	117·8	120·1	119·1	115·6[3]
Age of woman:						
Under 16 years	1·9	2·4	3·0	3·3	3·5[2]	3·5[4]
16 to 19 years	14·4	19·5	23·7	25·6	26·0[2]	23·9[4]
Under 20 years	16·3	22·0	26·7	28·9	29·5[2]	27·4[4]
20 to 34 years	48·9	60·3	69·1	69·6	67·2[2]	61·4[4]
35 to 44 years	14·5	17·4	19·5	19·2	18·2[2]	15·5[4]
45 years and over	0·4	0·5	0·5	0·6	0·5[2]	0·5[4]
Age unknown	1·6	1·9	2·0	1·9	1·6[2]	1·9[4]
Place of abortion:						
NHS hospitals	52·6	59·7	64·4	62·9	65·6	51·6[4]
Private hospitals and clinics	28·9	42·3	53·4	57·2	53·5	55·0[4]
Number of children[2]						
0	34·9	45·5	53·3	55·7	56·5	..
1	8·6	10·9	13·3	13·7	14·1	..
2	13·4	17·1	20·4	21·4	21·6	..
3	10·8	13·1	15·1	14·6	13·7	..
4 or more	12·7	13·7	14·0	12·5	11·0	..
Not stated	0·7	0·6	0·2	0·2	0·1	..

[1] Terminations carried out in England and Wales are occurrences and those in Scotland are notifications. No abortions are performed in Northern Ireland. [2] Excludes abortions in England and Wales to women whose country of usual residence was Scotland or Northern Ireland.
[3] Provisional. [4] Terminations carried out in England and Wales to women whose country of usual residence was England and Wales.

Source: Office of Population Censuses and Surveys, Scottish Home and Health Department

Statistics on personal problems

This group of tables and charts, 7.21–7.24, contains information on venereal diseases, alcoholism, dangerous drug addicts, and smoking habits. For the first two topics the tables simply show the numbers who have come into contact with various health services, and neither these numbers nor any trends necessarily reflect the total incidence. Thus Table 7.21 on venereal diseases refers to people who have been seen at hospital clinics and Chart 7.23 to people admitted to mental illness hospitals with a diagnosis of alcoholism. Table 7.24 lists numbers *registered* as drug addicts with the Home Office. The figures on smoking are self-reported from the *General Household Survey*, and estimate the total incidence in the population living in private households. A more detailed analysis of smoking habits can be found in the results of *The General Household Survey, 1973* (*HMSO 1976*).

Table 7.21 Venereal diseases: new patients seen at hospital clinics

	Great Britain					Thousands
	1949	1959	1969	1973	1974	1975
Cases (in all stages) dealt with for the first time at any centre:						
Syphilis						
Male	9	2	2	3	3	3
Female	7	2	1	1	1	1
Non-specific infections[1]						
Male	25	38	44	75	76	76
Female	10	14	..	15	15	17
Gonorrhoea						
Male	24	28	39	42	42	41
Female	5	7	16	23	23	24
Other conditions not requiring treatment						
Male	36	26	40	58	51	57
Female	17	10	21	32	33	35

[1] Includes chancroid.

Sources: Department of Health and Social Security; Scottish Home and Health Department

**Chart 7.22
Smoking habits, 1973**

**Chart 7.23
Alcoholism[1] : admissions to
mental illness hospitals and units**

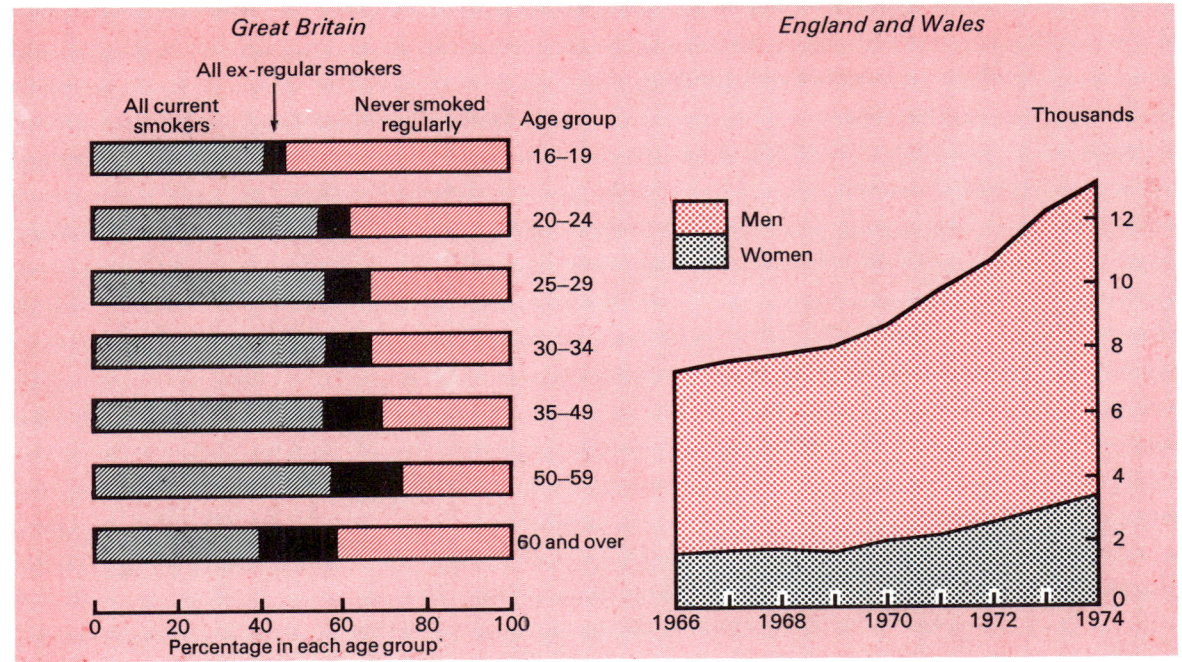

Great Britain

All ex-regular smokers

All current smokers — Never smoked regularly — Age group

16–19
20–24
25–29
30–34
35–49
50–59
60 and over

0   20   40   60   80   100
Percentage in each age group

Source: General Household Survey, 1973

England and Wales

Thousands

Men
Women

12
10
8
6
4
2
0

1966   1968   1970   1972   1974

[1] Figures are for hospitals and units under Regional Hospital Boards and teaching hospitals. They include patients whose first or second diagnosis was alcoholism or alcoholic psychosis.

Source: Department of Health and Social Security

Table 7.24   Dangerous drugs: registered addicts

United Kingdom   Numbers

	1970	1971	1972	1973	1974	1975
Number registered as taking drugs on						
31 December[1]	1,426	1,549	1,615	1,815	1,972	1,954
Males	1,051	1,133	1,194	1,369	1,459	1,438
Females	375	416	421	446	513	516
Age distribution:						
Under 20 years	142	118	96	84	64	39
20 and under 25	631	722	727	750	692	561
25 and under 30	237	288	376	530	684	754
30 and under 35	90	112	117	134	163	219
35 and under 50	112	112	118	136	163	169
50 and over	195	177	165	180	198	194
Age not stated	19	20	16	1	8	18
Type of drug[2]:						
Methadone	991	1,160	1,278	1,439	1,552	1,543
Heroin	437	385	338	378	392	316
Morphine	105	100	89	83	82	70
Pethidine	77	70	59	50	61	62
Cocaine	57	58	46	51	47	23
Dipipanone	45	49	37	48	76	133
Dextromoramide	28	35	32	49	64	70
Other drugs	13	9	7	8	11	7

Note: In 1975 there were 36 hospitals holding special clinics for the out-patient treatment of drug dependence, all having access to in-patient facilities. Treatment is also provided in general psychiatric units.

[1] Comparable figures for years before 1970 are not available.   [2] Addicts who are receiving more than one drug are shown against each drug they receive. Heroin and methadone are the drugs most commorly used together. In 1970 254 addicts were receiving both drugs: the figures for 1971, 1972, 1973 1974, and 1975 are 229, 201, 223, 243, and 212 respectively.

Source: Home Office

Table 7.25   Health visitor, home nursing, and chiropody services

	Great Britain			Thousands and rate per thousand	
	1971	1972	1973	1974	1975
Health visitors: cases attended					
Total:					
Thousands	5,158·5	5,317·9	5,047·9	4,957·6	4,658·9
Rate per thousand	95·4	98·0	92·8	91·1	85·6
Children aged under 1[1]					
Thousands	924·4	858·8	817·6	832·3	784·2
Children aged under 5					
Thousands	2,826·8	2,590·6	2,401·3	2,283·3	2,139·2
Rate per thousand	650·2	609·1	579·2	573·3	560·7
Persons aged 65 and over					
Thousands	518·1	636·5	660·1	677·9	632·5
Rate per thousand	72·2	87·2	88·9	89·8	82·6
Home nurses: cases attended					
Total:					
Thousands	1,265·2	2,146·9	2,408·3	2,481·8	2,775·4
Rate per thousand	23·4	39·6	44·3	45·6	51·0
Children aged under 5					
Thousands	43·9	161·1	172·8	160·0	180·2
Rate per thousand	10·1	37·9	41·7	40·2	47·2
Persons aged 65 and over					
Thousands	683·8	970·6	1,028·1	1,078·9	1,160·0
Rate per thousand	95·3	132·9	138·5	143·0	151·5
Chiropody services: persons treated					
Total:					
Thousands	1,122·2	1,203·4	1,284·5	1,560·6	1,374·2
Rate per thousand	20·8	22·2	23·6	28·7	25·2
Persons aged 65 and over					
Thousands	1,078·8	1,155·3	1,238·4	1,509·9	1,270·8
Rate per thousand	150·3	158·2	166·9	200·1	166·0

[1] All babies are visited by a health visitor immediately after birth.

Source: Health and Personal Social Services, Department of Health and Social Security

Table 7.26   Services provided for the disabled

	England				Numbers and rates	
	Households assisted (numbers)			Households assisted per 100,000 total household population		
	1972–73	1973–74	1974–75	1972–73	1973–74	1974–75
Telephone installation	16,759	21,813	22,025	36	47	47
Telephone attachments	707	1,109	1,617	2	2	3
Telephone rental	12,151	28,808	47,089	26	62	101
Television (supply)	2,242	2,545	2,205	5	5	5
Television licence	4,289	6,455	16,036	9	14	35
Radio (supply)	769	905	532	2	2	1
Other personal aids	118,211	142,453	159,386	255	307	343
Adaptations (all property)	28,374	39,173	41,255	61	84	89
Holidays[1]	80,860	89,817	104,835	174	193	226

[1] Relates to persons, not households.

Source: Department of Health and Social Security

Preventive medicine

Chart 7.27 and Table 7.28 show two aspects of preventive medicine: cervical cytology examinations and vaccinations carried out. Data are derived from administrative records of the services and although vaccinations are related to the population at risk this is not so easy for cervical cytology. Thus Chart 7.27 simply shows number of examinations and percentages requiring treatment.

**Chart 7.27
Cervical cytology: examinations and positive cases detected**

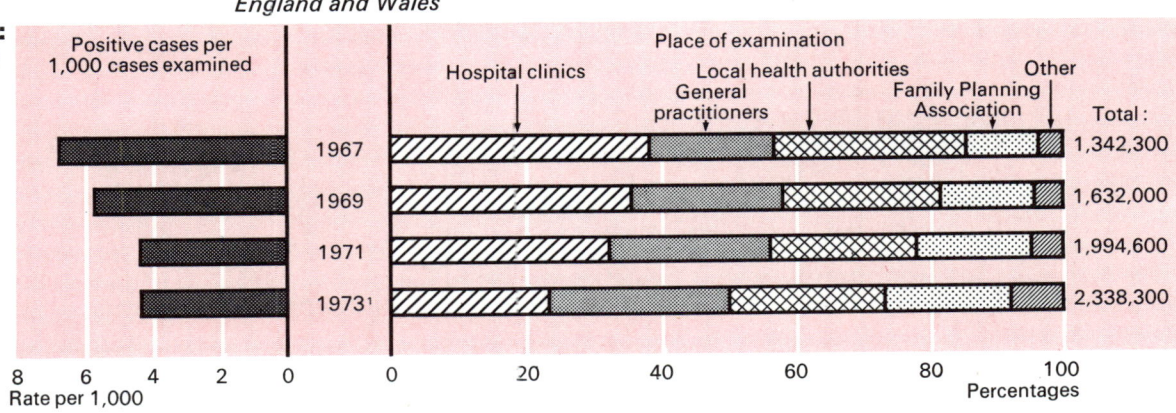

England and Wales

Positive cases per 1,000 cases examined

Place of examination

Hospital clinics — General practitioners — Local health authorities — Family Planning Association — Other

Year	Total:
1967	1,342,300
1969	1,632,000
1971	1,994,600
1973[1]	2,338,300

Rate per 1,000

Percentages

[1] Estimated numbers of cases examined based in part on a 20 per cent sample of negative smears taken during January 1973 and returned to the National Service Central Register.

Sources: Department of Health and Social Security; Welsh Office

Table 7.28 Preventive medicine: vaccination

Great Britain   Percentages and thousands

	Unit	1966	1968	1969	1970	1971	1972	1973	1974	1975
Smallpox Number vaccinated under age 2 as a percentage of live births during previous year	Per cent	37	37	30	32	–	–	–	–	–
Diphtheria Percentage of children born in preceding calendar year who were vaccinated by end of year stated	Per cent	73	78	67[1]	64[1]	65[1]	65[1]	64[1]	57[1]	57
Whooping cough Percentage of children born in preceding calendar year who were vaccinated by end of year stated	Per cent	72	76	66[1]	63[1]	64[1]	63[1]	61[1]	51[1]	32
Poliomyelitis Percentage of children born in preceding calendar year who were vaccinated by end of year stated	Per cent	69	74	65[1]	63[1]	64[1]	64[1]	62[1]	57[1]	57
Tetanus Percentage of children born in preceding calendar year who were vaccinated by end of year stated	Per cent	72	78	67[1]	64[1]	65[1]	65[1]	63[1]	57[1]	57
Measles Number of people under age 16 who were vaccinated[4]	Thousands	..	781·1[2]	428·7[3]	663·5	594·4	581·3	527·1	405·1	350·3
Rubella Number under age 16 who were vaccinated[5]	Thousands	..	..	..	131·0	439·4	322·2	295·3	287·9	298·1
Tuberculosis Number of people vaccinated	Thousands	564·0	590·3	602·5	597·2	659·3	645·1	679·4	646·1	684·2

[1] Low rate due to changes in the recommended schedule of vaccination and immunisation. [2] Figures for 9 months only. [3] There was a temporary reduction in the supply of vaccine in 1969 when the use of one manufacturer's product was suspended. [4] The data for Scotland are for people under the age of 7. [5] The data for Scotland are for people under the age of 15.

Source: Department of Health and Social Security

Table 7.29   Manpower in the health and local authority social services[1]

Great Britain   Thousands

	1971	1972	1973	1974	1975
Regional and Area Health Authorities/Boards[2]					
(wholetime equivalents):					
Medical and dental[3]	33	34	36	37	39
Nursing and midwifery (excluding agency staff)	339	360	367	373	..
Professional and technical (excluding works)[4]	47	49	52	53	..
Administrative and clerical	72	76	81	88	..
Other staff (including ancillary, works, maintenance, and ambulance)	260	263	257	256	..
Family practitioner services					
General medical practitioners	25	25	26	26	26
General dental practitioners	12	12	13	13	17
Other practitioners[5]	8	8	8	7	3
Dental Estimates Board and Prescription Pricing Authority/ Prescription Pricing Division (wholetime equivalents)	4	4	3	4	4
Local authority social services (wholetime equivalents)	145	160	179	197	..
Total	945	991	1,022	1,054	..

[1] The figures relate as closely as possible to 30 September.   [2] The figures include community health staff after reorganisation at 1 April 1974, and corresponding staff prior to 1974 but staff other than nursing staff in the community health service in Scotland are excluded in 1971–1973. Staff of the Family Practitioner Committees are included from 1974 as are corresponding staff prior to 1974 (except in Scotland). Staff of mass radiography units, blood transfusion centres, and Boards of Governors are included. Common Services Agency staff in Scotland are included for 1974 and 1975. Because of the reorganisation of the NHS at 1 April 1974 the figures for 1974 onwards are not truly comparable with earlier years.
[3] The figures exclude locums and paragraph 94 and 107 appointments. (See Appendix B.)   [4] Includes hospital social workers up to 1973 in England and Wales and up to 1974 in Scotland; thereafter these staff are included in local authority social services.   [5] Includes ophthalmic medical practitioners, ophthalmic opticians, and dispensing opticians. Pharmacists in the GPS are not included.

Sources: Department of Health and Social Security; Scottish Health Service Common Services Agency; Welsh Office

Table 7.30 Public expenditure on the health and personal social services[1]

United Kingdom   £ million and percentages

	1961 -62	1970 -71	1971 -72	1972 -73	1973 -74	1974 -75	1975 -76
Current expenditure							
Hospital, etc., services[2,3]	551	1,272	1,462	1,665	1,872	2,872	3,943
less Receipts from patients	−6	−11	−13	−16	−19	−19	−23
Local authority services:							
Health[3]	82	133	151	173	196	−	−
Personal social services[4]	56	252	298	377	503	739	999
School meals and milk:							
School milk	14	16	12	9	9	9	13
School meals	85	200	215	254	323	425	554
less Payments by parents	−35	−80	−91	−102	−111	−121	−155
Family practitioner services[2]	274	557	609	678	742	960	1,134
less Receipts from patients	−41	−50	−65	−74	−80	−92	−85
of which (net cost):							
Pharmaceutical services	*77*	*203*	*224*	*257*	*284*	*408*	*456*
General dental services	*52*	*91*	*96*	*102*	*113*	*165*	*200*
General ophthalmic services	*10*	*19*	*14*	*15*	*17*	*30*	*55*
General medical services	*88*	*181*	*196*	*212*	*228*	*265*	*338*
Welfare foods[2]	29	44	17	13	11	9	15
Departmental administration, other services, etc.	19	47	59	73	110	153	169
Total current expenditure	1,028	2,380	2,654	3,050	3,556	4,935	6,564
Capital expenditure							
Hospital, etc., services[3]	44	153	191	231	258	297	355
Local authority health[3] and personal social services	15	47	54	73	102	83	91
Other services	3	5	5	6	20	10	12
Total capital expenditure	62	205	250	310	380	390	458
Total public expenditure on health and personal social services	1,090	2,585	2,904	3,360	3,936	5,325	7,022
Capital and current expenditure (net) expressed as percentage of total expenditure on health and personal social services:							
Hospital, etc., services[3]	*54·0*	*54·7*	*56·5*	*56·0*	*54·1*	*59·5*	*61·2*
Local authority health services[3]	*8·1*	*5·6*	*5·7*	*5·7*	*5·8*	*−*	*−*
Local authority personal social services[4]	*6·0*	*11·1*	*11·6*	*12·7*	*13·6*	*15·4*	*15·5*
Pharmaceutical services	*7·1*	*7·9*	*7·7*	*7·6*	*7·2*	*7·7*	*6·5*
General dental services	*4·8*	*3·5*	*3·3*	*3·0*	*2·9*	*3·1*	*2·9*
General ophthalmic services	*0·9*	*0·7*	*0·5*	*0·4*	*0·4*	*0·6*	*0·8*
General medical services	*8·1*	*7·0*	*6·7*	*6·3*	*5·8*	*5·0*	*4·8*

[1] Including current expenditure on school meals and milk.
[2] Including administration.
[3] On 1 April 1974, local authority health services became the responsibility of central government and from that date are included in Hospital, etc., services. From the same date the school health service (formerly included in education) became part of the national health service.
[4] Including, from 1969–70, some services transferred from local authority health services.

Source: National Income and Expenditure, Central Statistical Office

Housing

General trends in recent years in the area of housing are covered in the Social Commentary on pages 27 to 29. The information in this section supplements the Commentary and goes beyond it in that it includes information on such aspects as rents and mortgages; housing characteristics of coloured people; government policies and public spending on housing; and people's satisfaction with housing.

Although the basic source of information on housing and housing conditions is the *Census of Population* last held in 1971, data for intercensal years are obtained from various government surveys, in particular the *General Household Survey* and *Family Expenditure Survey*, both annual, and the less regular *House Conditions Survey*. For further details the reader should refer to the detailed results of these surveys, published by HMSO.

Many other tables are obtained from routine administrative statistics. The first five tables and charts are of this type, and show stock and changes to the stock of dwellings. There are two tables on housing amenities, showing the trend over the years, and how amenities vary by colour of head of household. In this table, number 8.7, as well as in Chart 8.10, the colour of the head of household is as assessed by the *GHS* interviewer. In each table it is clear then, on this definition of 'coloured', coloured heads of household had generally poorer amenities, and live in more crowded accommodation. This is, of course, associated with the larger numbers of people living in such households, data on which can be found in the Households section on page 85.

Although this section deals with housing, we would also wish to extend it to include information on the homeless, and on such people as gipsies, squatters, caravan dwellers, etc. Very little information is available. A table on the number of gipsy sites is included in the next section on Environment on page 170, but there is no exact information on number of gipsies or squatters. Another area in which statistics are lacking is how existing housing is used; for example, under-occupation of larger houses; use of second homes, and holiday homes.

Chart 8.1
Stock of dwellings: by tenure

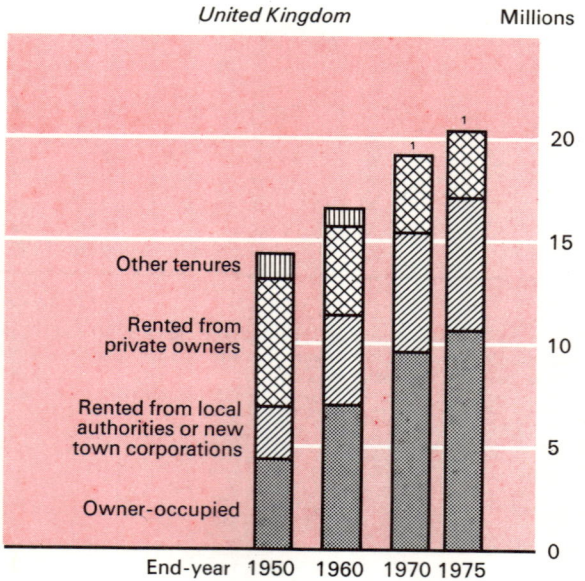

¹ For 1970 and 1975 includes dwellings 'rented from private owners' and 'other tenures'.

Source: Housing and Construction Statistics, Department of the Environment

Chart 8.2
Slum clearance

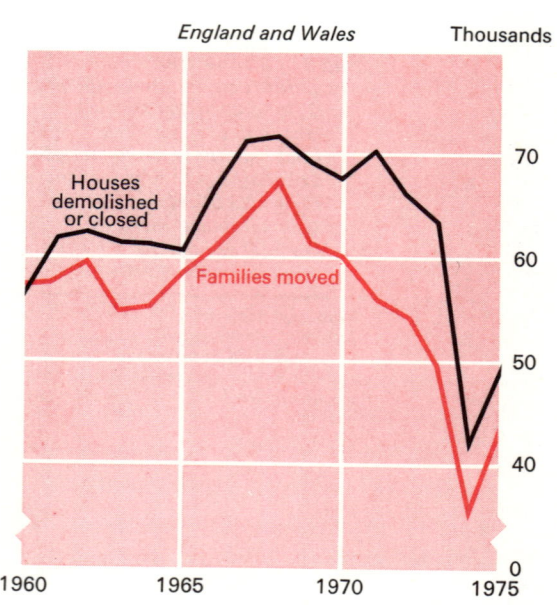

Source: Housing and Construction Statistics, Department of the Environment

Table 8.3 Stock of dwellings[1] : by region, December 1975

	Number of dwellings (millions)			Tenure of dwellings (percentages)			Age[2] of dwellings (percentages)			
					Rented from					
	In metro-politan counties[3]	Else-where	Total	Owner-occu-pied	Local[4] authority	Private[5] owner	Pre-1891	1891 to 1918	1919 to 1944	Post-1944
Standard regions										
North	0·44	0·71	1·15	45	40	15	15	17	21	47
Yorkshire and Humberside	1·25	0·56	1·80	53	32	15	17	17	24	42
East Midlands	–	1·37	1·37	55	29	16	17	14	22	47
East Anglia	–	0·67	0·67	55	27	18	25	9	16	50
South East	2·65	3·54	6·19	54	26	20	17	14	26	43
Greater London	2·65	–	2·65	46	29	25	20	19	31	30
Other South East	–	3·54	3·54	61	24	15	15	11	21	53
South West	–	1·58	1·58	61	22	17	24	11	19	46
West Midlands	0·96	0·86	1·82	54	34	12	14	13	25	48
North West	1·55	0·84	2·39	57	30	13	19	16	24	41
England	6·84	10·12	16·96	55	29	16	18	14	24	44
Wales	–	1·02	1·02	58	28	14	25	20	15	40
Scotland	..	1·89	1·89	33	54	13	14	17	19	50
Great Britain	6·84	13·03	19·87	53	31	16	18	15	22	45
Northern Ireland	–	0·48	0·48	49	37	14	13[6]	20[7]	16	51
United Kingdom	6·84	13·51	20·35	53	31	16	33		22	45

[1] See footnote 1 to Table 8.4 tenures.   [2] See note in Appendix A.   [3] Or Greater London.   [4] Or new town.   [5] Including other [6] Pre-1870.   [7] 1870 to 1919.

Source: Housing and Construction Statistics, Department of the Environment

Table 8.4 Stock of dwellings: change and tenure

United Kingdom   Thousands

	1951–60	1961–70	1971	1972	1973	1974	1975
Stock of dwellings—at end of period[1]							
Owner-occupied	6,967	9,567	9,809	10,095	10,357	10,539	10,725
Rented from local authorities or new town corporations	4,400	5,848	5,975	6,030	6,089	6,227	6,401
Rented from private owners	4,306 }	3,768	3,673	3,550	3,436	3,331	3,221
Other tenures	927 }						
Total	16,600	19,183	19,457	19,675	19,882	20,097	20,347
	Annual averages						
Annual net gain (+) or loss (−):							
Total	+234	+258	+242[2]	+218	+207	+215	+250
By nature of change:							
New construction—public sector	+189	+170	+168	+130	+114	+134	+167
of which							
local authorities	+169	+152	+141	+111	+94	+109	+134
new town corporations	+ 9	+ 9	+ 13	+ 10	+ 9	+ 12	+ 16
housing associations	+ 4	+ 4	+ 11	+ 8	+ 9	+ 10	+ 15
government departments	+ 7	+ 5	+ 3	+ 2	+ 2	+ 3	+ 2
private sector	+104	+198	+196	+201	+191	+146	+155
Other gains[3]	+ 10	+ 6	+ 8	+ 10	+ 12	+ 12	+ 10
Slum clearance[4]	− 51	− 86	− 99	− 92	− 85	− 59	− 64
Other losses[5]	− 18	− 30	− 31	− 31	− 25	− 18	− 18
By tenure:							
Owner-occupied	+277	+260	+242	+286	+261	+182	+186
Rented from local authorities or new town corporations	+187	+144	+127	+ 55	+ 59	+138	+174
Rented from private owners	−214 }	−146	−127	−123	−114	−105	−110
Other tenures	− 16 }						

[1]-[5] See notes in Appendix A.   *Source: Housing and Construction Statistics, Department of the Environment*

**Chart 8.5
Stock of
dwellings and
housing
completions:
by region, 1975**

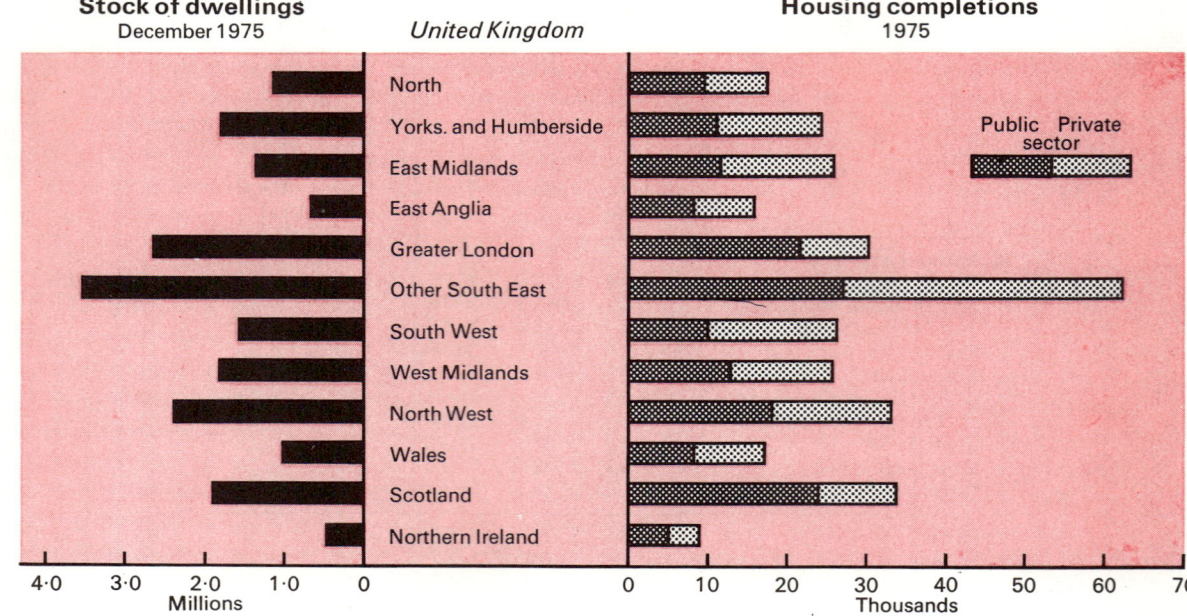

Stock of dwellings
December 1975

United Kingdom

Housing completions
1975

Source: Department of the Environment

Table 8.6   Housing conditions: availability of amenities

Great Britain   Percentages

	1951	1961	1966	1971
Percentage of all households entirely without certain amenities				
Fixed bath	37·6	22·4	15·4	9·1
Water closet:				
Internal or external	7·7	6·5[1]	1·7	1·1
Internal	..	..	18·3	11·5
Hot water tap	..	21·8	12·5	6·5
Percentage of all households sharing certain amenities				
Fixed bath	7·5	4·4	4·1	3·2
Water closet:				
Internal or external	14·9	6·7[1]	6·4	4·1
Internal	..	..	4·4	3·1
Hot water tap	..	1·8	2·0	1·9

[1] See note in Appendix A.   Source: Census of Population Reports, Office of Population Censuses and Surveys

Table 8.7   Housing amenities: by colour of head of household

Great Britain   Percentages and numbers

	1971		1972		1973	
	White	Coloured	White	Coloured	White	Coloured
Bath or shower (percentages):						
Sole use	88	67	89	73	89	72
Shared	3	21	3	17	3	20
None	9	12	8	10	8	8
Total sample size (=100%) (numbers)	11,050	200	10,904	211	10,855	251
Water closet (percentages):						
Sole use	96	76	96	81	96	79
Shared	3	24	3	19	3	20
None	1	–	1	–	1	1
Total sample size (=100%) (numbers)	10,978	198	10,893	210	10,832	251
Central heating (percentages):						
With	34	18	38	24	39	31
Without	66	82	62	76	61	69
Total sample size (=100%) (numbers)	11,050	200	10,914	208	10,810	251

Source: General Household Survey, 1971–1973

**Chart 8.8
Households:
tenure by type of
accommodation**

Great Britain   Percentages

Total sample size (= 100%) — Owner-occupied 5,818 / Rented 6,005 / Owner-occupied 5,663 / Rented 5,833 / Owner-occupied 5,635 / Rented 5,857

Detached houses — Semi-detached houses — Terraced houses — Flats and maisonettes[1] — Other accommodation

1971   1972   1973

[1] Purpose-built flats and maisonettes.

Source: *General Household Survey, 1971–1973*

Table 8.9   Households: tenure profile of heads, 1974

Great Britain   Percentages and numbers

			Tenure		
				Tenants	
	Outright owners	Mortgagors	Local authority	Unfurnished private	Furnished private
Age group (percentages):					
Under 30	1	19	9	12	60
30 to 44	9	46	23	13	19
45 and over	89	35	68	75	21
Socio-economic group (percentages):					
Professional and managerial	26	35	6	10	21
Intermediate and junior non-manual	26	22	14	22	32
Skilled manual, etc.	27	33	39	30	20
Semi-skilled manual, etc.	17	9	29	27	21
Unskilled	4	1	12	10	6
Income per week (percentages):					
Up to £30.00	59	13	60	68	51
£30.01 and over	41	87	40	32	49
Qualifications[1] (percentages):					
Degree or equivalent	6	11	1	3	14
Other higher + GCE 'A' level	10	21	3	7	24
Other	26	31	19	21	26
None	58	37	77	69	36
Total sample size[2] (=100%) (numbers)	2,685	2,831	3,504	1,120	319

[1] Limited to those aged 16–69.   [2] For age grouping. Somewhat lower sample sizes apply to other groupings.

Source: *General Household Survey, 1974*

Chart 8.10 Households: colour of head: by tenure and bedroom standard, 1971-1973

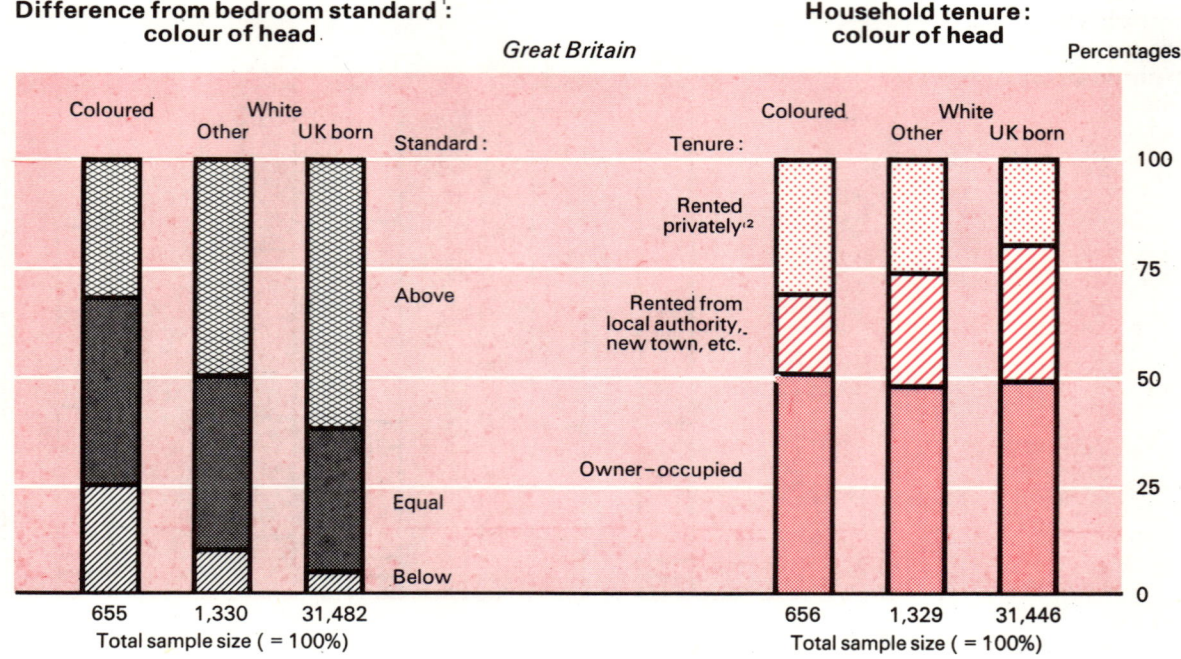

Difference from bedroom standard[1]: colour of head

Great Britain

Household tenure: colour of head

Percentages

Coloured — White Other — UK born — Standard:

Above

Equal

Below

655 — 1,330 — 31,482

Total sample size (= 100%)

Tenure:

Rented privately[1,2]

Rented from local authority, new town, etc.

Owner-occupied

Coloured — White Other — UK born

656 — 1,329 — 31,446

Total sample size (= 100%)

[1] See Appendix B, page 247.   [2] Includes 'rented with job/business' (5 per cent in each case).   *Source: General Household Survey, 1973*

Chart 8.11 Distribution of households: by income and tenure[1], 1974

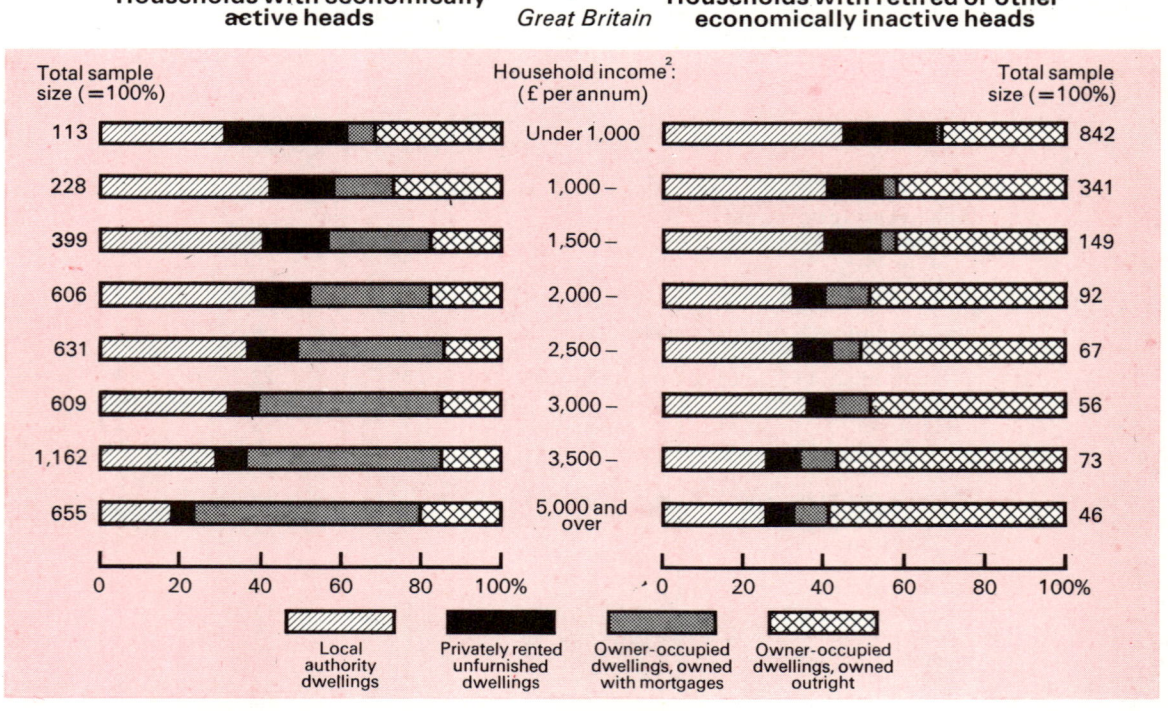

Households with economically active heads

Great Britain

Households with retired or other economically inactive heads

Total sample size (=100%)	Household income[2]: (£ per annum)	Total sample size (=100%)
113	Under 1,000	842
228	1,000 –	341
399	1,500 –	149
606	2,000 –	92
631	2,500 –	67
609	3,000 –	56
1,162	3,500 –	73
655	5,000 and over	46

0   20   40   60   80   100%   0   20   40   60   80   100%

Local authority dwellings — Privately rented unfurnished dwellings — Owner-occupied dwellings, owned with mortgages — Owner-occupied dwellings, owned outright

[1] Excluding privately rented furnished accommodation and accommodation occupied by virtue of employment.   [2] The income of owner-occupiers no longer includes a national estimate (based on rateable value of the dwelling) of income derived from ownership: this affects comparability with previous years.

Source: Department of the Environment from Family Expenditure Survey data

Table 8.12   Length of residence of head of household: by tenure, 1974

Great Britain   Percentages and numbers

	Tenure				Total sample size (=100%) (numbers)
	Outright owner	Mortgagor	Rented from local authority/ new town	Other rented	
Length of residence (years) (percentages):					
Under 1	8	28	26	38	735
1 to 2	9	39	29	23	671
2 to 3	12	37	31	19	796
3 to 4	14	36	34	16	794
4 to 5	14	36	32	17	660
5 to 6	18	29	39	14	559
6 to 10	19	33	35	13	2,095
11 to 20	31	24	35	10	2,380
21 to 30	37	8	38	17	936
31 to 40	47	6	19	28	829
41 or more	57	2	18	23	514
					10,969

Source: General Household Survey, 1974

Chart 8.13 Households: actual and potential movers

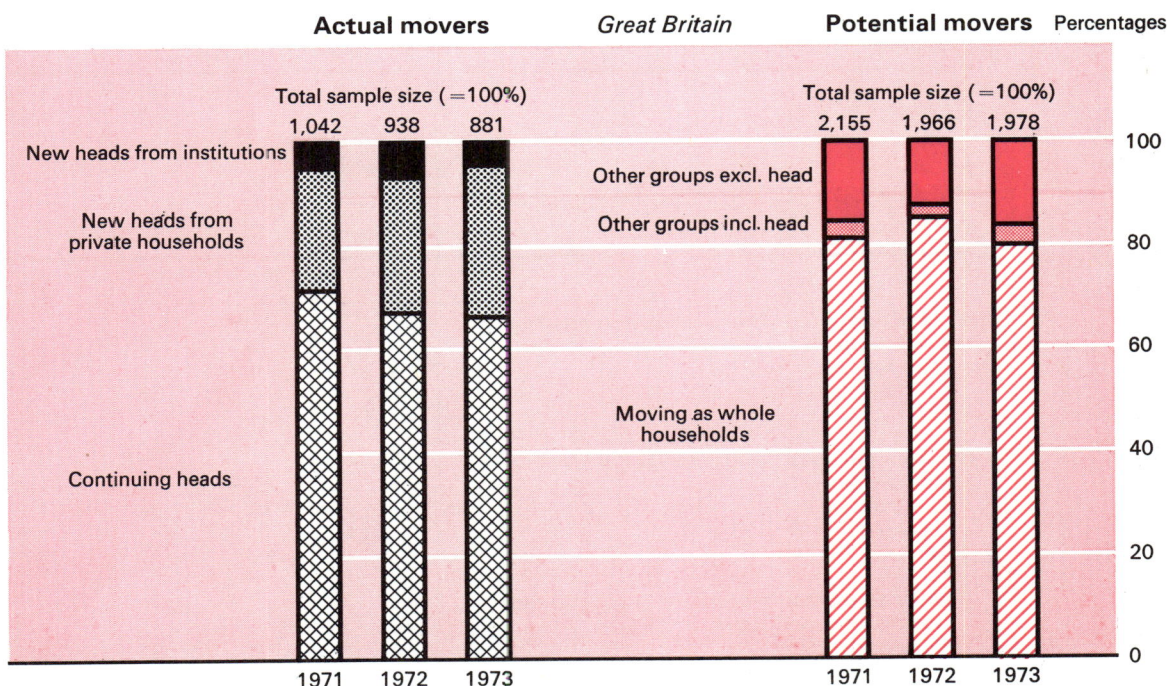

Source: General Household Survey, 1973

Table 8.14 Households: number of moves made by the head of household in the last five years: by current tenure

Great Britain   Percentages and numbers

	1971			1972			1973		
		Rented			Rented			Rented	
	Owner-occupied	From LA/new town	Other	Owner-occupied	From LA/new town	Other	Owner-occupied	From LA/new town	Other
Number of moves in last 5 years (percentages):									
0	66	65	61	67	63	59	69	69	59
1	25	24	19	24	26	20	21	23	18
2	6	6	9	5	7	8	6	5	10
3	2	3	6	2	3	5	2	2	6
4	1	1	3	1	1	3	1	1	3
5 or more	–	1	3	1	1	4	1	1	4
Total sample size (=100%) (numbers)	5,857	3,676	2,367	5,706	3,719	2,138	5,640	3,710	2,140

Source: General Household Survey, 1971–1973

Table 8.15 General improvement areas declared

England and Wales   Numbers

	1969	1971	1972	1973	1974	1975
Number of authorities	26	141	161	128	42	32
Number of general improvement areas	30	195	275	247	67	52
Number of dwellings:						
In declared areas	8,236	58,046	89,122	63,185	30,152	17,757
Improvement grants approved	52	5,453	18,239	32,621	15,799	12,318
Improvements completed	27	2,300	7,271	15,143	12,968	11,011

Source: Housing and Construction Statistics, Department of the Environment

Table 8.16 House renovation grants

United Kingdom   Thousand dwellings

	1961	1966	1972	1973	1974	1975
Grants approved[1] for local authorities[2]:						
Conversion	2	2	4	6	7	3
Improvement	9	16	129	178	112	58
Standard[3]	31	16	5	5	3	—
Total	43	34	137	189	122	61
Grants approved for owner-occupiers:						
Conversion	2	1	7	8	5	2
Improvement	24	15	108	150	107	62
Standard	39	40	43	30	16	9
Total	65	56	157	188	128	73
Grants approved for private landlords and housing associations:						
Conversion	2	2	21	20	14	8
Improvement	13	10	39	47	32	16
Standard	11	15	16	12	7	3
Total	26	27	76	79	53	27
All grants approved	134	117	371	456	303	161

[1] Northern Ireland figures are for grants completed.
[2] Including Scottish Special Housing Association, the Northern Ireland Housing Executive, and new town corporations.
[3] Not applicable to Scotland or to England and Wales from 1975.

Source: Housing and Construction Statistics, Department of the Environment

Regional variations

Table 8.17 and Chart 8.18 show the extensive regional variations in house prices, rents and mortgage payments. Although the rise in house prices has occurred in all regions, it has been uneven; for example, in Greater London average prices remained steady from 1974 to 1975, where those in Scotland and Northern Ireland rose sharply.

When interpreting these data it must be remembered that the general interest rate on mortgage loans has risen sharply in recent years; starting at 8 per cent in 1972, it rose to 11 per cent in 1973, falling briefly to $10\frac{1}{2}$ per cent in mid-1976, before rising to $12\frac{1}{4}$ per cent at the time of printing. Thus mortgage payments may have risen either because of extra payments on existing mortgages or due to the rise in house prices.

Table 8.17   House prices: by region

United Kingdom					Average purchase price (£ thousand)		
	1969	1970	1971	1972	1973	1974	1975
United Kingdom	4·6	5·0	5·6	7·4	9·9	11·0	11·8
North	3·7	3·9	4·4	5·4	7·4	8·4	9·6
Yorkshire and Humberside	3·4	3·6	4·0	4·9	7·1	8·2	9·0
East Midlands	3·8	4·0	4·4	5·6	8·2	9·2	10·0
East Anglia	4·3	4·5	5·0	7·0	9·8	11·0	11·9
South East:							
Greater London	6·2	6·9	7·9	11·1	14·4	14·9	14·9
Other South East	5·8	6·2	7·3	9·9	13·2	13·9	14·7
South West	4·5	4·9	5·6	7·8	10·9	11·5	11·9
West Midlands	4·3	4·5	4·9	6·2	8·8	10·1	10·6
North West	3·9	4·2	4·5	5·7	7·8	8·9	9·8
Wales	4·2	4·4	4·8	5·9	8·4	9·4	10·1
Scotland	4·6	5·0	5·4	6·2	8·6	9·8	11·1
Northern Ireland	3·9	4·4	4·6	4·9	6·2	8·7	10·0

Source: Housing and Construction Statistics, Department of the Environment

Chart 8.18 Rent and mortgage payments: by region, 1973

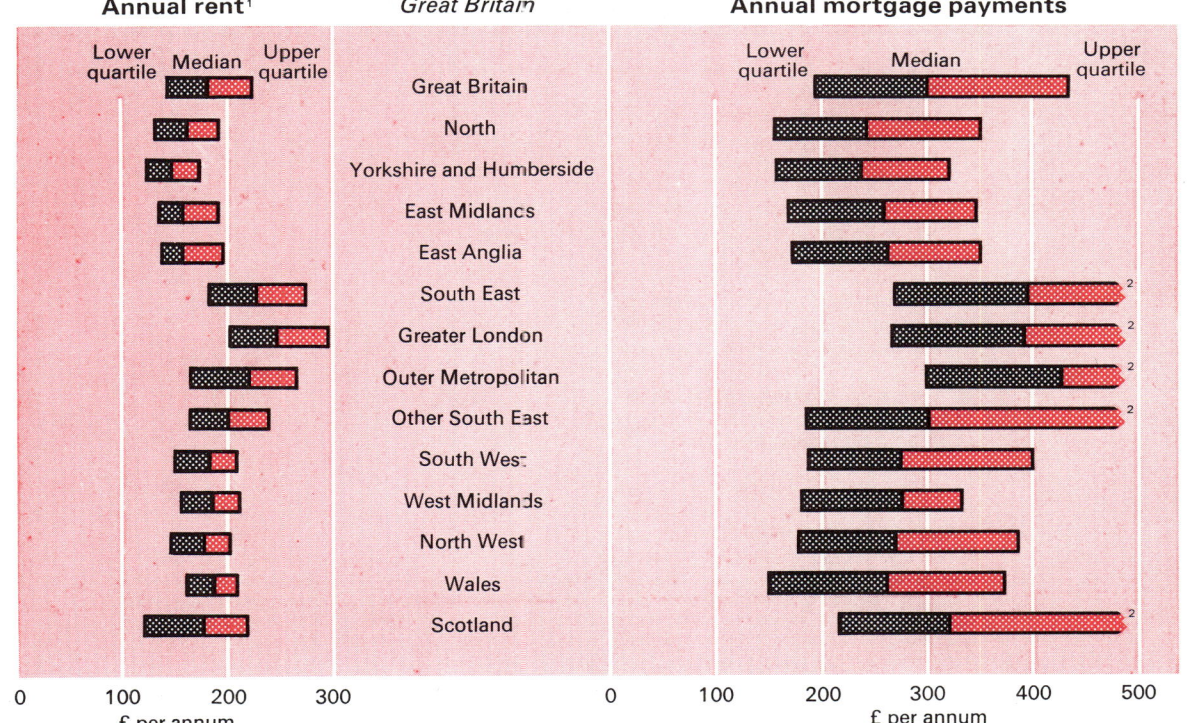

[1] Local authority/new town rents (before rebate, excluding rates).   [2] Open-ended band.   *Source: General Household Survey, 1973*

Table 8.19   Public expenditure on housing

United Kingdom | | | | | £ million and percentages

	1961 –62	1971 –72	1972 –73	1973 –74	1974 –75	1975 –76
Current expenditure						
Local authority housing:						
Loan charges	258	701	755	954	1,303	1,524
Other expenses	97	284	368	446	606	764
less Rents, etc., received	−232	−681	−828	−1,025	−1,109	−1,236
less Central government subsidies	−78	−232	−240	−315	−603	−863
Net expenditure before rent rebates	45	72	55	60	197	189
Rent rebates	–	–	94	153	167	189
Grants under the option mortgage scheme	–	18	28	51	75	109
Rent allowances	–	–	5	69	75	85
Central government housing subsidies:						
To local authorities[1]	78	231	240	315	603	863
To public corporations[2]	7	24	58	40	62	82
Other[3]	8	3	5	26	11	17
Total current expenditure	137	348	485	714	1,190	1,534
Capital expenditure						
Investment in housing:						
By local authorities	279	673	721	1,871	1,896	2,041
By public corporations	22	73	28	131	212	298
Improvement grants	14	53	109	169	176	75
Net lending for house purchase, etc.	114	118	263	409	825	552
Total capital expenditure	429	917	1,121	1,896	3,109	2,966
Total public expenditure on housing	566	1,265	1,606	2,610	4,299	4,500

[1] Includes some private housing associations: net of receipts for temporary housing.   [2] Mainly new towns.
[3] Includes, in 1973–74, grants for general relief of mortgage interest rates.   *Source: National Income and Expenditure, Central Statistical Office*

Table 8.20   Housing subsidies and tax relief on mortgages

United Kingdom | | | | | £ million and £

	1960–61	1971–72	1972–73	1973–74	1974–75
Housing subsidies					
Government contribution (£ million) towards:					
Conversion or improvement of existing dwellings					
By local authorities[1]	0·4	7·4	9·5	23·7	36·5
By private owners	2·9	17·7	25·5	41·4	62·2
Provision of permanent dwellings[2,3]	78·6	239·6	276·0	291·5	598·2
Local authority rate fund contribution to housing revenue					
account[4] (£ million)	32·9	79·6	60·7	114·2	219·8
Average contribution per dwelling (£)					
Government contributions towards permanent dwellings	19	41	46	48	96
Local authority rate fund contribution	8	15	11	20	39
Tax relief on mortgages (£ million)					
Tax relief	..	310	365	510	695
Option mortgage subsidy	..	18	28	51	75
Total	..	328	393	561	770
Average benefit to house mortgagors (£)[5]	..	61	70	98	133
Average benefit to all owner-occupiers (£)[6]	..	33	39	54	73

[1] Including the Scottish Special Housing Association, new town authorities, and the Northern Ireland Housing Executive.
[2] Contributions under all subsidy legislation including subsidies to the New Town Commission, development corporations and certain housing associations including the S.S.H.A. and grants towards its deficits on housing revenue account.
[3] Not including grants for remedial works to multi-storey flats.
[4] Excluding rent rebate subsidy of £69 million in 1972–73, £152 million in 1973–74, and £169 million in 1974–75. In these years rent allowance subsidy was £13 million, £16 million, and £36 million respectively.
[5] Calculated by reference to owner-occupiers in receipt of tax relief on mortgage interest or option mortgage subsidy.
[6] Calculated by reference to all owner-occupiers, including those not in receipt of tax relief or subsidy.

Source: Department of the Environment

Homelessness

The figures in Tables 8.21 to 8.24 refer to households who apply to a local authority for accommodation, stating that they are homeless. A household in this context is one person or a group of people who wish to form a household as defined on page 237. These figures are of interest, but they do not cover all people homeless in the strict sense of the term: some people who apply are not really homeless, but live in bad or inconvenient accommodation; conversely some people who are homeless do not apply to a local authority. The figures are drawn from new local authority returns which started in London at the beginning of 1974 and in the rest of England at the beginning of 1975.

Tables 8.21 and 8.22 summarise applications and acceptances during the first 18 months of the new returns.

Table 8.23 details the type of accommodation last lived in, and the reasons for loss of that accommodation. The different patterns between London and the rest of England are extremely interesting, particularly the high proportion in London, who were in privately rented furnished accommodation. Because of possible inconsistencies of reporting it is too early to say whether the trends in these tables, for example in private furnished accommodation, are meaningful.

Table 8.24 shows the types of household of those for whom a local authority accepted responsibility; it also shows that whereas, in London, 77 per cent of applications from households with dependent children were accepted, only 32 per cent of applicants from younger 1-person households were accepted.

Table 8.21 Homeless households: applications, acceptances, and action taken

England   Numbers

	London			Rest of England	England
	1974 1st half	1974 2nd half	1975 1st half	1975 1st half	1975 1st half
Applications during period:	7,460	8,270	8,790	16,340	25,120
Households accepted as homeless:					
In temporary homeless accommodation at start of period	..	4,640	4,940	..	..
New accpetances during period	5,720	5,640	6,280	10,960	17,240
Action taken during period:					
Permanent accommodation found	4,180	4,340	4,750	8,510	13,260
In temporary homeless accommodation at end of period	4,640	4,940	5,200	3,920	9,120
Not reported/needed:					
Lost contact[1]	120	280	390	210	600
Other[2]	..	720	880	..	..

[1] If a household, after the authority has accepted responsibility, leaves without contacting the authority and no further contact is made during the following six months, it is assumed that they are no longer homeless and the case is closed.   [2] Includes cases where no action was needed during period as well as some cases where temporary homeless accommodation or permanent accommodation was provided but not reported.
Source: Department of the Environment

Table 8.22 Homeless households: applicants housed: by type of permanent accommodation

England   Percentages and numbers

	London			Rest of England	England
	1974 1st half	1974 2nd half	1975 1st half	1975 1st half	1975 1st half
Rehoused by local authority (percentages):					
Local authority stock	75	74	73	58	64
Short life accommodation	11	11	12	17	15
Rehoused in other accommodation	5	6	4	8	7
Accommodated through own efforts	3	3	7	12	10
Returned to previous accommodation	6	6	4	5	4
All types of permanent accommodation	100	100	100	100	100
Returns received (=100%) (numbers)	2,243	3,188	3,887	5,469	9,356

Source: Department of the Environment

Table 8.23   Homeless households: by type of last accommodation and by reason for loss of accommodation

England Percentages and numbers

	London			Rest of England	England
	1974		1975	1975	1975
	First Half	Second Half	First Half	First Half	First Half
Type of last accommodation (percentages):					
Living with friends/relations	34	36	37	32	34
Owner-occupied	3	4	6	14	11
Local or public authority	6	6	7	10	9
Rented—private unfurnished	9	9	9	9	9
—private furnished	35	28	22	11	15
Housing association	1	1	1	–	1
Tied accommodation/rent free	6	6	7	15	12
Squat	2	3	5	1	2
All other tenures	5	5	7	9	8
Reason for loss of accommodation (percentages):					
Dispute: husband, wife, cohabitee	7	8	8	13	11
: other relatives	20	21	22	20	21
: other	7	7	8	7	7
Rent arrears	5	5	6	6	6
Illegal letting/unauthorised occupancy	6	6	5	3	4
Landlord requires/repossessed	28	24	18	10	12
All other cases	27	29	34	41	38
All reasons (=100%) (numbers)	4,273	3,978	4,891	8,255	13,146

Source: Department of the Environment

Table 8.24   Homeless households: applications for accommodation accepted; January–June 1975

England Numbers and percentages

	Household type				Total (=100%) (numbers)
	With dependent children	Elderly[1]	Adult[2]	One person (not elderly)	
Applications accepted (percentages):					
London	87	6	5	2	4,891
Rest of England	86	5	7	2	8,255
England	86	5	7	2	13,146
Percentages of applications for whom authorities accepted responsibility:					
London	77	72	50	32	
Rest of England	72	75	48	34	

[1] Households with no children and at least 1 person of pensionable age.   [2] Households with no children and no people of pensionable age.

Source: Department of the Environment

Environment

Although there has been a small improvement in the availability of statistics in this area, there are still many features of the environment where it is not possible to show any data. There is nothing on noise levels, or on the population who are subject to various levels of environmental nuisance. Data on derelict land are not very complete or accurate.

About half the tables or charts in this section are new. We have included for the first time charts on weather, sunshine and rain; two maps on pollution and conservation; a set of three tables on characteristics of conurbations; and new information on provision of sites for gipsies.

Weather

Charts 9.1 and 9.2 show the trends in sunshine and rain patterns over the last 15 years, and put into perspective recent dry spells.

The prolonged heat-wave in England during the summer of 1976 has prompted renewed assertions that weather patterns may be changing.

Chart 9.1
General values
of sunshine

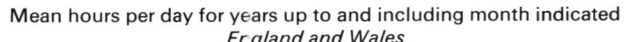
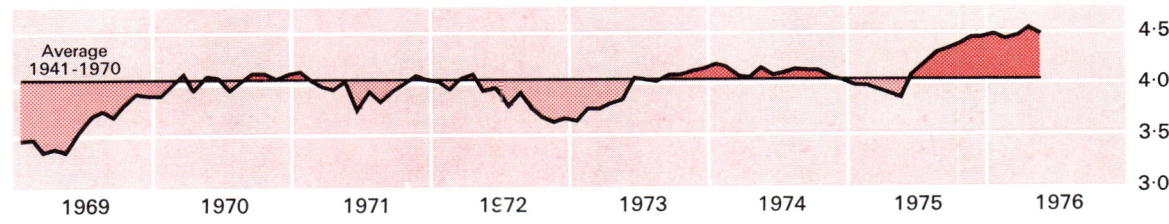

Mean hours per day for years up to and including month indicated
England and Wales

Source: Meteorological Office

Chart 9.2
Rainfall

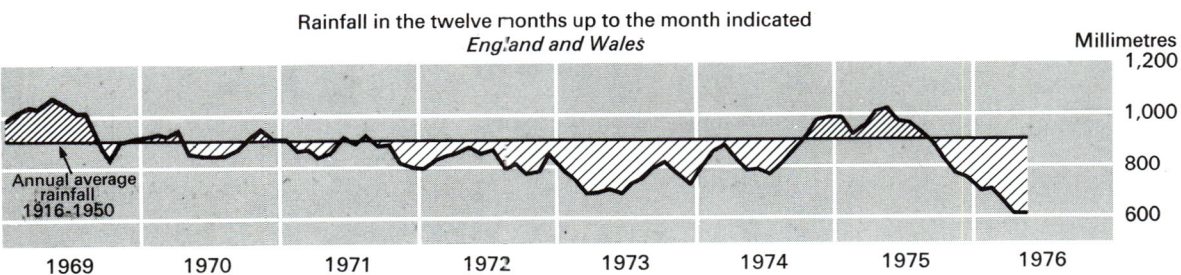

Rainfall in the twelve months up to the month indicated
England and Wales

Source: Meteorological Office

Pollution

There are seven tables or charts on pollution; air pollution is covered by the measurement of smoke or sulphur dioxide in the air, and by the emission of pollutants from the exhausts of road vehicles; radioactivity in milk, shown in Table 9.7, after a rise in 1964 following atmospheric bomb tests, has now fallen to a very low level. River pollution, as measured by the results of the three *River Pollution Surveys*, has dropped, although some rivers, particularly the Thames and the Lee, still show quite high concentration of nitrates. Pollution is a clear example of a highly localised indicator. In general there is less pollution now than twenty years ago; however, some specific pollutants are more in evidence, and in some local areas there are still very high concentrations. For more details, the reader is referred to the pollution reports shown in Appendix C.

**Chart 9.3
Cleaner air**

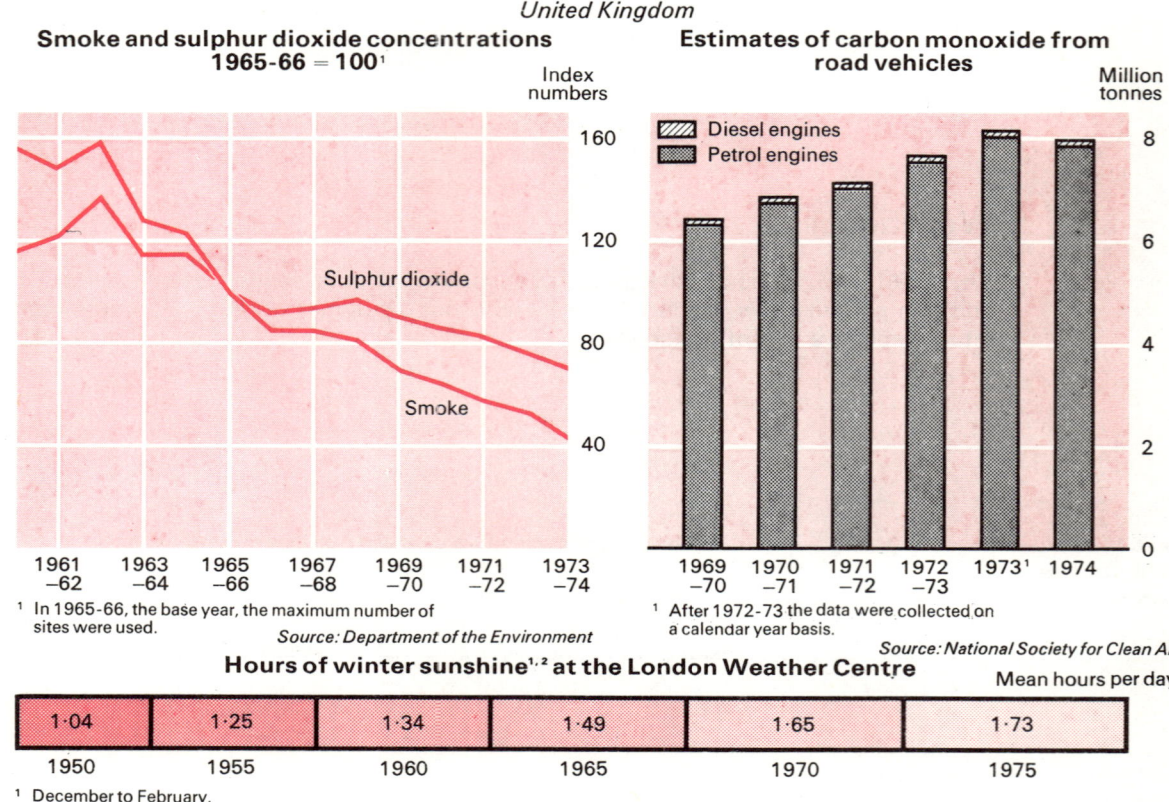

United Kingdom

Smoke and sulphur dioxide concentrations 1965-66 = 100[1]

Index numbers

Sulphur dioxide

Smoke

1961 –62 1963 –64 1965 –66 1967 –68 1969 –70 1971 –72 1973 –74

[1] In 1965-66, the base year, the maximum number of sites were used.

Source: Department of the Environment

Estimates of carbon monoxide from road vehicles

Million tonnes

Diesel engines
Petrol engines

1969 –70 1970 –71 1971 –72 1972 –73 1973[1] 1974

[1] After 1972-73 the data were collected on a calendar year basis.

Source: National Society for Clean Air

Hours of winter sunshine[1,2] at the London Weather Centre

Mean hours per day

1·04	1·25	1·34	1·49	1·65	1·73
1950	1955	1960	1965	1970	1975

[1] December to February.

[2] 10 year moving averages given.

Source: London Weather Centre

Table 9.4 Air pollution

	Unit	1952	1962	1970	1971	1972	1973	1974	1975
Emission of smoke and sulphur dioxide (*United Kingdom*)									
Smoke	Million metric tons	2·39	1·51	0·72	0·61	0·50	0·49	0·46	0·39[3]
Sulphur dioxide	,, ,, ,,	4·74	5·89	6·12	5·83	5·63	5·87	5·43	5·11[3]
Smoke control orders[1] in operation under the Clean Air Act 1956 (*Great Britain*)									
Orders—individual years	Number		154	172	237	330	377	336	164
—cumulative	,,		920	3,306	3,543	3,873	4,250	4,586	4,750
Area[2]—individual years	Thousand hectares	..	8·5	29·5	40·1	55·0	58·7	70·8	38·0
—cumulative	,, ,,	..	77	374	414	469	527	598	636

Note: In 1972, the National Coal Board carried out an exhaustive analysis of the sulphur content of their fuel as supplied for different purposes and in many instances have made changes which have in turn altered the estimates of the emission of sulphur dioxide from the values previously published.

[1,2] See notes in Appendix A.   [3] Provisional.

Sources: Emissions: Warren Spring Laboratory;
Smoke control orders: Department of the Environment

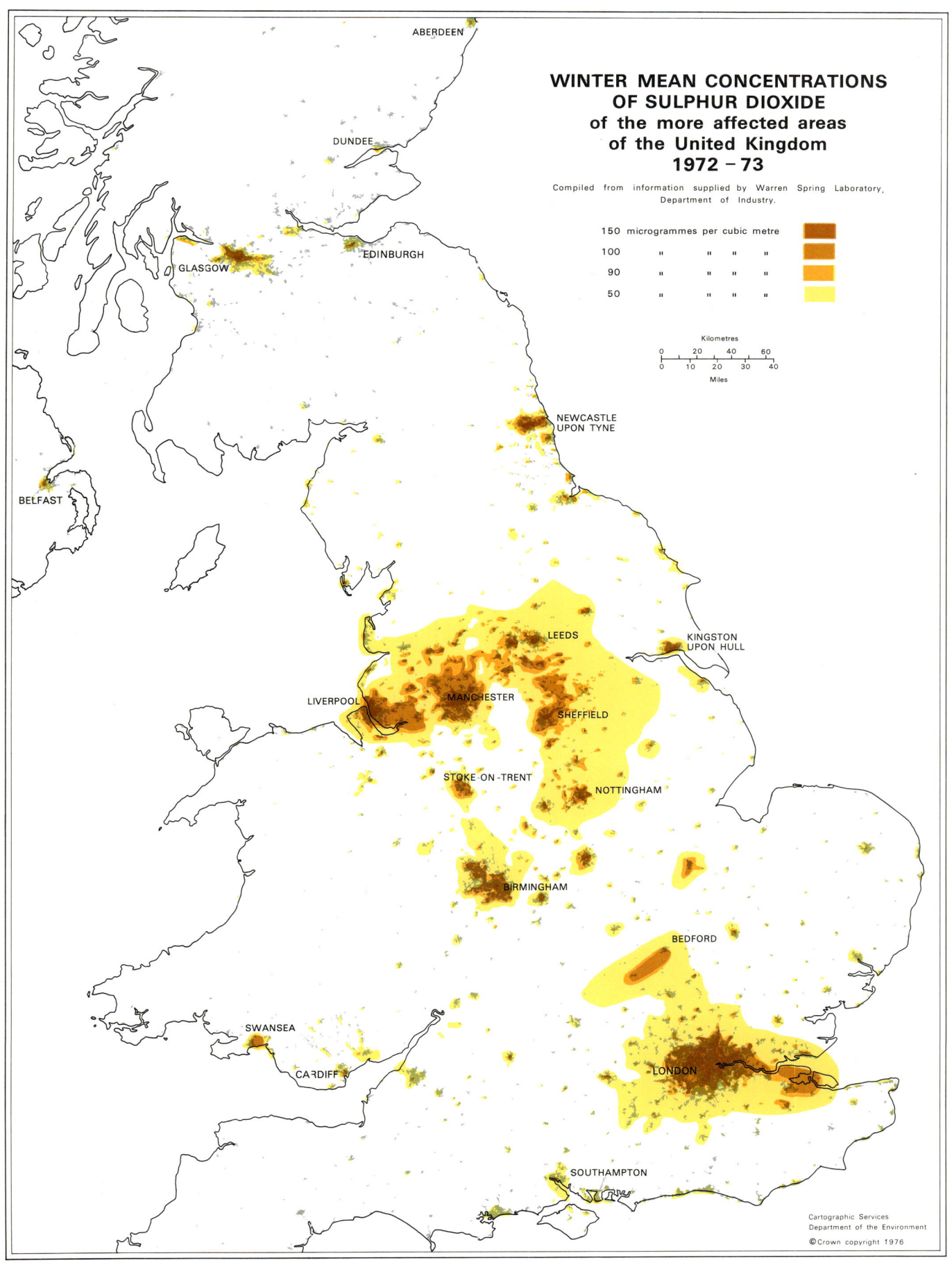

WINTER MEAN CONCENTRATIONS
OF SULPHUR DIOXIDE
of the more affected areas
of the United Kingdom
1972 – 73

Compiled from information supplied by Warren Spring Laboratory,
Department of Industry.

150	microgrammes per cubic metre
100	" " " "
90	" " " "
50	" " " "

Kilometres

Miles

ABERDEEN

DUNDEE

EDINBURGH

GLASGOW

BELFAST

NEWCASTLE
UPON TYNE

LEEDS

KINGSTON
UPON HULL

LIVERPOOL

MANCHESTER

SHEFFIELD

STOKE-ON-TRENT

NOTTINGHAM

BIRMINGHAM

BEDFORD

SWANSEA

CARDIFF

LONDON

SOUTHAMPTON

Cartographic Services
Department of the Environment

©Crown copyright 1976

163

Table 9.5 Air pollution: by region[1]

United Kingdom   Micrograms per cubic metre

	Smoke				Sulphur dioxide			
	1968/69	1972/73	1973/74	1974/75	1968/69	1972/73	1973/74	1974/75
North	108	74	55	37	97	91	72	59
Yorkshire and Humberside	97	65	44	38	140	108	89	88
East Midlands	77	55	44	35	102	88	77	62
East Anglia	51	40	35	25	87	77	66	52
South East								
Greater London	46	36	36	28	151	118	118	98
Other South East	39	27	27	19	78	62	64	57
South West	33	26	24	19	68	46	49	44
West Midlands	63	48	39	37	119	85	77	76
North West	109	65	49	39	147	97	93	90
Wales	39	29	30	23	62	54	69	60
Scotland	88	49	35	32	87	76	65	63
Northern Ireland	79	50	53	38	96	75	72	63

[1] See note in Appendix B, page 248.

Source: National Survey of Air Pollution, Warren Spring Laboratory

Table 9.6 Estimates of pollutants from road vehicles

United Kingdom   Million tonnes

	Petrol engines						Diesel engines					
	1969/70	1970/71	1971/72	1972/73	1973[1]	1974	1969/70	1970/71	1971/72	1972/73	1973[1]	1974
Pollutant												
Carbon monoxide	6·300	6·700	7·000	7·500	8·000	7·800	0·100	0·110	0·110	0·110	0·120	0·120
Hydrocarbons	0·320	0·340	0·360	0·380	0·390	0·380	0·020	0·021	0·022	0·022	0·024	0·023
Aldehydes	0·010	0·010	0·010	0·010	0·010	0·010	0·003	0·003	0·003	0·003	0·003	0·003
Oxides of nitrogen	0·220	0·230	0·246	0·250	0·250	0·240	0·060	0·070	0·080	0·080	0·080	0·070
Oxides of sulphur	0·025	0·025	0·015	0·016	0·015	0·013	0·040	0·040	0·030	0·030	0·030	0·040

[1] The annual basis for these estimates changed to calendar year from 1972/73.

Source: NSCA Yearbook, 1974, National Society for Clean Air

Table 9.7 Radioactivity in milk

United Kingdom

	1960	1962	1964	1966	1968	1970	1972	1974	1975
Mean ratio: Strontium-90/ calcium[1]:									
England	5·5	10·1	24·3	10·4	6·7	5·2	3·8	2·8	2·4
Wales	9·4	16·3	41·7	18·9	11·5	10·0	6·9	5·4	4·6
Scotland	8·3	16·8	36·7	16·3	9·6	7·6	6·3	4·1	3·6
Northern Ireland	9·9	16·4	39·2	15·2	8·6	7·7	5·5	4·1	3·4
United Kingdom average[2]	6·4	11·7	28·0	12·1	7·6	6·1	4·5	3·3	2·8
Mean concentration of Caesium-137[3]:									
England	..	51	130	39	14	14	11	8	6
Wales	..	97	218	72	22	24	17	12	9
Scotland	..	85	205	52	19	23	15	11	8
Northern Ireland	..	110	263	82	36	39	29	20	17
United Kingdom average[2]	..	62	153	46	16	17	13	9	7

[1] Units are picocuries per gram calcium.   [2] Weighted for production of milk.   [3] Units are picocuries per litre.

Source: Agricultural Research Council Letcombe Laboratory

Table 9.8   River pollution[1]

England and Wales Miles

Chemical classification:	Non-tidal rivers			Tidal rivers			Canals		
	1972	1973	Net[2] change	1972	1973	Net[2] change	1972	1973	Net[2] change
Unpolluted	17,282	17,449	+160	876	903	+27	706	739	+33
Doubtful	3,263	3,151	−117	419	397	−21	614	574	−36
Poor	932	935	+ 3	254	261	+ 7	148	151	+ 3
Grossly polluted	840	794	−46	235	221	−13	77	77	−
Total[3]	22,317	22,329	−	1,784	1,782	−	1,545	1,541	−

[1] The classification of river water quality refers to length of river irrespective of the volume of river flow, ie equal weight is given to large or small streams. It often happens, however, that it is in the lower reaches with their larger flows that the worst conditions are to be found and so the significance of these polluted stretches could be greater than the percentages would suggest.

[2] Net change is the net upgrading and downgrading due to changes in river quality. It does not include changes in mileage due to redefinition or other adjustments (eg straightening of river course). Hence net change is not the difference between the 1972 and 1973 mileages in each category.

[3] The adjustments referred to in footnote [2] caused slight changes in the total mileage of rivers and canals in the survey.

Source: National Survey of River Pollution, Department of the Environment

**Chart 9.9
River pollution**

Nitrate concentrations in River Lee and River Thames[1] Annual averages

Nitrate concentrations in parts per million

River Lee

River Thames

1958   1961   1964   1967   1970   1973 1975

[1] Samples taken at Chingford (Lee) and Walton (Thames).

Sources: For 1958 to 1973 data, Metropolitan Water Board, Lea Conservancy, Thames Conservancy. From 1974, Thames Water Authority

Tidal and non-tidal rivers

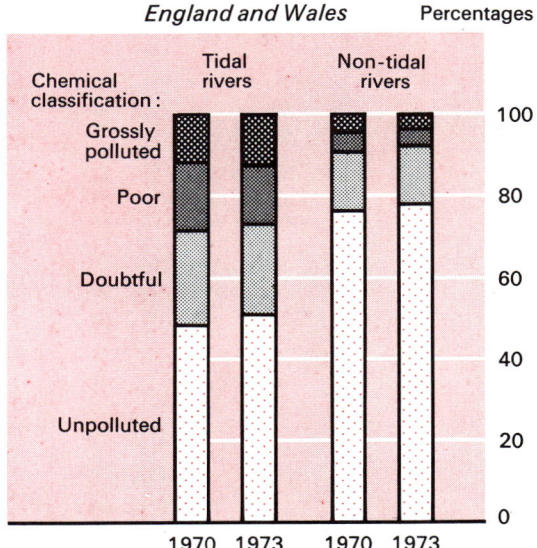

England and Wales Percentages

Chemical classification:
Grossly polluted
Poor
Doubtful
Unpolluted

Tidal rivers   Non-tidal rivers

1970 1973   1970 1973

Source: National Survey of River Pollution, Department of the Environment

Conurbations

Large metropolitan areas have many common characteristics not shared by the remainder of the country. The next two pages show some of these common features for seven metropolitan areas which have been denoted as conurbations in successive censuses of population. Greater London, Central Clydeside, Merseyside, South East Lancashire, Tyneside, West Midlands and West Yorkshire.

Population

These seven conurbations account for a major part of the population of Great Britain. In 1974 their total resident populations combined amounted to 17·3 millions. This compares with a total for Great Britain of 54·4 millions, so that in all about one-third of the population of Great Britain lives in these areas which themselves comprise less than 3% of the total land area.

Between 1951 and 1974 the total resident population of the conurbations declined by 7·5 per cent. With the exception of Greater London, each conurbation had a marginally greater population in 1961 than in 1951, whilst the population of the West Yorkshire conurbation continued to increase throughout the period. During the same period the total resident population of the rest of Great Britain increased by 23 per cent. Thus, as population has been dispersing from the conurbations to less densely populated areas, the latter have been accounting for an increasing proportion of the total resident population of Great Britain. These trends are detailed in Table 9.10.

This dispersal of population has been going on for a long time, certainly longer than is suggested by the crude figures for the conurbations. This is most obvious in the case of the London Metropolitan Region. Table 9.11 shows that Inner London has been losing population since the beginning of the century whereas outer London's decline is a post war phenomenon. The Outer Metropolitan Area meanwhile has experienced a rapid increase in population.

Table 9.10   Population in conurbations, 1951–1974

Great Britain   Thousands and percentages

	1951	1961	1966	1971	1974	Percentage change 1951–74
Greater London						
Population (thousands)	8,348	8,183	7,671	7,452	7,168	−14·1
As % of GB	17·1	16·0	14·7	13·8	13·2	
Central Clydeside						
Population (thousands)	1,758	1,802	1,766	1,728	1,658	− 5·7
As % of GB	3·6	3·5	3·4	3·2	3·0	
Merseyside						
Population (thousands)	1,382	1,384	1,338	1,267	1,207	−12·7
As % of GB	2·8	2·7	2·6	2·3	2·2	
South East Lancashire						
Population (thousands)	2,423	2,428	2,404	2,393	2,376	− 1·9
As % of GB	5·0	4·7	4·6	4·4	4·4	
Tyneside						
Population (thousands)	836	855	832	805	781	− 6·5
As % of GB	1·7	1·7	1·6	1·5	1·4	
West Midlands						
Population (thousands)	2,237	2,347	2,374	2,372	2,353	+ 5·2
As % of GB	4·6	4·6	4·5	4·4	4·3	
West Yorkshire						
Population (thousands)	1,693	1,704	1,708	1,728	1,737	+ 2·6
As % of GB	3·4	3·3	3·2	3·2	3·2	
All Conurbations						
Population (thousands)	18,677	18,703	18,093	17,745	17,280	− 7·5
As % of GB	38·2	36·5	34·6	32·9	31·8	
Rest of GB						
Population (thousands)	30,178	32,720	34,211	36,155	37,141	+23·1
As % of GB	61·8	63·8	65·4	67·3	68·2	

Source: Censuses of Population Reports 1951, 1961, 1966, 1971, Registrar General's Home Population Estimates, 1974

Table 9.11   Population in the London Metropolitan Region, 1901–1971

Thousands

	1901	1911	1921	1931	1939	1951	1961	1971
Inner London	4,533	4,517	4,481	4,393	4,010	3,346	3,198	2,772
Outer London	1,979	2,663	2,906	3,716	4,602	4,851	4,794	4,680
Greater London	6,507	7,160	7,387	8,110	8,615	8,197	7,992	7,452
Outer Metropolitan Area	1,691	1,967	2,174	2,511	2,916	3,458	4,457	5,307
Metropolitan Region	8,204	9,147	9,561	10,620	11,530	11,655	12,449	12,760

Source: 1973 Abstract of Greater London Statistics

Labour force

In the 20 years to 1971 the resident labour force of the conurbations fell from 9·2 millions to 8·7 millions, a reduction of about 5 per cent. In contrast that of the rest of Great Britain increased from 13·5 millions to 16·4 millions or about 22 per cent. Of the conurbations only one exhibited an increase in the labour forces during this period, the West Midlands. The difference between the conurbations and the rest of Great Britain is most clear cut in the case of the male labour force which reduced in number in all conurbations except the West Midlands where there was a marginal increase but increased elsewhere in the country (see Table 9.12).

The number of married women in the labour force has been increasing rapidly in all areas although generally less so in the conurbations than elsewhere. These increases have however been offset by reductions in the population of single widowed and divorced women and of economic activity rates among them.

Table 9.12   Resident labour force in conurbations, 1951–1971

Great Britain   Percentages

	Percentage change 1951–1971			
	Males	Single, widowed and divorced females	Married females	Total
Greater London	−14·6	−25·5	+ 43·2	− 8·3
Central Clydeside	−11·7	−31·9	+147·6	− 3·5
Merseyside	−14·2	−33·2	+ 89·0	− 7·6
South East Lancashire	− 9·1	−32·7	+ 25·9	− 7·0
Tyneside	−11·9	−26·9	+137·0	− 0·9
West Midlands	+ 0·5	−25·1	+ 62·4	+ 5·5
West Yorkshire	− 5·8	−32·1	+ 45·6	− 2·0
Rest of GB	+ 9·5	−16·0	+183·9	+22·1

Source: Census of Population Reports, 1951, 1971

ENVIRONMENT

Table 9.13   Population density

Great Britain   Thousands

				1931	1951	1961
Persons living in wards/parishes of density:						
0·00–0·02	persons/hectare[1]	(Virtually uninhabited)		16	19	23
0·02–0·10	„	„	(Very sparse)	248	255	271
0·10–0·20	„	„	(Sparse rural)	494	443	488
0·20–1·50	„	„	(Dense rural)	5,105	5,160	4,886
1·50–25·00	„	„	(Suburban)	14,443	16,993	18,633
25·00–100·00	„	„	(Urban)	13,307	18,789	21,774
100.00+	„	„	(Dense urban)	11,183	7,195	5,211
Total				44,795	48,854	51,284

[1] There are 259 hectares to a square mile.

Source: OPCS Studies on Medical and Population Subjects No. 30: Population Concentration and Distribution in Great Britain 1931–1961

The map opposite shows how much of the countryside is conserved by green belts, national parks, etc., and notes recent additions in the way of areas of scenic beauty, heritage coasts, etc. Table 9.14 and Chart 9.15 show trends in agricultural land use.

Table 9.14   Agricultural land in use[1]

United Kingdom   Thousand acres

	1951	1961	1971	1972	1973	1974	1975
Agricultural land in use (as at June Census):							
Total area	48,198	48,821	47,234	47,045	46,920	46,974	46,906
of which:							
Arable (including all grasses under five years old[2])	17,998	17,955	17,857	17,846	17,703	17,677	17,191
All grasses five years old and over[3]	13,134	12,683	12,172	12,132	12,143	12,157	12,538
Rough grazings—in sole right	17,066	18,183	13,713	13,557	13,541	13,435	13,415
—common rough grazing			2,788	2,785	2,779	2,784	2,783
Total woodland on agricultural holdings	..	..	380[4]	400[4]	406[4]	523[6]	556[6]
All other land on agricultural holdings	..	..	325[5]	326[5]	347[5]	397[6]	423[6]

[1] See note in Appendix B, page 249.
[2] Before 1975 collected as:
    in England and Wales – 'clover, sainfoin, and temporary grasses'
    in Scotland – 'grass under seven years old'
    in Northern Ireland – 'grass under four years old'.
[3] Before 1975 collected as:
    in England and Wales – 'permanent grass'
    in Scotland – 'grass seven years old and over'
    in Northern Ireland – 'grass four years old and over'.
[4] Collected as 'woodland ancillary to farming'.
[5] Collected as 'other land used for agriculture'.
[6] From June 1974 on figures are not comparable with those for earlier years (see footnotes 4 and 5).

Source: Ministry of Agriculture, Fisheries and Food

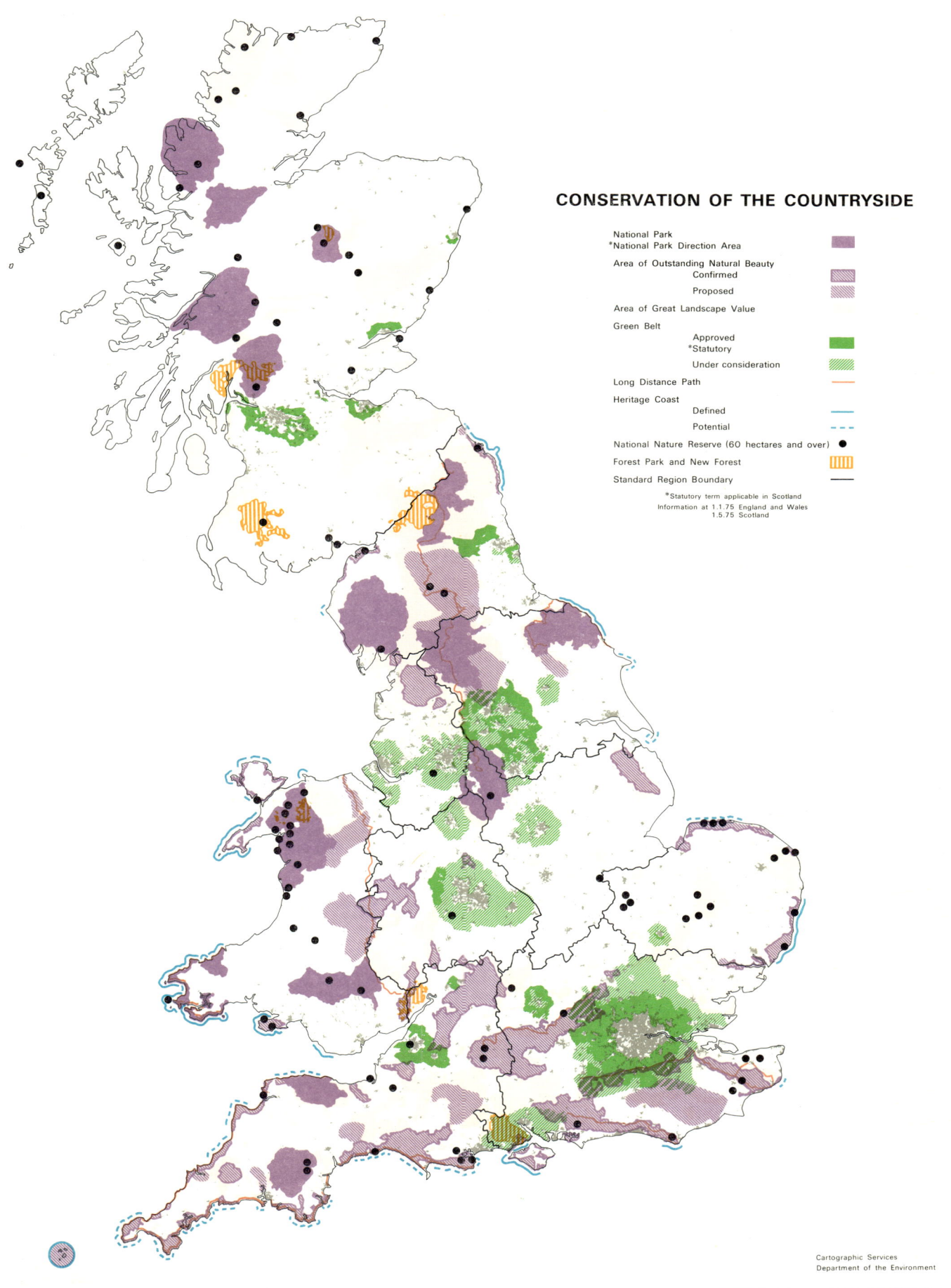

CONSERVATION OF THE COUNTRYSIDE

National Park
*National Park Direction Area

Area of Outstanding Natural Beauty
     Confirmed

     Proposed

Area of Great Landscape Value

Green Belt
     Approved
     *Statutory

     Under consideration

Long Distance Path

Heritage Coast
     Defined

     Potential

National Nature Reserve (60 hectares and over) ●

Forest Park and New Forest

Standard Region Boundary

*Statutory term applicable in Scotland
Information at 1.1.75 England and Wales
           1.5.75 Scotland

Cartographic Services
Department of the Environment

169

**Chart 9.15
Agricultural
land: changes¹**

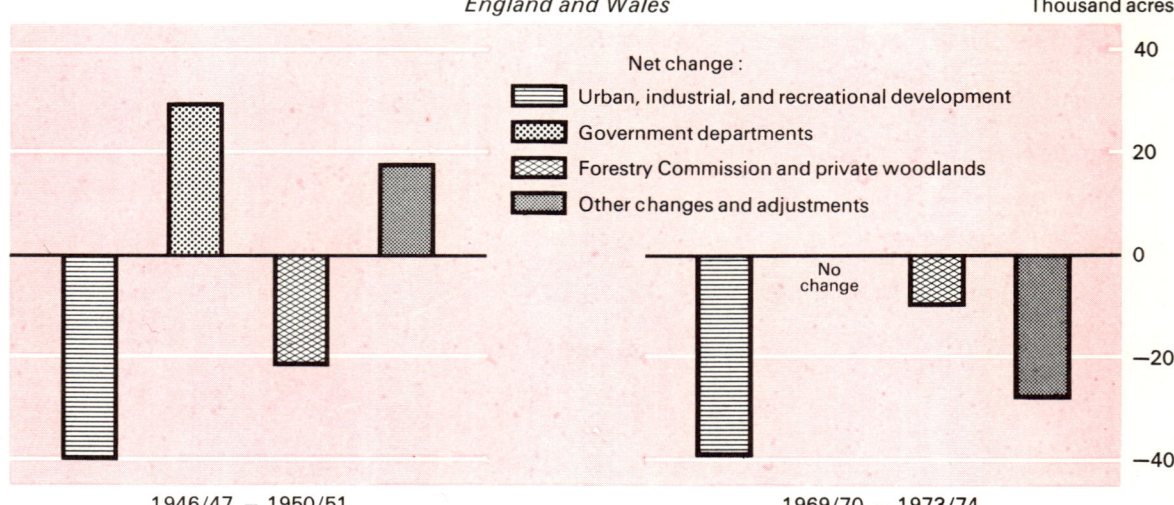

England and Wales   Thousand acres

Net change:
- Urban, industrial, and recreational development
- Government departments
- Forestry Commission and private woodlands
- Other changes and adjustments

No change

1946/47 — 1950/51   1969/70 — 1973/74

¹ Five year annual averages. Data are based on information collected during each year, and are by no means complete.

Source: Ministry of Agriculture, Fisheries and Food

Table 9.16 Gipsy site provision: by region, at 31 December 1975

England and Wales   Numbers

	Sites		Pitches	
	Permanent	Temporary	Permanent	Temporary
North	2	3	35	45
Yorkshire and Humberside	4	4	62	84
East Midlands	8	0	110	0
East Anglia	3	0	52	0
South East				
Greater London	14	11	250	155
Other South East	29	7	462	109
South West	13	2	192	49
West Midlands	9	2	138	25
North West	10	4	158	61
England	92	33	1,459	528
Wales	7	0	123	0
England and Wales	99	33	1,582	528

Source: Department of the Environment

Table 9.17 Accessibility of facilities, 1972

Outer Metropolitan Area   Minutes

	Median time in minutes		
	Walk	Bus	Car
Facility:			
'Weekend' shops:			
Urban	13	13	6
Rural	17	20	8
Nearest town centre:			
Urban	24	16	7
Rural	over 30	24	11
Nearest railway station:			
Urban	22	16	7
Rural	over 30	24	10
Nearest park or public open space:			
Urban	12	12	6
Rural	13	17	7
Own doctor:			
Urban	16	16	6
Rural	19	19	8

Source: 'Transport Realities and Planning Policy', Political and Economic Planning, forthcoming, M. Hillman, I. Henderson and A. Whalley

**Chart 9.18
Passenger
transport:
use and prices**

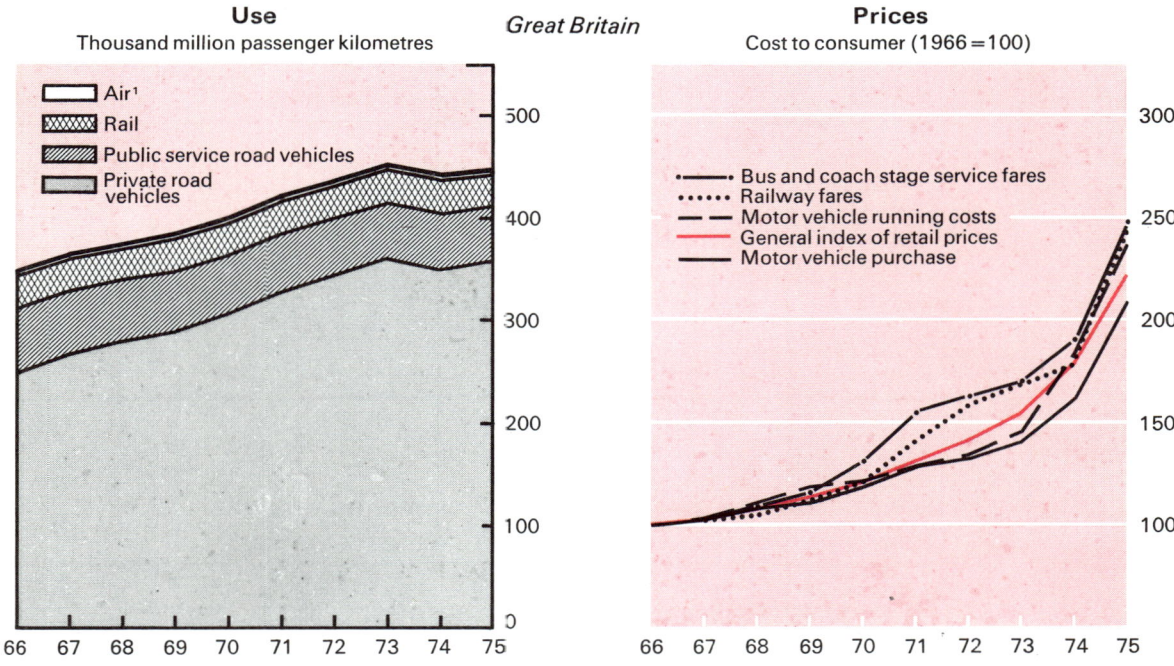

Use
Thousand million passenger kilometres

Great Britain

Prices
Cost to consumer (1966 = 100)

- Air[1]
- Rail
- Public service road vehicles
- Private road vehicles

- Bus and coach stage service fares
- Railway fares
- Motor vehicle running costs
- General index of retail prices
- Motor vehicle purchase

[1] Domestic journeys only including Northern Ireland and Channel Isles.

Source: Department of the Environment

Table 9.19   Passenger transport: use, resources, and prices

Great Britain

	Units	1966	1970	1971	1972	1973	1974	1975
Use								
Air[1]		1·8	1·9	1·9	2·1	2·4	2·3	2·2
Rail[2]	Thousand million passenger kilometres	35	36	36	35	35	36	35
Road:								
Public service vehicles		62	56	56	55	54	54	54
Private transport[3]		249	306	327	343	360	350	357
Total		348	400	421	435	451	442	448
Resources								
Railways[4]								
Routes open for passenger traffic	Kilometres	16,783	15,125	14,977	14,986	14,885	14,887	14,981
Passenger stations	Number	3,145	2,732	2,720	2,674	2,672	2,671	2,681
Rolling stock seating capacity	Thousands	1,503	1,349	1,326	1,296	1,299	1,295	1,295
Road: public transport—seating capacity[4]	Thousands	3,842	3,820	3,773	3,787	3,880	3,950	..
Road: private transport—								
Private cars and private vans[5]	Thousands	9,513	11,515	12,062	12,717	13,497	13,639	13,746
Percentage of households with regular use of:[6]								
One car	Percent-	39	44	44	44	45	45	45
Two or more cars	ages	6	8	8	9	9	10	10
Public roads—kilometres[7]								
Motorway		631	1,057	1,270	1,669	1,754	1,881	2,025
Trunk	Kilometres	13,415	13,441	13,433	13,451	13,449	13,472	13,478
Principal[8,9]		32,039	32,549	32,702	32,765	32,806	32,761	32,831
Prices								
Cost to the consumer of:								
Railway fares		100	121	140	159	170	187	247
Bus and coach stage service fares	1966=100	100	131	155	164	179	191	253
New and second-hand cars and motor cycles		100	118	128	133	141	164	208
Motor vehicle running costs		100	123	130	136	149	187	241

Domestic journeys only including Northern Ireland and Channel Isles.
British Railways, plus London Transport and Glasgow underground railways and other railways. The basis of calculating London Transport railways passenger kilometres has been revised from 1963 onwards from 'passenger kilometres paid for' to 'passenger kilometres travelled'.
Based on statistics of vehicle-kilometre derived from traffic counts and estimates of average numbers of persons per vehicle derived from the Motoring and National Travel Surveys.
End-year.   [5] Vehicles currently licensed in the July–September quarter.   [6] See also Chart 6.7 and Table 6.8.
1 April in England and Wales, 16 May in Scotland.   [8] 1961 and 1966 data are for Class 1 roads, thereafter the data are largely equivalent to the former Class 1 roads.

Source: Passenger Transport in Great Britain, Department of the Environment

Table 9.20 Recycling: quantities of selected materials recovered as a proportion of consumption, 1973

United Kingdom — Thousands of tonnes and percentages

	Ferrous[1] metals	Alu-minium	Copper	Lead	Zinc	Glass	Paper[1]	Rubber[2]	Lubricat-ing oil[1]
Production/consumption (thousands of tonnes):	23,200	668	718	364	395	3,100	7,200	450	1,029
Recovery (thousands of tonnes):	19,060	200	260	227	86	775	2,100	75	340
Recovery as a percentage of consumption	82	30	36	62	22	25	29	17	33

[1] Data relate to 1974.   [2] Data relate to 1972.   *Source: Department of the Environment*

Table 9.21 Public expenditure on environmental services

United Kingdom — £ million

	1961	1971	1972	1973	1974	1975
Water supply and conservation	47	99	98	120	138	126
Sewerage and sewage disposal	100	324	389	490	412	401
Refuse collection and disposal	49	154	172	186	242	352
Public health services[1]	25	63	70	75	100	150
Land drainage and coast protection[2]	19	41	49	56	37	30
Parks, pleasure grounds, etc.[3]	48	148	183	213	307	441
Town and country planning[4]	27	132	157	187	255	314
Other expenditure[5]	74	218	250	374	484	591
Total public expenditure on environmental services	389	1,179	1,368	1,701	1,975	2,405

[1] Including grants under the Clean Air Act.   [2] Including river pollution protection.   [3] Including local authority expenditure on swimming baths and public laundries and central government expenditure on Royal Parks, historic buildings, etc.   [4] Local authority expenditure under the Town and Country Planning Acts. Includes some expenditure under the Local Authorities (Historic Buildings) Act, 1972, the Local Authorities (Land) Act, 1963, and the Civil Amenities Act, 1967.   [5] Including expenditure on cemeteries, unallocated local government administration, and departmental administration.   *Source: National Income and Expenditure, Central Statistical Office*

Some idea of how satisfied people are with their environment can be seen from Table 9.22. This shows that, perhaps as one would expect, people are more satisfied the longer they live in an area. A longer discussion on people's satisfaction with their neighbourhood can be found on page 57.

Table 9.22 Satisfaction with district, by length of residence

England and Wales — Numbers

	1973			1975		
	Mean score[1]	Standard deviation[1]	Number in sample	Mean score[1]	Standard deviation[1]	Number in sample
Satisfaction by length of residence:						
Less than 2 years	7·14	2·52	83	6·85	2·77	59
2 but not 5 years	7·24	2·56	135	7·57	2·32	132
5 „ „ 10 „	7·50	2·55	133	8·01	1·99	134
10 „ „ 20 „	7·47	2·62	213	8·02	2·21	194
20 years or over	7·71	2·44	396	8·11	2·37	408
All lengths	7·52	2·52	960	7·92	2·33	927

[1] On a 0–10 scale, 0 = completely dissatisfied, 10 = completely satisfied.   *Source: Social Science Research Council Survey Unit*

Leisure

This section covers an area of growing interest and importance both to the individual and the administrator. Despite recent economic problems time available for leisure has continued to grow. However, the very concept of leisure is a matter of debate.

One view is that leisure consists of the complete area in which an individual can exercise choice over his activities – including the working environment. In this volume some data on the working environment are given in other chapters. The section on Public Safety includes some data on accidents at work; further information on working hours, days off for sickness and injury, and other aspects of working life are included in the sections on employment and health. This section, however, leans towards the idea of leisure as being carried out in free-time or non-work time. The section is thus divided into four sub-sections around this theme of free-time: leisure time, which approaches the question of the amount of time available to people for leisure activities; holidays and tourism, giving data about how people spend their holiday-time; leisure activities, including data on the membership of organisations; and, finally, individual leisure activities, where the data tend to be

proxy measures, for example, books published rather than books read. In this final group there are new tables on gambling and on public expenditure on libraries, museums, and the arts.

Leisure time

The question of leisure time is a complex one. To define it, it is first necessary to decide what activities can be regarded as being genuine leisure activities and which can not. In this section the general approach is to take leisure time available as being non-working time which is not already committed to some other necessary activity. This would include activities related to work, such as travel-to-work, and other necessary tasks such as eating and sleeping. It is estimated that 26 per cent of one's time is available for leisure in this definition of leisure time. Tables and charts 10.1–10.5 relate to working hours, paid holidays, journey times, and the types of transport used. These show a continuing fall in normal working hours not completely paralleled in actual hours worked, due to overtime working. Paid holiday time has also increased, with about 70 per cent of manual workers now having more than three weeks paid holiday.

Chart 10.1
Weekly hours of work[1]

Chart 10.2
Annual paid holiday[1]

United Kingdom

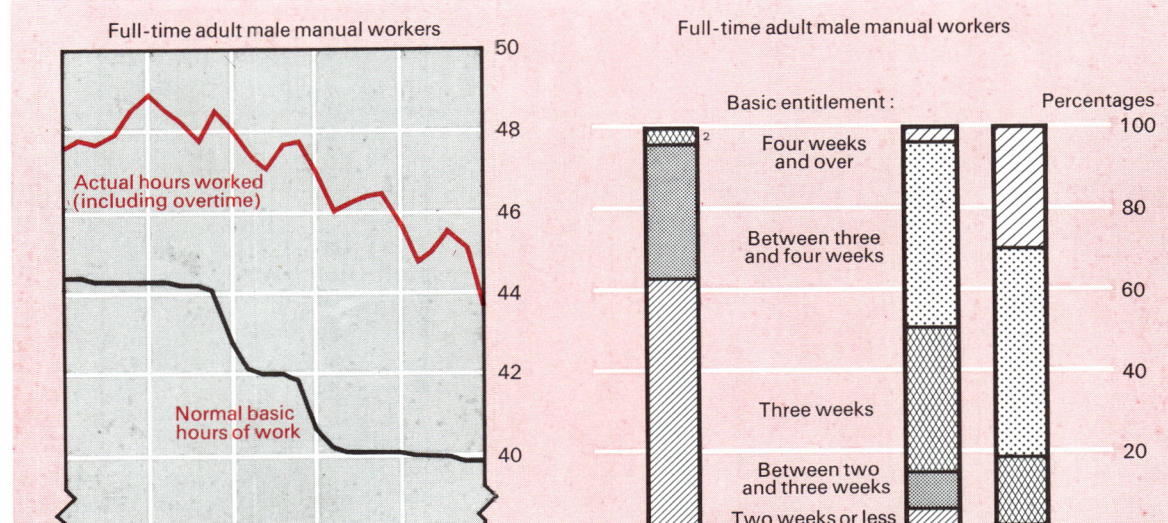

[1] As at October each year; the figures cover manufacturing and certain other industries only.
Source: Department of Employment

[1] Basic entitlement as at end-December each year.
[2] Three weeks and over.
Source: Department of Employment

Table 10.3   Weekly hours of work and paid holidays: manual workers

	United Kingdom					Numbers and percentages	
	1961	1966	1970	1971	1973	1974	1975
Weekly hours of work							
Men (21 years and over)							
working full-time:							
Normal basic hours of work[1]	42·1	40·2	40·1	40·0	40·0	40·0	40·0
Actual hours worked including overtime[1]	47·4	46·0	45·7	44·7	45·6	45·1	43·6
Paid holidays							
Percentage of all full-time workers having a							
basic entitlement[2] to annual holidays							
with pay of duration:							
Two weeks or less	97[3]	63	41	28	6	1	1
Between two and three weeks	1[3]	33	7	5	9	1	1
Three weeks	2[3]	4	49	63	36	30	17
Between three and four weeks	–	–	3	4	45	40	51
Four weeks and over	–	–	–	–	4	28	30

[1] At October; the figures cover manufacturing and certain other industries only.

[2] Figures are at end December. Moreover, a proportion of workers are covered by agreements and orders which provide for days of holiday additional to those shown in the table and dependent on length of service. This proportion rose from 4 per cent in 1951 to a quarter in 1970 falling to one-seventh in 1973, rising to about one quarter in 1975.

[3] 1960 data.

Source: Department of Employment

Journeys

In the definition of leisure time, time spent in travelling to work is classified as a work-time activity and so to be added to time spent at work. Table 10.4 looks at journey times and shows how those people living in the major conurbations tend to spend a longer time travelling to their work than those in smaller urban areas, a pattern which has remained fairly constant over time.

Chart 10.5 shows the movement away from public towards private transport which reflects increasing use of cars instead of buses. It is also interesting to note that there was a substantial fall from 1966 to 1973 in the number of people who cycled to work.

Table 10.4   Accessibility: journeys to work: time taken, 1966 and 1973

Great Britain

	Percentages of journeys to work taking (minutes)							
	1966				1973			
	Under[2] 15	15–30	30–60	Over 60	Under[2] 15	15–30	30–60	Over 60
Area of Residence								
Major urban areas								
London	12	26	42	20	18	29	37	16
Other[1]	14	33	43	10	25	37	33	5
Other urban areas								
Population of:								
250,000–1,000,000	30	46	20	5	23	47	28	3
100,000– 250,000	23	42	28	8	37	37	21	5
25,000– 100,000	39	34	20	6	35	42	20	3
3,000– 25,000	27	34	27	13	35	37	23	6
Non-urban areas	34	31	24	10	33	41	22	4
All areas	25	34	30	11	29	38	26	6

[1] Comprises Birmingham, Glasgow, Liverpool and Manchester.   [2] Includes short walks.

Source: National Travel Survey, Department of the Environment

**Chart 10.5
Journeys to
work: means of
travel, 1966
and 1971**

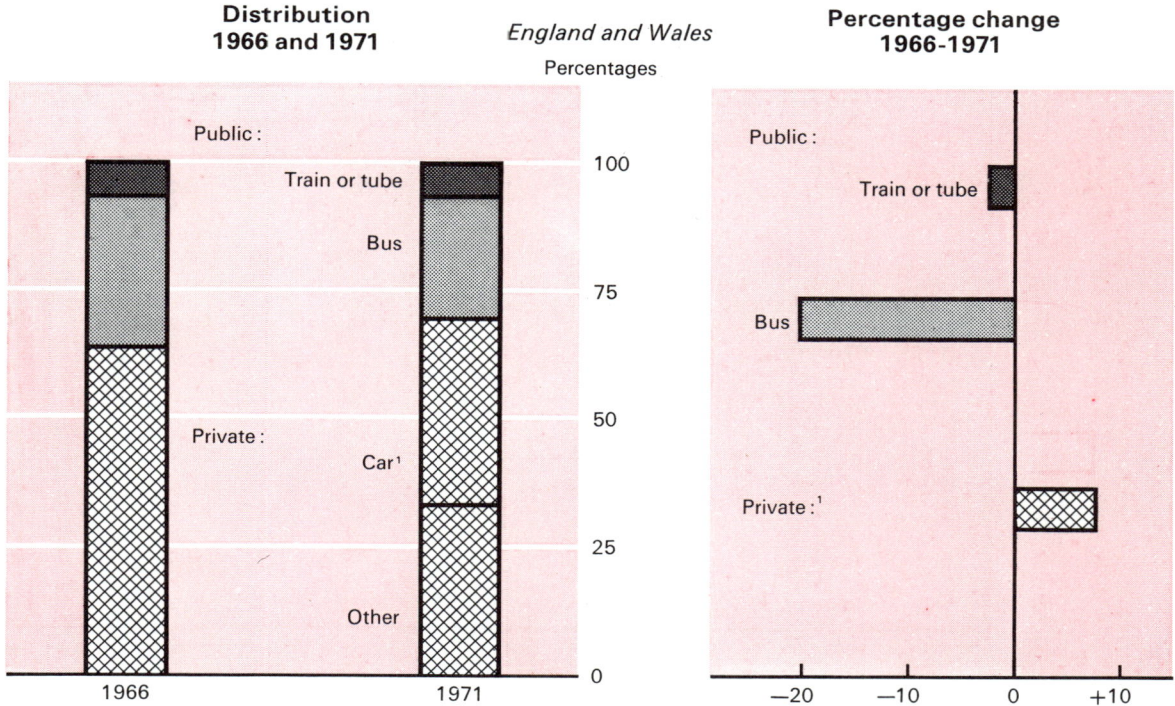

Distribution
1966 and 1971 — *England and Wales*
Percentages

Public:
Train or tube
Bus
Private:
Car[1]
Other

1966   1971

Percentage change
1966-1971

Public:
Train or tube
Bus
Private:[1]

−20   −10   0   +10

[1] No data for cars are available on a comparable basis for 1966. However, the increase in use of private means of getting to work is mostly attributable to cars.

Source: National Travel Survey, Department of the Environment

Tourism

The increased amount of holiday time has been a factor in the increase in leisure time available to people. Tables 10.6–10.10 are taken mainly from the British National Travel Survey, carried out by the British Tourist Authority, and show patterns of holiday taking. After falling in 1974, the total number of persons taking holidays increased again in 1975, the change being entirely due to a rise in holidays taken abroad. The figures on transport used need to be read in the light of an increasing number of people travelling overseas. Of these a marginally smaller proportion travelled by air. Package holidays increased however, with an increasing number using transport other than air. A new chart on holiday accommodation shows that, while for holidays in the United Kingdom the main form of accommodation used has tended to change from hotels or boarding houses towards the self catering holiday, hotels are still easily the most popular form of accommodation for overseas trips. However in 1975, 35 per cent of people still took no holidays away from home.

**Chart 10.6
Holidays[1]:
numbers taken
each year by
adults resident
in Great Britain**

Trend 1966-1975 — *Great Britain*   Social class, 1975   Percentages

No holiday
3 or more holidays
2 holidays
1 holiday

1966 1970 1974 1975   AB C1 C2 DE

[1] A holiday is defined as in footnote (1) of Table 10.7 at Appendix A.

Source: British National Travel Survey, British Tourist Authority

Table 10.7   Holidays

Millions and percentages

	1966	1970	1971	1972	1973	1974	1975
Holidays[1] taken by residents[2] of Great Britain (millions):							
In Great Britain	31	34½	34	37½	40½	40½	40
Abroad	5½	5¾	7¼	8½	8¼	6¾	8
Total	36½	40¼	41¼	46	48¾	47¼	48
Destination[3] of holiday abroad (percentages):							
France	14	11	10	12	11	10	14
Western Germany	7	5	6	5	4	5	5
Italy	17	10	8	9	8	7	7
Belgium and Luxembourg	4	2	3	2	2	2	2
Netherlands	3	2	3	2	2	3	2
Austria	7	8	7	5	5	3	3
Switzerland	7	4	4	4	3	2	3
Spain	22	30	34	35	35	35	34
Irish Republic	9	8	6	4	4	5	4
All in Europe	94	88	89	86	86	86	87
Total other countries	5	10	9	11	13	12	13

1–3 See notes in Appendix A.   *Source: British National Travel Survey, British Tourist Authority*

Chart 10.8 Profile of holidays[1] abroad taken by adults resident in Great Britain

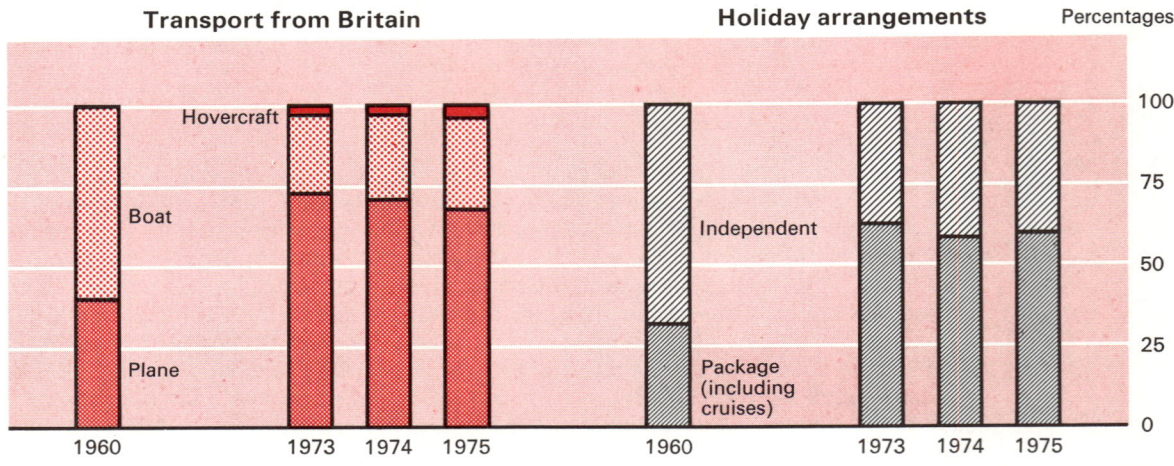

1 A holiday is defined as in footnote (1) of Table 10.7 at Appendix A.   *Source: British National Travel Survey, British Tourist Authority*

Chart 10.9 Holidays[1] taken by adults resident in Great Britain: accommodation used

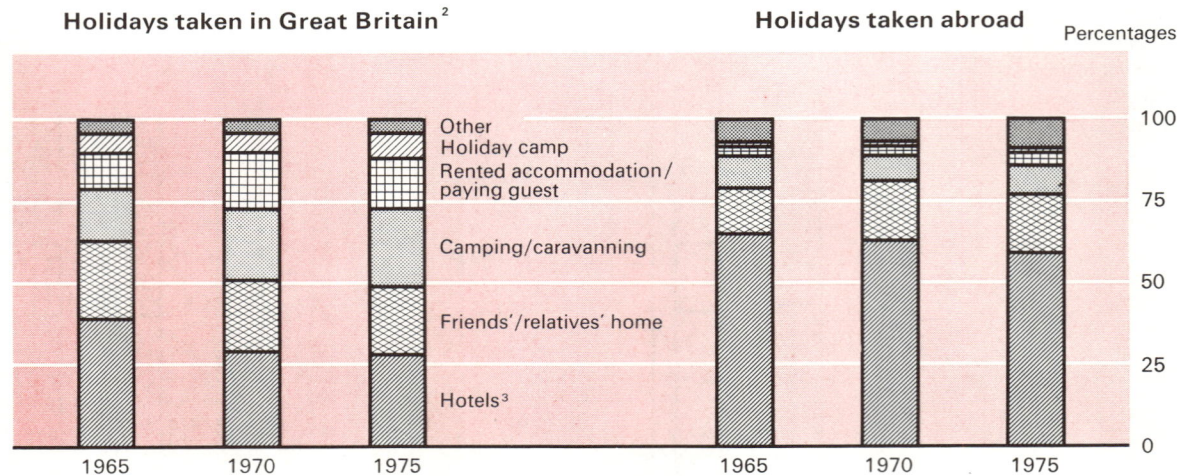

1 A holiday is defined as in footnote (1) of Table 10.7 at Appendix A.
2 Includes Isle of Man and Channel Isles.
3 Includes licensed and unlicensed hotels, motels, and boarding houses.
Source: British National Travel Survey, British Tourist Authority

Table 10.10   Overseas visitors

Thousands and percentages

	Number of holiday visits to the United Kingdom (thousands)							% share in world total	
	1973 total	1974 total	1975[1] total	1975[1] Q1	Q2	Q3	Q4	1974	1975[1]
Country of residence of visitors (selected countries)									
Belgium-Luxembourg	163	160	221	15	48	121	37	4·4	5·4
France	412	374	422	82	104	202	35	10·2	10·3
Germany (Fed. Rep.)	392	464	508	95	130	211	71	12·6	12·4
Italy	148	137	132	20	30	60	22	3·7	3·2
Netherlands	191	237	257	27	55	121	55	6·4	6·3
Spain	69	95	108	24	21	49	14	2·6	2·6
Switzerland	78	77	89	16	18	36	18	2·1	2·2
Australia	106	143	162	25	45	62	30	3·9	4·0
Canada	239	171	188	19	52	83	35	4·6	4·6
Japan	71	67	64	21	10	22	11	1·8	1·6
United States	936	735	707	76	185	313	133	20·0	17·3
World total[2]	3,717	3,678	4,084	608	972	1,823	681		

[1] Provisional.

Source: Department of Industry

Membership of organisations

Table 10.11 showing membership of clubs associated with outdoor activities this year covers an extended range of clubs. This is accompanied by a table on those clubs mainly concerned with young people, most of which show increases in the levels of membership, particularly among the youth club organisations and the Duke of Edinburgh's Award Scheme. This area is also mentioned in the Social Commentary, page 11.

Table 10.11   Outdoor activities: membership of organisations

Thousands

	1950	1960	1965	1970	1973	1975
Camping						
Camping Club of Great Britain and Ireland	14	52	92	110	144	157
Caravan Club[1]	11	44	41	84	138	174
Walking, climbing and riding						
Youth Hostels Association[2]	247	219	265	264	268	317
Ramblers' Association	9	11	14	22	29	32
British Horse Society	4	6	10	17	22	22
The Pony Club	20	30	29	33	42	28
British Mountaineering Council					12	30
Water Sports						
British Canoe Union	1	4	3	5	7	6
Royal Yachting Association	1	11	22	31	38	36
British Sub-Aqua Club	2[4]	4	7	14	19	21
Number of fishing licences issued by all river authorities	387[5]	977	1,269	1,216	1,231	..
Cycling						
British Cycling Federation	67	21	15	11	11	11
Cyclists Touring Club	54	26	22	19	21	25
Flying						
British Gliding Association[3]	–	5	6	8	9	12
Current private pilot licences issued	–	7[6]	14[7]	17	..	..

[1] Those holding full membership only; others of the family may hold affiliated membership.   [2] Includes Scottish Youth Hostels Association.
[3] Flying members only.   [4] Figure for 1956.   [5] Figure for 1952.   [6] Figure for 1961.   [7] Figure for 1966.

Source: Countryside Commission Digest of Countryside Recreation Statistics, 1975

LEISURE

Table 10.12 Organisations for young persons

United Kingdom

	1950	1960	1970	1975	1976
Membership					
Cub Scouts	187,887	243,062	254,539	289,144	..
Brownie Guides	170,539	275,689	368,615	404,715	..
Scouts[1]	239,706	277,947	212,017	219,605	..
Girl Guides[2]	222,408	257,832	311,173	335,045	..
Boys Brigade[3]	144,993	160,610	137,332	135,337	136,788
National Association of Youth Clubs[4]	152,705	173,395	302,182	456,462	519,271
of which female	88,045	84,195	128,965	205,106	243.024
Methodist Association of Youth Clubs[5]	120,345	109,635	115,240	..	..
Young Men's Christian Association[6]					
Registered members	..	41,708	52,539	90,595	..
of which female		6,128	14,437	28,178	..
Registered participants	..	..	59,090	183,218	..
Outward Bound Trust[7]	1,245	4,326	5,039	5,558	..
of which female	..	461	818	835	..
Air Training Corps	39,981	31,300	33,213	32,956	33,648
Sea Cadet Corps	20,851	19,465	17,556	18,092	20,679
Army Cadet Corps	50,000[10]	43,039	40,574	38,663	41,963
Combined Cadet Force	60,000[10]	73,775	45,939	40,579	42,629
Volunteer months					
Community Service Volunteers[8]	–	–	4,823	6,349[11]	6,237[11]
New entrants					
Duke of Edinburgh's Award[9]	–	30,360	61,315	73,767	..
of which female		4,460	25,935	31,672	..

Notes: No firm estimates exist for the number of young persons attending youth clubs. A report on the Youth Service in 1969 suggested 72% of boys and 58% of girls aged 14–20 attended a club of some sort (see Appendix C).   [1-11] See notes in Appendix A.

Sources: Air Training and Cadet Corps; Ministry of Defence. Other figures from Annual reports of the organisations concerned

Table 10.13 Church membership and attendance

	1964	1968	1970	1973	1974[8]
Church of England[1]					
Church membership					
Infants baptised in year—thousands	437	381	347	298	..
—percentage of live births	52·6	49·2	46·6	46·5	..
Total baptised membership—millions	27·5	27·8	27·7	27·5	
—percentage home population, all ages	61·3	60·3	59·7	58·9	..
Persons confirmed in year—thousands	157	125	113	100	..
—percentage home population aged 12–20 years	2·6	2·1	2·0	1·7	..
Total confirmed membership—millions	9·7	9·7	9·5	9·3	..
—percentage home population, all ages	21·7	21·0	20·5	20·0	..
Persons on church electoral rolls—thousands[2]	2,739	2,636	2,559	2,021	..
—percentage home population of appropriate age[2]	8·2	7·9	7·5	5·9	..
Church attendance					
Usual Sunday attendance at all services[3]—thousands		1,606	1,542	1,410	..
—percentage home population, all ages		3·5	3·3	3·0	..
Roman Catholic Church[4]					
Church membership					
Persons (up to age 7) baptised in year—thousands	138	121	108	86	81
—percentage of live births	15·7	14·7	13·8	12·8	12·6
Estimated Catholic population—millions	3·7	4·0	4·1	4·2	4·2
—percentage home population, all ages	8·5	8·5	8·5	8·5	8·5
Persons confirmed in year[5]—thousands	90	92	72	75	70
—percentage home population aged 9	13·9	12·7	9·3	9·1	8·5
Church attendance					
Attendance at Sunday Mass[6]—thousands	..	2,055	1,935	1,832	1,753
—percentage home population, all ages	..	4·3	4·0	3·7	3·6
Methodist Church[7]					
Membership at year end—thousands	..	651	617	..	..

[1-8] See notes in Appendix A.   Sources: Various, see Appendix C

178

Leisure activities

Together with the last section this part draws together some areas of leisure time activity. These are mainly approached through proxy measures, some of which take no direct account of the time spent on these activities or of the number of persons involved.

The numbers of new titles issued reflects people's interest in reading as does the circulation of newspapers. Other activities have been more directly measured, and include figures for attendances at art galleries, museums, and theatres, number of hours spent watching television, and the frequency of participation for a range of selected activities taken from the General Household Survey. Further details of this survey are given in Appendix B.

The number of new book titles published has risen with largest increases among school textbooks and science books, with fiction growing more slowly. Newspaper circulation figures have continued their decline, with the exception of the *Sun* which has continued to increase its circulation.

In addition to the papers shown in Table 10.16 there are now published in the United Kingdom 25 newspapers specially for ethnic minority groups. Of these 7 are published in English while there are 7 in Urdu, and 11 in other languages. No specific circulation figures are available for these, but it remains a significant development which reflects the growing diversity of society in the United Kingdom.

Table 10.15 shows a growing number of people visiting art galleries, museums, and theatres. There are also steadily increasing numbers of people visiting National Trust properties, rising from just over 1 million in 1960 to about 4½ million in 1975. The figure given for theatre attendances in 1974 is taken from a new survey carried out by the Theatres Advisory Council. This covers a large number of theatres not previously surveyed including all theatres 'mainly used for professional purposes'. The figure quoted is the reported total annual attendance at those theatres and so may well count the same group of theatre goers more than once. It has been estimated by the Theatres Advisory Council that in 1974 10 per cent of the population over 16 years of age visited a theatre once a month and 2 per cent once a week.

Immediately following are two tables on activities based on the General Household Survey. Although some of the classifications are a little crude, the pattern is one in which professional workers have a higher proportion of participation than any other

group with the exception of full-time students, and there is a steady gradient across the socio-economic groups. This may reflect the fact that professional workers may have more time and money to spend on leisure. The second table reveals some interesting patterns by age and sex. Football and gardening are predominantly male activities, while the others are fairly evenly balanced between the sexes. Also football and going to the cinema are mainly activities for young people and gardening and D.I.Y. are activities for the elderly. Going out for a meal or a drink is more associated with those in the age groups from 20 to 59, a bracket roughly equivalent to the duration of working life.

The patterns of television viewing which follow show a surprising drop for August of 1975 which may be attributable to a combination of the regular seasonal drop in viewing hours during the summer and a particularly warm August.

At the end of the section a step back is taken from the general concept of the earlier tables to focus on the area of central government provision for leisure facilities. The figures in Table 10.21 should be looked at in conjunction with both Table 10.15 and Table 6.1: in particular, expenditure on museums (Table 10.21) can be compared with attendances at museums (Table 10.15). However, such expenditure needs to be looked at in real terms, and, using the Public authority current expenditure index, it is estimated that public expenditure on museums increased in real terms by 38 per cent between 1970–71 and 1975–76. Even so the relationship between government expenditure on a given area and leisure activity in that area is extremely complex: for example, it will depend upon how much the increased subsidy will be able to actually increase accessibility to the population as a whole.

In general the pattern of leisure activities is a complex one and the interested reader may wish to refer to an article appearing in *Population Trends No. 3* on leisure patterns in Great Britain, in which there are more data on leisure pursuits and their inter-relationship. Other sources are given in Appendix C.

At the end of the section, and out of order, because data arrived later, is a table showing the proportion and characteristics of the population who own dogs.

Appendix B also contains some late figures on museums and art galleries.

Table 10.14 Books: number of titles issued[1]

Great Britain

	1950	1960	1970	1972	1973	1974	1975
Classification							
Fiction	3,697	4,209	4,449	3,685	4,145	4,154	4,198
Children's books	1,543	2,295	2,406	2,178	2,710	2,618	2,688
Political science	710	923	2,575	2,817	2,935	2,412	2,629[2]
Education and school textbooks	1,370	2,075	2,848	2,723	2,788	2,620	3,135
Medical science	614	1,116	1,285	1,388	1,550	1,466	1,844
History	253	412	1,556	1,570	1,478	1,193	1,324
Art and architecture	494	614	1,307	1,423	1,454	1,486	1,714
Natural sciences	276	372	928	1,125	1,044	1,091	1,130
Biography	522	566	940	1,031	1,120	1,024	1,211
Religion and theology	971	1,247	1,245	1,009	1,272	1,011	1,098
Poetry and drama	695	721	1,127	1,094	1,213	1,037	910
Sports, games, and pastimes	451	387	829	870	929	984	586[3]
Total	17,072	23,783	33,489	33,140	35,254	32,194	35,608

[1] Includes new books, reprints, and new editions.   [2] Includes Economics.   [3] Only includes sports and outdoor games.

Source: The Bookseller

Table 10.15 Attendances at art galleries, museums, and theatres

Thousands

	1971	1972	1973	1974[4]	1975
Art galleries					
National Gallery	1,859	1,774	1,616	1,629	2,046
Wallace Collection	153	135	122	108	134
Tate Gallery	936	913	879	881	813
National Portrait Gallery	513	423	371	355	350
Total art galleries	3,460	3,245	2,989	2,974	3,343
Museums					
British Museum (including Burlington Gardens)	2,680	2,885	2,449	2,234	3,314
London Museum[1]	512	376	500	392	148
Science Museum	1,942	1,936	2,312	2,052	2,404
Bethnal Green Museum	132	126	172	134	153
Imperial War Museum	557	586	669	914	654
National Maritime Museum	1,590	1,500[5]	1,500[5]	1,500[5]	1,300[5]
Victoria and Albert Museum	1,786	1,360	1,303	925	1,065
National Railway Museum, York[2]					567
Total museums	9,199	8,800[5]	8,900[5]	8,200[5]	9,600[5]
Theatres[3]	*4,620*	*4.925*	*4,905*	*37,000*	..

[1] Closed from 31 May 1975 on move to Barbican.   [2] Opened 24 September 1975.

[3] 1974 figures are attendances at theatres generally in professional use, as provided by the Theatre Advisory Council. Earlier figures refer to attendances at theatres subsidised by the Arts Council, which amounted to 5,080 in 1974. All figures refer to the financial year starting in April of the year given.

[4] From 1 January to 30 March, charges were made for entrance to museums and art galleries.

[5] Estimates only.

Sources: Arts Council; Department of Education and Science

Table 10.16   Circulation of newspapers

Great Britain   Thousands

	1960	1972	1973	1974	1975	1976
Average circulation per publishing day in January–June of each year						
Dailies						
Daily Mirror	4,565	4,289	4,262	4,192	4,018	3,864
Sun	1,407[2]	2,625	2,931	3,303	3,435	3,521
Daily Express	4,143	3,349	3,296	3,227	2,894	2,668
Daily Mail	2,066[3]	1,710	1,703	1,768	1,730	1,728
Daily Telegraph	. .	1,436	1,423	1,427	1,353	1,315
Guardian	199	341	344	365	336	308
Times	263	345	345	351	327	312
Financial Times	122	187	195	199	186	175
Sundays						
News of the World	6,456	6,614	5,950	5,872	5,646	5,231
Sunday Mirror	. .	4,473	4,496	4,571	4,284	4,090
Sunday People	5,323	4,615	4,429	4,387	4,219	4,089
Sunday Express	3,566	4,027	4,086	4,060	3,786	3,496
Sunday Times	943	1,450	1,504	1,505	1,396	1,388
Observer	704	798	795	833	761	686
Sunday Telegraph	. .	754	755	777	757	739
London Evenings[1]						
Evening News	1,156[4]	901	861	818	650	589
Evening Standard	584[4]	519	520	522	485	444

[1] Monday to Friday only.   [2] Daily Herald.   [3] Including News Chronicle circulation.   [4] Includes Saturday edition.
Source: Audit Bureau of Circulation

Table 10.17   Selected leisure activities: by age and sex, 1973[1]

Great Britain   Percentages

	Going to the cinema		Gardening		Do it yourself		Going out for a meal		Playing football	
	Males	Females	Males	Females	Males	Females	Males	Females	Males	Females
Percentage participating in activity by age:										
16–19	31	38	6	4	3	2	24	34	24	–
20–24	26	25	12	13	11	6	40	42	16	–
25–29	18	15	28	23	22	7	40	41	10	–
30–44	10	12	37	28	20	7	34	34	3	–
45–59	6	5	45	31	18	6	29	29	–	–
60–69	3	3	47	29	15	3	19	18	–	–
70 and over	1	1	41	18	7	1	10	10	–	–

[1] Individuals aged 16 and over taking part at least once during the four weeks immediately before the survey. Results from the four quarters of the year have been combined in the above table.
Source: General Household Survey, 1973

Table 10.18   Leisure activities: by socio-economic group[1], 1973

Great Britain   Percentages and numbers

	Total	Pro-fessional	Employers and managers	Inter-mediate non-manual	Junior non-manual	Skilled manual and own account non-professional	Semi-skilled manual and personal services	Unskilled	Full-time student
Percentages participating in leisure activity groups:									
Active outdoor sports and games	17	37	25	24	17	19	11	8	39
Active indoor sports and games	10	18	12	12	10	12	6	4	28
Watching sports and games	10	11	12	11	9	14	8	7	16
Open air outings[2]	21	31	26	30	25	20	16	13	21
Visits to buildings, museums, etc	9	19	13	17	11	6	5	3	15
Cultural outings[3]	18	27	20	27	22	14	13	10	48
Amateur music and dramatics	3	7	4	8	4	2	2	1	13
Going out for a meal or a drink, dancing, and bingo	56	68	65	62	58	61	50	46	65
Gardening, DIY, needle-work, hobbies	48	63	58	58	51	48	43	40	30
Social and voluntary activi-ties, visiting and enter-taining, and going to clubs	67	79	73	81	76	60	62	58	72
Betting, gambling, games of skill, and other activities	27	34	30	30	27	31	24	21	26
Total sample size (=100%) (numbers)	23,590	591	1,945	1,769	5,190	5,444	5,516	1,645	590

[1] Individuals aged 16 or over taking part at least once during the four weeks immediately before the survey. Results from the four quarters of the year have been combined in the above table. Individuals have been catagorised to socio-economic groups according to their current job or, if currently unemployed, to their last job. A special category exists for those who have never worked, including 823 individuals. These are included in the total sample, but are excluded from the main body of the table. Also excluded are members of the Armed Forces. The socio-economic classification used is the collapsed version, as used in the General Household Survey.   [2] Includes visits to parks, seaside, and country.
[3] Includes going to films, theatres, and operas.   *Source: General Household Survey, 1973*

Table 10.19   Gambling

Great Britain   Percentages

	January 1972	August 1975
Percentage of adult population saying they take part in activity 'these days'[1,2]		
Go in for football pools	40	35
Use betting shops or off-course bookmaker	12	13
Go to bingo where admission charge is made	11	9
Play cards or dice for money not in a casino	10	7
Put money on Tote	4	5
Use on-course bookmaker	3	4
Go to gambling club or casino	3	2

[1] Results from Gallup Polls. Sample sizes in 1972 and 1975 were about 1,000 for each year.   [2] Of those sampled 53 per cent took part in
some form of gambling in 1972 and 55 per cent in 1975.   *Source: Gallup Polls Limited*

Table 10.20   Television viewing

United Kingdom   Averages and millions

	February				August			
	1971	1973	1975	1976	1971	1973	1975	1976
Average weekly hours viewed								
Age group:								
5–14	20·7	24·5	24·0	22·0	18·8	22·7	14·7	19·0
15–19	16·6	16·8	17·3	18·4	13·9	13·0	13·3	13·9
20–29	17·0	18·1	18·2	19·1	14·0	13·7	12·2	14·0
30–49	18·4	18·4	18·4	19·0	14·2	13·4	11·9	13·2
50 and over	18·9	19·0	19·6	20·4	14·7	14·3	13·1	14·5
Social class of adults (15 and over)[1]								
A	14·0	15·0	14·0	16·6	12·7	11·2	10·1	11·3
B	16·8	16·8	16·6	17·7	13·1	12·8	11·3	12·5
C	19·1	19·3	20·0	20·3	15·0	14·4	13·2	14·6
Overall average weekly hours viewed by all persons aged 5 and over	18·6	19·3	19·7	19·9	15·0	15·3	13·9	14·7
Television broadcast licences current								
at 31 March (millions):								
Monochrome	15·3	13·8	10·1	9·1[2]				
Colour	0·6	3·3	7·6	8·6[2]				

[1] For definition of social class, see Appendix B, page 235.   [2] In 1976 there were about 90,000 more licences current than in 1975.

Source: British Broadcasting Corporation

Table 10.21   Public expenditure on libraries, museums, and the arts

United Kingdom   £ million

	1961 –62	1970 –71	1971 –72	1972 –73	1973 –74	1974 –75	1975 –76
Local libraries	27	68	80	95	105	131	161
Local museums and arts		7	10	11	19	34	51
National libraries and museums	5	16	19	25	36	38	51
Other arts	2	11	14	16	21	30	35
Total public expenditure on libraries, museums, and the arts	34	102	123	147	181	233	298
of which: Capital expenditure	*3*	*11*	*14*	*20*	*31*	*33*	*33*

Source: Central Statistical Office

Ownership of pets

A significant number of people in the United Kingdom keep pets in their homes. Although most of the data on such pets as gerbils, goldfish, pigeons, or tortoises are not available, a certain amount is known about the numbers of dogs and cats kept. Table 10.22 shows total populations of dogs and cats over the last decade: just over a quarter of all households own a dog and a little under a fifth own a cat. Estimates made of numbers of stray dogs are subject to large errors, but the number of stray dogs seized by the police in a recent 6-month period was over 80 thousand (see *Dogs in the United Kingdom*, report of the Joint Advisory Committee on Pets in Society, 1975).

Table 10.22   Ownership of pets

United Kingdom   Millions and percentages

	1962	1966	1969	1973	1975
Dogs:					
Population (millions)	..	5·02	4·96	5·83	..
Owned (millions)	4·16	..	..	5·77	..
Percentage of households owning	..	..	..	..	28
Cats:					
Population (millions)	..	4·22	3·86	4·45	..
Percentage of households owning	..	..	..	..	18

Source: Dogs in the United Kingdom, Joint Advisory Committee on Pets in Society

Public safety

This section puts together data on safety, with particular reference to crime, fire accidents, transport accidents, and industrial accidents. There is also some information on the situation in Northern Ireland.

This year the tables on crime have been cut down to five basic tables. This is because the subject of crime is covered extensively in the two articles;

Crime in England and Wales, by Dr Glennie, and *Crime in Scotland*, by Dr Bruce, on pages 32 and 43 of this issue. Tables 11.1 to 11.5, which supplement these articles, must be read in the light of the comments and caveats made in these articles. We have attempted to avoid breaks in the series due to changes in legislation by including data only on years 1971 to 1975. The main changes in the law during this period can be found in the Calendar of Events on pages 217 to 229.

Table 11.1   Crime: offences, persons proceeded against, and persons found guilty

United Kingdom Thousands

	1972	1973	1974	1975
Offences recorded as known to the police				
England and Wales				
Indictable offences recorded	1,690	1,658	1,963	2,106
Scotland				
Crimes	178	168	192	213[1]
Northern Ireland				
Indictable offences	36	32	33	38
Persons proceeded against				
England and Wales				
Indictable offences	373	366	406	439
Non-indictable offences	1,569	1,674	1,645	1,672
Scotland				
Crimes	34	33	36	39
Miscellaneous offences	182	202	205	199
Northern Ireland				
Indictable offences	3	4	5	5
Non-indictable offences	29	34	35	38
Persons found guilty and persons whose charge was otherwise proven				
England and Wales				
Indictable offences:				
Magistrates Courts	297	293	328	350
Crown Court	43	45	47	53
Non-indictable offences	1,486	1,591	1,559	1,586
Scotland				
Crimes	31	29	32	35
Miscellaneous offences	172	190	193	185
Northern Ireland				
Indictable offences	3	4	5	5
Non-indictable offences	26	31	32	35

[1] This figure has been adjusted on to a comparable basis to that in previous years. This was necessary due to changes in recording methods subsequent to the reorganisation of Scottish police forces on 16 May 1975.

Sources: *Criminal Statistics, Home Office; Criminal Statistics (Scotland), Scottish Home and Health Department; Ulster Year Book, Northern Ireland Office*

Table 11.2 Persons found guilty of indictable offences or crimes per 100,000 of the population: by age and sex

Great Britain				Numbers per 100,000 population
	1972	1973	1974	1975
England and Wales				
Males aged:				
Under 14	1,229	1,246	1,406	1,291
14 and under 17	4,597	4,738	5,418	5,229
17 „ „ 21	5,475	5,522	5,952	6,428
21 „ „ 30	2,427	2,349	2,509	2,714
30 and over	567	543	587	642
All ages	1,484	1,464	1,603	1,694
Females aged:				
Under 14	124	129	152	151
14 and under 17	490	505	626	656
17 „ „ 21	639	659	745	831
21 „ „ 30	368	356	400	462
30 and over	137	126	151	172
All ages	219	210	247	278
Scotland				
Males aged:				
Under 17	790	845	892	886
17 and under 21	4,663	4,248	4,642	5,005
21 „ „ 30	2,337	2,106	2,225	2,377
30 and over	585	535	603	633
All ages	1,181	1,102	1,206	1,278
Females aged:				
Under 17	64	74	83	98
17 and under 21	380	434	510	565
21 „ „ 30	297	294	280	365
30 and over	125	122	141	167
All ages	155	157	175	209

Sources: Home Office; Criminal Statistics (Scotland), Scottish Home and Health Department

Table 11.3 Persons found guilty of indictable offences: by age, sex, and type of offence, 1975

England and Wales — Percentages and numbers

			Age groups			
	All ages	Under 14	14 and under 17	17 and under 21	21 and under 30	30 and over
Percentage of males found guilty of indictable offences:						
Murder, manslaughter, or infanticide	0·1	—	—	0·1	0·1	0·2
Other offences of violence	9·7	2·6	6·4	10·0	12·3	10·9
Sexual offences	2·0	0·5	1·0	1·1	1·9	4·2
Burglary	19·5	40·5	33·7	19·3	15·3	8·4
Robbery	1·0	1·3	1·2	1·2	0·9	0·4
Theft and handling stolen goods	50·2	41·6	46·2	51·8	48·8	55·2
Fraud and forgery	4·6	0·6	1·0	3·0	6·6	7·7
Criminal damage	10·5	12·6	10·2	12·2	10·2	8·6
All indictable offences (=100%) (numbers)	342,125	21,434	60,166	90,598	88,161	81,766
Percentage of females found guilty of indictable offences:						
Murder, manslaughter, or infanticide	0·1	—	—	0·1	0·2	0·1
Other offences of violence	4·5	4·2	8·0	4·7	4·8	3·2
Sexual offences	0·1	—	0·1	0·1	0·1	0·1
Burglary	4·1	15·7	11·6	5·7	2·7	0·9
Robbery	0·3	1·2	0·8	0·6	0·3	0·1
Theft and handling stolen goods	77·7	72·2	70·4	73·5	73·6	84·6
Fraud and forgery	6·7	1·6	2·9	9·4	9·7	5·2
Criminal damage	4·2	4·9	5·9	4·5	4·7	3·2
All indictable offences (=100%) (numbers)	60,356	2,376	7,150	11,238	14,635	24,957

Source: Criminal Statistics, Home Office

Table 11.4 Receptions into prison establishments and population in custody

	England and Wales					Numbers
	1970	1971	1972	1973	1974	1975
Receptions						
Untried prisoners	43,042	47,731	44,501	46,144	51,422	52,967
Convicted prisoners awaiting sentence	27,671	27,729	23,917	23,770	23,683	24,936
Sentenced prisoners	62,019	60,429	57,738	51,777	56,558	64,313
Non-criminal prisoners:						
Aliens and immigrants[1]	1,100	745	1,161	1,521	846	715
Others	7,163	5,851	4,578	4,029	3,966	4,708
Average daily population						
Males	38,040	38,673	37,348	35,747	35,823	38,601
Females	988	1,035	980	1,027	1,044	1,219
Untried prisoners	2,671	2,749	2,858	2,792	3,213	3,573
Convicted prisoners awaiting sentence[2]	1,867	1,847	1,839	1,821	1,868	2,036
Sentenced prisoners:						
Imprisonment	25,634	26,775	25,887	24,831	24,274	25,877
Borstal training	6,478	6,071	5,509	5,307	5,409	6,006
Detention centre	1,762	1,730	1,738	1,527	1,713	1,850
Other sentences	36	–	–	–	–	–
Non-criminal prisoners:						
Aliens and immigrants[1]	95	74	110	160	77	96
Others	485	462	387	336	313	382

[1] Figures for 1970–1972 are of persons held under the Aliens Restrictions Acts 1914–1919 or under the Commonwealth Immigrants Acts 1962–1968; figures for 1973–1975 are of persons held under the Immigration Act 1971. [2] Includes persons remanded in custody while social and medical inquiry reports are prepared prior to sentence.

Source: Report on the Work of the Prison Department, Home Office

Chart 11.5 Adult male sentenced prison population, June 1975[1]

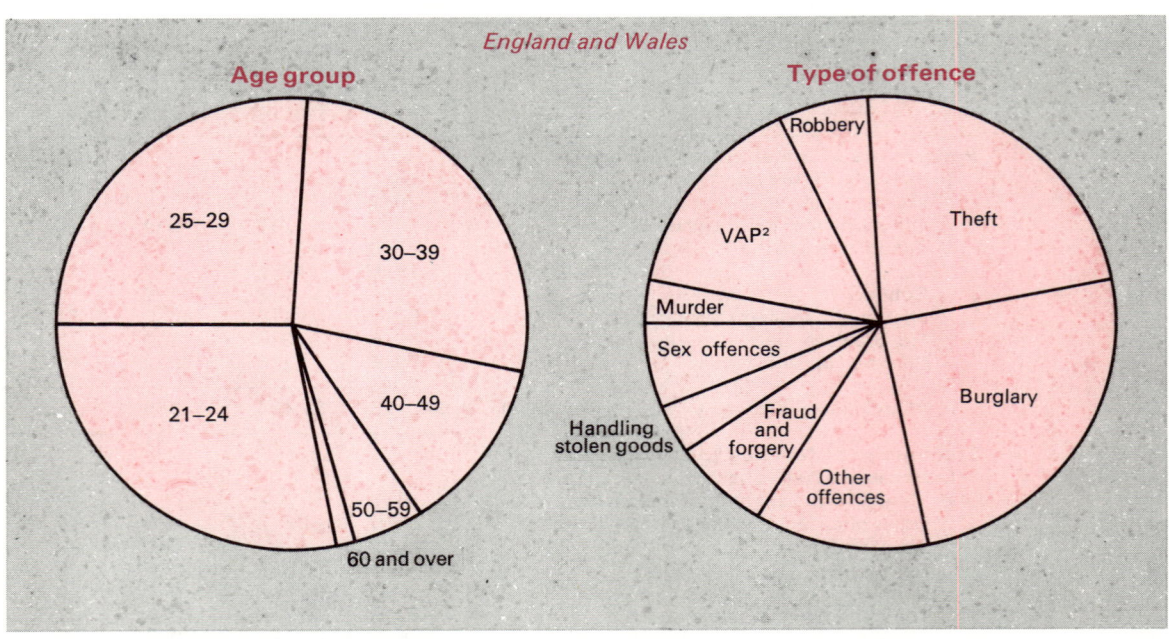

[1] Includes persons committed in default of payment of fines. manslaughter.

[2] Offences of violence against the person, excluding murder but including

Source: Home Office

Resources

Tables 11.6 and 11.7 show the growth in financial and manpower resources in the justice and law area. In addition to this it must be remembered that many of the tasks in the past carried out by the police are now carried out by other people, for example, traffic wardens, or private security firms. Thus, whereas in 1961 there were very few traffic wardens, in 1975 the number in England and Wales was 3,038 men, and 3,155 women.

Table 11.6 Public expenditure on justice and law

United Kingdom   £ million

	1951 –52	1961 –62	1970 –71	1971 –72	1972 –73	1973 –74	1974 –75	1975 –76
Police	73	156	411	474	507	593	749	1,018
Prisons[1]	7	23	64	84	98	122	157	213
Legal aid	–	4	19	23	29	35	48	62
Probation and after-care	} 8	} 23	14	17	21	27	35	50
Parliament and law courts			59	69	92	129	165	209
Total public expenditure on justice and law	88	206	567	667	747	906	1,154	1,552
of which: Capital expenditure	8	16	43	53	51	85	103	142

[1] Excluding approved schools and remand homes, expenditure on which forms part of personal social services.

Source: National Income and Expenditure, Central Statistical Office

Table 11.7 Strength of police forces

	United Kingdom		31 December			Number
	1961	1971	1972	1973	1974	1975
Regular police, England and Wales[1]						
Men	72,829	91,937	94,420	94,981	96,217	100,083
Women	2,332	3,822	4,140	4,239	4,709	5,775
Regular police, Scotland[2]						
Men	8,845	10,399	10,777	10,964	11,187	11,700
Women	285	412	453	488	532	676
Royal Ulster Constabulary, Northern Ireland[3]						
Men	2,943	3,942	4,078	4,172	4,281	4,549
Women	55	144	179	219	283	353

[1] Including additional constables in the Metropolitan Police Force. [2] Including additional regular police. [3] Excluding Royal Ulster Constabulary reserves.

Sources: Home Office; Scottish Home and Health Department; Northern Ireland Office

Accidents

The group of tables and charts from 11.7 to 11.13 deals with various types of accidents; road, rail, industrial, house, and accidents dealt with by the Air-sea rescue service. Table 11.8 and Chart 11.9 show that the total level of road casualties has kept very steady for many years, despite a doubling of the motor vehicle mileage between 1961 and 1976. Chart 11.10 shows how road accidents vary by the time of day, the number of casualties rising in the rush hour, and falling after midnight. Railway accidents, shown in Table 11.12 do not show quite such a clear pattern. The number of people killed has been gradually falling but, in any one year, a single accident, in which some 40 or 50 people were killed, for example, the Moorgate Underground accident of 1975, could double the number of deaths.

Table 11.13 on industrial accidents, shows a continuation in the general fall in the number of accidents which has followed improved safety regulations over many years. As in Table 11.12, however, a single works accident, in which many people were killed or injured, can cause substantial deviations from the trend. There is no clear trend in house accidents shown in Table 11.14; deaths due to gas poisoning have fallen due to the introduction of non-toxic North Sea gas, but other deaths show no particular movement.

Finally Table 11.15 is a new table showing MoD Air-sea rescue services.

Table 11.8   Road accident[1] casualties

Great Britain

	1961	1966	1971	1972	1973	1974	1975
Road motor vehicles with licences current (thousands)[2]	9,966	13,286	15,478	16,117	17,014	17,252	17,501
Index of motor vehicle kilometres (1966 = 100)	71	100	128	134	141	137	140
Casualties from road accidents (thousands):							
Killed	6·9	8·0	7·7	7·8	7·4	6·9	6·4
Seriously injured	82	100	91	91	89	82	77
Slightly injured	259	285	253	261	257	236	241
Total	350	392	352	360	353	325	325
Persons killed or seriously injured							
By class of road user (thousands):							
Pedestrians							
Under 15	8·3	10·6	11·1	11·5	10·5	9·3	8·2
15–59	7·0	9·3	8·4	8·7	8·3	7·9	6·9
60 and over	7·1	7·9	7·1	7·1	6·8	6·4	5·8
Pedal cyclists							
Under 15	2·9	2·5	2·5	2·3	2·0	1·9	2·1
15 and over	6·9	4·6	3·1	3·1	2·7	2·6	2·5
Motor cyclists (riders)							
Under 17	1·6	2·5	2·3	1·2	1·0	1·4	1·7
17–19	6·2	7·5	4·8	4·7	5·5	5·9	6·6
20 and over	14·6	8·8	6·3	6·5	6·6	6·2	6·8
Motor cycle passengers	4·6	3·3	2·2	1·8	1·5	1·3	1·6
Drivers of 4-wheeled motor vehicles							
Under 25	3·5	7·8	8·5	8·8	8·9	7·8	7·1
25 and over	10·2	16·3	17·8	18·6	18·9	17·2	15·2
Other passengers	17·7	25·8	24·5	24·8	24·1	21·1	19·2
Total all known ages	90·7	106·9	98·6	99·1	96·8	89·0	83·7
By class of road user per 100 million vehicle kilometres:							
Pedal cyclists	91	116	137	144	134	130	120
Riders of 2-wheeled motor vehicles	238	325	354	351	352	340	311
Drivers of other motor vehicles							
Cars and taxis	14	16	13	13	12	11	10
Goods vehicles	9	12	9	10	8	11	7
Public service vehicles	3	3	3	3	3	4	4
Per 100,000 age group population:							
Up to 4 years		77	77	72	68	59	56
5 to 9 years	110	164	156	160	151	133	119
10 to 14 years		147	141	143	131	121	114
15 to 19 years	463	557	501	471	469	452	458
20 to 24 years	409	405	352	381	387	340	317
25 to 29 years	224	228	214	216	224	194	182
30 to 59 years	136	151	140	142	135	126	114
60 years and over	137	147	140	138	130	120	108

[1] For definitions used in this table see Appendix A.   [2] This series has been revised to include all vehicles requiring a licence.

Source: Road Accidents, Department of the Environment

**Chart 11.9
Serious road
casualties:
traffic index**

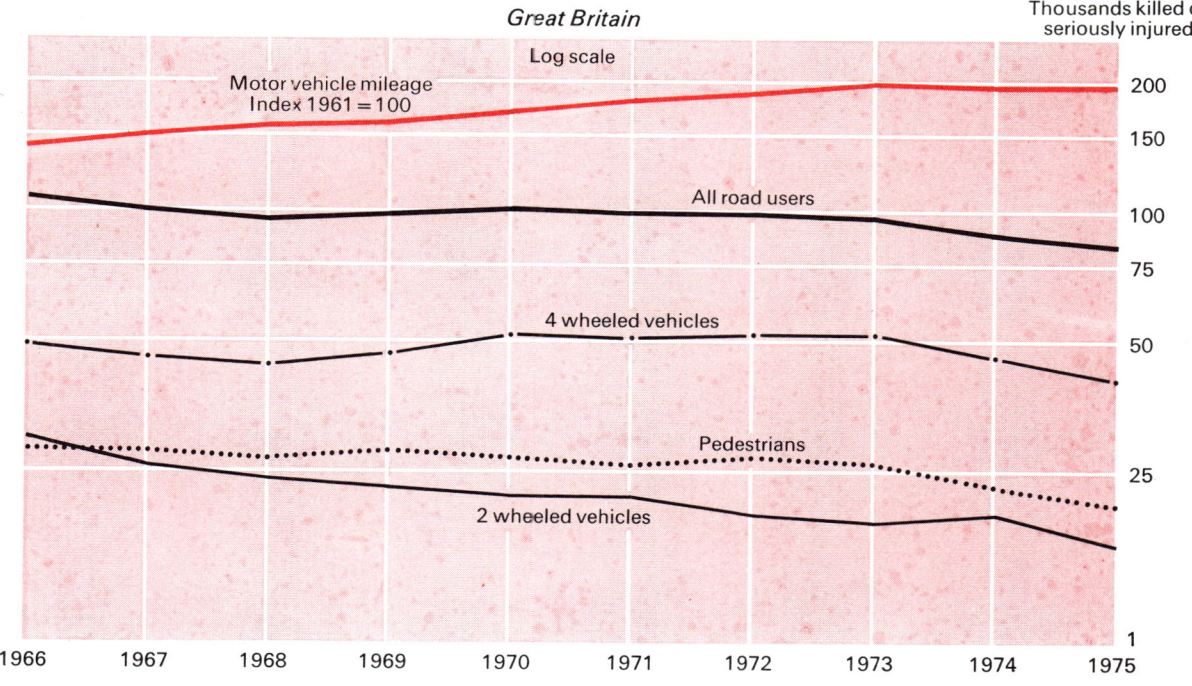

Great Britain

Thousands killed or
seriously injured

Log scale

Motor vehicle mileage
Index 1961 = 100

All road users

4 wheeled vehicles

Pedestrians

2 wheeled vehicles

200
150

100
75

50

25

1

1966   1967   1968   1969   1970   1971   1972   1973   1974   1975

Source: Department of the Environment

**Chart 11.10
Road accident
casualties:
averages by hour
of the day,
1973-1975**

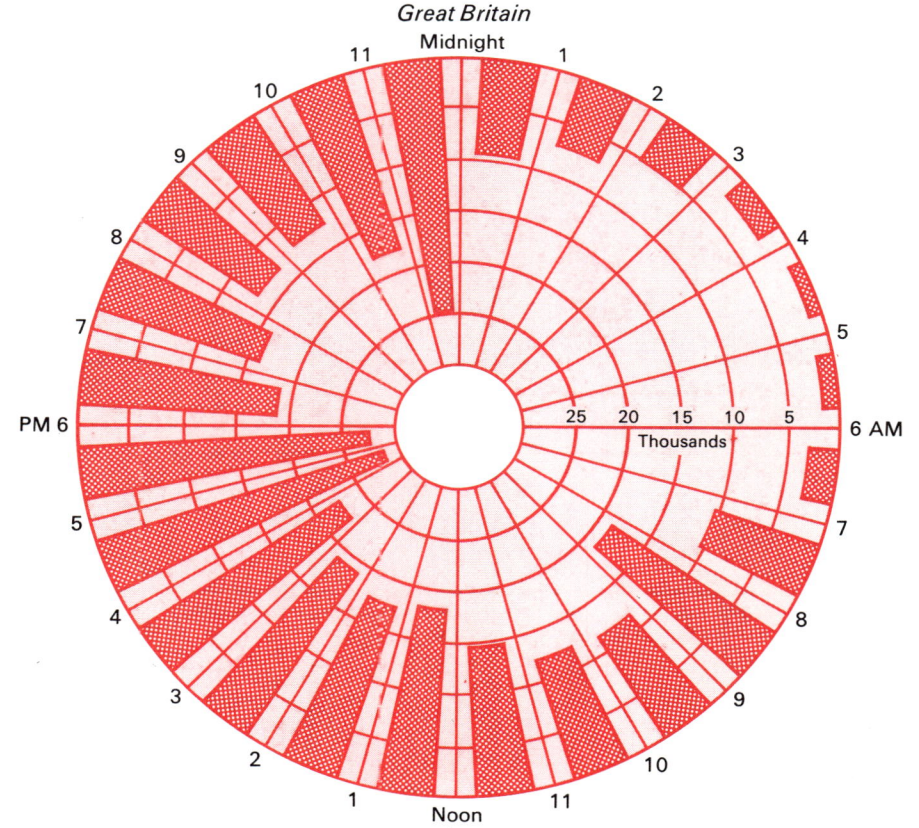

Great Britain
Midnight

Thousands

Noon

Source: Department of the Environment

**Chart 11.11
Serious road
casualties:
class and age
of user**

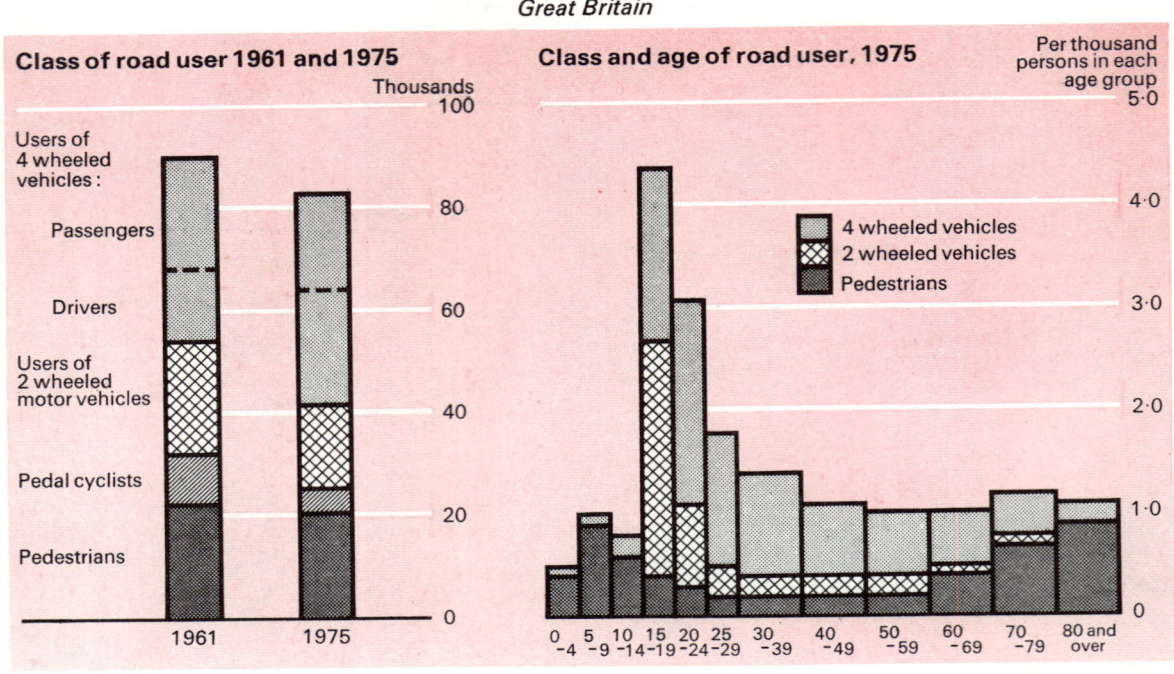

Source: Department of the Environment

Table 11.12   Railway accidents[1] : casualties

Great Britain   Numbers

	Killed					Injured				
	1970	1971	1972	1973	1974	1970	1971	1972	1973	1974
Passengers	55	47	30	42	26	5,625	5,428	5,367	5,560	5,350
Railway staff[2]	67	60	48	42	38	6,549	5,815	5,616	5,870	5,554
Other people	21	18	21	13	14	275	233	276	297	220
Total	143	125	99	97	78	12,449	11,476	11,259	11,727	11,124

[1] Includes British Rail, London Transport, and other smaller railway undertakings.
[2] Data on National Carriers Limited are not included.

Source: Railway Accidents, 1974, Department of the Environment

Table 11.13   Industrial accidents

Great Britain   Incidence per 100,000 employees

	1973		1974		1975[2]	
	Fatal accidents	All severe accidents	Fatal accidents	All severe accidents	Fatal accidents	All severe accidents
Food, drink and tobacco	2·7	710	3·7	560	1·4	620
Coal and petroleum products	15·7	930	9·7	590	19·4	900
Chemicals and allied industries	6·8	600	16·2[3]	660	6·0	610
Metal manufacture	17·2	930	14·0	1,120	10·0	920
Mechanical engineering	3·4	580	2·8	660	3·0	610
Instrument engineering	˙·0	280	1·0	270	2·0	270
Electrical engineering	0·7	360	0·5	280	1·5	270
Shipbuilding and marine engineering	13·4	830	10·3	860	13·1	780
Vehicles	2·3	410	1·8	440	1·8	400
Metal goods not elsewhere specified	4·1	720	3·4	640	2·5	690
Textiles	˙·7	560	4·0	420	1·5	430
Leather, leather goods and fur	2·5	380	2·6	540	–	390
Clothing and footwear	0·8	100	0·5	110	0·8	120
Bricks, pottery, glass, cement, etc.	6·4	790	6·4	660	6·0	640
Timber, furniture, etc.	2·8	620	6·1	850	4·8	610
Paper, printing and publishing	1·0	510	8·3	500	2·6	320
Other manufacturing industries	3·7	460	1·1	430	2·2	340
All manufacturing industries	3·9	550	4·2	550	3·3	510
Construction	21·1	700	15·7	740	17·2	710
Coalmining	25·4	..[1]	18·7	..[1]	24·7	..[1]
Railways	24·0	..[1]	18·0	..[1]	24·0	..[1]

[1] Comparable data not available.   [2] Provisional.   [3] Includes Flixborough.

Source: British Labour Statistics Yearbook, Department of Employment

Table 11.14   Deaths from accidents[1] occurring in the home and residential accommodation

England and Wales   Numbers

	1969		1970		1971		1972		1973		1974		
	Males	Females	Males	Females	Males	Females	Males	Females	Males	Females	Males	Females	Total
Poisoning: by solid/liquid substances	178	266	196	297	211	305	203	271	185	292	231	296	527
by gases and vapours	167	215	159	167	128	127	96	81	95	72	88	47	135
Falls	1,072	2,820	1,087	2,768	1,061	2,797	1,033	2,661	1,025	2,498	1,016	2,502	3,518
Fires and flames	269	432	294	439	268	369	263	417	331	411	289	412	701
Other	602	486	594	481	535	444	485	423	443	347	462	404	866
Total	2,288	4,219	2,330	4,152	2,203	4,042	2,080	3,853	2,079	3,620	2,086	3,661	5,747

[1] Excludes deaths undetermined whether accidentally or purposely inflicted.

Source: Mortality Statistics: accidents and violence, Series DH4, Office of Population Censuses and Surveys

Search and rescue services of the Ministry of Defence

The only forces currently dedicated to search and rescue duties are the Mountain Rescue Teams of the Royal Air Force and certain helicopter units of the Royal Navy and Royal Air Force which exist primarily to assist in military incidents. However, all the Services provide assistance in appropriate circumstances, including incidents also attended by civilian rescue services. Besides the incidents recorded in Table 11.15 other assistance is given by warships, by units such as the Joint Services Mountain Training Centres and by individuals; central records of such occasional ad hoc assistance are not kept. Search and rescue services also assist with urgent medical incidents (eg inter-hospital transfers) and these are included in the figures.

Table 11.15 Search and rescue operations at home

United Kingdom   Numbers

	1971[1]	1972	1973	1974	1975
Incidents[2]:					
Royal Navy	162	124	240	309	274
Royal Air Force	713	667	585	724	976
Total	864	768	816	1,028	1,245
Sorties[3]					
By aeroplanes:					
Royal Navy	..	1	1	2	1
Royal Air Force	91	74	69	48	48
Total	..	75	70	50	49
By helicopters:					
Royal Navy	..	189	278	366	319
Royal Air Force	650	613	490	781	1,026
Total	..	802	768	1,147	1,345
By marine craft (Royal Air Force only)	24	21	14	7	4
By mountain rescue teams (Royal Air Force only)	70	96	45	48	49
Persons assisted:					
By helicopters:					
Royal Navy	..	67	111	222	161
Royal Air Force	325	311	342	403	551
Total	..	378	453	625	712
By marine craft	2	9	6	7	—
By mountain rescue teams	48	71	15	30	20
Total	..	458	474	662	732

[1] An analysis of Royal Navy incidents for 1971 is not available. [2] Since both the Royal Navy and the Royal Air Force are involved in some incidents, the total may not be the sum of the incidents attended by the Services separately. [3] A sortie is a flight by an aeroplane or helicopter or a rescue mission by a marine craft or a mountain rescue team.

Source: Ministry of Defence

Fire

Table 11.16 and Chart 11.17 show casualties from fires and fireworks. There has been a slow upward trend in the numbers of fires and casualties from fires in recent years as these two tables show. On the other hand, the lower number of casualties from fireworks reflects more stringent regulations on their sale as well as a growing tendency to attend local municipally-organised displays rather than to set off one's own fireworks.

Table 11.16 Fatal fire casualties: by age and sex

United Kingdom   Numbers

	1970		1971		1972		1973		1974	
	Males	Females	Males	Females	Males	Females	Males	Females	Males	Females
Persons aged:										
Under 1	11	13	8	10	11	15	15	10	6	10
1–4	60	44	54	39	58	50	55	50	56	48
5–14	25	13	23	22	35	25	35	19	38	28
15–44	115	44	110	68	162	59	161	74	145	67
45–64	92	67	84	66	107	94	106	99	120	70
65–74	62	55	58	69	60	92	76	76	73	89
75 and over	76	145	78	116	94	191	75	167	87	179
Not stated	17	—	15	2	11	3	14	8	19	12
Total—United Kingdom	458	381	430	392	538	529	537	503	544	503

Source: UK Fire and Loss Statistics, Home Office

**Chart 11.17
Casualties from
fireworks**

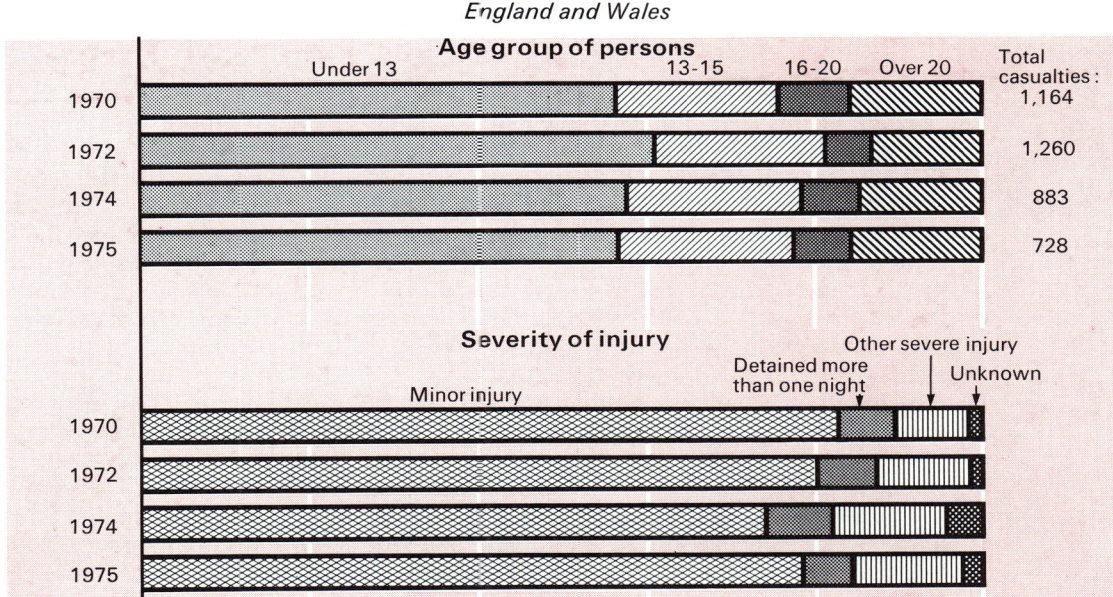

England and Wales

Source: Annual Report of HM Inspectors of Explosives

**Table 11.18   Northern Ireland: deaths and injuries connected with the civil disturbances,
1969–1976**

	Northern Ireland							Numbers
	1969	1970	1971	1972	1973	1974	1975	1976[1]
Deaths in Northern Ireland:								
The Army	—	—	43	103	58	28	14	6
Ulster Defence Regiment	—	—	5	26	8	7	6	7
Royal Ulster Constabulary	1	2	11	17	13	15	11	15
Civilians	12	23	115	322	171	166	216	146
Total	13	25	174	468	250	216	247	174
Persons injured in Northern Ireland:								
The Army	—	620	381	542	525	453	151	87
Ulster Defence Regiment	—	—	9	36	23	30	16	12
Royal Ulster Constabulary	711	191	317	466	291	235	263	121
Civilians	—	—	1,800	3,813	1,812	1,680	2,044	1,253
Total	711	811	2,507	4,857	2,651	2,398	2,474	1,473

[1] To end June.

Source: Northern Ireland Office

Social participation

The title of this section is also intended to cover the situation, not where the average person simply wishes to exercise his rights, but where he is happy to give his time to other people in the community; perhaps through representing his local area on a council or school board; perhaps by his membership of voluntary societies, charities, or churches. We are also interested in groups of people who band together to help others in society, for example, through the Citizens' Advice Bureaux, the Samaritans, or consumers' associations.

In this section we are concerned with the rights of the average person, and how he can attempt to exercise these rights, either at local or parliamentary elections; through organisations, either political or non-political; through the courts; or through pressure groups. The balance between these various ways is one which is changing gradually through time, and it is not at all easy to measure precisely what is happening. This section will be gradually developed during coming years, and we would welcome suggestions from readers as to additional sources of information.

Many of these ideas are, at best, only partly quantifiable, and it is certainly true that the section this year barely scratches the surface even of what is quantifiable. Some of the points are covered in the introduction to the Social Commentary, pages 8 to 31. Other points, mainly concerned with people's attitudes to democracy are covered in the article by John Hall on pages 47 to 60. In the 1975 survey carried out by the SSRC Survey Unit 24 per cent of all people claimed to belong to a club or organisation of some kind, and 15 per cent of all people claimed to be an office-holder, Treasurer, Secretary, etc. in such a club or organisation. There is no doubt that participation in organisations ranging from sporting to political, often on an informal basis, is a significant social characteristic of the present age in British society. It is hoped that in future years we will be able to monitor this, and it is with this end in view that we have made a start in *Social Trends No 7*.

There are four main groups of tables and charts: data on elections, parliamentary activities, and the background of MPs; membership of organisations; information on courts, tribunals, etc.; and finally data on legal aid.

Elections

The first group of four tables and charts shows the votes cast in various types of elections: general, parliamentary by-elections, and local elections. The general movement away from the two main parties is shown in all areas, and the increase in the proportion of votes given to nationalist parties such as Plaid Cymru in Wales, and the Scottish Nationalist Party is also apparent. Votes in by-elections tend to go against the government of the day. as can be seen in Table 12.2, although it must be remembered that by-elections do not occur in a valid statistical sample of constituencies.

A particular detail of interest in Table 12.1 is the increase in the 'other' vote. This is mainly a

definitional point (Ulster Unionist MPs are now included in 'other', as shown in the footnote), but it is also characterised by an increase in votes for such parties as the National Front; in the October 1974 election the National Front polled 113,579 votes (0·4 per cent of total) ccmpared to 17,426 votes for the Communist Party. Since that election the National Front increased its percentage poll; 2·8 per cent in all parliamentary by-elections from 1974 to July 1976, 5·9 per cent in the Rotherham by-election of June 1976, and 6·6 per cent in the Thurrock by-election in July 1976. In local areas smaller parties such as the National Front can do even better.

Table 12.1 Parliamentary elections, 1964 to 1974

United Kingdom   Various units

	15 October 1964	31 March 1966	18 June 1970	28 February 1974	10 October 1974
Number of electors[1] (millions)	35·89	35·96	39·62	39·80	40·26
Number of votes recorded[2]	27·66	27·26	28·34	31·33	29·19
As percentage of electorate	77·1	75·8	71·5	78·7	72·5
By party (millions):					
Communist	0·05	0·06	0·04	0·03	0·02
Conservative[3]	12·00	11·42	13·14	11·96	10·46
Labour	12·21	13·06	12·18	11·65	11·46
Liberal	3·09	2·33	2·12	6·06	5·35
Plaid Cymru	0·07	0·06	0·18	0·17	0·17
Scottish Nationalist	0·06	0·13	0·31	0·63	0·84
Other[3]	0·17	0·20	0·38	0·82	0·84
as percentage of votes cast:					
Communist	0·2	0·2	0·1	0·1	0·1
Conservative[3]	43·4	41·9	46·4	38·2	35·8
Labour	44·1	47·9	43·0	37·2	39·3
Liberal	11·2	8·6	7·5	19·3	18·3
Plaid Cymru	0·3	0·2	0·6	0·6	0·6
Scottish Nationalist	0·2	0·5	1·1	2·0	2·9
Other[3]	0·6	0·7	1·3	2·6	2·9
Members of Parliament elected (numbers):					
Conservative[3]	303	253	330	296	276
Labour	317	363	287	301	319
Liberal	9	12	6	14	13
Plaid Cymru	0	0	0	2	3
Scottish Nationalist	0	0	1	7	11
Other[3,4]	1	2	6	15	13
as percentage of Members of Parliament elected:					
Conservative[3]	48	40	52	46·6	43·5
Labour	50	58	46	47·4	50·2
Liberal	1	2	1	2·2	2·0
Plaid Cymru	0	0	0	0·3	0·5
Scottish Nationalist	0	0	0	1·1	1·7
Other[3]	0	0	1	2·4	2·0

[1] Voting age lowered to 18 from 16 February 1970. [2] Number of votes cast relates only to voting for contested seats. [3] Ulster Unionist MPs were included with Conservative numbers from 1964 to 1970, and with 'Other' in 1974. (There were 12 U.U. members in 1964, 11 in 1966, 8 in 1970, 11 United Ulster Unionists in February 1974 and 10 in October 1974.) [4] The Speaker is included in 'other'.

Source: Home Office

Table 12.2 Parliamentary by-elections

United Kingdom   Numbers and percentages

	Number of by-elections	Percentage of votes cast						Total votes cast (=100%) (Numbers)
		Conservative	Labour	Liberal	SNP	Plaid Cymru	Other	
1964–66	13	45·7	33·2	17·2	0·5	0·3	–	487,837
1966–70	38	47·0	32·8	9·4	3·0	3·0	4·7	1,339,218
1970–74	30	34·2	40·5	15·3	3·5	1·2	5·4	1,027,699

Source: Home Office

**Chart 12.3
General election
results**

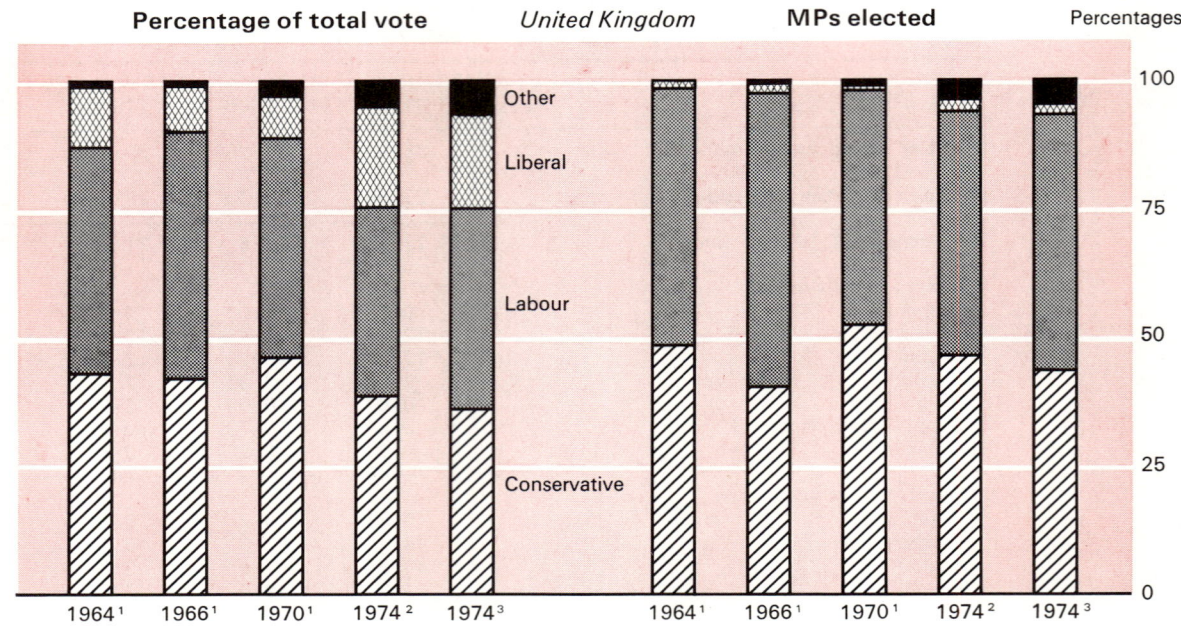

Percentage of total vote   *United Kingdom*   MPs elected   Percentages

1964[1]   1966[1]   1970[1]   1974[2]   1974[3]   1964[1]   1966[1]   1970[1]   1974[2]   1974[3]

[1] See footnote ([3]) of Table 12.1.   [2] February.   [3] October   *Source of data: Home Office*

Table 12.4   Local Elections, 1973 and 1976

England and Wales   Numbers

	1973				1976[1]	
	Counties		Districts		Districts	
	Metropolitan	Other	Metropolitan	Other	Metropolitan	Other
Party control						
Conservative	–	18	5	87	15	134
Labour	6	11	26	92	18	30
Liberal						
Other						62
No control	–	18	5	154	3	39
Seats						
Conservative	142	1,598	699	4,422	1,064	7,116
Labour	420	1,375	1,573	4,975	1,199	3,259
Liberal	49	210	178	961	151	625
Other	8	513	48	4,687	102	4,136

[1] Not all seats were 'at risk' in 1976. The figures for 1976 represent the total state of councils after the 1976 election.

Source: Compiled from figures published in "The Times" Newspaper

Table 12.5 Public Bills considered in Parliament: by session

United Kingdom   Numbers

	Session				
	1971–72	1972–73	1973–74	1974	1974–75
Public Bills					
Total number of Bills which received the Royal Assent[1]	84	83	17	50	99
of which:					
Introduced into the Commons	*48*	*50*	*13*	*27*	*48*
Introduced into the Lords	*28*	*22*	*2*	*15*	*35*
Provisional Order and Order Confirmation Bills	*8*	*11*	*2*	*8*	*16*
Total number of Bills introduced into, but not passed by, the Commons	63	66	53	33	78
Total number of Bills introduced into but not passed by, the Lords	9	6	15	13	10
Total number of Bills passed by the Commons, but not by the Lords	0	0	2	1	1
Total number of Bills passed by the Lords, but not by the Commons	2	4	5	2	4
Total number of Bills passed by both Houses, but Amendments not agreed to	0	0	0	0	1
Total Public Bills	158	159	92	99	193
Number of sitting days in the session[2]:					
House of Commons	180	164	60	87	198
House of Lords	141	128	45	67	165

[1] The number of pages of Public General Acts in the annual volumes of *Public General Acts and Measures* was in 1971, 2,107; in 1972, 2,527; in 1973, 2,236; and in 1974, 1,875.   [2] Including certain formal sittings at the beginning of each new Parliament but excluding sittings of the House of Lords in its judicial capacity.   *Sources: Public Bills, Returns for Sessions 1971–72 to 1974–75; Information Office, House of Lords*

Chart 12.6 Education of Conservative and Labour MPs

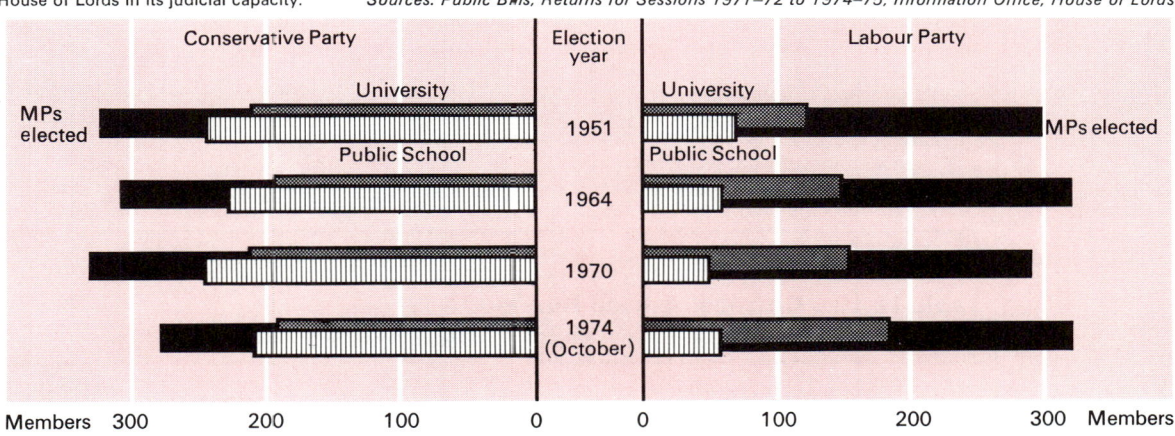

Source: British Political Facts, 1900–1975, Butler and Sloman

Table 12.7 Activities of charities and other organisations

United Kingdom   Various units

	1961	1971	1972	1973	1974	1975
Charities						
Oxfam (income, £ thousand)	1,627	4,613	4,082	4,586	4,821	6,662
Save the Children Fund (income, £ thousand)[1]	963	3,068	3,237	2,826	3,950	4,387
League Against Cruel Sports (income, £ thousand)	28	36	58	72	97	143
Christian Aid (income, £ thousand)[2]	678	3,096	2,885	3,122	3,786	4,207
The Samaritans Incorporated[3]						
Number of branches	17	130	140	143	151	160
New clients (thousands)	..	89	156	158	192	205
Volunteers (thousands)	..	15	16	17	18	19
Consumers' organisations						
Consumers' Association (membership, thousands)[4]	250	604	599	581	651	713

[1] For years ending 31 March.   [2] For years ending 30 September.   [3] These figures include branches in the Channel Isles (1 in 1961 and 2 from 1963) and the Irish Republic (1 in 1971, 2 from 1972, and 3 from 1974).   [4] At end March.

Source: Organisations concerned

**Chart 12.8
Trade unions:
membership**

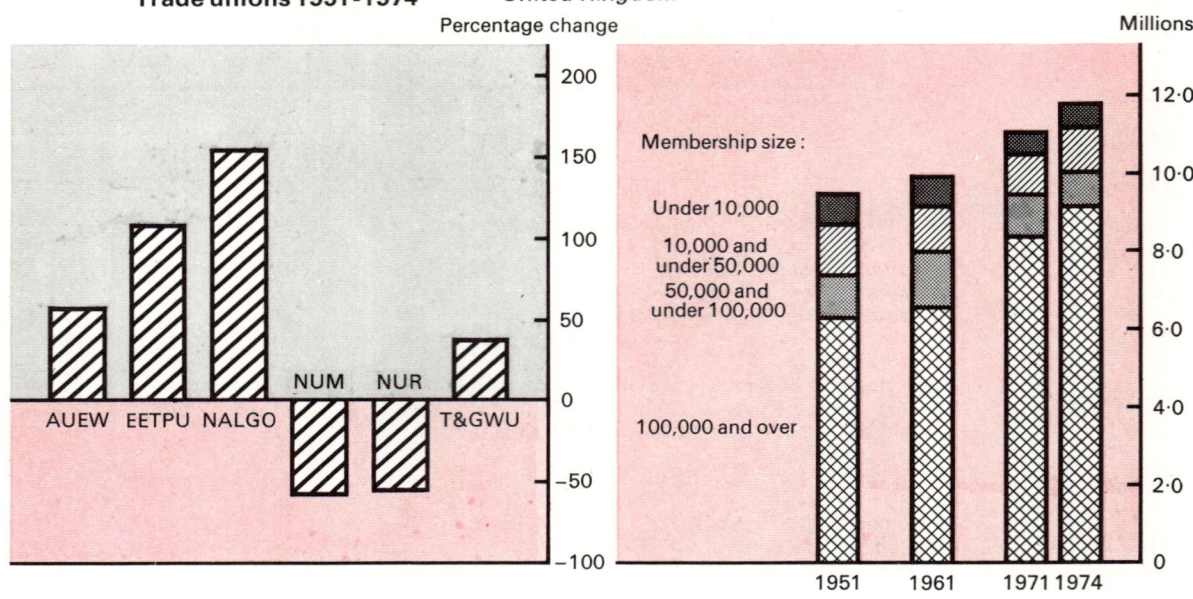

Change in membership of selected Trade unions 1951-1974 *United Kingdom*

Percentage change

Trade unions membership

Millions

Source: Trade Unions themselves

Table 12.9 Membership of trade unions

United Kingdom Numbers and percentages

Union:	1951	1974	Percentage change 1951–1974
Amalgamated Union of Engineering Workers	756,000	1,198,491	+58·5
Electrical Electronic Telecommunication and Plumbing	198,000	414,000	+109·1
National and Local Government Officers' Association	212,158	541,918	+155·4
National Union of Mineworkers	632,478	255,296	−59·6
National Union of Railwaymen	396,257	173,933	−56·1
Transport and General Workers	1,337,060	1,857,308	+38·9

Source: Trade Unions themselves

Table 12.10 Citizens' Advice Bureaux[1]

United Kingdom Numbers and thousands

	1961	1966	1971/72	1972/73	1973/74	1974/75	1975/76
Number of bureaux	416	473	529	566	614	619	670
Total enquiries (thousands)	1,112[2]	1,282	1,658	1,881	1,910	2,304	2,695
of which:							
Family and personal	..	354	381	414	402	471	546
National and international[3]	..	280	321	358	352	108	129
Housing, property, and land	..	287	332	387	391	453	517
Consumer, trade, and manufacture	..	104	173	219	247	399	463
Employment	..	84	114	118	116	142	195
Social security	..	39	96	109	101	118	167
Health and medical	..	50	79	86	84	177	112
Education and training	..	32	41	45	43	44	52
Communications and travel[4]	..	34	70	86	90	103	116
Taxes and duties[5]	..	..	37	42	40	55	90
Immigration and nationality[6]	–	–	–	–	–	20	20
Administration of justice[6]	–	–	–	–	–	152	214
Leisure activities[6]	–	–	–	–	–	62	72

[1] For 1961 and 1966 figures are for calendar years; for 1971/72 and subsequently, figures are for the twelve months commencing April.
[2] Contains a wider margin of error than the later figures.   [3] Previously known as 'Civic, local, and national information'.   [4] Includes transport and holidays.   [5] Prior to 1971/72 classified under other headings.   [6] Prior to 1974/75 classified under other headings.

Source: National Association of Citizens' Advice Bureaux Reports

Table 12.11 Civil justice: summary

Great Britain   Numbers

	1951	1961	1971	1973	1974	1975
Total number of proceedings commenced						
England and Wales						
Courts of First Instance						
High Court of Justice	159,781	173,208	303,728	312,359	382,392	399,437
County Courts[1]	535,374	1,683,581	1,538,874	1,554,243	1,776,321	1,841,112[5]
Other[2]	21,403	25,497	31,309	4,663	5,008	5,342
Total proceedings	716,558	1,882,287	1,873,911	1,871,265	2,163,721	2,245,891
Courts of Appeal						
Judicial Committee of the Privy Council	56	54	33	35	26	54
House of Lords[4]	35	59	50	51	34	64
Court of Appeal	711	690	922	1,094	1,176	1,302
High Court of Justice	507	455	784	722	784	917
Total proceedings	1,309	1,258	1,789	1,902	2,020	2,337
Scotland						
Courts of First Instance						
Court of Session	4,727	4,863	9,904	12,352	13,655	14,369
Sheriff Courts	14,383	36,282	37,260	46,520	62,267	67,948
Sheriff Small Debt Courts	50,247	143,567	145,413	107,862	114,388	109,513
Total proceedings[3]	73,390	189,825	193,357	166,991	190,310	191,830
Courts of Appeal						
House of Lords[4]	9	10	8	5	6	4
Court of Session, Inner House	108	132	100	94	115	94
Total proceedings	117	142	108	99	121	98

[1] Excluding divorce, information for which can be found in Table 1.12.   [2] Mayor's and City of London Court included in County Courts from 1 January 1972.   [3] Includes proceedings commenced in Justice of the Peace Small Debt Courts in 1951 (3,585); 1961 (4.711) and 1971 (600). JP Small Debt Courts ceased to function in 1973. Also ncludes proceedings commenced in the Sheriff Court of Chancery in 1951 (449); 1961 (402); 1971 (180); and 1973 (257). From 1974 functions of the Sheriff Court of Chancery were undertaken in the Sheriff Court. Figures for Court of Chancery proceedings are therefore included in the number of proceedings commenced in the Sheriff Courts thereafter.   [4] Scottish appeals are also included in the England and Wales figures.   [5] The nature of plaints included: 1,182,851 for goods sold and delivered, work done and materials supplied, professional fees; 171,799 for hire purchase, credit sale, conditional sale agreements (money claims and/or return of goods); 152,378 for other claims for debt (eg income tax, dishonoured cheques, arrears of rent (excluding hire purchase)); 82,700 for bank or finance house loans; and 22,020 claims for damages relating to personal injuries.

Sources: Civil Judicial Statistics, Lord Chancellor's Office; Civil Judicial Statistics (Scotland), Scottish Courts Administration

Table 12.12 Civil justice: County Courts

England and Wales   Numbers and thousands

	1951	1961	1971	1973	1974	1975
Class of proceedings commenced (thousands):						
By plaints issued for amounts:						
Not exceeding £100	457	1,587	1,276	1,184	1,267	1,215
Above £100 and not exceeding £500[1]	4	42	151	221	324	377
Above £500[1]	–	–	14	25	46	70
For recovery of land	31	26	56	77	90	109
Other plaints	36	23	33	40	42	62
Other proceedings commenced	7	6	8	7	7	8
Total proceedings commenced	535	1,684	1,538	1,554	1,776	1,841
Disposals (numbers):						
After trial[2]:						
Judge	23,947	20,153	20,274	23,788	24,414	25,164
Registrar	6,117	14,770	21,266	17,494	16,990	24,872
After arbitration[3]:						
Judge	–	–	–	104	60	88
Registrar					3,689	6,328
Others					22	31
In default of appearance or defence; on admission; by consent	309,042	1,173,806	998,715	968,524	1,091,541	993,257
Total[4]	339,106	1,208,729	1,040,255	1,009,910	1,136,716	1,049,740

[1] Jurisdiction of County Courts increased to £500 on 1 December 1966, to £750 on 26 May 1970 and to £1,000 on 1 October 1974.   [2] For 1951 and 1961 includes some cases determined on hearing out without trial.   [3] See Appendix B, page 252.   [4] Excludes actions paid-up, struck-out, withdrawn, or otherwise disposed of.

Source: Civil Judicial Statistics, Lord Chancellor's Office

**Chart 12.13
Civil justice:
County Courts**

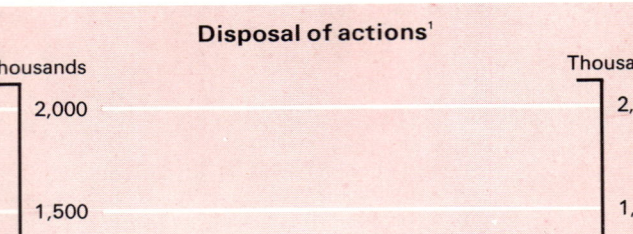

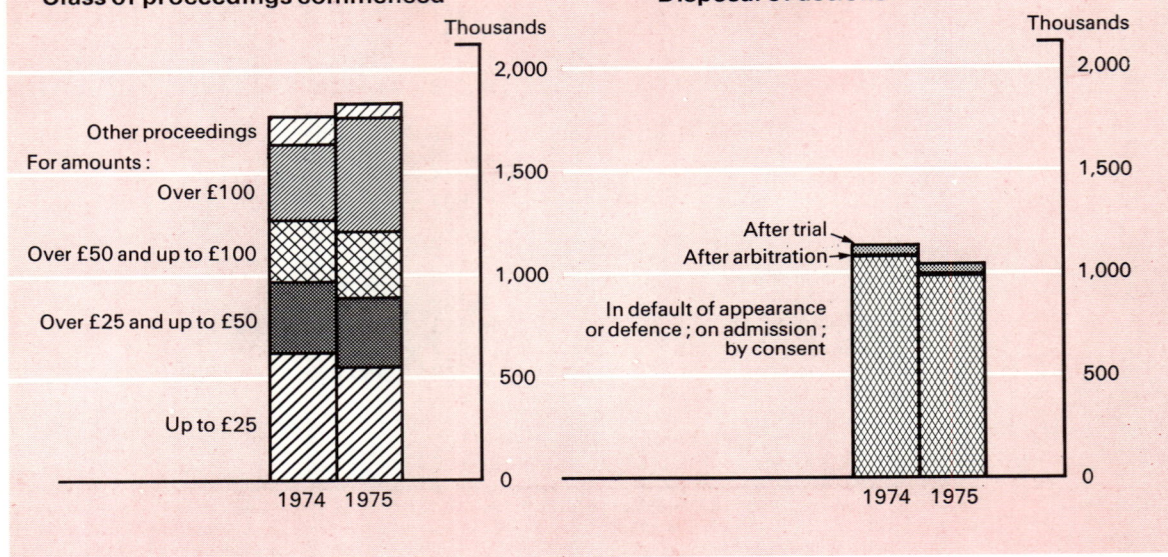

England and Wales

Class of proceedings commenced

Disposal of actions[1]

Thousands

Other proceedings

For amounts :

Over £100

Over £50 and up to £100

Over £25 and up to £50

Up to £25

After trial

After arbitration

In default of appearance
or defence ; on admission ;
by consent

1974 1975

1974 1975

[1] Excludes actions paid-up, struck out, withdrawn or otherwise disposed of.

Source: Lord Chancellor's Office

Table 12.14   Civil justice: Sheriff Courts[1]

	Scotland						Thousands
	1951	1961	1971	1972	1973	1974	1975
Disposal							
By final judgment or decree							
in foro[2]	15	22	20	15	13	11	12
in absence of defendant	36	121	110	108	98	113	110
Otherwise disposed of	13	35	53	49	43	49	52
Total actions disposed of	64	179	183	172	154	173	174
Class of actions disposed of by final judgment or decree							
Ordinary Court							
Debts	8	26	24	26	30	43	47
Other actions	3	3	4	4	5	5	5
Small Debt Court							
Debts	39	109	92	89	74	74	69
Rent sequestration	1	4	9	2	–	–	–
Other	1	2	1	2	1	2	1
Total disposals by final judgment or decree	51	144	130	123	110	124	122

[1] Including Small Debt Court.   [2] A decree *in foro* is a decree granted in a case in which the defender has appeared.

Source: Civil Judicial Statistics (Scotland), Scottish Courts Administration

**Chart 12.15
Civil justice:
Sheriff Courts**

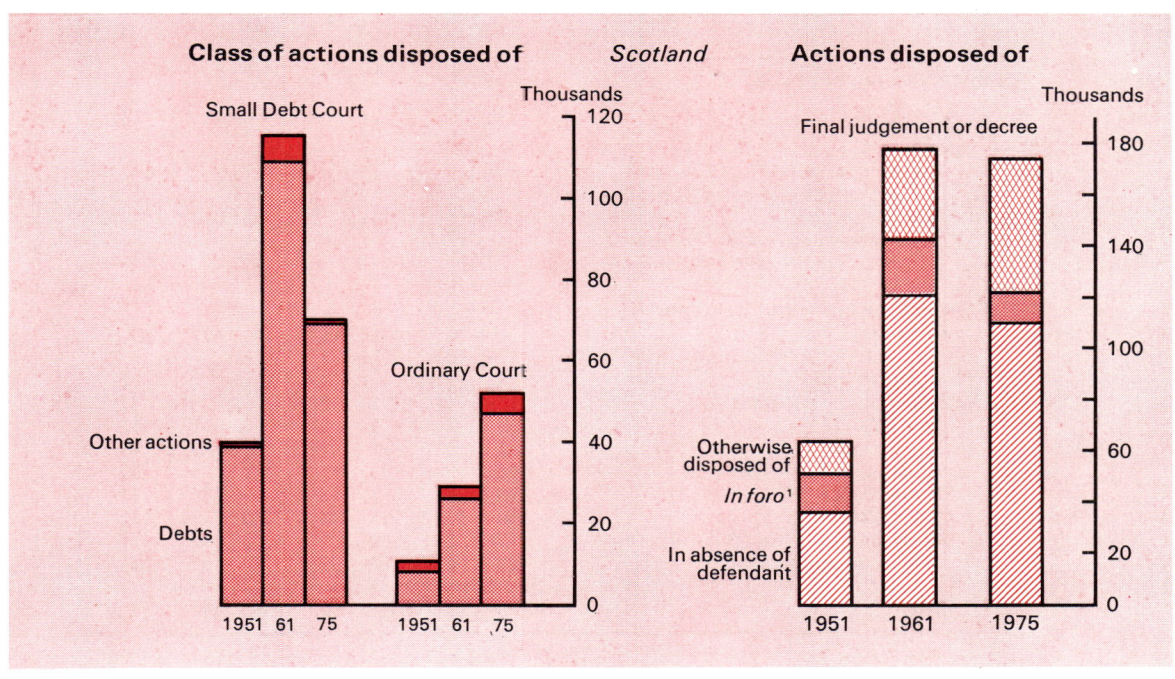

¹ A decree *in foro* is a decree granted in a case in which the defender has appeared.

Source: Scottish Courts Administration

**Chart 12.16
Crown Court:
persons tried by
type of plea**

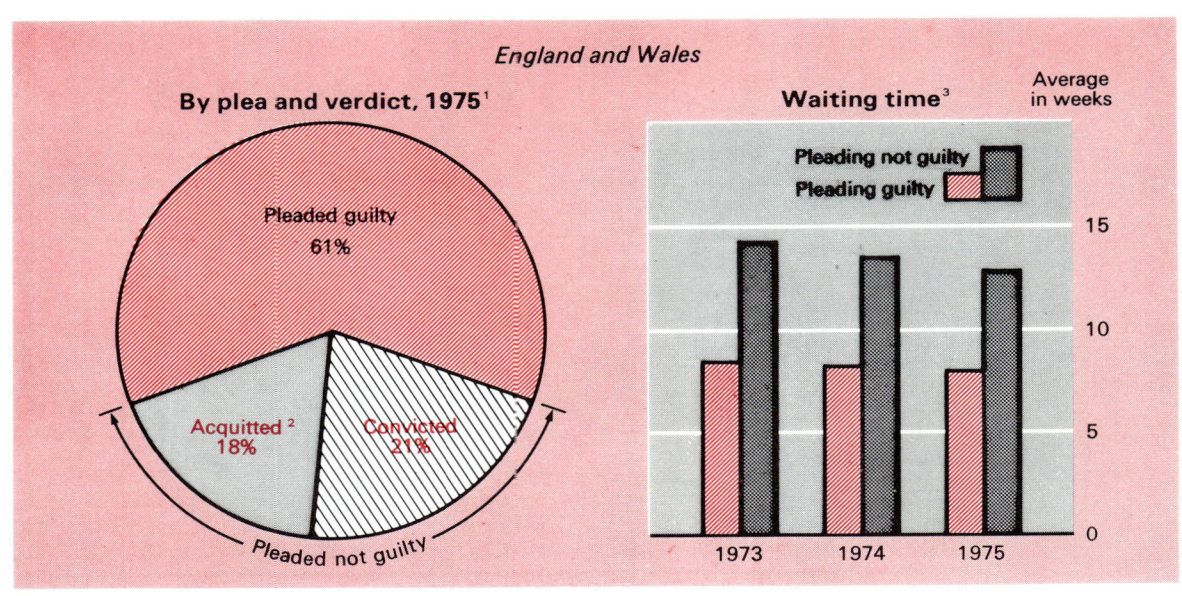

¹ In addition, there were 1,596 defendants for whom no plea was recorded.   ² Of these, 65 per cent were acquitted by the jury and 17 per cent by the judge. Of the remainder, the prosecution offered no evidence or the case was not proceeded with.   ³ The average waiting time for defendants refers to the length of time between the date of committal by the magistrates' courts and the start of the hearing by the Crown Court. It does not include any time spent in waiting before the case was committed to the Crown Court.

Source: Statistics on Judicial Administration, Lord Chancellor's Office

Table 12.17 Complaints to Parliamentary Commissioner for Administration

	United Kingdom[1]					Numbers
	1970	1971	1972	1973	1974	1975
Received during year	645	548	573	571	704	928
Dealt with during year	651	516	596	536	653	916
of which:						
Rejected as outside jurisdiction[2]	362	295	318	285	374	576
Discontinued after partial investigation	30	39	17	12	27	19
Reported upon	259	182	261	239	252	321
of which contained elements of maladministration leading to injustice	59	67	79	88	94	167

Complaints analysed by departments/ ministries[3]	(a)	(b)	(a)	(b)	(a)	(b)	(a)	(b)	(a)	(b)	(a)	(b)
Agriculture, Fisheries and Food	13	3	7	1	2	1	2	–	7	2	8	–
Customs and Excise	6	3	–	–	5	–	5	2	11	2	4	–
Education and Science	12	1	12	3	16	3	12	3	6	–	8	–
Employment	9	3	3	2	9	1	10	2	14	5	9	1
Environment	52	5	31	2	58	15	51	14	54	17	46	9
Health and Social Security	49	6	29	11	51	14	52	15	51	23	75	39
Home Office	23	–	11	3	6	1	11	2	20	7	41	34
Inland Revenue	56	32	62	39	70	37	65	39	60	32	49	27
Trade and Industry (Board of Trade)	17	2	10	3	13	3	15	8	8	3	58	51
Other departments, etc.	22	4	17	3	31	4	16	3	21	3	23	6
Total	259	59	182	67	261	79	239	88	252	94	321	167

[1] Excludes complaints concerning actions by Northern Ireland Government departments.   [2] Of which Schedule 2 department not involved. 1970: 123; 1971: 130; 1972: 132; 1973: 100; 1974: 142; 1975: 192.   [3] (a) complaints reported on (b) cases of maladministration. The Parliamentary Commissioner also holds the posts of Health Service Commissioner for England, for Wales, and for Scotland. Details are not shown in the above table, but can be found in Appendix B on page 252.   *Source: Parliamentary Commissioner for Administration*

Table 12.18 Administrative tribunals[1]

	Great Britain				Number of cases
	1960	1961	1971	1973	1974
Children's Hearings	–	–	5,243	11,275	15,108
Civil Aviation[2]	–	2,104	4,284	5,037	1,574
Immigration Adjudicators	–	–	1,944	4,140	6,573
Industrial Tribunals	–	–	10,048	15,376	15,205
Lands Tribunal§	1,121	467	1,108	1,304	1,225
Local Valuation Courts and *Valuation Appeal Committees*	. .	. .	24,922	30,057	39,945
Mental Health Review Tribunals§	1	830	1,021	956	952
National Health Service Executive Councils and Service Committees	1,292	1,300	845	944	805
National Insurance, etc.:					
Commissioners	2,775	2,421	2,261	2,039	1,916
Local Tribunals	41,139	39,731	29,334	29,477	28,510
Medical Appeal Tribunals	19,775	19,820	17,614	15,197	12,710
Patents, designs, and trade marks	5,652	7,334	7,208	6,769	7,910
Pensions Appeal Tribunals	5,434	2,576	3,760	3,869	3,833
Rent Assessment Committees	–	–	4,300	9,838	9,559
Rent Tribunals	4,730	5,998	16,107	26,545	23,203
Revenue:					
General Commissioners[3]	. .	. .	910,000	1,067,694	1,227,442
Special Commissioners	1,985	3,042	3,357	4,076	3,763
Road Traffic:					
Licensing Authorities	8,530	8,706	5,770	4,303	4,275
Traffic Commissioners	13,507	14,408	17,212	18,862	17,142
Supplementary Benefit Appeal Tribunals	7,757	14,922	29,648	26,002	27,242

[1] Figures are taken from the Annual Reports of the Council on Tribunals. They cover Scotland as well as England and Wales and relate only to those tribunals under the supervision of the Council and its Scottish Committee which deal with the greatest number of cases. Where tribunals have a separate appellation in Scotland this is given in italics. Tribunals which exist only for England and Wales are marked with the symbol §. The criterion taken for inclusion of tribunals in the table is whether they heard more than 1,000 cases in 1972.   [2] Up to 1971, the figures are for cases dealt with by the Air Transport Licensing Board; from 1972, they are for cases dealt with by the Civil Aviation Authority. [3] Figures relate only to England and Wales and, in 1971, were estimated.   *Source: Annual Report of the Council on Tribunals*

Table 12.19   Crime: legal aid applications

Great Britain   Numbers

	1972		1973		1974		1975	
	Ordered	Refused	Ordered	Refused	Ordered	Refused	Ordered	Refused
England and Wales								
By magistrates' courts:								
For proceedings before magistrates' courts	147,181	17,372	175,636	17,714	215,113	19,758	249,611	24,724
For appeals to the Crown Court	4,006	504	3,338	317	3,594	302	3,952	367
For persons committed to the Crown Court	52,575	288	52,750	359	61,206	354	69,323	362
By the Crown Court								
For proceedings before the Crown Court	10,204	40	9,327	69	9,556	40	9,237	40
For appeals to the Crown Court	2,063	118	2,290	59	2,648	48	3,229	66
By Court of Appeal, Criminal Division	984	4,443	989	4,428	871	3,384	1,016	4,428
Scotland[1,2]								
For solemn proceedings in the High Court and Sheriff Court	4,444	253	4,020	154	4,024	244	4,879	128
For summary proceedings in the Sheriff Court	8,844	3,046	10,595	3,255	11,114	3,656	12,586	3,597
For appeal proceedings (all courts)	130	180	137	239	145	205	188	219

[1] Year ending 31 March.
[2] Figures in the 'refused' columns include abandoned cases.

Sources: Home Office; Scottish Home and Health Department

Table 12.20   Civil justice: legal aid

Great Britain
Years April to March   Numbers

	1961/62	1966/67	1971/72	1972/73	1973/74	1974/75
Number of legal aid certificates issued						
England and Wales						
Courts of First Instance						
High Court of Justice[1]	39,246	54,691	119,492	108,042	105,731	123,130
County Courts[2]	4,432	4,915	5,945	5,943	5,598	8,093
Magistrates Courts[2]	28,515	49,362	76,872	71,981	67,490	68,234
Total cases	72,193	108,968	202,309	185,966	178,819	199,457
Out of court claims[3]	2,701	1,810	572	398	—	—
Courts of Appeal						
House of Lords	16	14	18	14	16	15
Court of Appeal	295	224	292	266	270	296
Other	497	644	912	735	624	564
Total cases	808	882	1,222	1,015	910	875
Scotland						
All courts						
House of Lords	5	4	4	1	2	2
Courts of Session	2,574	5,193	8,536	8,676	8,548	8,436
Sheriff Courts	2,280	2,706	3,422	3,394	3,282	3,092

[1] Cases which may be brought in the High Court, including matrimonial cases brought in the County Court.
[2] Legal aid came into effect in magistrates' courts on 8 May 1961 and in the County Courts on 1 January 1956.
[3] Bringing and defending claims without court procedure. *Section 5.* Such claims have not been allowed since 1972/73.

Sources: Lord Chancellor's Office; Scottish Home and Health Department

Immigration appeals

Table 12.21 supplements the data in Table 12.18 on Administrative tribunals for the Immigration Adjudicators. It shows, for the years 1973, 1974, and 1975 combined the appeals dealt with under the Immigration Act 1971.

Table 12.21   Immigration Act 1971: appeals disposed of, 1973 to 1975[1]

	Great Britain				Numbers
	Appeals allowed	Appeals dismissed	Appeals withdrawn	No jurisdiction	Total
Disposed of by adjudicators	2,179	11,076	5,316	50	18,621
Disposed of by Immigration Appeal Tribunal:					
Immigrants' appeals	54	193	126	6	379
Home Office appeals	38	15	39	–	92

[1] Calendar years 1973, 1974, and 1975.   Source: Home Office

Marriages

The final chart is on a rather different topic. It shows that during the last 10 years there has been a substantial change in the pattern of marriages solemnised in church or registry office. However, the proportion married in a registry office has risen substantially mainly because of the rise in the proportion of marriages which are second or later marriages for at least one partner. More detail can be found in an article in *Population Trends No.3, 1976.*

Chart 12.22 Marriages[1]: manner of solemnisation

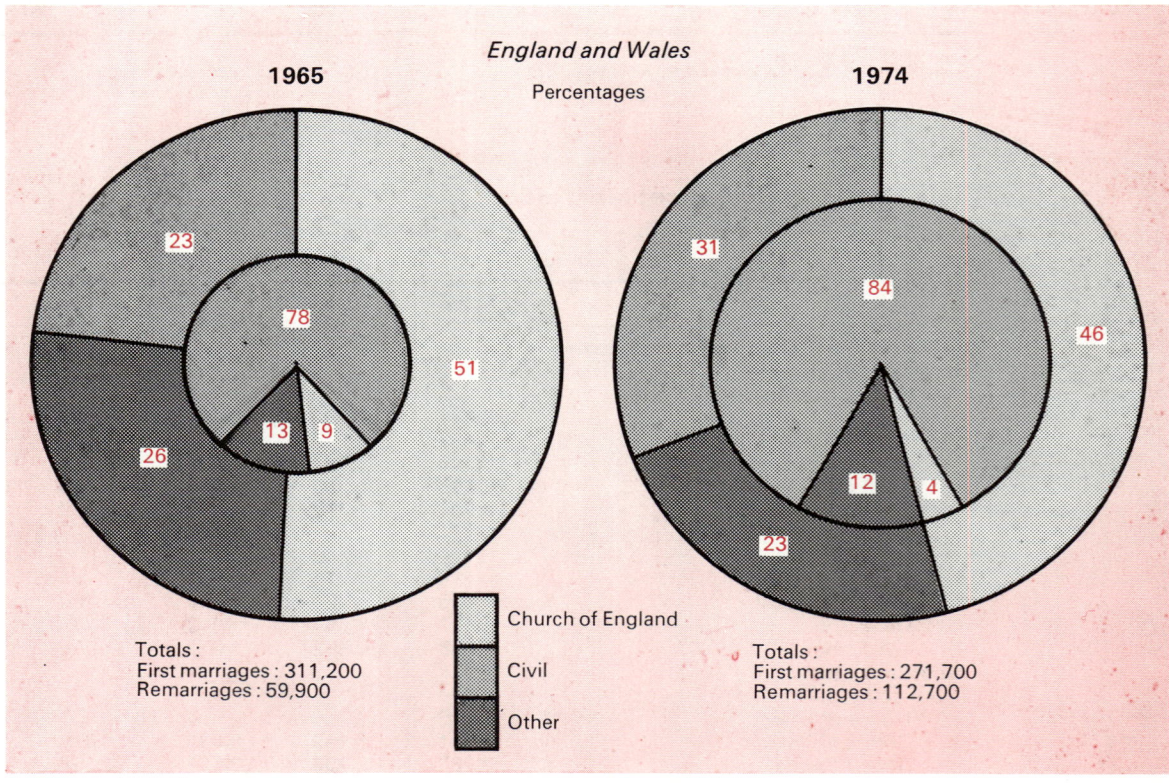

England and Wales

Percentages

1965

1974

23
78
51
13   9
26

31
84
46
12   4
23

Church of England
Civil
Other

Totals:
First marriages: 311,200
Remarriages: 59,900

Totals:
First marriages: 271,700
Remarriages: 112,700

[1] Outer band represents first marriages of both partners. Inner circle represents remarriages of at least one partner.
Source: *Population Trends No. 3, Office of Population Censuses and Surveys*

Resources

This section includes a very small number of basic tables on public expenditure, showing amounts spent on the various social services by both central and local government, and the sources of the money. Most of the tables in this section last year have been included this year in the relevant subject section, for example, public expenditure on education is included in the section on Education and Employment.

There are two tables and a chart on public expenditure, followed by the same number on local authority finance. The analysis by function Tables 13.3 and 13.5 are the most interesting as they show the changing patterns in public spending on different areas over the last 10 to 15 years. Table 13.7 shows the percentage annual increase in both local authority and public expenditure for the years 1961–72, and 1972–75. Detailed notes on definitions and terms used in this section are given at Appendix B. The reader is also referred to *National Income and Expenditure*, CSO, annual, for more detail on central government expenditure, and to the publications of the Chartered Institute of Public Finance and Accounting (CIPFA), especially *Local Government Trends,* annual, for more detail on local government expenditure.

**Chart 13.1
Pattern and
source of public
expenditure,
1974**

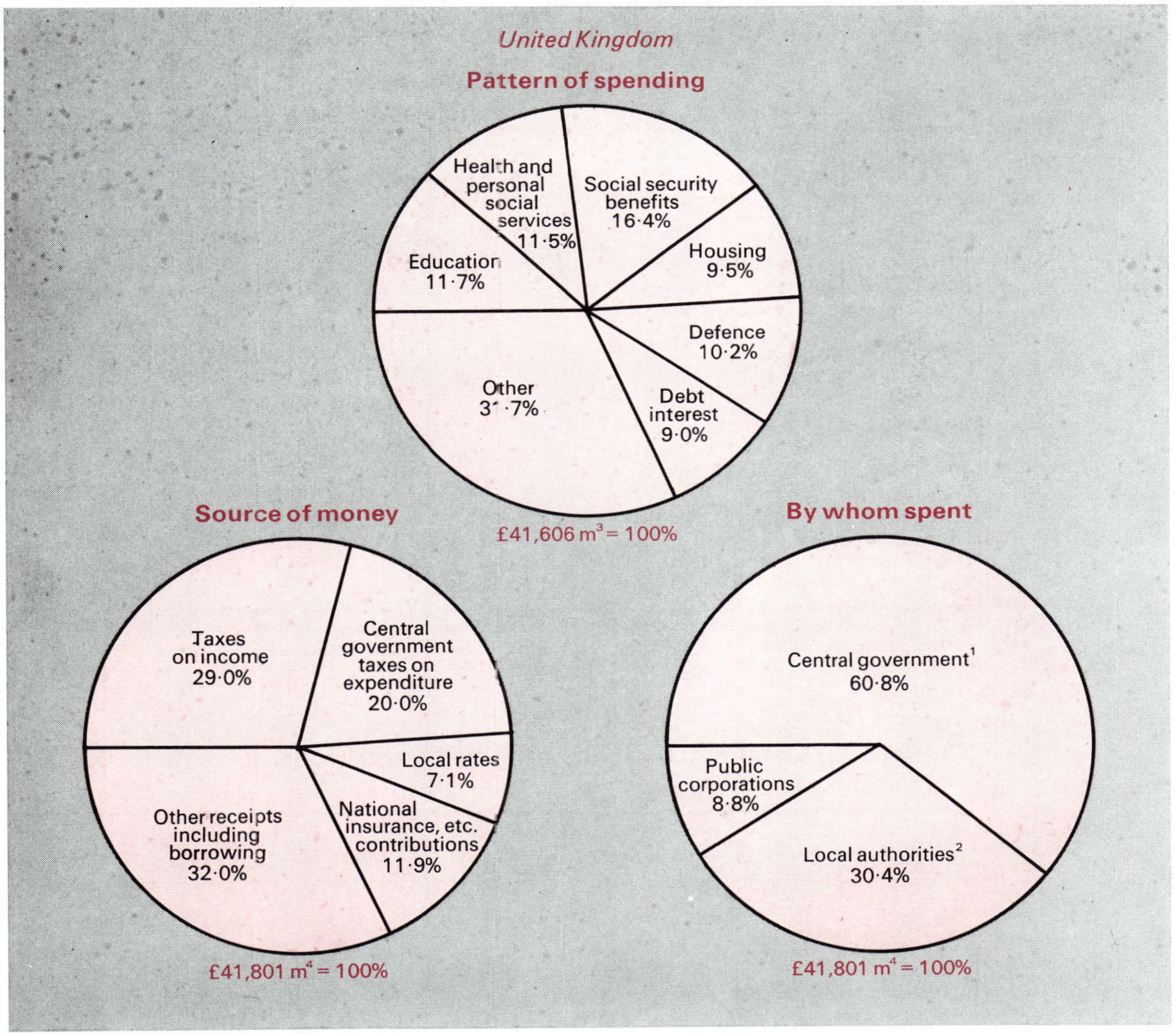

United Kingdom

Pattern of spending

Health and personal social services 11·5%

Social security benefits 16·4%

Education 11·7%

Housing 9·5%

Defence 10·2%

Other 31·7%

Debt interest 9·0%

£41,606 m[3] = 100%

Source of money

Taxes on income 29·0%

Central government taxes on expenditure 20·0%

Local rates 7·1%

Other receipts including borrowing 32·0%

National insurance, etc. contributions 11·9%

£41,801 m[4] = 100%

By whom spent

Central government[1] 60·8%

Public corporations 8·8%

Local authorities[2] 30·4%

£41,801 m[4] = 100%

[1,2] See notes in Appendix A.   [3] *National Income Blue Book* 1975 figures.
[4] Revised figures in *Economic Trends* No. 270 April 1976

Source: Central Statistical Office

205

Table 13.2 Public expenditure summary: analysis by economic category

United Kingdom   £ million and £

	1961	1966	1971	1972	1973	1974	1975
Expenditure on goods and services (£ millions):							
Current expenditure	4,584	6,572	10,344	11,772	13,403	16,578	22,907
Capital expenditure[1]	1,842	3,208	4,628	4,760	5,879	7,576	9,687
Total	6,426	9,780	14,972	16,532	19,282	24,154	32,594
Current grants to personal sector (£ millions)	1,708	2,825	4,784	5,853	6,445	7,873	10,208
Other public expenditure[2] (£ millions)	2,185	2,712	4,571	4,990	6,589	9,903	11,663
Total public expenditure (£ millions) (including debt interest)	10,319	15,317	24,327	27,375	32,316	41,930	54,465
Value per head of population (£)	195	280	437	490	577	748	971
Expenditure on goods and services[3] as percentage of gross national product at factor cost	26·3	29·2	30·2	29·8	29·7	32·3	34·6
Current grants to personal sector as percentage of total personal income	7·5	8·8	10·0	10·8	10·3	10·4	10·7

[1] Gross domestic fixed capital formation and increase in value of stocks (including stock appreciation). [2] Includes subsidies, other current and capital grants, and net expenditure on financial assets and debt interest. [3] Includes stock appreciation.

Source: National Income and Expenditure, Central Statistical Office

Table 13.3 Public expenditure summary: analysis by function[1]

United Kingdom   £ million and percentages

	1961	1971	1972	1973	1974	1975	Percentages 1961	Percentages 1975
Social services:								
Social security	1,628	4,309	5,119	5,531	6,837	8,918	15·8	16·4
Health and personal social services	1,088	2,784	3,219	3,743	4,917	6,707	10·5	12·3
Education	1,012	3,023	3,559	4,083	4,746	6,840	9·8	12·5
Housing and environmental services:								
Housing	555	1,240	1,463	2,394	4,118	4,291	5·4	7·9
Environmental services	389	1,179	1,368	1,701	1,975	2,405	3·8	4·4
Libraries, museums, and the arts	34	117	137	171	220	289	0·3	0·5
Justice and law	204	634	714	843	1,063	1,454	2·0	2·7
Roads and public lighting	276	846	936	1,085	1,176	1,502	2·7	2·8
Transport and communication	526	1,010	1,021	1,360	1,942	2,495	5·1	4·5
Commerce and industry	1,206	3,180	3,103	3,633	5,337	7,825	11·7	14·4
Defence and external relations	1,859	3,164	3,495	4,065	4,800	5,876	18·0	10·8
Other expenditure	285	628	821	754	962	1,350	2·7	2·5
Debt interest	1,257	2,213	2,420	2,953	3,837	4,513	12·2	8·3
Total	10,319	24,327	27,375	32,316	41,930	54,465	100·0	100·0

[1] This functional classification is consistent with the analysis of public expenditure given in the *National Income and Expenditure* Blue Book and the tables which follow show in more detail the content of social services, housing, environmental services justice, and law and libraries, museums and the arts expenditure.

Source: National Income and Expenditure, Central Statistical Office

Table 13.4 Local authority income: by source

United Kingdom   £ million and percentages

	1963	1972	1973	1974	1975[2]	Percentages 1963	Percentages 1975
Source of income:							
Rates	1,014	2,377	2,617	2,966	3,893	30·9	22·3
Government grants	1,093	3,441	4,309	5,135	8,087	33·3	46·3
Loans	605	1,387	2,365	3,377	2,810	18·4	16·1
Other capital receipts	24	288	73	−156	80	0·8	0·5
Miscellaneous income[1]	545	1,413	1,753	2,150	2,586	16·6	14·8
Total income (=100%)	3,281	8,906	11,117	13,472	17,456	100·0	100·0

[1] Including rents, tolls, fees, interest, and gross trading surplus. [2] Provisional.

Source: National Income and Expenditure, Central Statistical Office

Table 13.5   Local authority expenditure summary: analysis by function[1]

United Kingdom   £ million

	1961	1972	1973	1974	1975	Percentages 1961	Percentages 1975
Social services:							
Health and personal social services	212	744	955	1,061	1,427	8·2	8·7
Education	891	3,018	3,442	3,992	5,928	34·4	36·3
Housing and environmental services:							
Housing	395	1,088	1,835	2,815	3,202	15·3	19·6
Environmental services	379	1,329	1,625	1,581	1,845	14·6	11·3
Libraries, museums, and the arts	27	102	116	150	202	1·0	1·2
Justice and law	162	526	596	725	1,021	6·3	6·2
Roads and public lighting	207	631	715	728	941	8·0	5·8
Transport and communication	22	35	29	20	42	0·8	0·3
Commerce and industry	26	67	89	94	82	1·0	0·5
Other expenditure	58	160	175	226	324	2·2	2·0
Debt interest[2]	211	716	948	1,301	1,320	8·2	8·1

[1] This functional classification is consistent with the analysis of public expenditure given in the National Income and Expenditure Blue Book.
[2] Excluding payments to central government.   Source: National Income and Expenditure, Central Statistical Office

Chart 13.6 Local authority income and expenditure

Income   United Kingdom   Expenditure   Percentages

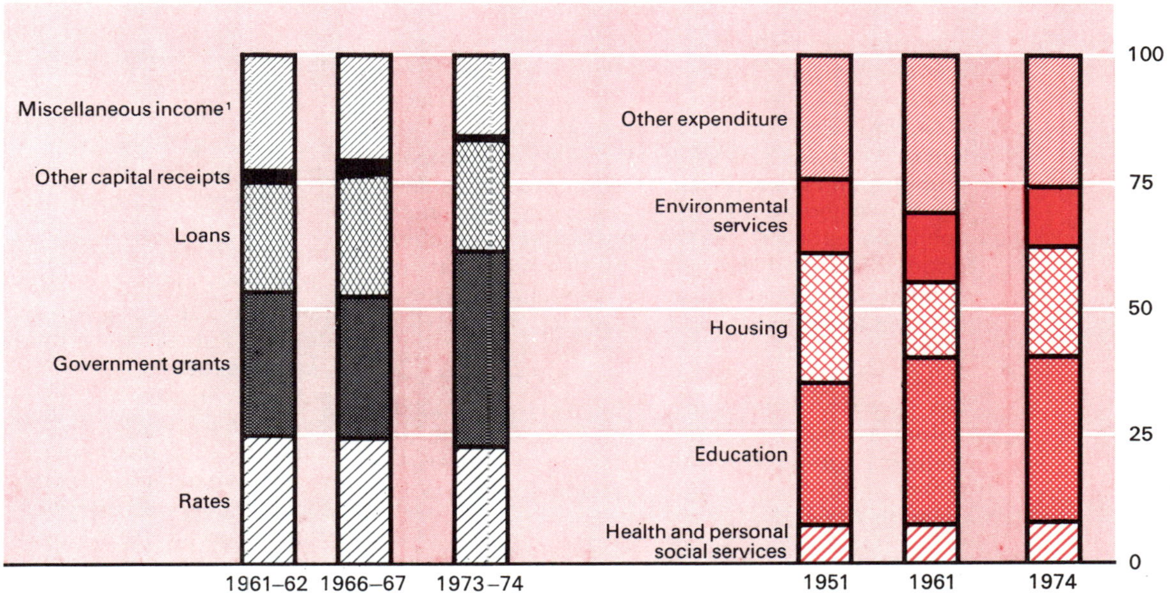

[1] Including rents, tolls, fees, and interest.   Sources: Central Statistical Office; Department of the Environment

Table 13.7   Public spending: annual average rates of increase

United Kingdom   Percentages

	Public expenditure			
	1951–1961	1961–1971	1971–1973	1973–1975
Social services				
Social security	9·0	10·2	13·3	27·0
Health and personal social services	6·4	9·9	16·0	33·9
Education	9·8	11·6	16·2	29·4
Housing and environmental services				
Housing	3·2	8·4	38·9	33·9
Environmental services	7·3	11·7	20·1	18·9
Libraries, museums, and the arts	10·1	13·2	20·9	30·0
Justice and law	9·6	12·0	15·3	31·3
Total Public spending	5·9	9·0	15·3	29·8

Source: National Income and Expenditure, Central Statistical Office

International

This section is concerned with the comparison of social trends and conditions in the United Kingdom with trends in other countries. The main comparisons are with the other members of the European Community, but comparisons are also made with four of the major industrially developed countries: Canada, Japan, the United States of America, and the USSR. Alongside these is now a wider selection from other countries with varying demographic and social patterns. From Europe Sweden is added, while Brazil and India represent countries with rapidly growing populations and less developed industrialisation. As further contrast, where possible, the tables also contain data from one of the more developed African countries, Kenya, and one of the younger nations of the world, the Philippines.

The nature of international statistics is one in which comparability is often very difficult, and this together with the availability of data has meant that not all countries are included. The tables follow the pattern of *Social Trends* itself, including data on population and birth rates. Areas of health are covered through infant mortality and life expectancy. There are also tables on the standard of living, showing consumer spending patterns and the possession of durable goods, followed by some further information relating to working life, active population, unemployment, and industrial disputes.

In recent years, as the interest in social statistics has grown, other countries have produced volumes similar to this, which give a range of statistics comparable with those appearing elsewhere in this volume. A list of some of these is given in Appendix C.

Demographic information

The major demographic statistics are gathered in these tables to provide a backcloth for the remaining tables and charts. It is always useful to examine patterns of population alongside other data in making comparisons between the countries. Perhaps the most important chart is that giving birth rates, which shows that all the European countries, with the exception of the Republic of Ireland, are experiencing a fall in the number of births per thousand population. This is also true for the United States and Canada, while for Japan and USSR birth rates have been fairly constant in recent years (chart 14.3).

In these tables, as in all the tables in this section, there are comparability problems and the reader is advised to refer to the source documents which explain in further detail some of the differences in the definitions used. In population statistics, for example there are often problems in defining the resident population. Different procedures can be adopted to obtain this figure: a major problem in this context is whether the count refers to persons actually resident on the Census day or includes persons normally resident but temporarily absent — possibly overseas. Generally the censuses carried out in different countries will use differing definitions, and reference should be made to the original sources. There will also be the problem of defining the dwelling unit they may be considered to be resident in: this includes the statistical classification of persons in institutions at the time of the Census.

Income and expenditure

This section roughly parallels the income and expenditure chapters earlier in this volume. Although no direct measure of income is actually given some comparison is possible of the *per capita* gross domestic product. This measure is widely accepted as a measure of general economic well-being in the country concerned, and as such may be thought to represent the level of individual economic well-being.

In the other tables care should be taken in interpreting the figures to take into account the different conditions which may exist in different countries. For example Britain's low figure for consumer expenditure on health in Table 14.7 as compared with that of France partly reflects the differing health systems in those two countries, UK having a comprehensive state scheme. The data for ownership of durables is taken from the European Economic Community (EEC) Consumer Attitude Survey (see Appendix B) and show different patterns of ownership of some major durables. Ownership in the table does not include rented equipment.

Education

This is always an area of difficulty in comparison across international boundaries because of the disparities in the educational systems. The age-groups contained within primary, secondary, and higher education can vary from country to country. However broad patterns of educational experience are shown in Table 14.11.

Further international comparisons of education statistics may be found by referring to the Organisation of Economic Co-operation and Development (*OECD*) *Educational Yearbook*, and the *UNESCO Statistical Yearbook*. Some of the other international publications listed in Appendix C include data on education.

Employment

There is some information on the work force in each country. Of particular interest are the figures for female activity which have been increasing in most Western European countries in the last few years, as also in the United States of America.

The unemployment data should be interpreted with some care, as indicated by the large number of footnotes. Different practices by organised labour groups in the various countries concerned affect the figures on industrial disputes, which relate mainly to the mining, manufacturing, construction, and transport industries. United Kingdom has suffered a slightly higher than median number of days lost over the ten-year period, while during the second five-year period all but Ireland had more days lost than in the first five-year period.

Table 14.1 Population and population density: 1950–1975

Thousands and numbers

	Estimates of mid-year population (thousands)					Population: (Number per square km) (1974)
	1950	1960	1973	1974	1975[3]	
United Kingdom	50,330	52,372	55,933	55,965	55,962	230
Belgium	8,639	9,153	9,757	9,772	9,788[4]	321
Denmark	4,271	4,581	5,025	5,045	5,059	117
France	41,736	45,684	52,130	52,507	52,743	96
Germany (Fed. Rep.)[1]	47,847	53,224	61,967	62,041	61,832	250
Irish Republic	2,969	2,834	3,029	3,086	3,127	44
Italy	46,603	49,642	54,888	55,361	55,812	184
Luxembourg	297	314	350	356	357[4]	132
Netherlands	10,114	11,480	13,348	13,541	13,654	332
Sweden	7,014	7,480	8,137	8,161	8,200[5]	18
Canada	13,712	17,909	22,125	22,479	22,830[5]	2
Japan[2]	82,990	94,216	108,346	109,671	110,950[5]	295
USA	152,264	180,684	210,404	211,909	213,610[5]	23
USSR	180,080	214,238	249,749	252,064	254,380[5]	11
Brazil	51,976	69,730	101,707	104,243	107,140[5]	12
India	358,293	429,016	574,216	586,056	598,100[5]	179
Kenya	5,579	8,115	12,482	12,912	13,400[5]	22
Philippines	19,910	27,410	40,219	41,457	42,510	138

Note: The population per square kilometre relates to total population per square kilometre of total area including inland water as well as such uninhabited or uninhabitable land as may lie within the national boundaries. Density figures are very rough indices as they do not take account of the concentration or dispersion of the population within countries.
[1] Includes West Berlin. [2] Including Okinawa. [3] Estimates. [4] As at 1 January 1975. [5] Rounded to nearest 10,000.

Sources: UNESCO Statistical Year Book 1972; United Nations Demographic Yearbook 1973 and 1974; UN monthly bulletin

**Chart 14.2
Population
changes,
1950-1974**

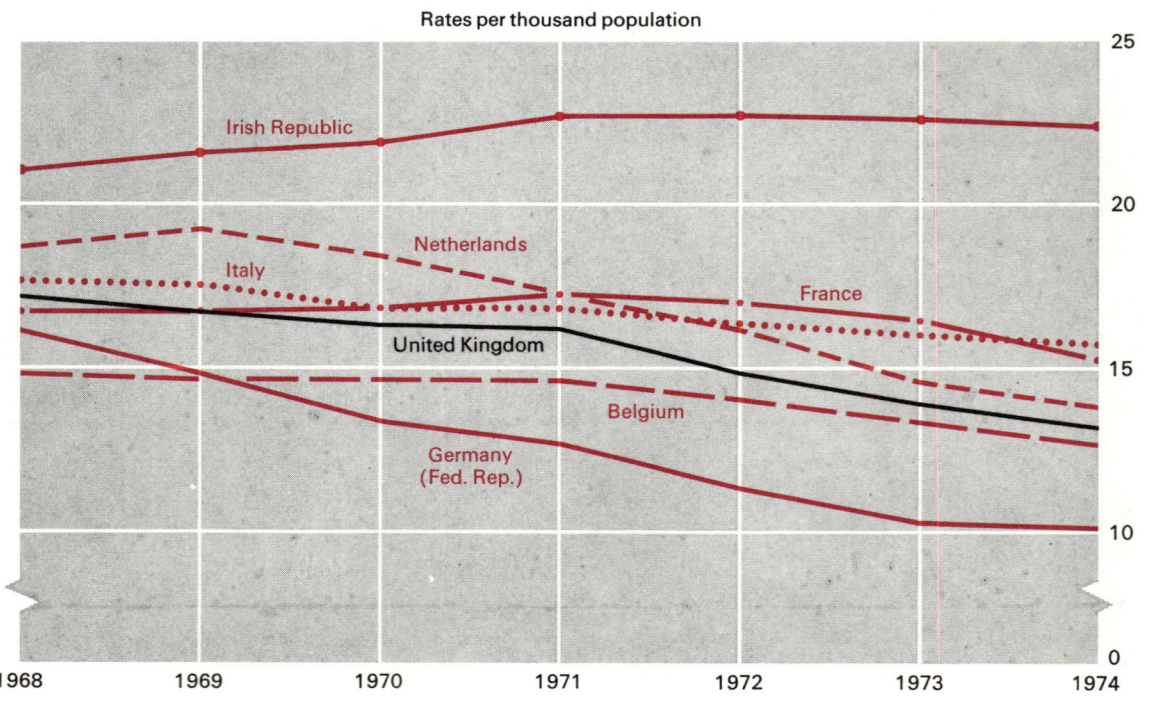

Population changes, 1950-1974 (Percentages):

United Kingdom
Belgium[1]
Denmark
France[2]
Germany (Fed. Rep.)[3]
Irish Republic[2]
Italy[2]
Netherlands
Sweden[2]
Canada[2]
Japan
USA
USSR[2]
Brazil
India
Kenya
Philippines

Legend: 1950–60 1960–70 1970–74

Percentages: −20   0   20   40   60   80   100   120   140

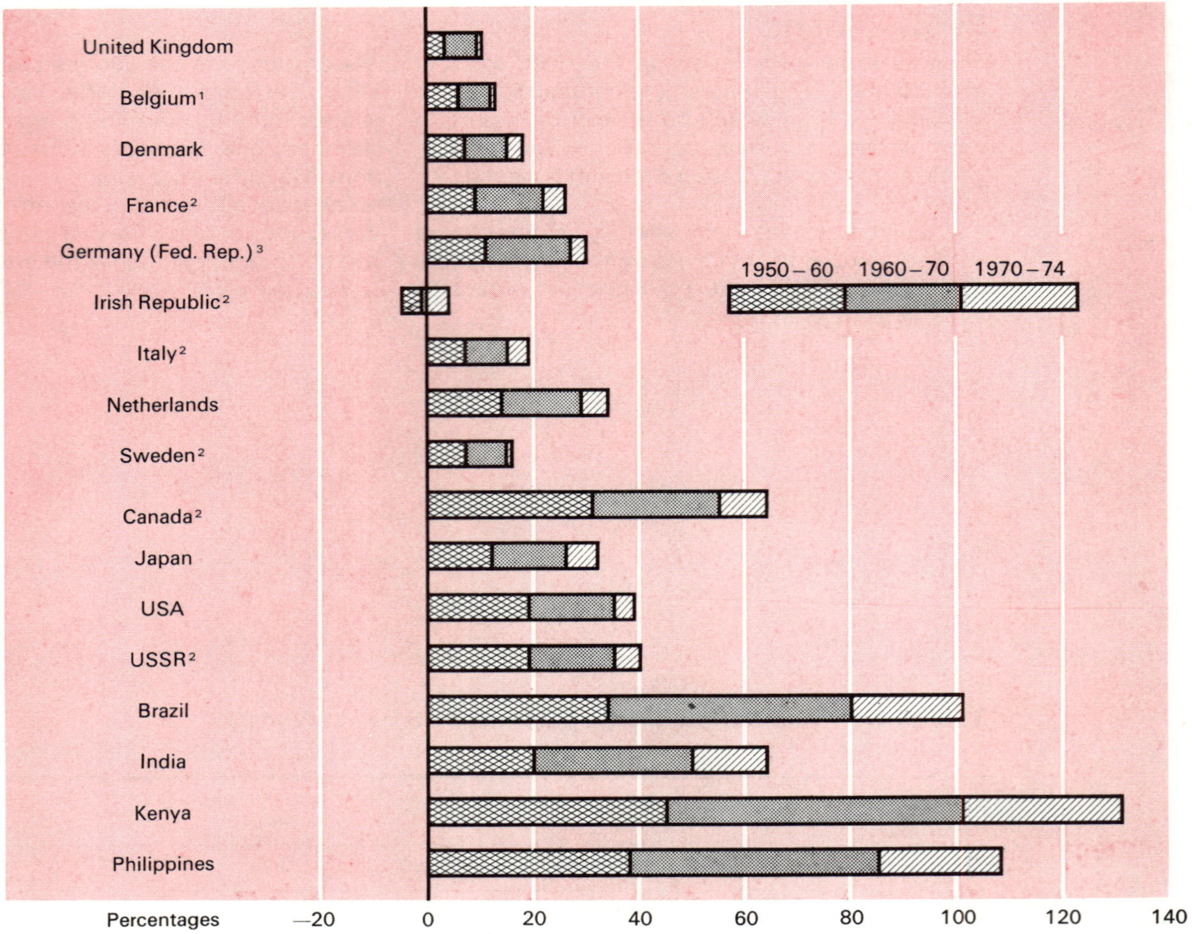

[1] 1974 data are UN estimate.   [2] Provisional data for 1974.   [3] 1970 and 1974 data include West Berlin.

Source: UN Demographic Yearbook, 1974

**Chart 14.3
Birth rates**

Rates per thousand population

Irish Republic
Netherlands
Italy
United Kingdom
France
Belgium
Germany (Fed. Rep.)

Scale: 25 20 15 10 0

Years: 1968   1969   1970   1971   1972   1973   1974

Source: UN Demographic Yearbook, 1974

**Chart 14.4
Infant
mortality**

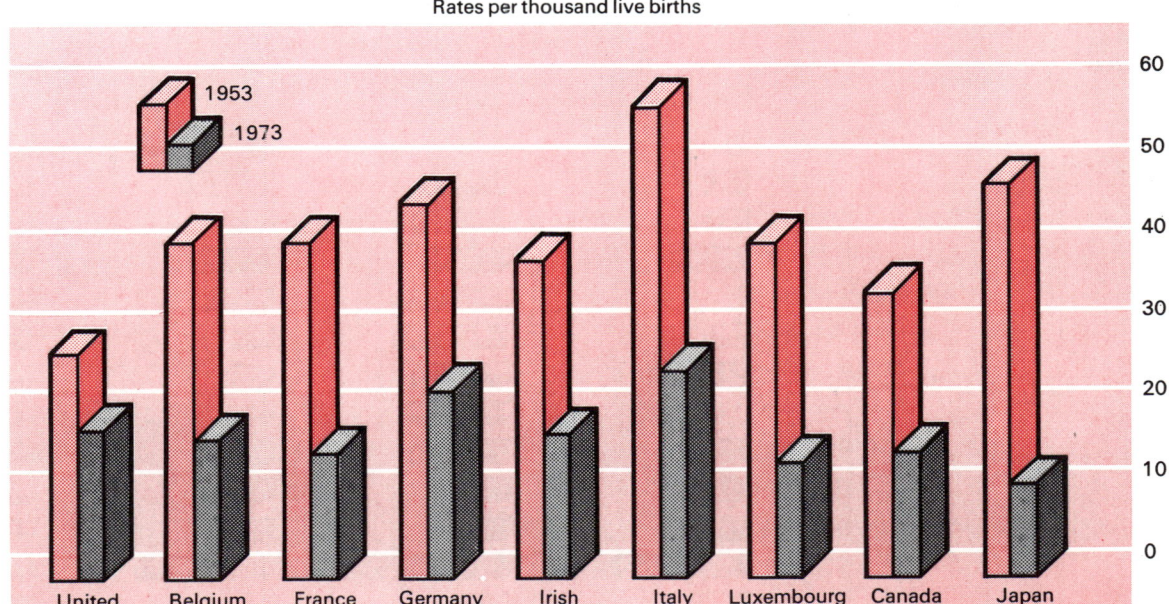

Rates per thousand live births

Source: UN Demographic Yearbook, 1974

Table 14.5 Life expectation

Years and rates

	Year	Expectation of life at specified age (years)						Increase in life expectation (years) due to eliminating deaths from:		Rate of accidental death per 1,000 live births
		0	10	20	40	60	80	Acci-dent	Cancer	
England and Wales	1973	72·4	63·9	54·2	35·0	18·0	6·5	0·6	2·9	27·0
Belgium	1972	71·4	63·2	53·5	34·6	17·6	6·2	1·3	2·8	52·7
Denmark	1973	73·8	65·0	55·3	36·2	19·1	6·9	1·0	3·2	42·1
France	1973	73·4	64·7	55·0	36·2	19·5	7·1	1·5	2·9	66·4
Germany (Fed. Rep.)	1973	71·3	63·3	53·7	34·8	17·8	6·1	1·1	2·6	46·5
Irish Republic	1972	70·9	62·6	52·9	33·8	17·0	5·6	0·9	2·4	39·4
Italy	1972	72·1	64·4	54·8	35·7	18·5	6·6	1·0	2·7	43·4
Luxembourg	1974	71·1	62·5	52·8	33·8	17·3	6·2	1·3	2·5	49·1
Netherlands	1974	74·7	65·9	56·2	37·0	19·5	7·1	0·9	3·4	44·5
Canada	1973	73·0	64·5	55·0	36·2	19·4	7·4	1·6	2·9	51·2
Japan	1973	73·6	64·9	55·2	36·2	18·8	6·3	0·9	2·3	35·3
USA	1973	71·4	63·1	53·5	35·0	18·7	7·5	1·4	2·7	44·6

Source: World Health Organisation

Chart 14.6
Per capita
domestic
product

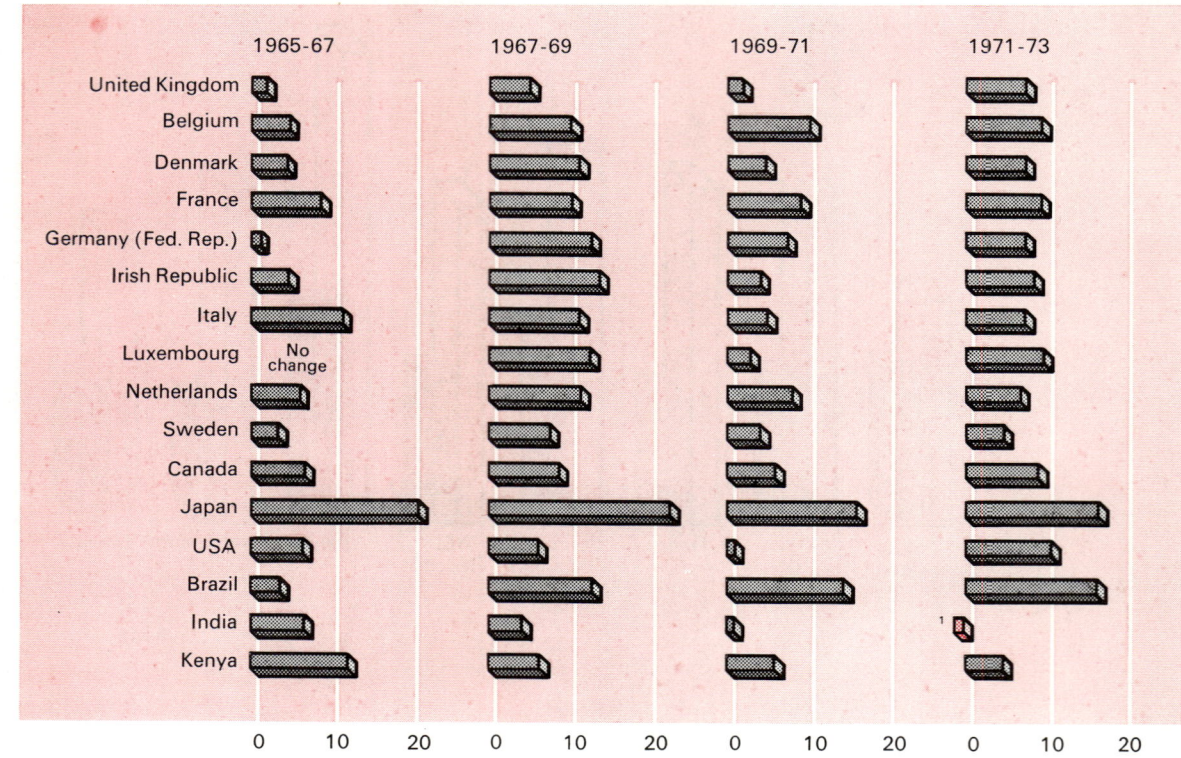

Percentage change at constant prices, 1970 = 100

[1] Fall of 1·0 per cent in 1971-73

Source: UN Yearbook of National Accounts Statistics, 1974

Table 14.7   Consumer spending at current prices, 1973

Percentages of total consumer spending

	Food, drink, and tobacco	Clothing and footwear	Rent, fuel, and power	House- hold goods[1]	Medical care and health	Transport and communi- cation	Recrea- tion, entertain- ment, edu- cation, and cultural services	Miscel- laneous
United Kingdom	31	9	18	8	1	14	10	10
Belgium	29	7	13	16	6	11	4	13
Denmark	29	6	12	13	..	13	..	27[3]
France[2]	33	9	14	9	11	11	8	7
Germany (Fed. Rep.)	28	11	15	13	3	12	7	11
Irish Republic	44	10	10	9	2	11	5	9
Italy	41	9	12	7	8	11	5	6
Luxembourg	29	9	18	10	7	12	4	11
Netherlands	26	10	14	13	10	10	8	10
Canada	23	9	19	9	3	15	9	14
Japan	32	11	15	9	..	..	..	33[3,4]
USA	18	9	18	9	10	16	10	11

[1] Includes furniture, furnishings, and household equipment.   [2] 1972 data.   [3] Includes 'Medical care and health' and 'Recreation,
entertainment, education, and cultural services'.   [4] Includes transport.

Source: OECD National Accounts 1962–1973

**Chart 14.8
Consumer
spending,
1963-1973**

Percentage increase at constant (1970) prices

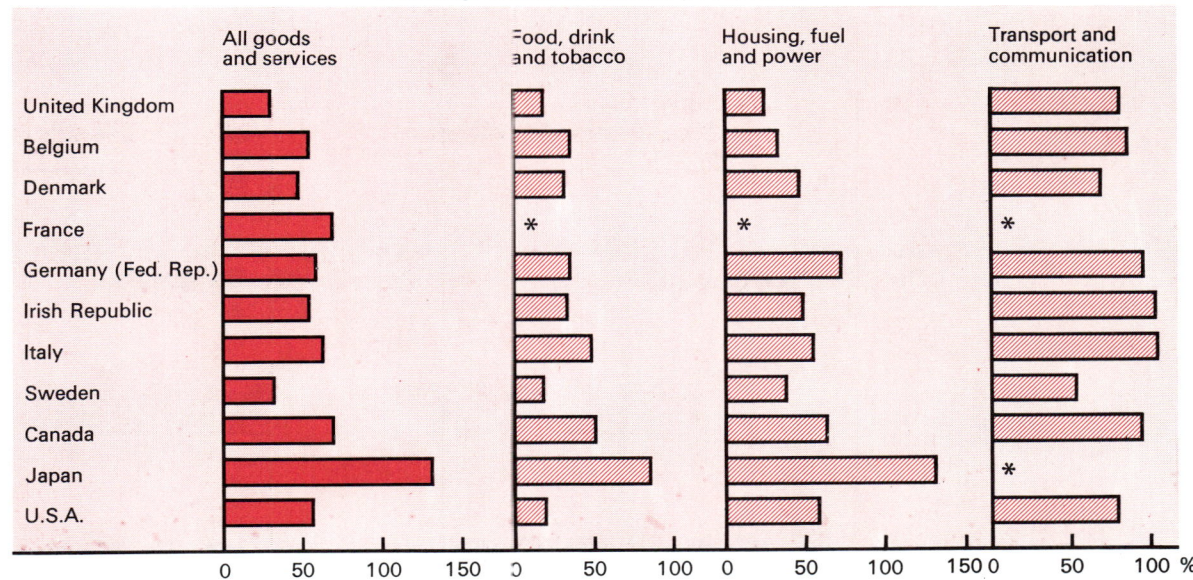

* Not available.

Source: OECD National Accounts, 1962–1973

Table 14.9 Consumer price index numbers

Index numbers and percentages

	Consumer price index numbers, all items (1970 = 100)						Annual percentage increase
	1970	1971	1972	1973	1974	1975	1970–1975
United Kingdom	100	109	117	128	148	184	13·0
Belgium[1]	100	104	110	118	133	150	8·5
Denmark	100	106	113	123	142	156	9·3
France	100	106	112	120	137	152	8·7
Germany (Fed. Rep.)[2]	100	105	111	119	127	135	6·2
Irish Republic	100	109	118	132	154	186	13·2
Italy	100	105	111	123	146	171	11·3
Netherlands	100	108	116	125	137	151	8·6
Canada	100	103	108	116	129	143	7·4
Japan	100	106	111	124	154	172	11·4
USA	100	104	108	114	127	139	6·8
Brazil	100	121	143	165	..	..	18·2[4]
India	100	103	110	128	165	..	13·4[5]
Philippines[3]	100	123	143	153	215	..	21·1[5]

[1] Excluding rent from 1 January, 1972. [2] Including West Berlin. [3] Middle income group only. [4] 1970–73 only.
[5] 1970–74 only.

Sources: UN Monthly Bulletin of Statistics; UN Statistical Yearbook

**Chart 14.10
Cars, freezers
and
dishwashers,
May 1975**

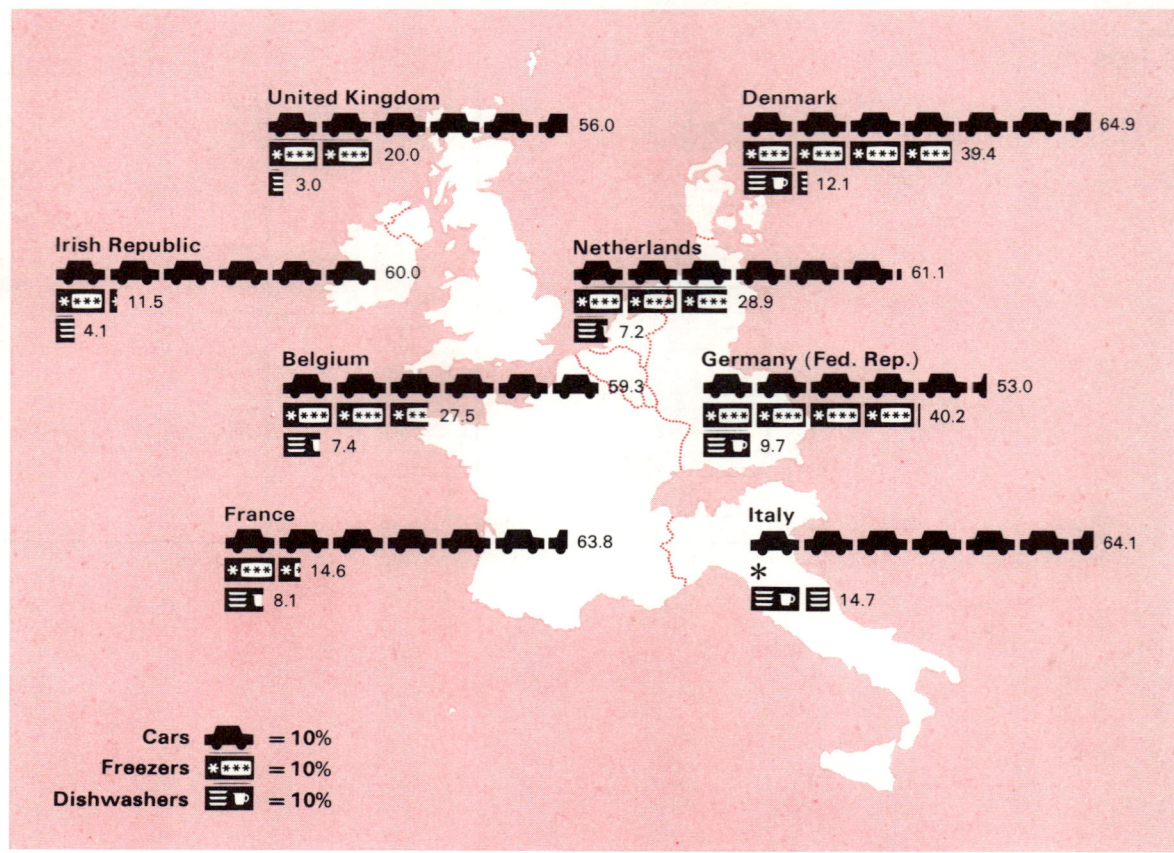

Percentage of households in possession of:

Source: Consumer Attitudes and Intentions Survey, SOEC

Table 14.11   Average formal educational experience of population

Years

	Year	Age 25–34				Age 65–74			
		Total years	of which:			Total years	of which:		
			primary	secondary	higher		primary	secondary	higher
United Kingdom[1]	1971	11·0	6·0	4·6	0·4	9·3	6·0	3·2	0·1
Belgium[1,2]	1971	11·3	6·0	4·3	0·9	8·5	6·0	2·3	0·2
Denmark[1,2]	1971	10·2	5·0	4·5	0·6	8·6	5·0	3·4	0·1
France	1968	10·1	5·0	4·6	0·5	7·9	5·0	2·8	0·1
Germany (Fed. Rep.)[1]	1970	9·4	4·0	5·2	0·2	8·0	4·0	3·9	0·1
Irish Republic	1966	9·8	6·0	3·3	0·5	8·8	6·0	2·6	0·2
Italy[1]	1971	7·9	4·6	3·0	0·3[3]	4·6	3·6	1·0	0·1[3]
Netherlands	1970	9·7	6·0	3·1	0·5	7·3	6·0	1·1	0·2
Canada[1]	1971	11·0	5·8	4·7	0·5[3]	8·1	5·4	2·5	0·1[3]
Japan[4]	1970	11·1	6·0	4·7	0·5	7·4	5·7	1·5	0·1
USA	1970	12·0	5·9	5·1	1·0	8·9	5·5	3·0	0·4

The standardised OECD educational classification is used. Where earlier data only were available an assumed linear growth of education between
1945 and 1970 was used to estimate later values.
[1] Estimates.   [2] Age groups 20–29 and 60–69.   [3] Excludes non-university higher education.   [4] Age group 65 and over.

Source: OECD Yearbook of Education Statistics, 1974

Table 14.12 Economically active population

	Year	Population aged 15 and over (millions)	Percentage economically active			Females as percentage of total economically active	Average number of hours worked in manufacturing industry, 1972 (per week)
			Aged 15–64	Aged 65 and over	Total population		
United Kingdom	1971	42·3	64	8	46	37	45[1]
Belgium	1970	7·4	59	4	41[2]	33[2]	38
Denmark	1970	3·8	70	13	48[2]	40[2]	33
France	1968	37·9	63	12	42[3]	36[3]	44
Germany (Fed. Rep.)	1970	46·6	66	10	44[2]	37[2]	43
Irish Republic	1971	2·0	60	26	37[2]	26	42
Italy	1971	37·1[4]	57[4]	7	36[2]	27[2]	34[5]
Luxembourg	1970	0·3	57	7	44[2]	26	42
Netherlands	1971	9·4	58	7	37	26	43
Canada	1961	12·0	59	17	36	27	40
Japan	1970	78·9	70	35	49[2]	39[2]	42
USA	1970	145·2	63	16	41	37	41
Brazil	1970	54·0	53	28	32	21	..
India	1971	317·7	55	43	33	17	..
Philippines	1970	20·8	57	37	34	32	44

Notes: The economically active population is the total of employed and unemployed persons and does not include students, women occupied solely with domestic duties, persons living entirely on their own means or wholly dependent upon others. Treatment of armed forces, inmates of institutions persons seeking work for the first time, seasonal and part-time workers varies from country to country. Comparability is also hampered by differences in the detail of definitions used and the method of collection and tabulation (censuses, labour force surveys, etc.). Full details of all these differences are given in the *ILO Year Book.*

[1] Males only.   [2] 1973 data.   [3] 1974 data.   [4] Age limit 20 not 15.   [5] Estimated

Source: ILO Year Book of Labour Statistics 1974

Table 14.13 Unemployment

		Annual averages					Thousands and percentages				
	Code[1]	Thousands					Percentages				
		1971	1972	1973	1974	1975	1971	1972	1973	1974	1975
United Kingdom[2]	a	799	886	630	631	870	3·4	3·8	2·7	2·7	3·7
Belgium[3]	a	71	87	92	105	162	2·9	3·4	3·6	4·0	6·1
Denmark[4]	b	30	30	20	44	84	3·7	3·6	2·4	5·2	9·1
France	a	338	384	394	498	738	..	..	..	..	..
Germany (Fed. Rep.)	a	185	246	273	582	1,002	0·8	1·1	1·2	2·6	4·4
Irish Republic[5]	c	42	48	44	48	74	7·2	8·1	7·2	7·9	12·1
Italy	d	609	697	668	560	667[7]	3·2	3·7	3·5	2·9	3·4[7]
Netherlands	a	62	108	110	135	176	1·6	2·7	2·7	4·4	4·3
Canada	d	552	562	520	525	704	6·4	6·3	5·6	5·4	6·8
Japan	d	640	730	670	720	920	1·2	1·4	1·3	1·4	1·7
USA	d	4,993	4,840	4,304	5,076	8,569	5·9	5·6	4·9	5·6	9·1
India	a	4,602	5,928	7,714	8,378	8,791	..	..	..	..	..
Philippines[6]	d	636	983	624	725	..	4·8	6·9	4·4	4·8	..

[1] Codes: a. Registered unemployed. Employment Office Statistics. b. Statistics of trade unions and union benefit fund statistics. c. Compulsory unemployment insurance statistics. d. Labour force sample surveys.   [2] Excludes temporarily stopped.   [3] Wholly unemployed receiving insurance benefits.   [4] Unemployment among members of trade union insurance funds.   [5] Excluding agriculture, fishing and private domestic services.   [6] At May of each year.   [7] At April.

Source: ILO Yearbook of Labour Statistics 1975 and Quarterly Bulletins

**Chart 14.14
Industrial
disputes**

Average number of working days lost per thousand employed

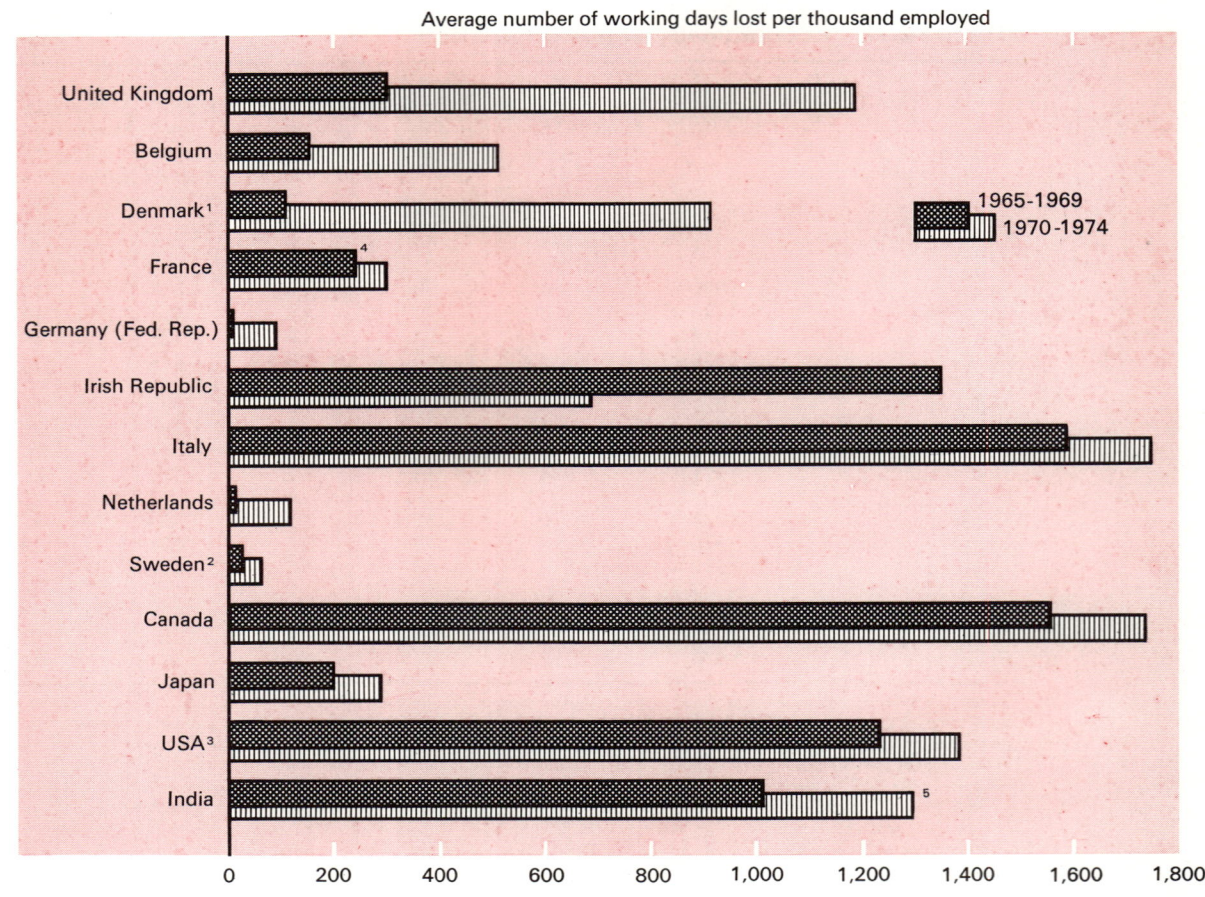

¹ Manufacturing industry only.   ² All industries included to 1971 only.   ³ Includes electricity, gas, and sanitary services.
⁴ 1968 excluded from average.   ⁵ 1970–1973 only.

Source: Department of Employment Gazette, December 1975, Department of Employment

Calendar of events

Social Trends attempts to monitor social conditions by means of articles, tables, and charts. However, there are many social changes which are difficult to fit into this framework and are more easily incorporated into a calendar of events. For example, it is important to have a record of the timing of new laws which may affect the interpretation of statistics. The housing field is a particular example. Administrative acts such as the setting up of the Health and Safety Commission or the introduction of the Family Income Supplement will also be important. Other measures such as the Sex Discrimination Act may be indicators of change in the social climate even if they do not directly affect the contents of the tables in the other sections of this volume. Finally there are many other events, such as the introduction of commercial radio stations, whose precise dates may be of value.

The choice of events covered has had to be limited. The calendar below covers the period January 1970 to December 1975 and indicates events which have had a direct social influence on the people of the United Kingdom or are important as indicators of social attitudes or change. Economic events may be of great and far-reaching social importance, but since there are so many of these and because they are covered in other calendars it was not felt necessary to include them in this calendar. There are a number of alternative reference works complementary to or partially overlapping this calendar. For economic and related events calendars are printed in the January issue of *Economic Trends*, and quarterly in the *National Institute Economic Review*, while the *Journal of Social Policy Digest* fulfils a similar function for social administration. More generally, *Keesings Contemporary Archives* and the series of official handbooks on Britain produced annually by the Reference Division of the Central Office of Information may also be found useful.

One event may often have a number of dates associated with it. For example, legislation may involve the publication of a White Paper and a Bill followed by the passage of the Bill through Parliament and the granting of the Royal Assent. The Act will come into force on later dates (usually specified in the Act). These later dates have the most relevance for the interpretation of statistics and will normally be the ones given. If, at the time of publication, the Act had not come into effect then the date of the Royal Assent is given.

Most Acts mentioned refer to the United Kingdom as a whole, with perhaps minor exceptions. When the major part of an Act or Bill is restricted to a part of the United Kingdom this is made clear, if necessary, by putting (GB) or (E and W) after the item.

In this issue the information is presented differently than heretofore in that Government legislation is grouped as the introductory item for each year. Key words appearing in the calendar are, for the first time, included in the Index.

Coding system. For convenience the following system has been used. It should be remembered that frequently an event could have repercussions in more areas than those indicated.

A.   Arts, Sports, and Media.
C.   Consumer Affairs and Prices.
D.   Housing.
E.   Education.
F.   Fiscal, Taxation, etc.
H.   Health.
J.   Justice and Crime.
L.   Local Government.
M.   Employment and Industrial Relations.
N.   National Insurance and Social Security.
P.   Population and Immigration.
R.   Personal Rights.
S.   Personal Social Services.
T.   Transport and Communications.
V.   Environment.
X.   Public Safety.
NI. Northern Ireland.
Sc. Scotland.

1970

Legislation

Rent (Control of Increases) Act 1969 limiting rent increases in Great Britain for local authority houses and privately rented dwellings subject to regulated tenancies came into effect. (*January 1*)

Local Employment Act 1970 empowered the designation of areas for which grant assistance could be given for improvement of basic services and derelict land clearance following the Hunt report 'The Intermediate Areas' of April 24 1969. (GB) (*February 26*)

The Law Reform (Miscellaneous Provisions) Act 1970 abolished action for breach of promise, the right to claim damages for adultery, and various other actions for enticement. (E & W) (*Royal Assent May 29*)

1970 *Legislation (continued)*

The Matrimonial Proceedings and Property Act 1970 altered substantially the law relating to financial provision in matrimonial proceedings. (E & W) (Royal Assent, *May 29*)

The Chronically Sick and Disabled Persons Act 1970 required local authorities to find out how many such persons lived in their areas and make provision for them. The various sections of the Act came into force during the next 2 years. (Royal Assent, *May 29*)

The Local Authority Social Services Act 1970, following the report of the Seebohm Committee on 24 July 1968, required local authorities in England and Wales to set up a Social Services Committee to assume responsibility on 1 January 1971 and appoint Directors of Social Services. (Royal Assent, *May 29*)

Equal Pay Act 1970 to prevent discrimination between men and women regarding terms and conditions of employment. The Act came into effect on 29 December 1975. (GB) (Royal Assent, *May 29*)

The Social Needs (Grants) Act (NI) 1970 made provision for the authorisation of the payment of grants towards expenditure incurred due to special social need in urban areas. (Royal Assent, *June 9*)

Employers' share of national insurance contributions increased under the National Health Service Contributions Act 1970. (GB) (*July 6*)

Section 2 of the Chronically Sick and Disabled Persons Act 1970 came into force requiring local authorities in England and Wales to make arrangements for provision of certain welfare services where needed. (*August 29*)

Supplementary benefits increased and old persons' (over 80s') pensions introduced under the National Insurance Act 1970. (*November 2*)

Section 4 of the Chronically Sick and Disabled Persons Act 1970 relating to access to public buildings came into force. (GB) (*November 29*)

January

P, R	1	Persons aged 18–21 allowed to marry without their parents' consent. (E & W)
A, F	1	Currency restrictions on foreign travel by United Kingdom residents lifted.
H, X	1	Use of cyclamates as a food additive prohibited.

CON 330   LAB 287

June

	18	General Election resulted in Conservative majority of 30.
	29	EEC entry talks commenced.
D	29	Restrictions on sales of council dwellings lifted in England and Wales by Ministry of Housing and Local Government circular 54/70.
Sc, E	30	Department of Education and Science circular 10/70 issued which withdrew the previous request to local education authorities to submit plans for the reorganisation of secondary education on comprehensive lines; the Scottish Education Department circular 760 of 2 July made similar provision for Scotland.

October

| C, E, F | 27 | White Paper (Cmnd 4515) on public expenditure published, containing *inter alia* a 5 year plan to replace and improve the worst of Victorian primary schools, and announcing the discontinuation of the grant to the Consumer Council. |

November

| D, L, V | 12 | Ministries of Housing and Local Government, Public Building and Works, and Transport unified into a single Department of the Environment to be responsible for a whole range of functions which affect people's living environment. |

December

| M | 3 | Industrial Relations Bill published proposing the establishment of a National Industrial Relations Court, a 60-day cooling-off period, all labour agreements to be legally binding unless otherwise stated, safeguards against unfair dismissal, and unions to register with a Registrar with powers to vet their rules. |

1971

Legislation

Divorce Reform Act 1969 amending the grounds for divorce and judicial separation and facilitating reconciliation in matrimonial matters came into force; divorce was granted for irretrievable breakdown of marriage including separation of the partners for two or five years with or without consent respectively. (E & W) (*January 1*)

Responsibility for child care services in England and Wales, including youth treatment centres and community homes, transferred from the Home Office to the Department of Health and Social Security, under the provisions of the Children and Young Persons Act 1969. Part I (other than sections 4 and 5) also came into effect, ending the powers of the Courts to send children and young persons to approved schools and remand homes. These powers were replaced by the power to commit to the care of a local authority. (*January 1*)

Creation of additional special development areas announced, under the Local Employment Act 1970. (GB) (*February 18*)

Electoral Law Act (NI) 1971 – annual register of parliamentary and local government electors to be prepared and published. Local government elections for 1971 postponed until 1972. (Royal Assent, *February 25*)

The Housing Executive Act (NI) 1971 set up the Northern Ireland Housing Executive. This centralised the functions of the former housing authorities and established a province-wide organisation with powers and duties covering the entire field of housing. (Royal Assent, *February 25*)

Section 13 of Health Services and Public Health Act 1968 for England and Wales and Section 13 of the Social Work (Scotland) Act 1968 came into effect making it the duty of local authorities to provide a home-help service. (*April 1*)

Education (Handicapped Children) Act 1970 came into effect in England and Wales requiring local education authorities to take responsibility for the education in normal schools of severely mentally handicapped children who were hitherto considered to be unsuitable for education at school. (*April 1*)

Land Commission (Dissolution) Act 1971 abolished the betterment levy (from 22 July 1970) and dissolved the Land Commission (on 1 May 1971). (GB) (Royal Assent, *April 8*)

The system of children's panels and children's hearings provided in Part III of the Social Work (Scotland) Act 1968 came into operation. Juvenile courts ceased to exist in Scotland, though children could still be dealt with in the Sheriff Court or the Court of Session in specified circumstances. (*April 15*)

Unsolicited Goods and Services Act 1971 gave greater protection to persons receiving unsolicited goods through the post. (GB) (Royal Assent, *May 12*)

Fire Precautions Act 1971 introduced the need for fire certificates for premises put to designated uses; eg hotels. (GB) (Royal Assent, *May 27*)

The Law Reform (Miscellaneous Provisions) Act 1971 abolished control by the court of widows' damages and provided that prospects of remarriage would be disregarded in assessing such damages. (GB) (Royal Assent, *July 1*)

Highways Act 1971 authorised *inter alia* the provision of picnic sites for travellers in England and Wales. (Royal Assent, *July 1*)

Sheriff Courts (Scotland) Act allowed cases involving small debts to be dealt with by the Sheriff Courts. (Royal Assent, *July 27*)

Education (Scotland) Act came into effect restoring the power to education authorities to charge fees in a limited number of schools. (*August 1*)

Education (Milk) Act 1971 came into force in Scotland restricting the provision of free school milk by education authorities to primary pupils up to August 1 immediately following their seventh birthday, to older pupils on health grounds, and to pupils receiving special education. It also empowered authorities to sell milk to pupils. (*August 1*)

Administration of Justice Act 1970 came into effect. This Act redistributed the business of the High Court, restricted imprisonment for debt, and introduced penalties for the unlawful harassment of debtors. It also extended the powers of courts to order payments due under maintenance orders etc. to be made directly by deductions from earnings (which had been consolidated by the Attachment of Earnings Act 1971). (*August 2*)

Family income supplement introduced under the Family Income Supplement Act 1970. (GB) (*August 3*)

Industrial Relations Act 1971 provided *inter alia* for National Industrial Relations Court and a Registrar of trade unions and employers' associations. (GB) (Royal Assent, *August 5*)

New regulations limiting benefits paid to strikers and their dependants came into effect under the Social Security Act 1971. (*August 5*)

Housing Act 1971 increased improvement grants in Great Britain for development and intermediate areas (the effective date for implementation of the Act had been 23 June 1971). (Royal Assent, *August 5*)

Education (Milk) Act 1971 came into force restricting the provision of free school milk by local education authorities to primary pupils below the age of 8, to older pupils on health grounds and to pupils receiving special education. It also empowered authorities to sell milk to pupils. (E & W and NI) (*September 1*)

Higher pensions for old persons under the National Insurance Acts 1970 and 1971 and for public service pensioners under the Pensions (Increase) Act 1971 came into effect. (*September 1*)

Section 1 of the Chronically Sick and Disabled Persons Act 1970 came into effect, requiring local authorities in England and Wales to obtain information about the numbers of disabled persons in their area. (*October 1*)

The Central Council for Education and Training in Social Work came into being under the Health Visiting and Social Work (Training) Act 1962 as amended by Section 11 of the Local Authority Social Services Act 1970, to give training in all branches of social work. (*October 1*)

Criminal Damage Act 1971 revising the offence of damage against property and introducing the concept of criminal damage came into effect. (*October 14*)

Immigration Act 1971 gave certain persons described as 'patrial' the 'right of abode' in the United Kingdom. (Royal Assent, *October 28*)

January

A, E	3	First broadcast by the Open University.
H	5	Royal College of Physicians report on Smoking and Health published indicating the health hazards of tobacco smoking.
T, V	22	Roskill Commission recommended Cublington as the site for a third London Airport.

February

M	4	Receiver appointed for Rolls Royce.
F	15	Decimal currency system introduced.
NI	20	J Chichester-Clark resigned as Prime Minister of Northern Ireland. On March 23 Brian Faulkner was elected in his place.

March

D	1	Francis Committee on the Rent Act (Cmnd 4609) recommended bringing controlled tenancies into the fair rent system, increasing the penalties for harassment, and the setting up of housing aid centres in stress areas in Great Britain.
H	16	Voluntary agreement established with the tobacco industry for cigarette packets to carry a government health warning.
M	18	One-day protest strike against Industrial Relations Bill.
C	24	Crowther Committee on Consumer Credit (Cmnd 4596) recommended reform of the law, appointment of a consumer credit commissioner, and that the real annual rate of interest be quoted on all loans.
M	31	National Board for Prices and Incomes disbanded.

April

E, H	1	Cheap milk provision came to an end but 700,000 school children remained entitled to free milk.
N	5	Age related widows' pensions introduced.
P	25	1971 Census of Population held covering Great Britain and Northern Ireland.

May

A	10	Last edition of *Daily Sketch* published.

July

Sc, M	30	Upper Clyde Shipbuilders shop stewards took over the yards and announced a 'work-in' in protest against redundancies and liquidation of UCS.

August

NI, J	9	Northern Ireland Government introduced internment under Special Powers Act. Over 300 men arrested for questioning and possible internment. This sparked off prolonged period of rioting and gave rise to a rent and rates strike.
M, N	16	Payment of sickness, unemployment, and injury benefit discontinued for the first 3 days of interruption of employment.

September

NI, J	19	A new internment camp was opened at Long Kesh, near Lisburn, Northern Ireland, for people suspected of terrorist activities.
H, N	23	Invalidity benefit introduced for the chronically sick.
H, V	30	Restrictions on the use of the insecticide DDT came into effect.

October

A	3	BBC announced the establishment of an independent complaints commission.
	31	Re-introduction of British Summer Time caused clocks to be put one hour forward in the summer months, as compared with British Standard Time.

November

H		Plans published to replace many old style mental hospitals over the next 20 years and to introduce new psychiatric units in general hospitals as well as extending out-patient treatment on the lines of the White Paper *Better Services for the Mentally Handicapped* (Cmnd 4683) of 23 June. (E & W)

December

M	1	First session of the National Industrial Relations Court (NIRC) took place.
H, N	6	Attendance allowance introduced for severely handicapped persons needing constant attendance.
N	16	Annual review of national insurance retirement pensions to protect their purchasing power announced.
T, X	16	Minimum age of riding motor cycles and motor scooters raised from 16 to 17 years.
T, V	22	A major link (M4) in the motorway network opened providing continuous motoring between London and South Wales.

1972

Legislation

The Courts Act 1971 replacing assizes and quarter sessions in England and Wales by the Crown Court came into effect. The central government through the Lord Chancellor assumed responsibility for the administration of all courts above the level of magistrates' courts. (*January 1*)

Employers Liability (Compulsory Insurance) Act 1969 came into effect requiring employers to insure against their civil liability for personal injury to their employees. (GB) (*January 2*)

Deposit of Poisonous Waste Act 1972 made it an offence to create an environmental hazard by depositing poisonous waste. (GB) (Royal Assent, *March 30*)

Employment Medical Advisory Service Act 1972 provided for the establishment of an employment medical advisory service. (GB) (Royal Assert, *May 11*)

Sound Broadcasting Act 1972 came into effect extending the functions of the Independent Television Authority to include local commercial radio stations and renaming it the Independent Broadcasting Authority. (*July 12*)

The Housing Finance Act 1972 through which was introduced a new system of housing subsidies. It also provided for rent rebate and rent allowances schemes to be administered by local authorities, and amended the law (Rent Act 1968) to make other provision as to housing finance. The provisions came into effect over a period of time. (E & W) (Royal Assent, *July 27*)

The Chronically Sick and Disabled Persons (Scotland) Act 1972 extended sections 1 and 2(i) of the CS & DP Act 1970 to Scotland with amendments to relate them to the Social Work (Scotland) Act 1968. (Royal Assent, *July 27*)

Legal Advice and Assistance Act 1972 provided for better facilities for advice and assistance at an early stage in a dispute and (provisions not yet in force) for solicitors employed by the Law Society to advise and act for those receiving legal aid. (GB) (Royal Assent, *July 27*)

National Health Service (Scotland) Act 1972 unified the Health Service in Scotland, setting up 15 Health Boards and the Common Services Agency. This unification included the transfer of personal health services from local authorities, the placing of the provision of family planning services under the NHS (from 1 April 1974) and the appointment of a Health Service Commissioner to investigate complaints in relation to the NHS. The various sections of the Act came into effect during the next two years. (Royal Assent, *August 9*)

The Health and Personal Social Services (NI) Order 1972 provided a new administrative structure to the health and personal social services in Northern Ireland. (*August 14*)

The Electoral Law (NI) Order 1972 provided for the election and terms of office of members of district councils and for the holding of the first elections to district councils according to the principles of proportional representation on the basis of transferable votes, and for the appointment of a Chief Electoral Officer for Northern Ireland; the first such elections were held for district councils taking office with effect from 1 October 1973. (*August 15*)

Provisions of the Housing Finance Act 1972 came into force, providing rent rebate and allowance schemes and introducing a new system of housing subsidies for housing authorities including increases in rent for many council tenants. This was the date by which local authorities should have introduced rent rebate schemes. (*October 1*)

National Health Service (Family Planning) Amendment Act 1972 permitted voluntary vasectomy to be performed by local health authorities. (Royal Assent, *October 26*)

The Detention of Terrorists (NI) Order 1972 replaced and revoked the Special Powers Regulations relating to detention and internment. The Order contained new provision for the appointment of legally qualified commissioners to ascertain whether a person's detention is necessary for the protection of the public. (*November 7*)

January

M	9	Coalminers' strike started.
Sc	21	Royal Charter granted to the Scottish Sports Council to foster the knowledge and practice of sport and physical recreation and the provision of facilities.
	22	Common Market treaty of accession signed.
E, Sc, NI	25	Report of the James Committee *Teacher Education and Training* published on the content of courses and the role of further education institutions in the training of teachers in England and Wales.
		A closely related report was published by the Lelievre Committee on 4 December 1973 for Northern Ireland, and a report on the training of graduates for secondary education in Scotland was published on 28 November 1972.
NI, X	30	'Bloody Sunday'. Thirteen people killed by Army at Civil Rights march in Londonderry. Widgery Tribunal, appointed to enquire into the incident, reported on 19 April 1974 'no general lack of discipline'.

February

M	9	State of Emergency declared to conserve power supplies during coalminers' strike.
M	14	Restricted work began for most of industry.
M	18	Wilberforce court of enquiry (Cmnd 4902) recommended pay increase for coalminers, and they returned to work on 28 February.
X	22	Terrorist explosion at Parachute Brigade HQ in Aldershot killed 7 people.

221

1972 *continued*

March

NI 30 Northern Ireland Parliament prorogued. Northern Ireland (Temporary Provisions) Act 1972 provided for government of the Province.

April

M 20 National Industrial Relations Court fined Transport and General Workers' Union £50,000 for contempt of court.

H 26 Enquiry set up under Baroness Sharp to look into the ways of helping people whose mobility was reduced by severe physical disablement.

May

T, V 24 Final section of M6 near Birmingham opened completing its link with the M1, Britain's first motorway.

July

R 12 Younger Committee on Privacy (Cmnd 5012) recommended greater protection for individual privacy in certain areas but decided against a general right in all circumstances.

H, M, X 19 Robens Committee on Safety and Health at Work report (Cmnd 5034) published.

M 21 NIRC ordered 5 London dockers to prison (they were released on 26 July after the intervention of the Official Solicitor).

NI, X 21 'Bloody Friday'. Twenty-two IRA bomb explosions in Belfast, 9 killed and 130 injured.

M 28 National Dock Strike began (finished 18 August).

NI, X 31 British troops moved into the barricaded areas in Andersonstown, Belfast, and the Bogside area of Londonderry and occupied positions in all hitherto 'no-go' areas. The army code-named this 'Operation Motorman'.

August

M 3 State of Emergency declared due to dock strike.

E 4 Improved staffing standards in primary schools and a more comprehensive structure of promoted posts for teachers in secondary schools came into effect.

M 7 Training Opportunities Scheme (TOPS) introduced by Department of Employment.

P 18 Uganda Resettlement Board set up in order to plan the orderly reception and resettlement of UK passport holders mainly of Asian origin whose expulsion from Uganda within 3 months had been announced by President Amin on 5 August. It consisted of representatives of Government, Race Relations organisations, and voluntary bodies.

September

E 1 School leaving age raised from 15 to 16.

November

M 6 White Paper *A Programme for Controlling Inflation: The First Stage* (Cmnd 5125) announced a 90-day prices, wages, and private rents standstill; a special £10 Christmas bonus would be paid to old age pensioners and the review period for entitlement to FIS was changed from 6 to 12 months. These measures were taken under the Counter-Inflation (Temporary Provision) Act 1972 which received the Royal Assent on 30 November.

December

R 19 Royal Commission on Civil Liability and Compensation for Personal Injury set up under Lord Pearson.

E 6 Education White Papers for England and Wales, *A Framework for Expansion* (Cmnd 5174) and for Scotland, *A Statement of Policy* (Cmnd 5175) published.

1973

Legislation

Criminal Justice Act 1972 came into effect in England and Wales giving new sentencing powers to the courts, including powers to order an offender to perform community service and attend a day training centre, and extended the court's power to order an offender to pay compensation for personal injury, loss, or damage. (*January 1*)

The Immigration Act 1971 came fully into force: work permit holders from the Commonwealth admitted to the United Kingdom on the same terms as work permit holders from foreign countries outside the EEC. (*January 1*)

Rent allowance scheme for private tenants in unfurnished accommodation introduced under the Housing Finance Act 1972. (E & W) (*January 1*)

A new system of community homes for children came into effect. This was as provided for under the Children and Young Persons Act 1969 and ended the formal distinction between remand homes, children's homes, and approved schools. (E & W) (*April 1*)

1973 Legislation (continued)

Part I of Legal Advice and Assistance Act 1972 came into effect enabling solicitors to assist persons with the preparation of their cases before tribunals. (GB) (*April 2*)

The Furnished Lettings (Rent Allowances) Act 1973 came into effect enabling furnished tenants to apply for rent allowances. (This section came into effect in Scotland on 1 October.) (*April 29*)

Land Compensation Act increased compensation for persons displaced by public development projects. (GB) (Royal Assent, *May 23*)

The main provisions of the Misuse of Drugs Act 1971 came into effect. It reclassified drugs subject to control, imposed new range of penalties for misuse, placed new responsibilities on doctors, dentists, manufacturers, and chemists. The Advisory Council on the Misuse of Drugs, established by this Act, came into effect in January 1972. (*July 1*)

The British Library was created under the British Library Act 1972, by merging a number of large national libraries with the object of providing comprehensive reference, lending and bibliographic services on a national scale. (*July 1*)

The Northern Ireland Constitution Act 1973 provided for the government of Northern Ireland and defined powers and functions of the Northern Ireland Assembly. (Royal Assent, *July 18*)

The Northern Ireland (Emergency Provisions) Act 1973 amended the law relating to detention and provided for trial without a jury for certain types of offence. (Royal Assent, *July 25*)

Fair Trading Act 1973 increased powers to protect the consumer against unfair trading practices by the appointment of a Director-General of Fair Trading (from 1 November) and a Consumer Protection Advisory Committee. (Royal Assent, *July 25*)

Local Government (Scotland) Act 1973 provided for the reorganisation of local authorities in Scotland in May 1975. (Royal Assent, *October 25*)

Divorce without a judicial hearing became available, where both parties have lived apart for two years, and consent, and there are no children of the family under 18; the decree is, however, pronounced in open court but neither party need be present or represented. (E & W) (*December 1*)

January

	1	Britain joined European Economic Community.
Sc, H, S	26	Scottish Information Service for the Disabled established.

February

C, F, M	1	Common Agricultural Policy of the EEC introduced.

March

P	1	Report of the Population Panel (Cmnd 5258) submitted to the Lord President of the Council. The Panel's task was to assess the available evidence about the significance of population growth in Great Britain now and in the future, and to make recommendations about further work required.
X	8	Terrorist car bombs exploded in London near Whitehall and Central Criminal Court.
NI	8	Border Poll — majority in favour of maintaining link with Great Britain.
C, M	31	Pay and dividend standstill under Phase I ended.

April

H	1	The Family Fund began work. A Treasury grant of £3 million was paid into a trust fund administered by the Joseph Rowntree Memorial Trust. Parents of very severely congenitally handicapped children who were caring for their children at home could apply to the fund for financial help.
C, F, M	1	Phase II of counter-inflation policy commenced, under the Counter-Inflation (Price and Pay Code) Act of 22 March. Wage and price restrictions were controlled by a new Pay Board and Price Commission respectively.
F	1	Value Added Tax introduced at 10 per cent.
S	24	Responsibility for adoption in England and Wales was transferred from the Secretary of State for the Home Office to the Secretaries of State for Social Services and for Wales.

May

C, M	1	Controlled price increases in Phase II replaced Phase I standstill.
M	1	One-day strike by $1\frac{1}{2}$ million workers in protest at government wage controls.
C, N	7	Two subsidy schemes announced for butter. First a general consumer subsidy. Second a butter token scheme for 'those in need' which came into effect on 1 July 1973. (Other food subsidies shown in the entry for 25 March 1974.)
M	23	Opening of the first new-style Job Centre replacing Employment Exchanges, as part of the modernised manpower service. Payment of unemployment benefit was made by Giro rather than at Exchanges from 2 July.

June

T, X	1	Regulations making the wearing of crash helmets by motor cyclists compulsory came into force.
N	4	The new lower rate attendance allowance introduced for those aged 16 to 64. The lower rates for those aged under 15 and those over 65 were introduced on 1 October and 3 December respectively.

1973 *continued*

July

S 15 The Leader of the House of Lords, Lord Windlesham, given special responsibility for voluntary social service organisations. (In April 1974 the Prime Minister asked the Home Secretary to assume this responsibility.)

30 Settlement between Distillers Company and representatives of Britain's thalidomide children approved in High Court.

August

E 13 Department of Education and Science announced £34 million building programme for nursery schools in 1974/75 and 1975/76. (E & W)

September

T 23 London Transport introduced free bus passes for all OAPs resident in Greater London; paid for by GLC ratepayers, 875,000 passes were issued by the end of 1973.

October

C, J 1 Small claims, of less than £75, could be dealt with in a less formal manner within the County Court system from this date. Rules of evidence and requirements of legal representation were relaxed to make it viable to claim such small sums under the County Court Act 1959 as amended by the Administration of Justice Act 1973. (E & W)

NI, L 1 A wide-ranging reconstruction of local government in Northern Ireland became effective.

H 1 The Parliamentary Commissioner took over the role of the Health Service Commissioner to investigate complaints against the health service.

A 8 London Broadcasting Company, Britain's first commercial radio station, started broadcasting.

Sc, L 31 The Kilbrandon Report on the Constitution published (Cmnd 5460). The majority report recommended a degree of devolution of functions to Scotland, Wales, and English regions.

November

C, M 1 Phase III of counter-inflation policy came into effect restricting price increases under the Counter-Inflation (Price and Pay Code) Act 1973.

F, M 7 Phase III of counter-inflation policy came into effect restricting wage increases.

M 12 Coalminers started overtime ban.

M 13 State of Emergency declared to conserve fuel supplies.

N 26 £10 Christmas bonus paid to pensioners.

T 29 Petrol coupons issued as precaution against fuel shortage due to cutback in supplies by primary producers.

December

T 5 Government announced further heating and lighting restrictions to conserve fuel supplies.

T, X 8 Government announced 50 mph maximum speed on all roads (later changed).

M 31 Three-day working week started for most of British industry.

1974

Legislation

The Manpower Services Commission established under the Employment and Training Act 1973 with responsibility for the public employment services and for promoting training for employment. (*January 1*)

The Local Government Act 1974 *inter alia* made further provision for the payment of rate support grants to local authorities in England and Wales and extended the powers of the Countryside Commission to give financial assistance. (Royal Assent, *February 8*)

Implementation of Local Government Act 1972, Water Act 1973, and National Health Reorganisation Act 1973. Local government in England and Wales reorganised with a reduction in number of local authorities from 1,425 to 457, England having 6 metropolitan and 39 non-metropolitan counties and Wales 8 counties. Local government water and sewerage services transferred to regional water authorities; local authority health (other than public health) services transferred to NHS. (*April 1*)

Under the Criminal Justice Act 1972 all persons between the ages of 18 and 65, registered as local government electors and not otherwise ineligible or disqualified, became liable for jury service in England and Wales. (*April 1*)

The Guardianship Act 1973, Parts I and III, came into force giving both parents equal parental rights over their children. (E & W) (*May 8*)

Legal Aid Act 1974 came into force raising the upper disposable income limit for eligibility for civil legal aid. The sum was fixed at £1,380 per annum on 1 September. (*May 8*)

The Prices Act 1974, authorised the payment of food subsidies and abolished the Pay Board as from 26 July, ending all statutory wage controls. (Royal Assent, *July 9*)

The Housing (Scotland) Act 1974 provided for the definition of a Housing Action Area in which a local authority may give grants of up to 75 per cent of the cost of improvement with an Exchequer contribution of 90 per cent of grants paid. In other areas grants of up to 50 per cent may be paid with an Exchequer contribution of 75 per cent. (Royal Assent, *July 31*)

The Health and Safety at Work, etc. Act 1974 made further provision for securing the health, safety, and welfare of persons at work, for controlling the keeping and use and preventing the unlawful acquisition and possession of dangerous substances, and for controlling certain emissions into the atmosphere. (Royal Assent, *July 31*) The Health and Safety Commission was set up under this Act on 1 October.

The Consumer Credit Act 1974 established for the protection of consumers in the United Kingdom a new system of licensing and other control of traders concerned with the provision of credit, or the supply of goods on hire or hire-purchase. (Royal Assent, *July 31*)

The Town and Country Amenities Act 1974 controlled development in conservation areas. (Royal Assent, *July 31*)

Control of Pollution Act 1974, containing new and more stringent provisions, to be introduced in stages covering waste disposal, water pollution, noise, and air pollution in Great Britain. (Royal Assent, *July 31*)

The Road Traffic Act 1974 *inter alia* fixed liability for the vehicle on the owner in respect of certain fixed penalty offences such as parking offences. (Royal Assent, *July 31*)

The Rent Act 1974 extended protection under the Rent Acts to furnished tenancies where the landlord does not live in the same building, excepting certain categories of people such as students. (Royal Assent, *July 31*)

The Trade Union and Labour Relations Act 1974 repealed the Industrial Relations Act 1971. (Royal Assent, *July 31*)

The Rehabilitation of Offenders Act 1974 rehabilitates offenders who have not been reconvicted of any serious offence for certain periods of years, the periods varying according to their original sentence; it also penalises the unauthorised disclosure of these. (Royal Assent, *July 31*)

Prevention of Terrorism (Temporary Provisions) Act 1974 came into force, proscribing the IRA and giving wider powers to the police. (*November 29*)

House renovation, housing action area, and priority neighbourhood provisions of the Housing Act 1974 came into effect. (*December 2*)

January

A	1	Museum charges came into effect. (Abolished 30 March.)
NI	1	'Reserved' powers devolved to the Northern Ireland Assembly.
A	1	New Year's Day became a Bank Holiday in England and Wales.
X	5	Bombs exploded at the Boat Show, Earl's Court, and Madame Tussaud's in London.
M	14	The energy crisis and three-day working week led to about $2\frac{1}{4}$ million people unemployed or on short-time working.

February

LAB 301   Others 38   CON 296

X	4	A bomb was planted in a coach carrying servicemen and their families along the M62 motorway from Manchester to Catterick. Twelve people were killed.
D	7	A joint DOE/DHSS/Welsh Office circular on Homelessness (DHSS 4/74) recommended that housing authorities should increasingly undertake the prime responsibility for homeless people and their accommodation. (E & W)
M	10	After three months of industrial action the coalminers' national strike started in support of a pay claim.
M	17	Mr Wilson, the Leader of the Labour Party, offered a new 'Social Compact' between the TUC and Labour Party.
	28	General Election resulted in Labour minority government with 301 of 635 seats.

March

M	8	From midnight, British industry returned to five-day working week.
D	8	Council, private, and housing association rents in Great Britain frozen for the remainder of the year (later extended to Spring 1975).
M	11	The State of Emergency was ended on the coalminers' return to work.
C, F	25	A bread subsidy was introduced. Subsidies which followed later in the year were on milk on 21 April, cheese on 6 May, and tea and household flour on 2 September.
H	25	Report by the Baroness Sharp on Mobility of Physically Disabled People published (see entry for 26 April 1972). Government statement on 13 September proposed the introduction of a mobility allowance.

April

S	1	Free family planning service made available at NHS hospitals and clinics.
H, R	3	The Lane Committee recommended greater opportunity for women to seek advice on abortion and to obtain treatment under the NHS (Cmnd 5579).
Sc, E	16	Scottish Education Department circular 898 re-affirmed Government policy to continue the reorganisation of secondary education on comprehensive lines. Authorities were asked for plans to eliminate remaining pockets of selection (subject to investment being available for new buildings).
R	29	A Royal Commission was announced to study problems in community service arising from clashes between public duty and private interests.

1974 *continued*

May

E	6	Proposals for increased payments to teachers at schools in areas of social deprivation announced·
NI	15	Ulster Workers' Council strike in Northern Ireland.
J	21	Publication of the Report of the Home Secretary's Advisory Council (the Younger Committee) on the Penal System *Young Adult Offenders*, recommending that present custodial sentences for offenders aged between 17 and 21 – imprisonment, borstal training, and detention centre – should be replaced by a new form of custodial sentence – the Custody and Control Order – and a new non-custodial sentence – the Supervision and Control Order.
NI	27–30	The province-wide strike called by the Ulster Workers' Council necessitated the implementation of a contingency plan for distributing petrol and oil to essential users. Oil terminals and filling stations were requisitioned and manned by Department of Commerce staff with the assistance of the Army.
NI	28	Resignation of Chief Executive and fall of the Executive in Northern Ireland.
NI	29	The Northern Ireland Assembly prorogued. The Northern Ireland Act 1974 provided for legislation at Westminster by Order in Council during period of prorogation.

June

X	1	An explosion and fire at a chemical plant in Flixborough, Lincolnshire, killed 29 people. The village was reduced to ruins.
X	17	Westminster Hall was damaged and 11 people injured in a bomb explosion.

July

F, N	2	The Finer Committee Report on one-parent families (Cmnd 5629) was published. It recommended a Guaranteed Maintenance Allowance of £9.50 plus £1.00 for each child at 1972–73 prices, costing about £85 million.
X	17	Forty people were injured and one killed in a bomb explosion at the Tower of London.
F	18	A Royal Commission on the Distribution of Income and Wealth was announced, with a standing reference to analyse and report on the current distribution and past trends.
Sc, J	30	Lord Advocate decided that court proceedings should not be commenced against Scottish children under 13 years of age without his authority, or against children alleged to have committed offences while acting along with an adult unless circumstances make joint prosecution essential.
J	30	The Home Secretary announced proposals to introduce an independent element into the procedure for handling complaints against the police.
L	30	Announcement of establishment of committee of inquiry into local government finance under the chairmanship of Mr Frank Layfield QC.

August

F	8	A Green Paper was published setting out the Government's plans for a wealth tax.
A, T	15	The major travel and aviation companies of the Court Line group collapsed.
J	22	The Home Secretary announced that from April 1975 all probation and after-care committees in England and Wales will be authorised to make community service orders, which makes it possible for an offender aged 17 or over who is convicted of an offence punishable by imprisonment to be ordered to carry out unpaid work of benefit to the community.
E	28	Education White Paper *Educational Disadvantage and the Educational Needs of Immigrants* presented to Parliament, announced the setting-up of two new units within DES on Educational Disadvantage and the Assessment of Performance.
P, R	29	A change in the Immigration Rules was made to enable husbands and fiancés of women settled in the United Kingdom to join their wives and fiancées in the United Kingdom.

September

M	2	The independent Conciliation and Arbitration Service was established under a council chaired by Mr J E Mortimer to provide conciliation in industrial disputes, make facilities available for arbitration, provide advisory and information services to industry, and undertake investigations for improvement of collective bargaining. Now called the Advisory, Conciliation, and Arbitration Service.
M	4	The Trade Union Congress voted to support the Social Compact.
R	6	A White Paper *Equality for Women: a proposal for equal opportunity* (Cmnd 5724) was published, promising legislation to make sex discrimination unlawful in employment; training; education; housing; the provision of goods, services, and facilities to the public, and related advertising.
V	11	A Green Paper *War on Waste* (Cmnd 5727) launched a national drive towards the reduction and reclamation of waste materials.
F, N	11	A White Paper on a new state scheme designed to fully protect earnings-related pensions against inflation was published (Cmnd 5713). The paper announced full equality of treatment for pensionable women, and preferential treatment for the old and the low-paid worker.
S	13	Government proposals announced for new non-contributory benefits for the chronically sick and disabled.
Sc	17	*Democracy and Devolution: proposals for Scotland and Wales* (Cmnd 5732) proposed directly elected assemblies for Scotland and Wales.

1974 *continued*

October

J	1	Upper limit of claims in contract and tort in County Court was raised to £1,000. Registrar's jurisdiction raised to £100.
J	1	'Intermediate Treatment' (ie, recreational, educational, or cultural activities to which children and young persons are directed in a Supervision Order) available to juvenile courts in all areas in England and Wales.
X	5	Bombs exploded at two public houses in Guildford, Surrey, used by soldiers, killing 5 and injuring 65.
	10	General Election resulted in an overall Labour majority of three.
C	28	First Maximum Price Order (for subsidised bread) came into effect.
S	30	The £10 Christmas bonus was extended to include widows, the chronically sick, and the disabled, where these people were already receiving social security benefits.

November

X	21	Bombs exploded in two bars in the centre of Birmingham killing 21 people and injuring about 120.

1975

Legislation

Offshore Petroleum Development (Scotland) Act 1975 provided for the acquisition of land for the purposes of offshore petroleum development. The Act also provides for the reinstatement of land used for this purpose. (*March 13*)

Education (Mentally Handicapped Children) (Scotland) Act 1974 ended the designation of severely mentally handicapped children as unsuitable for education and training and placed responsibility for making provision for such school age children on education authorities. (*May 16*)

The Rehabilitation of Offenders Act 1974 which rehabilitated offenders who have not been reconvicted of any serious offence for certain periods of years, the periods varying according to their original sentence, and penalises the unauthorised disclosure of these, came into effect. (GB) (*July 1*)

The Conservation of Wild Creatures and Wild Plants Act 1975 provided for the protection and conservation of wild creatures and plants growing wild. (GB) (Royal Assent, *August 1*)

The Safety of Sports Grounds Act 1975 made provision for safety at sports stadia and other sports grounds. (GB) (Royal Assent, *August 1*)

The Remuneration, Charges and Grants Act 1975 came into force. (*August 3*)

The Social Security Pensions Act carried into law the new earnings-related pension scheme which came into operation in April 1976. (Royal Assent, *August 7*)

The Criminal Jurisdiction Act 1975 *inter alia* created extra-territorial offences under the law of Northern Ireland and provided for obtaining evidence in Northern Ireland for the trial of offences in the Republic of Ireland. (Royal Assent, *August 7*)

Regulations to phase out direct grant schools over seven years, from September 1976, came into effect. (*August 21*)

The Northern Ireland (Emergency Provisions) (Amendment) Act 1975 revised the provisions of the 1973 Act in the light of the Report of the Committee, under the Chairmanship of Lord Gardiner, to consider measures to deal with terrorism in Northern Ireland in the context of civil liabilities and human rights. It removed the limitations on the power to grant bail. (*August 21*)

The Community Land Act 1975 is primarily designed to give local authorities new powers and duties to make land available for private development. (GB) (Royal Assent, *November 12*)

The Inheritance (Provision for Family and Dependants) Act 1975 empowered courts to order financial provision from the estate of a deceased person for various dependants of that person. It came into effect on 1 April 1976. (E & W) (Royal Assent, *November 12*)

The Policyholders Protection Act 1975 set up the Policyholders Protection Board. The Act enabled the Board to raise money from the insurance industry so that the Board could meet the liabilities of an individual insurance company in the event of that company failing. (Royal Assent, *November 12*)

The Children Act 1975 made it the duty of local authorities to establish and maintain within their area a comprehensive adoption service; it also altered the provisions relating to the custody of children and children in care. (GB) (Royal Assent, *November 12*)

The Employment Protection Act 1975 set up the Advisory Conciliation and Arbitration Service; it made dismissal on the grounds of pregnancy an unfair dismissal and introduced maternity pay paid by the employer; it also amended the law relating to workers' rights, trade unions, and employers' associations. (GB) (Royal Assent, *November 12*)

The Sex Discrimination Act 1975 rendered unlawful certain kinds of sex discrimination and discrimination on the grounds of marriage; it also established the Equal Opportunities Commission which works towards the elimination of such discrimination and the promotion of equality of opportunity between men and women generally. (GB) (*December 29*)

1975 *continued*

January

T, V	20	Abandonment of the Channel Tunnel announced. (Work halted on 25 January.)
X	27	25 people were injured in bomb explosions in London and Manchester.
A, R	29	Greater London Council voted against the abolition of film censorship.
NI, R, X	30	The Gardiner Report on anti-terrorism in Northern Ireland recommended the abolition of special category status for Ulster prisoners.

February

E	18	*A Language for Life*, the Report of the Bullock Committee (1972) on reading and the use of English in schools, was published.
N	20	The Supplementary Benefits Commission introduced certain changes in the payment of rents in line with the recommendations of the Finer Report on One-Parent Families.
NI, E	27	The Minister of State responsible for education in Northern Ireland announced a study of the practicalities and possibilities of introducing a non-selective system of secondary education within the present buildings.
X	28	Forty-three people were killed in the Moorgate Underground train accident.

March

M	7	A workers' cooperative at Meriden began producing motorcycles.
Sc, E	14	Publication of the Report of the Alexander Committee on Adult Education in Scotland – *Adult Education: The Challenge of Change*.
R	20	Important changes in the law of libel, slander, and defamation were recommended by the committee (1971) chaired by Mr Justice Faulks.

April

NI, X	7	Ten people were killed in weekend violence in Ulster.
P	15	Cancellation of the proposed 1976 Population Census announced.
M	24	The Government accepted the recommendation that it take over British Leyland.

May

NI	2	The United Ulster Unionist Coalition obtained an overall majority over other parties in the Northern Ireland elections.
M, X	12	The enquiry into the Flixborough disaster (January 1975) reported that it was caused by the failure of a temporary pipe.
H	13	The Secretary of State for Social Services announced a 10 per cent cut in pay beds in England by July.
M	14	The Government took $62\frac{1}{2}$ per cent control of Ferranti.
S	14	The Government announced free family planning service provided by GPs would start on 1 July.

June

F	2	The first index-linked National Savings bonds (for retirement pensioners) went on sale at the Post Office.
	5	EEC Referendum day. In a 64·5 per cent UK turnout, 67·2 per cent voted for the United Kingdom to stay in the EEC.
A	9	Experimental broadcasting of the House of Commons began, and ended on 4 July.
V	17	Britain's first North Sea oil was brought ashore in the Thames estuary.

July

	7	Labour Party delegates from the Commons and the Lords took their seats for the first time in the European Parliament.
F	11	The Government's measures to combat inflation were published in the White Paper *The Attack on Inflation* (Cmnd 6151): from 1 August, a limit of £6 per week on pay rises; no rises for those earning £8,500 plus per annum; more subsidies for food and council housing.
R	30	The Government rejected the Ombudsman's criticism of its handling of the Court Line failure.
F	30	The first report of the Royal Commission on the Distribution of Income and Wealth was published.

August

H	11	The Government issued a consultative document on the phasing out of private practice from NHS hospitals.
X	27	Bomb explosion at Caterham, Surrey; 40 people were injured.
X	28	Bomb explosion at Oxford Street, London; 7 people were injured. In the following months there were several such incidents: a bomb disposal expert was killed on 29 August; 2 people were killed and 62 injured in a bomb explosion at the London Hilton Hotel on 5 September; a man was killed in Green Park on 9 October; a cancer expert was killed on 23 October; 18 people were injured in Mayfair, London, on 29 October; another man was killed on 12 November (all in bomb explosions). The writer Ross McWhirter was shot dead on 27 November.

1975 *continued*

September

NI, X	2	Seven people were killed by terrorist activity in South Armagh.
F	3	The TUC voted to support the £6 per week pay increase limitation.
R	11	Publication of the White Paper on Racial Discrimination (Cmnd 6234).
F, H, M	18	The Review Body on Doctors' and Dentists' Remuneration recommended a new pay structure for junior hospital doctors. Some junior doctors began restricted services in many hospitals on 9 October in support of their pay and hours claim. Agreement was reached in this dispute on 12 December. The junior hospital doctors' leaders recommended the suspension of their industrial action on 23 December.
F, M	24	The Government announced a £175m package of measures to check unemployment.

October

NI, X	2	Widespread sectarian violence in Northern Ireland resulted in 11 deaths.
	15	Iceland extended its fishing limits from 50 miles to 200 miles and on 17 November talks between Great Britain and Iceland broke down. Following harassment of British trawlers, the Royal Navy was ordered into Icelandic waters on 25 November. Iceland immediately closed its ports and airspace to the British. The first clash between the Royal Navy frigates and the harassing Icelandic gunboats occurred on 11 December.
H	20	A Royal Commission on the Health Service was announced.
M	21	Unemployment rose to over 1 million for the first time since the Second World War.

November

M, X	4	Five men were killed in an explosion at the British Steel Corporation plant at Scunthorpe.
NI	4	The Secretary of State for Northern Ireland indicated in a statement in the House of Commons that he would be introducing an Order regarding a number of new measures for treatment of offenders, including release at half-sentence and phasing out of special category status.
N	17	Increased rates of social security benefits came into effect and some 12 million claimants received bigger benefits. These increases were announced in Parliament by the Chancellor on 22 May, 1975.
M	19	The National Enterprise Board came into being.
NI, X	22	Three soldiers were killed in South Armagh.
J	25	A Committee (1973) chaired by Lord Justice James recommended the end of trial by jury in drink and driving cases.
	27	Publication of the White Paper on Devolution – *Our Changing Democracy* (Cmnd 6348).
R	29	A register listing the interests of MPs was published.

December

H, M	1	Industrial action was initiated by hospital consultants in protest against the proposal to exclude private practice from the National Health Service.
J, R	10	The Advisory group, chaired by Mrs Justice Heilbron, proposed that complainants of rape should remain anonymous.
	11	The House of Commons voted by 361 to 232 not to restore the death penalty.
R	16	Publication of two White Papers on Computers and Privacy (Cmnds 6353 and 6354).

Appendix A Statistical notes

Population

Table 1.10 (also Chart 1.9)

(1) The estimates for the Alien, Commonwealth, and United Kingdom streams are adjusted in the light of other available information such as the statistics collected under the Immigration Act. Migrants to and from the Irish Republic are not included in the International Passenger Survey.

Table 1.12

(1) These figures relate to dissolutions and annulments of marriage.
(2) Scottish figures relate only to marriages which took place in Scotland.
(3) England and Wales only: all children born of the marriage who were alive at time of petition, irrespective of age, including children legitimised by marriage: adopted children are also included.

Households

Table 2.14

(1) Maintained by local authorities or voluntary bodies under agency arrangements under Section 22 of the National Health Service Act, 1946. For Scotland includes maximum places at all day nurseries except those provided specifically for mentally handicapped children.
(2) Includes most pre-school playgroups. The Pre-school Playgroups Association estimate for England and Wales a membership of approximately 9,100 groups in March 1975 and the number of children on register was about 280,000. In Scotland at the end of 1974 there were approximately 1,600 playgroups catering for about 47,000 children.
(3) Persons registered under the Nurseries and Child Minders Regulation Act, 1948 (as amended by Section 60 of the Health Services and Public Health Act 1968) which may include a few play-groups.
(4) Children aged 2 and under 5 in nursery schools and other schools (excluding special schools).
(5) See also Tables 3.1 to 3.4.
(6) Includes the severely subnormal children for whom responsibility was transferred to the education service on 1 April 1971.
(7) Figures are for 1973.
(8) Data relate to 31 March 1974.

Table 2.15

(1) For the year ending 31 March for England, Northern Ireland, and Wales and 31 December for Scotland.
(2) Certain children who change their legal status during the year may be entered under more than one heading.
(3) On 1 January 1971, the power of the courts in England and Wales to commit to an approved school or to the care of a fit person was abolished and replaced by the power to commit to the care of a local authority. Children and young persons aged under 19 then subject to approved school orders or to supervision after release from an approved school, were deemed from 1 January 1971 to be subject to care orders. On the same date the system of remand to a remand home was replaced by committal to care under an interim care order or remand to care.

(4) For England and Wales, interim fit person orders (April–December 1970) or interim care orders or on remand to care (January 1971 onwards).
(5) Scottish total includes 5,500 children placed under non-residential supervision and 1,500 placed under residential supervision.

Table 2.16

(1) For year ending 31 March for England and Wales, and Northern Ireland and, 31 December for Scotland.
(2) Figures prior to 1974 are not strictly comparable as, on April 1973, the community house system, established in accordance with the provisions of the Children and Young Persons Act, 1969, came into operation. This system integrated the previously separate systems of approved schools, remand homes, children's homes, and hostels.
(3) The Scottish figures apply to children in care or under supervision and the types of accommodation only roughly correspond with those for England and Wales.
(4) 5–11 years of age.
(5) 12 years of age and over.
(6) The system in Northern Ireland differs from that of England and Wales.

Chart 2.19

(1) Small homes are homes with fewer than 35 places prior to 1966 and with fewer than 31 places thereafter. Medium homes are homes with more than 34 places but fewer than 70 places prior to 1966 and with more than 30 places but less than 70 places thereafter. Large homes are homes with more than 70 places. From 1966 joint-user premises owned by the local authorities have been excluded.

Table 2.20

(1) Figures for England and Wales relate to 31 December before 1972, and to 31 March thereafter.
(2) Accommodation provided under Sections 21(1) (a) and 26 of the National Assistance Act 1948 in homes owned by local authorities or in joint-user premises shared with hospitals.
(3) In accommodation provided on behalf of local authorities in voluntary or private homes.
(4) Because of a change in the form of statistics collected, 1973 and 1974 figures are not comparable with those for earlier years.
(5) For England and Wales, the number of persons served in their own homes in one week in November (mainly the elderly). For Scotland, the number of persons receiving meals during a typical week.
(6) Under Section 29 of the National Assistance Act, 1948 (not all persons who could register do so).
(7) Accommodation in Scotland is provided under Section 59(1) of the Social Work (Scotland) Act 1968.

Education

Chart 3.3

(1) From 1961 to 1973 inclusive part-time pupils were counted as 0·5. From 1974 they are counted as 1.
(2) England and Wales data for 1961 to 1963 exclude part-time pupils in direct grant lower and all independent schools.
(3) England and Wales age data for 1964 to 1966 exclude part-time pupils in direct grant lower schools, and independent primary, primary, and secondary schools.
(4) United Kingdom 1975 data are estimated.

Table 3.13

(1) The public sector and assisted establishments are major establishments providing a substantial number of day courses. Universities (including colleges of advanced technology), colleges of education, colleges of music, and independent establishments not recognised as efficient are not included. In Scotland, students attending full-time courses of advanced further education in Social Work/Youth Leadership organised by certain colleges of education are included.

Table 3.15

(1) Includes Fellowship for higher degree graduates.
(2) Includes temporary UK employment.
(3) Includes those not available for employment, those believed to be unemployed, those whose economic activities are unknown, and those whose further study/employment is arranged but not due to commence until after 31 December.

Employment

Table 4.3

(1) The population figures for Great Britain aged 15 and over were taken from the 100% results in 1971 and from the 10% sample figures in 1961 and 1966. The 1966 figures do not include foreign visitors unless they had a place of work in Great Britain. No adjustment has been made for the bias in the 1961 figures or for the possible under-enumeration in 1966.
(2) Final 1971 Census figures.
(3) A limited breakdown for Northern Ireland is:

	1961	1966	1971
Males			
Self-employed *and* employers *plus* employees	373,733	376,956	370,197
Out of employment (sick or other)	41,479	39,121	41,549
Females			
Self-employed *and* employers *plus* employees	171,969	184,219	190,994
Out of employment (sick or other)	15,119	11,160	9,501

(4) In the 1961 and 1966 Censuses 'part-time' workers were those persons in employment who reported that their job in the previous week was not full-time, irrespective of the number of hours they actually claimed to have worked. In the 1971 Census they were those who said they were working normal hours of less than 30 hours per week. Persons whose job was normally full-time but who worked less than their normal hours because of sickness, holidays, short-time working, or labour disputes are not included.
(5) Figures not comparable with those for earlier years due to change in Census forms and possibly to changes in the way in which questions were interpreted by respondents.

Table 4.6

(1) Full-time students who worked in the reference week are not regarded as economically active.
(2) 16–17 for 1973 and 1974 owing to the raising of the school-leaving age in 1972. See Appendix 3, page 235.
(3) Sample size too small.
(4) The 'unmarried females' category comprises those who are single, widowed, divorced, or separated.

Personal income and wealth

Table 5.23

(5) Contains unidentifiable elements of all other groups apart from unemployed, eg any blind, tuberculosis, and hospital cases and accommodation provided under Part III of the National Assistance Act.
(6) The 'wage stopped' are those recipients of supplementary benefit whose benefit is restricted so that they receive no more net income when unemployed than they normally do when in full-time work. The 'wage stop' was abolished in April 1975.

Table 5.29

(2) See note (2) to Table 5.31.

Table 5.31

(2) Net weekly income = Weekly income *plus* Family Allowance *plus* Family Income Supplement *less* Tax *less* National Insurance contributions

Disposable income = Net weekly income *less* (rent *less* rent rebate) *less* (rates *less* rate rebate) *less* work expenses

Total income support = Disposable income *plus* the value of free school meals *plus* the value of free welfare milk

Net resources = Disposable income *less* supplementary benefit scale rate(s)

Because of differences between the calculation of net resources and the calculation of supplementary benefit for claimants, Table 5.31 does not indicate the proportion of persons entitled to but not receiving supplementary benefit. For example, a family could have had a disposable income above supplementary benefit level but could nonetheless be entitled to supplementary benefit if some of the income such as earnings, occupational pensions, or disability pension attracted a disregard. On the other hand a family with capital whose disposable income was below supplementary benefit level could have had no entitlement to benefit because calculations for entitlement to supplementary benefit impute a certain income from capital holdings over a certain level. The calculations for the table take account of stated income from capital and do not consider the imputed income.

The estimates shown in the table relate to December 1975 and are based on the *Family Expenditure Survey* (FES) for 1975 whose sampling fraction is approximately 1 in 3,000 families. (The estimates in the analysis of the FES are based on families as income units. This allows the calculation of disposable income to be consistent with the treatment of claims for social security benefits. In this respect this analysis differs from the household analysis of the FES mentioned elsewhere in this publication.) Some of the data from FES are subject to considerable sampling error. The largest sampling errors are likely in the figures for single parent families and some of the groups living within 20 per cent of the supplementary benefit level. Families below the supplementary benefit level are those with negative net resources. Those defined as being above supplementary benefit level but within 20 per cent of it are those whose net resources are positive and less than 20 per cent of the appropriate scale rate.

(3) This column shows the number of people dependent on supplementary benefit. These figures are derived from a supplementary benefit sample enquiry for November 1975. The sampling fraction for this enquiry was 1 in 40 for beneficiaries under pensionable age and 1 in 160 for beneficiaries over pensionable age. Because the analysis of the FES treats respondents according to their normal income and employment situation within the three months preceding the interview, these figures exclude persons who have received supplementary benefit for less than three months in order that the information should be consistent with that obtained from the FES.

Health

Table 7.3 (also Chart 7.4)

(1) These SMRs show the change over the years but the relative importance of causes in any year are indicated by the actual number of deaths. Thus in the table the rise in the SMR for lung cancer from 1968 to 1974 has been greater among females than among males but in 1974 there were still four times as many male deaths.

Table 7.7

(1) Chronic sickness can be defined as long-standing illness or limiting long-standing illness. See notes in Appendix B
(2) Great Britain = 100. See note in Appendix B page 234 on age-standardisation.
(3) Based on 10 or fewer observations.

Table 7.8

(1) Acute sickness is defined as restricted activity due to illness or injury in a two-week reference period. See note in Appendix B
(2) Great Britain = 100. See note in Appendix B page 234 on age-standardisation.
(3) Based on 10 or fewer observations.

Table 7.16

(1) Figures are not equivalent to consultations because respondents could have consulted more than once in the 2-week reference period. See note in Appendix B.
(2) Great Britain = 100. See note in Appendix B page 234 on age-standardisation.
(3) Based on 10 or fewer observations.

Housing

Table 8.3

(2) Department of the Environment estimates based on census data from 1851, estimated rates of new construction before 1919 and assumed ages of dwellings lost from housing stock.

Table 8.4

(1) Estimates based upon Census data. See Appendix B.
(2) In addition to the estimated net gain of 242,000 dwellings in 1971, changes in the dwelling definition used in the 1971 Census resulted in an increase of 32,000 dwellings in the 'privately rented and other tenures' category.
(3) Conversions.
(4) Estimated number of separate dwellings.
(5) Losses from obsolescence, fire, flood and other damage, or redevelopment: removal of temporary dwellings.

Table 8.6

(1) The 1961 Census enumerated water closets only if inside or attached to the building. Houses with, or sharing, a water closet not attached to the building are therefore shown as lacking this amenity in 1961.

Environment

Table 9.4

(1) Orders in operation are orders confirmed by the Secretary of State which have come into operation on the date specified in the order.
(2) Sometimes an order is made which contains an area already included in a smoke control order. There is therefore a small element of double-counting of the acreage and number of premises in these figures, both in individual years and cumulatively. Some orders are made in anticipation of development and may contain few premises and a relatively large acreage. Subsequent construction or demolition of premises after confirmation of an order is not reflected in the figures.

Leisure

Table 10.7

(1) A holiday is defined as a period of four or more nights away from home which is considered by the respondent to be a holiday. When only one holiday is taken during the year this is the main holiday; when two or more holidays are taken the main holiday is the longest, or the one nearest to the peak summer period if two or more were of equal length.
(2) Total numbers of holidays taken count both adults and children going on holiday. The percentage figures in the lower part of the table represent adult visitors only.
(3) Countries of destination are defined to be countries which were visited for at least 4 nights during the holiday. The total figure sometimes does not add to 100 per cent due to small numbers of persons on training holidays.

Table 10.12

(1) 1950 and 1960 figures include the categories of Senior Scouts (15–18 years) and Rover Scouts (18–24 years); the later years figures replace the latter by the new category of Venture Scouts (18–20 years).
(2) Girl Guide figures include Ranger Guides (14–18 years) and Young Leaders (16–18 years).
(3) There have been minor changes in areas catered for in the period 1950–1975. Figures relate to the British Isles.
(4) Figures relate to ages 13–25; in 1973 there were over 35,000 younger members under the age of 13.
(5) Numbers trained in the United Kingdom.
(6) Approximate figures.
(7) The Community Service Volunteers Organisation places young persons in full-time community service for periods from 4 to 12 months. The figures given are the number of months of full-time service undertaken by volunteers.
(8) Figures relate to the number of new entrants to the scheme, which covers ages 14–23 in the United Kingdom. It is estimated that there are approximately two persons working towards their awards for every new entrant; thus in 1975 there were about 147,500 young persons working towards their awards of which a little over 30,000 were gained in that year.
(9) YMCA figures are for total registered membership under 20 years of age; registered participants are those who use YMCA services for a major part of the year. These figures are in addition to members.
(10) Four local associations operate either full or part-time systems by which their services are available to a further 48,600 young people.
(11) These figures are calculated on a new basis and are not comparable with previous years figures.

Table 10.13

(1) Figures refer to the Church of England's area in the provinces of Canterbury and York.
(2) 1957 was the first year that persons of 17 years of age were included on the electoral rolls. In previous years the minimum age was 18.
(3) Statistics relating to the estimates of numbers usually attending Sunday services were not collected prior to 1968.
(4) Figures refer to England and Wales.
(5) These statistics fluctuate from year to year and are related to the number of episcopal visitations and the size of the parishes visited in the year. In the 5 years 1970–74 confirmations averaged 77,000.
(6) Based on a count at all churches on one Sunday in the year.
(7) Great Britain.

Public safety

Table 11.8

(1) The statistics of accidents and casualties in this table were derived from reports submitted by the Police to the Department of the Environment and to the Scottish Development Department. Estimates of traffic are based on roadside traffic counts taken for the Department of the Environment.

Road accident: an accident on the public highway in which a moving vehicle was involved and in which at least one person was injured.

Killed: killed outright or died within 30 days of an accident.

Serious injury: an injury after which a person was detained in hospital as an 'inpatient' or any of the following injuries whether or not the casualty was detained in hospital: fractures, concussion, internal injuries, crushings, severe cuts and lacerations, severe general shock requiring medical treatment.

Slight injury: an injury of a minor character such as a sprain, bruise or a cut or laceration not judged to be severe.

Resources

Chart 13.1

Pattern and source of public expenditure, 1974

(1) Excluding grants and lending to local authorities and public corporations.

(2) Including expenditure financed by grants received from central government.

Appendix B Definitions and terms

STATISTICAL TERMS

Measures of location and dispersion

The *median* is the value which divides a distribution into two equal parts so that one half of the values fall below and one half above this central value: it thus differs from the mean or average value of the items (except where the distribution is symmetrical).

Distributions can similarly be divided by *quartiles, quintiles, deciles, percentiles, etc.* The lower (upper) quartile, for example, is that value which has 25 per cent of all values falling below (above) it: the lowest (highest) quintile is that value which has 20 per cent of all values falling below (above) it, etc.

The Gini coefficient of concentration measures the degree of inequality in a distribution — usually of income or wealth. On page 244 it is given as a percentage with theoretical limits of 0 for absolute equality, and 100 for absolute inequality, where one unit has all the income (or wealth). It is defined as 'the mean of the differences between all pairs of values (of all incomes), divided by twice the mean value (income)'.

Age standardisation

Comparison of rates reflecting the incidence of deaths, sickness etc. between groups of people either at different times or in different places is affected by their age composition. This factor can be minimised by relating these rates to a population with a standard age structure.

In Table 7.3 standard mortality ratios are based on the mortality rates of the population in 1968. The standard mortality ratio (the SMR) is equal to the number of deaths in a given year taken as a percentage of the number of deaths that would have taken place in that year if the age-specific mortality rates of the base year 1968 had been applied to the population of the given year.

For example SMR for 1970 =

$$\frac{\text{Deaths in 1970}}{\text{Death rates } 1968 \times \text{relevant population in 1970,}}\times 100$$
summed over the age groups

GENERAL PURPOSE SOURCES

Three main sources of general purpose information exist which are used in various sections of *Social Trends*.

The Census of Population

The Census of Population has been held every 10 years since 1801 (except 1941) with the last one taking place in 1971. (In 1966 there was a 10 per cent sample census in Great Britain and a full census in Northern Ireland.) Completion of census returns is universal and compulsory. The census provides information on demographic characteristics, country of birth, previous addresses at particular points in time, marriages, births, occupations, education, housing, etc. As well as use of the census for policy and research it also provides benchmarks for other surveys, bases for projections, grossing up factors, etc.

General Household Survey

This multi-purpose survey which started in October 1970 is designed to provide information on a large number of topics about private households in Great Britain. The continuing nature of the survey makes it possible to obtain trend data during the intercensal period for both administrative and research purposes. A stratified sampling frame, clustered in a number of geographical areas, is used, giving an effective annual sample size of about 12,000 households. The form of the questionnaire is flexible to meet specific needs, but the results may differ from those obtained from other sources owing to different definitions (eg unemployment and sickness) as well as to sampling error. Results from the GHS have been used in this publication in sections on Population, Households, Employment, Health, Education, Housing, and Leisure. Specific points are dealt with individually in the definitions for each of these sections. Although the survey does not include the institutional population and is therefore representative of the private household population only, and the sample size means that for some groups of interest data may need to be aggregated over a number of years, this survey nevertheless gives the fullest information about a wide class of socio-economic variables and their inter-relationship yet obtained on a continuous basis. For further information and results see *The General Household Survey Introductory Report* (HMSO 1973), *The General Household Survey, 1972* (HMSO 1975), and *The General Household Survey, 1973* (HMSO 1976)[1].

Family Expenditure Survey

The Family Expenditure Survey is a continuing enquiry into the expenditure pattern of private households of all types in the United Kingdom, and has been in operation since 1957. Members of households co-operating in the survey give details of their expenditure during a two-week period, and information about their income. Each year a stratified random sample of about 11,000 addresses is selected. The effective sample is about 10,400 private households, of which about 70 per cent co-operate. In addition the Family Expenditure Survey sample includes an appropriate number of private households in Northern Ireland, selected at random from the sample of addresses for the similar survey conducted by the Statistics and Economics Unit of the Department of Finance in Northern Ireland.

The results of the survey are used in calculation of the weights given to the various items of the Indices of Retail Prices, as a source of consumers' expenditure data, and in the study of the redistributive effects of taxation and social benefits on the incomes of various types of households. Information from the survey indicates how the expenditure patterns of many different kinds of households vary. It throws light on the relationship between household income and circumstances of households, and the extent to which the various members contribute to the household income. Results are published in annual *Family Expenditure Survey Reports* which give a general account of the survey and full definitions of terms and classifications used. A separate publication *Family Expenditure Survey, Handbook on the Sample, Field Work, and Coding Procedures* gives a full description of these aspects of the survey.

The effect of any minor changes in survey methods and definitions made from time to time is described in the subsequent annual report. These sometimes affect comparisons between results for different years.

A *household* is defined as including all those who live at the same address, having meals prepared together and with common housekeeping. The members of a household thus defined are not necessarily related by blood or marriage. Resident domestic servants are included. As the survey covers only private households, people living in hostels,

---

[1] Some of the 1974 results and all 1975 results quoted in some tables are based on preliminary analysis and are subject to revision.

hotels, boarding houses, or institutions are excluded. Households are not excluded if some or all members are not British subjects, but no attempt is made to obtain records from households containing members of the diplomatic service of another country or of the United States armed forces.

Household income is used mainly for classification purposes and is the aggregate of the gross incomes of the individual members of the household before deduction of income tax, national insurance contributions, and any other deductions at source. Income as thus defined excludes money other than wages received by one member from another member of the household, proceeds from the sale of cars, furniture, or other capital assets, and receipts from legacies, maturing insurance policies, and windfalls. With the exceptions of imputed income from owner-occupied and from rent-free accommodation, and the value of meal vouchers, and of non-recurrent bills paid from outside the household, income in kind is also excluded.

Expenditure is defined as representing current expenditure on goods and services. It excludes savings or investments (eg purchase of national savings certificates or shares; life insurance premiums; contributions to pension funds). Income tax payments, national insurance contributions, and mortgage and other payments for purchase of, or major additions to, dwellings are also excluded.

A *child* was defined as a member of a household under 16 years of age to 1972. From 1973 a child is a member of a household who is under 18 years of age and unmarried.

A *worker* is a person who is gainfully employed as an employee or is an employer or is self-employed.

Retired or unoccupied persons are those other than workers.

Occupation. A classification by broad occupational group is used which is based on, but not completely identical with, the *Classification of Occupations, 1970.* The groups include professional and technical workers; administrative and managerial workers; teachers; clerical workers; shop assistants; manual workers; and members of H.M. Forces. If a person has several jobs, the most remunerative is used for classification.

SSRC Quality of Life Surveys

The Social Science Research Council Survey Unit carried out a pilot survey of 213 people in March 1971, and three full surveys of 593 people in November 1971, 966 people in October 1973, and 932 people in March 1975. People were asked their subjective feelings about various areas of their life, and their objective conditions were also recorded. The results of these surveys, and details of how they were carried out, are shown in the article by John Hall on page 47.

PROJECTIONS

Population projections

Each year the Government Actuary's Department in consultation with the Registrars General produces a set of population projections for the United Kingdom (by aggregating separate projections for England and Wales, Scotland, and Northern Ireland). The latest available estimate of total population is used as the base population. These projections are used as the basis of many other projections as well as being important in their own right.

The basic principle used in making these projections is that the population at a point in time is the population one year previously *plus* the number born in that annual period *less* the number of deaths *plus or minus* the net number of migrants. These four elements in the calculation must each be considered and the population subdivided into fairly homogeneous groups eg by age, sex, marital condition, or whatever combination is judged necessary. The fullest published account of the methods and assumptions is in the booklet *Population Projections 1974–2014* (HMSO).

Labour force projections

Projections of the labour force for Great Britain and the United Kingdom are prepared for males, married females, and non-married females. They are calculated by multiplying total population projections produced by the Government Actuary's Department by activity rates prepared by the Department of Employment.

Activity rate projections are based on past trends shown by activity rates of people classified as economically active in the *Census of Population.* For non-married females, the rates are obtained by combining separate projections for single females and widowed, and divorced females. For the age groups 16 to 24, for males and non-married females only, projections are based initially on activity rates including students, as these rates have remained reasonably stable over time; the projected numbers of students supplied by the Department of Education and Science are then subtracted from the labour force projections.

Formerly projections were prepared for the working population (for the distinction with economically active see: the notes under Employment). For a fuller description see *Department of Employment Gazette* April 1974 and December 1975.

Household projections (*see* note on page 237)

School population projections

The projections of the school population are based on the population projections prepared by the Government Actuary's Department in consultation with the Registrars General. They also include the following assumptions:

School leaving age. The statutory school leaving age was increased by one year to 16 in the educational year 1972–73. In England and Wales the first effect of this was that in January 1974 pupils whose 16th birthdays fell on or after 1st September 1973 were required to remain in school at least to Easter 1974.

Staying on beyond the statutory school leaving age. The proportions of children who stay on at school after the compulsory school age, which had been accelerating up to 1969, have since tended to slow down and in some cases there has actually been some decline. The projections of future numbers of 16–18 year olds in school assume a resumption of the pattern of a steady growth in the staying-on rates.

Pupils below the compulsory school age. The recent upward trend of the number of children in nursery classes and schools in the public sector is assumed to continue.

SOCIAL CLASS

Social and economic breakdowns of the population by social and/or economic factors may be made in a number of ways. Some of the methods used in official publications are detailed below. A detailed discussion was given in the *Social Commentary, Social Trends 6,* page 10.

Social class: Census definition

The following broad categories of social class are based on the unit groups of the Occupational Classification:

Class I		Professional and similar occupations
„	II	Intermediate occupations
„	III (N)	Skilled occupations (non-manual)
„	III (M)	Skilled occupations (manual)
„	IV	Partly skilled occupations
„	V	Unskilled occupations
NC		Not classified

The basic criterion used in selecting the occupations which make up each social class has been their general standing within the community. This criterion is associated with other factors such as education and economic environment, but it has no direct relationship to the average level of remuneration of particular occupations. Each occupational unit group has been assigned as a whole to a social class and no account taken of the standing of any specific individual. The allocation of occupations to the five groups has varied from census to census in accordance with changes in economic conditions so as to reflect prevailing attitudes towards status rather than literal continuity.

Social class: B.B.C. definition

Class A. Members of families in which the chief wage earner is a doctor, professor, clergyman, lawyer, architect; owner, director, senior executive of a large commercial or industrial organisation; senior civil servant; or high ranking industrial technician such as scientist or consulting engineer. This group covers about five per cent of the population.

Class B. Members of families in which the chief wage earner is a bank clerk, more senior office worker, teacher, small employer; manager or shopkeeper of larger shops; supervisor in a factory; professional worker not coming into class A. Class B covers about 25 per cent of the population.

Class C. The remaining 70 per cent of the population.

Socio-economic groups: Census definition

The socio-economic groups are intended to classify together people whose social, cultural, and recreational standards and behaviour are similar. In the absence of direct information on these subjects in the census, people have been allocated to socio-economic groups according to their employment status and occupation. The seventeen groups used in the 1961, 1966, and 1971 Censuses are based on the recommendations of the Conference of European Statisticians sponsored jointly by the Statistical Commission and Economic Commission for Europe (*European Programme for National Population Censuses*, Conf. Eur. Stats. WG.6/8 Geneva 1959). Full details of the allocation of combinations of occupation unit groups and employment status to the appropriate socio-economic group are given in *Classification of Occupations, 1970* published by HMSO.

Socio-economic class

Since the social class and socio-economic group classifications are not directly comparable, the latter was sub-divided in the 1971 Census to make this possible. The sub-divisions are referred to as socio-economic classes, and details are given in *Classification of Occupations 1970*, HMSO.

The *occupational classification* used in Chart 3.2 and other tables is a collapsed version of the General Household Survey socio-economic grouping (SEG). The collapsed categories are:

No.	SEG numbers	Definition
1	3, 4	Professional
2	1, 2, 13	Employers and managers
3	5, 6	Intermediate and junior non-manual
4	8, 9, 12, 14	Skilled manual (including foremen and supervisors) and own account non-professional
5	7, 10, 15	Semi-skilled manual and personal service
6	11	Unskilled manual

POPULATION

Population

Figures of population are given on two bases, *home* population and *total* population. The *home* population includes members of British, Commonwealth, and foreign armed forces in the United Kingdom. The *total* population includes members of H.M. Forces only, wherever stationed.

The mid-year estimates are based on the latest Census of Population prior to the mid-year concerned, with allowance for births, deaths, migration into and out of the country, and variation in the disposition of the armed forces since the Census was taken. No adjustment is made, however, for the purely temporary seasonal net increase in visitors to the country in the summer months.

The mid-year population estimates for 1971 to 1975 take account of the final results of the 1971 Census.

Population rates

Where statistics are expressed in terms of rates of the population, the figures used are usually the *home* population. In some cases, however, where it is conceptually more correct to do so, as in the section on public expenditure and that on personal income and expenditure, the figures used are those for the *total* population.

Births

Births are those registered or those occurring in each calendar year. For Scotland and Northern Ireland figures throughout are those registered. For England and Wales figures up to and including 1938 are for those registered and later figures are for those occurring in each year. Still-births are excluded.

Deaths

Deaths are those registered during the calendar year. Still births are excluded. They include those of members of the armed forces in the United Kingdom but exclude any which occur abroad. The crude death rate gives the total number of deaths as a ratio of the total population. Since age and the probability of death are related, the crude death rate and the age structure of the population are not independent. To compare the general level of mortality over time, or between areas, age standardised rates or the expectation of life may be used.

Cohort

A cohort in these tables is a group of persons born or married in a particular period.

Divorce

The grounds for divorce in England and Wales were altered by the Divorce Reform Act 1969, which came into effect on 1 January 1971. From this date divorce could be granted for irretrievable breakdown of marriage including separation after two years with the consent of both parties or after five years separation. The decree nisi is granted by the court at the time of the hearing, and normally becomes absolute after 6 weeks. From the date that the decree is made absolute, the parties are free to give notice of re-marriage. The law in Scotland will not change until the coming into effect of the Divorce Reform Act (Scotland) 1976.

Citizenship

This refers to the passport held at the time of entering or leaving the country. Some persons who entered on foreign passports, an increasing number who entered on Commonwealth passports, and all born in the Republic of Ireland could later emigrate on United Kingdom passports.

New Commonwealth and Pakistani ethnic origin: persons born in the New Commonwealth and Pakistan who are not of UK descent, plus children born in Great Britain to parents of NCW and Pakistani ethnic origin, including children with only one such parent.

International Passenger Survey

From 1964, information about migrants has been gathered from the International Passenger Survey which is made up of a stratified random sample of passengers entering or leaving Great Britain (excluding journeys to and from the Irish Republic and Northern Ireland). The survey gathers information on a continuous basis, not only on migration but also on tourism.

The coverage of the sample varies. More attention is paid to long route passengers, both air and sea, of whom normally about 4 per cent are interviewed. The corresponding figure for short route travellers is about 1 per cent. Because of the volume of peak traffic in the summer months and the difficult circumstances in which interviews have to be conducted (eg on cross-channel ferries), the sampling fraction may vary between 7 per cent and 0·3 per cent. In 1975 from a total passenger traffic in both directions of approximately $42\frac{1}{2}$ million, a sample of about 271 thousand were interviewed, of which the migration element was $7\frac{1}{4}$

thousand. The survey defines an immigrant as a passenger who declares an intention to stay in the United Kingdom for an unbroken period of 12 months or more, having resided outside the United Kingdom for a year or more (and vice-versa for an emigrant).

HOUSEHOLDS
Private households
The definition of a private household in this section and in the housing section relates to that used in the 1961. 1966, and 1971 Censuses of Population. The definition used in the section on personal income and expenditure is d fferent and is based on the Family Expenditure Survey.

In the Census a private household is defined as—

Any group of persons, whether related or not, who live together and benefit from a common housekeeping; or Any person living alone who is responsible for providing his or her own meals.

A person living but not taking meals with a private house-hold is treated as a separate household, but if that person has at least one meal a day with the household he is re-garded as part of that household. Breakfast counts as a meal for this purpose.

A household has to have at least one room. Two or more people living in one room are regarded as one household regardless of whether or not they have their meals together or share a common housekeeping.

Household projections
In Table 2.3, various different types of households or families are mentioned. The definitions are:

Married couple households
All households headed by a married couple. Only a married man can head this type of household.

Lone parent households
Households headed by a lone parent living with one or more never-married children of any age.

One-person households
All one-person households, whether sharing a dwelling or not.

Other households
Brothers, sisters, or unrelated people living together, or a lone parent living with a child who is or has been married.

Married couple families
All families headed by a married couple whether or not they form separate households. This category therefore includes all married couple households. Only a married man can head a married couple family.

Lone parent families
A lone parent living with one or more never-married children, whether or not the lone parent heads a household. This category therefore includes all lone parent households.

Numbers of households in the above six categories are calculated by the use of headship rates. Numbers in the following category are derived directly from the total projected number of one-person households. All figures have been derived from the 1973-based (with migration) population projections, using head-ship rates projected from 1961, 1966, and 1971 Census data.

One-person potential households
All one-person households apart from a proportion of those sharing a dwelling.

Census-type households: These include Married couple households; Lone parent households; One-person house-holds; Other households.

Potential households: These include Married couple families; Lone parent households; One-person potential households; and Other households.

Family
A family is a married couple, alone or with the r never married child or children (of any age). A family may also be a lone parent with his/her never married child or children. A lone parent is a married parent whose spouse does not reside in the same household; or any single, widowed, or divorced parent. This term 'child' also includes step-child or adopted child (but not foster child) and also a grandchild (without parents) or great grandchild (without parents or grandparents).

Child
As described in the note above the term child has a rather special meaning in the household or family context. The more usual definition is that for a dependent child.

Dependent child
In the 1966 and 1971 Censuses dependent children are defined as children in families who are either under 15 years of age or are between 15 and 24 years and classified as a student (that is, a person who would be in full-time attendance at an educational establishment in the term following the Census). Only never-married children in families are included.

In the 1961 Census dependent children are defined as all children under 15 years of age and all students of 15 years and over, whether in families or not. Students of any age. married or single, who are living alone or with other students are still classified as dependent children.

Children in care
The Children Act 1948 created a separate local authority child care service to care for children who for one reason or another are deprived of a normal home life, either per-manently or for a comparatively short period, for example during some family crisis. Under the Local Authority Social Services Act 1970 these functions were taken over by the newly formed social services departments.

Under the Children and Young Persons Acts 1933 to 1969, local authorities are responsible for children committed to their care or placed under their supervision by the courts. The Children and Young Persons Act 1963 also made it an express duty of local authorities to develop preventive work designed to reduce the need to take children into care or bring them before a court. The authorities have other responsibilities, for example, in connection with adoption and private fostering.

The Children and Young Persons Act 1969 provided for the replacement of the former fit person and approved school orders by care orders committing to the care of the local authority; and for the integration of the former separate children's homes, approved schools, and remand homes into a comprehensive system of community homes organ-ised on a regional basis and managed by local authorities or by voluntary organisations in collaboration with local authorities.

Remand homes were provided by local authorities and were designed in the main for the temporary accommoda-tion of children or young people who were appearing before the courts, during intervals in court proceedings. Before the coming into force of the Children and Young Persons Act 1969, children were remanded directly to these homes by the courts, but they are now remanded to the care of the local authorities. Remand homes have been integrated into the community home system.

Approved schools were designed for the accommodation of children and young people committed to them by the courts under approved school orders. These orders have now been replaced by committal to the care of a local authority, and the approved schools have also been integrated into the community home system. The schools are provided and managed by local authorities, religious bodies, or voluntary organisations.

Child health centres
Child welfare centres are provided by Health Boards to give a preventive and advisory service. They offer medical supervision to expectant and nursing mothers and young children (eg vaccination, dental services). Medical staff

carry out educational work with parents and give mothers advice on practical subjects such as child care.

Day nurseries, registered nurseries, and child minders

Some local authorities provide day nurseries for children under 5 who have special health or social needs, for example if their mother is the breadwinner or because they come from bad home conditions. Local authorities are also obliged under the Nurseries and Child Minders Regulations Act to keep a register of persons who, in their own homes and for reward, mind 3 or more children under 5, and of premises where children are received to be looked after. They have power to impose specified requirements as a condition of registration and power to inspect premises. A proportion of registered child minders are in fact self-help groups or voluntary bodies providing play groups.

The children's hearings system (Scotland)

Part III of the Social Work (Scotland) Act 1968 was brought into operation on 15 April 1971. The system of children's hearings replaced the former juvenile courts, though children could still be prosecuted in the Sheriff Court or the Court of Session in specified circumstances.

Elderly

The Elderly are defined as those people over the normal retirement age, which is 65 for men and 60 for women.

Residential accommodation

Local authorities have a duty to provide residential accommodation for people who, because of age, infirmity, or other circumstances, are in need of care and attention which is not otherwise available to them. An authority may arrange for a person to be accommodated in premises managed by another authority, and contributions can be made to the funds of any voluntary organisation providing such accommodation.

Home helps

Local authorities can provide domestic help for households requiring it owing to the presence of any person who is ill, lying-in, an expectant mother, aged, or is a child not over compulsory school age. They may make charges for these services depending on the means of the recipient.

'Meals on wheels'

Local authorities can provide meals at home for those who are house-bound or have difficulty in shopping, and in lunch clubs for those who are able to get about.

EDUCATION

A great deal of time and attention has been given over the past few years to bring common definitions and classifications into general educational use. A detailed subject classification system has, for instance, been set up and adopted by a number of educational bodies and now forms the basis of their published statistics. But despite a growing uniformity of treatment there is still some way to go before all the problems have been satisfactorily resolved even within government departments themselves. The statistics appearing in this section of the publication follow the definitions and classifications currently in use in the educational departments.

Main categories of educational establishment

Educational establishments in the United Kingdom may be administered and financed in one of three different ways:

Public sector: by local education authorities, which form part of the structure of local government.

Assisted: by governing bodies which have a substantial degree of autonomy from public authorities but which receive grants direct from central government sources.

Independent: by the private sector, including individuals, companies, and charitable institutions.

Stages of education

There are three stages of education: primary (including nursery), secondary, and further (including higher) education. The first two stages are compulsory for all children between the ages of five and sixteen years (fifteen before 1972/73); and the transition from primary to secondary education is usually made between ten and a half and twelve years. The third stage of education is voluntary and includes all education provided after full-time schooling ends.

Primary education

Primary education includes three age ranges: nursery, under five years of age; infant, five to seven or eight years; and junior, seven or eight to eleven or twelve years. The great majority of public sector primary schools take both boys and girls in mixed classes. In Scotland the distinction between infant and primary schools is generally not made.

Middle schools

In England and Wales middle schools take children from first schools and generally lead on, in turn, to comprehensive upper schools. They cover varying age ranges between 8 and 14. Depending on their individual age range they are deemed either primary or secondary by Order of the Secretary of State for Education and Science or (for age range 9 to 13) by choice of the Local Education Authority. Scotland has only two middle schools.

Secondary education

Provision of secondary education in an area may include any combination of types of schools. The pattern is a reflection of historical circumstance and of the policy adopted by the local education authority. There is a growing trend to comprehensive schools, on a variety of patterns as to forms of organisation and the age range of the pupils attending. In their 'pure' form, comprehensive schools admit pupils without reference to ability and aptitude, and cater for all the children in a neighbourhood; but many co-exist with selective schools for pupils of the highest academic attainment and thus under-represent the ablest sector of the age group. In some areas there still persists the post-1944 pattern of selective 'grammar' schools and non-selective 'secondary modern' schools. The number of technical schools is small and decreasing. Scotland has some schools which are part comprehensive/part selective.

Special schools, either day or boarding, provide education exclusively for children who are so seriously handicapped, physically or mentally, that they cannot profit fully from education in normal schools.

Higher education

The term 'higher education' as used in this section (Table 3.14) includes all students in universities and colleges of education together with students in further education colleges on courses leading to advanced level qualifications, ie qualifications above General Certificate of Education 'A' levels, Scottish Certificate of Education 'H' grade, and Ordinary National Diploma or Ordinary National Certificate.

Further education

The term 'further education' may be used in a general sense to cover all education after the period of compulsory education. More commonly it excludes those staying on at secondary school and those studying at universities or colleges of education (teacher training). It is in this latter sense that it is used in this section. The figures in Table 3.13 cover only public sector and assisted establishments and exclude throughout Colleges of Advanced Technology and Scottish central institutions which have obtained university status. Those in Table 3.14 on higher education are confined to students on courses leading to advanced level qualifications.

Class size

From January 1970 information about registered classes was collected only from primary schools (excluding middle deemed primary). These figures do not represent the size of classes as taught, which may include relatively large assemblies for some purposes (eg physical education or music) and much smaller groups for others (eg remedial teaching). The average size of taught classes is substantially below the registered size. For secondary schools classes or groups of pupils being taught together at a particular point in the school timetable are used. This information has been obtained from each school for a selected period on the day of enumeration (in January); for this purpose, in England and Wales secondary schools were sub-divided into five groups of equal size, and these groups made returns in respect of the 1st, 3rd, 4th, 5th, and last periods of the day respectively; for Scotland and Northern Ireland the class size refers to the 3rd period on the day of enumeration.

At any period in the timetable, a proportion of these groups will be found to be of a particularly large size. Such groups are usually assembled for special purposes (physical education, religious instruction, choir practice, etc.).

School leaving qualifications

In England and Wales, the two main examinations for older school pupils are the Certificate of Secondary Education (CSE) and the General Certificate of Education (GCE). The GCE is available at Ordinary ('O') and Advanced ('A') levels. The CSE is usually taken at 16 and is available in a very wide range of subjects. Each entry is awarded a Grade (1 to 5, with Grade 1 considered the equivalent of an 'O' level pass) or is ungraded. GCE 'O' level is also usually taken at 16.

At age 18 a more advanced stage, GCE Advanced ('A') level, may be taken by, for example, those wishing to enter higher education. At the 'A' level stage the pupil is usually specialising in a few selected subjects. There are 5 'pass' grades.

In Scotland there is no counterpart to the first type of examination (ie the CSE in England and Wales). The counterpart to the GCE examination is the Scottish Certificate of Education (SCE). The SCE Ordinary ('O') grade course leads to an examination of approximately equivalent standard to the GCE 'O' level) at the end of the fourth year of secondary schooling, which in Scotland, starts at age 12. From the 1973 examination, results, in a wide range of subjects, are awarded in a 5-band, A–E structure, awards in bands A–C corresponding in essence to what were previously rated passes. The examination on the higher ('H') grade requires, basically, one further year of study and may be taken at the end of the fifth or sixth year. For the better 'H' grade candidates the range of subjects covered may be almost as wide as on the 'O' grade – it is not unusual for candidates to study five or six subjects spanning both arts and science. The breadth of study inevitably means that an individual subject in the 'H' grade course is not taken to the same depth as the more specialised GCE 'A' level course.

The first CSE examinations were held in Northern Ireland in 1973. The Northern Ireland GCE, which is equivalent to that of England and Wales, has the same 'O' and 'A' levels normally taken at ages 16 and 18 respectively.

Passes in GCE or SCE examinations provide the normal minimum entry requirements for the majority of courses in further and higher education. Two GCE Advanced level passes together with appropriate passes at GCE Ordinary level are usually regarded as the minimum qualification necessary for starting a university education, but the conditions of entry to particular courses vary and depend, in part, on the balance of supply and demand for places. Where competition is strong, correspondingly strong candidates will be chosen by the universities. On the other hand, for some courses fewer candidates are forthcoming and those having lower academic qualifications may be admitted.

As already mentioned, the GCE examination at the Ordinary level and the SCE examination at the Ordinary grade are of approximately equivalent standard. Moreover, on the basis of qualifications which are accepted as the minimum for entry to degree level courses in higher education, it is reasonable and convenient to equate two GCE 'A' levels and three SCE 'H' grade passes.

General Household Survey

Highest educational qualifications are equivalent to Census levels a, b, and c – ie degrees/university or college diplomas or certificates/professional qualifications – above GCE 'A' level standard.

Other educational qualifications are all other qualifications of GCE 'A' level standard or below, including apprenticeships and foreign qualifications.

The Open University

The Open University provides part-time degree courses by means of broadcasts, correspondence, tutorials at local study centres, and summer schools. No formal entrance qualifications are required and it is possible to obtain a degree in four to six years although some students, with exemptions for previous study, do graduate in as little as 2 years. The first courses were offered in January 1971 and the first students graduated in 1972. The number of students is usually quoted in two parts, *finally registered new students*, ie first year students who are still studying two months after the start of the course (when there is a high drop-out rate), and *continuing students*, ie those who have completed their first year and go on to further study. Many students never graduate, or take a very long time to do so.

University students

Numbers: In 1965/66 a change was made in the basis on which student numbers in university institutions were measured. Since that year the student population has been measured by reference to the number of registered students at the end of the autumn term; only those students effective in the university at that date are included. Returns from the universities for previous years gave overall numbers for each academic year as assessed at the end of the academic year. This led to an apparent fall in part-time student numbers in 1965/66.

Coverage: It should be noted that degrees are not only awarded to university students. Tables do not include degrees awarded by London University to external students, degrees awarded by universities to students working through other institutions, eg polytechnics, B.Ed. degrees awarded to students at colleges of education, Council for National Academic Awards (CNAA) degrees, and Open University degrees.

EMPLOYMENT

Estimates of economically active population and working population

The two estimates of economically active population as published in the Census of Population and the total working population as published by the Department of Employment are compiled on different bases. The main differences are summarised below.

Economically active: Census definition

This is defined as those persons aged 15 and over who were in employment at any time during the week before the Census day together with those who were out of employment during that week but who were intending to get work. *In employment* means having a job or being self-employed. Temporary, part-time, or casual employment are included. Persons absent from their employment due to holidays, strikes, lock-outs, short-time working, or temporary stoppage are regarded as in employment. Persons off work due to sickness are regarded as in employment if their jobs are waiting for them on return. All students are excluded whether or not they worked in the week before the Census. *Out of Employment* means seeking work, prevented from seeking work by temporary sickness, or having obtained an appointment which has not yet been taken up.

Economically inactive: Census definition

Retired means wholly retired from employment and no longer seeking paid work. Married women engaged on unpaid home duties are not regarded as retired but treated as *others economically inactive.*

Students are persons in full-time attendance or about to commence full-time attendance next term at an educational establishment, irrespective of whether or not they have part-time or seasonal employment.

Other persons economically inactive includes all others not in employment and not seeking it. Persons of independent means, engaged entirely in unpaid domestic duties, or unable to work because of disability, and the permanently sick are included. Also included are housewives and women employed on unpaid domestic duties even though they may have had paid work at some time.

Working population: Department of Employment definition

The working population includes employees in employment, the registered unemployed, employers and self-employed persons, and members of HM Forces (both at home and overseas).

From 1971 the employees in employment estimates are based on an annual census of employment taken in June each year which excludes private domestic servants and civil servants temporarily stationed outside the United Kingdom.

For the years before 1971, estimates of employees in employment are taken from the continuous employment series which was published in the March 1975 issue of the *Department of Employment Gazette.* This continuous series removed discontinuities which occurred in previously published series.

The unemployed

The figures relate to persons who on the day of the monthly count are registered for employment at local employment offices of the Employment Service Agency or careers offices of the local education authorities and who on that day have no job and are capable of and available for work. They exclude adult students (aged over 18) registered for temporary employment during the vacation, at the end of which they intend to continue in full-time education. Unemployed school leavers (aged under 18) who have not been in insured employment since terminating full-time education are included. The figures do not include temporarily stopped workers (that is those who are suspended from work by their employer but expect to resume work with the same employer and are regarded as still having a job), nor severely disabled persons considered unlikely to obtain work other than under special conditions.

PEP Survey of racial minorities, 1974 (Table 4.25)

This survey was very complex both technically and administratively and involved the development of new techniques, particularly in the field of sampling. The group from which the sample was drawn covered adults (aged 16 or over) who were black or brown by race and whose families originated from the West Indies, India, Pakistan, or Bangladesh. People of mixed race and people born in this country if their family originally came from those four countries were included. Black Africans and Asians not originating from the Indian sub-continent (eg Chinese and Japanese) were excluded.

Scotland was excluded from the Survey because negligible numbers of Asians and West Indians live there.

The enumeration was carried out in January, February, and March 1974, during which time 40,000 households were contacted; the main fieldwork was carried out between May and December 1974.

At the same time a survey of the white male population of England and Wales aged 16 or over was carried out for comparison. This was not a straightforward survey, but the results were weighted. Full details are given on page 7 of the survey report: *The facts of racial disadvantage: a national survey*, D J Smith, Political and Economic Planning.

PERSONAL INCOME AND WEALTH

The personal sector (excluding private non-profit-making bodies) is a subsector of the personal sector as defined in the national accounts. It includes households, individuals living in institutions, unincorporated private businesses, private trusts, and life assurance funds. More information is shown in the Blue Book *National Income and Expenditure 1965–75*, including a reconciliation with the distribution of income tables. Details of the methods used to subdivide the personal sector, and the statistical sources, are given in an article in *Economic Trends*, May 1975. The definitions of the items are given in the Blue Book, and in more detail in *National Accounts Statistics: Sources and Methods*, HMSO, 1968.

Real personal disposable income

Personal disposable income is equal to the total current income of the personal sector less payments of UK taxes on income, national insurance contributions, transfers abroad, and taxes paid abroad. It is revalued at constant prices by the deflator implied by estimates of total consumers' expenditure at current and constant prices.

Survey of Personal Incomes

Table 5.5 is derived from the Survey of Personal Incomes carried out by the Inland Revenue Department. The survey covers all personal incomes reviewed for tax purposes including those found to be not liable to tax through the operation of tax allowances. The table, however, only includes incomes above a level which for each year corresponds approximately to the effective exemption limit for single persons whose income is wholly earned. Incomes below these levels are not shown because information about them is incomplete especially in the PAYE field.

The levels below which incomes are excluded were:

	£ pa
1949–50	135
1954–55	155
1959–60	180
1964–65	275
1969–70	330
1970–71	420
1971–72	420
1972–73	595
1973–74	595
1974–75	625

The income shown is as computed for tax purposes. Those types of income that are specifically exempt from tax, eg small amounts of Savings Bank interest (under £15 up to 1970–71; under £21 for 1971–72 to 1973–74 inclusive;

under £40 for 1974–75 onwards), certain National Insurance benefits, etc., are excluded.

Table 5.5 shows the sources of total income. This table differs from Table 5.1 which relates to the whole of the personal sector as defined in the National Accounts, but excluding non-profit-making bodies serving persons. Table 5.1 includes the types of income mentioned above as being not liable to tax, and the incomes of those whose incomes are below the limits mentioned above. Table 5.5 relates to individuals. It does not include the income of non-profit-making bodies serving persons, but does include incomes paid by these bodies to individuals, eg pensions paid by superannuation funds. Such pensions are not included in Table 5.1.

'Total income' is taxable income (before tax) from all sources before deduction of interest payments or other tax reliefs or allowances except as detailed in the descriptions of the components of income given below.

'Profits and professional earnings' are shown after deduction of capital allowances and losses. In general the figures relate to profits earned in accounting periods ending in the year before the income tax year shown at the head of the column.

'Employment Income' is shown after deduction of expenses but, in the years up to and including 1971–72, before deduction of employees' superannuation contributions. The spread in recent years of arrangements whereby employers deduct contributions before determining tax under PAYE has caused the estimate of the amount of employment income to become less accurate. For 1972–73, only the amount after deduction of superannuation contributions is known.

'Pensions' include National Insurance retirement and widows' pensions and pensions from occupational pension schemes.

'Investment income' includes all income that is not treated as earned income for income tax purposes. Up to 1959–60, the imputed income from owner-occupied houses was included. Such income however ceased to be chargeable with income tax from 1963–64 onwards. Income tax at the composite rate on interest paid by Building Societies is included from 1969–70 onwards.

Household incomes

Information on household income is derived from the *Family Expenditure Survey* which is described more fully on page 235.

Redistribution of income

Estimates of the incidence of taxes and benefits on households of different types and in different income groups, based on the Family Expenditure Survey, are published by the Central Statistical Office in *Economic Trends*. The most recent article, covering 1974, appears in the issue for February 1976, and contains details of the definitions and methods used. The notes below summarise some of the more important items.

Benefits include both those in cash (eg family allowances) and those in kind (eg education, national health).

Direct taxes include employees' national insurance contributions as well as income tax and surtax. Prior to 1969 employers' insurance contributions were also included.

Indirect taxes include those on both final and intermediate goods and services. Since 1969, indirect taxes on intermediate goods and services have included employers' contributions to national insurance and national health services, as well as the selective employment tax.

Original income is the sum of the incomes in cash and kind (as measured in the Survey) of all members of the household before the deduction of all taxes and before the addition of State benefits. Thus original income differs from the term *gross income* as used in the Family Expenditure Survey, since the latter includes national insurance and other cash benefits and excludes most forms of income in kind.

The changes, as from 1969, in the treatment of employers' contributions to national insurance and national health services affect both original income and income after all taxes and benefits. For households which include no employees, original income is unaffected; for other households, original income is lower than on the old definition. The consequential effect on income after all taxes and benefits is, in general, smaller because only part of the employers' contribution is included in indirect taxes on consumers' expenditure, the rest falling on government expenditure, investment and exports.

New Earnings Survey

The New Earnings Survey is an annual survey of the earnings of employees in Great Britain carried out by the Department of Employment under the Statistics of Trade Act, 1947. A separate similar survey is made in Northern Ireland. Information on earnings and hours for a reference pay-period in April and other characteristics of individual employees in a random sample is obtained from their employers. Resulting analyses of the levels, distributions, and make-up of earnings in the major wage-negotiation groups and the various occupational, industrial, age, and regional groups in April and changes since the previous April are the main objectives of the survey, but information on other topics such as holidays with pay, membership of pension schemes and sick-pay schemes, and vocational training has been obtained from the survey.

The results are based on returns for about 170,000 employees each year; returns for about three-quarters of these – known as a matched sample – were also received in the previous survey. The matched sample is used for deriving estimates of increases in average earnings since the previous April. The detailed analyses on earnings concentrate on full-time men aged 21 and over and full-time and part-time women aged 18 and over excluding those whose pay for the reference pay-period was affected by absence or related to employment for only part of the period; but younger employees are covered in analyses of earnings by age.

The *List of Key Occupations for Statistical Purposes* (KOS) is used for classifying employees by occupation. Manual and non-manual employees are generally distinguished in the results. Some results for counties, Scottish regions, and Greater London boroughs are obtained.

Results are published in an annual volume *New Earnings Survey*. This is now issued in six parts, but, up to 1973, was a single volume. Only streamlined and summary analyses of earnings and hours are published regularly in the *Department of Employment Gazette* (October or November issue); up to 1973 many detailed analyses were published in the Gazette in the first instance. Occasional articles on special topics, such as holidays with pay, are published in the Gazette.

The *earnings* comprise all payments for the particular period, regardless of when they were paid, and so may include an appropriate share of annual and other bonuses. They are gross, before PAYE, national insurance, superannuation, or other deductions. They exclude the value of benefits in kind; exceptionally for agricultural, catering, and other workers whose employers provide accommodation, meals, etc., for which reckonable values for pay purposes are laid down in wages regulation orders, these amounts are included. Gratuities and tips received by the employee but not shown in the employer's pay records are not reported. The earnings relate to a particular job with a particular employer and so will be less than the total income from employment if the individual has more than one source of such income.

The *components of earnings* which are separately identified are (i) overtime pay, (ii) payments-by-results, bonuses, commission and other incentive payments, (iii) premium payments for shift, night and weekend work, (iv) all other payments, which generally include basic pay and miscellaneous allowances.

The employee's *normal weekly basic hours*, if specified, are reported – in other cases the employer reports whether the employee is regarded as full-time or part-time. *Overtime hours* for which overtime pay was paid are also reported for the reference period; these combined with normal basic hours are described as *total hours,* for employees whose pay for the period was not affected by absence. They exclude main meal breaks but may differ from hours actually worked if either there were unpaid overtime hours or the employee was paid under guaranteed week and overtime schemes, for example, for some hours not actually worked.

Department of Employment October Earnings Enquiry

This source was used to provide the basis of the earnings data in Table 5.21. The enquiry is made in October only and includes returns furnished on a voluntary basis for about 40,000 establishments employing over 5 million manual workers. The information relates to manual workers at work during the whole or part of 1 pay week in October. Full details and analyses are given in articles in the Department of Employment Gazette, of which the most recent was published in February 1976.

National insurance benefits

Entitlement to national insurance benefits depends, among other things, upon specified contribution conditions being satisfied. The general scheme provides flat-rate benefits for unemployment, sickness, injury, maternity, retirement, widowhood, death, and orphanhood. In addition to flat-rate unemployment and sickness benefits and widow's allowance, an earnings related supplement may be payable.

This is paid to any person who is under the age of 65 (60 years for a woman), is entitled to flat-rate sickness or unemployment benefit, and has reckonable earnings of £450 a year or more in the relevant tax year. The supplement was one-third of average weekly earnings between £9 and £30 for supplements based on earnings in tax years up to 1971–72; for supplements based on earnings in the 1972–73 tax year they were one-third of average weekly earnings between £10 and £30, plus 15 per cent between £30 and £42, for supplements based on earnings in 1973–74 tax year they were one-third of average weekly earnings between £10 and £30 plus 15 per cent between £30 and £48, and for supplements based on earnings in the 1974–75 tax year they were one-third of average weekly earnings between £10 and £30 plus 15 per cent between £30 and £54. The supplement is subject to a maximum total benefit of 85 per cent of average weekly earnings. It is payable after 12 waiting days for up to 156 days (six months excluding Sundays), unemployment, sickness and injury benefit and maternity allowance being aggregated for this purpose.

For the purposes of the National Insurance Act the insured population is divided into three classes. These are: employed (class 1), self-employed (class 2) and non-employed (class 3). In general only employed persons are insurable under the Industrial Injuries Act. Persons in each of the three classes – and their employers in the case of those in class 1 – are generally liable to pay weekly flat-rate contributions.

Unemployment benefit

Class 1 contributors can qualify for unemployment benefit when out of work. To be entitled a claimant must be unemployed, capable of and available for employment, and free from certain grounds for disqualification or disallowance. Flat-rate benefit is payable for a year.

Sickness benefit

Class 1 and class 2 contributors may qualify for flat-rate sickness benefit. To be entitled, a claimant must show he is incapable of work by reason of some specific disease or bodily or mental disablement. He usually does this by submitting medical certificates obtained from his doctor. The benefit is normally replaced by invalidity benefit after 168 days. People who do not qualify for invalidity benefit may continue to receive sickness benefit for up to 312 days (a year excluding Sundays) in any period of interruption of employment.

Invalidity benefit (Introduction with effect from 23 September 1971).

People who have paid at least 156 contributions as employed persons (class 1) or self-employed persons (class 2) qualify for invalidity pension if their incapacity continues after they have been entitled to sickness benefit for 168 days in any period of interruption of employment. As with sickness benefit, claims are supported by evidence of incapacity for work. Invalidity allowance may be paid in addition to the pension at one of three weekly rates according to the claimant's age when incapacity began.

Retirement pension

Retirement pensions are payable on retirement from regular work provided that pension age (65 for men, 60 for women) has been reached and that the necessary conditions are satisfied. Increments to flat-rate pension are earned where retirement is deferred after pension age. After age 70 (65 for a woman) retirement pension can be paid whether a person has retired or not. A married woman can receive a pension on her husband's insurance, or on her own insurance if she is separately insured, whichever is more favourable. In addition to the flat-rate pension, graduated pension may also be payable according to the graduated contributions paid. In 1970 old persons' pensions were introduced for men aged 87 and women aged 82, who were too old to become insured under the national insurance scheme when it began in 1948. In 1971 these pensions were extended to people over age 80.

Widow's benefits

A benefit, known as widow's allowance, is payable for the first 26 weeks of widowhood. Thereafter, payment of widow's benefit depends on individual circumstances such as children and age. The various benefits are as follows:

Widowed mother's allowance: Payable so long as the widow has a son or daughter under 19 living with her or dependent upon her.

Widow's pension: Payable to a widow who does not qualify for widowed mother's allowance but who was over 40 when her husband died. If she is between age 40 and 50 a reduced rate is payable. The pension is also paid to a widow who is over 40 when her widowed mother's allowance ends, a reduced rate being payable if she is between age 40 and 50.

Widow's basic pension: This pension is paid to women who do not qualify for widowed mother's allowance or widow's pension but who were married before 5 July 1948 to men insured immediately before that date under the old Contributory Pensions Act.

Guardian's allowance

A benefit paid in respect of children whose parents are dead. Special rules apply to adopted children, to illegitimate children, to children of divorced parents and to children one of whose parents is dead and the other serving a long period of imprisonment.

Child's special allowance

An allowance which a divorced woman with a child may qualify for on her former husband's death if he had been contributing towards the child's maintenance.

Injury benefit

A flat-rate weekly benefit paid for a maximum period of six months to persons incapable of work as a result of an industrial injury or prescribed disease.

Industrial injuries disablement benefit

A long-term benefit paid for disablement due to an industrial injury or disease. It normally follows a period of injury benefit. Depending on a medical assessment of the degree of disablement the basic benefit takes the form of either a pension or a lump sum gratuity.

Family allowances

Family allowance is payable to a family with two or more children below the age limits. The basic age limit is the upper limit of compulsory school age which was 15 and is now 16. For a child continuing at school or college, or a child who is an apprentice with low earnings, the age limit is extended to 19. Family allowance is a non-contributory benefit. From 8 April 1975 the rates payable per week were £1.50 for the second and each subsequent child. Thus, for example, a family with only one child under sixteen and with other children at work would not receive family allowances.

Family income supplement (introduced with effect from 3 August 1971)

Family Income Supplement is a non-contributory benefit administered by the Supplementary Benefits Commission which is payable to a family with one or more children if the normal gross weekly income of the family is less than the amount prescribed, and if the head of the family is in full-time remunerative work and is normally so. It can be paid to a family with two parents or with one parent and in the case of a couple it is the man who must be in full-time work.

Supplementary benefit

Supplementary benefit can be claimed by a person aged 16 or over who is in Great Britain and is not in full-time work if his resources, if any, are less than his requirements. Broadly, the amount of benefit payable is the amount needed to bring a claimant's resources up to his requirement. On the resources side of the sum, certain income and capital is not taken into account ("disregarded") wholly or in part, and an income is attributed to other capital according to a prescribed "tariff". On the other side, requirements comprise the scale rates for the claimant and his dependants and an allowance for rent. The amount so assessed may be modified where there are exceptional circumstances.

Weekly rates of principal benefits

The standard rates of national insurance benefits introduced in November 1975 are, for retirement pension, widow's pension and invalidity benefit, £13.30 for a single person, with increases of £7.90 for one adult dependant, £6.50 for the first child, and £5.00 for each subsequent child. An invalidity allowance of 85p, which rises to £2.80 if the incapacity begins before age 35, is payable in addition to invalidity benefit. For unemployment or sickness benefit the standard rate is £11.10 for a single person, £6.90 for one adult dependant, £3.50 for the first child, and £2.00 for each subsequent child. Family allowances are £1.50 for the second and each subsequent child. The 100 per cent rate for industrial disablement benefit is £21.80, and the injury benefit is £13.85. Weekly rate of supplementary benefits are given in the following table:

Scale rates at November 1975 (£)

	Ordinary	Long-term	
		Claimant and wife aged less than 80	Claimant or wife aged 80 or over
Married couple	17·75	21·55	21·80
Single householder	10·90	13·70	13·95
Any other person aged:			
18 or over	8·70	11·00	11·25
16–17	6·70		
13–15	5·60		
11–12	4·60		
5–10	3·75		
Under 5	3·10		

These are scale rates for requirements, as prescribed by the Supplementary Benefit Act 1966, as amended. Special rates are provided for blind people aged 16 and over.

Long-term scale rate

A sum added to the requirements of:

i. People who are entitled to a supplementary pension, (ie those over pensionable age unless they are in hospital or local authority residential accommodation) and

ii. People who have received a supplementary allowance for a continuous period of 2 years, and whose allowance is not, and was not at any time during that period, subject to the condition of registration for employment.

Attendance allowance

Attendance allowance is a non-contributory benefit which is payable to a person who is severely disabled, physically or mentally, and requires frequent attention or continual supervision. There are tests for residence and presence in Great Britain. Claims are assessed by the Attendance Allowance Board.

Families

The definition of the family used in the tables in this section in Tables 5.28, 5.29, 5.30 and 5.31 differs substantially from that used in the Population and Households sections. As defined here, a family consists of a single person or couple, with or without dependent children under 19, living in the same private household, who would be treated as a single unit for Supplementary Benefit assessment. A child is defined as being either under 16 years of age, or 16 but under 19 and undergoing full-time education. Non-dependent children are counted as separate families under this definition.

In Table 5.31, under the heading 'married couples', 'Families over pension age' refers to married couples where the husband is aged 65 or over. Under the heading 'single persons', 'Families over pension age' refers to men aged 65 or over, or to women aged 60 or over.

Personal wealth

The official estimates of the wealth of individuals are derived from estate duty statistics. They are subject to fairly wide margins of error and are in some respects incomplete. The method of estimation involves applying the reciprocals of the population's death rates for the various country, sex, and age groups to the statistics of estates on which duty was paid or for which grants of representation were issued in the financial year ending three months later. This method assumes, amongst other things, that the estates passing on death are a representative sample both in number and value of the property of individuals.

Assets are valued at current market prices, except for life assurance policies which are valued at the sum assured *plus* bonuses. Their surrender values are usually much less. The estimates cover about 90 per cent of all wealth held by individuals. The major omissions are:

(a) Surviving spouse settlements and accumulating trusts;

(b) Much of the capital held in discretionary trusts, particularly for years before 1969;

(c) many small holdings of certain assets such as National Savings Certificates, small amounts of which can be transferred on death without formalities; and

(d) gifts, joint property, and property settled by the deceased where their total value together with the free estate does not exceed the point at which duty becomes payable.

On the other hand, as life assurance policies are included at their insured value, their value in the hands of the living is overestimated.

During 1965 the amount transferable without formality of such assets as National Savings Certificates was increased to £500 from, in most cases, £100. After 1964 therefore a smaller proportion of estates was covered by the estate duty statistics than in earlier years and this is reflected in a decrease in the percentages in the range *not over £1,000*.

A fuller account of the method of estimation and the scope of the estimates is given in *Inland Revenue Statistics 1975*.

The Gini coefficient has been mentioned in the introduction to this section (page 126) and defined statistically on page 234. It is a measure of the concentration of wealth, and the trend over time of the value of this coefficient shows how the concentration of wealth is changing. Two different series of Gini coefficients have been calculated. Series A is calculated without taking into account assets of wealth holders not covered by the wealth estimates. This tends to underestimate the concentration of wealth for the population as a whole. Series B is calculated for the whole population aged 15 and over, making the assumption that all those with wealth of the kind not covered by the estimates have no wealth at all. The figures in this second series are higher than the true figures for the actual distribution of wealth in the adult population because they ignore the individually small amounts of wealth owned by a large part of the population.

The two different series are compared below.

Gini coefficients of wealth distribution		*Percentages*
Year	Series A	Series B
1960	73	87
1961	72	87
1962	72	87
1963	73	87
1964	72	86
1965	70	86
1966	67	86
1967	67	86
1968	68	87
1969	65	85
1970	65	85
1971	64	84
1972	66	86
1973	65	84
1974	63	83

The trend in series B, though less pronounced than in series A, is in the same direction in spite of the Administration of Estates (Small Payments) Act 1965, which for several years from 1965 increased the section of the population that is treated as having no wealth. In 1972 this trend was reversed mainly because of the very big upsurge in Stock Exchange prices which considerably increased the wealth of the rich but had much less effect on other wealth-holders. Although the coefficients for individual years are probably not very reliable because of the limitations of the basic data, nevertheless the trends of the two series are thought to provide a reliable indication of the long-term trend towards greater equality in the distribution of identified personal wealth.

PERSONAL EXPENDITURE

Consumers' expenditure consists of personal expenditure on goods and services, including expenditure by private non-profit-making bodies, but does not include consumer spending by the non-personal sector. It includes durable goods which might also be considered as capital purchases but excludes the purchase of land and buildings. The former purchases are deemed to take place at the moment of acquisition rather than the actual payment for the item.

For further details see *National Accounts Statistics: Sources and Methods*.

The general index of retail prices

This index measures the changes month by month in the level of prices of the commodities and services purchased by all types of household in the United Kingdom, with the exception of certain higher income households and households of retired persons mainly dependent on social security benefits.

The weights which are used to calculate the index are based on the pattern of household expenditure derived from the continuing Family Expenditure Survey. From 1963 onwards the weights have been revised in January of each year. When calculating these weights the expenditure of certain households is excluded. These households are:

(a) the three or four per cent where the head has a recorded gross income exceeding a certain amount (£125 a week in the second half of 1975 and £130 a week in the first half of 1976) and

(b) those in which at least three-quarters of the total income was derived from national insurance retirement or similar pensions and/or supplementary pensions or allowances paid in supplementation or instead of such pensions. Such households will include at least one person over the national insurance retirement age, and it is estimated that about one-third of all national insurance retirement pensioners live in pensioner households as defined above.

For expenditure coming within the scope of the index a selection of commodities and services for pricing is made. The prices of these items are collected at regular intervals in such a way as to give adequate representation to types of locality throughout the country. The prices collected are those actually charged to the consumer. As far as possible they relate to goods and services of unchanged quality at successive dates; and when the quality changes an appropriate adjustment is made to the price index.

An explanation of the methods used in calculating the Retail Prices Index is contained in the October 1975 issue of the Department of Employment *Gazette*. More full details will be contained in *Method of Construction and Calculation of the Index of Retail Prices*. Studies in Official Statistics No. 6 (HMSO) to be published in the Spring/Summer of 1977.

Retail price indices for one-person and two-person pensioner households

Expenditure patterns for those pensioner households which are excluded from the General Index of Retail Prices (see (b) above) differ from those upon which the General Index is based. Therefore indices have been designed to measure price changes for such pensioner households from January 1962 and quarterly indices are published in the *Department of Employment Gazette*. They are chain indices constructed in the same way as the General Index of Retail Prices. It should however be noted that these indices *exclude* housing costs.

National Food Survey (*Ministry of Agriculture, Fisheries and Food*)

The National Food Survey is a continuous enquiry into the domestic food consumption and expenditure of private households in Great Britain. In the course of a year the National Food Survey investigates the food budgets of about 7,000–8,000 households in 46 parliamentary constituencies, selected by means of a three-stage stratified random sampling scheme so as to be representative of Great Britain as a whole. In each household surveyed, the housewife keeps a record of all food purchased, or entering the household without payment (garden, allotment produce etc.). The information which the housewife is asked to provide must be within her knowledge and thus the Survey excludes those items which other members of the family often purchase for themselves.

Detailed results are published in the Annual Reports of the National Food Survey Committee. Summarised quarterly results are published in the *Monthly Digest of Statistics* as soon as they become available, for all households, income groups, and types of family. Estimates of consumption and expenditure for all households are also published each quarter in *Trade and Industry* together with some nutritional data.

Personal credit

There are no continuing surveys in this field but the Crowther Committee on personal credit carried out a survey in 1969 which is the most recent source of information on this topic.

HEALTH

Expectation of life

The expectation of life at a given age is the number of further years of life that has been calculated for the population of that age, assuming the rates of mortality then being experienced continue in future.

Certified sickness

In order to claim benefit from the National Insurance scheme it is normally necessary for a certificate of medical sickness to be signed by a medical practitioner. Sickness benefit is not normally paid for the first 3 days of sickness. Persons who do not participate in the National Insurance scheme, particularly the three-quarters of all married women in employment who have chosen not to pay contributions for this benefit, will not appear in statistics relating to claims under the National Insurance scheme. The data are further limited by the nature of the information on cause of incapacity as certified by the doctor; what is written may not be a specific diagnosis but may merely record the symptoms described by the patient, eg headache. The data, which are thus most useful for an analysis of long-term sickness, are estimated from a 2·5 per cent sample of persons claiming sickness benefit.

Infant and maternal mortality

Stillbirth refers to a child which has issued forth from its mother after the 28th week of pregnancy and which did not breathe or show any other sign of life.

Perinatal mortality refers to stillbirths and deaths in the first week of life.

Neonatal mortality refers to deaths in the first four weeks of life.

Postneonatal mortality refers to deaths after the first four weeks but before the end of the first year.

Infant mortality refers to all deaths in the first year of life.

Maternal mortality refers to death of the mother owing to complications of pregnancy, childbirth, and puerperium including abortion. Associated maternal mortality refers to deaths associated with, but not directly attributable to, pregnancy or abortion.

General Household Survey

Chronic sickness (long-standing illness)

Information on chronic sickness is obtained for the first half of 1973 from the following 2-part question: "Do you have any long-standing illness, disability or infirmity?" If 'Yes': "Does this limit your activities compared with most people of your own age?" For the second half of 1973 the age comparison phrase was omitted from the question and informants were asked whether their long-standing illness limited their activities "in any way". The omission of the age comparison resulted only in a slight increase in the rates of nearly all age groups, so the two sets of 6-monthly data were combined. Long-standing illness is defined as a positive answer to the first part only of the 1973 question and is not affected by the mid-year change to the question.

In Table 7.17 those who report both a "long-standing illness" and "acute sickness" will be included in both categories and addition of these will, therefore, involve some double counting. As the survey is confined to households these results will understate the very sick in the older age groups who are more likely to be confined to institutions.

Acute sickness (restricted activity)

Results on acute sickness are obtained from replies to the question: "During the two weeks ending last Sunday, did you have to cut down on the things you usually do because of illness or injury?" The two-week period enabled leisure activities to be included as well as work activities.

GP consultations

The data relate to consultations with National Health Service General Medical Practitioners and include visits to the surgery, home visits, and telephone conversations, but exclude contacts with a receptionist or nurse.

Smoking habits

Results are from individuals' own descriptions of their smoking habits.

Age standardisation

Tables 7.7, 7.8, and 7.16 show age standardised data in a form similar to standardised mortality ratios. The observed sickness and consultation rates for a particular population have been expressed as percentages of the expected rates for that population — that is, the rates that would have been obtained if they had experienced sickness or consulted a doctor at the national rate. (See also the note on age standardisation at the beginning of Appendix B, page 234.)

International Classification of Diseases

Figures in Tables 7.3, 7.4, and 7.5 are based upon the eighth revision of the International Classification of Diseases. The B list classification used in these tables is given below:

B List No.	ICD Categories (Eighth revision)	Cause Title
B.1	000	Cholera
B.2	001	Typhoid fever
B.3	004, 006	Bacillary dysentery, amoebiasis
B.4	008, 009	Enteritis and other diarrhoeal diseases
B.5	010–012	Tuberculosis of respiratory system
B.6 (Pt)	0190	Late effects of respiratory tuberculosis
B.6 (Rem)	Rem 013–019	Other tuberculosis
B.7	020	Plague
B.8	032	Diphtheria
B.9	033	Whooping cough
B.10	034	Streptococcal sore throat, scarlet fever
B.11	036	Meningococcal infection
B.12	040–043	Acute poliomyelitis
B.13	050	Smallpox
B.14	055	Measles
B.15	080–083	Typhus and other rickettsioses
B.16	084	Malaria
B.17	090–097	Syphilis and its sequelae
B.18	Rem 000–136	Other infective and parasitic diseases
B.19 (Pt)	140–149	Malignant neoplasm buccal cavity etc
B.19 (Pt)	150	Malignant neoplasm oesophagus
B.19 (Pt)	151	Malignant neoplasm stomach
B.19 (Pt)	152–154	Malignant neoplasm intestine
B.19 (Pt)	161	Malignant neoplasm larynx
B.19 (Pt)	162	Malignant neoplasm lung, bronchus
B.19 (Pt)	174	Malignant neoplasm breast
B.19 (Pt)	180	Malignant neoplasm cervix uterus
B.19 (Pt)	Rem 180–182	Other malignant neoplasm of uterus
B.19 (Pt)	185	Malignant neoplasm prostate
B.19 (Pt)	204–207	Leukaemia
B.19 (Rem)	Rem 140–209	Other Malignant neoplasms, etc
B.20	210–239	Benign and unspecified neoplasms
B.21	250	Diabetes mellitus
B.22	260–269	Avitaminoses, etc
B.46 (Pt)	Rem 240–279	Other endocrine etc diseases
B.23	280–285	Anaemias
B.46 (Pt)	Rem 280–289	Other diseases of blood, etc

B List No.	ICD Categories (Eighth revision)	Cause Title
B.46 (Pt)	Rem 290–315	Mental disorders
B.24	320	Meningitis
B.46 (Pt)	340	Multiple sclerosis
B.46 (Pt)	Rem 320–389	Other diseases of nervous system, etc
B.25	390–392	Active rheumatic fever
B.26	393–398	Chronic rheumatic heart disease
B.27	400–404	Hypertensive heart disease
B.28	410–414	Ischaemic heart disease
B.29	420–429	Other forms of heart disease
B.30	430–438	Cerebrovascular disease
B.46 (Pt)	Rem 440–458	Other diseases of circulatory system
B.31	470–474	Influenza
B.32	480–486	Pneumonia
B.33 (Pt)	490–492	Bronchitis and Emphysema
B.33 (Pt)	493	Asthma
B.46 (Pt)	Rem 460–519	Other diseases of respiratory system
B.34	531–533	Peptic ulcer
B.35	540–543	Appendicitis
B.36	550–553, 560	Intestinal obstruction and hernia
B.37	571	Cirrhosis of liver
B.46 (Pt)	Rem 520–577	Other diseases of digestive system
B.38	580–584	Nephritis and nephrosis
B.39	600	Hyperplasia of prostate
B.46 (Pt)	Rem 580–629	Other diseases, genito-urinary system
B.40	640–645	Abortion
B.41	630–639, 650–678	Other complications of pregnancy, etc
B.46 (Pt)	680–709	Diseases of skin, subcutaneous tissue
B.46 (Pt)	710–738	Diseases of musculo-skeletal system
B.42	740–759	Congenital anomalies
B.43	764–768, 772, 776	Difficult delivery and/or anoxic condition
B.44	Rem 760–779	Other causes of perinatal mortality
B.45	780–796	Symptoms and ill-defined conditions
BE.47	E810–823	Motor vehicle accidents
BE.48	Rem E800–949	All other accidents
BE.49	E950–959	Suicide and self-inflicted injuries
BE.50	E960–999	All other external causes

National Health Service Statistics

Annual Returns

All NHS hospitals and specialist clinics return information annually on patients, staffing, etc. For these purposes an in-patient is a person who has gone through the full admission procedure and is occupying a bed in the in-patient department at the hour of the fixed count. Day cases are persons attending as non-resident who yet require some provision of accommodation and services. Out-patients are persons attending an out-patient department who do not require the fuller facilities of day cases. Regular day patients are persons who attend hospital regularly as part of a planned course and return home at night. They are similar to in-patients but have not gone through the full admission procedure.

Mental Health Enquiry/Mental Health Statistics – Scotland

This consists of an analysis of individual in-patient records of admission to and discharge from (or death in) psychiatric hospitals and psychiatric units in other hospitals. Diagnosis refers to the psychiatric diagnosis for which the patient was admitted.

Hospital In-patient Enquiry/Scottish Hospital In-patient Statistics

This enquiry (Department of Health and Social Security in conjunction with the Office of Population Censuses and Surveys) is based on a one in ten sample in England and Wales of in-patient records for non-psychiatric NHS hospitals with the exception of private patients and patients in psychiatric units and convalescent hospitals (psychiatric patients in general wards are normally included).

In Scotland there is full coverage of in-patient records for NHS hospitals (which are analysed by Information Services Division of the Scottish Health Service Common Services Agency).

It should be noted that the above sources for admissions, discharges, and attendances do not distinguish between single spells of in-patient treatment (or attendance at out-patient departments) occurring to different patients and multiple spells (or attendances) occurring to the same patient. Further details are given in *Health and Personal Social Services Statistics for England 1975*.

Appointments under paragraphs 94 and 107 of the Terms and Conditions

The medical staff to whom paragraph 94 of the Terms and Conditions of Service of Hospital Medical and Dental staff apply are mainly general practitioners acting as part-time medical officers at convalescent homes, general practitioner maternity hospitals or other hospitals or carrying out occasional work in the Blood Transfusion Service. Dental staff holding similar appointments are engaged under paragraph 107 of the Terms and Conditions.

Family Planning Services

Family planning services, previously provided by local health authorities directly or under agency arrangements, became the responsibility of the Area Health Authorities on the re-organisation of the National Health Service (NHS). Clinic services and domiciliary services provided by the Family Planning Association on an agency basis were to be transferred to the NHS by the end of September 1976. A free family planning service became available to all, irrespective of age, sex, or marital status through NHS family planning clinics from April 1974 and through hospital and family planning doctors from July 1975 when the terms under which the latter two services were to be provided had been settled.

Dangerous drugs: addicts

For the purpose of Home Office statistics, a drug addict is a person for whom a notification under the Dangerous Drugs (Notification of Addicts) Regulations 1968 or the Misuse of Drugs (Notification of and Supply to Addicts) Regulations, 1973 has been received and who is known to be licitly receiving drugs.

Health Service Commissioners

The function of the Health Service Commissioners, who are statutory independent officers appointed by the Crown, is to investigate complaints of failure in provision or execution in a service provided by a health authority, or maladministration by or on behalf of these authorities. The authorities concerned include Regional Health Authorities, Area Health Authorities, Boards of Governors, and Family Practitioner Committees. A complaint may be made directly to the appropriate Commissioner only after it has been brought to the attention of the relevant health authority, and an adequate opportunity given to that authority to investigate it and reply. Matters outside jurisdiction include action taken solely in the exercise of clinical or medical judgment by doctors, dentists, pharmacists, and opticians.

There are three Health Service Commissioners, for England, for Wales, and for Scotland; all three posts are at present held by the Parliamentary Commissioner.

The Commissioners report annually from April to the following March and as they see fit.

HOUSING

Dwellings

Department of the Environment estimates of the stock of dwellings have been based on data from the Censuses of Population, with adjustments for enumeration errors and for definitional changes.

In censuses before 1971 a dwelling was defined in terms of structurally separate living accommodation (not necessarily with a bathroom and WC) contained behind its own front door, with independent access to the street so that occupants could get out without passing through anyone else's living quarters. In the 1971 Census a different approach was adopted, based on whether households shared either any rooms, or any corridors or other circulation areas. The accommodation occupied by households which shared access space in order to move between their rooms or which shared rooms, was grouped together and defined as a dwelling; a household which did not share in either of these ways was enumerated as occupying a single unshared dwelling. Rooms, as in previous censuses, did not include bathrooms, WCs, sculleries not used for cooking, store rooms, landings, halls, etc.; on the other hand, whereas in 1966 all kitchens had been counted as rooms, those less than 6 feet wide were excluded under the 1971 definition.

Among the results of the change in definition of a dwelling, bedsitting rooms or one-room flatlets whose occupiers had to share the use of a bath and a WC with other households were counted as dwellings in 1971 while they had been specifically excluded in earlier censuses. An adjustment has, therefore, been made to the 1971 Census count of dwellings by excluding those of only one room which lacked exclusive use of a fixed bath or shower; however, in some cases, applying the definition used in earlier censuses, a dwelling would be composed entirely of such one-room units and, although the number of these cases can not be derived from the 1971 Census data, a small offsetting allowance has been made. Overall, the 1971 enumeration of dwellings in England and Wales has been reduced by 130,000.

The estimates also include an estimate of 'reasonably separate' dwellings, that is household spaces which though not separate dwellings by the strict census definition do provide adequate family accommodation with the exclusive use of basic amenities. The figures include vacant dwellings and temporary dwellings occupied as a normal place of residence. The estimated distribution by tenure is based on information from the 1961, 1966, and 1971 Censuses, certain assumptions having been made about the tenure distribution of gains and losses in the housing stock before and since the census dates. Although expressed to the nearest thousand the figures should not be regarded as accurate to the last digit.

Estimates of the age distribution of the dwelling stock have been made by the Department of the Environment using data from the Census reports from 1851 together with estimated rates of new construction and demolition for periods before these were recorded, and assumptions about the ages of dwellings lost from the housing stock.

Unfit dwellings

An unfit house is one which is deemed to be so far defective in one or more of the matters specified in Section 4, Housing Act 1957 (as amended) as to be not reasonably suitable for occupation. The matters so specified are repair, stability, freedom from damp, internal arrangement, natural lighting, ventilation, water supply, drainage and sanitary conveniences, and facilities for preparation and cooking of food and for the disposal of waste water.

Local authority housing

The figures relate to new housing schemes for local authorities and new towns in England and Wales (excluding the Greater London Council) for which tenders or direct labour estimates have been approved by the authority during the year stated. A "scheme" for this purpose may include dwellings on more than one site or relate to a part only of a site which is to be developed by a series of separate schemes over a period of time.

Homelessness

Tables 8.21 to 8.24 relate to the first results from a new system of statistical returns on homelessness made by local authorities in England to the Department of the Environment. The returns record the number of applications to authorities for accommodation by homeless people and the action taken to rehouse them. The returns replace those formerly made by local authorities to the Department of Health and Social Security. The earlier returns to the DHSS (related to the provision of temporary accommodation under the National Assistance Act 1949 and the Children and Young Persons Act 1963) did not provide a complete record of those homeless households who were directly rehoused in permanent accommodation, and the figures most often quoted were the number of households recorded as resident in local authority temporary accommodation. These first figures from the new returns contain some estimates from local authorities and may be subject to revision.

Applications include only those households who applied for help on the grounds that they were homeless or in danger of becoming homeless within one month. Households applying more than one month from the likely date of homelessness were not reported if and until they were likely to become homeless within a month. The applications are counted in the quarter in which the authority decided whether or not to accept responsibility. At the start of the system, authorities were asked to complete returns for all applicants 'claiming to be homeless or in danger of becoming so'; this was found difficult for the local authorities to apply in practice and so the former definition of an application was used. Some authorities have been unable to give any information on applicants for whom they do not accept responsibility.

Acceptances are those households for whom the authority undertakes to ensure that suitable accommodation is found (this does not necessarily imply the provision of local authority accommodation).

Permanent accommodation is recorded when the (accepted) household has found or been provided with accommodation which the authority considers suitable.

A household is recorded as being in a *temporary homeless accommodation* between the date of acceptance of responsibility and the date on which it moves into permanent accommodation.

Some authorities with *short life dwellings* use them only for temporary accommodation before the household is rehoused in an ordinary council dwelling. Other authorities consider some or all of their short life property to be of sufficient standard to constitute permanent accommodation – permanent in the sense that when the property comes to the end of its life (or earlier) the authority will move the household to other suitable accommodation.

Households with dependent children include all households with children who have not yet completed their full-time education.

Elderly households are households with no dependent children and at least one person over pensionable age ie a man aged 65 or over, or a woman aged 60 or over.

Adult households include households of more than one person, none of whom is a dependent child or a person of pensionable age.

One person households are households consisting of one adult living alone, who is not of pensionable age. Persons of pensionable age living alone are included with elderly households.

GHS bedroom standard

This is assessed as: a bedroom is required for each married couple, and for each person aged 21 or more; each two members of the household less than 21 share a bedroom with the proviso that those aged 10 to 20 should share with someone of the same sex. The actual number of bedrooms available for the sole use of the household is compared with this standard.

Renovation grants

House renovation grants are given to encourage owners to provide modern services and amenities in sound older houses or alternatively to increase the stock of satisfactory dwellings by converting out-moded houses and other buildings into modern housing use. The notes below refer to the grants available under the legislation current at the time of the latest figures shown.

Grants to private owners take the form of a cash payment by the local authority of a percentage of the approved eligible costs of the works which are subject to prescribed maxima. The appropriate percentage of eligible expense to be paid is 75 per cent for dwellings in housing action areas, 60 per cent for those in general improvement areas (England and Wales only) and 50 per cent for those elsewhere.

They may be made either at the discretion of the local authority (and commonly known as 'discretionary grants') for the improvement of existing houses or for the provision of new dwellings by conversion, or intermediate grants which are available as of right, if certain statutory requirements are fulfilled, for the provision of any of the five standard amenities that are lacking in the dwelling. The standard amenities are a fixed bath or shower, a wash-hand basin, hot and cold water supply at three points, a WC, and a sink.

Similar assistance is available for the improvement of local authority owned dwellings, the 'grant' in this case taking the form of a government subsidy or contribution.

A housing association may receive either the cash grant as a private owner or, provided the association is registered with the Housing Corporation, a housing association grant based on the deficit expected to arise in carrying out the approved works.

Similar assistance is available for the improvement of local authority owned dwellings, the 'grant' in this case taking the form of a government contribution.

A housing association may receive either the cash grant as a private owner, or, acting under arrangements with a local authority, the government contribution on the same terms as a housing authority. Grants for housing associations are here included with the figures for private owners.

General improvement areas

Part II of the Housing Act 1969, which came into operation on 25 August 1969, confers powers on local authorities in England and Wales to deal with the improvement of living conditions in predominantly residential areas by declaring general improvement areas and improving the amenities of such areas, or dwellings therein, or both.

Grants approved relate to the total of improvement, conversion, intermediate, repairs and special grants approved by or for local authorities for the improvement areas and these grants are also included in the house renovation grant table.

House prices and building society mortgages

The figures of house prices, mortgage advances, and incomes of borrowers have been obtained from the 5 per cent sample survey of building society mortgages. They relate to mortgage advances for the purchase of single dwellings which are to be used wholly or partly for owner-occupation. The changes in average house prices do not necessarily indicate changes in the price of comparable dwellings.

Income of borrowers is the total recorded income; but it should be noted that there is considerable variation in the details recorded by individual societies.

Option mortgages

Under the option mortgage scheme, introduced by the Housing Subsidies Act 1967, borrowers have been able to choose between a normal mortgage, under which the interest payments are allowed as a reduction from income for tax purposes, or an option mortgage, under which the interest payments are not allowed as a deduction from income for tax purposes but the rate of interest applied is lower than on a normal mortgage.

General Household Survey

The tenure category 'unfurnished' includes housing associations and accommodation provided by an employer or rented with a business.

Temporary accommodation

Local authorities are obliged to provide temporary accommodation for people who are in urgent need because of circumstances which could not reasonably have been foreseen, such as fire or floods, or in such other circumstances as the authority may in any particular case determine. These discretionary powers have been used in particular to provide accommodation for families made homeless because of a shortage of housing or eviction.

ENVIRONMENT

The National Survey of River Pollution, England and Wales 1970, 1972, and 1973

The survey was planned to cover all rivers and streams having a summer flow of 1 million gallons per day and above, and any smaller streams considered by the river authority to be significant. All canals were included. The controlled waters omitted were the River Humber, The Wash, The Solent, the controlled parts of the Bristol Channel, the Menai Straits, part of Morecambe Bay, and the Solway Firth. These were not considered as coming within the term 'river' as covered by the survey, but arrangements were made for a similar survey of these waters. The survey covers 22,000 miles of non-tidal river, 1,800 miles of tidal river, and 1,540 miles of canal. This survey, with minor amendments in coverage, was repeated in 1972, and again in 1973.

National Survey of Air Pollution

Smoke and sulphur dioxide concentrations have been measured systematically since 1960 for the National Survey of Air Pollution. Daily measurements are made by local authorities and other bodies at some 1,170 sites of which about 80 per cent are in urban areas, and the results are collated by the Warren Spring Laboratory of the Department of Industry. Grit and dust are also measured at some 600 sites. While they do not constitute a national survey, they have been of considerable help in the control of local problems.

Sulphur dioxide, whilst occurring naturally in low concentrations, is released when fuels containing sulphur are burnt. It may combine with water in the atmosphere and oxidise to form dilute sulphuric acid, which is corrosive and can damage many substances, including metals, stone, and textiles. In sufficient concentrations, sulphur dioxide can be an irritant to the respiratory system of both men and animals and can damage plants.

Smoke control orders

Smoke control orders in operation under the Clean Air Act 1956 are orders confirmed by the Secretary of State which have come into operation on the date specified in the order.

Radioactivity in milk

A measure of the radiation doses which the population of the United Kingdom receives in its diet from world-wide fallout is given in Table 9.7, because the ratio of strontium-90 to calcium in milk is close to that in a normal mixed diet. Measurements have been conducted since 1958, samples being collected on a random basis from about 80 depots which handle over one-quarter of total milk production in the United Kingdom. Measurements are also made of caesium-137, the other major long-lived nuclide, and iodine-131, which is a short-lived nuclide only present for a short period after nuclear explosions in the atmosphere. For a further discussion see *The Agricultural Research Council Letcombe Laboratory Annual Report 1975*.

Conurbation centres
The definitions used for the centres of conurbations in Tables 9.10 and 9.12 are:

Greater London – Census definition of the inner area – this does not correspond to any local authority boundaries, but is roughly the area within the main terminal railway stations of Waterloo, Victoria, Euston, Kings Cross, and Liverpool Street.

Tyneside Conurbation – Newcastle-upon-Tyne CB.

West Midlands Conurbation – Birmingham CB.

S.E. Lancashire Conurbation – Manchester CB.

Mersyside Conurbation – Liverpool CB.

West Yorkshire Conurbation – Centred on Leeds and Bradford.

Clydeside Conurbation – Glasgow CC.

Agricultural land in use
Up to 1969, the figures for Great Britain relate to agricultural holdings exceeding one acre in extent; but in June 1968, about 47,000 holdings were excluded from the census in England and Wales on the grounds that they were not statistically significant. In Scotland, 16,000 holdings were excluded on the same grounds with effect from June 1970.

Up to 1972, figures for Northern Ireland relate to holdings of one acre or more. From June 1973, some 8,000 statistically insignificant holdings were excluded from their census.

The definition of agricultural holdings was widened to include, as from June 1970, some 2,300 statistically significant holdings on one acre or less of agricultural and in Great Britain.

From June 1973, the threshold of significance in Great Britain was raised from 26 to 40 standard man-days (a standard man-day (smd) represents 8 hours productive work by an adult male worker under average conditions), excluding from the census a further 8,000 or so holdings on about 185,000 acres of land, mostly permanent grass and rough grazing. The net result of this change, together with the elimination of 6,000 or so holdings in Northern Ireland, has been to exclude some 14,000 holdings on about 225,000 acres of land in the United Kingdom.

The UK figures now relate to all known holdings with 40 smd or more; in England and Wales and Northern Ireland holdings with less than 40 smd are included only if they have 10 acres or more of crops and grass or at least one regular whole-time worker.

Changes to agricultural land
The figures are based on acreages returned by farmers at June each year, but, to preserve comparability with previous years, they are adjusted to discount changes in the coverage of the census since 1968. Five year average figures are given as information collected throughout the year is by no means exhaustive and figures for individual years are not considered to be reliable.

Passenger transport
Air travel statistics are based on published accounts and returns made by British Airways Board and private airlines and cover scheduled services only.

Rail travel information is derived from the Annual Report and Accounts of the British Railways Board, from supplementary information provided by the Railways Board and the London Transport Executive, and from returns rendered by other rail undertakings.

Road transport: Public service road transport statistics are based on returns made by operators of these vehicles. Estimates of travel by private transport are based on statistics of vehicle-mileages derived from roadside traffic counts and estimates of average numbers of persons per

vehicle derived from the Motoring and National Travel Surveys. Estimates of household car ownership are derived from a number of sources, published and unpublished, including the Motoring and National Travel Surveys, the Family Expenditure Survey, the General Household Survey, and the Censuses of Population.

Passenger transport prices
The chart shows implied consumer price indices for individual items of consumers' expenditure on passenger transport. These are calculated by dividing the consumers' expenditure at current prices for each item by the corresponding estimate at constant prices. More detailed information can be found in Chapter VI of *National Accounts Statistics: Sources and Methods*.

LEISURE
Hours of work
The statistics of hours of work relate to male manual workers aged 21 years and over.

Normal weekly hours are the recognised hours set out by national collective agreements or statutory wages regulation orders beyond which overtime rates become payable. *Average hours worked* relate to actual hours at work and are affected by changes in the amount of overtime or short time and by absences for other reasons.

National Travel Survey
The 1972 National Travel Survey was carried out by the Office of Population Censuses and Surveys for the Department of the Environment in the period April 1972 to March 1973 following the previous survey in the period 1964–66. An effective sample of 7,000 households in Great Britain was obtained using a multi-stage stratified sampling method. Information was recorded on 20,000 individuals, 4,300 vehicles, and 233,000 journeys. The recording period for each household was one week. All journeys were recorded except those made by professional drivers during the course of their work and short walks under one mile. Data on short walks and travel times were recorded for each journey on the final day of the recording period in order to reduce the load on the interviewer. Uses of the survey are to obtain information on car ownership and utilisation and travel in general, together with their dependence on a wide range of demographic, socio-economic, and other factors. Data are also obtained on the relative benefits of public and private transport and to fill in other gaps in national transport data.

British National Travel Survey
Whereas the British Home Tourism Survey covers mainly trips of one or more nights taken for all purposes in Britain, this survey concentrates on foreign holidays and those lasting four nights or more in Britain. In 1975 about 17,000 contacts were made on a random basis to provide information on 2,000 holidays abroad.

General Household Survey
Questions on leisure were included for the first time in 1973 and took the form: *We are interested in the things people do in their leisure time – when they are not working, at school or college, or looking after the house and family. Can you tell me what sort of things* **you** *have done in your spare time in the four weeks ending last Sunday ?*

This was followed by showing a prompt card and asking: *Apart from those you have already mentioned, have you done any of the activities listed on this card in the four weeks ending last Sunday ?*

The GHS sample is taken continuously throughout the year, but results for a full quarter are a balanced sample, so that although the question refers to the four weeks preceding the week of the interview, the rates and frequencies of participation over any four weeks within a quarter are assumed to be representative of the quarter as a whole. Only persons 16 years or over were questioned. Two measures were used: the proportion of adults (taken as those aged 16 or over) interviewed who had taken part and the frequency with which an activity was undertaken. Both these were aggregated over the year to produce annual figures. More details of this process and of other limitations of the data are given in the *General Household Survey, 1973* report (available from HMSO at £4) along with details of the questionnaire.

Gallup 'Omnibus' Survey

This is run weekly by Gallup Polls Ltd. It includes a wide range of questions on politics, consumer attitudes, and ownership of goods. It is run on a sample of approximately 1,000 people each week; 100 sampling points are selected, stratified by region and by town size. Individuals are selected randomly from passers-by or by household calls, but only interviewed if they fulfil quota requirements set by sex, age, social class, and employers. The standard error of the results is estimated by Gallup to be about 3 per cent.

PUBLIC SAFETY

Criminal courts in England and Wales

The courts of ordinary criminal jurisdiction in England and Wales are the magistrates' courts which try the less serious offences, and the Crown Court which deals with the serious cases. The Crown Court was established by The Courts Act 1971, which came into effect on 1 January 1972. From that date the former courts of assize and quarter sessions were abolished.

Offences fall into two main categories: indictable offences which are serious offences triable by jury at the Crown Court, and summary offences which are dealt with in magistrates' courts. In addition magistrates' courts may also try certain indictable offences if the accused foregoes his right to trial by jury, although this option is not available for the more serious offences. About 98 per cent of the trials of all cases take place in the magistrates' courts.

During the court hearing at a magistrates' court or the Crown Court, it may be necessary to adjourn the hearing, eg for medical or social reports to be prepared or for further criminal investigations to be made. In these cases, or when a person is committed from a magistrates' court to the Crown Court for trial or sentence, a person may be remanded by the court in custody or on bail.

Criminal courts in Scotland

These fall into two categories, courts of solemn jurisdiction (that is, where proceedings are taken on indictment and the judge sits with a jury) and courts of summary jurisdiction (which sit without a jury). The courts of solemn jurisdiction, where the more serious cases are tried, are the High Court of Justiciary and the Sheriff Courts. The courts of summary jurisdiction, where the majority of cases are dealt with, are the Sheriff Court (which tries cases under solemn and also summary procedure), and the (District) Court.

Social Work (Scotland) Act 1968

Part III of the Act and consequential provisions came into force on 15 April 1971 effecting radical changes to the measures for dealing with children detected in criminal offences. It introduced new non-criminal procedures for the application of compulsory measures to children under 16, abolished juvenile courts as such, and limited prosecution of children under 16 to prosecutions on the instructions of the Lord Advocate, or at his instance. It also modified the disposals available to the Sheriff and High Courts where children are prosecuted.

Sentences and orders

The following sentences may be imposed upon those persons found guilty at the magistrates' court or the Crown Court. For the more serious offences magistrates' courts, having found a person guilty of an offence, may commit him to the Crown Court for sentence, if they feel their powers are inadequate; certain offences can only be dealt with at the Crown Court. The Criminal Justice Act 1972, which came into effect from 1 January 1973, gave the courts the power to defer a sentence for a period of up to 6 months.

Absolute and conditional discharge

A court may make an order discharging a person absolutely or (except in Scotland) conditionally where it is inexpedient to inflict punishment and a probation order is not appropriate. An order for conditional discharge runs for such period of not more than three years as the court specifies, the condition being that the offender does not commit another offence within the period so specified.

Attendance centres

This is a form of treatment for boys and youths in England, Wales, and Northern Ireland which involves deprivation of free time. The boys and youths are mainly between the ages of 10 and 16 (but there are two centres for boys aged 17–20) found guilty of offences for which an adult could be sentenced to imprisonment. Attendance is on Saturday mornings or afternoons for up to three hours on any one occasion and for a total of not more than 24 hours and (normally) not less than 12. The activities include physical training and instruction in handicrafts or other practical subjects.

Probation orders and probation orders with day training centre order

Probation is designed to secure the rehabilitation of an offender while he remains at liberty and under the supervision of a probation officer ('social worker' in Scotland) whose duty it is to advise, assist, and befriend him. A cardinal feature of the service is that it relies on the co-operation of the offender. Before making a probation order, the court must explain its effects and make sure that the probationer understands that if he fails to comply with the requirements of the order he will be liable to be dealt with for the original offence. A probation order cannot be made without the consent of the person concerned. The order usually requires the probationer to keep in regular touch with the probation officer, to be of good behaviour, and to lead an industrious life. It may also require him to live in a specified place, to submit to treatment for mental condition, or attend a day training centre. A probation order is made for not less than one year and not more than three years. From 1 January 1971, probation is no longer applicable to juveniles under the age of 17 (in England and Wales). See note below on *Supervision orders and care orders*.

The Criminal Justice Act 1972, which came into force on 1 January 1973, gave the courts the power to require an offender to attend a day training centre as a condition of a probation order.

Community service

An offender over the age of 17 who is convicted of an offence punishable with imprisonment may be required to perform unpaid work for not more than 240 hours.

Detention centres

Detention centres are intended to provide a method of custodial treatment for young offenders who have committed an offence for which an adult could be sentenced to imprisonment and for whom a long period of residential training in borstal does not seem necessary but who cannot be taught respect for the law by such methods as fines or probation. Detention is for any term of not less than 3 and not more than 6 months. There are junior centres for boys aged 14 and under 17 and senior centres for those aged 17 and under 21; there is no longer a centre for girls. The regime in the centres is brisk and firm; there is an emphasis on hard work but also on the establishment of relationships between staff and trainees. There is a maximum remission of one-third of the sentence for those aged 17 and over and a maximum remission of one-half of the sentence for those aged under 17. There is 12 months compulsory supervision after discharge. In Scotland there is one detention centre for males aged not less than 16 but under 21; and there is a fixed period of detention of three months, one-third of the sentence being remitted subject to good conduct and industry.

Borstal training

The borstal training system, which is available for offenders who have reached the age of 15 but are not yet 21, and who have been convicted of an offence punishable in the case of an adult with imprisonment, comprises borstals specialising in treatment of different types of young offender, classified according to such criteria as age, intelligence, and type of offence. A person who is under 17 may not be sent for borstal training unless the court considers that no other method of dealing with him is appropriate. The period of detention ranges from 6 months to 2 years and is followed by supervision for 2 years. The system is essentially remedial and educational based on personal training by a carefully selected staff. Emphasis is placed on vocational training in skilled trades; there is much freedom of movement and many borstals are open establishments. In Scotland the minimum age for borstal training is 16 and the period of training is for a maximum of two years. In practice the average period served is less than two years, discharge depending on response to and progress during training. The period of compulsory supervision following release is one year.

The statutory provisions for borstal training in Northern Ireland are similar to those in Scotland with the exception that, at 15, training (approved) school inmates may be committed to borstal for serious misconduct or absconding.

Suspended sentences and suspended sentences with supervision order

In England, Wales, and Northern Ireland sentences of imprisonment of two years or less may be suspended. The period for which a sentence may be suspended is between one and two years at the discretion of the court. The result of suspending a sentence is that it will not take effect unless during the period specified the offender is convicted of another offence punishable with imprisonment and thereafter a court having power to do so orders that the suspended sentence shall take effect. An offender whose sentence of imprisonment is suspended may, in certain circumstances, be placed under supervision for a period not longer than the period for which his sentence is suspended. This form of sentence is not available to courts in Scotland.

The Criminal Justice Act 1972, which came into force on 1 January 1973, gave the courts power, on passing a suspended sentence of over 6 months, to impose a 'suspended sentence with supervision order' placing the offender under the supervision of a probation officer for a specified period not longer than the period of suspension.

Imprisonment

The custodial sentence for adult offenders is imprisonment or, in the case of mentally abnormal offenders, hospital orders with or without restrictions on when the offender may be discharged. The length of sentence is determined by the court, subject to the maximum prescribed by law for that particular offence of which the offender has been convicted, although an extended sentence may exceed the prescribed maximum for the offence if the offender's criminal record satisfies certain conditions. One-third of a prisoner's sentence is remitted subject to good conduct and industry; and those serving sentences of over 18 months may be released under the parole scheme after serving one year or one-third of that sentence whichever is the longer. A life sentence prisoner may be released on licence subject to supervision and is always liable to recall. Prisoners are classified into groups, according to the length of sentence, their character and potentialities, and the risk they present to security, and assigned, so far as circumstances permit, to the establishment best suited to their needs. Untried prisoners are segregated from convicted prisoners, and, as far as practicable, those under 21 are separated from adults.

Young offenders institutions: Scotland

The Criminal Justice (Scotland) Act, 1963 laid down that Young Offenders Institutions should be provided to ensure that young persons under the age of 21 and not less than 16 for whom neither borstal nor detention training was appropriate, but who still required custodial treatment, would no longer be sent to prison. The first Young Offenders Institution was opened in January 1965 and there are now five such establishments, four for males and one for females, providing accommodation, work, and training more suited to this younger age group.

Fines

Fines are monetary payments and may be imposed with or without the option of imprisonment.

Supervision orders and care orders: England and Wales

From 1 January 1971 in criminal proceedings against persons under 17, probation orders, approved school orders, fit person orders, and orders committing to a remand home were replaced by supervision orders and care orders. Both orders may also be used in care proceedings. A supervision order places a juvenile under the supervision of a probation officer or local authority; it is the duty of the supervisor to advise, assist, and befriend the juvenile. A care order commits the juvenile to the care of a local authority who, by virtue of that order, acquire, in general terms, the powers and duties of the parent or guardian. These two forms of order are not available to courts in Scotland.

Road accident casualties

These figures are compiled from information received by the Department of the Environment and the Scottish Development Department from police forces throughout Great Britain. Only those casualties from road accidents occurring on a public highway are included.

Severe industrial accidents

These are accidents which result in absence from normal work for more than three days where the injury is both severe (ie a serious fracture, amputation, concussion, etc.) and unambiguously the direct and undoubted result of an accident at work. These figures relate only to premises covered by the Factories Act.

SOCIAL PARTICIPATION
Elections

Parliamentary elections

General elections are normally held not more than 5 years apart. The United Kingdom is divided into 635 constituencies, each of which returns one member to the House of Commons. To ensure equitable representation, four permanent Boundary Commissions (for England, Wales, Scotland, and Northern Ireland) make periodic reviews of constituencies and recommend any redistribution of seats that may seem necessary in the light of population movements or for some other reason.

Local elections

The term of office of a councillor elected to any form of local government is usually four years. In England and Wales county council elections take place every four years. Metropolitan district elections are held for a third of the seats in each year when there is no county council election; the non-metropolitan district councils have either adopted the same procedure or opted to hold whole council elections in 1976, 1979 and every fourth year thereafter. In London the next Greater London Council elections will be held in 1977 and elections to the London borough councils will take place in 1978. In Scotland the next elections for the regions will be in 1978 and for the districts in 1977. Elections are held every four years in Northern Ireland.

Members of Parliament

Members of the House of Commons are elected to represent one constituency. They usually belong to a political party, although occasionally an independent MP will be elected. They are under no obligation to give up their job or profession, although many do so. MPs sit until the next general election, or until they resign or die. There is no upper age limit. Members of the House of Lords are comprised of hereditary peers (some of whom give up their right generally to take part in debates or votes) and of life peers appointed by a Prime Minister. Life peers sit for life, but there is no inheritance of these peerages. The government is drawn almost exclusively from members of both houses.

Civil courts in England and Wales

The main civil courts in England and Wales are the County Courts, which are the courts for the lesser cases, and the High Court, where the more important cases are heard. Magistrates' courts have limited civil jurisdiction covering such matters as matrimonial proceedings for separation and maintenance orders, adoption, and affiliation and guardianship orders and care proceedings. Most appeals in civil cases go to the Court of Appeal (Civil Division) and from there may go to the House of Lords.

County Courts are presided over by a paid judge, who almost always sits alone, although he may in a very limited number of cases sit with a jury consisting of eight persons if either party wishes it and the court makes an order to that effect. The jurisdiction of the county courts covers: actions founded upon contract and tort (except libel and slander) where the amount claimed is not more than £1,000; equity matters, such as trusts and mortgages, where the amount does not exceed £5,000; and actions concerning land where the net annual value for rating does not exceed £1,000. Cases outside these limits may be tried in the county court by consent of the parties, or may be transferred to the High Court.

Other matters dealt with by the county courts include adoption cases, bankruptcies (which are dealt with in certain courts outside the London Bankruptcy Districts); undefended divorce cases (which are heard and determined by County Courts designated as divorce County Courts); and complaints of racial discrimination brought by the Race Relations Board (which are dealt with by specially designated courts sitting with two assessors, having knowledge and experience of race).

Civil courts in Scotland

The Court of Session is the supreme civil court in Scotland. As a general rule it has original jurisdiction in all civil cases and appellate jurisdiction over all civil courts, unless such jurisdiction, original or appellate is expressly excluded by statute. The Court is divided into two parts, the Inner House and the Outer House. The Inner House exercises appellate jurisdiction on reclaiming motions from the Outer House and on appeals from the inferior courts. Appeals from the Court of Session may go to the House of Lords.

The Sheriff Court is the principal local court of civil, as well as criminal, jurisdiction in Scotland. Its civil jurisdiction is comparable with that of the County Courts in England and Wales but is more extensive in certain directions. There is no limit to the sum which may be sued for in the Sheriff Court. The Sheriff's jurisdiction does not extend to actions of divorce, or declarator of marriage or to actions of declarator involving the personal status of individuals or to certain other actions: but with these exceptions, the civil jurisdiction of the Court is generally similar in scope to that of the Court of Session. In addition, the Sheriff deals with a mass of quasi-judicial and administrative business, some of which is similar to that dealt with in County Courts in England and Wales but of which a large part is peculiar to the Scottish system.

Legal aid

Free legal aid in civil cases is available to persons with small incomes and capital, and contributory legal aid to those with larger but still limited means. Applicants must show that they have reasonable grounds for asserting or disputing a claim. Certain types of action, including libel and slander, are excluded from the scheme.

In the criminal courts in England and Wales a legal aid order may be made by the court or courts concerned if this appears desirable in the interests of justice and the defendant's means are such that he requires financial help in meeting the costs of the proceedings in which he is involved. No limit of income or capital above which a person is ineligible for legal aid is specified, but the court has power to order applicants to pay a reasonable contribution towards the cost of the case according to their means.

In general, legal aid in Scotland follows the same pattern, except that when legal aid is granted in criminal courts, successful applicants are not required to pay contributions towards the cost.

Persons who are eligible for legal aid may also obtain the normal services provided by a solicitor, short of actual representation in court and tribunal proceedings, either free or on payment of a small contribution under the Legal Advice and Assistance Schemes.

Administrative tribunals

Administrative tribunals are persons or bodies exercising judicial or quasi-judicial functions outside the ordinary hierarchy of the courts, and their constitution, functions, and procedure are governed by statutory provisions. With the continuing expansion of governmental activity and involvement in the social and economic affairs of the nation, the number and importance of tribunals has grown very substantially. It is fairly typical for their chairmen to be lawyers appointed by the Lord Chancellor (in Scotland by the Lord President of the Court of Session), and for their members to be appointed by the Minister concerned with their field of operation. In many cases there is a right of appeal from their decisions on a point of law to the High Court, or, in Scotland, to the Court of Session. The tribunals currently under the supervision of the Council of Tribunals are listed in Schedule 1 to the Tribunals and Inquiries Act 1971, and the application of that Act may be extended or varied by orders made jointly by the Lord Chancellor and the Lord Advocate.

Parliamentary Commissioner for Administration

The Parliamentary Commissioner is a statutory independent officer appointed by the Crown. His function is to investigate complaints of maladministration brought to his notice by members of Parliament on behalf of members of the public. His powers of investigation extend to actions taken by central government departments in the exercise of their administrative functions, but not to policy decisions (which are the concern of the Government). Certain administrative actions are, however, outside his jurisdiction; these include matters affecting relations with other countries, contractual matters, hospitals (but see the note on the Health Service Commissioners), and personnel questions of the armed forces and the civil services. The Commissioner cannot investigate any matter where the complainant has exercised a right of appeal to a tribunal or court of law. However, he may, at his discretion, conduct an investigation if such a right of appeal exists and it is held that the complainant has, with good reason, not resorted to that right.

In the performance of his duties, the Parliamentary Commissioner has access to all departmental papers, and reports his findings to the member of Parliament who presented the case. The Commissioner reports annually to Parliament and may submit such other reports as he thinks fit. A Select Committee has been appointed to consider these reports.

RESOURCES

The definitions used in this section follow those in the *National Income and Expenditure* Blue Book. The following notes are intended as a general guide to the definitions adopted. A detailed description of sources, methods and definitions is given in *National Accounts Statistics: Sources and Methods* (HMSO 1968) and is brought up to date in the notes to *National Income and Expenditure, 1965–75*.

The tables analyse the expenditure on current and capital account of central government, local authorities, and public corporations. All operating expenditure by public corporations and other public trading bodies is excluded, but subsidies from central government or local authorities to meet deficits on trading activities, including housing, are included in current expenditure.

The definitions used in the functional summary are the same as those in the Blue Book. As in the Blue Book, current expenditure on administration includes the cost of common services (ie accommodation, stationery and printing, superannuation, etc.) which is not borne by the department administering each service. Debt interest is included in total only as it cannot be allocated satisfactorily by function.

The coverage of the present set of tables is slightly wider than in the *Annual Abstract of Statistics* in that it includes details of expenditure on environmental services, on 'justice and law', and on libraries, museums, and the arts.

The functional classification for the social and related services used here differs from that followed in the White Paper *Public Expenditure to 1978–79* (Cmnd. 5879) where expenditure on school meals and milk and on libraries is included under Education. The White Paper also includes expenditure on the fire services under Law and Order, whereas in this section it is included in 'Other expenditure'. Imputed rents for the use of assets owned and used by public authorities are included here but not in the White Paper.

The notes below indicate briefly some of the more important points relating to the main items appearing in the section.

Economic classification

Current expenditure on goods and services: This comprises purchases of those goods which are not regarded as fixed assets, payments for the services of public authority employees, and payments for other services. Imputed rents for the use of assets owned and used by public authorities are also included.

Gross domestic fixed capital formation: This includes both expenditure on new assets and the purchase (*less* sales) of land and existing buildings. Fixed capital formation on the social services relates mainly to buildings, but expenditure on capital equipment in hospitals, for example, is also included.

Current grants to the personal sector: These consist predominantly of social security benefits; other important items are scholarships, students' maintenance allowances, and grants towards the current expenditure of universities, colleges, etc.

Gross national product at factor cost: This is the value of the goods and services produced by United Kingdom residents together with net property income from abroad. It includes only those incomes of residents which are derived directly from the current production of goods and services. Incomes arising from payments for which no goods or services are received in return, such as social security benefits, are 'transfer' payments and are excluded.

Personal income: This is the total of all incomes accruing to United Kingdom residents, whether from current production or by transfer of income from others through government grants or through receipts of interest and dividends.

Functional classification[1]

Social security benefits: Non-contributory pensions and national assistance grants ceased after 26 November 1966, when they were replaced by supplementary benefits. The analysis by type of supplementary benefit is not exact. The estimates are derived from average numbers in receipt of benefit and average amounts paid.

The health services include expenditure by hospital authorities, executive councils, and health departments on hospital, general medical, and other health services. The

---

[1] These notes relate to public expenditure data that are to be found in the relevant sections of the Tables and Charts sections.

expenditure by local authorities on the provision of health centres, health visiting, home nursing, ambulance services, vaccination, and immunisation, etc. was transferred to central government on 1 April 1974. Only the net costs of providing these services are included in total public expenditure. Receipts from patients are shown separately in Table 7.30.

Personal social services include local authority expenditure on the aged, handicapped, and homeless; approved schools, remand homes, and other children's homes; care of mothers and young children; mental health; and domestic help. Expenditure on sheltered employment is, however, excluded and included in 'Commerce and Industry'. Figures before 1969/70 refer to the former services of child care and local welfare services.

School meals, milk, and welfare foods covers the cost of providing these services at reduced prices to children and expectant mothers; only the net costs are included in total public expenditure. Payments by the recipients of school meals and milk are shown separately in Table 7.30. Local authority capital expenditure on school canteens is included with Education.

Education: This covers expenditure by the education departments and local education authorities in schools, training colleges, technical institutions, and universities.

Housing: This covers subsidies paid by the central government towards the provision of housing by local authorities, development corporations, and housing associations; net current expenditure by local authorities on housing after deducting rents and central government subsidies; capital expenditure by the public sector on the provision of houses for letting; grants by local authorities towards the cost of conversions and improvements of privately-owned houses; and net lending by the public sector for private house purchase and improvement.

Justice and law: This covers expenditure on police, prisons, probation and after-care (except in Scotland), legal aid, Parliament, and the law courts.

Libraries, museums, and the arts: This covers expenditure on national and local libraries, museums and art galleries, expenditure by the Arts Council, and other grants for the arts.

Environmental services: mainly local authorities' current and capital expenditure on the group of services shown in Table 9.21. Includes related expenditure by the central government, mainly departmental administrative costs, and related capital expenditure by the new town corporations.

Social services manpower

Health and personal social services

Health and personal social services, apart from medical, nursing, and midwifery services, include mainly home helps, ambulance staff, and those employed in residential homes and temporary accommodation except those relating to the residential care of children. Also included are nursery staff, mental health social workers, and staff of homes and centres for the physically or mentally handicapped. The table has been redrafted to take into account the reorganisation of the health services on 1 April 1974. The figures shown for health and personal social services omit agency staff and those employed by voluntary organisations.

INTERNATIONAL
European Economic Community Consumer Attitude Survey

This survey was instituted in 1965 and covers 40,000 households taken from all the countries of the Community. The survey asks questions about attitudes to the general economic situation, about intentions on saving, and on the purchase of durable goods. The ownership of goods is asked in relation to this last point and specifically defines ownership to include only equipment actually purchased and not rentals. This has a marked effect on the figures for televisions, for which rental figures are high in the United Kingdom.

Appendix C Sources and further references

Subject and table or chart numbers	Department (if appropriate)	Publication[1], or source of data	Frequency/date of publication[2]

Sources of tables and charts

Population

1.1, 1.3–1.6	Government Actuary's Department	Population Projections Variant Population Projections	Annual 1975
1.1–1.12	Office of Population Censuses and Surveys	Census of Population Reports (England and Wales)	1951, 1961, 1966, 1971
1.13	Office of Population Censuses and Surveys	General Household Survey[3]	Annual
1.14–1.22		Registrar General's Statistical Review of England and Wales, Parts I and II, Tables[4]	Annual (until 1973)
		Registrar General's Quarterly Return (England and Wales)[4]	Quarterly (until 1974)
		Population Trends	Quarterly (from 1975)
	General Register Office (Scotland)	Census of Population Reports (Scotland)	1951, 1961, 1966, 1971
	General Register Office (Northern Ireland)	Annual Report of the Registrar General for Scotland, Part II Census of Population Reports (Northern Ireland)	Annual 1951, 1961, 1966, 1971

Households

2.1, 2.2, 2.9, 2.28	Office of Population Censuses and Surveys	Census of Population Reports (England and Wales)	1951, 1961, 1966, 1971
	General Register Office (Scotland)	Census of Population Reports (Scotland)	1951, 1961, 1966, 1971
2.3	Department of the Environment	Derived from 1973 based population projections	
2.4–2.8, 2.12, 2.13, 2.25–2.27	Office of Population Censuses and Surveys	General Household Survey[3]	Annual
2.10, 2.11, 2.18	Government Actuary's Department Office of Population Censuses and Surveys	Variant Population Projections	1975
2.14–2.17, 2.19, 2.20	Department of Health and Social Security Welsh Office Department of Education and Science Scottish Education Department – Social Work Services Group	Health and Personal Social Services Statistics for England Health and Personal Social Services Statistics for Wales Statistics of Education, Volume 1 Scottish Social Work Statistics	Annual Annual Annual Annual
2.21, 2.23, 2.24	Department of Employment	Family Expenditure Survey	Annual
2.22	Department of Health and Social Security	Calculated from Family Expenditure Survey data	Annual

Education

3.1, 3.3, 3.4, 3.5, 3.13	Department of Education and Science Scottish Education Department Department of Education, Northern Ireland	Education Statistics for the United Kingdom Scottish Education Statistics	Annual Annual
3.2	Office of Population Censuses and Surveys	General Household Survey[3]	Annual

3.6, 3.8–3.10, 3.12, 3.14, 3.16	Department of Education and Science	Statistics of Education: (England and Wales)
		   Volume 1 Schools
		    „ 2 School leavers, GCE and CSE
		    „ 3 Further Education
		    „ 4 Teachers
		    „ 5 Finance and Awards
		    „ 6 Universities (United Kingdom)
			Annual

3.7	University Grants Committee Scottish Education Department Department of Education, Northern Ireland	Scottish Education Statistics Northern Ireland Education Statistics	Annual Annual
3.11	Department of Education and Science	School Intentions Survey	
3.15	University Grants Committee	First Destination of University Graduates	Annual
3.17	Central Statistical Office	National Income and Expenditure	Annual
3.18	Social Science Research Council Survey Unit		

Employment

4.1, 4.4, 4.16, 4.17	Department of Employment	Department of Employment Gazette	Monthly
4.2	Department of Education and Science	Statistics of Education – Volume 3 Further Education	Annual
4.3, 4.5, 4.10, 4.11, 4.14, 4.23, 4.24	Office of Population Censuses and Surveys General Register Office (Scotland)	Census of Population Reports (England and Wales) Census of Population Reports (Scotland)	1951, 1961, 1966, 1971

Subject and table or chart numbers	Department (if appropriate)	Publication[1], or source of data	Frequency/date of publication[2]
Sources of tables and charts			
4.5, 4.6, 4.12, 4.13, 4.15, 4.22	Office of Population Censuses and Surveys	General Household Survey[3]	Annual
4.4, 4.7, 4.8	Central Statistical Office	Economic Trends, February 1976	
4.9	Institute of Manpower Studies	First Employment of University Graduates	Annual
4.17	Department of Employment Department of Manpower Services, Northern Ireland		
4.18	Training Services Agency		
4.19	Open University		
4.20, 4.21	Department of Employment	New Earnings Survey	
4.25	Political and Economic Planning	Facts of Racial Discrimination in Britain	
Personal income and wealth			
5.1, 5.2,	Central Statistical Office	National Income and Expenditure	Annual
5.3, 5.4, 5.6, 5.11–5.14	Central Statistical Office		
5.5	Board of Inland Revenue	Survey of Personal Incomes	Annual
5.7–5.10	Department of Employment	Family Expenditure Survey	Annual
5.15–5.20	Department of Employment	New Earnings Survey	Annual
5.21	Board of Inland Revenue	Derived from Department of Employment data	
5.22–5.33	Department of Health and Social Security	Social Security Statistics	Annual
5.34	Central Statistical Office Department of Health and Social Security		
5.35–5.37	Board of Inland Revenue	Inland Revenue Statistics	Annual
5.38	Department of Employment	New Earnings Survey	Annual
		Family Expenditure Survey	Annual
	Department of Health and Social Security Office of Population Censuses and Surveys		
	Central Statistical Office	Regional Statistics	Annual
Personal expenditure			
6.1, 6.2	Department of Employment	Department of Employment Gazette	Monthly
6.3	Central Statistical Office	Derived from retail price index, quarterly press notice	Quarterly
6.4, 6.5, 6.7	Department of Employment	Family Expenditure Survey	Annual
6.6	Central Statistical Office	National Income and Expenditure	Annual
6.8	Social Science Research Council Survey Unit (see article on page 47)		
6.9	Customs and Excise (Inland Revenue)		
6.10, 6.11	Ministry of Agriculture, Fisheries and Food	Household Food Consumption and Expenditure	Annual
Health			
7.1	Government Actuary's Department with	Registrar General's Decennial Supplement, 1961, Life Tables (England and Wales)[4]	Decennial
	Office of Population Censuses and Surveys	Registrar General's Quarterly Return, 2nd quarter (England and Wales)[4]	Quarterly
	General Register Office (Scotland)	Supplement to the 114th Annual Report of the Registrar General: Life Tables (Scotland)	Annual
		Registrar General's Quarterly Return (Scotland)	Quarterly
7.2–7.5	Office of Population Censuses and Surveys	Registrar General's Statistical Review of England and Wales, Part I[4]	Annual
	General Register Office (Scotland)	Annual Report of the Registrar General for Scotland	Annual
7.6–7.8, 7.16, 7.22	Office of Population Censuses and Surveys	General Household Survey[3]	Annual
7.9, 7.15	Department of Health and Social Security Scottish Health Service, Common Services Agency, Information Services Division Welsh Office Department of Health and Social Services, Northern Ireland	Health and Personal Social Services Statistics for England Scottish Health Statistics Health and Personal Social Services Statistics for Wales	Annual Annual Annual
7.10	Department of Health and Social Security Scottish Health Service, Common Services Agency, Information Services Division	Report on Hospital In-patient Enquiry (England and Wales), Part 1 Tables Scottish Hospital In-patient Statistics Scottish Health Statistics	Annual Annual Annual
7.11, 7.14, 7.18, 7.19, 7.21, 7.25, 7.28, 7.29	Department of Health and Social Security Scottish Health Service, Common Services Agency, Information Services Division Welsh Office	Health and Personal Social Services Statistics for England Scottish Health Statistics Health and Personal Social Services Statistics for Wales	Annual Annual Annual
7.12	Department of Health and Social Security	Mental Health Enquiry	Annual
7.13	Department of Health and Social Security	UK Private Medical Care: Provident Schemes Statistics	

Subject and table or chart numbers	Department (if appropriate)	Publication[1], or source of data	Frequency/date of publication[2]
Sources of tables and charts			
7.17	Department of Health and Social Security	Health and Personal Social Services Statistics for England	Annual
	Office of Population Censuses and Surveys	General Household Survey[3]	Annual
	Scottish Health Service, Common Services Agency, Information Services Division	Scottish Health Statistics	Annual
	Welsh Office	Digest of Welsh Statistics	Annual
	Office of Population Censuses and Surveys	Registrar General's Statistical Review of England and Wales, Part I[4]	Annual
	General Register Office (Scotland)	Annual Report of the Registrar General for Scotland	Annual
7.20	Office of Population Censuses and Surveys	Registrar General's Statistical Review of England and Wales, Supplement on Abortion (until 1973)[4]	Annual
		OPCS Monitor, Reference AB[6]	Monthly
	Scottish Home and Health Department	Health Bulletin	Quarterly
7.24	Home Office		
7.23, 7.27,	{ Department of Health and Social Security	Health and Personal Social Services Statistics for England	Annual
	Welsh Office	Health and Personal Social Services Statistics for Wales	Annual
7.26	Department of Health and Social Security	Health and Personal Social Services Statistics for England	Annual
7.30	Central Statistical Office	National Income and Expenditure	Annual
Housing			
8.1, 8.3–8.5, 8.16, 8.17, 8.20	{ Department of the Environment Scottish Development Department	Housing and Construction Statistics	Quarterly
	Ministry of Development (Northern Ireland)	Housing Return for Northern Ireland	Quarterly up to September 1973
	Department of Housing, Local Government and Planning	Digest of Housing Statistics for Northern Ireland	Quarterly from December 1973
8.2, 8.15	Department of the Environment	Housing and Construction Statistics	Quarterly
8.6	{ Office of Population Censuses and Surveys General Register Office (Scotland)	Census of Population Reports (separate series for England and Wales, and for Scotland)	1951, 1961, 1966, 1971
8.7–8.10, 8.12–8.14, 8.18	Office of Population Censuses and Surveys	General Household Survey[3]	Annual
8.11	Department of the Environment	Derived from Family Expenditure Survey data	Annual
8.19	Central Statistical Office	National Income and Expenditure	Annual
8.21–8.24	Department of the Environment		
Environment			
9.1, 9.2	Meteorological Office		
9.3–9.5	{ Department of the Environment	National Survey of Air Pollution	Annual since 1970
	Department of Trade and Industry Scottish Development Department		
9.3, 9.6	National Society for Clean Air		
9.7	Agricultural Research Council	Letcombe Laboratory Annual Report	Annual
9.8, 9.9	Department of the Environment Welsh Office	Report of a River Pollution Survey of England and Wales, Vols I and II	1972 and 1973
9.9	Thames Water Authority		
9.10–9.12	Office of Population Censuses and Surveys	Census of Population Reports	1931, 1951, 1961, 1966, and 1971
9.13	Office of Population Censuses and Surveys	Studies on Medical and Population Subjects No. 30. Population Concentration and Distribution in Great Britain 1931–1961	
9.14, 9.15	Ministry of Agriculture, Fisheries and Food		
9.16	Department of the Environment		
9.17	Political and Economic Planning	Transport Realities and Planning Policy	1972
9.18, 9.19	Department of the Environment	Passenger Transport in Great Britain	Annual
		Highway Statistics	Annual
9.20	Royal Commission on Environmental Pollution	Fourth Report, Cmnd 5780	1974
9.21	Central Statistical Office	National Income and Expenditure	Annual
9.22	Social Science Research Council Survey Unit		
Leisure			
10.1–10.3	Department of Employment	Department of Employment Gazette	Monthly
10.4, 10.5	Department of the Environment	National Travel Survey	1966, 1973
10.6–10.9	British Tourist Authority	British National Travel Survey	Annual
10.10	Department of Industry	International Passenger Survey	Quarterly
10.11	Countryside Commission	Digest of Countryside Recreation Statistics	1968, 1974
10.12	Ministry of Defence (for Air Training and Cadet Corps). All other figures obtained from Annual reports of the organisations concerned		

Subject and table or chart numbers	Department (if appropriate)	Publication[1], or source of data	Frequency/date of publication [2]
Sources of tables and charts			
10.13	Church of England Statistics Unit Catholic Education Council Methodist Archives and Research Centre		
10.14	The Bookseller	The Bookseller	Weekly (Data published monthly)
10.15	The Arts Council; Department of Education and Science		
10.16	Audit Bureau of Circulation		
10.17, 10.18	Office of Population Censuses and Surveys	General Household Survey[3]	Annual
10.19	Gallup Polls Ltd		
10.20	British Broadcasting Corporation		
10.21	Central Statistical Office	National Income and Expenditure	Annual
10.22	Joint Advisory Committee on Pets in Society	Dogs in the United Kingdom	
Public safety			
11.1, 11.7	Home Office	Criminal Statistics	Annual
	Scottish Home and Health Department	Criminal Statistics (Scotland)	Annual
	Northern Ireland, Ministry of Home Affairs	Report on the Administration of Home Office Services	Annual
11.2, 11.3	Home Office	Criminal Statistics	Annual
	Scottish Home and Health Department	Criminal Statistics (Scotland)	Annual
11.4, 11.5	Home Office	Report on the Work of the Prison Department	Annual
11.6	Central Statistical Office	National Income and Expenditure	Annual
11.8–11.11	Department of the Environment Scottish Development Department Welsh Office	Road Accidents	Annual
11.12	Department of the Environment	Railway Accidents	Annual
11.13	Department of Employment	British Labour Statistics: Historical Abstract 1886–1968 British Labour Statistics Year Book Department of Employment Gazette	Annual Monthly
11.14	Office of Population Censuses and Surveys	Registrar General's Statistical Review for England and Wales[4]	Annual
11.15	Ministry of Defence		
11.16	Home Office Department of the Environment Scottish Development Department	United Kingdom Fire and Loss Statistics	Annual
11.17	Department of Employment	Report of Her Majesty's Inspectors of Explosives	Annual
11.18	Northern Ireland Office		
Social participation			
12.1–12.3, 12.21	Home Office		
12.4	The Times Newspaper	Compiled from published data	
12.5	Houses of Parliament, Information Office	Public Bills	Sessional
12.6	MacMillan and Co Ltd	British Political Facts, 1900–1975	
12.7	Various organisations		
12.8, 12.9	Various Trade Union Organisations		
12.10	National Association of Citizens' Advice Bureaux	Annual Reports	Annual
12.11–12.13, 12.16	Lord Chancellor's Office	Civil Judicial Statistics	Annual
12.11, 12.14–12.15	Scottish Courts Administration	Civil Judicial Statistics (Scotland)	Annual
12.17	Parliamentary Commissioner for Administration	Annual Report	Annual
12.18	Council on Tribunals	Annual Report	Annual
12.19	Home Office Scottish Home and Health Department		
12.20, 12.21	Lord Chancellor's Office Scottish Home and Health Department The Law Society	Annual Report on Legal Aid and Advice	Annual
12.22	Office of Population Censuses and Surveys	Population Trends No. 3	Quarterly

Resources

All data in the tables and charts are taken from *National Income and Expenditure* published annually by the Central Statistical Office.

International   The sources of figures used are indicated on the respective tables.

[1] *The Annual Abstract of Statistics* and the *Monthly Digest of Statistics* published by the Central Statistical Office are further general sources of many statistics in *Social Trends*.

[2] The Census of Population Reports refer to the year of the Census and are published during the several years following the Census.

[3] The General Household Survey is carried out by the Social Survey Division of the Office of Population Censuses and Surveys (OPCS). The first report on the General Household Survey from OPCS was published in July 1973, the second in June 1975 and the third in March 1976.

[4] *The Registrar General's Statistical Review* ceased publication in 1973 and the Quarterly Returns ceased in 1974. These were replaced by a number of smaller volumes, published annually, and in which the medical and population tables are subdivided. These volumes are supplemented by a series of OPCS Monitors. (See page 258)

[5] Some data have been revised since publication of *Economic Trends No. 268* of February 1976.

[6] Available from the Office of Population Censuses and Surveys and not HMSO.

Further references

Title	Frequency/date of publication	Source
General		
Annual Abstract of Statistics	Annual	Central Statistical Office
Britain: an official handbook	Annual	Central Office of Information
Regional Statistics	Annual	Central Statistical Office
Digest of Welsh Statistics	Annual	Welsh Office
Scottish Abstract of Statistics	Annual	Scottish Office
Digest of Statistics, Northern Ireland	Bi-annual	Department of Finance, Northern Ireland
The Ulster Year Book	Annual	Northern Ireland Information Service HMSO Belfast
Statistical returns on children's services, education, local health services, welfare services, and public libraries	Annual	Chartered Institute of Public Finance and Accountancy
List of Principal Statistical series and publications (Studies in Official Statistics No. 20)	1974	Central Statistical Office
Facts in Focus	1972, 1974, 1975	Central Statistical Office / Penguin Books
Britain in Figures – A F Sillitoe, 2nd Edition	1973	Penguin Books
The British Economy 1900–1970	1972	Times Newspapers Ltd.
Trends in British Society since 1900 – ed. A H Halsey	1972	MacMillan
An Analysis of Regional Economic and Social Statistics – E Hammond	1968	University of Durham, Rowntree Research Unit
The Changing Social Structure of England and Wales 1871–1961 D C Marsh	1965	Routledge and Kegan Paul Ltd
Social and Economic Trends in Northern Ireland	1975, 1976	
Population		
Corresponding annual, quarterly and weekly publications are produced for Scotland and Northern Ireland		General Register Office (Scotland) / General Register Office (Northern Ireland)
Population Projections: England and Wales, Wales, Scotland, Great Britain, Northern Ireland, United Kingdom	Annual	Office of Population Censuses and Surveys for Government Actuary's Department
Long-Term Population Distribution in Great Britain – A study	1971	Department of the Environment
First Report, Population of the United Kingdom, H.C. 379–1	1971	
Observations by the Government, Cmnd. 4748	1971	Select Committee on Science and Technology
Fifth Report, Population Policy, H.C. 335	1972	
Report of the Population Panel, Cmnd. 5258	1973	

The publications of the Office of Population Censuses and Surveys were changed in 1975. A series of Annual Volumes and various more frequent monitors is being introduced. The quarterly Population Trends first appeared in 1975.

Annual Series[1]		
Births	FM1	
Marriage and Divorce	FM2	
Mortality statistics	DH1	
„ „ : causes	DH2	
„ „ : childhood	DH3	
„ „ : accidents and violence	DH4	
„ „ : area	DH5	
Morbidity: cancer statistics	MB1	
„ : statistics of infectious diseases	MB2	
Population estimates (mid-year, local areas)	PP1	
„ projections – national	PP2	
„ „ – subnational	PP3	
Abortion statistics	AB	
Migration statistics	MN	
Local authority vital statistics	VS	
Electoral statistics	EL	

OPCS Monitors[1]		
Births (detailed analysis)	FM1	Ad hoc
Adoptions	FM3	Monthly
Deaths	DH1	Ad hoc
Deaths by cause	DH2	Quarterly
Deaths from accidents	DH4	Monthly
Population estimates and projections	PP	Annual
Abortions notified	AB	Monthly
Migration	MN	Quarterly
Births, deaths, natural increase for England and Wales	VS	Weekly
Electoral statistics	EL	Annual
Weekly Return (births, deaths, infectious diseases, and weather)	WR	Weekly

Further references

Title	Frequency/date of publication	Source

Employment

Title	Frequency/date of publication	Source
Studies of Technological Manpower: No. 3, Persons with qualifications in engineering, technology and science 1959–68	1971	Department of Trade and Industry
Social Services Manpower: Dr S Rosenbaum – *Social Trends No. 2*	1971	Central Statistical Office
Qualified manpower: Statistical sources: E G Whybrew – *Statistical News 17*	1972	Central Statistical Office
Census 1966 Qualified Manpower Tables	1971	Office of Population Censuses and Surveys
Qualified manpower in Great Britain; Studies in Official Statistics No. 18 and No. 29	1971	Central Statistical Office

Leisure

Title	Frequency/date of publication	Source
Report and Accounts of the Arts Council of Great Britain	Annual	Arts Council of Great Britain
Report of Countryside Commission	Annual	Countryside Commission
Report of Countryside Commission for Scotland	Annual	Countryside Commission for Scotland
Business Monitor; Miscellaneous Series: M2, Cinemas	Annual	Department of Trade and Industry
Pilot National Recreation Survey Reports: No. 1	1967	British Travel Association
No. 2	1969	Keele University
Report on opera and ballet in the United Kingdom	1969	Arts Council of Great Britain
Private motoring in England and Wales – P G Gray	1969	Government Social Survey
Standing Commission on Museums and Galleries: Eighth Report 1965–1969	1970	Standing Commission on Museums and Galleries
Report on orchestral resources in Great Britain	1970	Arts Council of Great Britain
The theatre today in England and Wales	1970	Arts Council of Great Britain
A survey of municipal entertainment in Great Britain for the year ending 31st March 1969	1970	Institute of Municipal Entertainment
Digest of Tourist Statistics	Annual	British Tourist Authority
Provision for Sport	1972	The Sports Council
Levy Board's Racing Statistical Information Digest	1972	Horse Race Betting Levy Board
National Parks Statistics	1973	Pembrokeshire County Council
Second Homes in England and Wales	1973	Countryside Commission
British Waterways: Recreation and Amenity Cmnd. 3401	1967	
Sport in Britain. Reference pamphlet (R4296/72) No. 107	1972	Central Office of Information

Personal income and wealth

Title	Frequency/date of publication	Source
Report on War Pensioners	Annual	Department of Health and Social Security
Time Rates of Wages and Hours of Work	Annual	Department of Employment
Reports on finances of National Insurance and Industrial Injuries schemes	Various	Government Actuary's Department
Reports of National Board for Prices and Incomes, Appendices and Statistical Supplements (Supplement to Board's fifth and final general report, Cmnd. 4649, includes summaries of the 170 reports)	Various	National Board for Prices and Incomes
Two parent families – a study of their resources and needs in 1968, 1969 and 1970	1971	Department of Health and Social Security
Families receiving supplementary benefit – a study comparing the circumstances of some fatherless families and families of the long-term sick and unemployed	1972	
Family Benefits and Pensions	1972	
Report of the Committee on One Parent Families (Finer Report)	1974	Department of Health and Social Security
The distribution of wealth and the relevance of age	1975	*Statistical News*, February 1975, CSO
Estimated Wealth of Individuals in GB 1973	1975	Inland Revenue
First report of the Royal Commission on the Distribution of Income and Wealth	1975	

Health

Title	Frequency/date of publication	Source
Statistical and Research Report Series	Various	Department of Health and Social Security
Reports on Public Health and Medical Subjects	Various	
Reports on Health and Social Subjects	Various	
On the State of the Public Health	Annual	
Digest of Pneumoconiosis Statistics	Annual	Department of Trade and Industry
National Health Service – Hospital Costing Returns	Annual	Department of Health and Social Security
Health Services in Scotland	Annual	Scottish Home and Health Department
Annual Report of the Department of Health and Social Security	Annual	Department of Health and Social Security
The Registrar General's Statistical Review of England and Wales, Supplements (series on eg Cancer; Abortion)	Various	Office of Population Censuses and Surveys
Scottish Health Service Studies	Various	Scottish Home and Health Department
Misuse of drugs in Scotland	1972	Scottish Home and Health Department

Further references

Title	Frequency/date of publication	Source
Adult Dental Health in England and Wales in 1968	1970	Department of Health and Social Security Office of Population Censuses and Surveys
The Committee on Local Authority and Allied Personal Services (Seebohm Report) Cmnd. 3703	1968	
Social Welfare for the Elderly	1968	Government Social Survey
Statistics of Smoking	1971	Tobacco Research Council
Handicapped and Impaired in Great Britain (2 vols.)	1971	Office of Population Censuses and Surveys
Social work in Scotland	Annual	Scottish Education Department – Social Work Services Group
The Family Planning Association Annual Report and Accounts	Annual	} Family Planning Association
Family Planning Association Fact Sheets	Various	

Education

Title	Frequency/date of publication	Source
Annual Report of University Central Council of Admissions (Statistical supplement is published in a separate volume)	Annual	University Central Council on Admissions
Statistics of Science and Technology last edition 1970	Annual	Department of Education and Science Ministry of Technology
Education in Scotland – A Report of the Secretary of State for Scotland	Annual	} Scottish Education Department
Scottish Educational Statistics	Annual	
Education in Northern Ireland	Annual	Department of Education, Northern Ireland
First employment of University graduates	Annual	} University Grants Committee
Surveys of the University Grants Committee	Annual	
Statistics of Education Special Series:		
No. 1: Survey of the Curriculum and Deployment of Teachers (Secondary Schools):		
Part 1—Deployment of Teachers	1968	
Part 2—The Curriculum	1971	
No. 2: Survey of in-service training for teachers, 1967	1970	
No. 3: Survey of earnings of qualified manpower in England and Wales 1966–67	1971	Department of Education and Science
Education Planning Papers:		
No. 1: Output budgeting for the Department of Education and Science	1970	
No. 2: Student numbers in higher education in England and Wales	1970	
Secondary School Staffing Survey 1970: Volumes 1–3	1972–3	Scottish Education Department
Education: a framework for expansion, Cmnd. 5174	1972	
Report on Secondary School Staffing	1973	Scottish Education Department
Education in Scotland: A statement of policy, Cmnd. 5175	1972	
The Educational System of England and Wales. H C Dent	1971	University of London Press
The First Teaching Year of the Open University: Report of the Vice-Chancellor	1971	Open University

Housing

Title	Frequency/date of publication	Source
Rate Rebates in England and Wales	Annual	} Department of the Environment
Rates and Rateable Values in England and Wales	Annual	
Local Housing Statistics: England and Wales	Quarterly	
Rates and Rateable Values in Scotland	Annual	Scottish Development Department
Housing statistics (England and Wales)		
Part I Rents		} Chartered Institute of Public Finance and Accountancy
Part II Revenue and repairs accounts	Annual	
Housing Survey Reports, No. 1–9, (West Midlands, South East Lancashire, Merseyside, Tyneside and West Yorkshire conurbations and West Yorkshire movers survey and House Condition Survey 1971 England and Wales)[1]	1969 to 1973	Department of the Environment
Welsh House Condition Survey 1968	1969	Welsh Office
Council Housing: purposes, procedures and priorities (Cullingworth Committee)	1969	Ministry of Housing and Local Government
London's Housing Needs up to 1974 (Report No. 3 of the Standing Working Party on London Housing)[2]	1970	
Statistics for Town and Country Planning Series III[3], Population and Households, No. 1, Projecting growth patterns in regions	1970	Department of the Environment
Housing in Clydeside, 1970	1971	Scottish Development Department
Homelessness in London. J Greve	1971	Scottish Academic Press
Homelessness near a thousand homes: A study of homeless families in South Wales and the West of England. B Glastonbury	1971	Allen and Unwin
Housing Executive – Annual Report	Annual	Northern Ireland Housing Executive
Report of the Committee on the Rent Acts, Cmnd. 4609	1971	

Further references

Title	Frequency/date of publication	Source
Environment		
Annual Report on Railway Accidents	Annual	Department of the Environment
Report on Grit and Dust Emissions (Hicks Report)	1967	
Report on Needs of New Communities (Cullingworth Report)	1967	Ministry of Housing and Local Government
Report on Intermediate Areas (Hunt Report) Cmnd. 3998	1969	
People and Planning (Skeffington Report)	1969	
Royal Commission on Environmental Pollution:		
First Report Cmnd. 4585	1971	
Second Report Cmnd. 4894	1972	
Third Report Cmnd. 5054	1972	
Fourth Report Cmnd. 5780	1974	
Annual National Surveys of Smoke and Sulphur Dioxide	Annual	⎫
Annual Reports of the Chief Alkali Inspector	Annual	⎬ Warren Spring Laboratory
The National Survey of Air Pollution 1961–71	1972	⎭
Basic Road Statistics	Annual	British Roads Federation
Towards Cleaner Water, Report of a River Pollution Survey of Scotland	1972	Scottish Development Department
Public safety		
Offences of Drunkenness	Annual	⎫
Offences Relating to Motor Vehicles	Annual	⎪
Report of the Parole Board	Annual	⎪
Report of the Criminal Injuries Compensation Board	Annual	⎬ Home Office
Report of Her Majesty's Chief Inspector of Constabulary	Annual	⎪
Report of the Commissioner of Police of the Metropolis	Annual	⎭
Report of the Parole Board, Scotland	Annual	⎫
Report of the Criminal Injuries Compensation Board	Annual	⎬ Scottish Home and Health Department
Report of Her Majesty's Chief Inspector of Constabulary for Scotland	Annual	⎭
Children in trouble Cmnd. 3601	1968	Home Office
People in Prison (England and Wales) Cmnd. 4214	1969	⎫
Reports on the Work of the Probation and After-Care Department:		⎪
1966–1968 Cmnd. 4233	1969	⎬ Home Office
1969–1971 Cmnd. 5158	1972	⎪
Research studies	Various	⎭
Report of Departmental Committee on Criminal Statistics Cmnd. 3448	1967	
Report of the Committee on Civil Judicial Statistics Cmnd. 3684	1968	Lord Chancellor's Office
Report of Departmental Committee on Crime Recording Cmnd. 3705	1968	Scottish Home and Health Department
Justice out of reach; a case for small claims courts	1970	The Consumer Council
Supplementary Statistics relating to Crime[4]	Annual	Home Office
Murder 1957 to 1968	1969	Home Office
Civil administration		
Report of the Parole Board	Annual	Home Office
Report of the Parole Board, Scotland	Annual	Scottish Home and Health Department
People in Prison (England and Wales) Cmnd. 4214	1969	⎫
Reports on the Work of the Probation and After-Care Department:		⎪
1966–1968 Cmnd. 4233	1969	⎬ Home Office
1969–1971 Cmnd. 5158	1972	⎭
Health Service Commissioners for England, Wales and Scotland Annual Reports	Annual	
Return of Election Expenses	Occasional	HMSO
British Parliamentary Election Results 1950–1970. F W S Craig	1971	MacMillan
The Times Guide to the House of Commons	Occasional	The Times Newspaper
British Parliamentary Election Statistics 1918–1968. F W S Craig 2nd ed.	1971	MacMillan
The British General Election of 1964. D Butler and A King	1965	⎫
" " " " " 1966. D Butler and A King	1966	⎪
" " " " " 1970. D Butler and M Pinto-Duschinsky	1971	⎬ MacMillan
" " " " " February 1974. D Butler and D Kavanagh	1974	⎪
" " " " " October 1974. D Butler and D Kavanagh	1975	⎭
Public expenditure		
Local Government Financial Statistics (England and Wales)	Annual	⎧ Department of the Environment / Welsh Office
Local Financial Returns, Scotland	Annual	Scottish Development Department
Local Authority Financial Returns, Northern Ireland	Annual	Department of Environment, Northern Ireland

Further references

Title	Frequency/date of publication	Source
Public Expenditure White Papers	Annual	
Public expenditure: planning and control Cmnd. 2915	1966	
A Selection of Unit Costs in Public Expenditure	1968	
Public expenditure: a new presentation Cmnd. 4017	1969	H.M. Treasury
New policies for public spending Cmnd. 4515	1970	
Public Expenditure White Papers Handbook on Methodology	1972	
The future shape of local government finance, Cmnd. 4741	1971	Department of the Environment
Statistics of the British Economy. F M M Lewes	1967	Allen & Unwin

Households

Title	Frequency/date of publication	Source
Services for the Elderly at Home	1972	National Old People's Welfare Council (N.C.S.S.)
Care of the Elderly in Britain, Reference Paper No. 121	1974	Central Office of Information
The Census of residential accommodation 1970 Vol. I 'Residential Accommodation for the Elderly and for the Younger Physically Handicapped' [5]	1975	Department of Health and Social Security
Children in care in England and Wales	Annual	HMSO
Children in Britain: Reference Pamphlet R5236/73 No. 34	1973	Central Office of Information (HMSO)
The Youth Service and Similar Provision for Young People by Margaret Bone assisted by Elizabeth Ross	1972	Office of Population Censuses and Surveys, Social Survey Division

International

Other countries have produced publications which are similar to 'Social Trends', and contain many statistics which can be compared to those in this volume. The main publications of the type include:

USA	— 'Social Indicators', 1973 (1977 edition planned)
	— The USA has also recently (July 1976) started producing a monthly 'Status', similar to a combination of the UK *Economic Trends* and *Social Trends*
France	— 'Données Sociales', 1973 and 1974
Germany	— 'Geselleschaftliche Daten', 1973
Canada	— 'Perspective Canada', 1974 (two editions, 1 English, 1 French)
Japan	— 'The Life & its Quality in Japan', 1972 (English)
Netherlands	— 'Social en Cuturaal Rapport', 1974
Norway	— 'Social Survey', 1974
Sweden	— 'Social Survey', 1974
Italy	— 'Statische Sociale', 1975
Malaysia	— 'Socio-economic Indicators and National Policy', 1974
Philippines	— 'Measuring the Quality of Life, Philippines Social Indicators', 1975

[1] These publications are available from the Office of Population Censuses and Surveys and not HMSO.
[2] Housing Survey Reports No. 1–5 are available from HMSO and No. 6–9 are available from the Department of the Environment.
[3] These publications are available from the Department of the Environment and not HMSO.
[4] These publications are available from the Home Office and not HMSO.
[5] A printed report is available from the Department of Health and Social Security

Index

The numbers in this index refer to table and chart numbers. Chart numbers are in italics. The references in Appendix B are to definitions and methodology.

abortions *1.19*, 7.20
academic qualifications of population 4.10–4.13
accessibility of facilities 9.17
accidents
   see casualties and injuries
activity rates 4.6
administrative tribunals 12.18, 12.21
age standardisation, App. B page 234
agricultural land 9.14, *9.15*, App. B page 249
Agricultural Policy (EEC), Calendar, page 223
air pollution *9.3–9.6*, map on page 163
Air Pollution Survey, App. B page 248
air-sea rescue operations 11.15
alcoholic drinking
   consumption of *6.9*
   expenditure on *6.4–6.6*
   retail price index *6.1*, 6.2
alcoholism *7.23*
annual paid holiday, male manual workers *10.2*, 10.3
art galleries
   attendance figures 10.15
arts, public expenditure on 10.21, 13.3, 13.5, 13.7
attendance allowance, App. B page 243
attitudes, pages 47–60
   to district 9.22
   to durables 6.8
   to education 3.11, 3.18

bedroom standard, *8.10*, App. B page 247
benefits, related to income 5.11–*5.14*, 5.32
birth rates 1.7
   international comparison *14.3*
births
   at home and in hospital 7.18
   live
      by country of birth of mother 1.21
      by number of previous liveborn children 1.18
      illegitimate 1.7
      legitimate 1.7, 1.18
      New Commonwealth 1.20, 1.21
      premarital conceptions 1.7
   maternity services 7.18
blind population 2.20
books
   titles, number issued 10.14
borstals, population of 11.4
breach of promise, Calendar, page 217
British National Travel Survey, App. B page 249

cars, ownership by household *6.7*
   international comparison *14.10*
casualties
   fire 11.16
   from fireworks *11.17*
   from industrial accidents 11.13
   Northern Ireland 11.18
   railway accidents 11.12
   road accidents 11.8–*11.11*
Census of Population 1.1, 1.14, 2.1, 2.2, 2.9, 2.23, 4.3, *4.5*, 4.10, 4.11, 4.14, 4.23, 4.24, 8.6, 9.10, 9.12, Calendar, page 220, App. B page 234
certified sickness 7.17, App. B page 245
cervical cytology *7.27*

charities
   turnover 12.7
child care
   children's services 2.14
   detention centres 11.4
   health centres 2.14
   local authority care 2.15–*2.17*
   special schools 2.14, 3.4, 3.16, 3.17
childless women *1.17*
child minders 2.14
child offenders 11.2, 11.3
   borstals, detention centres 11.4
   receptions into institutions 2.15
children
   allowances 5.22
   by age group 2.9–2.13
   by household accommodation 2.13
   by socio-economic group of parent *3.2*
   circumstances under which received into care 2.15
   in care of local authorities 2.15–*2.17*, App. B page 237
   in families receiving family allowances 5.26, 5.30
   in households 1.14, 2.6, 2.12
   of dissolved marriages 1.12
   (previous) of mothers having an abortion 7.20
   under 5 at school 3.1–3.5
   see also child care, child offenders, schools
chiropody 2.20, 7.25
church membership and attendance 10.13
Chronically Sick and Disabled Persons Act 1970, Calendar, page 218
circulation of newspapers 10.16
Citizens' Advice Bureaux 12.10
civil administration
   see administrative tribunals, civil justice, elections, Parliamentary Commissioner, prisons
civil justice
   County Courts
      class of proceedings and disposals 12.12, *12.13*
      number of proceedings 12.11
   Courts of Appeal 12.11
   Courts of First Instance 12.11
   legal aid 12.20
   proceedings 12.11–*12.16*
   Sheriff Courts 12.14, *12.15*
   summary 12.11
clean air
   hours of winter sunshine *9.3*
   orders under Clean Air Act 9.4
clothing
   expenditure on *6.4–6.6*
   retail price index *6.1*, 6.2
coalminers' strike, Calendar, pages 221, 225
colleges of education 3.14
coloured population
   in households 2.25–2.27
   in work 4.23–4.25
Common Agricultural Policy, Calendar, page 223
community homes 2.16, *2.17*
conservation, map on page 169
construction
   of dwellings 8.4
consumer price index numbers
   international comparison 14.9
Consumers' Association 12.7
consumers' expenditure, App. B page 244
   analysis by types of goods or services:
      shares of total at constant prices 6.6
   average weekly household *6.4*, 6.5
   international comparison 14.7, *14.8*

conurbations
  labour force of 9.12
  population 9.10
    in London Metropolitan Region 9.11
convictions *see* crime
County Courts, proceedings in 12.11–*12.13*, *12.16*,
  App. B page 252
Courts of Appeal
  civil proceedings 12.11
Courts of First Instance
  number of proceedings 12.11
crime (*see* article on page 32)
  indictable offences
    age groups of persons found guilty 11.2
    pattern of offence by age 11.3
    persons found guilty 11.1–11.3
  legal aid 12.19
  non-indictable offences
    persons found guilty 11.1
  offences known to the police 11.1
  persons proceeded against 11.1
  Scotland (*see* article on page 43)
Criminal Damage Act 1971, Calendar, page 219
Crown Court, App. B page 250
  type of plea *12.16*

day nurseries, App. B page 238
day-release courses 4.2
deaf population 2.20
death grants, public expenditure on 5.34
death rates 1.8, 7.1–7.5, 7.17
  by age 1.8, 7.5
  by selected causes 7.3–7.5
  by regions 7.17
  by sex 1.8, 7.3–7.5
  standardised mortality ratios 7.1, 7.3, *7.4*
deaths
  and net population changes 1.3
  by cause and sex 7.3–7.5
  from fire 11.16
  home accidents 11.14
  industrial accidents 11.13
  infant mortality 1.8, 7.1, *7.2*, 7.5, 7.17, *14.4*
  maternal mortality 7.1, *7.2*
  Northern Ireland emergency 11.18
  railway accidents 11.12
  road accidents 11.8
defence, public expenditure on *13.1*, 13.3
dentists *7.15*, 7.17, 7.29, 7.30
dependent children 1.14, 2.6, 2.12
disabled 7.26
disabled and sick receiving supplementary benefit 5.23
divorce 1.12
  children of dissolved marriages 1.12
Divorce Reform Act 1969, Calendar, page 218
doctors *7.15*–7.17, 7.29, 7.30
drug addiction, App. B page 246
  number of addicts, by age and drug taken 7.24
durables, possession of *6.7*, 6.8
  attitudes toward 6.8
  retail price index *6.1*, 6.2
dwellings *8.1–8.5*
  see also households, App. B page 237

earnings
  cumulative distribution of 5.17
  gross weekly 5.15, *5.16*, 5.18, *5.19*
    by age 5.18
    median and decile points 5.15, *5.16*
  percentage increase 5.20
  related supplement 5.22
economically active population 4.3–*4.8*, App. B page 240
  international comparison 14.12
  qualifications 4.10–4.13
  see also labour force *and* working population

education
  colleges of 3.14
  examination passes 3.8, *3.9*, 3.11, *3.13*
  for the under-fives 3.1–3.5
  further 3.12–3.14, 3.16, 3.17
  higher 3.14
  highest achievement 4.12, 4.13
  international comparison 14.11
  manpower in 3.16
  nursery 2.14, 3.1–3.5, 3.16, 3.17
  primary 3.4, 3.5, 3.16, 3.17
  public expenditure on 3.17, *13.1*, 13.3, 13.5–13.7
  secondary 3.4–3.11, 3.16, 3.17
  special schools 2.14, 3.4, 3.16, 3.17
elderly
  expenditure *2.21*, 2.24
  income 2.22, *2.23*
  in residential accommodation *2.19*, 2.20
  local authority accommodation *2.19*, 2.20
  population 2.18
  residential services 2.20
elections
  by-election results 12.2
  general election results 12.1, *12.3*, Calendar, pages
    218, 225, and 227
  local election results 12.4
emigration *1.9*, 1.10
employees
  earnings 5.17
  hours of work *10.1*, 10.3
  paid holidays *10.2*, 10.3
  summary table 4.3
  total in employment 4.3–4.7
employment, young persons entering 4.1
energy crisis, Calendar, page 224
environment
  agricultural land 9.14, *9.15*
  Clean Air Act 9.4
  facilities, accessibility of 9.17
  pollution
    from road vehicles 9.6
    of air *9.3*–9.6, map on page 163
    of rivers 9.8, *9.9*
  population
    density 9.13
    in conurbations 9.10, 9.11
  radioactivity in milk 9.7
  rain *9.2*
  recycling of materials 9.20
  sunshine *9.1*, *9.3*
  transport *9.18*, 9.19
environmental services
  public expenditure on 9.21, 13.3, 13.5–13.7
Equal Pay Act 1970, Calendar, page 218
European Economic Community, Calendar, pages 218
  and 223
examinations *see* education
expectation of life 7.1, App. B page 245
  international comparison 14.5
expenditure
  by local authorities 13.5, *13.6*
  by public authorities *13.1*–13.7
  elderly *2.21*, 2.24
  households *2.21*, 2.24, *6.4*, 6.5

facilities, accessibility of 9.17
families 1.14, 2.1, 2.3, 2.6
  average size for various years of marriage 1.15
  benefits from additional £1 of earnings 5.28
  by size 1.14–1.16
  homeless 8.21–8.24
  in households 2.1, 2.3, 2.6, 2.7
  non-family households 2.1, 2.2
  with low net resources 5.29, 5.31
family allowances 5.30, 5.34
  public expenditure on 5.34

Family Expenditure Survey *2.21*–2.24, *6.4*, 6.5, *6.7*, 8.11
family income supplement 5.26, *5.27*, Calendar, page 243
family planning 7.19
Family Planning Association, App. B page 246
fertility rates 1.7
fire casualties
 fatal 11.16
fireworks
 injuries from *11.17*
food
 consumption 6.11
  changes in *6.10*
 expenditure on *6.4*–6.6
 retail price index *6.1*, 6.2
freezers
 numbers owned
  international comparison *14.10*
further education
 advanced level passes *3.12*
 manpower in 13.16
 public expenditure on 3.17
 students 3.13, 3.14
 summary 3.13
 type of course 3.13

gambling 10.19
GCE examination passes 3.8, *3.9*, 3.11, *3.12*
general dental services
 public expenditure 7.30
General Household Survey 1.13, 2.4–2.8, 2.12, 2.13,
 2.25–2.27, *3.2*, 4.4, *4.5*, 4.12, 4.13, 4.15, *7.6*–7.8,
 7.16, 7.17, 8.7–*8.10*, 8.12–8.14, *8.18*, 10.17, 10.18,
 App. B page 234
general improvement areas 8.15
general medical practitioners 7.29
 by region 7.17
 payments to *7.15*
 persons consulting 7.16
general medical services
 public expenditure on 7.30
Gini coefficient, App. B page 234
gipsies 9.16
government training schemes *4.18*
graduates, employment of 3.15, *4.9*
grants, government
 as source of personal income 13.2
 house renovation 8.16
 housing 8.19
 to personal sector 13.2
guardians' allowances 5.22

handicapped
 residential and other services 2.20
health
 abortions *1.19*, 7.20
 centres *7.14*
 certified sickness, days lost through 7.17
 drug addiction 7.24
 family planning 7.19
 general medical practitioners 7.16, 7.17, 7.29
 hospitals 7.9–7.12
 life expectation 7.1
  international comparison 14.5
 maternity services 7.18
 private insurance *7.13*
 regional statistics 7.17
 service commissioners, App. B page 246
 service, manpower in 7.29
 smoking habits *7.22*
 venereal disease *7.21*
 see also births, deaths, hospitals, and morbidity
Health and Safety at Work, etc Act 1974, Calendar,
 page 225
health visitors 7.25

higher education
 age of students 3.14
 number of students 3.14
holidays *10.6*–10.10
 abroad *10.6*, 10.7, *10.8*, *10.9*
 in Great Britain *10.6*, 10.7, *10.9*, 10.10
 manual workers' paid *10.2*, 10.3
 number of tourist visits 10.10
home accidents
 deaths in the home and residential
  accommodation 11.14
home helps 2.20, App. B page 238
home nursing 2.20, 7.25
homelessness 8.21–8.24
hospitals
 alcoholism *7.23*
 beds 7.9, *7.11*
 births in 7.18
 in-patient enquiry, App. B page 246
 maternity services 7.18
 non-psychiatric illnesses 7.10
 patients 7.9, *7.11*
 psychiatric illnesses 7.12
 summary table 7.9
hours
 weekly hours of work 4.20, *4.21*, *10.1*, 10.3
household accommodation
 type lived in by children 2.13
households 2.1–2.8
 age of head of 2.5
 by country of birth (excluding UK) of chief economic
  supporter 2.28
 by family type 2.6
 by income and tenure *8.11*
 by number of families 2.1
 by size 2.1, 2.4
 by type 2.7
 coloured population 2.25–2.27
 expenditure
  average weekly *2.21*, 2.24, *6.4*, 6.5
  on goods and services *6.4*–6.6
  pattern *6.4*
  pensioner *2.21*, 2.24
 food consumption 6.11
  changes in *6.10*
 income *2.23*
  active and non-active households *5.8*, *5.9*
  average weekly by source 5.10
  by household type 5.7
  by region 5.38
  pensioner 2.22, *2.23*
  redistribution through taxes and benefits 5.11–*5.14*
 moves
  actual and potential movers *8.13*
  number in last 5 years 8.14
 projections 2.3
 socio-economic group of head 2.8
 tenure
  by colour of head *8.10*
  by type of accommodation *8.8*
  profile of head 8.9
 with women and children 2.12
 see also App. B page 237
housing
 amenities 8.6, 8.7, *8.10*
  by colour of head 8.7
 average purchase price 8.17
 bedroom standard *8.10*
 central government expenditure 8.19
 colour of head *8.10*
 completions *8.5*
 conditions 8.6
 expenditure on *6.4*–6.6
 grants to personal sector 8.19
 improvement areas 8.15
 improvement/renovation grants 8.15, 8.16, 8.20
 length of residence 8.12

loans and mortgages *8.18*, 8.19, 8.20
local authority expenditure 8.19
moves in 5 years 8.14
new construction 8.4
public expenditure 8.19, *13.1*, 13.3, 13.5, 13.7
rents and mortgages *8.18*
retail price index *6.1*, 6.2
slum clearance *8.2*, 8.4
stock of dwellings *8.1*, 8.3–*8.5*
  by tenure *8.1*, 8.4
  change in 8.4
subsidies 8.19, 8.20
tenure *8.1*, 8.4, *8.8*–*8.12*
type of accommodation *8.8*

illegitimacy, percentage of live births 1.7
immigration *1.9*, 1.10, Calendar, page 222
Immigration Act 1971, 12.21, Calendar, pages 219, 222
improvement grants, housing 8.15, 8.16, 8.20
  see also house renovation grants, App. B page 248
income
  household *2.23*, 5.7–*5.14*
  local authority 13.4, *13.6*
  percentage represented by social security payments
    to sick men 5.33
  personal *see* personal income
  personal sector 5.1
  persons over retirement age 2.22, *2.23*
  redistribution of 5.11–*5.14*
industrial
  accidents 11.13, App. B page 251
  death benefit 5.22
  disablement benefit 5.22
  disputes
    as cause of stoppages *Figure VIII* page 19
    international comparison *14.14*
  injuries
    benefits
      persons receiving 5.22
      public expenditure 5.34
  tribunals 12.18
infant mortality 1.8, 7.1, *7.2*, 7.5, 7.17, App. B page 245
  international comparison *14.4*
injuries from
  fire 11.16
  fireworks *11.17*
  home accidents 11.14
  industrial accidents 11.13
  Northern Ireland civil disturbances 11.18
  railway accidents 11.12
  road accidents 11.8–*11.11*
injury benefit 5.22
institutional population 2.2
  children in care of local authorities 2.15–*2.17*
International Classification of Diseases, App. B page 245
International Passenger Survey, App. B page 236
invalidity benefits 5.22

job mobility 4.15
job satisfaction 4.22
journeys
  to work: means of travel *10.5*
      time taken 10.4
justice and law
  public expenditure 11.6, 13.3, 13.5, 13.7
  see also administrative tribunals, civil justice, crime, *and*
    Parliamentary Commissioner for Administration
juvenile delinquency *see* child offenders

labour force 4.1–4.7
  contribution of immigrants 4.23–4.25
  of conurbations 9.12
  projections and age distributions, App. B page 235

see also economically active population, working
  population
land, agricultural 9.14, *9.15*
land tribunals 12.18
legal aid, App. B page 252
  civil cases 12.20
  criminal cases 12.19
  public expenditure on 11.6
Legal Aid Act 1974, Calendar, page 224
leisure
  activities: by age and sex 10.17
        by socio-economic group 10.18
  church membership and attendance 10.13
  expenditure on 6.6
  holidays *10.6*–10.10
  membership of organisations
    outdoor activities 10.11
    young persons 10.12
  television viewing 10.20
libraries, public expenditure on 10.21, 13.3, 13.5, 13.7
life expectation 7.1
  international comparison 14.5
local authorities
  children in care of 2.15–*2.17*
  children's services 2.14
  elderly and handicapped services 2.20
  expenditure 13.5, *13.6*
  health authorities, expenditure 7.30
  house loans 8.19
  housing
    expenditure on 8.19
  income 13.4, *13.6*
  maternity services 7.18
  personal social services expenditure 7.30
  residential accommodation for elderly *2.19*, 2.20
  school meals and milk 3.17

manpower
  in education 3.16
  in health and personal social services 7.29
marginal net benefits ('poverty trap') *5.27*, 5.28
marriage 1.11–1.13, 1.15–*1.17*
  manner of solemnisation *12.22*
  marital condition by age and sex *1.2*
  parental consent, Calendar, page 218
  percentage of remarriages 1.11
maternity benefits 5.22
  public expenditure on 5.34
  services 7.18
maternal mortality 7.1, *7.2*, App. B page 245
meals on wheels 2.20, App. B page 238
median, App. B page 234
mental health 7.12
migration
  flows *1.9*, 1.10
  net changes 1.3, *1.4*
morbidity 7.6–7.8
mortality 7.1–7.5
  infant mortality 1.8, 7.1, *7.2*, 7.5, 7.17
    international comparison *14.4*
  maternal 7.1, *7.2*
  ratios, standardised 7.1, 7.3, *7.4*
  see also deaths
mortgages
  payments, by region *8.18*
  tax relief on 8.20
motor vehicles 6.7, 6.8
  expenditure on *6.4*–6.6
  international comparison *14.10*
  retail price index *6.1*, 6.2
mountain rescue teams 11.15
MPs
  education of *12.6*
museums
  attendance figures 10.15

266

charges, Calendar, page 225
public expenditure on museums and galleries 10.21, 13.3, 13.5, 13.7

national assistance *see* supplementary benefits
National Food Survey *6.10*, 6.11, App. B page 244
national health service *see* health
national insurance benefits 5.22, 5.34
   as source of personal income 5.22
   attendance allowances 5.34
   death grants 5.34
   earnings-related supplement 5.22
   guardians' allowances 5.22, 5.34
   industrial injuries benefits 5.22, 5.34
      industrial death benefit 5.22
      industrial disablement benefit 5.22
      injury benefit 5.22
   invalidity benefits 5.22
   maternity allowance 5.22
   maternity benefits 5.34
   persons receiving 5.22
   public expenditure on 5.34
   regional analysis 5.38
   retirement pensions 5.22, 5.34
   sickness benefits 5.22, 5.34
   unemployment benefits 5.22, 5.34
   widows' benefits 5.22, 5.34
      see also social security, App. B page 242
National Travel Survey, App. B page 249
New Commonwealth ethnic origin
   population 1.20
New Earnings Survey, 4.20, *4.21*, 5.15–5.20, 538, App. B page 241
newspapers, circulation of 10.16
nitrate concentrations in rivers *9.9*
non-contributory old-age pensions
   public expenditure on 5.34
non-psychiatric hospitals 7.10
Northern Ireland civil disturbances
   deaths and injuries 11.13
nursery schools 2.14, 3.1–3.4
nurses, qualified 7.29
nursing, home 2.20, 7.25

occupational change 4.14
Ombudsman 12.17, App. B page 252
Open University 4.19, App. B page 239, Calendar, page 220
option mortgages, App. B page 248
organisations
   for young persons 10.12
   membership of 10.11–10.13, 12.7–12.9
orphans' pensions 5.22
outdoor activities, membership of 10.11
owner-occupied dwellings
   by region 8.3
   stock of *8.1*, 8.4
ownership of pets 10.22
ownership of vehicles *6.7*, 6.8

paid holiday, manual male workers *10.2*, 10.3
Parliamentary Commissioner for Administration 12.17, Calendar, page 252
parity of mother 1.18
part-time workers 4.20, *4.21*
passenger transport, App. B page 249
   prices *9.18*, 9.19
   resources 9.19
   use *9.18*, 9.19
pensioner households
   average weekly expenditure *2.21*, 2.24
   average weekly income *2.22*, *2.23*
   retail price index 6.2
pensioners on supplementary benefit 5.23, *5.24*

pensions
   industrial disablement 5.22
   non-contributory old-age 5.34
   retirement 5.22, 5.34
   war 5.34
   widows' 5.22, 5.34
personal expenditure
   analysis of consumers' expenditure 6.6
   average weekly household *2.21*, 2.24, *6.4*, 6.5
   of elderly *2.21*, 2.24
personal income, App. B page 240, 5.1–*5.6*
   by highest qualification level 4.13
   composition 5.1, 5.5
   distribution before and after tax *5.3*, 5.4
   of elderly *2.22*, *2.23*
   quantile shares *5.6*
   real disposable *5.2*
   redistribution through taxes and benefits 5.11–*5.14*
   sources 5.1, 5.5, 5.10
   see also earnings
personal social services
   child welfare
      children's services 2.14
      local authority care 2.15–*2.17*
   chiropody 2.20, 7.25
   Citizens' Advice Bureaux 12.10
   disabled 7.26
   elderly 2.20
   handicapped 2.20
   health visitors 2.20, 7.25
   home helps 2.20
   home nursing 2.20, 7.25
   local authority expenditure 7.30
   manpower in 7.29
   meals on wheels 2.20
   public expenditure 7.30, *13.1*, 13.3, 13.5–13.7
   residential services 2.20
   school meals and milk 7.30
   special schools 2.14, 3.4, 3.16, 3.17
   welfare foods 7.30
pets, ownership of 10.22
police
   public expenditure on 11.6
   strength of forces 11.7
Pollution Act 1974, Control of, Calendar, page 225
pollution
   from road vehicles 9.6
   of air *9.3*–9.6, map on page 163
   of rivers 9.8, *9.9*
population
   abortions *1.19*, 7.20
   age distribution 1.1, *1.2*
   births 1.3, *1.4*, 1.7, 1.18, 1.20, 1.21
   changes 1.3, *1.4*
   children 2.9–2.11
   density 9.13
      international comparison 14.1
   elderly 2.18
   emigration *1.9*, 1.10
   geographical distribution 1.22
   immigration *1.9*, 1.10
   in conurbations 9.10, 9.11
   in new standard regions 1.22, *Figure III* on page 12
   institutional 2.2
   international comparison 14.1, *14.2*
   marital status *1.2*, 1.13
   metropolitan counties *Figure IV* on page 13
   migration
      flows *1.9*, 1.10
   New Commonwealth ethnic origin 1.20
   projections 1.1, 1.3–*1.6*, 1.22, *2.10*, 2.11, 2.18
   regional 1.22
   sex and age structure 1.1, *1.2*
   sex ratio 1.1
   total population 1.1
   variant projections 1.5, *1.6*
   working 4.3–*4.8*

in conurbations 9.12
see also births, deaths, and App. B page 234
'Poverty Trap' *5.27*, 5.28
preventive medicine *7.27*, 7.28
primary schools *see* schools
prisons
    population 11.4, *11.5*
    male inmates
        by age *11.5*
        male sentenced *11.5*
    receptions into 11.4
private medical insurance *7.13*
probation
    public expenditure on 11.6
projections
    children *2.10*, 2.11
    households 2.3
    population 1.1, 1.3–*1.6*, 1.22
        elderly 2.18
    school population 3.4, 3.5
    variant population 1.5, *1.6*
    see also App. B page 235
prosecutions *see* crime
psychiatric illness 7.12
public expenditure *13.1*–13.7
    administration of social security 5.34
    annual rates of increase 13.7
    death grants 5.34
    defence *13.1*, 13.3
    dental services 7.30
    education 3.17, *13.1*, 13.3, 13.5–13.7
    environmental services 9.21, 13.3, 13.5–13.7
    family allowances 5.34
    fixed capital formation 13.2
    general medical and dental services 7.30
    goods and services 13.2
    grants to personal sector 13.2
    health 7.30, *13.1*, 13.3, 13.5–13.7
    hospital, etc. services 7.30
    house loans 8.19
    housing 8.19, 8.20, *13.1*, 13.3, 13.5–13.7
    housing subsidies 8.19, 8.20
    industrial injuries benefits 5.34
    justice and law 11.6, 13.3, 13.5, 13.7
    libraries, museums, and arts 10.21, 13.3, 13.5, 13.7
    local health authority services 7.30
    local personal social services 7.30
    maternity benefits 5.34
    national insurance benefits 5.34
    non-contributory old-age pensions 5.34
    ophthalmic services 7.30
    personal social services 7.30, *13.1*, 13.3, 13.5–13.7
    pharmaceutical services 7.30
    police 11.6
    pollution 9.21
    prisons 11.6
    probation and after-care 11.6
    retirement pensions 5.34
    sewerage 9.21
    social security 5.34, *13.1*, 13.3, 13.7
    supplementary benefits 5.34
    teacher training 3.17
    unemployment benefits 5.34
    universities 3.17
    war pensions 5.34
    widows' benefits 5.34
public sector employment *4.4*, 4.7–*4.9*
public transport *9.18*, 9.19
pupils
    age distribution 3.5
    as a percentage of age group population 3.1, *3.3*, 3.5
    projections 3.4, 3.5
    school leavers *3.9*–3.11
    summary by type of school 3.4
purchasing power of the pound (internal) 6.3

qualified population 4.10–4.13

radioactivity in milk 9.7, App. B page 248
rain *9.2*
recreation *see* leisure
recycling of materials 9.20
redistribution of income 5.11–*5.14*
regional statistics (most statistics on a regional basis are
        included in a separate CSO annual volume *Regional
        Statistics*)
    air pollution 9.5
    distribution of income 5.38
    health 7.17
    household income 5.38
    house prices 8.17
    housing stock 8.3
    infant mortality 7.17
    median earnings 5.38
    mortgages *8.18*
    population 1.22
    rented accommodation 8.3
    rent payments *8.18*
    social security benefits 5.38
Rehabilitation of Offenders Act 1974, Calendar, page 225
remarriages 1.11
    manner of solemnisation *12.22*
rented accommodation
    by region 8.3
    stock of *8.1*, 8.4
rent, received by local authorities 8.19
rent payments *8.18*
    by region *8.18*
residential services 2.20
restricted activity
    by marital status *7.6*, 7.7
retail price index *6.1*, 6.2, App. B page 244
retirement pensions
    compared with earnings and retail prices 5.32
    persons receiving 5.22, *5.25*
    public expenditure 5.34
river pollution 9.8, *9.9*
River Pollution Survey, App. B page 248
road accidents 11.8–*11.11*, App. B page 251
Royal Air Force rescues 11.15
Royal Naval rescues 11.15

Satisfaction with
    district 9.22
    education 3.18
    work 4.22
schools 3.1–3.11
    courses taken 3.8
    examinations 3.8, *3.9*, 3.11, *3.12*
    intentions of school children 3.11
    leavers
        by qualification *3.9*, 3.11
        by type of school *3.9*, 3.10,
        destination 3.10
        examination achievement *3.9*, 3.11
    meals and milk, public expenditure 3.17
    nursery 2.14, 3.1–3.4
    primary, public expenditure 3.17
    pupils
        number 3.1, 3.4, 3.5
        projected numbers 3.4, 3.5
    secondary 3.4–3.11, 3.16, 3.17
        public expenditure 3.17
        Scotland and Northern Ireland 3.7
    special 2.14, 3.4, 3.16, 13.17
    under fives at 3.1–3.5
search and rescue operations 11.15
self-employment 4.3
sentences, of courts, App. B pages 250, 251
Sheriff Courts 12.14, *12.15*
shiftworking 4.25
sickness benefit 5.22
    public expenditure 5.34
sickness, acute *7.6*, 7.8

sickness, certified 7.17
sickness, chronic 7.6, 7.7
skill centres 4.18
slum clearance 8.2, 8.4
smoke control orders 9.4, App. B page 248
smoking habits 7.22
social class, App. B page 235
social security
    administrative costs 5.34
    family allowances 5.30, 5.34
    industrial injuries benefits 5.34
        industrial death benefit 5.22
        industrial disablement benefit 5.22
        injury benefit 5.22
    non-contributory old-age pensions 5.34
    payments as percentage of income, for unemployed
      or sick 5.33
    public expenditure 5.34, *13.1*, 13.3, 13.7
    regional analysis 5.38
    war pensions 5.34
    see also national insurance *and* supplementary benefits
Social Services Act 1970, Calendar, page 219
socio-economic groups
    of head of household 2.8
    of parents of school children *3.2*
SSRC Survey Unit 3.18, 6.8, 9.22
standardised mortality ratios 7.1, 7.3, *7.4*
State of Emergency, Calendar, pages 221, 225
students
    evening courses 3.13
    further education 3.13
    higher education 3.14
    part-time 3.14
    university 3.14
subjective indicators 3.11, 3.18, 6.8, 9.22
sunshine *9.1*, *9.3*
supplementary benefits
    families with net resources less than 120 per cent
      of 5.29, 5.31
    percentage of NI beneficiaries receiving 5.22
    persons receiving 5.22–*5.24*
    public expenditure on 5.34
    related to net earnings 5.32
    wage stopped 5.23
    see also, App. B page 243

taxation 5.11–*5.14*
    personal incomes, before and after tax *5.3*, 5.4
    redistribution of income 5.11–*5.14*
    tax relief on mortgages 8.20
teachers
    training, public expenditure 3.17
    see also colleges of education
television
    licences issued in UK 10.20
    viewing hours by age and social class 10.20
theatres – attendance figures 10.15
three-day working week, Calendar, page 225
tobacco
    expenditure on *6.4*–6.6
    retail price index *6.1*, 6.2
trade unions
    membership *12.8*, 12.9
training, government schemes *4.18*
transport *9.18*, 9.19
travel
    expenditure on *6.4*–6.6
    retail price index *6.1*, 6.2
tribunals, administrative 12.18, App. B page 252

Uganda Resettlement Board, Calendar, page 222
unemployed *4.16*, 4.17, App. B page 240
unemployment
    benefits 5.22

international comparison 14.13
public expenditure 5.34
universities
    employment of graduates 3.15, *4.9*
    manpower in 3.16
    Open University students 4.19
    public expenditure 3.17

vaccination 7.28
Value Added Tax, Calendar, page 223
vehicles
    ownership *6.7*, 6.8
    pollution from 9.6
venereal disease 7.21
vital statistics 1.1–1.11, 7.1–7.5
    birth rates 1.7
    births, live
        average annual numbers 1.3, *1.4*
        illegitimate 1.7
    death rates
        by age and sex 1.8
        infant 1.8, 7.1, *7.2*, 7.5, 7.17
    deaths
        and net population changes 1.3
        by age, cause, and sex 7.1–7.5
        by selected causes 7.3–7.5
        standardised mortality ratios 7.1, 7.3, *7.4*
        see also births, deaths, and marriages
    families 1.14–1.16
    infant mortality 1.8, 7.1, *7.2*, 7.5, 7.17
        international comparison *14.4*
    life expectation 7.1
        international comparison 14.5
    marriages 1.11
    remarriages 1.11
    standardised mortality ratios 7.1, 7.3, *7.4*
voluntary homes 2.16, *2.17*, *2.19*, 2.20

wage stopped supplementary benefits 5.23
war pensions, public expenditure 5.34
wealth 5.35–5.37, App. B pages 243–4
    by asset value 5.37
    distribution
        among adult population 5.36
        among owners 5.35
weather
    rain *9.2*
    sunshine *9.1*, *9.3*
weekly hours
    of work 4.20, *4.21*, *10.1*, 10.3
weekly rates of benefit, App. B page 243
widows' benefit
    persons receiving 5.22
    public expenditure 5.34
wives *1.2*
    receiving supplementary benefit 5.23
women
    childless *1.17*
    with children in household 2.12
working days lost *Figure VIII* on page 19
    international comparison *14.14*
working population 4.3–*4.8*
    in conurbations 9.12
work, journeys to
    means of travel *10.5*
    time taken 10.4
work stoppages due to industrial disputes *Figure VIII* on
    page 19

young persons entering employment 4.1
young persons on day-release courses 4.2
young persons' organisations 10.12

CENTRAL STATISTICAL OFFICE

Guide to official statistics

This publication, which is published by Her Majesty's Stationery Office, is the result of several years' work by the Central Statistical Office in conjunction with other government departments.

The aim has been to compile a detailed guide to statistics available from all official and important non-official publications – and to make it as comprehensive as possible.

The following broad areas are covered: general sources of statistics; area, climate, environment; population and vital statistics; social statistics; labour; agriculture; production industries; transport; distribution and other services; public services; prices; the economy; general and public finance; financial and business institutions; overseas transactions. Altogether 800 areas are covered in some 350 pages and around 2,500 sources are identified. An important feature is that the Guide points readers not only to regular publications but also to special reports, articles etc. with significant statistical content published over the last ten years.

The price is £7.50 (net) and it is available from any Government bookshop (see addresses on back cover) or through booksellers.

Printed in England for Her Majesty's Stationery Office by Burgess & Son (Abingdon) Ltd.
Station Road Abingdon Oxfordshire   Dd. 496693 K52 12/76